TOYOTA CELICA 1994-98 REPAIR MANUAL

CHILTON'S

President	Dean F. Morgantini, S.A.E.
Vice President–Finance	Barry L. Beck
Vice President–Sales	Glenn D. Potere
Executive Editor	Kevin M. G. Maher, A.S.E.
Manager–Consumer Automotive	Richard Schwartz, A.S.E.
Manager–Marine/Recreation	James R. Marotta, A.S.E.
Production Specialists	Brian Hollingsworth, Melinda Possinger
Project Managers	Will Kessler, A.S.E., S.A.E., Thomas A. Mellon, A.S.E., S.A.E., Richard Rivele, Todd W. Stidham, A.S.E., Ron Webb
Editor	Dawn M. Hoch, S.A.E.

CHILTON™ *Automotive Books*

PUBLISHED BY **W. G. NICHOLS, INC.**

Manufactured in USA
© 1999 Chilton Nichols
1020 Andrew Drive
West Chester, PA 19380
ISBN 0-8019-8959-0
Library of Congress Catalog Card No. 99-072521
1234567890 8765432109

www.chiltononline.com

Contents

Contents

DRIVE TRAIN   **7**

SUSPENSION AND STEERING   **8**

BRAKES   **9**

BODY AND TRIM   **10**

GLOSSARY

MASTER INDEX

See last page for information on additional titles

SAFETY NOTICE

Proper service and repair procedures are vital to the safe, reliable operation of all motor vehicles, as well as the personal safety of those performing repairs. This manual outlines procedures for servicing and repairing vehicles using safe, effective methods. The procedures contain many NOTES, CAUTIONS and WARNINGS which should be followed, along with standard procedures to eliminate the possibility of personal injury or improper service which could damage the vehicle or compromise its safety.

It is important to note that repair procedures and techniques, tools and parts for servicing motor vehicles, as well as the skill and experience of the individual performing the work vary widely. It is not possible to anticipate all of the conceivable ways or conditions under which vehicles may be serviced, or to provide cautions as to all possible hazards that may result. Standard and accepted safety precautions and equipment should be used when handling toxic or flammable fluids, and safety goggles or other protection should be used during cutting, grinding, chiseling, prying, or any other process that can cause material removal or projectiles.

Some procedures require the use of tools specially designed for a specific purpose. Before substituting another tool or procedure, you must be completely satisfied that neither your personal safety, nor the performance of the vehicle will be endangered.

Although information in this manual is based on industry sources and is complete as possible at the time of publication, the possibility exists that some car manufacturers made later changes which could not be included here. While striving for total accuracy, NP/Chilton cannot assume responsibility for any errors, changes or omissions that may occur in the compilation of this data.

PART NUMBERS

Part numbers listed in this reference are not recommendations by Chilton for any product brand name. They are references that can be used with interchange manuals and aftermarket supplier catalogs to locate each brand supplier's discrete part number.

SPECIAL TOOLS

Special tools are recommended by the vehicle manufacturer to perform their specific job. Use has been kept to a minimum, but where absolutely necessary, they are referred to in the text by the part number of the tool manufacturer. These tools can be purchased, under the appropriate part number, from your local dealer or regional distributor, or an equivalent tool can be purchased locally from a tool supplier or parts outlet. Before substituting any tool for the one recommended, read the SAFETY NOTICE at the top of this page.

ACKNOWLEDGMENTS

Chilton expresses appreciation to Toyota Motor Co. for their generous assistance.

A special thanks to the fine companies who supported the production of this book. Hand tools, supplied by Craftsman, were used during all phases of vehicle teardown and photography. Many of the fine specialty tools used in procedures were provided courtesy of Lisle Corporation. Lincoln Automotive Products has provided their industrial shop equipment including jacks, engine stands and shop presses. A Rotary lift, the largest automobile lift manufacturer in the world offering the biggest variety of surface and inground lifts available, was also used.

1

GENERAL INFORMATION AND MAINTENANCE

HOW TO USE THIS BOOK

Chilton's Total Car Care manual for the Toyota Celica is intended to help you learn more about the inner workings of your vehicle while saving you money on its upkeep and operation.

The beginning of the book will likely be referred to the most, since that is where you will find information for maintenance and tune-up. The other sections deal with the more complex systems of your vehicle. Operating systems from engine through brakes are covered to the extent that the average do-it-yourselfer becomes mechanically involved. This book will not explain such things as rebuilding a differential for the simple reason that the expertise required and the investment in special tools make this task uneconomical. It will, however, give you detailed instructions to help you change your own brake pads and shoes, replace spark plugs, and perform many more jobs that can save you money, give you personal satisfaction and help you avoid expensive problems.

A secondary purpose of this book is a reference for owners who want to understand their vehicle and/or their mechanics better. In this case, no tools at all are required.

Where to Begin

Before removing any bolts, read through the entire procedure. This will give you the overall view of what tools and supplies will be required. There is nothing more frustrating than having to walk to the bus stop on Monday morning because you were short one bolt on Sunday afternoon. So read ahead and plan ahead. Each operation should be approached logically and all procedures thoroughly understood before attempting any work.

All sections contain adjustments, maintenance, removal and installation procedures, and in some cases, repair or overhaul procedures. When repair is not considered practical, we tell you how to remove the part and then how to install the new or rebuilt replacement. In this way, you at least save labor costs. "Backyard" repair of some components is just not practical.

Avoiding Trouble

Many procedures in this book require you to "label and disconnect . . ." a group of lines, hoses or wires. Don't be lulled into thinking you can remember where everything goes—you won't. If you hook up vacuum or fuel lines incorrectly, the vehicle may run poorly, if at all. If you hook up electrical wiring incorrectly, you may instantly learn a very expensive lesson.

You don't need to know the official or engineering name for each hose or line. A piece of masking tape on the hose and a piece on its fitting will allow you to assign your own label such as the letter A or a short name. As long as you remember your own code, the lines can be reconnected by matching similar letters or names. Do remember that tape will dissolve in gasoline or other fluids; if a component is to be washed or cleaned, use another method of identification. A permanent felt-tipped marker or a metal scribe can be very handy for marking metal parts. Remove any tape or paper labels after assembly.

Maintenance or Repair?

It's necessary to mention the difference between maintenance and repair. Maintenance includes routine inspections, adjustments, and replacement of parts which show signs of normal wear. Maintenance compensates for wear or deterioration. Repair implies that something has broken or is not working. A need for repair is often caused by lack of maintenance. Example: draining and refilling the automatic transaxle fluid is maintenance recommended by the manufacturer at specific mileage intervals. Failure to do this can shorten the life of the transmission/transaxle, requiring very expensive repairs. While no maintenance program can prevent items from breaking or wearing out, a general rule can be stated: MAINTENANCE IS CHEAPER THAN REPAIR.

TOOLS AND EQUIPMENT

♦ **See Figures 1 thru 15**

Naturally, without the proper tools and equipment it is impossible to properly service your vehicle. It would also be virtually impossible to catalog every tool that you would need to perform all of the operations in this book. Of course, It would be unwise for the amateur to rush out and buy an expensive

Two basic mechanic's rules should be mentioned here. First, whenever the left side of the vehicle or engine is referred to, it is meant to specify the driver's side. Conversely, the right side of the vehicle means the passenger's side. Second, screws and bolts are removed by turning counterclockwise, and tightened by turning clockwise unless specifically noted.

Safety is always the most important rule. Constantly be aware of the dangers involved in working on an automobile and take the proper precautions. See the information in this section regarding SERVICING YOUR VEHICLE SAFELY and the SAFETY NOTICE on the acknowledgment page.

Avoiding the Most Common Mistakes

Pay attention to the instructions provided. There are 3 common mistakes in mechanical work:

1. Incorrect order of assembly, disassembly or adjustment. When taking something apart or putting it together, performing steps in the wrong order usually just costs you extra time; however, it CAN break something. Read the entire procedure before beginning disassembly. Perform everything in the order in which the instructions say you should, even if you can't immediately see a reason for it. When you're taking apart something that is very intricate, you might want to draw a picture of how it looks when assembled at one point in order to make sure you get everything back in its proper position. We will supply exploded views whenever possible. When making adjustments, perform them in the proper order. One adjustment possibly will affect another.

2. Overtorquing (or undertorquing). While it is more common for overtorquing to cause damage, undertorquing may allow a fastener to vibrate loose causing serious damage. Especially when dealing with aluminum parts, pay attention to torque specifications and utilize a torque wrench in assembly. If a torque figure is not available, remember that if you are using the right tool to perform the job, you will probably not have to strain yourself to get a fastener tight enough. The pitch of most threads is so slight that the tension you put on the wrench will be multiplied many times in actual force on what you are tightening. A good example of how critical torque is can be seen in the case of spark plug installation, especially where you are putting the plug into an aluminum cylinder head. Too little torque can fail to crush the gasket, causing leakage of combustion gases and consequent overheating of the plug and engine parts. Too much torque can damage the threads or distort the plug, changing the spark gap.

There are many commercial products available for ensuring that fasteners won't come loose, even if they are not torqued just right (a very common brand is Loctite®). If you're worried about getting something together tight enough to hold, but loose enough to avoid mechanical damage during assembly, one of these products might offer substantial insurance. Before choosing a threadlocking compound, read the label on the package and make sure the product is compatible with the materials, fluids, etc. involved.

3. Crossthreading. This occurs when a part such as a bolt is screwed into a nut or casting at the wrong angle and forced. Crossthreading is more likely to occur if access is difficult. It helps to clean and lubricate fasteners, then to start threading the bolt, spark plug, etc. with your fingers. If you encounter resistance, unscrew the part and start over again at a different angle until it can be inserted and turned several times without much effort. Keep in mind that many parts, especially spark plugs, have tapered threads, so that gentle turning will automatically bring the part you're threading to the proper angle. Don't put a wrench on the part until it's been tightened a couple of turns by hand. If you suddenly encounter resistance, and the part has not seated fully, don't force it. Pull it back out to make sure it's clean and threading properly.

Be sure to take your time and be patient, and always plan ahead. Allow yourself ample time to perform repairs and maintenance. You may find maintaining your car a satisfying and enjoyable experience.

set of tools on the theory that he/she may need one or more of them at some time.

The best approach is to proceed slowly, gathering a good quality set of those tools that are used most frequently. Don't be misled by the low cost of bargain tools. It is far better to spend a little more for better quality. Forged wrenches, 6 or 12-point sockets and fine tooth ratchets are by far preferable to their less expensive counterparts. As any good mechanic can tell you, there are few worse experiences than trying to work on a vehicle with bad tools. Your monetary savings will be far outweighed by frustration and mangled knuckles.

Begin accumulating those tools that are used most frequently: those associated with routine maintenance and tune-up. In addition to the normal assortment of screwdrivers and pliers, you should have the following tools:

• Wrenches/sockets and combination open end/box end wrenches in sizes 3mm–19mm 13/16 inch or 5/8 inch spark plug socket (depending on plug type).

➡If possible, buy various length socket drive extensions. Universal-joint and wobble extensions can be extremely useful, but be careful when using them, as they can change the amount of torque applied to the socket.

• Jackstands for support.
• Oil filter wrench.

• Spout or funnel for pouring fluids.
• Grease gun for chassis lubrication (unless your vehicle is not equipped with any grease fittings—for details, please refer to information on Fluids and Lubricants, later in this section).
• Hydrometer for checking the battery (unless equipped with a sealed, maintenance-free battery).
• A container for draining oil and other fluids.
• Rags for wiping up the inevitable mess.

In addition to the above items there are several others that are not absolutely necessary, but handy to have around. These include Oil Dry® (or an equivalent oil absorbent gravel—such as cat litter) and the usual supply of lubricants, antifreeze and fluids, although these can be purchased as needed. This is a basic list for routine maintenance, but only your personal needs and desire can accurately determine your list of tools.

After performing a few projects on the vehicle, you'll be amazed at the other tools and non-tools on your workbench. Some useful household items are: a large turkey baster or siphon, empty coffee cans and ice trays (to store parts),

Fig. 1 All but the most basic procedures will require an assortment of ratchets and sockets

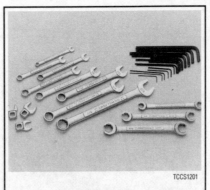

Fig. 2 In addition to ratchets, a good set of wrenches and hex keys will be necessary

Fig. 3 A hydraulic floor jack and a set of jackstands are essential for lifting and supporting the vehicle

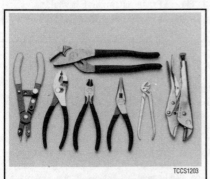

Fig. 4 An assortment of pliers, grippers and cutters will be handy for old rusted parts and stripped bolt heads

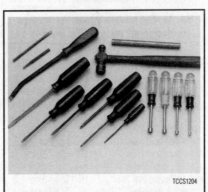

Fig. 5 Various drivers, chisels and prybars are great tools to have in your toolbox

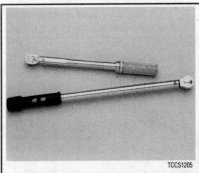

Fig. 6 Many repairs will require the use of a torque wrench to assure the components are properly fastened

Fig. 7 Although not always necessary, using specialized brake tools will save time

Fig. 8 A few inexpensive lubrication tools will make maintenance easier

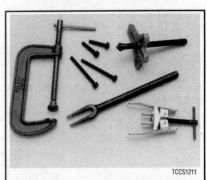

Fig. 9 Various pullers, clamps and separator tools are needed for many larger, more complicated repairs

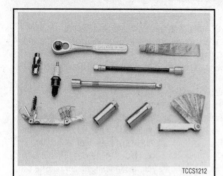

Fig. 10 A variety of tools and gauges should be used for spark plug gapping and installation

Fig. 11 Inductive type timing light

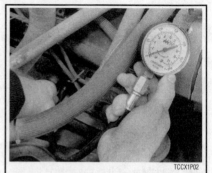

Fig. 12 A screw-in type compression gauge is recommended for compression testing

Fig. 13 A vacuum/pressure tester is necessary for many testing procedures

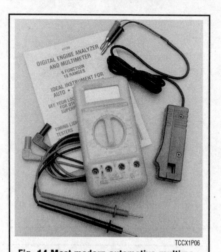

Fig. 14 Most modern automotive multimeters incorporate many helpful features

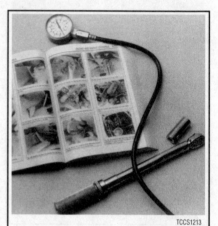

Fig. 15 Proper information is vital, so always have a Chilton Total Car Care manual handy

ball of twine, electrical tape for wiring, small rolls of colored tape for tagging lines or hoses, markers and pens, a note pad, golf tees (for plugging vacuum lines), metal coat hangers or a roll of mechanics's wire (to hold things out of the way), dental pick or similar long, pointed probe, a strong magnet, and a small mirror (to see into recesses and under manifolds).

A more advanced set of tools, suitable for tune-up work, can be drawn up easily. While the tools are slightly more sophisticated, they need not be outrageously expensive. There are several inexpensive tach/dwell meters on the market that are every bit as good for the average mechanic as a professional model. Just be sure that it goes to a least 1200–1500 rpm on the tach scale and that it works on 4, 6 and 8-cylinder engines. The key to these purchases is to make them with an eye towards adaptability and wide range. A basic list of tune-up tools could include:

- Tach/dwell meter.
- Spark plug wrench and gapping tool.
- Feeler gauges for valve adjustment.
- Timing light.

The choice of a timing light should be made carefully. A light which works on the DC current supplied by the vehicle's battery is the best choice; it should have a xenon tube for brightness. On any vehicle with an electronic ignition system, a timing light with an inductive pickup that clamps around the No. 1 spark plug cable is preferred.

In addition to these basic tools, there are several other tools and gauges you may find useful. These include:

- Compression gauge. The screw-in type is slower to use, but eliminates the possibility of a faulty reading due to escaping pressure.

- Manifold vacuum gauge.
- 12V test light.
- A combination volt/ohmmeter
- Induction Ammeter. This is used for determining whether or not there is current in a wire. These are handy for use if a wire is broken somewhere in a wiring harness.

As a final note, you will probably find a torque wrench necessary for all but the most basic work. The beam type models are perfectly adequate, although the newer click types (breakaway) are easier to use. The click type torque wrenches tend to be more expensive. Also keep in mind that all types of torque wrenches should be periodically checked and/or recalibrated. You will have to decide for yourself which better fits your pocketbook, and purpose.

Special Tools

Normally, the use of special factory tools is avoided for repair procedures, since these are not readily available for the do-it-yourself mechanic. When it is possible to perform the job with more commonly available tools, it will be pointed out, but occasionally, a special tool was designed to perform a specific function and should be used. Before substituting another tool, you should be convinced that neither your safety nor the performance of the vehicle will be compromised.

Special tools can usually be purchased from an automotive parts store or from your dealer. In some cases special tools may be available directly from the tool manufacturer.

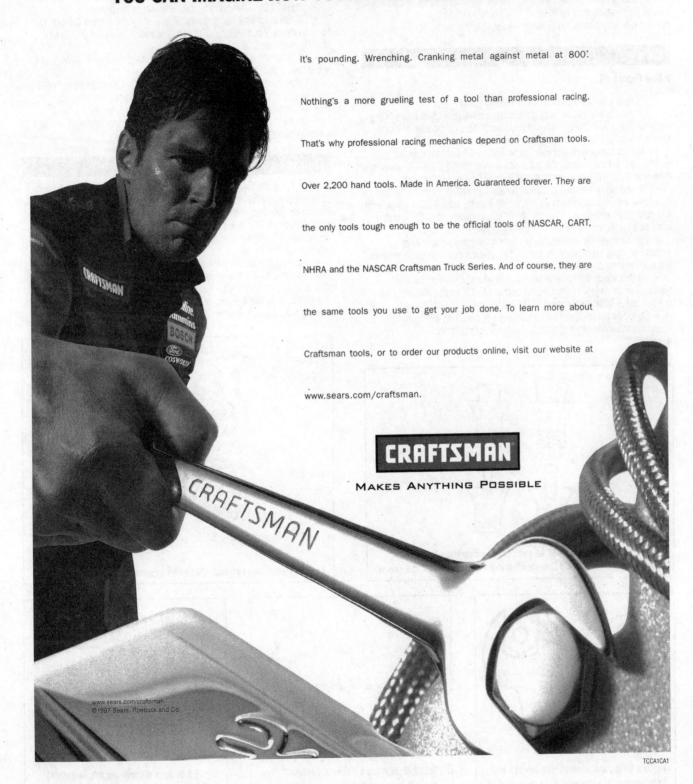
TCCA1CA1

SERVICING YOUR VEHICLE SAFELY

▶ **See Figures 16, 17, 18 and 19**

It is virtually impossible to anticipate all of the hazards involved with automotive maintenance and service, but care and common sense will prevent most accidents.

The rules of safety for mechanics range from "don't smoke around gasoline," to "use the proper tool(s) for the job." The trick to avoiding injuries is to develop safe work habits and to take every possible precaution.

Do's

▶ **See Figure 20**

- Do keep a fire extinguisher and first aid kit handy.
- Do wear safety glasses or goggles when cutting, drilling, grinding or prying, even if you have 20–20 vision. If you wear glasses for the sake of vision, wear safety goggles over your regular glasses.
- Do shield your eyes whenever you work around the battery. Batteries contain sulfuric acid. In case of contact with the eyes or skin, flush the area with water or a mixture of water and baking soda, then seek immediate medical attention.
- Do use safety stands (jackstands) for any undervehicle service. Jacks are for raising vehicles; jackstands are for making sure the vehicle stays raised until you want it to come down. Whenever the vehicle is raised, block the wheels remaining on the ground and set the parking brake.
- Do use adequate ventilation when working with any chemicals or hazardous materials. Like carbon monoxide, the asbestos dust resulting from some brake lining wear can be hazardous in sufficient quantities.
- Do disconnect the negative battery cable when working on the electrical system. The secondary ignition system contains EXTREMELY HIGH VOLTAGE. In some cases it can even exceed 50,000 volts.
- Do follow manufacturer's directions whenever working with potentially hazardous materials. Most chemicals and fluids are poisonous if taken internally.

- Do properly maintain your tools. Loose hammerheads, mushroomed punches and chisels, frayed or poorly grounded electrical cords, excessively worn screwdrivers, spread wrenches (open end), cracked sockets, slipping ratchets, or faulty droplight sockets can cause accidents.
- Likewise, keep your tools clean; a greasy wrench can slip off a bolt head, ruining the bolt and often harming your knuckles in the process.
- Do use the proper size and type of tool for the job at hand. Do select a wrench or socket that fits the nut or bolt. The wrench or socket should sit straight, not cocked.
- Do, when possible, pull on a wrench handle rather than push on it, and adjust your stance to prevent a fall.
- Do be sure that adjustable wrenches are tightly closed on the nut or bolt and pulled so that the force is on the side of the fixed jaw.
- Do strike squarely with a hammer; avoid glancing blows.
- Do set the parking brake and block the drive wheels if the work requires a running engine.

Don'ts

- Don't run the engine in a garage or anywhere else without proper ventilation—EVER! Carbon monoxide is poisonous; it takes a long time to leave the human body and you can build up a deadly supply of it in your system by simply breathing in a little every day. You may not realize you are slowly poisoning yourself. Always use power vents, windows, fans and/or open the garage door.
- Don't work around moving parts while wearing loose clothing. Short sleeves are much safer than long, loose sleeves. Hard-toed shoes with neoprene soles protect your toes and give a better grip on slippery surfaces. Jewelry such as watches, fancy belt buckles, beads or body adornment of any kind is not safe working around a vehicle. Long hair should be tied back under a hat or cap.

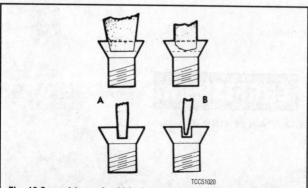

Fig. 16 Screwdrivers should be kept in good condition to prevent injury or damage which could result if the blade slips from the screw

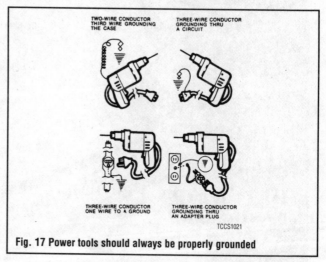

Fig. 17 Power tools should always be properly grounded

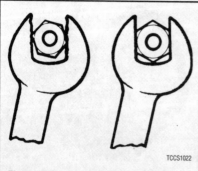
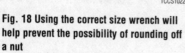

Fig. 18 Using the correct size wrench will help prevent the possibility of rounding off a nut

Fig. 19 NEVER work under a vehicle unless it is supported using safety stands (jackstands)

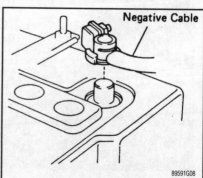

Fig. 20 Always disconnect the negative battery cable prior to working on any electrical component

• Don't use pockets for toolboxes. A fall or bump can drive a screwdriver deep into your body. Even a rag hanging from your back pocket can wrap around a spinning shaft or fan.

• Don't smoke when working around gasoline, cleaning solvent or other flammable material.

• Don't smoke when working around the battery. When the battery is being charged, it gives off explosive hydrogen gas.

• Don't use gasoline to wash your hands; there are excellent soaps available. Gasoline contains dangerous additives which can enter the body through a cut or through your pores. Gasoline also removes all the natural oils from the skin so that bone dry hands will suck up oil and grease.

• Don't service the air conditioning system unless you are equipped with the necessary tools and training. When liquid or compressed gas refrigerant is released to atmospheric pressure it will absorb heat from whatever it contacts. This will chill or freeze anything it touches.

• Don't use screwdrivers for anything other than driving screws! A screwdriver used as an prying tool can snap when you least expect it, causing injuries. At the very least, you'll ruin a good screwdriver.

• Don't use an emergency jack (that little ratchet, scissors, or pantograph jack supplied with the vehicle) for anything other than changing a flat! These jacks are only intended for emergency use out on the road; they are NOT designed as a maintenance tool. If you are serious about maintaining your vehicle yourself, invest in a hydraulic floor jack of at least a 1½ ton capacity, and at least two sturdy jackstands.

FASTENERS, MEASUREMENTS AND CONVERSIONS

Bolts, Nuts and Other Threaded Retainers

▶ See Figures 21, 22, 23 and 24

Although there are a great variety of fasteners found in the modern car or truck, the most commonly used retainer is the threaded fastener (nuts, bolts, screws, studs, etc). Most threaded retainers may be reused, provided that they are not damaged in use or during the repair. Some retainers (such as stretch bolts or torque prevailing nuts) are designed to deform when tightened or in use and should not be reinstalled.

Whenever possible, we will note any special retainers which should be replaced during a procedure. But you should always inspect the condition of a retainer when it is removed and replace any that show signs of damage. Check all threads for rust or corrosion which can increase the torque necessary to achieve the desired clamp load for which that fastener was originally selected. Additionally, be sure that the driver surface of the fastener has not been com-

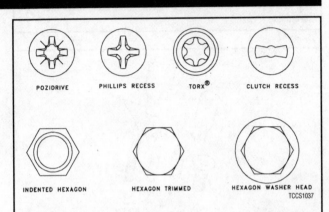

Fig. 21 Here are a few of the most common screw/bolt driver styles

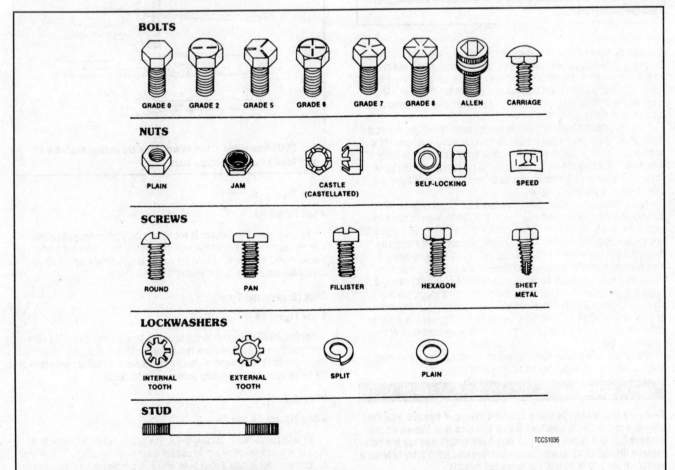

Fig. 22 There are many different types of threaded retainers found on vehicles

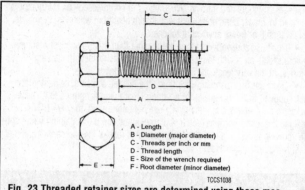

A - Length
B - Diameter (major diameter)
C - Threads per inch or mm
D - Thread length
E - Size of the wrench required
F - Root diameter (minor diameter)

TCCS1038

Fig. 23 Threaded retainer sizes are determined using these measurements

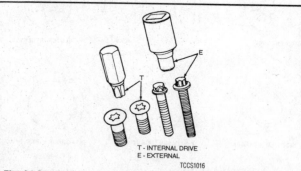

T - INTERNAL DRIVE
E - EXTERNAL

TCCS1016

Fig. 24 Special fasteners such as these Torx® head bolts are used by manufacturers to discourage people from working on vehicles without the proper tools

promised by rounding or other damage. In some cases a driver surface may become only partially rounded, allowing the driver to catch in only one direction. In many of these occurrences, a fastener may be installed and tightened, but the driver would not be able to grip and loosen the fastener again. (This could lead to frustration down the line should that component ever need to be disassembled again).

If you must replace a fastener, whether due to design or damage, you must ALWAYS be sure to use the proper replacement. In all cases, a retainer of the same design, material and strength should be used. Markings on the heads of most bolts will help determine the proper strength of the fastener. The same material, thread and pitch must be selected to assure proper installation and safe operation of the vehicle afterwards.

Thread gauges are available to help measure a bolt or stud's thread. Most automotive and hardware stores keep gauges available to help you select the proper size. In a pinch, you can use another nut or bolt for a thread gauge. If the bolt you are replacing is not too badly damaged, you can select a match by finding another bolt which will thread in its place. If you find a nut which threads properly onto the damaged bolt, then use that nut to help select the replacement bolt. If however, the bolt you are replacing is so badly damaged (broken or drilled out) that its threads cannot be used as a gauge, you might start by looking for another bolt (from the same assembly or a similar location on your vehicle) which will thread into the damaged bolt's mounting. If so, the other bolt can be used to select a nut; the nut can then be used to select the replacement bolt.

In all cases, be absolutely sure you have selected the proper replacement. Don't be shy, you can always ask the store clerk for help.

✳✳ WARNING

Be aware that when you find a bolt with damaged threads, you may also find the nut or drilled hole it was threaded into has also been damaged. If this is the case, you may have to drill and tap the hole, replace the nut or otherwise repair the threads. NEVER try to force a replacement bolt to fit into the damaged threads.

Torque

Torque is defined as the measurement of resistance to turning or rotating. It tends to twist a body about an axis of rotation. A common example of this would be tightening a threaded retainer such as a nut, bolt or screw. Measuring torque is one of the most common ways to help assure that a threaded retainer has been properly fastened.

When tightening a threaded fastener, torque is applied in three distinct areas, the head, the bearing surface and the clamp load. About 50 percent of the measured torque is used in overcoming bearing friction. This is the friction between the bearing surface of the bolt head, screw head or nut face and the base material or washer (the surface on which the fastener is rotating). Approximately 40 percent of the applied torque is used in overcoming thread friction. This leaves only about 10 percent of the applied torque to develop a useful clamp load (the force which holds a joint together). This means that friction can account for as much as 90 percent of the applied torque on a fastener.

TORQUE WRENCHES

▶ See Figures 25, 26 and 27

In most applications, a torque wrench can be used to assure proper installation of a fastener. Torque wrenches come in various designs and most automotive supply stores will carry a variety to suit your needs. A torque wrench should be used any time we supply a specific torque value for a fastener. A torque wrench can also be used if you are following the general guidelines in the accompanying charts. Keep in mind that because there is no worldwide standardization of fasteners, the charts are a general guideline and should be used with caution. Again, the general rule of "if you are using the right tool for the job, you should not have to strain to tighten a fastener" applies here.

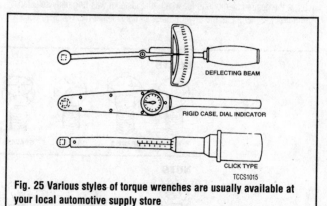

DEFLECTING BEAM

RIGID CASE, DIAL INDICATOR

CLICK TYPE

TCCS1015

Fig. 25 Various styles of torque wrenches are usually available at your local automotive supply store

Beam Type

▶ See Figure 28

The beam type torque wrench is one of the most popular types. It consists of a pointer attached to the head that runs the length of the flexible beam (shaft) to a scale located near the handle. As the wrench is pulled, the beam bends and the pointer indicates the torque using the scale.

Click (Breakaway) Type

▶ See Figure 29

Another popular design of torque wrench is the click type. To use the click type wrench you pre-adjust it to a torque setting. Once the torque is reached, the wrench has a reflex signaling feature that causes a momentary breakaway of the torque wrench body, sending an impulse to the operator's hand.

Pivot Head Type

▶ See Figures 29 and 30

Some torque wrenches (usually of the click type) may be equipped with a pivot head which can allow it to be used in areas of limited access. BUT, it must be used properly. To hold a pivot head wrench, grasp the handle lightly, and as you pull on the handle, it should be floated on the pivot point. If the handle

Fig. 26 Determining bolt strength of metric fasteners—NOTE: this is a typical bolt marking system, but there is not a worldwide standard

	Class	Mark
	4T	4 —
	5T	5 —
Bolt head No.	6T	6 —
	7T	7 —
	8T	8 —
	9T	9 —
	10T	10 —
	11T	11 —

	Class	Mark
Hexagon head bolt	4T	No mark
Hexagon flange bolt w/ washer hexagon bolt	4T	No mark
Hexagon head bolt	5T	Two protruding lines
Hexagon flange bolt w/ washer hexagon bolt	6T	Two protruding lines
Hexagon head bolt	7T	Three protruding lines
Hexagon head bolt	8T	Four protruding lines

	Class	Mark
Stud bolt	4T	No mark
	6T	Grooved
Welded bolt	4T	

Fig. 27 Typical bolt torques for metric fasteners—WARNING: use only as a guide

Class	Diameter mm	Pitch mm	Hexagon head bolt N·m	kgf·cm	ft-lbf	Hexagon flange bolt N·m	kgf·cm	ft-lbf
4T	6	1	5	55	48 in.·lbf	6	60	52 in.·lbf
	8	1.25	12.5	130	9	14	145	10
	10	1.25	26	260	19	29	290	21
	12	1.25	47	480	35	53	540	39
	14	1.5	74	760	55	84	850	61
	16	1.5	115	1,150	83	—	—	—
5T	6	1	6.5	65	56 in.·lbf	7.5	75	65 in.·lbf
	8	1.25	15.5	160	12	17.5	175	13
	10	1.25	32	330	24	36	360	26
	12	1.25	59	600	43	65	670	48
	14	1.5	91	930	67	100	1,050	76
	16	1.5	140	1,400	101	—	—	—
6T	6	1	8	80	69 in.·lbf	9	90	78 in.·lbf
	8	1.25	19	195	14	21	210	15
	10	1.25	39	400	29	44	440	32
	12	1.25	71	730	53	80	810	59
	14	1.5	110	1,100	80	125	1,250	90
	16	1.5	170	1,750	127	—	—	—
7T	6	1.25	10.5	110	8	12	120	9
	8	1.25	25	260	19	28	290	21
	10	1.25	52	530	38	58	590	43
	12	1.5	95	970	70	105	1,050	76
	14	1.5	145	1,500	108	165	1,700	123
	16	1.5	230	2,300	166	—	—	—
8T	8	1.25	29	300	22	33	330	24
	10	1.25	61	620	45	68	690	50
	12	1.25	110	1,100	80	120	1,250	90
9T	8	1.25	34	340	25	37	380	27
	10	1.25	70	710	51	78	790	57
	12	1.25	125	1,300	94	140	1,450	105
10T	8	1.25	38	390	28	42	430	31
	10	1.25	78	800	58	88	890	64
	12	1.25	140	1,450	105	155	1,600	116
11T	8	1.25	42	430	31	47	480	35
	10	1.25	87	890	64	97	990	72
	12	1.25	155	1,600	116	175	1,800	130

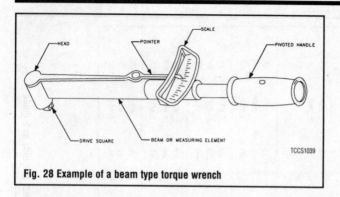

Fig. 28 Example of a beam type torque wrench

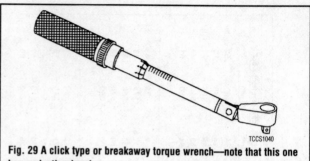

Fig. 29 A click type or breakaway torque wrench—note that this one has a pivoting head

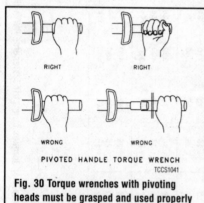

Fig. 30 Torque wrenches with pivoting heads must be grasped and used properly to prevent an incorrect reading

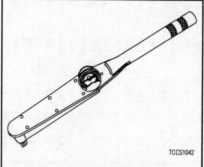

Fig. 31 The rigid case (direct reading) torque wrench uses a dial indicator to show torque

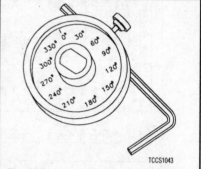

Fig. 32 Some specifications require the use of a torque angle meter (mechanical protractor)

comes in contact with the yoke extension during the process of pulling, there is a very good chance the torque readings will be inaccurate because this could alter the wrench loading point. The design of the handle is usually such as to make it inconvenient to deliberately misuse the wrench.

➡️**It should be mentioned that the use of any U-joint, wobble or extension will have an effect on the torque readings, no matter what type of wrench you are using. For the most accurate readings, install the socket directly on the wrench driver. If necessary, straight extensions (which hold a socket directly under the wrench driver) will have the least effect on the torque reading. Avoid any extension that alters the length of the wrench from the handle to the head/driving point (such as a crow's foot). U-joint or wobble extensions can greatly affect the readings; avoid their use at all times.**

Rigid Case (Direct Reading)

▶ See Figure 31

A rigid case or direct reading torque wrench is equipped with a dial indicator to show torque values. One advantage of these wrenches is that they can be held at any position on the wrench without affecting accuracy. These wrenches are often preferred because they tend to be compact, easy to read and have a great degree of accuracy.

TORQUE ANGLE METERS

▶ See Figure 32

Because the frictional characteristics of each fastener or threaded hole will vary, clamp loads which are based strictly on torque will vary as well. In most applications, this variance is not significant enough to cause worry. But, in certain applications, a manufacturer's engineers may determine that more precise clamp loads are necessary (such is the case with many aluminum cylinder heads). In these cases, a torque angle method of installation would be specified. When installing fasteners which are torque angle tightened, a predetermined seating torque and standard torque wrench are usually used first to remove any compliance from the joint. The fastener is then tightened the specified additional portion of a turn measured in degrees. A torque angle gauge (mechanical protractor) is used for these applications.

CONVERSION FACTORS

LENGTH-DISTANCE

Inches (in.)	x 25.4	= Millimeters (mm)	x .0394	= Inches
Feet (ft.)	x .305	= Meters (m)	x 3.281	= Feet
Miles	x 1.609	= Kilometers (km)	x .0621	= Miles

VOLUME

Cubic Inches (in3)	x 16.387	= Cubic Centimeters	x .061	= in3
IMP Pints (IMP pt.)	x .568	= Liters (L)	x 1.76	= IMP pt.
IMP Quarts (IMP qt.)	x 1.137	= Liters (L)	x .88	= IMP qt.
IMP Gallons (IMP gal.)	x 4.546	= Liters (L)	x .22	= IMP gal.
IMP Quarts (IMP qt.)	x 1.201	= US Quarts (US qt.)	x .833	= IMP qt.
IMP Gallons (IMP gal.)	x 1.201	= US Gallons (US gal.)	x .833	= IMP gal.
Fl. Ounces	x 29.573	= Milliliters	x .034	= Ounces
US Pints (US pt.)	x .473	= Liters (L)	x 2.113	= Pints
US Quarts (US qt.)	x .946	= Liters (L)	x 1.057	= Quarts
US Gallons (US gal.)	x 3.785	= Liters (L)	x .264	= Gallons

MASS-WEIGHT

Ounces (oz.)	x 28.35	= Grams (g)	x .035	= Ounces
Pounds (lb.)	x .454	= Kilograms (kg)	x 2.205	= Pounds

PRESSURE

Pounds Per Sq. In. (psi)	x 6.895	= Kilopascals (kPa)	x .145	= psi
Inches of Mercury (Hg)	x .4912	= psi	x 2.036	= Hg
Inches of Mercury (Hg)	x 3.377	= Kilopascals (kPa)	x .2961	= Hg
Inches of Water (H₂O)	x .07355	= Inches of Mercury	x 13.783	= H₂O
Inches of Water (H₂O)	x .03613	= psi	x 27.684	= H₂O
Inches of Water (H₂O)	x .248	= Kilopascals (kPa)	x 4.026	= H₂O

TORQUE

Pounds-Force Inches (in-lb)	x .113	= Newton Meters (N·m)	x 8.85	= in-lb
Pounds-Force Feet (ft-lb)	x 1.356	= Newton Meters (N·m)	x .738	= ft-lb

VELOCITY

Miles Per Hour (MPH)	x 1.609	= Kilometers Per Hour (KPH)	x .621	= MPH

POWER

Horsepower (Hp)	x .745	= Kilowatts	x 1.34	= Horsepower

FUEL CONSUMPTION*

Miles Per Gallon IMP (MPG)	x .354	= Kilometers Per Liter (Km/L)	
Kilometers Per Liter (Km/L)	x 2.352	= IMP MPG	
Miles Per Gallon US (MPG)	x .425	= Kilometers Per Liter (Km/L)	
Kilometers Per Liter (Km/L)	x 2.352	= US MPG	

*It is common to covert from miles per gallon (mpg) to liters/100 kilometers (1/100 km), where mpg (IMP) x 1/100 km = 282 and mpg (US) x 1/100 km = 235.

TEMPERATURE

Degree Fahrenheit (°F)	= (°C x 1.8) + 32
Degree Celsius (°C)	= (°F – 32) x .56

TCCS1044

Fig. 33 Standard and metric conversion factors chart

Standard and Metric Measurements

▶ See Figure 33

Throughout this manual, specifications are given to help you determine the condition of various components on your vehicle, or to assist you in their installation. Some of the most common measurements include length (inch or cm/mm), torque (ft. lbs., inch lbs. or Nm) and pressure (psi, inch Hg, kPa or mm Hg). In most cases, we strive to provide the proper measurement as determined by the manufacturer's engineers.

Though, in some cases, that value may not be conveniently measured with what is available in your toolbox. Luckily, many of the measuring devices which are available today will have two scales so the Standard or Metric measurements may easily be taken. If any of the various measuring tools which are available to you do not contain the same scale as listed in the specifications, use the accompanying conversion factors to determine the proper value.

The conversion factor chart is used by taking the given specification and multiplying it by the necessary conversion factor. For instance, looking at the first line, if you have a measurement in inches such as "free-play should be 2 inch" but your ruler reads only in millimeters, multiply 2 inch by the conversion factor of 25.4 to get the metric equivalent of 50.8mm. Likewise, if the specification was given only in a Metric measurement, for example in Newton Meters (Nm), then look at the center column first. If the measurement is 100 Nm, multiply it by the conversion factor of 0.738 to get 73.8 ft. lbs.

SERIAL NUMBER IDENTIFICATION

Vehicle

▶ See Figures 34, 35, 36 and 37

All models have the vehicle identification number stamped on a plate attached to the left side of the instrument panel. The plate is visible by looking through the windshield from the outside. The VIN is also stamped on the manufacturer's plate in the engine compartment which is usually located on the firewall cowl panel and on the certification regulation plate affixed to the driver's door post.

The serial number consists of a series of 17 digits including the six digit serial or production number. The first three digits are the World Manufacturer Identification number. Corolla models are made in Japan, the US and Canada, these first three digits with designate the location of production. The next five digits are the Vehicle Description Section. The remaining nine digits are the production numbers including various codes on body style, trim level (base, luxury, etc.) and safety equipment or other information.

Example:
- JT2FG02T1T025886
- First three digits—JT2—Manufacturing; Japan Toyota car
- Fourth digit—F—body type; 2 door convertible
- Fifth digit—G—engine; 5S-FE engine
- Sixth digit—0—series; ST204L
- Seventh digit—2—restraint system; Manual seat belts with air bag
- Eighth digit—T—line; Celica
- Ninth digit—1—check digit
- Tenth digit—T—model year; 1996
- Eleventh digit—0—Plant manufacture; Tahara
- Twelfth—Seventeenth—serial number; 025886

Engine

▶ See Figures 38 and 39

Each engine is referred to by both its family designation, such as 5S-FE, and its production or serial number. The serial number can be important when ordering parts. Certain changes may have been made during production of the

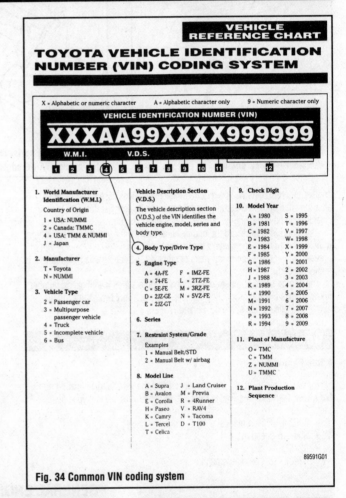

Fig. 34 Common VIN coding system

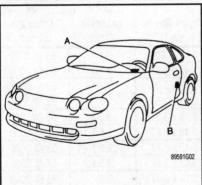

Fig. 35 View of the common VIN plate locations

Fig. 36 There is a metal VIN tag attached to the drivers side of the dash, seen through the windshield

Fig. 37 Another label is attached to the hood of most vehicles

VEHICLE IDENTIFICATION CHART

Engine Code						Model Year	
Engine Series (ID/VIN)	Engine Displacement Liters (cc)	Cubic Inches	No. of Cylinders	Fuel System	Eng. Mfg.	Code	Year
5S-FE	2.2 (2164)	132	4	EFI	Toyota	R	94
7A-FE	1.8 (1762)	107	4	EFI	Toyota	S	95
						T	96
						V	97
						W	98

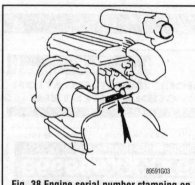

Fig. 38 Engine serial number stamping on the block—5S-FE engine

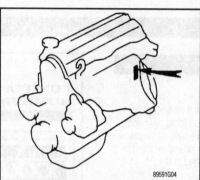

Fig. 39 Engine serial number stamping on the block—7A-FE engine

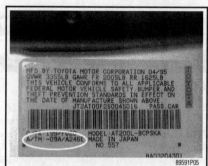

Fig. 40 The transaxle code can be found on the drivers door tag along with other important information

engine; different parts will be required if the engine was assembled before or after the change date. Generally, parts stores and dealers list this data in their catalogs, so have the engine number handy when you go.

It's a good idea to record the engine number while the vehicle is new. Jotting it inside the cover of the owner's manual or similar easy-to-find location will prevent having to scrape many years of grime off the engine when the number is finally needed.

The engine serial number consists of an engine series identification number, followed by a 6–digit production number. There are only two engines in the 1994–98 Celica models, the 5S-FE and 7A-FE.

Transaxle

♦ See Figure 40

Transaxle identification codes are located on the vehicle identification number under the hood. The Toyota Celica is equipped with several types of transaxles.

- C-52—5 speed manual
- S54—5-speed manual
- A245E—4-speed automatic
- A140E—4-speed automatic

Body

♦ See Figure 41

A body code is engraved into the firewall of the vehicle. The code will start with the body style code; AT200 is Celica. The last digits are the serial number of the vehicle.

Fig. 41 A body code is engraved into the firewall of the vehicle as shown here

GENERAL ENGINE SPECIFICATIONS

Year	Engine ID/VIN	Engine Displacement Liters (cc)	Fuel System Type	Net Horsepower @ rpm	Net Torque @ rpm (ft. lbs.)	Bore x Stroke (in.)	Compression Ratio	Oil Pressure @ rpm
1994	7A-FE	1.8 (1762)	EFI	110 @ 5600	115 @ 2800	3.19 x 3.37	9.5:1	53 @ 3000
	5S-FE	2.2 (2164)	EFI	135 @ 5400	145 @ 4400	3.43 x 3.58	9.5:1	53 @ 3000
1995	7A-FE	1.8 (1762)	EFI	110 @ 5600	115 @ 2800	3.19 x 3.37	9.5:1	53 @ 3000
	5S-FE	2.2 (2164)	EFI	135 @ 5400	145 @ 4400	3.43 x 3.58	9.5:1	53 @ 3000
1996	7A-FE	1.8 (1762)	EFI	105 @5200	117 @ 2800	3.19 x 3.37	9.5:1	53 @ 3000
	5S-FE	2.2 (2164)	EFI	135 @ 5400	145 @ 4400	3.43 x 3.58	9.5:1	53 @ 3000
1997	7A-FE	1.8 (1762)	EFI	105 @5200	117 @ 2800	3.19 x 3.37	9.5:1	53 @ 3000
	5S-FE	2.2 (2164)	EFI	135 @ 5400	145 @ 4400	3.43 x 3.58	9.5:1	53 @ 3000
1998	7A-FE	1.8 (1762)	EFI	105 @5200	117 @ 2800	3.19 x 3.37	9.5:1	53 @ 3000
	5S-FE	2.2 (2164)	EFI	135 @ 5400	145 @ 4400	3.43 x 3.58	9.5:1	53 @ 3000

89591C01

ENGINE IDENTIFICATION

Year	Model	Engine Displacement Liters (cc)	Engine Series (ID/VIN)	Fuel System	No. of Cylinders	Engine Type
1994	Celica	1.8 (1762)	7A-FE	EFI	4	DOHC
	Celica	2.2 (2164)	5S-FE	EFI	4	DOHC
1995	Celica	1.8 (1762)	7A-FE	EFI	4	DOHC
	Celica	2.2 (2164)	5S-FE	EFI	4	DOHC
1996	Celica	1.8 (1762)	7A-FE	EFI	4	DOHC
	Celica	2.2 (2164)	5S-FE	EFI	4	DOHC
1997	Celica	1.8 (1762)	7A-FE	EFI	4	DOHC
	Celica	2.2 (2164)	5S-FE	EFI	4	DOHC
1998	Celica	1.8 (1762)	7A-FE	EFI	4	DOHC
	Celica	2.2 (2164)	5S-FE	EFI	4	DOHC

89591C04

ROUTINE MAINTENANCE AND TUNE-UP

Proper maintenance and tune-up is the key to long and trouble-free vehicle life, and the work can yield its own rewards. Studies have shown that a properly tuned and maintained vehicle can achieve better gas mileage than an out-of-tune vehicle. As a conscientious owner and driver, set aside a Saturday morning, say once a month, to check or replace items which could cause major problems later. Keep your own personal log to jot down which services you performed, how much the parts cost you, the date, and the exact odometer reading at the time. Keep all receipts for such items as engine oil and filters, so that they may be referred to in case of related problems or to determine operating expenses. As a do-it-yourselfer, these receipts are the only proof you have that the required maintenance was performed. In the event of a warranty problem, these receipts will be invaluable.

The literature provided with your vehicle when it was originally delivered includes the factory recommended maintenance schedule. If you no longer have this literature, replacement copies are usually available from the dealer. A maintenance schedule is provided later in this section, in case you do not have the factory literature.

Air Cleaner (Element)

▶ See Figure 42

The element should be replaced at the recommended intervals shown in the Maintenance Intervals chart later in this section. If your car is operated under severely dusty conditions or severe operating conditions, more frequent changes will certainly be necessary. Inspect the element at least twice a year. Early spring and early fall are always good times for inspection. Remove the element and check for any perforations or tears in the filter. Check the cleaner housing for signs of dirt or dust that may have leaked through the filter element or in through the snorkel tube. Position a droplight on one side of the element and look through the filter at the light. If no light can be seen through the element material, replace the filter. If holes in the filter element are apparent or signs of dirt seepage through the filter are evident, replace the filter.

REMOVAL & INSTALLATION

▶ See Figures 43 and 44

1. Turn the ignition switch to the **LOCK** position.
2. Disconnect the negative battery cable. Wait at least 90 seconds once the batter cable is disconnected to hinder the air bag deployment.

✳ CAUTION

Models covered by this manual may be equipped with a Supplemental Restraint System (SRS), which uses an air bag. Whenever working near any of the SRS components, such as the impact sensors, the air bag module, steering column and instrument panel, disable the SRS, as described in Section 6.

➡ It may not be necessary to remove any wiring or cables depending on your model.

3. Disconnect the wiring, cables and hoses attached to the air cleaner housing in the way of top removal.
4. Lift the wire tabs, if equipped, to release the four retaining clips on the bottom of the housing and lift off the top cover.
5. Position the cover with the flexible hose off to the side.
6. Withdraw the air filter element from the housing and if it is too dirty, discard it. If it is only mildly dusty, it can be cleaned with low-pressure compressed air.

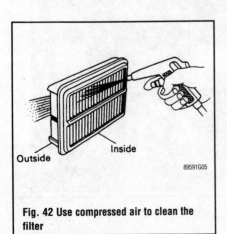

Fig. 42 Use compressed air to clean the filter

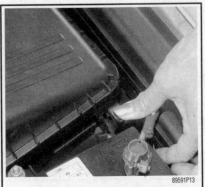

Fig. 43 Pull the tabs on the side of the air cleaner housing to lift up the cap

Fig. 44 Withdraw the filter from the air cleaner housing

UNDERHOOD MAINTENANCE COMPONENT LOCATIONS

1. Air cleaner
2. Battery
3. Radiator hose
4. Radiator cap
5. Fuse block
6. Spark plug wire
7. Fuel injector
8. Power steering reservoir
9. Washer fluid reservoir
10. Engine coolant reservoir
11. Distributor
12. Alternator
13. Brake master cylinder reservoir
14. Engine oil dipstick
15. Engine oil fill cap

To install:

7. With a clean rag, remove any dirt or dust from the front cover and also from the element seating surface.

8. Position and install the new filter element so that it seats properly in the housing.

9. Position the cover with the attached hose over the element. Secure it with the retaining clips. Reconnect the electrical wiring, cables ect. if disconnected.

✳✳ WARNING

Do not drive the vehicle with the air cleaner removed. Doing so will allow dirt and a variety of other foreign particles to enter the engine and cause damage and wear. Also, backfiring could cause a fire in the engine compartment.

Fuel Filter

REMOVAL & INSTALLATION

▶ **See Figures 45 and 46**

✳✳ CAUTION

Observe all applicable safety precautions when working around fuel. Whenever servicing the fuel system, always work in a well ventilated area. Do not allow fuel spray or vapors to come in contact with a spark or open flame. Keep a dry chemical fire extinguisher near the work area. Always keep fuel in a container specifically designed for fuel storage; also, always properly seal fuel containers to avoid the possibility of fire or explosion.

There are 2 types of fittings used on fuel filter connections. The banjo fitting or union bolt type uses a bolt and 2 washers to prevent leakage between an eye-

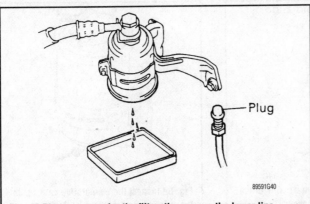

Fig. 45 Place a pan under the filter, the remove the lower line

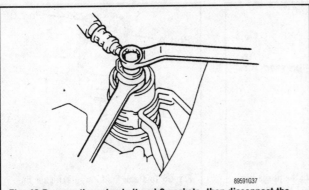

Fig. 46 Remove the union bolt and 2 gaskets, then disconnect the inlet hose from the fuel filter

let and the filter. The flare fitting type uses no washers or bolts. It uses a thread interference pattern to make a tight connection.

1. Unbolt the retaining screws and remove the protective shield (if equipped) for the fuel filter.

2. Place a pan under the delivery pipe (large connection) to catch the dripping fuel and SLOWLY loosen the banjo fitting bolt or flare fitting at the bottom of the filter to bleed off the fuel pressure.

✳✳ CAUTION

To avoid personal injury, remember that the fuel system is under pressure. Release pressure slowly and contain spillage. Wear eye protection and observe no smoking/no open flame precautions. Have a dry powder fire extinguisher within arm's reach at all times.

3. Remove the banjo bolt or flare fitting and drain the remaining fuel.
4. Disconnect and plug the inlet line.
5. Unbolt and carefully remove the fuel filter. It may still contain some fuel.

To install:

➡ **When tightening the fuel line bolts to the fuel filter, you must use a torque wrench. The tightening torque is very important, as under or over tightening may cause fuel leakage. Insure that there is sufficient clearance between the fuel filter, lines and any other parts.**

6. Coat the flare or banjo bolt threads along with the copper washers lightly with engine oil. Always use new washers.

7. Hand tighten the inlet line to the fuel filter.

8. Install the fuel filter then tighten the banjo type bolt to 22 ft. lbs. (29 Nm) or the flare fitting on the fuel pump side to 17 ft. lbs. (24 Nm) and all others to 22 ft. lbs. (30 Nm).

✳✳ WARNING

The fuel pump builds high pressure within the lines. If new gaskets are not used, a high-pressure leak may spray fuel onto the engine or other hot surface.

9. Run the engine for a few minutes and check for any fuel leaks.
10. Install the protective shield if removed.

PCV Valve

The Positive Crankcase Ventilation (PCV) valve regulates the release of crankcase vapors during various engine operating conditions. As the engine operates, some combustion gas will escape from the cylinder by passing the piston rings. These gasses accumulate in the oil pan. Since a small amount of vapor is added on every piston stroke, the pressure within the oil pan quickly builds. If these vapors are not allowed to escape through a planned path they will quickly find their own exit, usually by forcing a hole in an engine gasket.

Since the gasses contain hydrocarbons and other pollutants, they cannot simply be vented to the atmosphere. The PCV valve allows the release of the vapors under controlled conditions back into the intake air stream. The vapors are then mixed with the incoming air, reintroduced to the combustion chamber and reburned. At high vacuum (idle speed and partial load range) the PCV will open slightly and at low vacuum (full throttle) it will open fully. This causes vapor to be removed from the crankcase by the engine vacuum and then sucked into the combustion chamber where it is dissipated.

REMOVAL & INSTALLATION

▶ **See Figures 47, 48, 49, 50 and 51**

The PCV valve regulates crankcase ventilation during various engine operating conditions. Inspect the PCV valve system every 60,000 miles (96,000 km) or every 36 months. Toyota Motor Corporation recommends replacing the PCV valve every 15,000 miles (24,000 km).

1. Open and support the hood.

2. Locate the PCV valve in the valve cover or from the manifold-to-crankcase hose and remove it. Clean any gum deposits from the orifices by spraying the valve with carburetor or contact cleaner.

3. Visually inspect all hose connections and hoses for cracks, clogs or deterioration and replace as necessary.

4. Inspect the grommet the PCV valve sits in. Replace if necessary. If replacing, use a small amount of clean engine oil to help insert the grommet into the cover.

5. Install the PCV valve. Make sure all hose connections are tight.

Evaporative Canister

SERVICING

◆ **See Figures 52, 53, 54 and 55**

The canister cycles the fuel vapor from the fuel tank. The activated charcoal element within the canister acts as a storage device for the fuel vapors at times when the engine operating conditions do not allow efficient burning of the vapors.

The only required service for the canister is inspection at the intervals specified in the Maintenance Chart at the end of this section. If the charcoal element is saturated, the entire canister will require replacement. Label and disconnect the canister purge hoses, loosen the retaining bracket bolt(s) and lift out the canister. Installation is simply the reverse of the removal process. To check the canister:

1. Label and remove the vacuum lines leading to the canister.
2. Unfasten the retaining bolts from the canister.
3. Pull the lower hose off the tube attached to the lower portion of the canister.
4. Inspect the case for any cracking or damage.
5. Using low pressure compressed air, blow into the tank pipe (flanged end) and check that air flows freely from the other ports.
6. Blow into the purge pipe (next to tank pipe) and check that air does not flow from the other ports. If air does flow, the check valve has failed and the canister must be replaced.

Fig. 47 Grasp the clamp over the hose attached to the PCV valve . . .

Fig. 48 . . . next pull off the hose from the valve

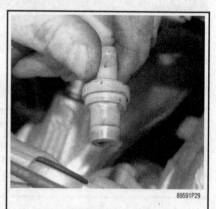
Fig. 49 The PCV valve pulls right out

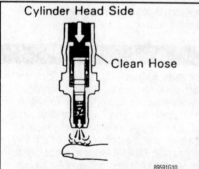
Fig. 50 Blow air into the cylinder head side of the PCV valve and check for air flow from the other end

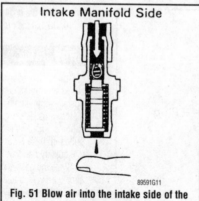
Fig. 51 Blow air into the intake side of the PCV, little air flow should occur

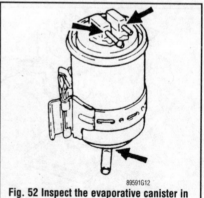
Fig. 52 Inspect the evaporative canister in these locations for cracks or damage

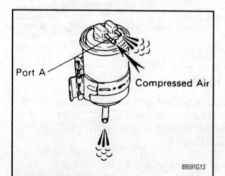
Fig. 53 Blow low pressure air into the tank pipe end and check for free air flow from the other ports

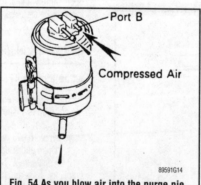
Fig. 54 As you blow air into the purge pie, limited air flow should come from the other ports

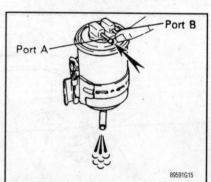
Fig. 55 To clean the filter, place your finger on the purge pipe, then apply air into the tank pipe

7. Never attempt to clean the canister with fluid or solvent. Low pressure air 43 psi (294 kPa) maximum may be used to evaporate any vapors within the canister. When applying the air, hold a finger over the purge pipe to force all the air out the bottom port.

8. No carbon should come out of the filter at any time. Loose charcoal is a sign of internal failure in the canister.

Battery

PRECAUTIONS

Always use caution when working on or near the battery. Never allow a tool to bridge the gap between the negative and positive battery terminals. Also, be careful not to allow a tool to provide a ground between the positive cable/terminal and any metal component on the vehicle. Either of these conditions will cause a short circuit, leading to sparks and possible personal injury.

Do not smoke, have an open flame or create sparks near a battery; the gases contained in the battery are very explosive and, if ignited, could cause severe injury or death.

All batteries, regardless of type, should be carefully secured by a battery hold-down device. If this is not done, the battery terminals or casing may crack from stress applied to the battery during vehicle operation. A battery which is not secured may allow acid to leak out, making it discharge faster; such leaking corrosive acid can also eat away at components under the hood.

Always visually inspect the battery case for cracks, leakage and corrosion. A white corrosive substance on the battery case or on nearby components would indicate a leaking or cracked battery. If the battery is cracked, it should be replaced immediately.

GENERAL MAINTENANCE

▶ See Figure 56

A battery that is not sealed must be checked periodically for electrolyte level. You cannot add water to a sealed maintenance-free battery (though not all maintenance-free batteries are sealed); however, a sealed battery must also be checked for proper electrolyte level, as indicated by the color of the built-in hydrometer "eye."

Always keep the battery cables and terminals free of corrosion. Check these components about once a year. Refer to the removal, installation and cleaning procedures outlined in this section.

Keep the top of the battery clean, as a film of dirt can help completely discharge a battery that is not used for long periods. A solution of baking soda and water may be used for cleaning, but be careful to flush this off with clear water. DO NOT let any of the solution into the filler holes. Baking soda neutralizes battery acid and will de-activate a battery cell.

Batteries in vehicles which are not operated on a regular basis can fall victim to parasitic loads (small current drains which are constantly drawing current from the battery). Normal parasitic loads may drain a battery on a vehicle that is in storage and not used for 6–8 weeks. Vehicles that have additional accessories such as a cellular phone, an alarm system or other devices that increase parasitic load may discharge a battery sooner. If the vehicle is to be stored for 6–8 weeks in a secure area and the alarm system, if present, is not necessary, the negative battery cable should be disconnected at the onset of storage to protect the battery charge.

Remember that constantly discharging and recharging will shorten battery life. Take care not to allow a battery to be needlessly discharged.

BATTERY FLUID

▶ See Figures 57 and 58

Check the battery electrolyte level at least once a month, or more often in hot weather or during periods of extended vehicle operation. On non-sealed batteries, the level can be checked either through the case on translucent batteries or by removing the cell caps on opaque-cased types. The electrolyte level in each cell should be kept filled to the split ring inside each cell, or the line marked on the outside of the case.

If the level is low, add only distilled water through the opening until the level is correct. Each cell is separate from the others, so each must be checked and filled individually. Distilled water should be used, because the chemicals and minerals found in most drinking water are harmful to the battery and could significantly shorten its life.

If water is added in freezing weather, the vehicle should be driven several miles to allow the water to mix with the electrolyte. Otherwise, the battery could freeze.

Although some maintenance-free batteries have removable cell caps for access to the electrolyte, the electrolyte condition and level on all sealed maintenance-free batteries must be checked using the built-in hydrometer "eye." The exact type of eye varies between battery manufacturers, but most apply a sticker to the battery itself explaining the possible readings. When in doubt, refer to the battery manufacturer's instructions to interpret battery condition using the built-in hydrometer.

➡Although the readings from built-in hydrometers found in sealed batteries may vary, a green eye usually indicates a properly charged battery with sufficient fluid level. A dark eye is normally an indicator of a battery with sufficient fluid, but one which may be low in charge. And a light or yellow eye is usually an indication that electrolyte supply has dropped below the necessary level for battery (and hydrometer) operation. In this last case, sealed batteries with an insufficient electrolyte level must usually be discarded.

Checking the Specific Gravity

▶ See Figures 59, 60 and 61

A hydrometer is required to check the specific gravity on all batteries that are not maintenance-free. On batteries that are maintenance-free, the specific gravity is checked by observing the built-in hydrometer "eye" on the top of the battery case. Check with your battery's manufacturer for proper interpretation of its built-in hydrometer readings.

✳✳ CAUTION

Battery electrolyte contains sulfuric acid. If you should splash any on your skin or in your eyes, flush the affected area with plenty of clear water. If it lands in your eyes, get medical help immediately.

Fig. 56 A typical location for the built-in hydrometer on maintenance-free batteries

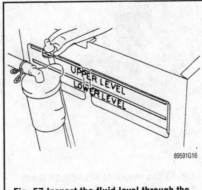

Fig. 57 Inspect the fluid level through the side of the battery

Fig. 58 Insert water in each low cell using a bulb type syringe

Fig. 59 On non-maintenance-free batteries, the fluid level can be checked through the case on translucent models; the cell caps must be removed on other models

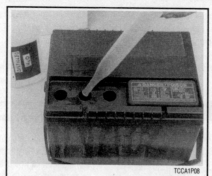

Fig. 60 If the fluid level is low, add only distilled water through the opening until the level is correct

Fig. 61 Check the specific gravity of the battery's electrolyte with a hydrometer

The fluid (sulfuric acid solution) contained in the battery cells will tell you many things about the condition of the battery. Because the cell plates must be kept submerged below the fluid level in order to operate, maintaining the fluid level is extremely important. And, because the specific gravity of the acid is an indication of electrical charge, testing the fluid can be an aid in determining if the battery must be replaced. A battery in a vehicle with a properly operating charging system should require little maintenance, but careful, periodic inspection should reveal problems before they leave you stranded.

As stated earlier, the specific gravity of a battery's electrolyte level can be used as an indication of battery charge. At least once a year, check the specific gravity of the battery. It should be between 1.20 and 1.26 on the gravity scale. Most auto supply stores carry a variety of inexpensive battery testing hydrometers. These can be used on any non-sealed battery to test the specific gravity in each cell.

The battery testing hydrometer has a squeeze bulb at one end and a nozzle at the other. Battery electrolyte is sucked into the hydrometer until the float is lifted from its seat. The specific gravity is then read by noting the position of the float. If gravity is low in one or more cells, the battery should be slowly charged and checked again to see if the gravity has come up. Generally, if after charging, the specific gravity between any two cells varies more than 50 points (0.50), the battery should be replaced, as it can no longer produce sufficient voltage to guarantee proper operation.

CABLES

▶ See Figures 62, 63, 64, 65 and 66

Once a year (or as necessary), the battery terminals and the cable clamps should be cleaned. Loosen the clamps and remove the cables, negative cable first. On batteries with posts on top, the use of a puller specially made for this purpose is recommended. These are inexpensive and available in most auto parts stores. Side terminal battery cables are secured with a small bolt.

Clean the cable clamps and the battery terminal with a wire brush, until all corrosion, grease, etc., is removed and the metal is shiny. It is especially important to clean the inside of the clamp thoroughly (an old knife is useful here), since a small deposit of foreign material or oxidation there will prevent a sound electrical connection and inhibit either starting or charging. Special tools are available for cleaning these parts, one type for conventional top post batteries and another type for side terminal batteries. It is also a good idea to apply some dielectric grease to the terminal, as this will aid in the prevention of corrosion.

After the clamps and terminals are clean, reinstall the cables, negative cable last; DO NOT hammer the clamps onto battery posts. Tighten the clamps securely, but do not distort them. Give the clamps and terminals a thin external coating of grease after installation, to retard corrosion.

Check the cables at the same time that the terminals are cleaned. If the cable insulation is cracked or broken, or if the ends are frayed, the cable should be replaced with a new cable of the same length and gauge.

CHARGING

✳✳ CAUTION

The chemical reaction which takes place in all batteries generates explosive hydrogen gas. A spark can cause the battery to explode and splash acid. To avoid serious personal injury, be sure there is proper ventilation and take appropriate fire safety precautions when connecting, disconnecting, or charging a battery and when using jumper cables.

A battery should be charged at a slow rate to keep the plates inside from getting too hot. However, if some maintenance-free batteries are allowed to discharge until they are almost "dead," they may have to be charged at a high rate to bring them back to "life." Always follow the charger manufacturer's instructions on charging the battery.

REPLACEMENT

When it becomes necessary to replace the battery, select one with an amperage rating equal to or greater than the battery originally installed. Deterioration and just plain aging of the battery cables, starter motor, and associated wires

Fig. 62 Maintenance is performed with household items and with special tools like this post cleaner

Fig. 63 The underside of this special battery tool has a wire brush to clean post terminals

Fig. 64 Place the tool over the battery posts and twist to clean until the metal is shiny

makes the battery's job harder in successive years. The slow increase in electrical resistance over time makes it prudent to install a new battery with a greater capacity than the old.

Belts

INSPECTION

▶ See Figures 67 thru 72

Inspect the belts for signs of glazing or cracking. A glazed belt will be perfectly smooth from slippage, while a good belt will have a slight texture of fabric visible. Cracks will usually start at the inner edge of the belt and run outward. All worn or damaged drive belts should be replaced immediately. It is best to replace all drive belts at one time, as a preventive maintenance measure, during this service operation.

ADJUSTMENT

Alternator

▶ See Figures 73 and 74

To adjust the tension of the alternator drive belt, loosen the pivot and mounting bolts on the alternator. These bolts should be either 12mm or 14mm. Using a wooden hammer handle or a broomstick, or even your hand if you're strong enough, move the alternator one way or the other until the tension is within acceptable limits.

✳✳ CAUTION

Never use a screwdriver or any other metal device such as a prybar, as a lever when adjusting the alternator belt tension!

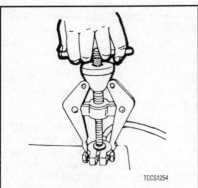

Fig. 65 A special tool is available to pull the clamp from the post

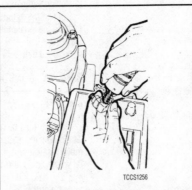

Fig. 66 The cable ends should be cleaned as well

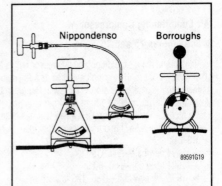

Fig. 67 Types of belt tension gauges used for checking belt tension

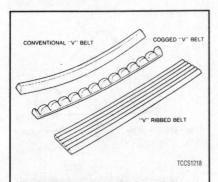

Fig. 68 There are typically 3 types of accessory drive belts found on vehicles today

Fig. 69 An example of a healthy drive belt

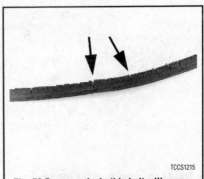

Fig. 70 Deep cracks in this belt will cause flex, building up heat that will eventually lead to belt failure

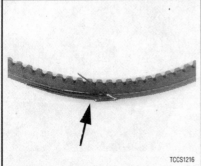

Fig. 71 The cover of this belt is worn, exposing the critical reinforcing cords to excessive wear

Fig. 72 Installing too wide a belt can result in serious belt wear and/or breakage

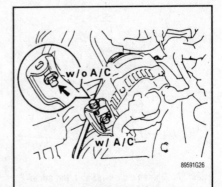

Fig. 73 Alternator adjusting bolt location—5S-FE engine

Tighten the mounting bolts securely. If a new belt has been installed, always recheck the tension after a few hundred miles of driving.

Alternator belt tension on all other engines is adjusted by means of a tension adjusting bolt with is usually a 12mm or 14mm. Loosen the alternator pivot bolt and the locking bolt, then turn the tension adjusting bolt until proper tension is achieved.

Tighten the mounting bolts securely. If a new belt has been installed, always recheck the tension after a few hundred miles of driving.

5S-FE:
- 1994 new belt w/AC—155–175 lb
- 1994–98 new belt w/o AC—100–150 lb
- 1994 used belt w/AC—100–120 lb
- 1994–98 used belt w/o AC—75–115 lb
- 1995–98 new belt w/AC—170–180 lb
- 1995–98 used belt w/AC—95–135 lb

7A-FE:
- 1994–98 new belt—170–180 lb
- 1994–98 used belt—95–135 lb

Air Conditioning Compressor

▶ **See Figures 75 and 76**

Tension on the air conditioning compressor belt is adjusted by means of an idler pulley. Loosen the lockbolt and then turn the adjusting bolt on the idler pulley until the desired tension is achieved. Retighten the idler pulley lockbolt. All of the bolts are either a 12mm or 14mm.

Tighten the lockbolt securely. If a new belt has been installed, always recheck the tension after a few hundred miles of driving.

5S-FE:
- 1994 new belt—140–150 lb
- 1994 used belt—60–80 lb
- 1995–98 new belt—135–185 lb
- 1995–98 used belt—100–120 lb

7A-FE:
- 1994 new belt—120–140 lb
- 1994 used belt—60–80 lb
- 1995–98 new belt—170–180 lb
- 1995–98 used belt—95–135 lb

Power Steering Pump

▶ **See Figure 77**

On some models, tension on the power steering pump belt is adjusted by means of an idler pulley. Loosen the lockbolt and then turn the adjusting bolt on the idler pulley until the desired tension is achieved. Retighten the idler pulley lockbolt. All of these bolts are usually a 12mm or 14mm.

Tighten the lockbolt securely. If a new belt has been installed, always recheck the tension after a few hundred miles of driving.

Power steering pump belt tension on other models is adjusted by means of a tension adjusting bolt. Loosen the power steering pump pivot bolt and then turn the tension adjusting bolt until proper tension is achieved.

Tighten the mounting bolts securely. If a new belt has been installed, always recheck the tension after a few hundred miles of driving.
- New belt—99–121 lb
- Used belt—44–77 lb

REMOVAL & INSTALLATION

▶ **See Figures 78, 79, 80, 81 and 82**

If a belt must be replaced, the driven unit must be loosened and moved to its extreme loosest position, generally by moving it toward the center of the motor. After removing the old belt, check the pulleys for dirt or built-up material which could affect belt contact. Carefully install the new belt, remembering that it is new and unused — it may appear to be just a little too small to fit over the pulley flanges. Fit the belt over the largest pulley (usually the crank-

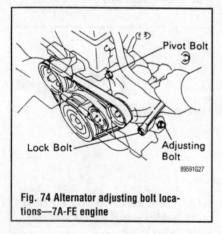

Fig. 74 Alternator adjusting bolt locations—7A-FE engine

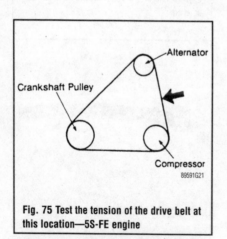

Fig. 75 Test the tension of the drive belt at this location—5S-FE engine

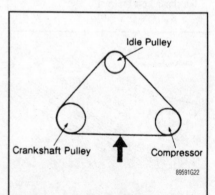

Fig. 76 Test the tension of the drive belt at this location—7A-FE engine

Fig. 77 Tighten the power steering pump once the drive belt tension is adjusted

Fig. 78 On some components a front pulley bolt must be loosened . . . .

Fig. 79 . . . then the upper bolt so you can . . .

Fig. 80 . . . lift up and remove the drive belt

Fig. 81 Once the front belt is removed you can access the other belts in need of replacement

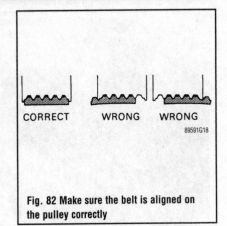

Fig. 82 Make sure the belt is aligned on the pulley correctly

shaft pulley at the bottom center of the motor) first, then work on the smaller one(s). Gentle pressure in the direction of rotation is helpful. Some belts run around a third or idler pulley, which acts as an additional pivot in the belt's path. It may be possible to loosen the idler pulley as well as the main component, making your job much easier. Depending on which belt(s) you are changing, it may be necessary to loosen or remove other interfering belts to get at the one(s) you want.

When buying replacement belts, remember that the fit is critical according to the length of the belt, the width of the belt, the depth of the belt and the angle or profile of the V shape (always match up old belt with new belt if possible). The belt shape should exactly match the shape of the pulley; belts that are not an exact match can cause noise, slippage and premature failure.

After the new belt is installed, draw tension on it by moving the driven unit away from the motor and tighten its mounting bolts. This is sometimes a three- or four-handed job; you may find an assistant helpful. Make sure that all the bolts you loosened get retightened and that any other loosened belts also have the correct tension. A new belt can be expected to stretch a bit after installation so be prepared to re-adjust your new belt.

➡️ After installing a new belt, run the engine for about 5 minutes and then recheck the belt tension.

Timing Belts

SERVICING

The 5S-FE and 7A-FE engines utilizes a timing belt to drive the camshaft from the crankshaft's turning motion and to maintain proper valve timing. Some manufacturer's schedule periodic timing belt replacement to assure optimum engine performance, to make sure the motorist is never stranded should the belt break (as the engine will stop instantly) and for some (manufacturer's with inter-

ference motors) to prevent the possibility of severe internal engine damage should the belt break.

Although the 5S-FE and 7A-FE engines are not listed as interference motors (it is not listed by the manufacturer as a motor whose valves might contact the pistons if the camshaft was rotated separately from the crankshaft) the first 2 reasons for periodic replacement still apply. Toyota publishes a replacement interval for these motors. The recommend interval is 60,000 miles (96,000 km). Refer to Section 3 for Removal & Installation.

It would be wise to check it periodically to make sure it has not become damaged or worn. Generally speaking, a severely worn belt may cause engine performance to drop dramatically, but a damaged belt (which could give out suddenly) may not give as much warning. In general, any time the engine timing cover(s) is(are) removed you should inspect the belt for premature parting, severe cracks or missing teeth.

Hoses

INSPECTION

◆ See Figures 83, 84, 85 and 86

Upper and lower radiator hoses along with the heater hoses should be checked for deterioration, leaks and loose hose clamps at least every 15,000 miles (48,000 km). It is also wise to check the hoses periodically in early spring and at the beginning of the fall or winter when you are performing other maintenance. A quick visual inspection could discover a weakened hose which might have left you stranded if it had remained unprepared.

Whenever you are checking the hoses, make sure the engine and cooling system are cold. Visually inspect for cracking, rotting or collapsed hoses, and replace as necessary. Run your hand along the length of the hose. If a weak or swollen spot is noted when squeezing the hose wall, the hose should be replaced.

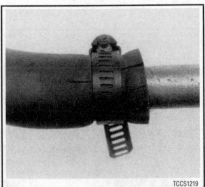

Fig. 83 The cracks developing along this hose are a result of age-related hardening

Fig. 84 A hose clamp that is too tight can cause older hoses to separate and tear on either side of the clamp

Fig. 85 A soft spongy hose (identifiable by the swollen section) will eventually burst and should be replaced

Fig. 86 Hoses are likely to deteriorate from the inside if the cooling system is not periodically flushed

REMOVAL & INSTALLATION

♦ See Figure 87

1. Remove the radiator pressure cap.

✳✳ CAUTION

Never remove the pressure cap while the engine is running, or personal injury from scalding hot coolant or steam may result. If possible, wait until the engine has cooled to remove the pressure cap. If this is not possible, wrap a thick cloth around the pressure cap and turn it slowly to the stop. Step back while the pressure is released from the cooling system. When you are sure all the pressure has been released, use the cloth to turn and remove the cap.

2. Position a clean container under the radiator and/or engine draincock or plug, then open the drain and allow the cooling system to drain to an appropriate level. For some upper hoses, only a little coolant must be drained. To remove hoses positioned lower on the engine, such as a lower radiator hose, the entire cooling system must be emptied.

✳✳ CAUTION

When draining coolant, keep in mind that cats and dogs are attracted by ethylene glycol antifreeze, and are quite likely to drink any that is left in an uncovered container or in puddles on the ground. This will prove fatal in sufficient quantity. Always drain coolant into a sealable container. Coolant may be reused unless it is contaminated or several years old.

3. Loosen the hose clamps at each end of the hose requiring replacement. Clamps are usually either of the spring tension type (which require pliers to squeeze the tabs and loosen) or of the screw tension type (which require screw or hex drivers to loosen). Pull the clamps back on the hose away from the connection.

4. Twist, pull and slide the hose off the fitting, taking care not to damage the neck of the component from which the hose is being removed.

➡If the hose is stuck at the connection, do not try to insert a screwdriver or other sharp tool under the hose end in an effort to free it, as the connection and/or hose may become damaged. Heater connections especially may be easily damaged by such a procedure. If the hose is to be replaced, use a single-edged razor blade to make a slice along the portion of the hose which is stuck on the connection, perpendicular to the end of the hose. Do not cut deep so as to prevent damaging the connection. The hose can then be peeled from the connection and discarded.

5. Clean both hose mounting connections. Inspect the condition of the hose clamps and replace them, if necessary.

To install:

6. Dip the ends of the new hose into clean engine coolant to ease installation.

7. Slide the clamps over the replacement hose, then slide the hose ends over the connections into position.

8. Position and secure the clamps at least ¼ inch (6.35mm) from the ends of the hose. Make sure they are located beyond the raised bead of the connector.

9. Close the radiator or engine drains and properly refill the cooling system with the clean drained engine coolant or a suitable mixture of ethylene glycol coolant and water.

10. If available, install a pressure tester and check for leaks. If a pressure tester is not available, run the engine until normal operating temperature is reached (allowing the system to naturally pressurize), then check for leaks.

✳✳ CAUTION

If you are checking for leaks with the system at normal operating temperature, BE EXTREMELY CAREFUL not to touch any moving or hot engine parts. Once temperature has been reached, shut the engine OFF, and check for leaks around the hose fittings and connections which were removed earlier.

CV-Boots

INSPECTION

♦ See Figures 88 and 89

The CV (Constant Velocity) boots should be checked for damage each time the oil is changed and any other time the vehicle is raised for service. These boots keep water, grime, dirt and other damaging matter from entering the CV-joints. Any of these could cause early CV-joint failure which can be expensive to repair. Heavy grease thrown around the inside of the front wheel(s) and on the brake caliper/drum can be an indication of a torn boot. Thoroughly check the boots for missing clamps and tears. If the boot is damaged, it should be replaced immediately. Please refer to Section 7 for procedures.

Fig. 87 Grasp the hose clamp. squeeze tightly and pull back

Fig. 88 CV-boots must be inspected periodically for damage

Fig. 89 A torn boot should be replaced immediately

Spark Plugs

▶ See Figure 90

A typical spark plug consists of a metal shell surrounding a ceramic insulator. A metal electrode extends downward through the center of the insulator and protrudes a small distance. Located at the end of the plug and attached to the side of the outer metal shell is the side electrode. The side electrode bends in at a 90° angle so that its tip is just past and parallel to the tip of the center electrode. The distance between these two electrodes (measured in thousandths of an inch or hundredths of a millimeter) is called the spark plug gap.

The spark plug does not produce a spark but instead provides a gap across which the current can arc. The coil produces anywhere from 20,000 to 50,000 volts (depending on the type and application) which travels through the wires to the spark plugs. The current passes along the center electrode and jumps the gap to the side electrode, and in doing so, ignites the air/fuel mixture in the combustion chamber.

SPARK PLUG HEAT RANGE

▶ See Figure 91

Spark plug heat range is the ability of the plug to dissipate heat. The longer the insulator (or the farther it extends into the engine), the hotter the plug will operate; the shorter the insulator (the closer the electrode is to the block's cooling passages) the cooler it will operate. A plug that absorbs little heat and remains too cool will quickly accumulate deposits of oil and carbon since it is not hot enough to burn them off. This leads to plug fouling and consequently to misfiring. A plug that absorbs too much heat will have no deposits but, due to the excessive heat, the electrodes will burn away quickly and might possibly lead to preignition or other ignition problems. Preignition takes place when plug tips get so hot that they glow sufficiently to ignite the air/fuel mixture before the actual spark occurs. This early ignition will usually cause a pinging during low speeds and heavy loads.

The general rule of thumb for choosing the correct heat range when picking a spark plug is: if most of your driving is long distance, high speed travel, use a colder plug; if most of your driving is stop and go, use a hotter plug. Original equipment plugs are generally a good compromise between the 2 styles and most people never have the need to change their plugs from the factory-recommended heat range.

REMOVAL & INSTALLATION

▶ See Figure 92

On the 7A-FE engine the spark plugs require replacement every 30,000 miles (48,000 km). On the 5S-FE engines the spark plugs are platinum and require replacement every 60,000 miles (96,000 km). In normal operation plug gap increases about 0.001 inch (0.025mm) for every 2500 miles (4000 km). As the gap increases, the plug's voltage requirement also increases. It requires a greater voltage to jump the wider gap and about two to three times as much voltage to fire the plug at high speeds than at idle. The improved air/fuel ratio control of modern fuel injection combined with the higher voltage output of modern ignition systems will often allow an engine to run significantly longer on a set of standard spark plugs, but keep in mind that efficiency will drop as the gap widens (along with fuel economy and power).

When you're removing spark plugs, work on one at a time. Don't start by removing the plug wires all at once, because, unless you number them, they may become mixed up. Take a minute before you begin and number the wires with tape.

1. Turn the ignition switch to the **LOCK** position.
2. Disconnect the negative battery cable, and if the vehicle has been run recently, allow the engine to thoroughly cool. Wait at least 90 seconds once the negative battery cable is disconnected to hinder air bag deployment.

✳✳ CAUTION

Models covered by this manual may be equipped with a Supplemental Restraint System (SRS), which uses an air bag. Whenever working near any of the SRS components, such as the impact sensors, the air bag module, steering column and instrument panel, disable the SRS, as described in Section 6.

3. Carefully twist the spark plug wire boot to loosen it, then pull upward and remove the boot from the plug. Be sure to pull on the boot and not on the wire, otherwise the connector located inside the boot may become separated.
4. Using compressed air, blow any water or debris from the spark plug well to assure that no harmful contaminants are allowed to enter the combustion chamber when the spark plug is removed. If compressed air is not available, use a rag or a brush to clean the area.

➡Remove the spark plugs when the engine is cold, if possible, to prevent damage to the threads. If removal of the plugs is difficult, apply a few drops of penetrating oil or silicone spray to the area around the base of the plug, and allow it a few minutes to work.

5. Using a spark plug socket that is equipped with a rubber insert to properly hold the plug, turn the spark plug counterclockwise to loosen and remove the spark plug from the bore. A 16mm socket is usually used to remove the spark plugs on these Celcia engines.

✳✳ WARNING

Be sure not to use a flexible extension on the socket. Use of a flexible extension may allow a shear force to be applied to the plug. A shear force could break the plug off in the cylinder head, leading to costly and frustrating repairs.

To install:
6. Inspect the spark plug boot for tears or damage. If a damaged boot is found, the spark plug wire must be replaced.
7. Using a wire feeler gauge, check and adjust the spark plug gap. When using a gauge, the proper size should pass between the electrodes with a slight drag. The next larger size should not be able to pass while the next smaller size should pass freely.
8. Carefully thread the plug into the bore with the (extension and socket) by hand. If resistance is felt before the plug is almost completely threaded, back the plug out and begin threading again. In small, hard to reach areas, an old spark plug wire and boot could be used as a threading tool. The boot will hold the plug while you twist the end of the wire and the wire is supple enough to twist before it would allow the plug to crossthread.

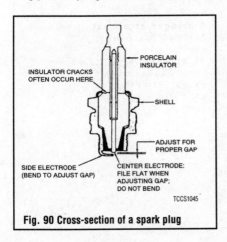

Fig. 90 Cross-section of a spark plug

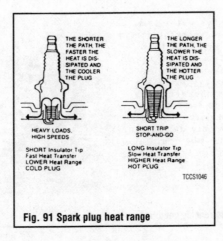

Fig. 91 Spark plug heat range

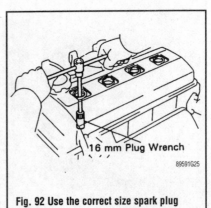

Fig. 92 Use the correct size spark plug wrench with socket to extract the plug

Do not use the spark plug socket to thread the plugs. Always carefully thread the plug by hand or using an old plug wire to prevent the possibility of crossthreading and damaging the cylinder head bore.

9. Using the 16mm socket, carefully tighten the spark plug. If the plug you are installing is equipped with a crush washer, seat the plug, then tighten about ¼ turn to crush the washer. If you are installing a tapered seat plug, tighten the plug to 13 ft. lbs. (18 Nm).

10. Apply a small amount of silicone dielectric compound to the end of the spark plug lead or inside the spark plug boot to prevent sticking, then install the boot to the spark plug and push until it clicks into place. The click may be felt or heard, then gently pull back on the boot to assure proper contact.

INSPECTION & GAPPING

▶ See Figures 93, 94, 95, 96 and 97

Check the plugs for deposits and wear. If they are not going to be replaced, clean the plugs thoroughly. Remember that any kind of deposit will decrease the efficiency of the plug. Plugs can be cleaned on a spark plug cleaning machine, which can sometimes be found in service stations, or you can do an acceptable job of cleaning with a stiff brush. If the plugs are cleaned, the electrodes must be filed flat. Use an ignition points file, not an emery board or the like, which will leave deposits. The electrodes must be filed perfectly flat with sharp edges; rounded edges reduce the spark plug voltage by as much as 50%.

Check spark plug gap before installation. All Toyota spark plugs from the

A **normally worn** spark plug should have light tan or gray deposits on the firing tip.

A **carbon fouled** plug, identified by soft, sooty, black deposits, may indicate an improperly tuned vehicle. Check the air cleaner, ignition components and engine control system.

This spark plug has been **left in the engine too long,** as evidenced by the extreme gap- Plugs with such an extreme gap can cause misfiring and stumbling accompanied by a noticeable lack of power.

An **oil fouled** spark plug indicates an engine with worn poston rings and/or bad valve seals allowing excessive oil to enter the chamber.

A **physically damaged** spark plug may be evidence of severe detonation in that cylinder. Watch that cylinder carefully between services, as a continued detonation will not only damage the plug, but could also damage the engine.

A **bridged or almost bridged** spark plug, identified by a build-up between the electrodes caused by excessive carbon or oil build-up on the plug.

TCCA1P40

Fig. 93 Inspect the spark plug to determine engine running conditions

manufacture are already pregapped, but do not assume that the gap is correct, check them anyway prior to installation. The ground electrode (the L-shaped one connected to the body of the plug) must be parallel to the center electrode and the specified size wire gauge (please refer to the Tune-Up Specifications chart for details) must pass between the electrodes with a slight drag.

➡**NEVER adjust the gap on a used platinum type spark plug.**

Always check the gap on new plugs as they are not always set correctly at the factory. Do not use a flat feeler gauge when measuring the gap on a used plug, because the reading may be inaccurate. A round-wire type gapping tool is the best way to check the gap. The correct gauge should pass through the electrode gap with a slight drag. If you're in doubt, try one size smaller and one larger. The smaller gauge should go through easily, while the larger one shouldn't go through at all. Wire gapping tools usually have a bending tool attached. Use that to adjust the side electrode until the proper distance is obtained. Absolutely never attempt to bend the center electrode. Also, be careful not to bend the side electrode too far or too often as it may weaken and break off within the engine, requiring removal of the cylinder head to retrieve it.

Spark Plug Wires

TESTING

▶ **See Figure 98**

At every tune-up/inspection, visually check the spark plug cables for burns cuts, or breaks in the insulation. Check the boots and the nipples on the distributor cap and/or coil. Replace any damaged wiring.

Every 50,000 miles (80,000 Km) or 60 months, the resistance of the wires should be checked with an ohmmeter. Wires with excessive resistance will cause misfiring, and may make the engine difficult to start in damp weather.

To check resistance, remove each plug wire and test one at a time. Connect one lead of an ohmmeter to the electrode within the wire on the cap end; connect the other lead to the corresponding spark plug terminal end of the wire. Replace any wire which shows a resistance of over 25,000 ohms.

REMOVAL & INSTALLATION

▶ **See Figures 99 thru 106**

Some California 5S-FE models were equipped with a coil wire.
1. Label and disconnect the wires from each spark plug one at a time. Some engines have spark plug wires which are labeled, No. 1, No. 2 ect. from the manufacture.

➡**If there is no tape around to label the wires. It may be a good idea to remove one spark plug wire at a time so not to mix them up during installation.**

2. Remove the spark plug wires from the distributor cap. On some models you may need to use a flat bladed tool to lift up the lock claw and disconnect the holder from the cap. Separate the wires at the grommet.

✳✳ WARNING

Do not pull on the plug wires to remove them, this may damage the conductor inside.

3. Pull the plug wires from the retaining clamps.
To install:
4. Attach the holder and grommet portion to the distributor cap. Make sure that the holder is installed correctly to the grommet and cap.
5. Check that the lock claw of the holder is engaged by lightly pulling on the holder.
6. On the coil wire (if equipped), insert the grommet and holder together.
7. Secure the wires with the clamps.

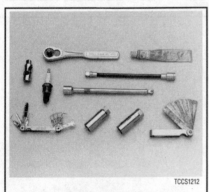

Fig. 94 A variety of tools and gauges are needed for spark plug service

TCCS1212

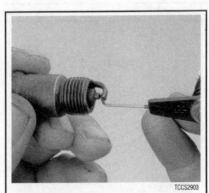

Fig. 95 Checking the spark plug gap with a feeler gauge

TCCS2903

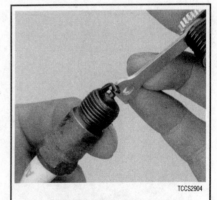

Fig. 96 Adjusting the spark plug gap

TCCS2904

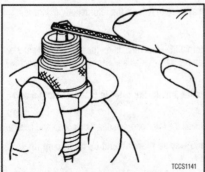

Fig. 97 If the standard plug is in good condition, the electrode may be filed flat—WARNING: do not file platinum plugs

TCCS1141

Fig. 98 Checking individual plug wire resistance with a digital ohmmeter

TCCS1009

Fig. 99 Grasp the plug wire from the cylinder head cover and pull upwards to extract

89591P24

Fig. 100 The cap is usually marked by Toyota with the ignition markings

Fig. 101 At the cap, use a screwdriver to lift up the lock claw and disconnect the holder

Fig. 102 Release this clip to withdraw the wire from the cap

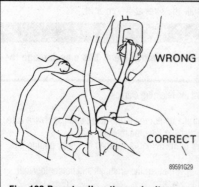

Fig. 103 Do not pull on the cords, it may damage the conductor inside

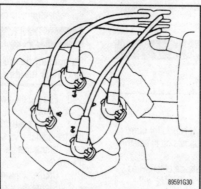

Fig. 104 Connect the holder and grommet portion to the cap . . .

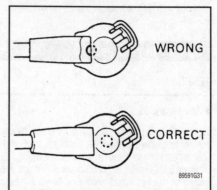

Fig. 105 . . . check that the holder is correctly installed as shown

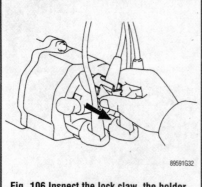

Fig. 106 Inspect the lock claw, the holder must be engaged. Lightly pull to inspect

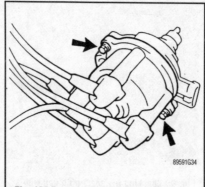

Fig. 107 Remove the bolts that secure the cap to the distributor

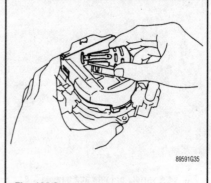

Fig. 108 Some rotors are removed by pulling up . . .

Distributor Cap and Rotor

REMOVAL & INSTALLATION

▶ **See Figures 107, 108, 109, 110 and 111**

1. Turn the ignition switch to the **LOCK** position.
2. If equipped, remove the distributor cap rubber boot.
3. On some models the air cleaner tube may need to be removed to access the distributor cap.
4. Loosen the screws securing the cap on the distributor. Depending on your engine you will have 2 or 3 screws.
5. Tag the wires leading to the cap for easy identification upon installation.
6. Lift the cap off the distributor. Pulling from the wire boot, remove the plug wires from the cap.
7. If necessary to remove the rotor, some models you simply lift it straight off the shaft. On others, you may need to remove the rotor retaining screws, then lift up the unit.

To install:

8. On the 1994–95 California 5S-FE engine, align the hollow of the signal rotor with the protrusion tab on the rotor. Install and secure the retaining screws of the rotor.

➡ **Do not tighten the screws too much, the rotor is made of plastic and could crack.**

9. On all other models, install the rotor onto the distributor shaft and secure.

➡ **The rotor only goes on one way so there should be no mix-up in replacement.**

10. Apply a small amount of dielectric grease on the tip of the rotor and the inside of the cap carbon ends.
11. Attach the tagged wires to their proper locations on the cap.
12. Fit the cap onto the distributor, then tighten the bolts securely.

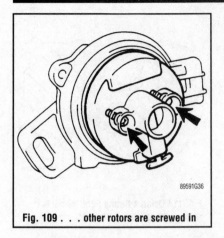

Fig. 109 . . . other rotors are screwed in

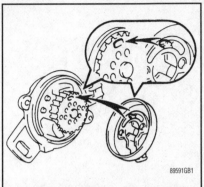

Fig. 110 Align the hollow of the signal rotor with the tab of the rotor when installing

Fig. 111 A cutout is on one side of the rotor, insert the rotor correctly

13. Make sure all the wires are secure on the cap and spark plugs.
14. Start the vehicle and check for proper operation.

INSPECTION

When inspecting a cap and rotor, look for signs of cracks, carbon tracking, burns and wear. The inside of the cap may be burnt or have wear on the carbon ends. On the rotor, look at the tip for burning and excessive wear.

Ignition Timing

GENERAL INFORMATION

Ignition timing is the measurement (in degrees) of crankshaft position at the instant the spark plug fires. Ignition timing is adjusted by loosening the distributor locking device and turning the distributor in the engine.

It takes a fraction of a second for the spark from the plug to completely ignite the mixture in the cylinder. Because of this, the spark plug must fire before the piston reaches TDC (top dead center, the highest point in its travel), if the mixture is to be completely ignited as the piston passes TDC. This measurement is given in degrees (of crankshaft rotation) before the piston reaches top dead center (BTDC). If the ignition timing setting for your engine is 10° BTDC, this means that the spark plug must fire at a time when the piston for that cylinder is 10° before top dead center of its compression stroke. However, this only holds true while your engine is at idle speed.

As you accelerate from idle, the speed of your engine (rpm) increases. The increase in rpm means that the pistons are now traveling up and down much faster. Because of this, the spark plugs will have to fire even sooner if the mixture is to be completely ignited as the piston passes TDC. To accomplish this, the distributor incorporates means to advance the timing of the spark as the engine speed increases.

On fuel injected vehicles there is no centrifugal advance or vacuum unit to advance the timing. All engine timing changes are controlled electronically by the ECU. This solid state "brain" ECU receives data from many sensors and commands changes in spark timing based on immediate driving conditions. This instant response allows the engine to be kept at peak performance and economy throughout the driving cycle. Basic timing and idle speed can still be checked and adjusted on these engines.

If the ignition timing is set too far advanced (BTDC), the ignition and expansion of the air/fuel mixture in the cylinder will try to force the piston down while it is still traveling upward. This causes engine ping, a sound which resembles marbles being dropped into an empty tin can. If the ignition timing is too far retarded (after, or ATDC), the piston will have already started down on the power stroke when the air/fuel mixture ignites and expands. This will cause the piston to be forced down only a portion of its travel. This results in poor engine performance and lack of power.

Ignition timing adjustment is checked with a timing light. This instrument is connected to the number one (No. 1) spark plug of the engine. The timing light flashes every time an electrical current is sent from the distributor through the No. 1 spark plug wire to the spark plug. The crankshaft pulley and the front cover of the engine are marked with a timing pointer and a timing scale.

When the timing pointer is aligned with the 0 mark on the timing scale, the piston in the No. 1 cylinder is at TDC of it compression stroke. With the engine running, and the timing light aimed at the timing pointer and timing scale, the stroboscopic (periodic) flashes from the timing light will allow you to check the ignition timing setting of the engine. The timing light flashes every time the spark plug in the No. 1 cylinder of the engine fires. Since the flash from the timing light makes the crankshaft pulley seem to stand still for a moment, you will be able to read the exact position of the piston in the No. 1 cylinder on the timing scale on the front of the engine.

If you're buying a timing light, make sure the unit you select is rated for electronic or solid-state ignitions. Generally, these lights have two wires which connect to the battery with alligator clips and a third wire which connects to the No. 1 plug wire. The best lights have an inductive pick-up on the third wire; this allows you to simply clip the small box over the wire. Older lights may require the removal of the plug wire and the installation of an in-line adapter. Since the spark plugs in the twin-cam engines are in deep wells, rigging the adapter can be difficult. Buy quality the first time and the tool will give lasting results and ease of use.

INSPECTION & ADJUSTMENT

1994–95 MODELS

▶ See Figures 112, 113, 114 and 115

This service procedure is for setting base ignition timing. Refer to underhood emission sticker for any additional service procedure steps and/or specifications.

These engines require a tachometer hook-up to the check connector—see illustrations. NEVER allow the tachometer terminal to become grounded; severe and expensive damage can occur to the coil and/or igniter.

Some tachometers are not compatible with this ignition system, confirm the compatibility of your unit before using.

1. Warm the engine to normal operating temperature. Turn off all electrical accessories. Do not attempt to check timing specification or idle speed on a cold engine.
2. Connect a tachometer (connect the tachometer (+) terminal to the terminal IG- of the check connector) and check the engine idle speed to be sure it is within the specification given in the Tune-Up Specifications chart or underhood emission sticker.
3. Remove the cap on the diagnostic check connector. Using a small jumper wire or Special Service Tool SST 09843-18020, short terminals TE1 (test terminal No. 1) and E1 (earth-ground) together.

➡If the timing marks are difficult to see, shut the engine OFF and use a dab of paint or chalk to make them more visible.

4. Connect a timing light according to the manufacturer's instructions.
5. Start the engine and use the timing light to observe the timing marks. With the jumper wire in the check connector the timing should be to specifications (refer to underhood emission sticker as necessary) with the engine fully warmed up (at correct idle speed) and the transaxle in correct position. If the timing is not correct, loosen the bolts at the distributor just enough so that the distributor can be turned. Turn the distributor to advance or retard the timing as required. Once the proper marks are seen to align with the timing light, timing is correct.

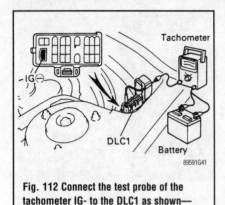

Fig. 112 Connect the test probe of the tachometer IG- to the DLC1 as shown—1994–95 models

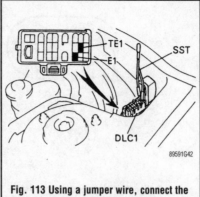

Fig. 113 Using a jumper wire, connect the TE1 and E1 of the DLC1 terminals

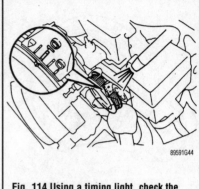

Fig. 114 Using a timing light, check the timing with the transaxle in Neutral

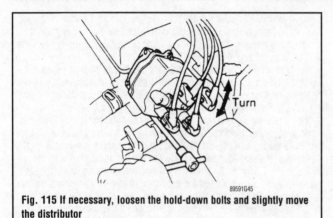

Fig. 115 If necessary, loosen the hold-down bolts and slightly move the distributor

6. Without changing the position of the distributor, tighten the distributor bolts and double check the timing with the light (check idle speed as necessary).

7. Disconnect the jumper wire or Special Service Tool (SST) at the diagnostic check connector.

➡This jumper will be used repeatedly during diagnostics in later sections. Take the time to make a proper jumper with correct terminals or probes. It's a valuable special tool for very low cost.

8. Refer to the underhood emission sticker for timing specification and any additional service procedure steps.

9. Recheck the timing, the mark ranges from 5°–15° BTDC on 7A-FE and 0–10 on 5S-FE at idle.

10. Shut the engine OFF and disconnect all test equipment. Roadtest the vehicle for proper operation.

1996–98 MODELS

♦ See Figure 116

➡Toyota's hand-held tester or an equivalent OBD-II scan tool must be used for this procedure.

1. Warm the engine to normal operating temperature.

2. Connect an OBD-II compliant scan tool to the DLC3 located under the dash on the driver's side. Refer to Section 4 for more information.

3. Connect the timing light to the engine as per manufactures instructions.

4. Using SST 09843-18020 or its equivalent jumper wire, connect terminals TE1 and E1 of the DLC1 under the hood.

5. After the engine speed is kept at about 1000–1500 rpm on the 7A-FE and 1000–1300 on the 5S-FE for 5 seconds, check that it returns to idle speed.

6. Check the ignition timing, the reading should be 10° BTDC at idle.

7. Remove the jumper wire from the DLC1.

8. Recheck the timing, the mark ranges from 5°–15° BTDC on 7A-FE and 0–10 on 5S-FE at idle.

9. Disconnect the scan tool.

10. Disconnect the timing light.

Valve Lash

GENERAL INFORMATION

➡**Check and adjust the valve clearance every 60,000 miles or 72 months.**

Valve clearance is one factor which determines how far the intake and exhaust valves will open into the cylinder. If the valve clearance is too large, part of the lift of the camshaft will be used up in removing the excessive clearance, thus the valves will not be opened far enough. This condition has two effects, the valve train components will emit a tapping noise as they take up the excessive clearance, and the engine will perform poorly, since the less the intake valve opens, the smaller the amount of air/fuel mixture that will be admitted to the cylinders. The less the exhaust valves open, the greater the back-pressure in the cylinder which prevents the proper air/fuel mixture from entering the cylinder.

If the valve clearance is too small, the intake and exhaust valves will not fully seat on the cylinder head when they close. When a valve seats on the cylinder head it does two things, it seals the combustion chamber so none of the gases in the cylinder can escape and it cools itself by transferring some of the heat it absorbed from the combustion process through the cylinder head and into the engine cooling system. Therefore, if the valve clearance is too small, the engine will run poorly due to gases escaping from the combustion chamber, and the valves will overheat and warp since they cannot transfer heat unless they are touching the seat in the cylinder head.

ADJUSTMENT

5S-FE Engine

♦ See Figures 117 thru 128

1. Remove the cylinder head (valve) cover.

2. Set the No. 1 cylinder to TDC by turning the crankshaft pulley and align its groove with the timing mark "0" of the No. 1 timing cover. Check that the valve lifters on the No. 1 are loose and the No. 4 are tight.

3. Inspect the valve clearance.

4. To inspect the valve clearance, check only the valves indicated.

   a. Using a thickness gage, measure the clearance between the valve lifter and camshaft. Record the out-of-specification valve clearance measurements. They will be used later to determine the required replacement adjusting shim.
   - Intake COLD: 0.007–0.011 inch (0.19–0.29mm)
   - Exhaust COLD: 0.011–0.015 inch (0.28–0.38mm)

   b. Turn the crankshaft pulley one revolution (360°) and align its groove with the timing mark "0" of the No. 1 timing cover. Check only the valve indicated in the illustration. Measure the valve clearance as specified earlier.

5. Remove the adjusting shim. turn the crankshaft so that the cam lobe of the camshaft on the adjusting valve points upward. Position the notch of the valve lifter facing the spark plug side.

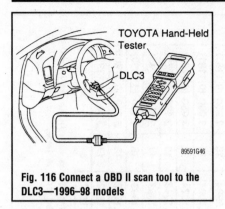

Fig. 116 Connect a OBD II scan tool to the DLC3—1996–98 models

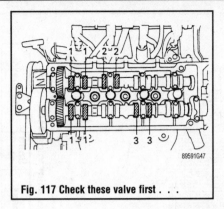

Fig. 117 Check these valve first . . .

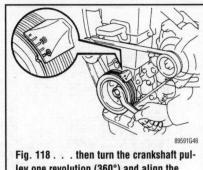

Fig. 118 . . . then turn the crankshaft pulley one revolution (360°) and align the groove with the timing mark

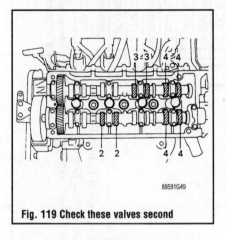

Fig. 119 Check these valves second

Fig. 120 Use a small flat-bladed tool to remove the shim . . .

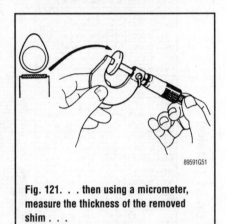

Fig. 121 . . . then using a micrometer, measure the thickness of the removed shim . . .

Fig. 122 . . . then position a new shim on the valve lifter

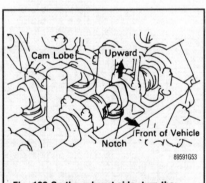
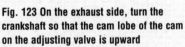

Fig. 123 On the exhaust side, turn the crankshaft so that the cam lobe of the cam on the adjusting valve is upward

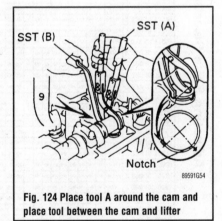

Fig. 124 Place tool A around the cam and place tool between the cam and lifter

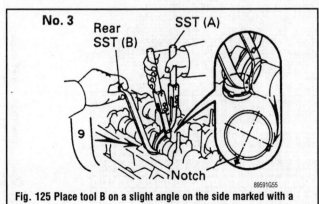

Fig. 125 Place tool B on a slight angle on the side marked with a "9"

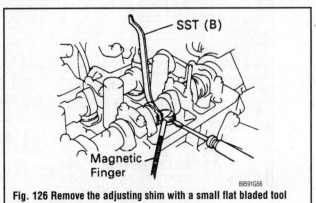

Fig. 126 Remove the adjusting shim with a small flat bladed tool and magnetic finger

Adjusting Shim Selection Chart (Intake)

Measured clearance mm (in.) \ Installed shim thickness mm (in.)	2.500 (0.0984)	2.520 (0.0992)	2.540 (0.1000)	2.550 (0.1004)	2.560 (0.1008)	2.580 (0.1016)	2.600 (0.1024)	2.620 (0.1031)	2.640 (0.1039)	2.650 (0.1043)	2.660 (0.1047)	2.670 (0.1051)	2.680 (0.1055)	2.690 (0.1059)	2.700 (0.1063)	2.710 (0.1067)	2.720 (0.1071)	2.730 (0.1075)	2.740 (0.1079)	2.750 (0.1083)	2.760 (0.1087)	2.770 (0.1091)	2.780 (0.1094)	2.790 (0.1098)	2.800 (0.1102)	2.810 (0.1106)	2.820 (0.1110)	2.830 (0.1114)	2.840 (0.1118)	2.850 (0.1122)	2.860 (0.1126)	2.870 (0.1130)	2.880 (0.1134)	2.890 (0.1138)	2.900 (0.1142)	2.910 (0.1146)	2.920 (0.1150)	2.930 (0.1154)	2.940 (0.1157)	2.950 (0.1161)	2.960 (0.1165)	2.970 (0.1169)	2.980 (0.1173)	2.990 (0.1177)	3.000 (0.1181)	3.010 (0.1185)	3.020 (0.1189)	3.030 (0.1193)	3.040 (0.1197)	3.050 (0.1201)	3.060 (0.1205)	3.080 (0.1213)	3.100 (0.1220)	3.120 (0.1228)	3.140 (0.1236)	3.150 (0.1240)	3.160 (0.1244)	3.180 (0.1252)	3.200 (0.1260)	3.220 (0.1268)	3.240 (0.1276)	3.250 (0.1280)	3.260 (0.1283)	3.280 (0.1291)	3.300 (0.1299)
0.000 – 0.020 (0.0000 – 0.0008)													1	1	1	1	1	1	1	1	2	2	2	2	2	3	3	3	3	3	4	4	4	4	4	5	5	5	5	5	6	6	6	6	6	7	7	7	7	7	8	8	8	9	9	9	10	10	10	11	11	11	12	12	12
0.021 – 0.040 (0.0008 – 0.0016)											1	1	1	1	1	1	1	1	2	2	2	2	2	3	3	3	3	3	4	4	4	4	4	5	5	5	5	5	6	6	6	6	6	7	7	7	7	7	8	8	8	8	9	9	10	10	10	10	11	11	12	12	12	12	13
0.041 – 0.060 (0.0016 – 0.0024)									1	1	1	1	1	1	1	1	2	2	2	2	2	3	3	3	3	3	4	4	4	4	4	5	5	5	5	5	6	6	6	6	6	7	7	7	7	7	8	8	8	8	8	9	9	10	10	10	10	11	11	12	12	12	12	13	13
0.061 – 0.080 (0.0024 – 0.0031)								1	1	1	1	1	1	1	2	2	2	2	2	3	3	3	3	3	4	4	4	4	4	5	5	5	5	5	6	6	6	6	6	7	7	7	7	7	8	8	8	8	8	9	9	9	10	10	10	11	11	11	12	12	12	13	13	13	14
0.081 – 0.100 (0.0032 – 0.0039)							1	1	1	1	1	1	2	2	2	2	2	3	3	3	3	3	4	4	4	4	4	5	5	5	5	5	6	6	6	6	6	7	7	7	7	7	8	8	8	8	8	9	9	9	9	10	10	10	11	11	11	12	12	12	13	13	13	14	14
0.101 – 0.120 (0.0040 – 0.0047)						1	1	1	1	1	2	2	2	2	2	3	3	3	3	3	4	4	4	4	4	5	5	5	5	5	6	6	6	6	6	7	7	7	7	7	8	8	8	8	8	9	9	9	9	9	10	10	10	11	11	11	12	12	12	13	13	13	14	14	14
0.121 – 0.140 (0.0048 – 0.0055)					1	1	1	1	2	2	2	2	2	3	3	3	3	3	4	4	4	4	4	5	5	5	5	5	6	6	6	6	6	7	7	7	7	7	8	8	8	8	8	9	9	9	9	9	10	10	10	10	11	11	12	12	12	12	13	13	14	14	14	14	15
0.141 – 0.160 (0.0056 – 0.0063)			1	1	1	1	1	2	2	2	2	3	3	3	3	3	4	4	4	4	4	5	5	5	5	5	6	6	6	6	6	7	7	7	7	7	8	8	8	8	8	9	9	9	9	9	10	10	10	10	10	11	11	12	12	12	12	13	13	14	14	14	14	15	15
0.161 – 0.180 (0.0063 – 0.0071)		1	1	1	1	1	2	2	2	3	3	3	3	3	4	4	4	4	4	5	5	5	5	5	6	6	6	6	6	7	7	7	7	7	8	8	8	8	8	9	9	9	9	9	10	10	10	10	10	11	11	11	12	12	12	13	13	13	14	14	14	15	15	15	16
0.181 – 0.189 (0.0071 – 0.0074)		1	1	1	1	1	2	2	3	3	3	3	3	4	4	4	4	4	5	5	5	5	5	6	6	6	6	6	7	7	7	7	7	8	8	8	8	8	9	9	9	9	9	10	10	10	10	10	11	11	11	11	12	12	13	13	13	13	14	14	15	15	15	15	16
0.190 – 0.290 (0.0075 – 0.0114)																																																																	
0.291 – 0.300 (0.0115 – 0.0118)	2	3	3	3	3	4	4	5	5	5	5	6	6	6	6	6	7	7	7	7	7	8	8	8	8	8	9	9	9	9	9	10	10	10	10	10	11	11	11	11	11	12	12	12	12	12	13	13	13	13	13	14	14	15	15	15	15	16	16	17	17	17	17	17	
0.301 – 0.320 (0.0119 – 0.0126)	2	3	3	3	4	4	4	5	5	5	6	6	6	6	6	7	7	7	7	7	8	8	8	8	8	9	9	9	9	9	10	10	10	10	10	11	11	11	11	11	12	12	12	12	12	13	13	13	13	13	14	14	14	15	15	15	16	16	16	17	17	17	17	17	
0.321 – 0.340 (0.0126 – 0.0134)	3	3	4	4	4	4	5	5	6	6	6	6	6	7	7	7	7	7	8	8	8	8	8	9	9	9	9	9	10	10	10	10	10	11	11	11	11	11	12	12	12	12	12	13	13	13	13	13	14	14	14	14	15	15	16	16	16	16	17	17	17	17	17		
0.341 – 0.360 (0.0134 – 0.0142)	3	4	4	4	4	5	5	6	6	6	6	7	7	7	7	7	8	8	8	8	8	9	9	9	9	9	10	10	10	10	10	11	11	11	11	11	12	12	12	12	12	13	13	13	13	13	14	14	14	14	14	15	15	16	16	16	16	17	17	17	17				
0.361 – 0.380 (0.0142 – 0.0150)	4	4	4	5	5	5	6	6	6	7	7	7	7	7	8	8	8	8	8	9	9	9	9	9	10	10	10	10	10	11	11	11	11	11	12	12	12	12	12	13	13	13	13	13	14	14	14	14	14	15	15	15	16	16	16	17	17	17	17	17					
0.381 – 0.400 (0.0150 – 0.0157)	4	4	5	5	5	6	6	6	7	7	7	7	8	8	8	8	8	9	9	9	9	9	10	10	10	10	10	11	11	11	11	11	12	12	12	12	12	13	13	13	13	13	14	14	14	14	14	15	15	15	15	16	16	16	17	17	17	17	17						
0.401 – 0.420 (0.0158 – 0.0165)	4	5	5	5	6	6	6	7	7	7	8	8	8	8	8	9	9	9	9	9	10	10	10	10	10	11	11	11	11	11	12	12	12	12	12	13	13	13	13	13	14	14	14	14	14	15	15	15	15	15	16	16	16	17	17	17	17	17							
0.421 – 0.440 (0.0166 – 0.0173)	5	5	6	6	6	6	7	7	8	8	8	8	8	9	9	9	9	9	10	10	10	10	10	11	11	11	11	11	12	12	12	12	12	13	13	13	13	13	14	14	14	14	14	15	15	15	15	15	16	16	16	16	17	17	17	17	17								
0.441 – 0.460 (0.0174 – 0.0181)	5	6	6	6	6	7	7	8	8	8	8	9	9	9	9	9	10	10	10	10	10	11	11	11	11	11	12	12	12	12	12	13	13	13	13	13	14	14	14	14	14	15	15	15	15	15	16	16	16	16	16	17	17	17	17										
0.461 – 0.480 (0.0181 – 0.0189)	6	6	6	7	7	7	8	8	8	9	9	9	9	9	10	10	10	10	10	11	11	11	11	11	12	12	12	12	12	13	13	13	13	13	14	14	14	14	14	15	15	15	15	15	16	16	16	16	16	17	17	17	17	17											
0.481 – 0.500 (0.0189 – 0.0197)	6	6	7	7	7	8	8	8	9	9	9	9	10	10	10	10	10	11	11	11	11	11	12	12	12	12	12	13	13	13	13	13	14	14	14	14	14	15	15	15	15	15	16	16	16	16	16	17	17	17	17	17	17												
0.501 – 0.520 (0.0197 – 0.0205)	6	7	7	7	8	8	8	9	9	9	10	10	10	10	10	11	11	11	11	11	12	12	12	12	12	13	13	13	13	13	14	14	14	14	14	15	15	15	15	15	16	16	16	16	16	17	17	17	17	17	17	17													
0.521 – 0.540 (0.0205 – 0.0213)	7	7	8	8	8	8	9	9	10	10	10	10	10	11	11	11	11	11	12	12	12	12	12	13	13	13	13	13	14	14	14	14	14	15	15	15	15	15	16	16	16	16	16	17	17	17	17	17	17	17	17														
0.541 – 0.560 (0.0213 – 0.0220)	7	8	8	8	8	9	9	10	10	10	10	11	11	11	11	11	12	12	12	12	12	13	13	13	13	13	14	14	14	14	14	15	15	15	15	15	16	16	16	16	16	17	17	17	17	17	17	17	17																
0.561 – 0.580 (0.0221 – 0.0228)	8	8	8	9	9	9	10	10	10	11	11	11	11	11	12	12	12	12	12	13	13	13	13	13	14	14	14	14	14	15	15	15	15	15	16	16	16	16	16	17	17	17	17	17	17	17	17																		
0.581 – 0.600 (0.0229 – 0.0236)	8	8	9	9	9	10	10	10	11	11	11	11	12	12	12	12	12	13	13	13	13	13	14	14	14	14	14	15	15	15	15	15	16	16	16	16	16	17	17	17	17	17	17	17	17																				
0.601 – 0.620 (0.0237 – 0.0244)	8	9	9	9	10	10	10	11	11	11	12	12	12	12	12	13	13	13	13	13	14	14	14	14	14	15	15	15	15	15	16	16	16	16	16	17	17	17	17	17	17	17	17																						
0.621 – 0.640 (0.0244 – 0.0252)	9	9	10	10	10	10	11	11	12	12	12	12	12	13	13	13	13	13	14	14	14	14	14	15	15	15	15	15	16	16	16	16	16	17	17	17	17	17	17	17	17																								
0.641 – 0.660 (0.0252 – 0.0260)	9	10	10	10	10	11	11	12	12	12	12	13	13	13	13	13	14	14	14	14	14	15	15	15	15	15	16	16	16	16	16	17	17	17	17	17	17	17	17																										
0.661 – 0.680 (0.0260 – 0.0268)	10	10	10	11	11	11	12	12	12	13	13	13	13	13	14	14	14	14	14	15	15	15	15	15	16	16	16	16	16	17	17	17	17	17	17	17	17																												
0.681 – 0.700 (0.0268 – 0.0276)	10	10	11	11	11	12	12	12	13	13	13	13	14	14	14	14	14	15	15	15	15	15	16	16	16	16	16	17	17	17	17	17	17	17	17																														
0.701 – 0.720 (0.0276 – 0.0283)	10	11	11	11	12	12	12	13	13	13	14	14	14	14	14	15	15	15	15	15	16	16	16	16	16	17	17	17	17	17	17	17	17																																
0.721 – 0.740 (0.0284 – 0.0291)	11	11	12	12	12	12	13	13	14	14	14	14	14	15	15	15	15	15	16	16	16	16	16	17	17	17	17	17	17	17	17																																		
0.741 – 0.760 (0.0292 – 0.0299)	11	12	12	12	12	13	13	14	14	14	14	15	15	15	15	15	16	16	16	16	16	17	17	17	17	17	17	17	17																																				
0.761 – 0.780 (0.0300 – 0.0307)	12	12	12	13	13	13	14	14	14	15	15	15	15	15	16	16	16	16	16	17	17	17	17	17	17	17	17																																						
0.781 – 0.800 (0.0307 – 0.0315)	12	12	13	13	13	14	14	14	15	15	15	15	16	16	16	16	16	17	17	17	17	17	17	17	17																																								
0.801 – 0.820 (0.0315 – 0.0323)	12	13	13	13	14	14	14	15	15	15	16	16	16	16	16	17	17	17	17	17	17	17	17																																										
0.821 – 0.840 (0.0323 – 0.0331)	13	13	14	14	14	14	15	15	16	16	16	16	16	17	17	17	17	17	17	17	17																																												
0.841 – 0.860 (0.0331 – 0.0339)	13	14	14	14	14	15	15	16	16	16	16	17	17	17	17	17	17	17	17																																														
0.861 – 0.880 (0.0339 – 0.0346)	14	14	14	15	15	15	16	16	16	17	17	17	17	17	17	17	17																																																
0.881 – 0.900 (0.0347 – 0.0354)	14	14	15	15	15	16	16	16	17	17	17	17	17	17	17																																																		
0.901 – 0.920 (0.0355 – 0.0362)	14	15	15	15	16	16	16	17	17	17	17	17	17																																																				
0.921 – 0.940 (0.0363 – 0.0370)	15	15	16	16	16	16	17	17	17	17	17																																																						
0.941 – 0.960 (0.0370 – 0.0378)	15	16	16	16	16	17	17	17	17																																																								
0.961 – 0.980 (0.0378 – 0.0386)	16	16	16	17	17	17	17	17																																																									
0.981 – 1.000 (0.0386 – 0.0394)	16	16	17	17	17	17	17																																																											
1.001 – 1.020 (0.0394 – 0.0402)	16	17	17	17	17	17																																																												
1.021 – 1.040 (0.0402 – 0.0409)	17	17	17	17	17																																																													
1.041 – 1.060 (0.0410 – 0.0417)	17	17	17																																																															
1.061 – 1.080 (0.0418 – 0.0425)	17	17																																																																	
1.081 – 1.090 (0.0426 – 0.0429)	17																																																																		

Intake valve clearance (Cold):
0.19 – 0.29 mm (0.007 – 0.011 in.)

EXAMPLE: The 2.800 mm (0.1102 in.) shim is installed, and the measured clearance is 0.450 mm (0.0177 in.). Replace the 2.800 mm (0.1102 in.) shim with a new No.11 shim.

New shim thickness mm (in.)

Shim No.	Thickness	Shim No.	Thickness
1	2.500 (0.0984)	10	2.950 (0.1161)
2	2.550 (0.1004)	11	3.000 (0.1181)
3	2.600 (0.1024)	12	3.050 (0.1201)
4	2.650 (0.1043)	13	3.100 (0.1220)
5	2.700 (0.1063)	14	3.150 (0.1240)
6	2.750 (0.1083)	15	3.200 (0.1260)
7	2.800 (0.1102)	16	3.250 (0.1280)
8	2.850 (0.1122)	17	3.300 (0.1299)
9	2.900 (0.1142)		

HINT: New shims have the thickness in millimeters imprinted on the face.

89591G59

Fig. 127 Adjusting shim chart—5S-FE intake

Adjusting Shim Selection Chart (Exhaust)

88591G60

New shim thickness — mm (in.)

Shim No.	Thickness	Shim No.	Thickness
1	2.500 (0.0984)	10	2.950 (0.1161)
2	2.550 (0.1004)	11	3.000 (0.1181)
3	2.600 (0.1024)	12	3.050 (0.1201)
4	2.650 (0.1043)	13	3.100 (0.1220)
5	2.700 (0.1063)	14	3.150 (0.1240)
6	2.750 (0.1083)	15	3.200 (0.1260)
7	2.800 (0.1102)	16	3.250 (0.1280)
8	2.850 (0.1122)	17	3.300 (0.1299)
9	2.900 (0.1142)		

HINT: New shims have the thickness in millimeters imprinted on the face.

Exhaust valve clearance (Cold):
0.28 – 0.38 mm (0.011 – 0.015 in.)

EXAMPLE: The 2.800 mm (0.1102 in.) shim is installed, and the measured clearance is 0.450 mm (0.0177 in.). Replace the 2.800 mm (0.1102 in.) shim with a new No.9 shim.

Installed shim thickness (mm / in.), across top of chart:
2.500 (0.0984), 2.520 (0.0992), 2.540 (0.1000), 2.560 (0.1008), 2.580 (0.1016), 2.600 (0.1024), 2.620 (0.1031), 2.640 (0.1039), 2.660 (0.1047), 2.680 (0.1055), 2.700 (0.1063), 2.710 (0.1067), 2.720 (0.1071), 2.730 (0.1075), 2.740 (0.1079), 2.750 (0.1083), 2.760 (0.1087), 2.770 (0.1091), 2.780 (0.1094), 2.790 (0.1098), 2.800 (0.1102), 2.810 (0.1106), 2.820 (0.1110), 2.830 (0.1114), 2.840 (0.1118), 2.850 (0.1122), 2.860 (0.1126), 2.870 (0.1130), 2.880 (0.1134), 2.890 (0.1138), 2.900 (0.1142), 2.910 (0.1146), 2.920 (0.1150), 2.930 (0.1154), 2.940 (0.1157), 2.950 (0.1161), 2.960 (0.1165), 2.970 (0.1169), 2.980 (0.1173), 2.990 (0.1177), 3.000 (0.1181), 3.010 (0.1185), 3.020 (0.1189), 3.030 (0.1193), 3.040 (0.1197), 3.050 (0.1201), 3.060 (0.1205), 3.080 (0.1213), 3.100 (0.1220), 3.120 (0.1228), 3.140 (0.1236), 3.150 (0.1240), 3.160 (0.1244), 3.180 (0.1252), 3.200 (0.1260), 3.220 (0.1268), 3.240 (0.1276), 3.250 (0.1280), 3.260 (0.1283), 3.280 (0.1291), 3.300 (0.1299)

Measured clearance (mm / in.), down left side of chart:
0.000 – 0.020 (0.0000 – 0.0008); 0.021 – 0.040 (0.0008 – 0.0016); 0.041 – 0.060 (0.0016 – 0.0024); 0.061 – 0.080 (0.0024 – 0.0031); 0.081 – 0.100 (0.0032 – 0.0039); 0.101 – 0.120 (0.0040 – 0.0047); 0.121 – 0.140 (0.0048 – 0.0055); 0.141 – 0.160 (0.0056 – 0.0063); 0.161 – 0.180 (0.0063 – 0.0071); 0.181 – 0.200 (0.0071 – 0.0079); 0.201 – 0.220 (0.0079 – 0.0087); 0.221 – 0.240 (0.0087 – 0.0094); 0.241 – 0.260 (0.0095 – 0.0102); 0.261 – 0.279 (0.0103 – 0.0110); 0.280 – 0.380 (0.0110 – 0.0150); 0.381 – 0.400 (0.0150 – 0.0157); 0.401 – 0.420 (0.0158 – 0.0165); 0.421 – 0.440 (0.0166 – 0.0173); 0.441 – 0.460 (0.0174 – 0.0181); 0.461 – 0.480 (0.0181 – 0.0189); 0.481 – 0.500 (0.0189 – 0.0197); 0.501 – 0.520 (0.0197 – 0.0205); 0.521 – 0.540 (0.0205 – 0.0213); 0.541 – 0.560 (0.0213 – 0.0220); 0.561 – 0.580 (0.0221 – 0.0228); 0.581 – 0.600 (0.0228 – 0.0236); 0.601 – 0.620 (0.0237 – 0.0244); 0.621 – 0.640 (0.0244 – 0.0252); 0.641 – 0.660 (0.0252 – 0.0260); 0.661 – 0.680 (0.0260 – 0.0268); 0.681 – 0.700 (0.0268 – 0.0276); 0.701 – 0.720 (0.0276 – 0.0283); 0.721 – 0.740 (0.0284 – 0.0291); 0.741 – 0.760 (0.0292 – 0.0299); 0.761 – 0.780 (0.0300 – 0.0307); 0.781 – 0.800 (0.0307 – 0.0315); 0.801 – 0.820 (0.0316 – 0.0323); 0.821 – 0.840 (0.0323 – 0.0331); 0.841 – 0.860 (0.0331 – 0.0339); 0.861 – 0.880 (0.0339 – 0.0346); 0.881 – 0.900 (0.0347 – 0.0354); 0.901 – 0.920 (0.0355 – 0.0362); 0.921 – 0.940 (0.0363 – 0.0370); 0.941 – 0.960 (0.0370 – 0.0378); 0.961 – 0.980 (0.0378 – 0.0386); 0.981 – 1.000 (0.0386 – 0.0394); 1.001 – 1.020 (0.0394 – 0.0402); 1.021 – 1.040 (0.0402 – 0.0409); 1.041 – 1.060 (0.0410 – 0.0417); 1.061 – 1.080 (0.0418 – 0.0425); 1.081 – 1.100 (0.0426 – 0.0433); 1.101 – 1.120 (0.0433 – 0.0441); 1.121 – 1.140 (0.0443 – 0.0449); 1.141 – 1.160 (0.0449 – 0.0457); 1.161 – 1.180 (0.0457 – 0.0465)

Fig. 128 Adjusting shim chart—5S-FE exhaust

a. Using a SST-A (09248–05410) or equivalent valve clearance and adjuster tool, press down the valve lifter and place SST-B 09248–05420 (or equivalent), between the camshaft and valve lifter. Remove the SST-A.

➡**Apply SST-B at a slight angle on the side marked with "9", at the position shown in the illustration.**

b. Remove the adjusting shim with a small flat bladed tool and magnetic finger.

6. Determine the replacement shim size by following the formula or the chart.

a. Using a micrometer, measure the thickness of the removed shim. Calculate the thickness of a new shim so that the valve clearance comes within the specified value.

- T: Thickness of the remove shim
- A: Measured value of clearance
- N: Thickness of the new shim
- Intake: N= T + (A—0.009 inch (0.24mm))
- Exhaust: N= T + (A—0.013 inch (0.33mm))

b. Select a new shim with a thickness as close as possible to calculate value. The shims are available in 17 sizes in increments of 0.0020 inch (0.05mm). They range from 0.0984 inch (2.50mm) to 0.1299 inch (3.30mm).

7. Install the new adjusting shim on the valve lifter. Using the SST-A or equivalent, press down the valve lifter and remove SST-B.

8. Recheck the valve clearance.

9. Install and secure the valve cover. Attach the spark plug wires.

7A-FE Engine

◆ **See Figures 117 thru 126 and 129 and 130**

➡**Inspect and adjust the valve clearance while the engine is cold.**

1. Remove the spark plug wires from the valve cover.
2. Remove the valve cover and gasket as described in Section 3.
3. Set the No. 1 cylinder to TDC by turning the crankshaft pulley and align its groove with the timing mark "0" of the No. 1 timing cover. Check that the hole of the camshaft timing pulley is aligned with the timing mark of the bearing cap. If not, turn the crankshaft one revolution (360°).
4. To inspect the valve clearance, check only the valves indicated.

a. Using a thickness gage, measure the clearance between the valve lifter and camshaft. Record the out-of-specification valve clearance measurements. They will be used later to determine the required replacement adjusting shim.
- Intake COLD: 0.006–0.010 inch (0.15–0.25mm)
- Exhaust COLD: 0.010–0.014 inch (0.25–0.35mm)

b. Turn the crankshaft pulley one revolution (360°) and align its groove with the timing mark "0" of the No. 1 timing cover. Check only the valve indicated in the illustration. Measure the valve clearance as specified earlier.

5. On the intake side to adjust the valve clearance the camshaft must be removed.

6. Remove the adjusting shim with a small flat bladed tool.

7. Determine the replacement adjusting shim size by following the formula or charts.

a. Using a micrometer, measure the thickness of the removed shim. Calculate the thickness of a new shim so that the valve clearance comes within the specified value.
- T: Thickness of the remove shim
- A: Measured value of clearance
- N: Thickness of the new shim
- Intake: N= T + (A—0.008 inch (0.20mm))

b. Select a new shim with a thickness as close as possible to calculate value. The shims are available in 16 sizes in increments of 0.0020 inch (0.05mm). They range from 1.0039 inch (2.55mm) to 0.1299 inch (3.30mm).

8. Install the new adjusting shim by placing the shim on the valve lifter.

9. Install the intake camshaft.

10. Recheck the valve clearance.

11. To adjust the exhaust valve clearance, turn the crankshaft so that the cam lobe of the camshaft on the adjusting valve is upward.

a. Position the notch of the valve lifter facing the front of the vehicle.

b. Using a SST-A (09248–05410) or equivalent valve clearance and adjuster tool, press down the valve lifter and place SST-B

09248–05420 (or equivalent), between the camshaft and valve lifter. Remove the SST-A.

➡**Apply SST-B at a slight angle on the side marked with "9", at the position shown in the illustration. When SST-B is inserted too deeply, it will get pinched by the shim. To prevent it from getting stuck, insert it gently from the intake side at a slight angle. The shape of the cam makes it difficult to insert SST-B from the intake side to the No. 3 rear. For this shim, it is best approached from the exhaust side instead.**

c. Remove the adjusting shim with a small flat bladed tool and magnetic finger.

12. Determine the replacement shim size by following the formula or the chart.

a. Using a micrometer, measure the thickness of the removed shim. Calculate the thickness of a new shim so that the valve clearance comes within the specified value.
- T: Thickness of the remove shim
- A: Measured value of clearance
- N: Thickness of the new shim
- Exhaust: N= T + (A—0.012 inch (0.30mm))

b. Select a new shim with a thickness as close as possible to calculate value. The shims are available in 16 sizes in increments of 0.0020 inch (0.05mm). They range from 1.0039 inch (2.55mm) to 0.1299 inch (3.30mm).

13. Install the new adjusting shim on the valve lifter. Using the SST-A or equivalent, press down the valve lifter and remove SST-B.

14. Recheck the valve clearance.

15. Install and secure the valve cover. Attach the spark plug wires.

Idle Speed Adjustment

INSPECTION & ADJUSTMENT

1994–95 Models

◆ **See Figure 131**

This engine requires a tachometer hook-up to the check connector-see illustrations. NEVER allow the tachometer terminal to become grounded; severe and expensive damage can occur to the coil and/or igniter. Some tachometers are not compatible with this ignition system, confirm the compatibility of your unit before using.

1. Idle speed adjustment is performed under the following conditions:
- Engine at normal operating temperature
- Air cleaner installed
- Air pipes and hoses of the air induction and EGR systems properly connected
- All vacuum lines and electrical wires connected and plugged in properly
- All electrical accessories in the **OFF** position
- Transaxle in the **N** position

2. Connect a tachometer to the engine. Connect the probe of the tachometer to terminal IG- of the check connector.

3. Run the engine at 2500 rpm for 90 seconds.

4. Check the idle speed. If the speed is not correct, check the Idle Air Control (IAC) system.

5. Disconnect the tachometer.

1996–98 Models

◆ **See Figure 116**

1. Idle speed adjustment is performed under the following conditions:
- Engine at normal operating temperature.
- Air cleaner installed.
- Air pipes and hoses of the air induction and EGR systems properly connected.
- All vacuum lines and electrical wires connected and plugged in properly.
- SFI system wiring connectors fully plugged
- All electrical accessories in the **OFF** position.

Adjusting Shim Selection Chart (Intake)

New shim thickness   mm (in.)

Shim No.	Thickness	Shim No.	Thickness
1	2.55 (0.1004)	9	2.95 (0.1161)
2	2.60 (0.1024)	10	3.00 (0.1181)
3	2.65 (0.1043)	11	3.05 (0.1201)
4	2.70 (0.1063)	12	3.10 (0.1220)
5	2.75 (0.1083)	13	3.15 (0.1240)
6	2.80 (0.1102)	14	3.20 (0.1260)
7	2.85 (0.1122)	15	3.25 (0.1280)
8	2.90 (0.1142)	16	3.30 (0.1299)

HINT: New shims have the thickness in millimeters imprinted on the face.

Intake valve clearance (Cold):
0.15 – 0.25 mm (0.006 – 0.010 in.)

EXAMPLE: The 2.800 mm (0.1102 in.) shim is installed, and the measured clearance is 0.450 mm (0.0177 in.). Replace the 2.800 mm (0.1102 in.) shim with a new No. 11 shim.

Fig. 129 Adjusting shim chart—7A-FE intake

89991G57

Adjusting Shim Selection Chart (Exhaust)

The installed shim thickness (mm / in.) runs across the top of the chart from 2.500 (0.0984) up to 3.300 (0.1299). The measured clearance (mm / in.) runs down the left side in ranges from 0.000–0.020 (0.0000–0.0008) down to 1.141–1.150 (0.0449–0.0453). The body of the chart gives the new shim number (1–16) to install.

New shim thickness mm (in.)

Shim No.	Thickness	Shim No.	Thickness
1	2.55 (0.1004)	9	2.95 (0.1161)
2	2.60 (0.1024)	10	3.00 (0.1181)
3	2.65 (0.1043)	11	3.05 (0.1201)
4	2.70 (0.1063)	12	3.10 (0.1220)
5	2.75 (0.1083)	13	3.15 (0.1240)
6	2.80 (0.1102)	14	3.20 (0.1260)
7	2.85 (0.1122)	15	3.25 (0.1280)
8	2.90 (0.1142)	16	3.30 (0.1299)

HINT: New shims have the thickness in millimeters imprinted on the face.

Exhaust valve clearance (Cold):
0.25 – 0.35 mm (0.010 – 0.014 in.)

EXAMPLE: The 2.800 mm (0.1102 in.) shim is installed, and the measured clearance is 0.450 mm (0.0177 in.). Replace the 2.800 mm (0.1102 in.) shim with a new No. 9 shim.

89591G58

Fig. 130 Adjusting shim chart—7A-FE exhaust

GASOLINE ENGINE TUNE-UP SPECIFICATIONS

Year	Engine ID/VIN	Engine Displacement Liters (cc)	Spark Plugs Gap (in.)	Ignition Timing (deg.) MT	AT	Fuel Pump (psi)	Idle Speed (rpm) MT	AT	Valve Clearance In.	Ex.
1994	7A-FE	1.8 (1762)	0.31	10 BTDC	10 BTDC	38-44	700	700	0.006-0.010	0.010-0.014
	5S-FE	2.2 (2164)	0.43	10 BTDC	10 BTDC	38-44	750	750	0.007-0.011	0.011-0.015
1995	7A-FE	1.8 (1762)	0.31	10 BTDC	10 BTDC	38-44	700	700	0.006-0.010	0.010-0.014
	5S-FE	2.2 (2164)	0.43	10 BTDC	10 BTDC	38-44	750	750	0.007-0.011	0.011-0.015
1996	7A-FE	1.8 (1762)	0.31	10 BTDC	10 BTDC	38-44	700	700	0.006-0.010	0.010-0.014
	5S-FE	2.2 (2164)	0.43	10 BTDC	10 BTDC	38-44	750	750	0.007-0.011	0.011-0.015
1997	7A-FE	1.8 (1762)	0.31	10 BTDC	10 BTDC	38-44	700	700	0.006-0.010	0.010-0.014
	5S-FE	2.2 (2164)	0.43	10 BTDC	10 BTDC	38-44	750	750	0.007-0.011	0.011-0.015
1998	7A-FE	1.8 (1762)	0.31	10 BTDC	10 BTDC	38-44	700	700	0.006-0.010	0.010-0.014
	5S-FE	2.2 (2164)	0.43	10 BTDC	10 BTDC	38-44	750	750	0.007-0.011	0.011-0.015

89591C02

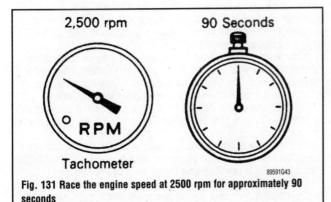

Fig. 131 Race the engine speed at 2500 rpm for approximately 90 seconds

- Ignition timing set correctly
- Transaxle in the **N** position.

2. Connect the hand held OBD II scan tool to the DLC3 under the drivers side lower dash panel.

3. Race the engine idle speed to 2500 rpm for approximately 90 seconds with the cooling fan off.

4. Check the idle speed. If the speed is not correct, check the Idle Air Control (IAC) system.

5. Disconnect the OBD II scan tool.

Air Conditioning System

SYSTEM SERVICE & REPAIR

➡It is recommended that the A/C system be serviced by an EPA Section 609 certified automotive technician utilizing a refrigerant recovery/recycling machine.

The do-it-yourselfer should not service his/her own vehicle's A/C system for many reasons, including legal concerns, personal injury, environmental damage and cost. The following are some of the reasons why you may decide not to service your own vehicle's A/C system.

According to the U.S. Clean Air Act, it is a federal crime to service or repair (involving the refrigerant) a Motor Vehicle Air Conditioning (MVAC) system for money without being EPA certified. It is also illegal to vent R-134a refrigerant into the atmosphere.

State and/or local laws may be more strict than the federal regulations, so be sure to check with your state and/or local authorities for further information. For further federal information on the legality of servicing your A/C system, call the EPA Stratospheric Ozone Hotline.

➡Federal law dictates that a fine of up to $25,000 may be levied on people convicted of venting refrigerant into the atmosphere. Additionally, the EPA may pay up to $10,000 for information or services leading to a criminal conviction of the violation of these laws.

When servicing an A/C system you run the risk of handling or coming in contact with refrigerant, which may result in skin or eye irritation or frostbite. Although low in toxicity (due to chemical stability), inhalation of concentrated refrigerant fumes is dangerous and can result in death; cases of fatal cardiac arrhythmia have been reported in people accidentally subjected to high levels of refrigerant. Some early symptoms include loss of concentration and drowsiness.

Also, refrigerants can decompose at high temperatures (near gas heaters or open flame), which may result in hydrofluoric acid, hydrochloric acid and phosgene (a fatal nerve gas).

R-134a refrigerant is a greenhouse gas which, if allowed to vent into the atmosphere, will contribute to global warming (the Greenhouse Effect).

It is usually more economically feasible to have a certified MVAC automotive technician perform A/C system service to your vehicle. While it is illegal to service an A/C system without the proper equipment, the home mechanic would have to purchase an expensive refrigerant recovery/recycling machine to service his/her own vehicle.

PREVENTIVE MAINTENANCE

Although the A/C system should not be serviced by the do-it-yourselfer, preventive maintenance can be practiced and A/C system inspections can be performed to help maintain the efficiency of the vehicle's A/C system. For preventive maintenance, perform the following:

• The easiest and most important preventive maintenance for your A/C system is to be sure that it is used on a regular basis. Running the system for five minutes each month (no matter what the season) will help ensure that the seals and all internal components remain lubricated.

➡Some newer vehicles automatically operate the A/C system compressor whenever the windshield defroster is activated. When running, the compressor lubricates the A/C system components; therefore, the A/C system would not need to be operated each month.

• In order to prevent heater core freeze-up during A/C operation, it is necessary to maintain a proper antifreeze protection. Use a hand-held coolant tester (hydrometer) to periodically check the condition of the antifreeze in your engine's cooling system.

➡Antifreeze should not be used longer than the manufacturer specifies.

• For efficient operation of an air conditioned vehicle's cooling system, the radiator cap should have a holding pressure which meets manufacturer's specifications. A cap which fails to hold these pressures should be replaced.

• Any obstruction of or damage to the condenser configuration will restrict air flow which is essential to its efficient operation. It is, therefore, a good rule to keep this unit clean and in proper physical shape.

➡Bug screens which are mounted in front of the condenser (unless they are original equipment) are regarded as obstructions.

• The condensation drain tube expels any water, which accumulates on the bottom of the evaporator housing, into the engine compartment. If this tube is obstructed, the air conditioning performance can be restricted and condensation buildup can spill over onto the vehicle's floor.

SYSTEM INSPECTION

▶ **See Figure 132**

Although the A/C system should not be serviced by the do-it-yourselfer, preventive maintenance can be practiced and A/C system inspections can be performed to help maintain the efficiency of the vehicle's A/C system. For A/C system inspection, perform the following:

The easiest and often most important check for the air conditioning system consists of a visual inspection of the system components. Visually inspect the air conditioning system for refrigerant leaks, damaged compressor clutch, abnormal compressor drive belt tension and/or condition, plugged evaporator drain tube, blocked condenser fins, disconnected or broken wires, blown fuses, corroded connections and poor insulation.

A refrigerant leak will usually appear as an oily residue at the leakage point in the system. The oily residue soon picks up dust or dirt particles from the surrounding air and appears greasy. Through time, this will build up and appear to be a heavy dirt impregnated grease.

For a thorough visual and operational inspection, check the following:

• Check the surface of the radiator and condenser for dirt, leaves or other material which might block air flow.
• Check for kinks in hoses and lines. Check the system for leaks.
• Make sure the drive belt is properly tensioned. When the air conditioning is operating, make sure the drive belt is free of noise or slippage.

• Make sure the blower motor operates at all appropriate positions, then check for distribution of the air from all outlets with the blower on **HIGH** or **MAX**.

➡Keep in mind that under conditions of high humidity, air discharged from the A/C vents may not feel as cold as expected, even if the system is working properly. This is because vaporized moisture in humid air retains heat more effectively than dry air, thereby making humid air more difficult to cool.

• Make sure the air passage selection lever is operating correctly. Start the engine and warm it to normal operating temperature, then make sure the temperature selection lever is operating correctly.

Windshield Wiper (Elements)

ELEMENT (REFILL) CARE & REPLACEMENT

▶ **See Figures 133 thru 142**

For maximum effectiveness and longest element life, the windshield and wiper blades should be kept clean. Dirt, tree sap, road tar and so on will cause streaking, smearing and blade deterioration if left on the glass. It is advisable to wash the windshield carefully with a commercial glass cleaner at least once a month. Wipe off the rubber blades with the wet rag afterwards. Do not attempt to move wipers across the windshield by hand; damage to the motor and drive mechanism will result.

To inspect and/or replace the wiper blade elements, place the wiper switch in the **LOW** speed position and the ignition switch in the **ACC** position. When the wiper blades are approximately vertical on the windshield, turn the ignition switch to **OFF**.

Examine the wiper blade elements. If they are found to be cracked, broken or torn, they should be replaced immediately. Replacement intervals will vary with usage, although ozone deterioration usually limits element life to about one year. If the wiper pattern is smeared or streaked, or if the blade chatters across the glass, the elements should be replaced. It is easiest and most sensible to replace the elements in pairs.

If your vehicle is equipped with aftermarket blades, there are several different types of refills and your vehicle might have any kind. Aftermarket blades and arms rarely use the exact same type blade or refill as the original equipment. Here are some typical aftermarket blades; not all may be available for your vehicle:

The Anco® type uses a release button that is pushed down to allow the refill to slide out of the yoke jaws. The new refill slides back into the frame and locks in place.

Some Trico® refills are removed by locating where the metal backing strip or the refill is wider. Insert a small screwdriver blade between the frame and metal backing strip. Press down to release the refill from the retaining tab.

Other types of Trico® refills have two metal tabs which are unlocked by squeezing them together. The rubber filler can then be withdrawn from the frame jaws. A new refill is installed by inserting the refill into the front frame jaws and sliding it rearward to engage the remaining frame jaws. There are usually four jaws; be certain when installing that the refill is engaged in all of them. At the end of its travel, the tabs will lock into place on the front jaws of the wiper blade frame.

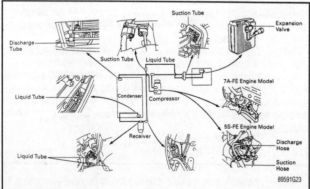

Fig. 132 Inspect the A/C hose and tube connections for leaks and looseness

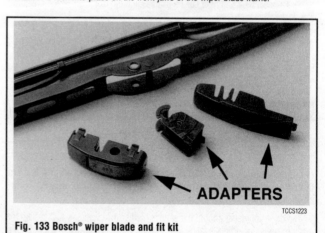

Fig. 133 Bosch® wiper blade and fit kit

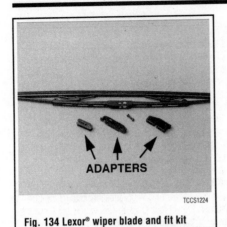

Fig. 134 Lexor® wiper blade and fit kit

Fig. 135 Pylon® wiper blade and adapter

Fig. 136 Trico® wiper blade and fit kit

Fig. 137 Tripledge® wiper blade and fit kit

Fig. 138 To remove and install a Lexor® wiper blade refill, slip out the old insert and slide in a new one

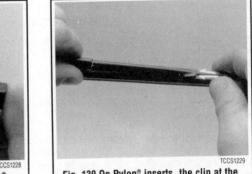

Fig. 139 On Pylon® inserts, the clip at the end has to be removed prior to sliding the insert off

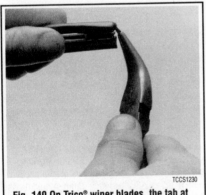

Fig. 140 On Trico® wiper blades, the tab at the end of the blade must be turned up . . .

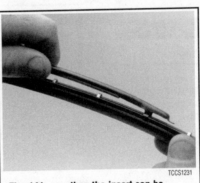

Fig. 141 . . . then the insert can be removed. After installing the replacement insert, bend the tab back

Fig. 142 The Tripledge® wiper blade insert is removed and installed using a securing clip

Another type of refill is made from polycarbonate. The refill has a simple locking device at one end which flexes downward out of the groove into which the jaws of the holder fit, allowing easy release. By sliding the new refill through all the jaws and pushing through the slight resistance when it reaches the end of its travel, the refill will lock into position.

To replace the Tridon® refill, it is necessary to remove the wiper blade. This refill has a plastic backing strip with a notch about 1 inch (25mm) from the end. Hold the blade (frame) on a hard surface so that the frame is tightly bowed. Grip the tip of the backing strip and pull up while twisting counterclockwise. The backing strip will snap out of the retaining tab. Do this for the remaining tabs until the refill is free of the blade. The length of these refills is molded into the end and they should be replaced with identical types.

Regardless of the type of refill used, be sure to follow the part manufacturer's instructions closely. Make sure that all of the frame jaws are engaged as the refill is pushed into place and locked. If the metal blade holder and frame are allowed to touch the glass during wiper operation, the glass will be scratched.

Tires and Wheels

Common sense and good driving habits will afford maximum tire life. Fast starts, sudden stops and hard cornering are hard on tires and will shorten their useful life span. Make sure that you don't overload the vehicle or run with incorrect pressure in the tires. Both of these practices will increase tread wear.

➡**For optimum tire life, keep the tires properly inflated, rotate them often and have the wheel alignment checked periodically.**

Inspect your tires frequently. Be especially careful to watch for bubbles in the tread or sidewall, deep cuts or underinflation. Replace any tires with bubbles in the sidewall. If cuts are so deep that they penetrate to the cords, discard the tire. Any cut in the sidewall of a radial tire renders it unsafe. Also look for uneven tread wear patterns that may indicate the front end is out of alignment or that the tires are out of balance.

TIRE ROTATION

♦ See Figures 143 and 144

Tires must be rotated periodically to equalize wear patterns that vary with a tire's position on the vehicle. Tires will also wear in an uneven way as the front steering/suspension system wears to the point where the alignment should be reset.

Rotating the tires will ensure maximum life for the tires as a set, so you will not have to discard a tire early due to wear on only part of the tread. Regular rotation is required to equalize wear.

When rotating "unidirectional tires," make sure that they always roll in the same direction. This means that a tire used on the left side of the vehicle must not be switched to the right side and vice-versa. Such tires should only be rotated front-to-rear or rear-to-front, while always remaining on the same side of the vehicle. These tires are marked on the sidewall as to the direction of rotation; observe the marks when reinstalling the tire(s).

Some styled or "mag" wheels may have different offsets front to rear. In these cases, the rear wheels must not be used up front and vice-versa. Furthermore, if these wheels are equipped with unidirectional tires, they cannot be rotated unless the tire is remounted for the proper direction of rotation.

➡ The compact or space-saver spare is strictly for emergency use. It must never be included in the tire rotation or placed on the vehicle for everyday use.

TIRE DESIGN

♦ See Figure 145

For maximum satisfaction, tires should be used in sets of four. Mixing of different types (radial, bias-belted, fiberglass belted) must be avoided. In most cases, the vehicle manufacturer has designated a type of tire on which the vehicle will perform best. Your first choice when replacing tires should be to use the same type of tire that the manufacturer recommends.

When radial tires are used, tire sizes and wheel diameters should be selected to maintain ground clearance and tire load capacity equivalent to the original specified tire. Radial tires should always be used in sets of four.

✳ CAUTION

Radial tires should never be used on only the front axle.

When selecting tires, pay attention to the original size as marked on the tire. Most tires are described using an industry size code sometimes referred to as P-Metric. This allows the exact identification of the tire specifications, regardless of the manufacturer. If selecting a different tire size or brand, remember to check the installed tire for any sign of interference with the body or suspension while the vehicle is stopping, turning sharply or heavily loaded.

Snow Tires

Good radial tires can produce a big advantage in slippery weather, but in snow, a street radial tire does not have sufficient tread to provide traction and control. The small grooves of a street tire quickly pack with snow and the tire behaves like a billiard ball on a marble floor. The more open, chunky tread of a snow tire will self-clean as the tire turns, providing much better grip on snowy surfaces.

To satisfy municipalities requiring snow tires during weather emergencies, most snow tires carry either an M + S designation after the tire size stamped on the sidewall, or the designation "all-season." In general, no change in tire size is necessary when buying snow tires.

Most manufacturers strongly recommend the use of 4 snow tires on their vehicles for reasons of stability. If snow tires are fitted only to the drive wheels, the opposite end of the vehicle may become very unstable when braking or turning on slippery surfaces. This instability can lead to unpleasant endings if the driver can't counteract the slide in time.

Note that snow tires, whether 2 or 4, will affect vehicle handling in all non-snow situations. The stiffer, heavier snow tires will noticeably change the turning and braking characteristics of the vehicle. Once the snow tires are installed, you must re-learn the behavior of the vehicle and drive accordingly.

➡ Consider buying extra wheels on which to mount the snow tires. Once done, the "snow wheels" can be installed and removed as needed. This eliminates the potential damage to tires or wheels from seasonal removal and installation. Even if your vehicle has styled wheels, see if inexpensive steel wheels are available. Although the look of the vehicle will change, the expensive wheels will be protected from salt, curb hits and pothole damage.

TIRE STORAGE

If they are mounted on wheels, store the tires at proper inflation pressure. All tires should be kept in a cool, dry place. If they are stored in the garage or basement, do not let them stand on a concrete floor; set them on strips of wood, a mat or a large stack of newspaper. Keeping them away from direct moisture is of paramount importance. Tires should not be stored upright, but in a flat position.

INFLATION & INSPECTION

♦ See Figures 146 thru 154

The importance of proper tire inflation cannot be overemphasized. A tire employs air as part of its structure. It is designed around the supporting strength of the air at a specified pressure. For this reason, improper inflation drastically reduces the tire's ability to perform as intended. A tire will lose some air in day-to-day use; having to add a few pounds of air periodically is not necessarily a sign of a leaking tire.

Two items should be a permanent fixture in every glove compartment: an accurate tire pressure gauge and a tread depth gauge. Check the tire pressure (including the spare) regularly with a pocket type gauge. Too often, the gauge on the end of the air hose at your corner garage is not accurate because it suffers too much abuse. Always check tire pressure when the tires are cold, as pressure increases with temperature. If you must move the vehicle to check the tire inflation, do not drive more than a mile before checking. A cold tire is generally one that has not been driven for more than three hours.

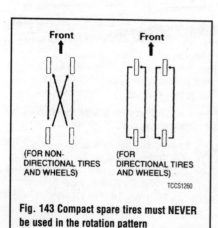

Fig. 143 Compact spare tires must NEVER be used in the rotation pattern

Fig. 144 Unidirectional tires are identifiable by sidewall arrows and/or the word "rotation"

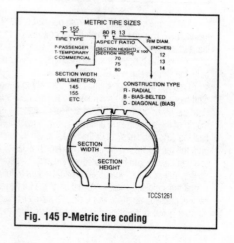

Fig. 145 P-Metric tire coding

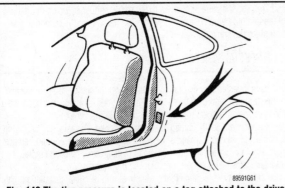

Fig. 146 The tire pressure is located on a tag attached to the drivers door jam

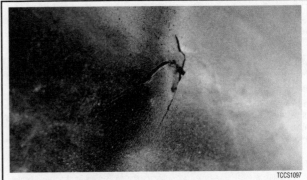

Fig. 147 Tires should be checked frequently for any sign of puncture or damage

Fig. 148 Tires with deep cuts, or cuts which bulge, should be replaced immediately

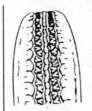

- DRIVE WHEEL HEAVY ACCELERATION
- OVERINFLATION

- HARD CORNERING
- UNDERINFLATION
- LACK OF ROTATION

Fig. 149 Examples of inflation-related tire wear patterns

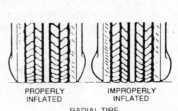

PROPERLY INFLATED   IMPROPERLY INFLATED

RADIAL TIRE

Fig. 150 Radial tires have a characteristic sidewall bulge; don't try to measure pressure by looking at the tire. Use a quality air pressure gauge

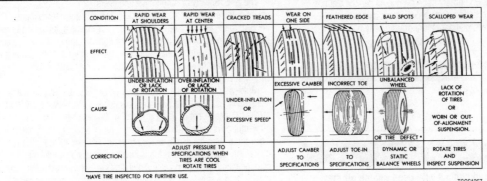

CONDITION	RAPID WEAR AT SHOULDERS	RAPID WEAR AT CENTER	CRACKED TREADS	WEAR ON ONE SIDE	FEATHERED EDGE	BALD SPOTS	SCALLOPED WEAR
EFFECT							
CAUSE	UNDER-INFLATION OR LACK OF ROTATION	OVER-INFLATION OR LACK OF ROTATION	UNDER-INFLATION OR EXCESSIVE SPEED*	EXCESSIVE CAMBER	INCORRECT TOE	UNBALANCED WHEEL OR TIRE DEFECT *	LACK OF ROTATION OF TIRES OR WORN OR OUT-OF-ALIGNMENT SUSPENSION.
CORRECTION		ADJUST PRESSURE TO SPECIFICATIONS WHEN TIRES ARE COOL ROTATE TIRES		ADJUST CAMBER TO SPECIFICATIONS	ADJUST TOE-IN TO SPECIFICATIONS	DYNAMIC OR STATIC BALANCE WHEELS	ROTATE TIRES AND INSPECT SUSPENSION

*HAVE TIRE INSPECTED FOR FURTHER USE.

Fig. 151 Common tire wear patterns and causes

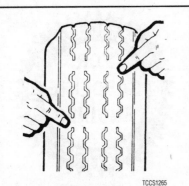

Fig. 152 Tread wear indicators will appear when the tire is worn

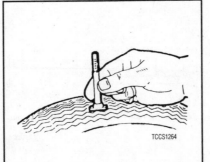

Fig. 153 Accurate tread depth indicators are inexpensive and handy

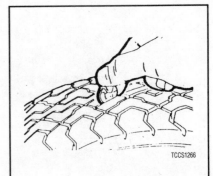

Fig. 154 A penny works well for a quick check of tread depth

A plate or sticker is normally provided somewhere in the vehicle (door post, hood, tailgate or trunk lid) which shows the proper pressure for the tires. Never counteract excessive pressure build-up by bleeding off air pressure (letting some air out). This will cause the tire to run hotter and wear quicker.

✳✳ CAUTION

Never exceed the maximum tire pressure embossed on the tire! This is the pressure to be used when the tire is at maximum loading, but it is rarely the correct pressure for everyday driving. Consult the owner's manual or the tire pressure sticker for the correct tire pressure.

Once you've maintained the correct tire pressures for several weeks, you'll be familiar with the vehicle's braking and handling personality. Slight adjustments in tire pressures can fine-tune these characteristics, but never change the cold pressure specification by more than 2 psi. A slightly softer tire pressure will give a softer ride but also yield lower fuel mileage. A slightly harder tire will give crisper dry road handling but can cause skidding on wet surfaces. Unless you're fully attuned to the vehicle, stick to the recommended inflation pressures.

All tires made since 1968 have built-in tread wear indicator bars that show up as ½ in. (13mm) wide smooth bands across the tire when 1/16 in. (1.5mm) of tread remains. The appearance of tread wear indicators means that the tires should be replaced. In fact, many states have laws prohibiting the use of tires with less than this amount of tread.

You can check your own tread depth with an inexpensive gauge or by using a Lincoln head penny. Slip the Lincoln penny (with Lincoln's head upside-down) into several tread grooves. If you can see the top of Lincoln's head in 2 adjacent grooves, the tire has less than 1/16 in. (1.5mm) tread left and should be replaced. You can measure snow tires in the same manner by using the "tails" side of the Lincoln penny. If you can see the top of the Lincoln memorial, it's time to replace the snow tire(s).

CARE OF SPECIAL WHEELS

If you have invested money in magnesium, aluminum alloy or sport wheels, special precautions should be taken to make sure your investment is not wasted and that your special wheels look good for the life of the vehicle.

Special wheels are easily damaged and/or scratched. Occasionally check the rims for cracking, impact damage or air leaks. If any of these are found, replace the wheel. But in order to prevent this type of damage and the costly replacement of a special wheel, observe the following precautions:

• Use extra care not to damage the wheels during removal, installation, balancing, etc. After removal of the wheels from the vehicle, place them on a mat or other protective surface. If they are to be stored for any length of time, support them on strips of wood. Never store tires and wheels upright; the tread may develop flat spots.

• When driving, watch for hazards; it doesn't take much to crack a wheel.

• When washing, use a mild soap or non-abrasive dish detergent (keeping in mind that detergent tends to remove wax). Avoid cleansers with abrasives or the use of hard brushes. There are many cleaners and polishes for special wheels.

• If possible, remove the wheels during the winter. Salt and sand used for snow removal can severely damage the finish of a wheel.

• Make certain the recommended lug nut torque is never exceeded or the wheel may crack. Never use snow chains on special wheels; severe scratching will occur.

FLUIDS AND LUBRICANTS

Fluid Disposal

Used fluids such as engine oil, transaxle fluid, antifreeze and brake fluid are hazardous wastes and must be disposed of properly. Before draining any fluids, consult with your local authorities; in many areas, waste oil, antifreeze, etc. is being accepted as a part of recycling programs. A number of service stations and auto parts stores are also accepting waste fluids for recycling.

Be sure of the recycling center's policies before draining any fluids, as many will not accept different fluids that have been mixed together.

Fuel and Engine Oil Recommendation

▶ **See Figures 155, 156 and 157**

OIL

✳✳ CAUTION

The EPA warns that prolonged contact with used engine oil may cause a number of skin disorders, including cancer! You should make every effort to minimize your exposure to used engine oil.

Protective gloves should be worn when changing the oil. Wash your hands and any other exposed skin areas as soon as possible after exposure to used engine oil. Soap and water, or waterless hand cleaner should be used.

The SAE (Society of Automotive Engineers) grade number indicates the viscosity of the engine oil; its resistance to flow at a given temperature. The lower the SAE grade number, the lighter the oil. For example, the mono-grade oils begin with SAE 5 weight, which is a thin light oil, and continue in viscosity up to SAE 80 or 90 weight, which are heavy gear lubricants. These oils are also known as "straight weight", meaning they are of a single viscosity, and do not vary with engine temperature.

Multi-viscosity oils offer the important advantage of being adaptable to temperature extremes. These oils have designations such as 10W-40, 20W-50, etc. The "10W-40" means that in winter (the "W" in the designation) the oil acts like a thin 10 weight oil, allowing the engine to spin easily when cold and offering rapid lubrication. Once the engine has warmed up, however, the oil acts like a straight 40 weight, maintaining good lubrication and protection for the engine's internal components. A 20W-50 oil would therefore be slightly heavier than and not as ideal in cold weather as the 10W-40, but would offer better protection at higher rpm and temperatures because when warm it acts like a 50 weight oil. Whichever oil viscosity you choose when changing the oil, make sure you are anticipating

Fig. 155 Look for the API oil identification label when choosing your engine oil

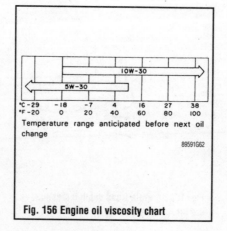

Fig. 156 Engine oil viscosity chart

Fig. 157 The International Lubricant Standardization and Approval Committee label

the temperatures your engine will be operating in until the oil is changed again. Refer to the oil viscosity chart for oil recommendations according to temperature.

The API (American Petroleum Institute) designation indicates the classification of engine oil used under certain given operating conditions. Only oils designated for use "Service SH" should be used. Oils of the SH type perform a variety of functions inside the engine in addition to the basic function as a lubricant. Through a balanced system of metallic detergents and polymeric dispersants, the oil prevents the formation of high and low temperature deposits and also keeps sludge and particles of dirt in suspension. Acids, particularly sulfuric acid, as well as other by-products of combustion, are neutralized. Both the SAE grade number and the APE designation can be found on top of the oil can.

Synthetic Oil

※※ WARNING

Operating the engine without the proper amount and type of engine oil will result in severe engine damage.

There are many excellent synthetic and fuel-efficient oils currently available that can provide better gas mileage, longer service life, and in some cases better engine protection. These benefits do not come without a few hitches, however. The main one is the price of synthetic oils, which is three or four times the price per quart of conventional oil.

Synthetic oil is not for every car and every type of driving, so you should consider your engine's condition and your type of driving. Also, check your car's warranty conditions regarding the use of synthetic oils.

Both brand new engines and older, high mileage engines are the wrong candidates for synthetic oil. The synthetic oils are so slippery that they can prevent the proper break-in of new engines; most manufacturers recommend that you wait until the engine is properly broken in (3000 miles) before using synthetic oil. Older engines with wear have a different problem with synthetics: they "use" (consume during operation) more oil as they age. Slippery synthetic oils get past these worn parts easily. If your engine is "using" conventional oil, it will use synthetics much faster. Also, if your car is leaking oil past old seals you'll have a much greater leak problem with synthetics.

Consider your type of driving. If most of your accumulated mileage is high speed, highway type driving, the more expensive synthetic oils may be a benefit. Extended highway driving gives the engine a chance to warm up, accumulating less acids in the oil and putting less stress on the engine over the long run. Under these conditions, the oil change interval can be extended (as long as your oil filter can last the extended life of the oil) up to the advertised mileage claims of the synthetics. Cars with synthetic oils may show increased fuel economy in highway driving, due to less internal friction. However, many automotive experts agree that 50,000 miles (80,000 km) is too long to keep any oil in your engine.

FUEL

※※ CAUTION

Observe all applicable safety precautions when working around fuel. Whenever servicing the fuel system, always work in a well ventilated area. Do not allow fuel spray or vapors to come in contact with a spark or open flame. Keep a dry chemical fire extinguisher near the work area. Always keep fuel in a container specifically designed for fuel storage; also, always properly seal fuel containers to avoid the possibility of fire or explosion.

It is important to use fuel of the proper octane rating in your car. Octane rating is based on the quantity of anti-knock compounds added to the fuel and it determines the speed at which the gas will burn. The lower the octane rating, the faster it burns. The higher the octane, the slower the fuel will burn and a greater percentage of compounds in the fuel prevent spark ping (knock), detonation and preignition (dieseling).

As the temperature of the engine increases, the air/fuel mixture exhibits a tendency to ignite before the spark plug is fired. If fuel of an octane rating too low for the engine is used, this will allow combustion to occur before the piston has completed its compression stroke, thereby creating a very high pressure rapidly.

Fuel of the proper octane rating, for the compression ratio and ignition timing of your car, will slow the combustion process sufficiently to allow the spark plug enough time to ignite the mixture completely and smoothly. Many non-catalyst

models are designed to run on regular fuel. The use of some super-premium fuel is no substitution for a properly tuned and maintained engine. Chances are that if your engine exhibits any signs of spark ping, detonation or pre-ignition when using regular fuel, the ignition timing should be checked against specifications or the cylinder head should be removed for decarbonizing.

Vehicles equipped with catalytic converters must use UNLEADED GASOLINE ONLY. Use of leaded fuel shortens the life of spark plugs, exhaust systems and EGR valves and can damage the catalytic converter. Most converter equipped models are designed to operate using unleaded gasoline with a minimum rating of 87 octane. Use of unleaded gas with octane ratings lower than 87 can cause persistent spark knock which could lead to engine damage.

Light spark knock may be noticed when accelerating or driving up hills. The slight knocking may be considered normal (with 87 octane fuel) because the maximum fuel economy is obtained under condition of occasional light spark knock. Gasoline with an octane rating higher than 87 may be used, but it is not necessary (in most cases) for proper operation.

If spark knock is constant, when using 87 octane fuel, at cruising speeds on level ground, ignition timing adjustment may be required.

➡**Your engine's fuel requirement can change with time, mainly due to carbon buildup, which changes the compression ratio. If your engine pings, knocks or runs on, switch to a higher grade of fuel. Sometimes just changing brands will cure the problem.**

If you plan to drive your car outside the United States or Canada, there is a possibility that fuels will be too low in anti-knock quality and could produce engine damage. It is wise to consult with local authorities upon arrival in a foreign country to determine the best fuels available.

Engine

※※ CAUTION

To avoid personal injury, avoid prolonged and repeated skin contact with used engine oil. Always follow these simple precautions when handling used motor oil:

- Avoid prolonged skin contact with used motor oil.
- Remove oil from skin by washing thoroughly with soap and water or waterless hand cleaner. Do not use gasoline, thinners or other solvents.
- Avoid prolonged skin contact with oil-soaked clothing.

OIL LEVEL CHECK

▶ **See Figures 158 and 159**

Every time you stop for fuel, check the engine oil as follows:
1. Park the car on level ground.
2. When checking the oil level it is best for the engine to be at operating temperature, although checking the oil immediately after a stopping will lead to a false reading. Wait a few minutes after turning off the engine to allow the oil to drain back into the crankcase.
3. Open the hood and locate the dipstick.
4. Pull the dipstick from its tube, wipe it clean and reinsert it.
5. Reinsert the dipstick, push it in as far as it will go or the reading will not be accurate.
6. Pull the dipstick out again and, holding it horizontally, read the oil level on the end of the stick. The oil should be between the **F** and **L** marks on the dipstick. If the oil is below the **L** mark, add oil of the proper viscosity through the capped opening on the top of the cylinder head cover.
7. Replace the dipstick and check the oil level again after adding any oil. Be careful not to overfill the crankcase. Approximately one quart of oil will raise the level from the **L** to the **F**. Excess oil will generally be consumed at an accelerated rate.

OIL & FILTER CHANGE

▶ **See Figures 160 thru 171**

Toyota recommends changing the oil filter with every other oil change; we suggest that the filter be changed with EVERY oil change. There can be up to 1 quart of dirty oil left remaining in an old oil filter if it is not changed.

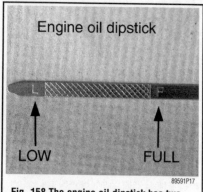

Fig. 158 The engine oil dipstick has two markings for LOW and FULL

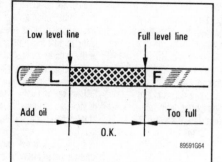

Fig. 159 Only read the engine oil dipstick level when the vehicle is at operating temperature

Fig. 160 The drain plug is located in the oil pan and the filter is close by

Fig. 161 Remove the oil cap, some are labeled with the type of oil to fill your crankcase with

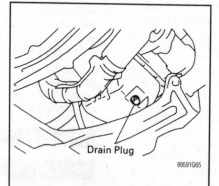

Fig. 162 The engine oil drain plug is located on the bottom of the pan

Fig. 163 Use inward pressure when removing the oil drain plug

Fig. 164 Always wipe the area clean before replacing the gasket and drain plug

Fig. 165 Place a strap wrench over the filter to loosen it . . .

Fig. 166 . . . then remove the filter with your hands

Fig. 167 Next wipe the filter mating area with a clean rag

Fig. 168 Before installing a new oil filter, lightly coat the rubber gasket with clean oil

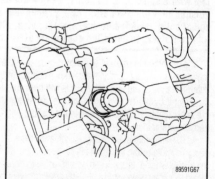

Fig. 169 Tighten the oil filter by hand until the gasket contacts the seat of the mounting

The oil drain plug is located on the bottom of the oil pan (the belly-like reservoir held on by many bolts). The oil filter is located on the front side of the engine.

The mileage figures given are the Toyota recommended intervals assuming normal driving and conditions. If your car is being used under dusty, polluted or off-road conditions, change the oil and filter more frequently than specified. The same goes for cars driven in stop-and-go traffic or only for short distances. Always drain the oil after the engine has been running long enough to bring it to normal operating temperature. Hot oil will flow easier and more contaminants will be removed along with the oil than if it were drained cold. To change the oil and filter:

1. Warm the oil by running the engine for a short period of time or at least until the needle on the temperature gauge rises above the **C** mark. This will make the oil flow more freely from the oil pan.

2. Park on a level surface, apply the parking brake and block the wheels. Stop the engine. Raise the hood and remove the oil filler cap from the top of the valve cover. This allows the air to enter the engine as the oil drains. Remove the dipstick, wipe it off and set it aside.

3. Position a suitable oil drain pan under the drain plug.

➡ **The engine holds approximately 4 quarts of oil, so choose a drain pan that exceeds this amount to allow for movement of the oil when the pan is pulled from under the vehicle. This will prevent time lost to the cleaning up of messy oil spills.**

4. With the proper size metric socket or closed end wrench (DO NOT use pliers or vise grips), loosen the drain plug. Back out the 12mm drain plug while maintaining a slight upward force on it to keep the oil from running out around it (and your hand). Allow the oil to drain into the drain pan.

✳✳ CAUTION

To avoid personal injury, remember that the engine oil will be hot. Keep your arms, face and hands away from the oil as it is draining

5. Remove the drain pan and wipe any excess oil from the area around the hole using a clean rag. Clean the threads of the drain plug and the drain plug gasket to remove any sludge deposits that may have accumulated.

6. With a filter wrench, loosen the oil filter counterclockwise and back the filter off the filter post the rest of the way by hand. Keep the filter end up so that the oil does not spill out. Tilt the filter into the drain pan to drain the oil.

7. Remove the drain pan from under the vehicle and place it aside.

8. With a clean rag, wipe off the filter seating surface to ensure a proper seal. Make sure that the old gasket is not stuck to the seating surface. If it is, remove it and thoroughly clean the seating surface of the old gasket material.

9. Open a container of new oil and smear some of this oil onto the rubber gasket of the new oil filter. Get a feel for where the filter post is and start the filter by hand until the gasket contacts the seat. Using the filter wrench, turn the filter the additional amount indicated on the filter box. This is usually 3/4 turn.

10. Install the drain plug and gasket. Be sure that the plug is tight enough that the oil does not leak out, but not tight enough to strip the threads. Over time you will develop a sense of what the proper tightness of the drain plug is. If a torque wrench is available, tighten the plug to 29 ft. lbs. (39 Nm).

➡ **Replace the drain plug gasket at every third or fourth oil change, or when the gasket does not create a drip-free seal.**

11. Through a suitable plastic or metal funnel, add clean new oil of the proper grade and viscosity through the oil filler on the top of the valve cover. Be sure that the oil level registers near the **F** (full) mark on the dipstick.

✳✳ WARNING

Operating the engine without the proper amount and type of engine oil will result in severe engine damage.

12. Install and tighten the oil filler cap.
13. Start the engine and allow it to run for several minutes.

➡ **Do not rev up the engine, since damage can occur, especially to a turbocharger, if equipped.**

14. Check for leaks at the filter and drain plug. Sometimes leaks will not be revealed until the engine reaches normal operating temperature.
15. Stop the engine and recheck the oil level. Add oil as necessary.

Manual Transaxle

LEVEL CHECK

♦ **See Figure 172**

➡ **Only SAE75W-90 fluid or an equivalent should be used in the manual transaxles.**

The oil in the manual transaxle should be checked at least every 15,000 miles (24,000 km) and replaced every 25,000–30,000 miles (40,000–48,000 km), even more frequently if driven in deep water.

1. Park the car on a level surface.
2. Raise the vehicle and support it properly on jackstands so that you can safely work underneath. You will probably not have enough room to work if the car is not raised.
3. On some models it will be necessary to remove the LH engine under cover.
4. Remove the 17mm hex filler plug from the front side of the transaxle housing.
5. If the lubricant begins to trickle out of the hole, there is enough. Otherwise, carefully insert your finger (watch out for sharp threads!) and check to see if the oil is up to the edge of the hole.
6. If not, add oil through the hole until the level is at the edge of the hole. Most gear lubricants come in a plastic squeeze bottle with a nozzle; making additions simple. You can also use a common everyday kitchen baster.
7. Replace the filler plug and tighten it to 36 ft. lbs. (49 Nm). Run the engine and check for leaks.

DRAIN & REFILL

♦ **See Figures 173 and 174**

➡ **The transaxle oil should be hot before it is drained. If the engine is at normal operating temperature, the transaxle oil should be hot enough.**

Fig. 170 Refill the crankcase with oil

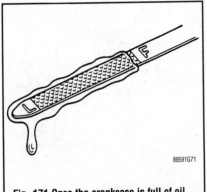

Fig. 171 Once the crankcase is full of oil, double check the level on the dipstick

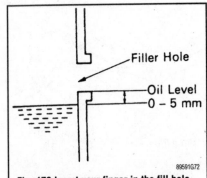

Fig. 172 Insert your finger in the fill hole and check that the oil level is 0–5mm below the lip of the hole

1. Raise the car and support it properly on jackstands so that you can safely work underneath. You will probably not have enough room to work if the car is not raised.

2. The drain plug is located on the bottom of the transaxle and usually 24mm. Place a pan under the drain plug and remove it. Keep a slight upward pressure on the plug while unscrewing it, this will keep the oil from pouring out until the plug is removed.

✳✳ CAUTION

To avoid personal injury, remember that the oil may be hot.

3. Allow the oil to drain completely. Clean off the plug and reinstall it, tightening it to 36 ft. lbs. (49 Nm).

4. Remove the filler plug from the side of the transaxle case. Most Celicas should have a 17mm hexagon filler plug. It is on the front side. There is usually a gasket underneath this plug. Replace it if damaged.

5. Fill the transaxle, with the proper lubricant, through the filler plug hole as detailed previously, using a suction gun. Refer to the Capacities Chart for the amount of oil needed to refill your transaxle.

6. The oil level should come right up to the edge of the hole. You can stick your finger in to verify this. Watch out for sharp threads!

7. Reinstall the filler plug and gasket, lower the car, and check for leaks. Dispose of the old oil in the proper manner.

Automatic Transaxle

FLUID RECOMMENDATIONS

The automatic transaxle on the Celica requires DEXRON®II ATF (or its superceding fluid type).

FLUID LEVEL CHECK

♦ **See Figures 175 and 176**

Check the automatic transaxle fluid level at least every 15,000 miles (24,000 km). The dipstick is in engine compartment. The fluid level should be checked only when the transaxle is hot (normal operating temperature). The transaxle is considered hot after about 20 miles of highway driving.

1. Park the car on a level surface with the engine idling. Shift the transaxle into **P** and set the parking brake.

2. Remove the dipstick, wipe it clean and reinsert if firmly. Be sure that it has been pushed all the way in. Remove the dipstick and check the fluid level while holding it horizontally. All models have a HOT and a COLD side to the dipstick.

• **COLD** : the fluid level should fall in this range when the engine has been running for only a short time.

• **HOT** : the fluid level should fall in this range when the engine has reached normal running temperatures.

3. If the fluid level is not within the proper area on either side of the dipstick, pour ATF into the dipstick tube. This is easily done with the aid of a fun-nel. Check the level often as you are filling the transaxle. Be extremely careful not to overfill it. Overfilling will cause slippage, seal damage and overheating. Approximately one pint of ATF will raise the level from one notch to the other.

➥**Always use DEXRON®II transaxle fluid (or its superceding type) when filling your car's transaxle. Always check with the owner's manual to be sure. The fluid on the dipstick should always be a bright red color. It if is discolored (brown or black), or smells burnt, serious transaxle troubles, probably due to internal slippage resulting in overheating, should be suspected. The transaxle should be inspected by a qualified service technician to locate the cause of the burnt fluid.**

DRAIN & REFILL

♦ **See Figures 177, 178, 179, 180 and 181**

The automatic transaxle fluid should be changed at least every 25,000–30,000 miles (40,000–48,000 km). If the car is normally used in severe service, such as stop-and-go driving, trailer towing or the like, the interval should be halved. The fluid should be hot before it is drained; a 20 minute drive will accomplish this.

➥**The removal of the transaxle oil pan drain plug requires the use a 10mm hex head socket.**

1. Remove the dipstick from the filler tube and install a funnel in the opening.

2. Position a suitable drain pan under the drain plug. Loosen the drain plug with a 10mm hex head socket and allow the fluid to drain.

3. Install and tighten the drain plug to:
• A140E—36 ft. lbs. (49 Nm)
• A246E—13 ft. lbs. (17 Nm)

4. Through the filler tube opening, add the proper amount of transaxle fluid as specified in the Capacities Chart.

5. Start the engine and shift the selector into all positions from **P** through **L**, and then shift into **P**. With the engine idling, check the fluid level. Add fluid up to the COOL level on the dipstick.

➥**Do not overfill.**

6. Recheck the level at the normal operating temperature and add as necessary.

PAN & FILTER SERVICE

♦ **See Figures 182 thru 187**

➥**The removal of the transaxle oil pan drain plug requires the use of Toyota special tool SST 09043-38100 or its equivalent (a 10mm hex head socket).**

1. To avoid contamination of the transaxle, thoroughly clean the exterior of the oil pan and surrounding area to remove any deposits of dirt and grease.

2. Position a suitable drain pan under the oil pan and remove the 10mm drain plug. Allow the oil to drain from the pan. Set the drain plug aside.

3. Loosen and remove all but two or four of the oil pan retaining bolts. The bolts are usually 10mm in size.

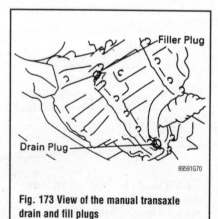

Fig. 173 View of the manual transaxle drain and fill plugs

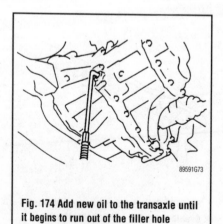

Fig. 174 Add new oil to the transaxle until it begins to run out of the filler hole

Fig. 175 Release the clip and pull the transaxle gauge out of the tube

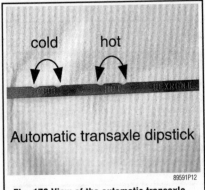

Fig. 176 View of the automatic transaxle dipstick

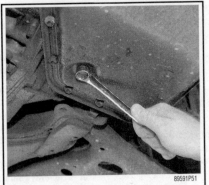

Fig. 177 Remove the drain plug from the bottom of the automatic transaxle pan

Fig. 178 Place slight pressure on the automatic drain plug as you loosen it

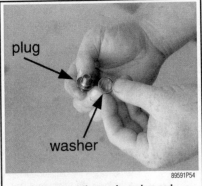

Fig. 179 Inspect the crush washer and plug and replace if needed

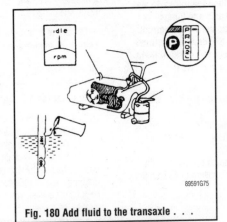

Fig. 180 Add fluid to the transaxle . . .

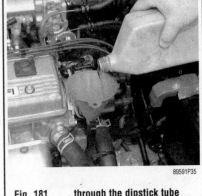

Fig. 181 . . . through the dipstick tube

Fig. 182 Leave a few bolts in the pan and allow the fluid to drain

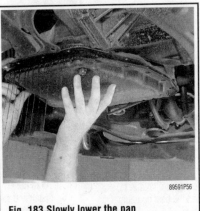

Fig. 183 Slowly lower the pan

Fig. 184 To lower the filter, remove these three screws

Fig. 185 The filter should be thrown away and replaced with a new one

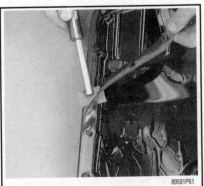

Fig. 186 Scrape the old gasket and discard from the pan

Fig. 187 Inspect and clean the magnets in the pan

4. Support the pan by hand and slowly remove the remaining two bolts. It may be heavy, so get in a stable position.

5. Carefully lower the pan to the ground. There will be some fluid still inside the pan, so be careful.

6. Remove the three oil strainer attaching bolts and carefully remove the strainer. The strainer will also contain some fluid.

→One of the three oil strainer bolts is slightly longer than the other two. Mark down where the longer bolt goes so that it will be reinstalled in the original position.

7. Discard the strainer. Remove the gasket from the pan and discard it.

8. Drain the remainder of the fluid from the oil pan and wipe the pan clean with a rag. With a gasket scraper, remove any old gasket material from the flanges of the pan and the transaxle. Remove the gasket from the drain plug and replace it with a new one.

→Depending on the year and maintenance schedule of the vehicle, there may be from one to three small magnets on the bottom of the pan. These magnets were installed by the manufacturer at the time the transaxle was assembled. The magnets function to collect metal chips and filings from clutch plates, bushings and bearings that accumulate during the normal break-in process that a new transaxle experiences. So, don't be alarmed if such accumulations are present. Clean the magnets and reinstall them. They are useful tools for determining transaxle component wear.

To install:

9. Install the new oil strainer. Install and tighten the retaining bolts in their proper locations to 7 ft. lbs. (10 Nm).

10. Install the new gasket onto the oil pan making sure that the holes in the gasket are aligned evenly with those of the pan. Position the magnets so that they will not interfere with the oil tubes.

11. Raise the pan and gasket into position on the transaxle and install the retaining bolts. Tighten the retaining bolts in a crisscross pattern to 45 inch lbs. (5 Nm).

12. Install and tighten the drain plug to:
- A140E—36 ft. lbs. (49 Nm)
- A246E—13 ft. lbs. (17 Nm)

13. Fluid is added only through the dipstick tube. Use only the proper automatic transaxle fluid; do not overfill.

14. Replace the dipstick after filling. Start the engine and allow it to idle. DO NOT race the engine!

15. After the engine has idled for a few minutes, shift the transaxle slowly through the gears and then return it to **P**. With the engine still idling, check the fluid level on the dipstick. If necessary, add more fluid to raise the level to where it is supposed to be.

Cooling System

FLUID RECOMMENDATIONS

The correct coolant is any permanent, high quality ethylene glycol antifreeze mixed in a 50/50 concentration with water. This mixture gives the best combination of antifreeze and anti-boil characteristics within the engine.

LEVEL CHECK

▶ See Figures 188, 189, and 190

❊❊ CAUTION

Never open, service or drain the radiator or cooling system when hot; serious burns can occur from the steam and hot coolant. Also, when draining engine coolant, keep in mind that cats and dogs are attracted to ethylene glycol antifreeze and could drink any that is left in an uncovered container or in puddles on the ground. This will prove fatal in sufficient quantities. Always drain coolant into a sealable container. Coolant should be reused unless it is contaminated or is several years old.

It's best to check the coolant level when the engine is COLD. The radiator coolant level should be between the LOW and the FULL lines on the reservoir tank when the engine is cold. If low, check for leakage and add coolant up to the FULL line but do not overfill.

→Check the freeze protection rating of the antifreeze at least once a year or as necessary with a suitable antifreeze tester.

DRAIN & REFILL

▶ See Figures 191 thru 197

1. Draining the cooling system is always done with the engine **COLD**.
2. Remove the reservoir tank cap.
3. Remove the engine under covers.
4. Position the drain pan under the draincock on the bottom of the radiator. Loosen the radiator and engine draincocks. These should be opened to aid in draining the cooling system completely. If for some reason the radiator draincock can't be used, you can loosen and remove the lower radiator hose at its joint to the radiator.

❊❊ CAUTION

When draining the coolant, keep in mind that cats and dogs are attracted by the ethylene glycol antifreeze, and are quite likely to drink any that is left in an uncovered container or in puddles on the ground. This will prove fatal in sufficient quantity. Always drain the coolant into a sealable container. Coolant should be reused unless it is contaminated or several years old.

5. When the system stops draining, close both draincocks as necessary.
6. Using a funnel if necessary, fill the reservoir tank with a 50/50 solution of antifreeze and water. Allow time for the fluid to run through the hoses and into the engine.
7. Start the engine and let it idle about 10 minuets; add the coolant/water mixture up to the FULL level.
8. Install and secure the engine under covers.
9. Securely tighten the cap.

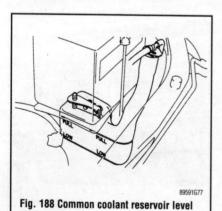
Fig. 188 Common coolant reservoir level indicators

Fig. 189 The coolant reservoir level indicators are hard to see, located under the battery in the 7A-FE engine

Fig. 190 If necessary, lift the cap and add coolant

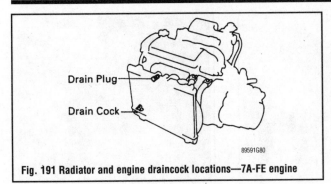

Fig. 191 Radiator and engine draincock locations—7A-FE engine

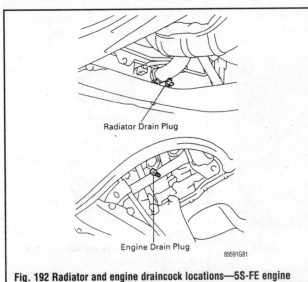

Fig. 192 Radiator and engine draincock locations—5S-FE engine

10. Race the engine 2000–3000 rpms for about 5 minutes, then stop the engine.

11. After the coolant drops, remove the cap and add coolant to the FULL level again.

FLUSHING & CLEANING THE SYSTEM

Proceed with draining the system as outlined above. When the system has drained, reconnect any hoses close to the radiator draincock. Move the temperature control for the heater to its hottest position; this allows the heater core to be flushed as well. Using a garden hose or bucket, fill the reservoir and allow the water to run out the engine drain cock. Continue until the water runs clear. Be sure to clean the expansion tank as well.

If the system is badly contaminated with rust or scale, you can use a commercial flushing solution to clean it out. Follow the manufacturer's instructions. Some causes of rust are air in the system, failure to change the coolant regularly, use of excessively hard or soft water, and/or failure to use the correct mix of antifreeze and water.

After the system has been flushed, continue with the refill procedures outlined above. Check the condition of the radiator cap and its gasket, replacing the radiator cap as necessary.

Brake Master Cylinder

FLUID RECOMMENDATIONS

All Celicas use DOT 3 or SAE J1703 brake fluid.

LEVEL CHECK

▶ See Figures 198, 199, 200 and 201

The brake master cylinder is located under the hood, in the left rear side of the compartment. It is made of translucent plastic so that the levels may be

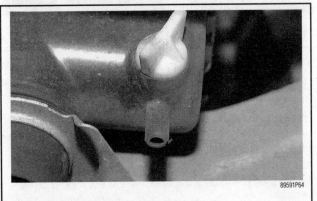

Fig. 193 The draincock can be loosened by hand

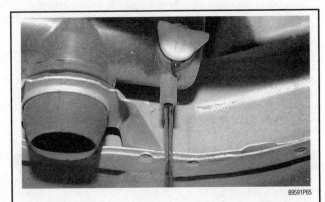

Fig. 194 Notice the coolant mixture will flow straight out of the hose

Fig. 195 Fill the cooling system through the radiator

Fig. 196 Using a funnel, top off the engine cooling system

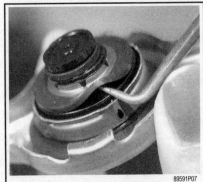

Fig. 197 Always inspect the radiator cap gasket for deterioration

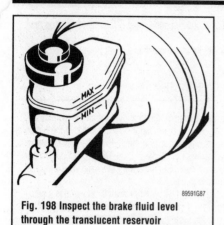

Fig. 198 Inspect the brake fluid level through the translucent reservoir

Fig. 199 The brake master cylinder cap specifies to clean it prior to removal

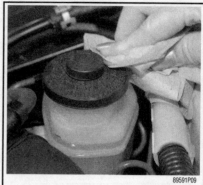

Fig. 200 Use a cloth to clean the master cylinder cap of any dirt before opening

Fig. 201 Carefully pour the brake fluid into the reservoir to top off the system

Fig. 202 Note the type of power steering fluid is labeled on the cap

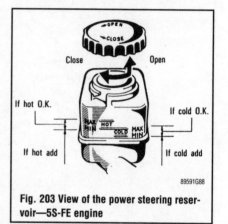

Fig. 203 View of the power steering reservoir—5S-FE engine

checked without removing the top. The fluid level in the reservoir should be checked at least every 15,000 miles (24,000km) or 1 year. The fluid level should be maintained at the uppermost mark on the side of the reservoir. Any sudden decrease in the level indicates a possible leak in the system and should be checked out immediately.

When adding fluid, use only fresh, uncontaminated brake fluid meeting or exceeding DOT 3 standards. Be careful not to spill any brake fluid on painted surfaces, as it eats the paint. Do not allow the brake fluid container or the master cylinder reservoir to remain open any longer than necessary; brake fluid absorbs moisture from the air, reducing its effectiveness and causing corrosion in the lines.

Clutch Master Cylinder

FLUID RECOMMENDATIONS

All vehicles use DOT 3 or SAEJ1703 brake fluid.

LEVEL CHECK

The clutch master cylinder is located under the hood, in the left rear section of the engine compartment near the brake master. The clutch master reservoir is made of a translucent plastic so that the levels may be checked without removing the top. The fluid level in the reservoir should be checked at least every 15,000 miles (24,000 km) or 1 year. The fluid level should be maintained at the uppermost mark on the side of the reservoir. Any sudden decrease in the level indicates a possible leak in the system and should be checked out immediately.

When adding fluid, use only fresh, uncontaminated brake fluid meeting or exceeding DOT 3 standards. Be careful not to spill any brake fluid on painted surfaces, as it eats the paint. Do not allow the brake fluid container or the master cylinder reservoir to remain open any longer than necessary; brake fluid absorbs moisture from the air, reducing its effectiveness and causing corrosion in the lines.

Power Steering Pump

FLUID RECOMMENDATIONS

◗ See Figure 202

All vehicles use DEXRON®II or III type automatic transmission fluid in the power steering system.

LEVEL CHECK

◗ See Figures 203, 204, 205, 206 and 207

Check the power steering fluid level every 6 months or 6000 miles (9600 km). The power steering pump is located on the right side of the vehicle near the firewall.

1. Make sure that the vehicle is level. If the reservoir is dirty, wipe it off.
2. Start the engine and allow it to idle.
3. With the engine at idle, move the steering wheel from LOCK to LOCK several times to raise the temperature of the fluid.
4. The power steering pump reservoir is translucent, so the fluid level may be checked without removing the cap. Look through the reservoir and check for foaming or emulsification.

➡Foaming or emulsification indicates the either there is air in the system or the fluid level is low.

5. Check the fluid level in the reservoir. The fluid should be within the **HOT LEVEL** of the reservoir. If the fluid is checked when cold, the level should be within the **COLD LEVEL** of the reservoir.
6. Add fluid as required until the proper level is reached. To add fluid, remove the filler cap by turning it counterclockwise and lifting up. After the proper amount of fluid is added, replace the cap making sure that the arrows on the cap are properly aligned with the arrows on the tank.
7. While your in the neighborhood, check the steering box case, vane pump

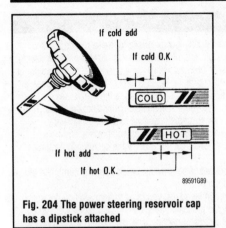

Fig. 204 The power steering reservoir cap has a dipstick attached

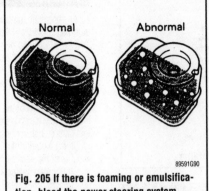

Fig. 205 If there is foaming or emulsification, bleed the power steering system

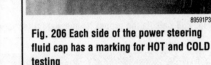

Fig. 206 Each side of the power steering fluid cap has a marking for HOT and COLD testing

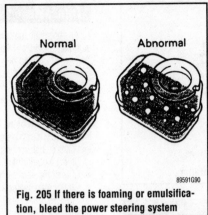

Fig. 207 Use a funnel to add power steering fluid to the pump

and hose connections for leaks and damage. Simple preventative maintenance checks like these can identify minor problems before turn into major problems and also increase your familiarity with the locations of steering system components.

Body Lubrication and Maintenance

There is no set period recommended by Toyota for body lubrication. However, it is a good idea to lubricate the following body points at least once a year, especially in the fall before cold weather.

TRAILER TOWING

General Recommendations

Your vehicle was primarily designed to carry passengers and cargo. It is important to remember that towing a trailer will place additional loads on your vehicles engine, drivetrain, steering, braking and other systems. However, if you decide to tow a trailer, using the prior equipment is a must.

Local laws may require specific equipment such as trailer brakes or fender mounted mirrors. Check your local laws.

Trailer Weight

The weight of the trailer is the most important factor. A good weight-to-horsepower ratio is about 35:1, 35 lbs. of Gross Combined Weight (GCW) for every horsepower your engine develops. Multiply the engine's rated horsepower by 35 and subtract the weight of the vehicle passengers and luggage. The number remaining is the approximate ideal maximum weight you should tow, although a numerically higher axle ratio can help compensate for heavier weight.

LOCK CYLINDERS

Apply graphite lubricant sparingly thought the key slot. Insert the key and operate the lock several times to be sure that the lubricant is worked into the lock cylinder.

DOOR HINGES & HINGE CHECKS

Spray a silicone lubricant or apply white lithium grease on the hinge pivot points to eliminate any binding conditions. Open and close the door several times to be sure that the lubricant is evenly and thoroughly distributed. When applying grease, the use of a small acid brush is very helpful in getting the grease to those hard to reach areas.

BODY DRAIN HOLES

Be sure that the drain holes in the doors and rocker panels are cleared of obstruction. A small screwdriver can be used to clear them of any debris.

Wheel Bearings

The Toyota Celica models are equipped with sealed bearing assemblies. The bearing assemblies are nonserviceable. If the assembly is damaged, the complete unit must be replaced. Refer to Section 8 for the bearing removal and installation procedure.

Hitch (Tongue) Weight

▶ See Figure 208

Calculate the hitch weight in order to select a proper hitch. The weight of the hitch is usually 9–11% of the trailer gross weight and should be measured with the trailer loaded. Hitches fall into various categories: those that mount on the frame and rear bumper, the bolt-on type, or the weld-on distribution type used for larger trailers. Axle mounted or clamp-on bumper hitches should never be used.

Check the gross weight rating of your trailer. Tongue weight is usually figured as 10% of gross trailer weight. Therefore, a trailer with a maximum gross weight of 2000 lbs. will have a maximum tongue weight of 200 lbs. Class I trailers fall into this category. Class II trailers are those with a gross weight rating of 2000–3000 lbs., while Class III trailers fall into the 3500–6000 lbs. category. Class IV trailers are those over 6000 lbs. and are for use with fifth wheel trucks, only.

When you've determined the hitch that you'll need, follow the manufacturer's installation instructions, exactly, especially when it comes to fastener torques. The hitch will subjected to a lot of stress and good hitches come with hardened bolts. Never substitute an inferior bolt for a hardened bolt.

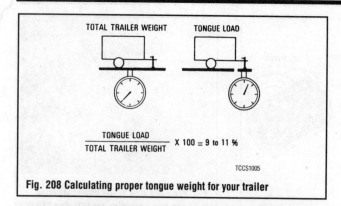

Fig. 208 Calculating proper tongue weight for your trailer

Engine

One of the most common, if not THE most common, problems associated with trailer towing is engine overheating. If you have a cooling system without an expansion tank, you'll definitely need to get an aftermarket expansion tank kit, preferably one with at least a 2 quart capacity. These kits are easily installed on the radiator's overflow hose, and come with a pressure cap designed for expansion tanks.

Aftermarket engine oil coolers are helpful for prolonging engine oil life and reducing overall engine temperatures. Both of these factors increase engine life. While not absolutely necessary in towing Class I and some Class II trailers, they are recommended for heavier Class II and all Class III towing. Engine oil cooler systems usually consist of an adapter, screwed on in place of the oil filter, a remote filter mounting and a multi-tube, finned heat exchanger, which is mounted in front of the radiator or air conditioning condenser.

JUMP STARTING A DEAD BATTERY

▶ See Figures 209 and 210

Whenever a vehicle is jump started, precautions must be followed in order to prevent the possibility of personal injury. Remember that batteries contain a small amount of explosive hydrogen gas which is a by-product of battery charging. Sparks should always be avoided when working around batteries, especially when attaching jumper cables. To minimize the possibility of accidental sparks, follow the procedure carefully.

✸✸ CAUTION

NEVER hook the batteries up in a series circuit or the entire electrical system will go up in smoke, including the starter!

Vehicles equipped with a diesel engine may utilize two 12 volt batteries. If so, the batteries are connected in a parallel circuit (positive terminal to positive terminal, negative terminal to negative terminal). Hooking the batteries up in parallel circuit increases battery cranking power without increasing total battery voltage output. Output remains at 12 volts. On the other hand, hooking two 12

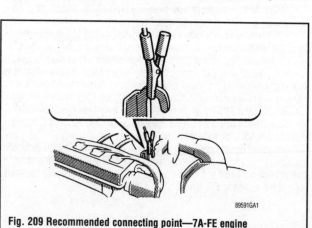

Fig. 209 Recommended connecting point—7A-FE engine

Transaxle

An automatic transaxle is usually recommended for trailer towing. Modern automatics have proven reliable and, of course, easy to operate, in trailer towing. The increased load of a trailer, however, causes an increase in the temperature of the automatic transaxle fluid. Heat is the worst enemy of an automatic transaxle. As the temperature of the fluid increases, the life of the fluid decreases.

It is essential, therefore, that you install an automatic transaxle cooler. The cooler, which consists of a multi-tube, finned heat exchanger, is usually installed in front of the radiator or air conditioning compressor, and hooked in-line with the transaxle cooler tank inlet line. Follow the cooler manufacturer's installation instructions.

Select a cooler of at least adequate capacity, based upon the combined gross weights of the vehicle and trailer.

Cooler manufacturers recommend that you use an aftermarket cooler in addition to, and not instead of, the present cooling tank in your radiator. If you do want to use it in place of the radiator cooling tank, get a cooler at least two sizes larger than normally necessary.

➥**A transaxle cooler can, sometimes, cause slow or harsh shifting in the transaxle during cold weather, until the fluid has a chance to come up to normal operating temperature. Some coolers can be purchased with or retrofitted with a temperature bypass valve which will allow fluid flow through the cooler only when the fluid has reached above a certain operating temperature.**

Handling A Trailer

Towing a trailer with ease and safety requires a certain amount of experience. It's a good idea to learn the feel of a trailer by practicing turning, stopping and backing in an open area such as an empty parking lot.

Fig. 210 Recommended connecting point—5S-FE engine

volt batteries up in a series circuit (positive terminal to negative terminal, positive terminal to negative terminal) increases total battery output to 24 volts (12 volts plus 12 volts).

Jump Starting Precautions

• Be sure that both batteries are of the same voltage. Vehicles covered by this manual and most vehicles on the road today utilize a 12 volt charging system.

• Be sure that both batteries are of the same polarity (have the same terminal, in most cases NEGATIVE grounded).

• Be sure that the vehicles are not touching or a short could occur.

• On serviceable batteries, be sure the vent cap holes are not obstructed.

• Do not smoke or allow sparks anywhere near the batteries.

• In cold weather, make sure the battery electrolyte is not frozen. This can occur more readily in a battery that has been in a state of discharge.

• Do not allow electrolyte to contact your skin or clothing.

Jump Starting Procedure

1. Make sure that the voltages of the 2 batteries are the same. Most batteries and charging systems are of the 12 volt variety.

2. Pull the jumping vehicle (with the good battery) into a position so the jumper cables can reach the dead battery and that vehicle's engine. Make sure that the vehicles do NOT touch.

3. Place the transmissions/transaxles of both vehicles in **Neutral** (MT) or **P** (AT), as applicable, then firmly set their parking brakes.

→**If necessary for safety reasons, the hazard lights on both vehicles may be operated throughout the entire procedure without significantly increasing the difficulty of jumping the dead battery.**

4. Turn all lights and accessories OFF on both vehicles. Make sure the ignition switches on both vehicles are turned to the **OFF** position.

5. Cover the battery cell caps with a rag, but do not cover the terminals.

6. Make sure the terminals on both batteries are clean and free of corrosion or proper electrical connection will be impeded. If necessary, clean the battery terminals before proceeding.

7. Identify the positive (+) and negative (−) terminals on both batteries.

8. Connect the first jumper cable to the positive (+) terminal of the dead battery, then connect the other end of that cable to the positive (+) terminal of the booster (good) battery.

9. Connect one end of the other jumper cable to the negative (−) terminal on the booster battery and the final cable clamp to an engine bolt head, alternator bracket or other solid, metallic point on the engine with the dead battery. Try to pick a ground on the engine that is positioned away from the battery in order to minimize the possibility of the 2 clamps touching should one loosen during the procedure. DO NOT connect this clamp to the negative (−) terminal of the bad battery.

✳✳ CAUTION

Be very careful to keep the jumper cables away from moving parts (cooling fan, belts, etc.) on both engines.

10. Check to make sure that the cables are routed away from any moving parts, then start the donor vehicle's engine. Run the engine at moderate speed for several minutes to allow the dead battery a chance to receive some initial charge.

11. With the donor vehicle's engine still running slightly above idle, try to start the vehicle with the dead battery. Crank the engine for no more than 10 seconds at a time and let the starter cool for at least 20 seconds between tries. If the vehicle does not start in 3 tries, it is likely that something else is also wrong or that the battery needs additional time to charge.

12. Once the vehicle is started, allow it to run at idle for a few seconds to make sure that it is operating properly.

13. Turn ON the headlights, heater blower and, if equipped, the rear defroster of both vehicles in order to reduce the severity of voltage spikes and subsequent risk of damage to the vehicles' electrical systems when the cables are disconnected. This step is especially important to any vehicle equipped with computer control modules.

14. Carefully disconnect the cables in the reverse order of connection. Start with the negative cable that is attached to the engine ground, then the negative cable on the donor battery. Disconnect the positive cable from the donor battery and finally, disconnect the positive cable from the formerly dead battery. Be careful when disconnecting the cables from the positive terminals not to allow the alligator clips to touch any metal on either vehicle or a short and sparks will occur.

JACKING

♦ **See Figures 211 and 212**

Your vehicle was supplied with a jack for emergency road repairs. This jack is fine for changing a flat tire or other short term procedures not requiring you to go beneath the vehicle. If it is used in an emergency situation, carefully fol-

low the instructions provided either with the jack or in your owner's manual. Do not attempt to use the jack on any portions of the vehicle other than specified by the vehicle manufacturer. Always block the diagonally opposite wheel when using a jack.

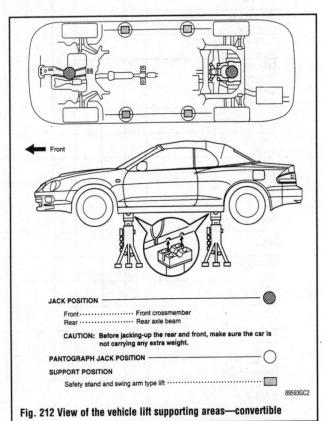

JACK POSITION

Front .... Front crossmember
Rear .... Rear axle beam
CAUTION: Before jacking-up the rear and front, make sure the car is not carrying any extra weight.

PANTOGRAPH JACK POSITION

SUPPORT POSITION
Safety stand and swing arm type lift ....

89593GC1

Fig. 211 View of the vehicle lift supporting areas—except convertible

JACK POSITION

Front ·················· Front crossmember
Rear ·················· Rear axle beam
CAUTION: Before jacking-up the rear and front, make sure the car is not carrying any extra weight.

PANTOGRAPH JACK POSITION

SUPPORT POSITION
Safety stand and swing arm type lift ··························

89593GC2

Fig. 212 View of the vehicle lift supporting areas—convertible

A more convenient way of jacking is the use of a garage or floor jack. You may use the floor jack to raise the front or rear of the vehicle, then place jackstands under the car for support.

Never place the jack under the radiator, engine or transaxle components. Severe and expensive damage will result when the jack is raised. Additionally, never jack under the floorpan or bodywork; the metal will deform.

Whenever you plan to work under the vehicle, you must support it on jackstands or ramps. Never use cinder blocks or stacks of wood to support the vehicle, even if you're only going to be under it for a few minutes. Never crawl under the vehicle when it is supported only by the tire-changing jack or other floor jack.

➡**Always position a block of wood or small rubber pad on top of the jack or jackstand to protect the lifting point's finish when lifting or supporting the vehicle.**

Small hydraulic, screw, or scissors jacks are satisfactory for raising the vehicle. Drive-on trestles or ramps are also a handy and safe way to both raise and support the vehicle. Be careful though, some ramps may be too steep to drive your vehicle onto without scraping the front bottom panels. Never support the vehicle on any suspension member (unless specifically instructed to do so by a repair manual) or by an underbody panel.

Jacking Precautions

The following safety points cannot be overemphasized:
- Always block the opposite wheel or wheels to keep the vehicle from rolling off the jack.
- When raising the front of the vehicle, firmly apply the parking brake.
- When the drive wheels are to remain on the ground, leave the vehicle in gear to help prevent it from rolling.
- Always use jackstands to support the vehicle when you are working underneath. Place the stands beneath the vehicle's jacking brackets. Before climbing underneath, rock the vehicle a bit to make sure it is firmly supported..

MAINTENANCE INTERVALS CHARTS

NORMAL RECOMMENDED MAINTENANCE INTERVALS (1994-95)

Component	6	12	18	24	30	36	42	48	54	60	66	72	78	84	90	96	Months
km (x1000) / Miles (x1000)	3.75	7.5	11.25	15	18.75	22.5	26.25	30	33.75	37.5	41.25	45	48.75	52.5	56.25	60	
Engine oil and filter	R	R	R	R	R	R	R	R	R	R	R	R	R	R	R	R	I: Every 6
Timing Belt																R	
Valve clearance										A						A	R: Every 72
Drive belts						I										I	
Engine coolant					I			R				I				R	I: Every 24
Exhaust pipes						I						I				I	I: Every 24
Air cleaner filter						R										R	I: Every 6
Fuel lines and connections								I								I	I: Every 36
Fuel tank cap gasket																R	R: Every 72
Spark plugs-non platinum								R								R	R: Every 36
Spark plugs-platinum																R	R: Every 72
Charcoal canister																I	I: Every 72
Brake linings and drums		I		I		I		I		I		I		I		I	I: Every 12
Brake pads and discs		I		I		I		I		I		I		I		I	I: Every 12
Brake line hose and connections			I					I				I				I	I: Every 24
Steering linkage	I		I		I		I		I		I		I		I		I: Every 12
SRS air bags																	I: Every 12
Ball joints and dust covers		I		I		I		I		I		I		I		I	I: Every 12
Drive shaft boots		I		I		I		I	I			I		I		I	I: Every 12
Transaxles			R					R			R					R	R: Every 24
Steering gear box			I					I				I				I	I: Every 24
Bolts and nuts on chassis and body		I			I			I			I			I		I	I: Every 24

I: Inspect
R: Replace
A: Adjust

89591C93

NORMAL RECOMMENDED MAINTENANCE INTERVALS (1996-98)

VEHICLE MAINTENANCE INTERVAL

Component / km (x1000)	6	12	18	24	30	36	42	48	54	60	66	72	78	84	90	96	Months
Miles (x1000)	3.75	7.5	11.25	15	18.75	22.5	26.25	30	33.75	37.5	41.25	45	48.75	52.5	56.25	60	
Engine oil and filter	R	R	R	R	R	R	R	R	R	R	R	R	R	R	R	R	I: Every 4
Timing Belt																R	
Valve clearance										A						A	R: Every 48
Drive belts								I		A						I	
Engine coolant					I			R				I				R	
Exhaust pipes								I				I				I	I: Every 24
Air cleaner filter		I		I		I		R		I		I		I		R	I: Every 6
Fuel lines and connections								I								I	I: Every 24
Fuel tank cap gasket																R	R: Every 72
Spark plugs-non platinum								R								R	R: Every 24
Spark plugs-platinum																R	R: Every 72
Charcoal canister																I	I: Every 48
Brake linings and drums		I		I		I		I		I		I		I		I	I: Every 12
Brake pads and discs		I		I		I		I		I		I		I		I	I: Every 12
Brake line hose and connections				I				I				I				I	I: Every 24
Steering linkage		I		I		I		I		I		I		I		I	I: Every 12
SRS air bags																	I: Every 12
Ball joints and dust covers		I		I		I		I		I		I		I		I	I: Every 12
Drive shaft boots		I		I		I		I		I		I		I		I	I: Every 12
Transaxles				R				R				R				R	R: Every 24
Steering gear box				I				I				I				I	I: Every 24
Bolts and nuts on chassis and body		I		I		I		I		I		I		I		I	I: Every 24

I: Inspect
R: Replace
A: Adjust

89591C94

SEVERE RECOMMENDED MAINTENANCE INTERVALS (1994-95)

Component	_	VEHICLE MAINTENANCE INTERVAL															Months
km (x1000)	6	12	18	24	30	36	42	48	54	60	66	72	78	84	90	96	
Miles (x1000)	3.75	7.5	11.25	15	18.75	22.5	26.25	30	33.75	37.5	41.25	45	48.75	52.5	56.25	60	
Engine oil and filter	R	R	R	R	R	R	R	R	R	R	R	R	R	R	R	R	I: Every 6
Timing Belt																R	
Valve clearance										A						A	R: Every 72
Drive belts										A						I	I: Every 72
Engine coolant						I						R				R	R: Every 24
Exhaust pipes								R								R	R: Every 36
Air cleaner filter								R								R	R: Every 36
Fuel lines and connections								-								-	I: Every 36
Fuel tank cap gasket												R				R	R: Every 72
Spark plugs-non platinum								R								R	R: Every 36
Spark plugs-platinum												-				R	R: Every 72
Charcoal canister												-				-	I: Every 72
Brake linings and drums				-				-				-				-	I: Every 24
Brake pads and discs				-				-				-				-	I: Every 24
Brake line hose and connections				-				-				-				-	I: Every 24
Steering linkage				-				-				-				-	I: Every 24
SRS air bags																-	I: Every 12
Ball joints and dust covers				-				-				-				-	I: Every 24
Drive shaft boots				-				-				-				-	I: Every 24
Transaxles				R				R				R				R	R: Every 24
Steering gear box				-				-				-				-	I: Every 24
Bolts and nuts on chassis and body	-			-				-				-			-	-	I: Every 24

I: Inspect
R: Replace
A: Adjust

89591C95

SEVERE RECOMMENDED MAINTENANCE INTERVALS (1996-98)

Component		VEHICLE MAINTENANCE INTERVAL															Months
km (x1000)	6	12	18	24	30	36	42	48	54	60	66	72	78	84	90	96	
Miles (x1000)	3.75	7.5	11.25	15	18.75	22.5	26.25	30	33.75	37.5	41.25	45	48.75	52.5	56.25	60	
Engine oil and filter	R	R	R	R	R	R	R	R	R	R	R	R	R	R	R	R	I: Every 4
Timing Belt																R	
Valve clearance										A						A	R: Every 48
Drive belts										A						I	
Engine coolant								R								R	
Exhaust pipes								-				-				-	I: Every 24
Air cleaner filter								R		-				-		R	I: Every 6
Fuel lines and connections								-				-				-	I: Every 24
Fuel tank cap gasket																R	R: Every 72
Spark plugs-non platinum								R								R	R: Every 24
Spark plugs-platinum												-				R	R: Every 72
Charcoal canister										-						-	I: Every 48
Brake linings and drums		-		-		-		-		-		-		-		-	I: Every 12
Brake pads and discs		-		-		-		-		-		-		-		-	I: Every 12
Brake line hose and connections				-				-				-				-	I: Every 24
Steering linkage		-		-		-		-		-		-		-		-	I: Every 12
SRS air bags																-	I: Every 12
Ball joints and dust covers		-		-		-		-		-		-		-		-	I: Every 12
Drive shaft boots		-		-		-		-		-		-		-		-	I: Every 12
Transaxles				R				R				R				R	R: Every 24
Steering gear box				-				-				-				-	I: Every 24
Bolts and nuts on chassis and body		R		-		-		-		-		-		-		-	I: Every 24

I: Inspect
R: Replace
A: Adjust

89591C96

ENGLISH TO METRIC CONVERSION: MASS (WEIGHT)

Current mass measurement is expressed in pounds and ounces (lbs. & ozs.). The metric unit of mass (or weight) is the kilogram (kg). Even although this table does not show conversion of masses (weights) larger than 15 lbs, it is easy to calculate larger units by following the data immediately below.

To convert ounces (oz.) to grams (g): multiply th number of ozs. by 28
To convert grams (g) to ounces (oz.): multiply the number of grams by .035

To convert pounds (lbs.) to kilograms (kg): multiply the number of lbs. by .45
To convert kilograms (kg) to pounds (lbs.): multiply the number of kilograms by 2.2

lbs	kg	lbs	kg	oz	kg	oz	kg
0.1	0.04	0.9	0.41	0.1	0.003	0.9	0.024
0.2	0.09	1	0.4	0.2	0.005	1	0.03
0.3	0.14	2	0.9	0.3	0.008	2	0.06
0.4	0.18	3	1.4	0.4	0.011	3	0.08
0.5	0.23	4	1.8	0.5	0.014	4	0.11
0.6	0.27	5	2.3	0.6	0.017	5	0.14
0.7	0.32	10	4.5	0.7	0.020	10	0.28
0.8	0.36	15	6.8	0.8	0.023	15	0.42

ENGLISH TO METRIC CONVERSION: TEMPERATURE

To convert Fahrenheit (°F) to Celsius (°C): take number of °F and subtract 32; multiply result by 5; divide result by 9

To convert Celsius (°C) to Fahrenheit (°F): take number of °C and multiply by 9; divide result by 5; add 32 to total

Fahrenheit (F)		Celsius (C)		Fahrenheit (F)		Celsius (C)		Fahrenheit (F)		Celsius (C)	
°F	°C	°C	°F	°F	°C	°C	°F	°F	°C	°C	°F
−40	−40	−38	−36.4	80	26.7	18	64.4	215	101.7	80	176
−35	−37.2	−36	−32.8	85	29.4	20	68	220	104.4	85	185
−30	−34.4	−34	−29.2	90	32.2	22	71.6	225	107.2	90	194
−25	−31.7	−32	−25.6	95	35.0	24	75.2	230	110.0	95	202
−20	−28.9	−30	−22	100	37.8	26	78.8	235	112.8	100	212
−15	−26.1	−28	−18.4	105	40.6	28	82.4	240	115.6	105	221
−10	−23.3	−26	−14.8	110	43.3	30	86	245	118.3	110	230
−5	−20.6	−24	−11.2	115	46.1	32	89.6	250	121.1	115	239
0	−17.8	−22	−7.6	120	48.9	34	93.2	255	123.9	120	248
1	−17.2	−20	−4	125	51.7	36	96.8	260	126.6	125	257
2	−16.7	−18	−0.4	130	54.4	38	100.4	265	129.4	130	266
3	−16.1	−16	3.2	135	57.2	40	104	270	132.2	135	275
4	−15.6	−14	6.8	140	60.0	42	107.6	275	135.0	140	284
5	−15.0	−12	10.4	145	62.8	44	112.2	280	137.8	145	293
10	−12.2	−10	14	150	65.6	46	114.8	285	140.6	150	302
15	−9.4	−8	17.6	155	68.3	48	118.4	290	143.3	155	311
20	−6.7	−6	21.2	160	71.1	50	122	295	146.1	160	320
25	−3.9	−4	24.8	165	73.9	52	125.6	300	148.9	165	329
30	−1.1	−2	28.4	170	76.7	54	129.2	305	151.7	170	338
35	1.7	0	32	175	79.4	56	132.8	310	154.4	175	347
40	4.4	2	35.6	180	82.2	58	136.4	315	157.2	180	356
45	7.2	4	39.2	185	85.0	60	140	320	160.0	185	365
50	10.0	6	42.8	190	87.8	62	143.6	325	162.8	190	374
55	12.8	8	46.4	195	90.6	64	147.2	330	165.6	195	383
60	15.6	10	50	200	93.3	66	150.8	335	168.3	200	392
65	18.3	12	53.6	205	96.1	68	154.4	340	171.1	205	401
70	21.1	14	57.2	210	98.9	70	158	345	173.9	210	410
75	23.9	16	60.8	212	100.0	75	167	350	176.7	215	414

TCCS1C01

ENGLISH TO METRIC CONVERSION: LENGTH

To convert inches (ins.) to millimeters (mm): multiply number of inches by 25.4

To convert millimeters (mm) to inches (ins.): multiply number of millimeters by .04

Inches		Decimals	Milli-meters	Inches to millimeters		Inches		Decimals	Milli-meters	Inches to millimeters	
				inches	mm					inches	mm
	1/64	0.051625	0.3969	0.0001	0.00254		33/64	0.515625	13.0969	0.6	15.24
1/32		0.03125	0.7937	0.0002	0.00508	17/32		0.53125	13.4937	0.7	17.78
	3/64	0.046875	1.1906	0.0003	0.00762		35/64	0.546875	13.8906	0.8	20.32
1/16		0.0625	1.5875	0.0004	0.01016	9/16		0.5625	14.2875	0.9	22.86
	5/64	0.078125	1.9844	0.0005	0.01270		37/64	0.578125	14.6844	1	25.4
3/32		0.09375	2.3812	0.0006	0.01524	19/32		0.59375	15.0812	2	50.8
	7/64	0.109375	2.7781	0.0007	0.01778		39/64	0.609375	15.4781	3	76.2
1/8		0.125	3.1750	0.0008	0.02032	5/8		0.625	15.8750	4	101.6
	9/64	0.140625	3.5719	0.0009	0.02286		41/64	0.640625	16.2719	5	127.0
5/32		0.15625	3.9687	0.001	0.0254	21/32		0.65625	16.6687	6	152.4
	11/64	0.171875	4.3656	0.002	0.0508		43/64	0.671875	17.0656	7	177.8
3/16		0.1875	4.7625	0.003	0.0762	11/16		0.6875	17.4625	8	203.2
	13/64	0.203125	5.1594	0.004	0.1016		45/64	0.703125	17.8594	9	228.6
7/32		0.21875	5.5562	0.005	0.1270	23/32		0.71875	18.2562	10	254.0
	15/64	0.234375	5.9531	0.006	0.1524		47/64	0.734375	18.6531	11	279.4
1/4		0.25	6.3500	0.007	0.1778	3/4		0.75	19.0500	12	304.8
	17/64	0.265625	6.7469	0.008	0.2032		49/64	0.765625	19.4469	13	330.2
9/32		0.28125	7.1437	0.009	0.2286	25/32		0.78125	19.8437	14	355.6
	19/64	0.296875	7.5406	0.01	0.254		51/64	0.796875	20.2406	15	381.0
5/16		0.3125	7.9375	0.02	0.508	13/16		0.8125	20.6375	16	406.4
	21/64	0.328125	8.3344	0.03	0.762		53/64	0.828125	21.0344	17	431.8
11/32		0.34375	8.7312	0.04	1.016	27/32		0.84375	21.4312	18	457.2
	23/64	0.359375	9.1281	0.05	1.270		55/64	0.859375	21.8281	19	482.6
3/8		0.375	9.5250	0.06	1.524	7/8		0.875	22.2250	20	508.0
	25/64	0.390625	9.9219	0.07	1.778		57/64	0.890625	22.6219	21	533.4
13/32		0.40625	10.3187	0.08	2.032	29/32		0.90625	23.0187	22	558.8
	27/64	0.421875	10.7156	0.09	2.286		59/64	0.921875	23.4156	23	584.2
7/16		0.4375	11.1125	0.1	2.54	15/16		0.9375	23.8125	24	609.6
	29/64	0.453125	11.5094	0.2	5.08		61/64	0.953125	24.2094	25	635.0
15/32		0.46875	11.9062	0.3	7.62	31/32		0.96875	24.6062	26	660.4
	31/64	0.484375	12.3031	0.4	10.16		63/64	0.984375	25.0031	27	690.6
1/2		0.5	12.7000	0.5	12.70						

ENGLISH TO METRIC CONVERSION: TORQUE

To convert foot-pounds (ft. lbs.) to Newton-meters: multiply the number of ft. lbs. by 1.3

To convert inch-pounds (in. lbs.) to Newton-meters: multiply the number of in. lbs. by .11

in lbs	N-m	in lbs	N-m	in lbs	N-m	in lbs	N-m	in lbs	N-m
0.1	0.01	1	0.11	10	1.13	19	2.15	28	3.16
0.2	0.02	2	0.23	11	1.24	20	2.26	29	3.28
0.3	0.03	3	0.34	12	1.36	21	2.37	30	3.39
0.4	0.04	4	0.45	13	1.47	22	2.49	31	3.50
0.5	0.06	5	0.56	14	1.58	23	2.60	32	3.62
0.6	0.07	6	0.68	15	1.70	24	2.71	33	3.73
0.7	0.08	7	0.78	16	1.81	25	2.82	34	3.84
0.8	0.09	8	0.90	17	1.92	26	2.94	35	3.95
0.9	0.10	9	1.02	18	2.03	27	3.05	36	4.0

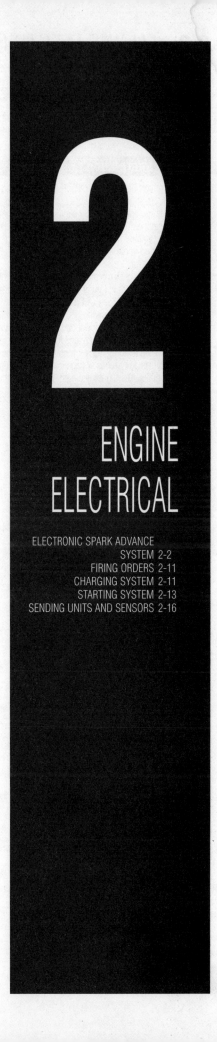

2

ENGINE
ELECTRICAL

ELECTRONIC SPARK ADVANCE SYSTEM

→For information on understanding electricity and troubleshooting electrical circuits, please refer to Section 6 of this manual.

General Information

The Electronic Spark Advance (ESA) system is used on all Toyota Celicas. The electronic ignition system offers many advantages over the conventional breaker points ignition system. By eliminating the points, maintenance requirements are greatly reduced. An electronic ignition system is capable of producing a much higher voltage which in turn aide in starting, reduces spark fouling and provides emission control. The 1996–98 models are all equipped with a crankshaft position sensor.

The ESA ignition system consists of a distributor with a signal generator, ignition coil (s), electronic igniter and a micro-computer called an Electronic Control Module (ECM). The ECM is programmed with data for optimum ignition timing for a wide range of driving and operating conditions. Using data provided by the various engine mounting sensors (intake air volume, engine temperature, rpm, etc.), the ECM converts the data into a reference voltage signal and sends this signal to the igniter mounted inside the distributor. The signal generator receives a reference voltage from the ECM and activates the components of the igniter. The signal generator consists of three main components: the

signal rotor, pick-up coil and the permanent magnet. The signal rotor revolves with the distributor shaft, while the pick-up coil and permanent magnet are stationary. as the signal; rotor spins the teeth on it pass a projection leading from the pick-up coil. When this occurs, voltage is allowed to flow through the system and fire the spark plugs. This process happens without physical contact or electrical arching; therefore, there is no need to replace burnt or worn parts.

Diagnosis and Testing

NO START TEST

♦ See Figures 1, 2, 3, 4 and 5

5S-FE Engines—California

1994–95 MODELS

    1. First, conduct a spark test as follows.
    2. Disconnect the coil wire from distributor. Hold the coil wire end about ½ inch (12.5mm) from a good body ground; check if spark occurs while engine is being cranked.

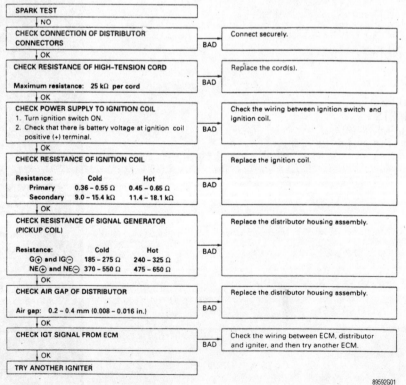

Fig. 1 No start test chart—1994-95 5S-FE engine except California

ON–VEHICLE INSPECTION
SPARK TEST

CHECK THAT SPARK OCCURS

(a) Disconnect the high–tension cord (from the ignition coil) from the distributor cap.

(b) Hold the end approx. 12.5 mm (0.50 in.) from the body ground.

(c) See if spark occurs while engine is being cranked.

HINT: To prevent gasoline from being injected from injectors during this test, crank the engine for no more than 1 – 2 seconds at time.

If the spark does not occur, perform the test as follows:

SPARK TEST		
↓ NO		
CHECK CONNECTION OF IGNITION COIL, IGNITER AND DISTRIBUTOR CONNECTOR	BAD →	Connect securely.
↓ OK		
CHECK RESISTANCE OF HIGH–TENSION CORD	BAD →	Replace the cord(s).
Maximum resistance: 25 kΩ per cord		
↓ OK		
CHECK POWER SUPPLY TO IGNITION COIL AND IGNITER	BAD →	Check the wiring between ignition switch, ignition coil and igniter.
1. Turn ignition switch to ON.		
2. Check that there is battery voltage at ignition coil positive (+) terminal.		
↓ OK		
CHECK RESISTANCE OF IGNITION COIL	BAD →	Replace the ignition coil.

Resistance:

	Cold	Hot
Primary	0.36 – 0.55 Ω	0.45 – 0.65 Ω
Secondary	9.0 – 15.4 kΩ	11.4 – 18.1 kΩ

↓ OK		
CHECK RESISTANCE OF SIGNAL GENERATOR (PICKUP COIL)	BAD →	Replace the distributor housing assembly.

Resistance:

	Cold	Hot
G1 and G⊖	125 – 200 Ω	160 – 235 Ω
G2 and G⊖	125 – 200 Ω	160 – 235 Ω
NE and G⊖	155 – 250 Ω	190 – 290 Ω

↓ OK		
CHECK AIR GAP OF DISTRIBUTOR	BAD →	Replace the distributor housing assembly.
Air gap: 0.2 – 0.5 mm (0.008 – 0.020 in.)		
↓ OK		
CHECK IGT SIGNAL FROM ECM	BAD →	Check the wiring between ECM, distributor and igniter, and then try another ECM.
↓ OK		
TRY ANOTHER IGNITER		

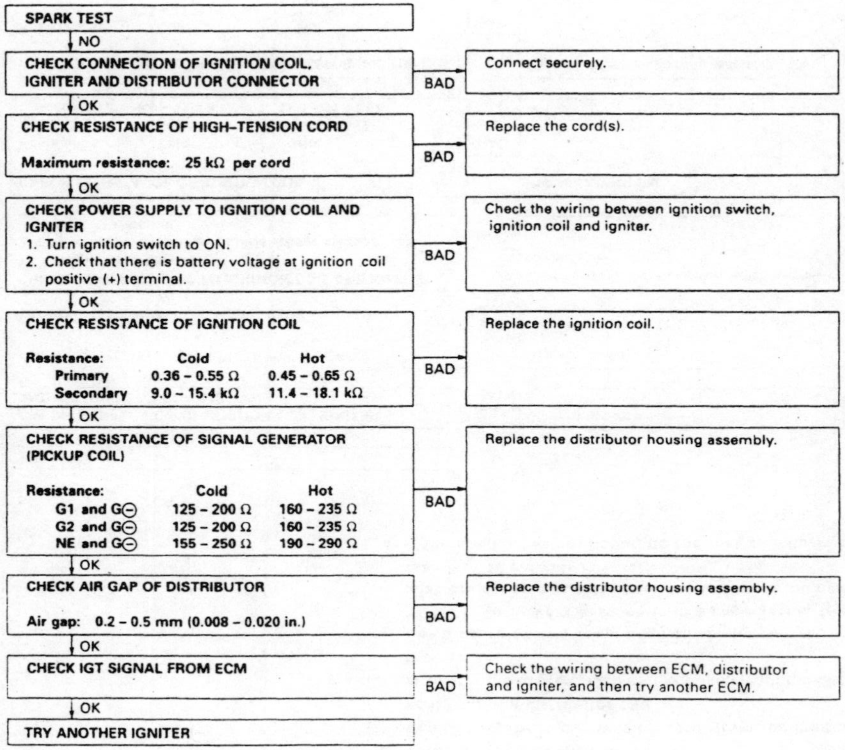

89592G02

Fig. 2 No start test chart—1994-95 5S-FE engine California

ON–VEHICLE INSPECTION
SPARK TEST

CHECK THAT SPARK OCCURS

(a) Disconnect the high–tension cords from the spark plugs.

(b) Remove the spark plugs.

(c) Install the spark plugs to the each high–tension cord.

(d) Ground the spark plug.

(e) Check if spark occurs while engine is being cranked.

HINT: To prevent gasoline from being injected from injectors during this test, crank the engine for no more than 1 – 2 seconds at a time.

If the spark does not occur, perform the test as follows:

SPARK TEST		
↓ NO		
CHECK CONNECTION OF IIA CONNECTORS	BAD →	Connect securely.
↓ OK		
CHECK RESISTANCE OF HIGH–TENSION CORD	BAD →	Replace the cord(s).
Maximum resistance: 25 kΩ per cord		
↓ OK		
CHECK POWER SUPPLY TO IGNITION COIL	BAD →	Check the wiring between ignition switch and ignition coil.
1. Turn ignition switch ON.		
2. Check that there is battery voltage at ignition coil positive (+) terminal.		
↓ OK		
CHECK RESISTANCE OF IGNITION COIL	BAD →	Replace the ignition coil.

Resistance:

	Cold	Hot
Primary	1.11 – 1.75 Ω	1.41 – 2.05 Ω
Secondary	9.0 – 15.7 kΩ	11.4 – 18.4 kΩ

↓ OK		
CHECK RESISTANCE OF SIGNAL GENERATOR (PICKUP COIL)	BAD →	Replace the distributor housing assembly.

Resistance:

	Cold	Hot
G⊕ and G⊖	185 – 275 Ω	240 – 325 Ω
NE⊕ and NE⊖	370 – 550 Ω	475 – 650 Ω

↓ OK		
CHECK AIR GAP OF DISTRIBUTOR	BAD →	Replace the distributor housing assembly.
Air gap: 0.2 – 0.4 mm (0.008 – 0.016 in.)		
↓ OK		
CHECK IGT SIGNAL FROM ECM	BAD →	Check the wiring between ECM and IIA, and then try another ECM.
↓ OK		
TRY ANOTHER IGNITER		

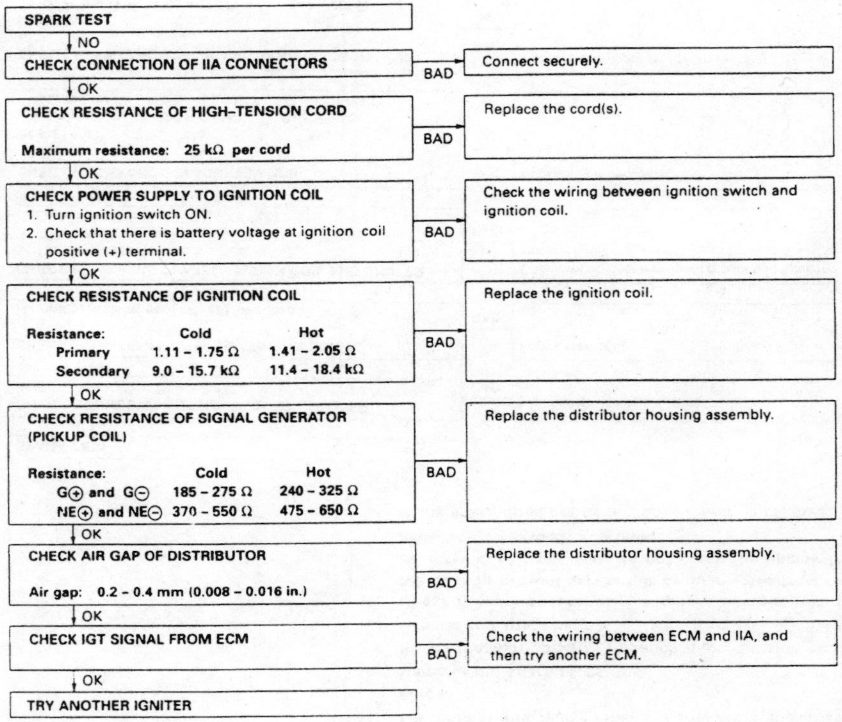

89592G03

Fig. 3 No start test chart—1994-95 7A-FE engine

ON-VEHICLE INSPECTION
SPARK TEST

CHECK THAT SPARK OCCURS

(a) Disconnect the high-tension cord (from the ignition coil) from the distributor cap.
(b) Hold the end approx. 12.5 mm (0.50 in.) from the body ground.
(c) See if spark occurs while engine is being cranked.
NOTICE: To prevent gasoline from being injected from injectors during this test, crank the engine for no more than 5 - 10 seconds at time.
If the spark does not occur, do the test as follows:

```
SPARK TEST
   │ NO
CHECK CONNECTION OF IGNITION COIL, IGNITER
AND DISTRIBUTOR CONNECTORS ──BAD──► Connect securely.
   │ OK
CHECK RESISTANCE OF HIGH-TENSION CORDS ──BAD──► Replace cord(s).
Maximum resistance: 25 kΩ per cord
   │ OK
CHECK POWER SUPPLY TO IGNITION COIL AND IGNITER ──BAD──► Check wiring between ignition switch to ignition coil and igniter.
1. Turn ignition switch to ON.
2. Check that there is battery positive voltage at ignition coil positive (+) terminal.
   │ OK
CHECK RESISTANCE OF IGNITION COIL ──BAD──► Replace ignition coil.
Resistance:   Cold            Hot
Primary       0.36 - 0.55 Ω   0.45 - 0.65 Ω
Secondary     9.0 - 15.4 kΩ   11.4 - 18.1 kΩ
   │ OK
CHECK RESISTANCE OF SIGNAL GENERATOR (PICKUP COIL) ──BAD──► Replace distributor housing assembly.
Resistance:   Cold        Hot
              135 - 220 Ω  175 - 255 Ω
   │ OK
CHECK RESISTANCE OF CRANKSHAFT POSITION SENSOR ──BAD──► Replace crankshaft position sensor.
Resistance:   Cold          Hot
              985 - 1,600 Ω  1,265 - 1,890 Ω
   │ OK
CHECK AIR GAP OF DISTRIBUTOR ──BAD──► Replace distributor housing assembly.
Air gap: 0.2 - 0.45 mm (0.008 - 0.018 in.)
   │ OK
CHECK IGT SIGNAL FROM ECM ──BAD──► Check wiring between ECM, distributor and igniter, and then try another ECM.
(See circuit inspection in Engine Troubleshooting)
   │ OK
TRY ANOTHER IGNITER
```

Fig. 4 No start test chart—1996-98 5S-FE engine

ON-VEHICLE INSPECTION
SPARK TEST

CHECK THAT SPARK OCCURS

(a) Disconnect the high-tension cords from the spark plugs.
(b) Remove the spark plugs.
(c) Install the spark plug to the each high-tension cord.
(d) Ground the spark plug.
(e) Check if spark occurs while engine is being cranked.
NOTICE: To prevent excess fuel being injected from the injectors during this test, do not crank the engine for more 5 - 10 seconds at a time.
If the spark does not occur, do the test as follows:

```
SPARK TEST
   │ NO
CHECK CONNECTION OF IGNITION COIL IGNITER
AND DISTRIBUTOR CONNECTOR ──BAD──► Connect securely.
   │ OK
CHECK RESISTANCE OF HIGH-TENSION CORD ──BAD──► Replace cord(s).
Maximum resistance: 25 kΩ per cord
   │ OK
CHECK POWER SUPPLY TO IGNITION COIL AND IGNITER ──BAD──► Check wiring between ignition switch to ignition coil and igniter.
1. Turn ignition switch to ON.
2. Check that there is battery voltage at ignition coil positive (+) terminal.
   │ OK
CHECK RESISTANCE OF IGNITION COIL ──BAD──► Replace ignition coil.
Resistance:   Cold            Hot
Primary       0.36 - 0.55 Ω   0.45 - 0.65 Ω
Secondary     9.0 - 15.4 kΩ   11.4 - 18.1 kΩ
   │ OK
CHECK RESISTANCE OF SIGNAL GENERATOR (PICKUP COIL) ──BAD──► Replace distributor housing assembly.
Resistance:          Cold        Hot
G ⊕ and G ⊖          185 - 275 Ω  240 - 325 Ω
   │ OK
CHECK RESISTANCE OF CRANKSHAFT POSITION SENSOR ──BAD──► Replace crankshaft position sensor.
Resistance:   Cold            Hot
              1,630 - 2,740 Ω  2,065 - 3,225 Ω
   │ OK
CHECK AIR GAP OF DISTRIBUTOR ──BAD──► Replace distributor housing assembly.
Air gap: 0.2 - 0.4 mm (0.008 - 0.016 in.)
   │ OK
CHECK IGT SIGNAL FROM ECM ──BAD──► Check wiring between ECM, distributor and igniter, and then try another ECM.
(See circuit inspection in Engine Troubleshooting)
   │ OK
TRY ANOTHER IGNITER
```

Fig. 5 No start test chart—1996-98 7A-FE engine

➡Crank the engine for no more than 2 seconds at a time to prevent flooding the engine with gasoline.

3. If good spark does not occur (should be bright blue), follow the correct diagnostic flow chart (engine and year) and necessary service procedures. If good spark does occur, the ignition system is probably not at fault.

7A-FE and except 1994–95 California 5S-FE Engines

1. Disconnect the plug wires from the spark plugs.
2. Remove the spark plugs.
3. Install each spark plug into each wire end.
4. Ground the plug.
5. Check that spark occurs while the engine is being cranked.

➡To prevent gasoline from being injected from the injectors during this test, crank the engine for no more than 1–2 seconds (1994–95 models) and 5–10 seconds for (1996–98 models) at a time.

6. If good spark does not occur (should be bright blue), follow the correct diagnostic flow chart (engine and year) and necessary service procedures. If good spark does occur, the ignition system is probably not at fault.

AIR GAP INSPECTION

▸ See Figures 6, 7 and 8

➡The air gap in the distributor should be check periodically. Distributor air gap may only be checked and can only be adjusted by component replacement.

Remove the hold-down bolts from the top of the distributor cap.
1. Remove the distributor cap from the housing without disconnecting the ignition wires.

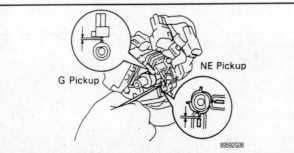

Fig. 6 Using a feeler gauge to measure the air gap between the signal rotor and pick-up coil projection—7A-FE engine

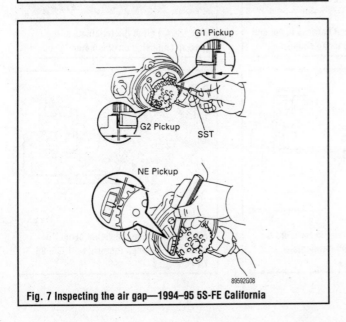

Fig. 7 Inspecting the air gap—1994–95 5S-FE California

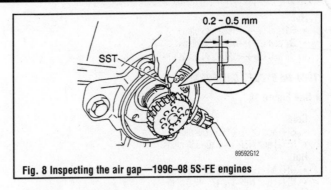

Fig. 8 Inspecting the air gap—1996–98 5S-FE engines

2. Pull the ignition rotor (not the signal rotor) straight up and remove it. If the contacts are worn, pitted or burnt, replace it. Do not file the contacts.

3. Turn the crankshaft (a socket wrench on the front pulley bolt may be used to do this) until a tooth on the signal rotor aligns with the projection of the pick-up coil.

4. Using a non-ferrous feeler gauge (brass, copper or plastic) measure the gap between the signal rotor and the pick-up coil projection. DO NOT USE AND ORDINARY METAL FEELER GAUGE! The gauge should just touch either side of the gap (snug fit). The acceptable range for the air gap is as follows:
   • 7A-FE—0.008–0.016 inch (0.2–0.4mm)
   • 1994–95 5S-FE except California—0.008–0.016 inch (0.2–0.4mm)
   • 1994–95 5S-FE California—0.008–0.020 inch (0.2–0.5mm)
   • 1996–98 5S-FE—0.008–0.018 inch (0.2–0.45mm)
5. If the air gap is not within specifications, replace the IIA distributor housing.
6. Check to make sure the housing gasket is in position on the housing.
7. Install the rotor.
8. Install the distributor cap with attached wiring. Attach the cap to the housing and tighten the hold-down bolts.

SIGNAL GENERATOR (PICK-UP COIL)

Using an ohmmeter, measure the resistance between the terminals. Refer to the following. If the resistance is not within specifications, replace the distributor housing assembly.

5S-FE Engine

1994–95 CALIFORNIA

▸ See Figure 9

Cold
   • G1 and G(–)—125–200 ohms
   • G2 and G(–)—125–200 ohms
   • NE and G(–)—155–250 ohms

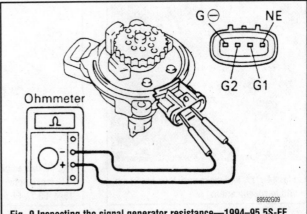

Fig. 9 Inspecting the signal generator resistance—1994–95 5S-FE California

Hot
- G1 and G(–)—160–235 ohms
- G2 and G(–)—160–235 ohms
- NE and G(–)—190–290 ohms

1994–95 EXCEPT CALIFORNIA

▶ See Figure 10

Cold
- G(+) and G(–)—185–275 ohms
- NE(+) and NE(–)—370–550 ohms

Hot:
- G(+) and G(–)—240–325 ohms
- NE(+) and NE(–)—475–650 ohms

1996–98 MODELS

▶ See Figure 11

Cold
- G(+) and G(–)—135–220 ohms

Hot
- G(+) and G(–)—175–255 ohms

7A-FE Engine

▶ See Figures 12, 13, 14, 15 and 16

Cold:
- G(+) and G(–)—185–275 ohms
- NE(+) and NE(–)—370–550 ohms

Hot:
- G(+) and G(–)—240–325 ohms
- NE(+) and NE(–)—475–650 ohms

➡The 1996–98 model 7A-FE engines only have G(+) and G(–) specifications.

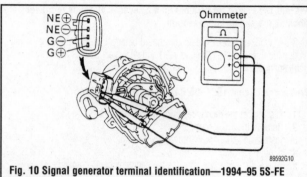

Fig. 10 Signal generator terminal identification—1994–95 5S-FE except California

IGNITER TEST

To test the igniter perform the ìOn Vehicle Inspection Spark Test". Check that spark occurs. If no spark occurs follow the correct diagnostic flow chart and necessary service procedures.

Adjustments

There are no adjustments possible inside the distributor. If the air gap between the signal rotor and the pickup coil projection is not within specifications, the distributor or distributor housing must be replaced.

Ignition Coil

▶ See Figure 17

The ignition coil is either located near the firewall with the igniter attached, or inside the distributor.

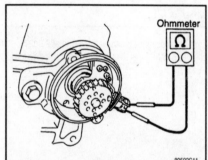

Fig. 11 Measuring the resistance of the signal generator terminals—1996–98 5S-FE engines

Fig. 12 The pick-up coil harness is the one with 6 wires attached to the connector

Fig. 13 Test all of the terminals of the pick-up coil using an ohmmeter . . .

Fig. 14 . . . and make sure they are within specifications

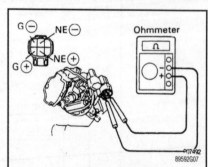

Fig. 15 Use an ohmmeter to measure the resistance between the terminals—1994–95 7A-FE engine

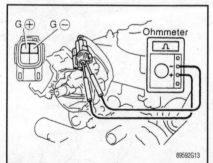

Fig. 16 Inspecting the signal generator resistance between terminals—1996–98 7A-FE engine

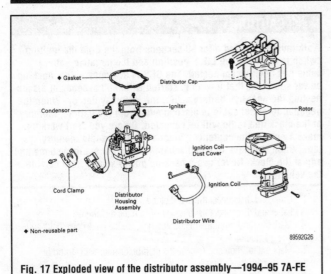

Fig. 17 Exploded view of the distributor assembly—1994–95 7A-FE engine

TESTING

◆ **See Figures 18 thru 23**

1. Disconnect the negative battery cable. Wait at least 90 seconds after the negative battery cable is disconnected before working on the vehicle to hinder air bag deployment.

✳✳ CAUTION

Models covered by this manual may be equipped with a Supplemental Restraint System (SRS), which uses an air bag. Whenever working near any of the SRS components, such as the impact sensors, the air bag module, steering column and instrument panel, disable the SRS, as described in Section 6.

2. Disconnect the plug wire from the ignition coil. A clip is on the tip of the wire, release the clip and pull to separate.
3. Clean and inspect for the following on the coil:
- Cracks or damages
- Check the terminals for carbon tracks
- Check the coil wire for holes or carbon deposits and corrosion
4. Using an ohmmeter, check the primary resistance between the positive and negative terminals. Resistance should be as follows when cold:

5S-FE engine:
- 0.36–0.55 ohms

7A-FE engine:
- 1994–95—1.11–1.75 ohms
- 1996–98—0.36–0.55 ohms

5. If the resistance is not within specifications, replace the coil.
6. To check the secondary resistance, measure the resistance between the positive terminal of the coil and the terminal. Resistance should be within the following when cold:

5S-FE engine:
- 9.0–15.4 kilohms

7A-FE engine:
- 1994–95—9.0–15.7 kilohms
- 1996–98—9.0–15.4 kilohms

7. If the resistance is not within specifications, replace the coil.
8. Connect the negative battery cable and reset any digital equipment such as the radio.

REMOVAL & INSTALLATION

External Coils

1. Turn the ignition key to the **OFF** position. Disconnect the negative battery cable. Wait at least 90 seconds from the time the negative battery was disconnected to start work.

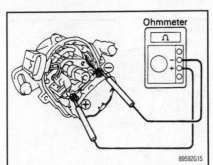

Fig. 18 Measure the resistance between the positive and negative terminals for primary resistance—1994–95 California 5S-FE engine

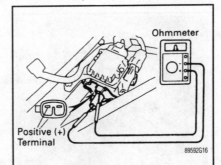

Fig. 19 Testing the primary coil resistance—1994–95 except California 5S-FE engine

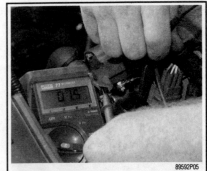

Fig. 20 Check the primary resistance of the ignition coil using an ohmmeter—1994–95 7A-FE engine

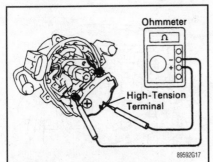

Fig. 21 Measuring the secondary resistance of the coil—1994–95 California 5S-FE engine

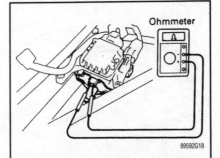

Fig. 22 Testing the secondary coil resistance—1994–95 except California 5S-FE engine

Fig. 23 Inspect the secondary resistance of the ignition coil using an ohmmeter—1994–95 7A-FE engine

Work must be started after 90 seconds from the time the ignition switch is turned to the LOCK position and the negative battery cable has been disconnected. The SRS is equipped with a back-up power source so that if work is started within 90 seconds of disconnecting the negative battery cable, the SRS may deploy. When the negative terminal cable is disconnected from the battery, memory of the clock and radio will be canceled. Before you start working, make a note of the contents memorized by the audio memory system. When you have finished working, reset the audio systems and adjust the clock. Never use a back-up power supply from outside the vehicle.

2. Disconnect the high tension wire or coil wire (running between the coil and the distributor) from the coil.
3. Disconnect the low tension wires from the coil.
4. Loosen the coil bracket and remove the coil.

To install:
5. Install the new coil and securely tighten the bracket.
6. Attach the low tension wires first, then the coil wire. Reconnect the battery cable.
7. Reset any various digital equipment such as radio memory and the clock if necessary.

Internal Coils

♦ See Figures 17 and 24 thru 31

The internal coil found within the distributor and can be changed without removing the distributor (a selection of various short screwdrivers may be required for access to the screws) but it is recommended to remove the distributor and then replace the coil assembly.

1. Turn the ignition key to the OFF position. Disconnect the negative battery cable. Wait at least 90 seconds once the battery cable has been disconnect to hinder air bag deployment.

Work must be started after 90 seconds from the time the ignition switch is turned to the LOCK position and the negative battery cable has been disconnected. The SRS is equipped with a back-up power source so that if work is started within 90 seconds of disconnecting the negative battery cable, the SRS may deploy. When the negative terminal cable is disconnected from the battery, memory of the clock and radio will be canceled. Before you start working, make a note of the contents memorized by the audio memory system. When you have finished working, reset the audio systems and adjust the clock. Never use a back-up power supply from outside the vehicle.

2. Label and disconnect the distributor wiring.
3. Label and disconnect the plug wires from the distributor.
4. Mark the location of the distributor. Remove the hold-down bolts and pull out the distributor.
5. Mark the location and remove the distributor rotor with O-ring (if equipped). Discard the O-ring.
6. Remove the dust cover over the ignition coil.

➡Note position and routing of all internal distributor assembly wiring.

7. Remove the nuts, then label and disconnect the wiring from the ignition coil.
8. Remove the screws and the ignition coil and gasket from the distributor.

To install:
9. Install the ignition coil, gasket, screws and secure its wiring. Again, watch the wiring positions.

➡When connecting the wires to the ignition coil, insert both properly into their grooves found on the side of the ignition coil. Be sure that the wires do not contact the signal rotor or distributor housing.

10. Install a new gasket to the housing when attaching the dust cover.
11. Install the distributor rotor.

Fig. 24 A dust cover is hiding most internal coils

Fig. 25 Remove the 2 nuts retaining the wiring to the coil terminals

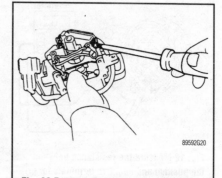

Fig. 26 Remove the screws to extract the ignition coil

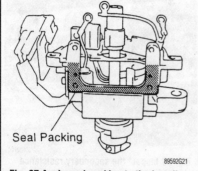

Fig. 27 Apply seal packing to the installation surface of the ignition coil housing

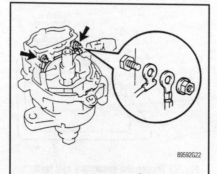

Fig. 28 Connect the wires to the coil terminals with the two nuts . . .

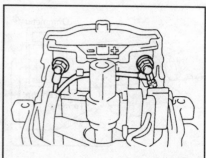

Fig. 29 . . . and be sure that the wires do not contact the signal rotor or distributor housing

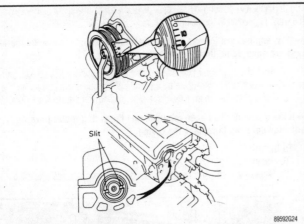

Fig. 30 Set the No. 1 cylinder to TDC and position the slit of the intake camshaft as shown

12. Set the No. 1 cylinder to TDC of the compression stroke. Turn the crankshaft clockwise, and position the slit of the intake camshaft as shown in distributor Removal and Installation.

13. Apply a light coat of engine oil to the new O-ring and install it to the distributor housing. align the cutout portion of the coupling with the protrusion of the housing. Insert the distributor, aligning the center of the flange with that of the bolt hole on the cylinder head. Lightly tighten the 2 mounting bolts.

14. Attach the spark plug wires to the distributor cap.

15. Connect the wiring to the distributor. Connect the negative battery cable.

16. Warm up the engine to reach operating temperature and adjust the timing.

17. Reset any digital equipment such as radio memory and the clock if necessary.

Igniter

REMOVAL & INSTALLATION

♦ See Figure 17

Depending on the engine and model year, some igniters are attached to the ignition coil and others are simply bolted to the body of the car. On 1994–95 7A-FE engines, the igniter is integrated with the distributor.

Internal

♦ See Figures 32 and 33

The distributor assembly must be removed to access the igniter assembly on the 1994–95 7A-FE engine.

1. Turn the ignition key to the **OFF** position. Disconnect the negative battery cable. Wait at least 90 seconds once the battery cable has been disconnect to hinder air bag deployment.

✳✳ CAUTION

Work must be started after 90 seconds from the time the ignition switch is turned to the LOCK position and the negative battery cable has been disconnected. The SRS is equipped with a back-up power source so that if work is started within 90 seconds of disconnecting the negative battery cable, the SRS may deploy. When the negative terminal cable is disconnected from the battery, memory of the clock and radio will be canceled. Before you start working, make a note of the contents memorized by the audio memory system. When you have finished working, reset the audio systems and adjust the clock. Never use a back-up power supply from outside the vehicle.

2. Label and disconnect the distributor wiring.

3. Label and disconnect the plug wires from the distributor.

4. Mark the location of the distributor. Remove the hold-down bolts and pull out the distributor.

5. Mark the location and remove the distributor rotor with O-ring (if equipped). Discard the O-ring.

6. Remove the ignition coil. Refer to the procedure in this section.

7. Remove the three screws, then label and disconnect the 3 wires from the igniter terminals.

➡ It is very important to label the wiring before disconnecting the igniter.

8. Unscrew the igniter and pull off of the distributor.

To install:

9. Insert the igniter into the distributor and secure with the retaining screws.

10. Attach the wiring to the correct locations.

11. Install the ignition coil.

12. Install and attach the rotor and distributor cap.

13. Set the No. 1 cylinder to TDC of the compression stroke. Turn the crankshaft clockwise, and position the slit of the intake camshaft as shown in distributor Removal and Installation.

14. Apply a light coat of engine oil to the new O-ring and install it to the distributor housing. align the cutout portion of the coupling with the protrusion of the housing. Insert the distributor, aligning the center of the flange with that of the bolt hole on the cylinder head. Lightly tighten the 2 mounting bolts.

15. Attach the spark plug wires to the distributor cap.

16. Connect the wiring to the distributor. Connect the negative battery cable.

17. Warm up the engine to reach operating temperature and adjust the timing.

18. Reset any digital equipment such as radio memory and the clock if necessary.

External

1. Separate the wiring harness connections.

2. Unbolt the igniter.

3. Loosen the nut holding the wire lead onto the coil if equipped.

4. Tag and disconnect the wire lead.

5. Lift the igniter off its mount.

To install:

6. Mount the igniter to the bracket.

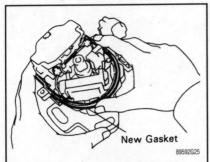

Fig. 31 Install a new gasket on the distributor housing before attaching the dust cover

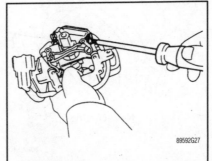

Fig. 32 Remove the 3 screws, then label and disconnect the wiring from the terminals of the igniter

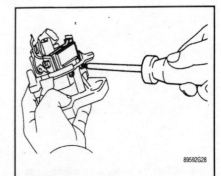

Fig. 33 Remove the 2 screws retaining the igniter

7. Attach the wire lead to the coil.
8. Connect the harness.
9. Connect the negative battery cable. Reset any digital equipment such as radio memory and the clock if necessary.

Distributor

REMOVAL & INSTALLATION

♦ See Figures 34 thru 42

1. On some models it may be necessary to remove the air cleaner cap.
2. Disconnect the wiring from the distributor.

3. Label and disconnect the spark plug wires from the spark plugs. Leave the wires connected to the distributor cap.

➥**Most engines are marked on the cap and wires, but in case the markings are gone, label them before removal.**

4. Mark the distributor flange in relation to the cylinder head. Loosen and remove the distributor hold-down bolt(s) and pull out the distributor assembly.
5. Remove the O-ring from the distributor housing and discard if deteriorated.

➥**If the distributor has been removed and the O-ring replaced recently, you may not need to replace the O-ring.**

To install:
6. Remove the RH engine under cover.
7. Before the distributor can be installed (especially in cases where the

Fig. 34 Disconnect the distributor harnesses

Fig. 35 The cap is usually labeled . . .

Fig. 36 . . . as are the spark plug wires

Fig. 37 Loosen and remove the two distributor mounting bolts . . .

Fig. 38 . . . and pull the unit from the cylinder head

Fig. 39 Use a pick to pull the O-ring off the distributor, but do not scratch the surface

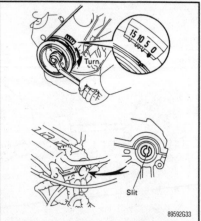
Fig. 40 Turn the crankshaft clockwise, and position the slit of the intake camshaft as shown

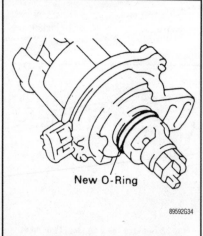
Fig. 41 Install the O-ring lubricated with clean engine oil to ease application

Fig. 42 When installing the distributor, align the cutout of the coupling with the groove of the housing

engine has been disturbed, cranked or dismantled), set the No. 1 piston at TDC by performing the following: with a socket wrench or equivalent, turn the crankshaft clockwise and position the slit in the intake camshaft as shown in the accompanying illustrations. Also the timing mark on the crankshaft pulley should be aligned with the **0** mark on the No. 1 timing belt cover indicator.

8. Coat the new distributor housing O-ring with clean engine oil and install the O-ring.

9. Align the cut-out of the coupling with the line of the housing.

10. Insert the distributor into the cylinder head by aligning the center of the flange with the bolt hole in the cylinder head. Now align the flange with the match mark made previously on the cylinder head. Lightly tighten the hold-down bolts.

11. Connect the spark plug wires to their respective spark plugs.

12. Connect the distributor wiring.

13. Connect the negative battery cable. Reset any digital equipment such as radio memory and the clock if necessary.

14. Connect a tachometer and timing light to the engine and adjust the ignition timing.

15. Tighten the hold-down bolts to 15 ft. lbs. (20 Nm).

16. Install the air cleaner cap if removed.

17. Recheck the ignition timing.

18. Disconnect the timing light and tachometer.

19. Reinstall the RH engine under cover.

Crankshaft Position Sensor

Refer to Electronic Engine Controls in Section 4 for information on servicing the crankshaft position sensor.

FIRING ORDERS

▶ **See Figures 43 and 44**

➡**To avoid confusion, remove and tag the spark plug wires one at a time, for replacement.**

If a distributor is not keyed for installation with only one orientation, it could have been removed previously and rewired. The resultant wiring would hold the correct firing order, but could change the relative placement of the plug towers in relation to the engine. For this reason it is imperative that you label all wires before disconnecting any of them. Also, before removal, compare the current wiring with the accompanying illustrations. If the current wiring does not match, make notes in your book to reflect how your engine is wired.

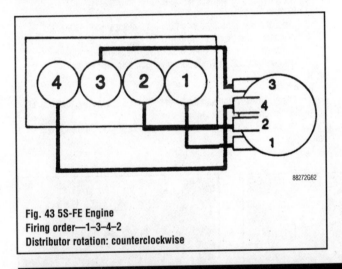

Fig. 43 5S-FE Engine
Firing order—1–3–4–2
Distributor rotation: counterclockwise

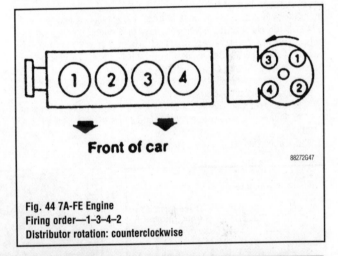

Front of car

Fig. 44 7A-FE Engine
Firing order—1–3–4–2
Distributor rotation: counterclockwise

CHARGING SYSTEM

General Information

The charging system is a negative (–) ground system which consists of an alternator, a regulator, a charge indicator lamp, a storage battery, circuit protection and wiring connecting the components.

The alternator is belt-driven from the engine. Energy is supplied from the alternator (with integral regulator) to the rotating field through brushes to slip-rings. The slip-rings are mounted on the rotor shaft and are connected to the field coil. This energy supplied to the rotating field from the battery is called excitation current and is used to initially energize the field to begin the generation of electricity. Once the alternator starts to generate electricity, the excitation current comes from its own output rather than the battery.

The alternator produces power in the form of alternating current. The alternating current is rectified by diodes into direct current. The direct current is used to charge the battery and power the rest of the electrical system. When the ignition key is turned on, current flows from the battery, through the charging system indicator light on the instrument panel, to the voltage regulator, and to the alternator. Since the alternator is not producing any current, the alternator warning light comes on. When the engine is started, the alternator begins to produce current and turns the alternator light off.

As the alternator turns and produces current, the current is divided in two ways: charging the battery and powering the electrical components of the vehicle. Part of the current is returned to the alternator to enable it to increase its output. In this situation, the alternator is receiving current from the battery and from itself. A voltage regulator is wired into the current supply to the alternator to prevent it from receiving too much current, which would cause it to overproduce current. Conversely, if the voltage regulator does not allow the alternator to receive enough current, the battery will not be fully charged and will eventually go dead.

The battery is connected to the alternator at all times, whether the ignition key is turned on or off. If the battery were shorted to ground, the alternator would also be shorted. This would damage the alternator. To prevent this, circuit protection (usually in the form of a fuse link) is installed in the wiring between the battery and the alternator. If the battery is shorted, the circuit protection will protect the alternator.

Alternator Precautions

To prevent damage to the alternator and regulator, the following precautionary measures must be taken when working with the electrical system.

• Never reverse the battery connections. Always check the battery polarity visually. This is to be done before any connections are made to ensure that all of the connections correspond to the battery ground polarity of the car.

• Booster batteries must be connected properly. Make sure the positive cable of the booster battery is connected to the positive terminal of the battery which is getting the boost.

• Disconnect the battery cables before using a fast charger; the charger has a tendency to force current through the diodes in the opposite direction for which they were designed.

• Never use a fast charger as a booster for starting the car.

• Never disconnect the voltage regulator while the engine is running, unless as noted for testing purposes.

• Do not ground the alternator output terminal.

• Do not operate the alternator on an open circuit with the field energized.

• Do not attempt to polarize the alternator.

• Disconnect the battery cables and remove the alternator before using an electric arc welder on the car.

• Protect the alternator from excessive moisture. If the engine is to be steam cleaned, cover or remove the alternator.

Alternator

TESTING

▶ See Figure 45

A voltmeter and ammeter are necessary for testing.

1. Make sure the battery terminals are not loose or corroded. Check the fusible link for continuity.

2. Inspect the drive belt for excessive wear. Check the drive belt tension. If necessary adjust the drive belt.

3. Check the fusible link, H°fuses, M°fuses, and fuses for continuity.

4. Visually check alternator wiring and listen for abnormal noises.

5. Check that the discharge warning light comes ON when the ignition switch is turned **ON**. Start the engine. Check that the warning light goes out.

6. Check the charging circuit WITHOUT A LOAD.

   a. Disconnect the wire from terminal B of the alternator and attach it to the negative lead of the ammeter.

   b. Connect the positive lead of the ammeter to terminal B of the alternator.

   c. Connect the positive lead of the voltmeter to terminal B of the alternator.

   d. Ground the negative lead of the voltmeter.

e. To check the charging circuit, run the engine from idle to 2000 rpms and check the reading on the ammeter and voltmeter. Standard amperage is 10 amps or less. Standard voltage is as follows:

• 77°F (25°C)—14.0–15.0 volts
• 239°F (115°C)—13.5–14.3 volts

   f. If the voltmeter reading is more than standard voltage, replace the voltage regulator. If the voltmeter reading is less than standard, check the alternator.

7. Check the charging circuit WITH A LOAD.

   a. With the engine running at 2000 rpm, turn on high beams and heater fan to HI.

   b. Check the standard amperage, it should be 30 amps or more. If the ammeter is less than standard, replace the alternator.

8. Replace the necessary parts. Recheck the charging system.

➡ **If a battery is fully charged, sometimes the indication will be less than 30 amps.**

REMOVAL & INSTALLATION

▶ See Figures 46 thru 59

1. Disconnect the negative battery cable.

2. On some models it is necessary to remove the fuse/relay block located near the alternator.

3. Loosen the adjusting lock bolt, adjusting bolt and pivot bolt.

4. Remove the drive belt.

5. Label and disconnect the wire from the 2 clamps on the alternator.

6. Disconnect the alternator wiring.

7. Remove rubber cap and nut, then detach the alternator wire.

8. Remove the adjusting lock bolt, pivot bolt and nut, then extract the alternator.

To install:

9. Attach the alternator with the pivot bolt, nut and adjusting lock bolt. Do not tighten the drive belt at this time.

10. Install the drive belt with the pivot bolt, adjusting lock bolt and adjusting bolt.

11. Adjust the drive belt.

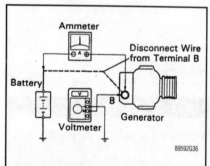

89592G36

Fig. 45 Connections of components when checking the charging circuit without a load

89592P09

Fig. 46 Lift up the fuse/relay block and set aside

89592P10

Fig. 47 Unbolt and remove the retaining bracket for the fuse/relay bracket

89592P11

Fig. 48 Loosen the adjusting lock bolt . . .

89592P12

Fig. 49 . . . the adjusting bolt . . .

89592P13

Fig. 50 . . . and pivot bolt

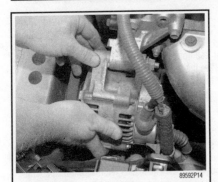

Fig. 51 Next, pull the alternator aside far enough to . . .

Fig. 52 . . . slip the drive belt off the pulley

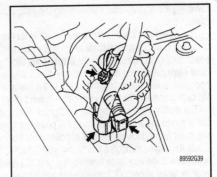

Fig. 53 Disconnect any wiring from the alternator and loosen any clamps

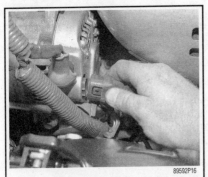

Fig. 54 Disconnect the wiring at the back of the alternator

Fig. 55 Lift the rubber cap and . . .

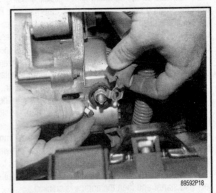

Fig. 56 . . . remove the nut and wire

Fig. 57 Take the lower and . . .

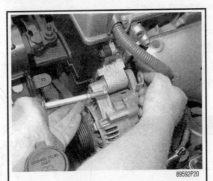

Fig. 58 . . . upper bolts off of the alternator

Fig. 59 Extract the alternator from the engine

12. Tighten the pivot bolt and adjusting bolts:
- 5S-FE engine—Pivot bolt—40 ft. lbs. (54 Nm)
- Adjusting bolt—14 ft. lbs. (19 Nm)
- 7A-FE engine—Pivot bolt—45 ft. lbs. (61 Nm)
- Adjusting bolt—14 ft. lbs. (19 Nm)

13. Connect the alternator wiring.
14. Attach the alternator wire with the nut and rubber cap.
15. Install the wire to the clamp on the rear end cover.
16. Connect the negative battery cable.
17. Inspect all electrical connections.

STARTING SYSTEM

General Information

The battery is the first link in the chain of mechanisms which work together to provide cranking of the automobile engine. The battery is a lead/acid electrochemical device consisting of six 2V subsections connected in series so the unit is capable of producing approximately 12V of electrical pressure. Each subsection, or cell, consists of a series of positive and negative plates held a short distance apart in a solution of sulfuric acid and water. The two types of plates are of dissimilar metals. This causes a chemical reaction to be set up, and it is this reaction which produces current flow from the battery when its

positive and negative terminals are connected to an electrical appliance such as a lamp or motor. The continued transfer of electrons would eventually convert the sulfuric acid in the electrolyte to water, and make the two plates identical in chemical composition. As electrical energy is removed from the battery, its voltage output tends to drop. Thus, measuring battery voltage and battery electrolyte composition are two ways of checking the ability of the unit to supply power. During the starting of the engine, electrical energy is removed from the battery. However, if the charging circuit is in good condition and the operating conditions are normal, the power removed from the battery will be replaced by the alternator which will force electrons back through the battery, reversing the normal flow, and restoring the battery to its original chemical state.

The battery and starting motor are linked by very heavy electrical cables designed to minimize resistance to the flow of current. Generally, the major power supply cable that leaves the battery goes directly to the starter, while other electrical system needs are supplied by a smaller cable. During starter operation, power flows from the battery to the starter and is grounded through the car's frame and the battery's negative ground strap.

The starting motor is a specially designed, direct current electric motor capable of producing a very great amount of power for its size. One thing that allows the motor to produce a great deal of power is its tremendous rotating speed. It drives the engine through a tiny pinion gear (attached to the starter's armature), which drives the very large flywheel ring gear at a greatly reduced speed. Another factor allowing it to produce so much power is that only intermittent operation is required of it. This, little allowance for air circulation is required, and the windings can be built into a very small space.

A magnetic switch mounted on the starter housing, is supplied by current from the starting switch circuit of the ignition switch. This magnetic action of the switch mechanically engages the starter clutch assembly and electrically closes the heavy switch which connects it to the battery. The starting switch circuit consists of the starting switch contained within the ignition switch, a transmission neutral safety switch or clutch pedal switch, and the wiring necessary to connect these in series with the starter solenoid or relay.

A pinion, which is a small gear, is mounted to a one-way drive clutch. This clutch is splined to the starter armature shaft. When the ignition switch is moved to the **START** position, the solenoid plunger slides the pinion toward the flywheel ring gear via a collar and spring. If the teeth on the pinion and flywheel match properly, the pinion will engage the flywheel immediately. If the gear teeth butt one another, the spring will be compressed and will force the gears to mesh as soon as the starter turns far enough to allow them to do so. As the solenoid plunger reaches the end of its travel, it closes the contacts that connect the battery and starter and then the engine is cranked.

As soon as the engine starts, the flywheel gear begins turning fast enough to drive the pinion at an extremely high rate of speed. At this point, the one-way clutch begins allowing the pinion to spin faster than the starter shaft so that the starter will not operate at excessive speed. When the ignition switch is released from the starter position, the solenoid is de-energized, and a spring contained within the solenoid assembly pulls the gear out of mesh and interrupts the current flow to the starter.

The starter uses a separate relay, mounted on the left hand cowl, to switch the motor and magnetic switch current on and off. The relay is used to reduce the amount of current the starting switch must carry.

Starter

TESTING

✱✱ WARNING

This tests must be performed within 3 to 5 seconds to avoid burning out the coil.

Pull-in

◆ See Figure 60

Disconnect the field coil lead from the terminal C. Connect the battery to the solenoid switch as shown. See if the clutch pinion gear movement is outward. If the gear does not move perform the hold-in test.

Hold-in

◆ See Figure 61

Attach the battery to the starter as shown and with the clutch pinion gear out, disconnect the negative lead from terminal C. Check to make sure the pinion gear stays in the outward position. If the clutch gear returns inwards, perform the clutch pinion gear return test.

Clutch Pinion Gear Return

◆ See Figure 62

Disconnect the negative lead from the solenoid body. Check the clutch pinion gear returns inward. If not perform the no-load test.

No-load

◆ See Figure 63

Attach a battery and ammeter to the starter. Check that the starter rotates smoothly and steadily with the pinion gear moving out. Check the ammeter shows the correct current. 90 amps or less at 11.5 volts on gasoline engines and 180 amps or less at 11.0 volts on diesel engines. If not replace the starter.

REMOVAL & INSTALLATION

◆ See Figures 64, 65, 66 and 67

1. Disconnect the negative battery cable.
2. Remove the air cleaner assembly.
3. On the 5S-FE engine remove the battery if necessary.

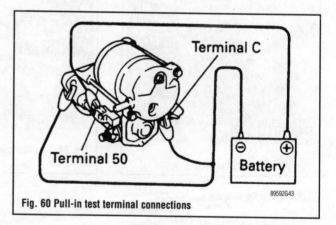

Fig. 60 Pull-in test terminal connections

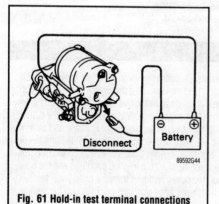

Fig. 61 Hold-in test terminal connections

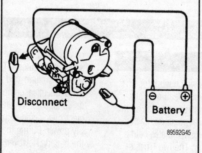

Fig. 62 Clutch pinion gear return terminal connections

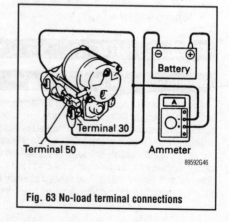

Fig. 63 No-load terminal connections

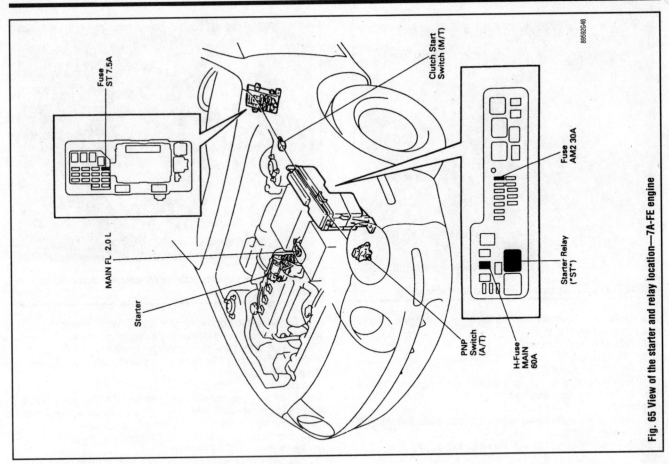

Fig. 65 View of the starter and relay location—7A-FE engine

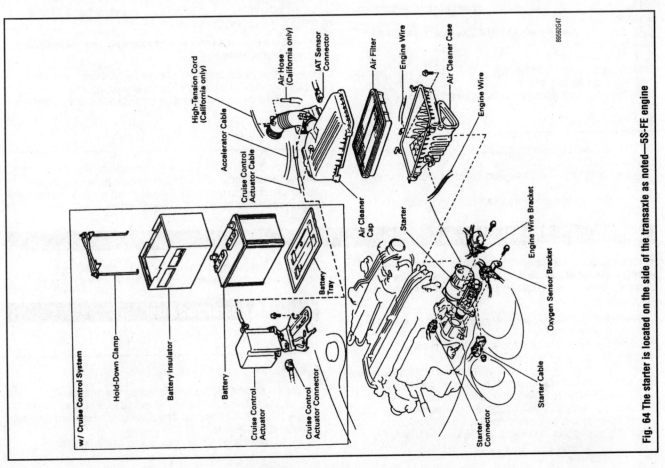

Fig. 64 The starter is located on the side of the transaxle as noted—5S-FE engine

Fig. 66 From under the vehicle, disconnect the starter wiring

Fig. 67 Once the mounting bolts are removed, the starter can be removed from the vehicle

4. On models equipped with cruise control, disconnect the cruise control actuator from the body bracket.

5. Disconnect the starter wiring.

6. Remove the nut, then disconnect the starter cable.

7. Remove the 2 starter bolts.

8. Remove the oxygen sensor wiring harness from the engine wire brackets and starter. Extract the starter from the engine.

To install:

9. Attach the starter and oxygen sensor wiring and brackets. tighten the two bolts to 29 ft. lbs. (39 Nm).

10. Attach the starter cable and tighten the nut. Attach all other starter wiring.

11. On cruise control models, install the actuator with the 3 bolts, then connect the wiring.

12. If removed, install the battery. Face the arrow mark on the hold-down clamp forward.

13. Install the air cleaner.

14. Connect the negative battery cable.

15. Check that the engine starts.

16. Reset any electrical components such as the radio and clock.

SOLENOID REPLACEMENT

The starter solenoid (magnetic switch) is an integral part of the starter assembly.

1. Remove the starter from the van. Remove the heat insulator from the starter assembly, if equipped.

2. Disconnect the wire lead from the magnetic switch terminal.

3. Remove the two long, through bolts holding the field frame to the magnetic switch. Pull out the field frame with the armature from the magnetic switch.

4. To separate the starter housing from the magnetic switch assembly, remove the two screws and the starter housing with the pinion gear (1.6 kW), idler and clutch assembly.

To install:

5. If necessary, install the gears and clutch assembly to the starter housing. Apply grease to the gear and clutch assemblies and place the clutch assembly, idler gear, bearing and pinion gear (1.6 kW) in the starter housing.

6. Insert the spring into the clutch shaft hole and place the starter housing onto the magnetic switch. Install the two screws.

7. Install the field frame with the armature onto the magnetic switch assembly and install the two through bolts. Tighten the bolts on the 1.4 kW to 52 inch lbs. (6 Nm) and on the 1.6 kW to 82 inch lbs. (9 Nm).

➡There is a protrusion or tab on each part; make sure you line them up correctly during assembly.

8. Connect the wire to the terminal on the magnetic switch and tighten the nut to 52 inch lbs. (6 Nm). Install the heat insulator, if equipped.

9. Reinstall the starter on the vehicle. Check starter system for proper operation.

RELAY REPLACEMENT

The starter relay is located in the engine compartment relay box. Disconnect the negative battery cable. Wait at least 90 seconds after the cable is disconnected to hinder airbag deployment. Remove the relay box cover and extract the relay. The relay should simply pull out with a slight hindrance.

SENDING UNITS AND SENSORS

➡This section describes the operating principles of sending units, warning lights and gauges. Sensors which provide information to the Electronic Control Module (ECM) are covered in Section 4 of this manual.

Instrument panels contain a number of indicating devices (gauges and warning lights). These devices are composed of two separate components. One is the sending unit, mounted on the engine or other remote part of the vehicle, and the other is the actual gauge or light in the instrument panel.

Several types of sending units exist, however most can be characterized as being either a pressure type or a resistance type. Pressure type sending units convert liquid pressure into an electrical signal which is sent to the gauge. Resistance type sending units are most often used to measure temperature and use variable resistance to control the current flow back to the indicating device. Both types of sending units are connected in series by a wire to the battery (through the ignition switch). When the ignition is turned **ON**, current flows from the battery through the indicating device and on to the sending unit.

Coolant Temperature Sensor

TESTING

♦ See Figure 68

Using an ohmmeter, measure the resistance between the terminals.

1. Check that there is no continuity between the terminals when the sensor is above 199 °F (93 °C). Check that there is continuity between terminals when the temperature is below 181 ° (83 °C).

2. If the continuity is not within specifications, replace the switch.

3

ENGINE AND ENGINE OVERHAUL

ENGINE MECHANICAL

5S-FE ENGINE MECHANICAL SPECIFICATIONS

Description		English Specifications	Metric Specifications
Compression Pressure			
STD		178 psi	1226 kPa
Limit		142 psi	981 kPa
Idler Pulley Tension Spring			
Free length		1.811 inch	46.0mm
Installed load @ 1.988 inch (50.5mm)		7.2-8.3 lbf	32-37 N
Cylinder Head			
Cylinder block side warpage		0.020 inch	0.05mm
Manifold side warpage		0.031 inch	0.08mm
Valve seat			
refacing angle		30, 45, 75°	30, 45, 75°
contacting angle		45°	45°
contacting width		0.039-0.055 inch	1.0-1.4mm
Valve Guide Bushing			
Inner diameter		0.2366-0.2374 inch	6.01-6.03mm
Outer diameter STD		0.4331-0.4342 inch	11.000-11.027mm
O/S 0.5		0.4350-0.4361 inch	11.050-11.077mm
Valve			
Overall length STD	intake	3.8425 inch	97.60mm
	exhaust	3.8760 inch	98.45mm
limit	intake	3.823 inch	97.1mm
	exhaust	3.853 inch	98.0mm
Face angle		44.5°	44.5°
Stem diameter	intake	0.2350-0.2356 inch	5.970-5.985mm
	exhaust	0.2348-0.2354 inch	5.965-5.980mm
Stem oil clearance STD	intake	0.0010-0.0024 inch	0.025-0.060mm
	exhaust	0.0012-0.0026 inch	0.030-0.065mm
limit	intake	0.0031 inch	0.08mm
	exhaust	0.0039 inch	0.10mm
Margin thickness STD		0.031-0.047 inch	0.8-1.2mm
limit		0.020 inch	0.5mm
Valve Spring			
Deviation limit		0.079 inch	2.0mm
Free length		1.6520-1.6531 inch	41.96-41.99mm
Installed tension @ 1.366 inch (34.7mm)		36.8-42.5 lbf	164-189 N
Valve Lifter			
Lifter diameter		1.2191-1.2195 inch	30.966-30.976mm
Lifter bore diameter		1.2205-1.2213 inch	31.000-31.018mm
Oil clearance STD		0.0009-0.0020 inch	0.024-0.052mm
limit		0.0028 inch	0.07mm
Camshaft			
Thrust clearance STD	intake	0.0018-0.0039 inch	0.045-0.100mm
	exhaust	0.0012-0.0033 inch	0.030-0.085mm
limit	intake	0.0047 inch	0.12mm
	exhaust	0.0039 inch	0.10mm

89593C05

5S-FE ENGINE MECHANICAL SPECIFICATIONS

Description		English Specifications	Metric Specifications
Camshaft—continued			
Journal oil clearance STD		0.0010-0.0024 inch	0.025-0.062mm
limit		0.0039 inch	0.10mm
Journal diameter		1.0614-1.0620 inch	26.969-26.975mm
Circle runout		0.0016 inch	0.04mm
Cam lobe height STD	intake	1.6539-1.6579 inch	42.01-42.11mm
	exhaust	1.5772-1.5811 inch	40.06-40.16mm
limit	intake	1.6496 inch	41.90mm
	exhaust	1.5728 inch	39.95mm
Camshaft gear backlash STD		0.0008-0.0079 inch	0.020-0.200mm
limit		0.0188 inch	0.30mm
Camshaft—continued			
Camshaft gear spring end free distance		0.886-0.902 inch	22.5-22.9mm
Manifold			
limit		0.0118 inch	0.30mm
Cylinder Block			
Head surface warpage		0.0020 inch	0.05mm
Cylinder bore STD	Mark 1	3.4252-3.4256 inch	87.000-87.010mm
	Mark 2	3.4256-3.4260 inch	87.010-87.020mm
	Mark 3	3.4260-3.4264 inch	87.020-87.030mm
maximum	STD	3.4342 inch	87.23mm
	O/S 0.50	3.4350 inch	87.73mm
Piston and Rings			
Piston diameter STD	Mark 1	3.4193-3.4197 inch	86.850-86.860mm
	Mark 2	3.4197-3.4201 inch	86.860-86.870mm
	Mark 3	3.4201-3.4205 inch	86.870-86.880mm
	O/S 0.50	3.4390-3.4402 inch	87.350-87.380mm
Piston oil clearance STD		0.0055-0.0063 inch	0.14-0.016mm
limit		0.0071 inch	0.18mm
Piston ring groove clearance	No. 1	0.0016-0.0031 inch	0.0012-0.0028mm
	No. 2	0.0012-0.0028 inch	0.030-0.070mm
Piston ring end-gap STD	No. 1	0.0106-0.0197 inch	0.270-0.500mm
	No. 2	0.0138-0.0234 inch	0.350-0.600mm
	oil	0.0079-0.0217 inch	0.200-0.550mm
Limit	No. 1	0.0433 inch	1.10mm
	No. 2	0.0472 inch	1.20mm
	oil	0.0453 inch	1.15mm
Connecting Rod			
Thrust clearance STD		0.0063-0.0123 inch	0.160-0.312mm
limit		0.0118 inch	0.35mm

89593C06

Troubleshooting Basic Starting System Problems

Problem	Cause	Solution
Starter motor rotates engine slowly	• Battery charge low or battery defective	• Charge or replace battery
	• Defective circuit between battery and starter motor	• Clean and tighten, or replace cables
	• Low load current	• Bench-test starter motor. Inspect for worn brushes and weak brush springs.
	• High load current	• Bench-test starter motor. Check engine for friction, drag or coolant in cylinders. Check ring gear-to-pinion gear clearance.
Starter motor will not rotate engine	• Battery charge low or battery defective	• Charge or replace battery
	• Faulty solenoid	• Check solenoid ground. Repair or replace as necessary.
	• Damaged drive pinion gear or ring gear	• Replace damaged gear(s)
	• Starter motor engagement weak	• Bench-test starter motor
	• Starter motor rotates slowly with high load current	• Inspect drive yoke pull-down and point gap, check for worn end bushings, check ring gear clearance
	• Engine seized	• Repair engine
Starter motor drive will not engage (solenoid known to be good)	• Defective contact point assembly	• Repair or replace contact point assembly
	• Inadequate contact point assembly ground	• Repair connection at ground screw
	• Defective hold-in coil	• Replace field winding assembly
Starter motor drive will not disengage	• Starter motor loose on flywheel housing	• Tighten mounting bolts
	• Worn drive end busing	• Replace bushing
	• Damaged ring gear teeth	• Replace ring gear or driveplate
	• Drive yoke return spring broken or missing	• Replace spring
Starter motor drive disengages prematurely	• Weak drive assembly thrust spring	• Replace drive mechanism
	• Hold-in coil defective	• Replace field winding assembly
Low load current	• Worn brushes	• Replace brushes
	• Weak brush springs	• Replace springs

TCCS2C01

Troubleshooting Basic Charging System Problems

Problem	Cause	Solution
Noisy alternator	• Loose mountings	• Tighten mounting bolts
	• Loose drive pulley	• Tighten pulley
	• Worn bearings	• Replace alternator
	• Brush noise	• Replace alternator
	• Internal circuits shorted (High pitched whine)	• Replace alternator
Squeal when starting engine or accelerating	• Glazed or loose belt	• Replace or adjust belt
Indicator light remains on or ammeter indicates discharge (engine running)	• Broken belt	• Install belt
	• Broken or disconnected wires	• Repair or connect wiring
	• Internal alternator problems	• Replace alternator
	• Defective voltage regulator	• Replace voltage regulator/alternator
Car light bulbs continually burn out—battery needs water continually	• Alternator/regulator overcharging	• Replace voltage regulator/alternator
Car lights flare on acceleration	• Battery low	• Charge or replace battery
	• Internal alternator/regulator problems	• Replace alternator/regulator
Low voltage output (alternator light flickers continually or ammeter needle wanders)	• Loose or worn belt	• Replace or adjust belt
	• Dirty or corroded connections	• Clean or replace connections
	• Internal alternator/regulator problems	• Replace alternator/regulator

TCCS2C02

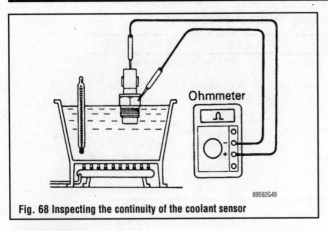

Fig. 68 Inspecting the continuity of the coolant sensor

REMOVAL & INSTALLATION

▶ **See Figure 69**

1. Locate the coolant temperature sending unit on the engine.
2. Disconnect the sending unit electrical wiring.
3. Drain the engine coolant below the level of the switch.
4. Unfasten and remove the sending unit from the engine. Discard the old gasket if equipped.

To install:

5. Coat the new sending unit with Teflon® tape or electrically conductive sealer. Place a new gasket on the sender.
6. Install the sending unit and tighten to 18 ft. lbs. (24 Nm).
7. Attach the sending unitís electrical connector.
8. Fill the engine with coolant.
9. Start the engine, allow it to reach operating temperature and check for leaks.
10. Check for proper sending unit operation.

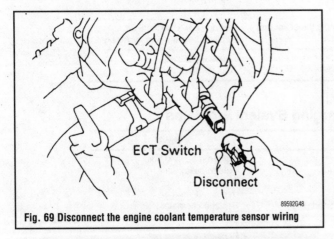

Fig. 69 Disconnect the engine coolant temperature sensor wiring

Oil Pressure Sensor

TESTING

A quick way to determine if the gauge (idiot light) or sending unit is faulty is to disconnect the sending unit electrical harness and ground it (if two terminal, jumper between the terminals). If the gauge responds, the sending unit may be faulty. Proceed with the sending unit test.

1. Disconnect the sending unit electrical harness.
2. Using an ohmmeter, check continuity of the sending unit terminals (sending unit terminal and ground).
3. With the engine stopped, continuity should exist.
4. With the engine running, continuity should not exist.
5. If continuity does not exist as stated, the sending unit is faulty.

REMOVAL & INSTALLATION

▶ **See Figures 70 and 71**

1. Locate the oil pressure sending unit on the engine.
2. Disconnect the sending unit electrical harness.
3. Unfasten and remove the sending unit from the engine.

To install:

4. Coat the new sending unit with Teflon® tape or electrically conductive sealer.
5. Install the sending unit and tighten to 11 ft. lbs. (15 Nm).
6. Attach the sending unitís electrical connector.
7. Start the engine, allow it to reach operating temperature and check for leaks.
8. Check for proper sending unit operation.

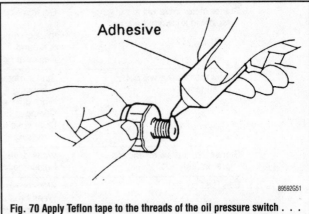

Fig. 70 Apply Teflon tape to the threads of the oil pressure switch . . .

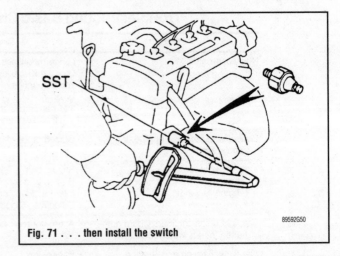

Fig. 71 . . . then install the switch

5S-FE ENGINE MECHANICAL SPECIFICATIONS

Description			English Specifications	Metric Specifications
Connecting Rod—continued				
Connecting rod bearing wall thickness				
Reference	STD Mark 1		0.0584-0.0586 inch	1.484-1.488mm
	STD Mark 2		0.0586-0.0587 inch	1.488-1.492mm
	STD Mark 3		0.0587-0.0589 inch	1.492-1.496mm
Connecting rod oil clearance				
	STD		0.0009-0.0022 inch	0.024-0.055mm
	U/S	0.25	0.0009-0.0027 inch	0.023-0.069mm
	limit		0.0031 inch	0.08mm
Rod twist				
limit per 3.94 inch (100mm)			0.0059 inch	0.15mm
Piston pin diameter			0.8660-0.8665 inch	21.997-22.009mm
Piston pin oil clearance				
STD			0.0002-0.0004 inch	0.005-0.011mm
limit			0.0020 inch	0.005mm
Connecting rod bolt outside diameter				
STD			0.3094-0.3150 inch	7.860-8.000mm
limit			0.2992 inch	7.60mm
Crankshaft				
Thrust clearance				
STD			0.0008-0.0087 inch	0.020-0.220mm
maximum			0.0118 inch	0.30mm
Thrust washer thickness			0.0961-0.0980 inch	2.440-2.490mm
Main journal oil clearance				
STD No. 3			0.0010-0.0017 inch	0.025-0.044mm
	U/S	0.25	0.0011-0.0026 inch	0.027-0.067mm
others	STD		0.0006-0.0013 inch	0.015-0.034mm
	U/S	0.25	0.0007-0.0023 inch	0.019-0.059mm
limit			0.0031 inch	0.08mm
Main journal diameter				
STD			2.1653-2.1655 inch	54.988-55.003mm
	U/S	0.25	1.8797-1.8801 inch	54.0745-54.755mm
Main journal wall thickness				
STD No. 3	Mark 1		0.0784-0.0785 inch	1.992-1.995mm
	Mark 2		0.0785-0.0787 inch	1.995-1.998mm
	Mark 3		0.0787-0.0788 inch	1.998-2.001mm
	Mark 4		0.0788-0.0789 inch	2.001-2.004mm
	Mark 5		0.0789-0.0790 inch	2.004-2.007mm
STD others	Mark 1		0.0788-0.0787 inch	1.997-2.000mm
	Mark 2		0.0787-0.0789 inch	2.000-2.003mm
	Mark 3		0.0789-0.0790 inch	2.003-2.006mm
	Mark 4		0.0790-0.0791 inch	2.006-2.009mm
	Mark 5		0.0791-0.0792 inch	2.009-2.012mm
Crank pin diameter				
STD			2.0466-2.0472 inch	51.985-52.000mm
U/S 0.25			2.0372-2.0376 inch	51.745-51.755mm
Circle run-out			0.0024 inch	0.06mm

89593C07

7A-FE ENGINE MECHANICAL SPECIFICATIONS

Description			English Specifications	Metric Specifications
Compression Pressure				
STD			191 psi	1320 kPa
Limit			142 psi	981 kPa
Cylinder Head				
Cylinder block side warpage			0.020 inch	0.05mm
Manifold side warpage			0.039 inch	0.10mm
Valve seat	refacing		30, 45, 60°	30, 45, 60°
	contacting angle		45°	45°
	contacting width		0.039-0.055 inch	1.0-1.4mm
Valve Guide Bushing				
Inner diameter			0.2366-0.2374 inch	6.01-6.03mm
Outer diameter	STD		0.4331-0.4341 inch	11.000-11.027mm
	O/S 0.5		0.4350-0.4361 inch	11.050-11.077mm
Valve				
Overall length	STD	intake	3.4429 inch	103.45mm
		exhaust	3.4583 inch	103.45mm
	limit	intake	3.4232 inch	103.60mm
		exhaust	3.4386 inch	103.90mm
Face angle			44.5°	44.5°
Stem diameter		intake	0.2350-0.2356 inch	5.970-5.985mm
		exhaust	0.2348-0.2354 inch	5.965-5.980mm
Stem oil clearance	STD	intake	0.0010-0.0024 inch	0.025-0.060mm
		exhaust	0.0012-0.0026 inch	0.030-0.065mm
	limit	intake	0.0031 inch	0.08mm
		exhaust	0.0039 inch	0.10mm
Margin thickness			0.031-0.047 inch	0.8-1.2mm
Valve Spring				
Free length			1.5185 inch	38.57mm
Installed tension @ 1.248 inch (31.7mm)			37.3 lbf	166 N
Camshaft				
Thrust clearance	STD	intake	0.0012-0.0033 inch	0.030-0.085mm
		exhaust	0.0014-0.0035 inch	0.035-0.090mm
	limit		0.0043 inch	0.11mm
Journal oil clearance	STD		0.0014-0.0028 inch	0.035-0.762mm
	limit		0.0039 inch	0.10mm
Journal diameter	exhaust No. 1		0.9822-0.9829 inch	24.949-24.965mm
	others		0.9035-0.9041 inch	22.949-22.965mm
Circle runout			0.0016 inch	0.04mm
Cam lobe height	intake		1.6776-1.6815 inch	42.610-42.710mm
	exhaust		1.6520-1.6560 inch	41.960-42.060mm
Camshaft gear backlash	STD		0.0008-0.0079 inch	0.020-0.200mm
	limit		0.0188 inch	0.30mm

89593C08

7A-FE ENGINE MECHANICAL SPECIFICATIONS

Description		English Specifications	Metric Specifications
Camshaft-continued			
Camshaft gear spring end free distance		0.669-0.693 inch	17.0-17.6mm
Valve Lifter			
Lifter diameter		1.219-1.2195 inch	30.966-30.976mm
Lifter bore diameter		1.2205-1.2215 inch	31.000-31.025mm
Oil clearance	STD	0.0009-0.0023 inch	0.024-0.059mm
	limit	0.0028 inch	0.07mm
Manifolds			
Warpage	intake	0.0079 inch	0.20mm
	exhaust	0.0118 inch	0.30mm
Cylinder Block			
Head surface warpage		0.0020 inch	0.05mm
Cylinder bore STD	Mark 1	3.1890-3.1894 inch	81.000-81.010mm
	Mark 2	3.1894-3.1898 inch	81.010-81.020mm
	Mark 3	3.1898-3.1902 inch	81.020-81.030mm
maximum	STD	3.1982 inch	81.23mm
	O/S 0.50	3.2177 inch	81.73mm
Main journal bore diameter	Mark 1	2.0482-2.0485 inch	52.025-52.031mm
	Mark 2	2.0485-2.0487 inch	52.031-52.037mm
	Mark 3	2.0487-2.0489 inch	52.037-52.043mm
Piston and Rings			
Piston diameter STD	Mark 1	3.1852-3.1856 inch	80.905-80.915mm
	Mark 2	3.1856-3.1860 inch	80.915-80.925mm
	Mark 3	3.1860-3.1864 inch	80.925-80.935mm
	O/S 0.50	3.2049-3.2061 inch	81.405-81.435mm
Piston oil clearance	STD	0.0003-0.0031 inch	0.008-0.080mm
	limit	0.0012-0.0028 inch	0.030-0.070mm
Piston ring groove clearance	No. 1	①	①
	No. 2	①	①
Piston ring end-gap STD	No. 1	0.0098-0.0138 inch	(0.250-0.350mm)
	No. 2	0.0138-0.0197 inch	(0.350-0.500mm)
	oil	0.0039-0.0157 inch	(0.100-0.400mm)
Limit	No. 1	0.0413 inch	1.05mm
	No. 2	0.0472 inch	1.20mm
	oil	0.0433 inch	1.10mm
Connecting Rod			
Thrust clearance	STD	0.0059-0.0098 inch	0.15-0.25mm
	limit	0.0118 inch	0.30mm
Connecting rd bearing wall thickness			
Reference	STD Mark 1	0.0685-0.0687 inch	1.486-1.490mm
	STD Mark 2	0.0687-0.0688 inch	1.490-1.494mm
	STD Mark 3	0.0688-0.0690 inch	1.494-1.498mm

89593C09

7A-FE ENGINE MECHANICAL SPECIFICATIONS

Description		English Specifications	Metric Specifications
Connecting Rod-continued			
Connecting rod oil clearance	STD	0.0008-0.0019 inch	0.020-0.048mm
	U/S 0.25	0.0007-0.0022 inch	0.019-0.058mm
	limit	0.0031 inch	0.08mm
Rod twist			
limit per 3.94 inch (100mm)		0.0020 inch	0.05mm
Rod bolt outside diameter	STD	0.3488-0.3543 inch	8.860-9.000mm
	limit	0.3386 inch	8.60mm
Crankshaft			
Thrust clearance	STD	0.0006-0.0087 inch	0.015-0.220mm
	maximum	0.0118 inch	0.30mm
Thrust washer thickness		0.0961-0.0980 inch	2.440-2.490mm
Main journal oil clearance	STD	0.0006-0.0013 inch	2.440-2.490mm
	U/S 0.25	0.0006-0.0013 inch	0.015-0.033mm
	limit	0.0006-0.0022 inch	0.016-0.059mm
Main journal diameter	STD	1.8891-1.8898 inch	47.982-48.000mm
	U/S 0.25	1.8797-1.8801 inch	47.745-47.755mm
Main journal wall thickness STD	Mark 1	0.0788-0.0789 inch	2.002-2.005mm
	Mark 2	0.0789-0.0791 inch	2.005-2.008mm
	Mark 3	0.0791-0.0792 inch	2.008-2.011mm
	Mark 4	0.0792-0.0793 inch	2.011-2.014mm
	Mark 5	0.0793-0.0794 inch	2.014-2.017mm
Crank pin diameter	STD	1.8893-1.8898 inch	47.988-48.000mm
	U/S 0.25	1.8797-1.8801 inch	47.745-47.555mm
Circle run-out		0.0012 inch	0.03mm

① 1994-95 No. 1: 0.0003-0.0031 inch (0.008-0.080mm)
No. 2: 0.0012-0.0028 inch (0.030-0.070mm)
1996-98 No.1: 0.0018-0.0033 inch (0.045-0.085mm)
No. 2: 0.0012-0.0028 inch (0.030-0.070mm)

89593C10

Engine

REMOVAL & INSTALLATION

▶ **See Figures 1 thru 6**

In the process of removing the engine, you will come across a number of steps which call for the removal of a separate component or system, such as "disconnect the exhaust system" or "remove the radiator." In most instances, a detailed removal procedure can be found elsewhere in this manual.

It is virtually impossible to list each individual wire and hose which must be disconnected, simply because so many different model and engine combinations have been manufactured. Careful observation and common sense are the best possible approaches to any repair procedure.

Removal and installation of the engine can be made easier if you follow these basic points:

• If you have to drain any of the fluids, use a suitable container.

• Always tag any wires or hoses and, if possible, the components they came from before disconnecting them.

• Because there are so many bolts and fasteners involved, store and label the retainers from components separately in muffin pans, jars or coffee cans. This will prevent confusion during installation.

• After unbolting the transmission or transaxle, always make sure it is properly supported.

• If it is necessary to disconnect the air conditioning system, have this service performed by a qualified technician using a recovery/recycling station. If the system does not have to be disconnected, unbolt the compressor and set it aside.

Fig. 1 Engine under covers should be removed to access all underneath components

• When unbolting the engine mounts, always make sure the engine is properly supported. When removing the engine, make sure that any lifting devices are properly attached to the engine. It is recommended that if your engine is supplied with lifting hooks, your lifting apparatus be attached to them.

• Lift the engine from its compartment slowly, checking that no hoses, wires or other components are still connected.

• After the engine is clear of the compartment, place it on an engine stand or workbench.

• After the engine has been removed, you can perform a partial or full teardown of the engine using the procedures outlined in this manual.

➡ **The engine and transaxle assembly must be removed as a single unit.**

1. Disconnect the negative battery cable. Wait at least 90 seconds after the battery cable is disconnected to hinder air bag deployment.

❊❊ CAUTION

Work must be started after 90 seconds from the time the ignition switch is turned to the LOCK position and the negative battery cable has been disconnected. The SRS is equipped with a back-up power source so that if work is started within 90 seconds of disconnecting the negative battery cable, the SRS may deploy. When the negative terminal cable is disconnected from the battery, memory of the clock and radio will be canceled. Before you start working, make a note of the contents memorized by the audio memory system. When you have finished working, reset the audio systems and adjust the clock. Never use a back-up power supply from outside the vehicle.

2. Remove the battery.

3. With the aid of an assistant, unbolt and remove the hood.

4. Raise and safely support the front of the vehicle securely on jackstands. Remove the engine undercovers.

5. Drain and recycle the engine coolant.

6. Drain the engine oil from the crankcase.

7. Drain the transaxle case fluid.

8. Disconnect and label any wiring associated with removal of the air cleaner. Unclamp, disconnect the air hose then unbolt and remove the air cleaner assembly.

9. Disconnect the accelerator cable from the throttle body and cable bracket.

10. Disconnect the cruise control actuator cable from its clamps.

11. On Canadian models, disconnect the relay box for the daytime running lights system from the radiator.

12. Remove the radiator. Be sure to label all wiring and hoses and pipes.

13. Disvonnect the following wiring:

   a. Manifold Absolute Pressure (MAP) sensor vacuum hose from the gas filter on the intake manifold

   b. Power steering air hose from the intake manifold

   c. Power steering hose from the air pipe

   d. Brake booster vacuum hose from the intake manifold

   e. A/C idle-up valve connector

   f. A/C idle-up valve hose from the intake manifold

   g. A/C idle-up valve hose from the air pipe

Fig. 2 Only a few bolts retain the left engine cover

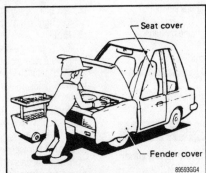

Fig. 3 Place a fender and seat covers on the car before working to spare exterior scratches and a soiled interior

Fig. 4 Be careful when removing the ECM

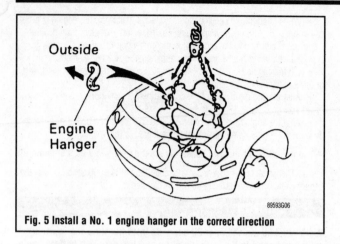

Fig. 5 Install a No. 1 engine hanger in the correct direction

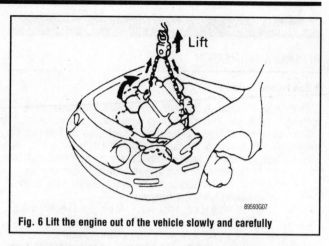

Fig. 6 Lift the engine out of the vehicle slowly and carefully

h. Data Link Connector (DLC1) from the bracket
i. Engine wire protector with bracket
j. Ground cable and strap from body
k. 2 heater hoses from the water inlet housing
l. Fuel inlet hose from the fuel filter
m. Fuel return hose from return pipe
n. EVAP hose from charcoal canister

14. Disconnect and labile the engine wire from the engine compartment relay box.
15. Remove the scuff plate, cowl side trim and lower instrument finish panel.
16. Disconnect the engine wire from the clamp of the ECM bracket, the ECM connections, circuit opening relay wiring and A/C amplifier connection.
17. Detach the MAP sensor wiring and separate from the bracket.
18. Unclamp the engine wire from the bracket.
19. Remove the nuts holding the engine wire retainer to the cowl panel.
20. Pull out the engine wire from the cabin.
21. Remove the front exhaust pipe.
22. Remove both driveshafts.
23. Remove the alternator drive belt.
24. Separate, suspend and secure the A/C compressor from the engine but do not disconnect any lines.
25. Separate, suspend and secure the power steering pump from the engine but do not disconnect any lines.
26. On the 5S-FE engine, remove the starter motor assembly.
27. Remove the bolts, and disconnect the A/C relay box.
28. On manual transaxles, disconnect the clutch slave cylinder.
29. Disconnect the transaxle control cables.
30. On automatics, disconnect the transaxle control cable from the engine mounting center member.
31. Remove the exhaust pipe support bracket.
32. Remove the engine mounting center crossmember 2 dust covers from the rear.
a. Disconnect the A/C pipe from the bracket.
b. Remove the bolt and nut holding the front engine mounting bracket to the mounting insulator.
c. Remove the bolt holding the rear engine mounting bracket to the mounting insulator.
d. Remove the bolt and the 2 nuts holding the rear engine mounting insulator to the front suspension crossmember.
e. Remove the bolts and the rear engine mounting bracket.
f. Remove the bolts holding the center member and rear engine mounting insulator.
33. Attach the No. 1 engine hanger in the correct direction. Attach the engine chain hoist to the hanger.

✳✳ CAUTION

Do not attempt to hang the engine by hooking the chain to any other component.

34. Remove the 2 bolts and nut, then disconnect the LH engine mounting bracket from the insulator. Remove the through bolt and LH engine insulator.
35. Disconnedct the ground strap connector. Remove the bolt and nuts, then disconnect the RH engine bracket from the insulator.

➡ **Make sure the engine is clear of all wiring, hoses and cables.**

36. Place the engine and transaxle assembly onto the stand.
37. Separatre the engine from the transaxle.
38. Install and attach all components to the engine and transaxle in the reverse order of removal. Make sure to tighten all components securely, refer the Torque Specifications chart at the end of this section. Pay particular attention the following:
a. Secure the engine to the transaxle and tighten the retaining bolts to:
• 12mm—17 ft. lbs. (23 Nm)
• 14mm—34 ft. lbs. (46 Nm)
• 17mm—47 ft. lbs. (64 Nm)
39. Attach the chain hoist to the engine hangers. Slowly lower the engine assembly into the engine compartment. Tilt the transaxle downward, lower the engine and clear the LH body mounting.
40. Keep the engine level, and align the RH and LH mountings with the body mountings.
41. Attach the RH engine mounting bracket to the insulator, then temporarily install the nuts. Temporarily install the LH engine mounting insulator to the body with the through bolt. Attach the LH mounting bracket to the insulator and secure with the bolts and nut. Tighten the through bolt retaining the LH engine mount insulator to the body. Tighten the nuts holding the RH engine mounting bracket to the insulator.
42. Attach the ground strap wiring, remove the engine chain hoist, bolt and engine No. 1 hanger.
43. Install the engine center mounting crossmember. Attach the member together with the rear engine mounting insulator to the front suspension member. Temporarily install the 2 bolts holding the center member to the body. Install the rear engine mounting bracket with the two bolts. Tighten them to 58 ft. lbs. (78 Nm).
44. Temporarily install the bolt and 2 nuts holding the rear engine mounting insulator to the front suspension member. Temporarily install the bolt holding the rear engine mounting bracket to the insulator. Temporarily install the bolt and nut holding the front engine mounting bracket to the insulator.
45. Tighten the 2 bolts holding the center member to the body to 26 ft. lbs. (35 Nm).
46. Tighten the bolt and 2 nuts holding the rear engine mounting insulator to the front suspension member to 59 ft. lbs. (80 Nm).
47. Tighten the bolt holding the rear engine mounting bracket to the insulator to 65 ft. lbs. (88Nm).
48. Tighten the bolt and nut holding the front engine mounting bracket to the insulator to 65 ft. lbs. (88 Nm). Install and secure all other components.
49. Install the battery.
50. Attach the battery cables.
51. Fill the cooling system, engine crankcase and transaxle with the correct types and amounts of fluids. Start the engine and check for leaks. Perform engine adjustments as necessary.

✻✻✻ WARNING

Operating the engine without the proper amount and type of engine oil will result in severe engine damage.

52. Install the engine under covers and hood. Road test the vehicle and recheck the fluid levels.

Rocker Arm (Valve) Cover

REMOVAL & INSTALLATION

◆ See Figures 7 thru 16

1. Disconnect the spark plug wires from the clamp on the valve cover.
2. Label the spark plug wires and extract them at the rubber boot end.

➡Pulling on or bending the plug wires may damage the conductor inside.

3. Disconnect the accelerator cable from the throttle body, then pull the cable from the clamp on the intake manifold.
4. Disconnect the throttle control cable from the throttle body.
5. Remove the PCV hose.
6. Unbolt the cable bracket from the intake manifold.
7. On some models, disconnect the engine wire protector from the mounting bolts of the No. 2 timing belt cover in the sequence shown.
8. Remove the nuts, grommets, valve cover and gasket.

➡If the grommets are being reused, arrange them in the same order as they had been removed. Leakage can occur if a grommet is placed in the wrong position.

9. Pull off the gasket from the crease of the valve cover.
10. Clean the valve cover and cylinder head mating area thoroughly.

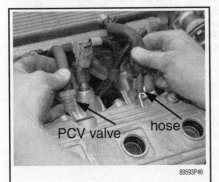

Fig. 7 Pull the PCV valve and assorted hoses from the valve cover

Fig. 8 Remove the engine wire protector from the mounting bolts for the No. 2 timing belt cover in this sequence

Fig. 9 Then lift the cover off and set the harness aside

Fig. 10 Remove the 4 nuts to extract the . . .

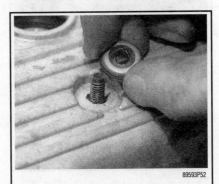

Fig. 11 . . . grommets. Be sure to arrange them in the order of removal

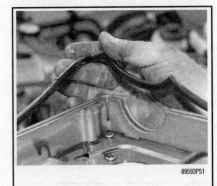

Fig. 12 Lift the entire valve cover off the cylinder head to . . .

Fig. 13 . . . pull off the seal inset into the valve cover

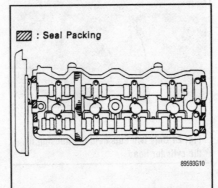

Fig. 14 Apply seal packing to the cylinder head at these areas

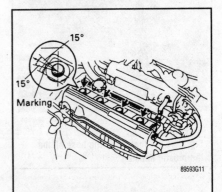

Fig. 15 Be sure to install the grommets with the markings in the correct position

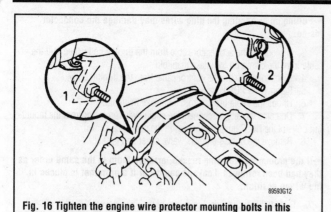

Fig. 16 Tighten the engine wire protector mounting bolts in this order

To install:

11. Apply seal packing to the cylinder head as shown in the illustration.

12. Install the gasket to the valve cover. Install the valve cover and position the 4 grommets and nuts.

13. Uniformly tighten the nuts in several passes to 17 ft. lbs. (23 Nm).

➡**Install the grommets so that their markings are as shown.**

14. If removed, install the engine wire protector to the mounting bolts of the No. 2 timing belt cover in the sequence shown.

15. Connect all the cables and hoses detached previously. Tighten the accelerator bracket.

16. Install and secure the plug wires. Attach the wires into the clamp.

Thermostat

REMOVAL & INSTALLATION

♦ **See Figures 17 thru 27**

The thermostat is located in the water inlet housing that is connected to the lower radiator hose.

➡**The thermostat is equipped with a by-pass valve. If the engine tends to overheat, removal of the thermostat would cause a decrease in cooling system efficiency.**

❋❋ CAUTION

Never open, service or drain the radiator or cooling system when hot; serious burns can occur from the steam and hot coolant. Also, when draining engine coolant, keep in mind that cats and dogs are attracted to ethylene glycol antifreeze and could drink any that is left in an uncovered container or in puddles on the ground. This will prove fatal in sufficient quantities. Always drain coolant into a sealable container. Coolant should be reused unless it is contaminated or is several years old.

1. Position a suitable drain pan under the radiator drain cock and drain the cooling system.

2. On the 7A-FE engine disconnect the engine coolant temperature switch harness from the water inlet housing.

3. Remove the oil filter on 5S-FE engines.

4. Loosen the hose clamp and disconnect the lower radiator hose from the water inlet housing.

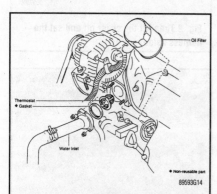

Fig. 17 The oil filter must be removed to access the thermostat on the 5S-FE engine

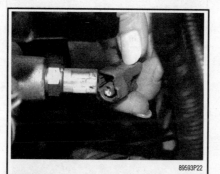

Fig. 18 Disconnect the engine coolant temperature switch wiring located on the side of the thermostat housing

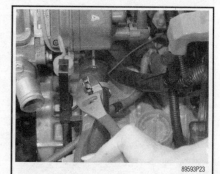

Fig. 19 Loosen the radiator hose clamp . . .

Fig. 20 . . . then slide the hose off the thermostat housing

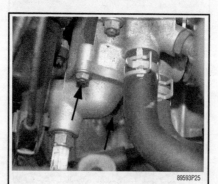

Fig. 21 Only two nuts hold the housing to the cylinder head

Fig. 22 Pull the housing straight out to remove

Fig. 23 Then pull the thermostat and gasket out

Fig. 24 Sometimes the gasket is stuck and has to be pried out of the head

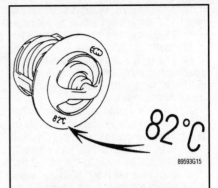

Fig. 25 Only use the correct temperature range thermostat when for replacement

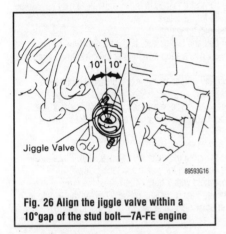

Fig. 26 Align the jiggle valve within a 10°gap of the stud bolt—7A-FE engine

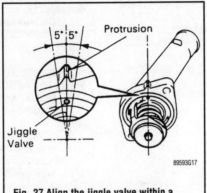

Fig. 27 Align the jiggle valve within a 5°gap of the stud bolt—5S-FE engine

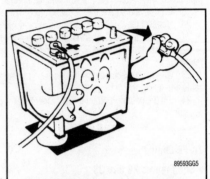

Fig. 28 Always disconnect the negative battery cable to prevent an accidental short circuit

5. Remove the two nuts from the water inlet housing and remove the housing from the water pump studs.

6. Remove the thermostat and rubber O-ring gasket from the water inlet housing.

To install:

7. Make sure all the gasket surfaces are clean. Clean the inside of the inlet housing and the radiator hose connection with a rag.

8. Install the new rubber O-ring gasket onto the thermostat. On 5S-FE engines, align the jiggle valve with the upper side of the stud bolt. Insert the thermostat into the housing.

9. Position the water inlet housing with the thermostat over the studs on the water pump and install the two nuts. Tighten the two nuts to 78–82 inch lbs. (9–10 Nm).

➡Don't forget to install a new O-ring onto the water inlet pipe. Apply soapy water to the O-ring prior to installation.

10. Connect the lower radiator hose to the inlet housing and install the hose clamp.

11. Attach the water temperature switch connector.

12. Install the oil filter and check the oil level if removed.

13. Fill the cooling system with a good brand of ethylene glycol based coolant.

14. Start the engine and inspect for leaks.

Intake Manifold

REMOVAL & INSTALLATION

5S-FE Engine

◆ **See Figure 28**

1. Turn the ignition key to the **OFF** position. Disconnect the negative battery cable. Wait at least 90 seconds from the time the negative battery was disconnected to start work.

2. Position a suitable drain pan under the radiator drain cock and drain the cooling system.

⁕⁕ CAUTION

Work must be started after 90 seconds from the time the ignition switch is turned to the LOCKposition and the negative battery cable has been disconnected. The SRS is equipped with a back-up power source so that if work is started within 90 seconds of disconnecting the negative battery cable, the SRS may deploy. When the negative terminal cable is disconnected from the battery, memory of the clock and radio will be canceled. Before you start working, make a note of the contents memorized by the audio memory system. When you have finished working, reset the audio systems and adjust the clock. Never use a back-up power supply from outside the vehicle.

3. Remove the accelerator cable return spring along with the cable and bracket from the throttle body.

4. Loosen the clamp and disconnect the air cleaner hose.

5. Disconnect the throttle position sensor harness.

6. Disconnect, label and plug the following hoses:
- Two water by-pass hoses.
- PCV hoses from the throttle body.
- Inlet hose to the air valve.
- All emission vacuum hoses attached to the throttle body.
- Vacuum hose between the EGR valve and modulator.
- Power steering pump air hose (if equipped).

7. Remove the bolts attaching the throttle body to the intake manifold. Remove the throttle body and gasket.

8. Loosen the union nut of the EGR pipe. Remove the two bolts, EGR valve modulator and gasket. Remove the bolt and the EGR valve.

9. Remove the intake manifold stays and on the No. 1 air intake chamber.

10. Disconnect the vacuum sensing hose.

11. Remove the two nuts and six bolts that attach the intake manifold to the cylinder head.

12. Remove the bolt, vacuum hose bracket and the main engine wire harness. On California models, remove the wire bracket.

13. Remove the intake manifold and gasket from the cylinder head.

To install:

14. Thoroughly clean the intake manifold and cylinder head surfaces. Using a machinist's straight edge and a feeler gauge, check the surface of the intake manifold for warpage. If the warpage is greater than 0.0118 inch (0.300mm), replace the intake manifold.

15. Place a new gasket onto the intake manifold and position the intake manifold onto the cylinder head with the proper amount of nuts and bolts. Tighten the nuts and bolts to 14 ft. lbs. (19 Nm).

16. Install the intake manifold stays. Tighten the 12mm bolts to 14 ft. lbs. (19 Nm) and the 14mm bolts to 31 ft. lbs. (42 Nm).

17. Place a new gasket onto the throttle body and attach the unit to the intake manifold with the four bolts. Uniformly tighten the bolts in several passes to 14 ft. lbs. (19 Nm).

18. Install the EGR valve with new gasket and the modulator. Tighten the pipe union nut to 43 ft. lbs. (59 Nm) and the bolts to 9 ft. lbs. (13 Nm).

19. Unplug and connect all hoses along with attaching any related wiring.

20. Connect the throttle position sensor and ISC valve wiring.

21. Connect the air cleaner hose and tighten the hose clamp.

22. Attach the throttle cable with bracket onto the throttle body. Install the return spring.

23. On vehicles equipped with automatic transaxle, connect the accelerator cable and adjust it.

24. Fill the cooling system to the proper level and connect the negative battery cable.

25. Start the engine and inspect for leaks.

7A-FE Engine

▶ See Figures 29 thru 38

1. Disconnect the negative battery cable. On vehicles equipped with an air bag, wait at least 90 seconds before proceeding.

❊❊ CAUTION

Fuel injection systems remain under pressure after the engine has been turned OFF. Properly relieve fuel pressure before disconnecting any fuel lines. Failure to do so may result in fire or personal injury.

2. Drain the engine coolant into a suitable container.

3. Disconnect the throttle body from the air intake chamber.

4. Disconnect the ground strap harness.

5. Tag and disconnect the hoses from the intake chamber.

6. On vehicles with A/C remove the hose from the idle-up valve.

7. On vehicles with P/S remove the air hose from the air pipe.

8. Using a 6mm hexagon wrench, remove the 3 bolts, 2 nuts, and the air intake chamber cover and gasket.

9. If equipped with EGR, remove the EGR VSV.

10. Remove the intake manifold stay.

11. Unbolt and remove the air pipe.

12. The engine wiring harness attached to the cylinder head may need to be disconnected to access bolts for the intake manifold.

13. Disconnect the fuel injector wiring.

14. Remove the union bolt and two gaskets and disconnect the fuel inlet hose from the delivery pipe. Place a shop towel under the connection to absorb the fuel.

15. Disconnect the fuel return hose from the fuel pressure regulator and the air hose from the IAC valve to the air pipe.

16. Remove the two bolts and the delivery pipe together with the four injectors.

17. Remove the 7 bolts, 4 nuts, ground strap, intake manifold and the two gaskets.

To install:

18. Place a new intake manifold gasket to the cylinder head. Place a new EGR gasket to the cylinder head, with the protrusion facing down.

19. Install the intake manifold with 7 bolts, 4 nuts, and the ground strap. Uniformly tighten the bolts and nuts in several passes. Tighten the **A** nuts to 9 ft. lbs. (13 Nm). Tighten all other nuts and bolts to 14 ft. lbs. (19 Nm).

Fig. 29 It is advisable to disconnect the hoses attached to the air intake chamber

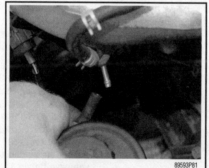

Fig. 30 Disconnect the power steering hose from the air pipe

Fig. 31 Remove the bolts and nuts retaining the air intake chamber

Fig. 32 When lifting the lid, remove the gasket

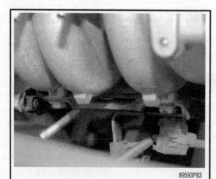

Fig. 33 Unbolt the air pipe located under the intake manifold

Fig. 34 Remove the 7 bolts and 2 nuts for the intake manifold . . .

Fig. 35 . . . then lift the intake off the cylinder head

Fig. 36 Be sure to remove the whole gasket, sometime parts get attached to the manifold or cylinder head

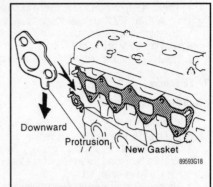

Fig. 37 Place the new intake manifold gasket on their mating areas correctly

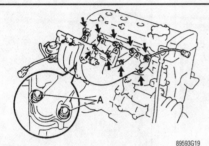

Fig. 38 Uniformly tighten the bolts and nuts in several passes on the intake manifold

20. Install the injectors and the delivery pipe.
21. If equipped with EGR, install the EGR VSV.
22. Install the air intake chamber cover with a new gasket.
23. Install the throttle body.
24. Install the air pipe and fuel inlet hose with the two bolts and nut. Install new gaskets on the fuel inlet hose and secure the clamp of the inlet hose to the intake manifold.
25. Connect the fuel return hose to the pressure regulator and the air hose from the IAC valve to the air pipe.
26. Install the intake manifold stay. Tighten the 12mm head bolt to 14 ft. lbs. (19 Nm) and the 14mm head bolt to 29 ft. lbs. (39 Nm).
27. Connect the hoses to the intake chamber.
28. If equipped, install the air hoses the idle-up valve and the air pipe.
29. Connect the ground strap connector and connect the fuel injector connectors.
30. Refill the cooling system with coolant and connect the negative battery cable. Start the engine, check for leaks, and road test the vehicle for proper operation.

Exhaust Manifold

REMOVAL & INSTALLATION

5S-FE Engine

1. Turn the ignition key to the **OFF** position. Disconnect the negative battery cable. Wait at least 90 seconds from the time the negative battery was disconnected to start work.

✳✳ CAUTION

Work must be started after 90 seconds from the time the ignition switch is turned to the LOCK position and the negative battery cable has been disconnected. The SRS is equipped with a back-up power source so that if work is started within 90 seconds of disconnecting the negative battery cable, the SRS may deploy. When the negative terminal cable is disconnected from the battery, memory of the

clock and radio will be canceled. Before you start working, make a note of the contents memorized by the audio memory system. When you have finished working, reset the audio systems and adjust the clock. Never use a back-up power supply from outside the vehicle.

2. Raise the front of the vehicle and support safely.
3. Disconnect the oxygen sensor wiring.
4. Loosen the two bolts and disconnect the front exhaust pipe bracket. Disconnect the exhaust pipe from the catalytic converter. Remove the gasket and discard it.
5. Remove the upper manifold heat insulator by removing the retaining bolts.
6. Remove the two manifold stays.
7. Remove the six nuts and lower the exhaust manifold. Discard the nuts and replace with new ones.
8. Remove the four bolts and lift off the lower heat insulator.
9. To separate the exhaust manifold from the converter, proceed as follows:
   a. Remove the 5 bolts and the lower heat insulator.
   b. Remove the 8 bolts and 2 converter heat insulators.
   c. Remove the 3 bolts, 2 nuts, converter, gasket, retainer and cushion.
10. Thoroughly clean the exhaust manifold and cylinder block to remove any carbon or gasket material deposits. Replace the exhaust manifold gaskets, catalytic converter gasket, retainer and cushion.

To install:
11. To assemble the exhaust manifold to the converter on California models, attach these components in this order:
   a. Three-way catalytic converter
   b. Cushion
   c. Retainier
   d. Gasket
   e. Exhaust manifold
   f. Bolts and nuts, tighten the nuts to 22 ft. lbs. (29 Nm).
   g. Heat insulators
   h. Eight bolts
   i. Manifold lower heat insulator
   j. Three bolts
12. Then for California models, install a new gasket, the exhaust manifold and catalytic converter assembly with the six nuts. Uniformly tighten the nuts in several passes to 36 ft. lbs. (49 Nm).
   a. Install the manifold stay with the bolt and nut and tighten to 31 ft. lbs. (42 Nm). Install the No. 1 manifold stay and tighten to 31 ft. lbs. (42 Nm).
   b. Install the manifold upper heat insulator with the four bolts and attach the two oxygen sensor wiring harnesses.
13. On non-California models perform the following:
   a. Install the lower heat insulator with the four bolts securely.
   b. Install a new gasket and attach the exhaust manifold with six new nuts, uniformly tighten them to 36 ft. lbs. (49 Nm).
   c. Attach the manifold stay with the bolt and nut and tighten to 31 ft. lbs. (42 Nm).
   d. Attach the No. 1 manifold stay and tighten that to 31 ft. lbs. (42 Nm).
   e. Attach the manifold upper heat insulator with six new bolts and tighten them securely. Connect the oxygen sensor wiring.

14. Place a new gasket onto the exhaust pipe and attach the pipe. Tighten the nuts to 46 ft. lbs. (62 Nm). Install the clamp and the bracket.

15. Lower the vehicle and connect the negative battery cable.

16. Start the engine and inspect for leaks.

17. Reset any electronic components such as the radio.

7A-FE Engine

▶ **See Figures 39 thru 45**

1. Disconnect the negative battery cable. On vehicles equipped with an air bag, wait at least 90 seconds before proceeding.

2. Raise and safely support the vehicle.

3. Working from under the vehicle, remove the bolts holding the front exhaust pipe to the mounting bracket.

4. Using a 14mm deep socket wrench, remove the nuts and the gasket and disconnect the front exhaust pipe from the manifold.

5. Remove the main oxygen sensor connector.

6. Remove the bolts and extract upper heat insulator.

7. Remove the nuts, exhaust manifold, and the gasket.

8. Remove the bolts and lower heat insulator from the exhaust manifold.

To install:

9. Install the lower heat insulator to the exhaust manifold with the bolts and tighten to 82 inch lbs. (9 Nm).

10. Install a new gasket and the exhaust manifold with the nuts. Uniformly tighten the nuts in several passes. Tighten the nuts to 25 ft. lbs. (34 Nm).

11. Install the upper heat insulator with the bolts and tighten to 82 inch lbs. (9 Nm).

12. Install the front exhaust pipe with a new gasket to the exhaust manifold. Install the nuts using a 14mm deep socket wrench. Tighten the nuts to 46 ft. lbs. (62 Nm).

13. Secure the front exhaust pipe to the exhaust pipe bracket with the bolts.

14. Connect the main oxygen sensor connector.

Fig. 39 Remove the four bolts holding the heat shield—7A-FE engine shown

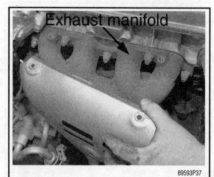

Fig. 40 Remove the heat shield to expose the exhaust manifold

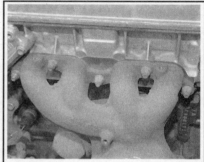

Fig. 41 Note the exhaust manifold is bolted to the side of the cylinder head

Fig. 42 The manifold is heavy, use care when removing

Fig. 43 Pull off the old gasket material from the head . . .

Fig. 44 . . . use a coarse cloth to remove any rust or dirt on the head . . .

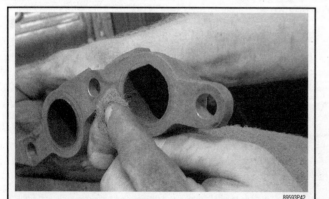

Fig. 45 . . . and the manifold

15. Lower the vehicle safely and reconnect the negative battery cable.

16. Start the engine and make sure that there are no exhaust leaks.

Radiator

REMOVAL & INSTALLATION

▶ **See Figures 46 thru 55**

❄ **CAUTION**

Never open, service or drain the radiator or cooling system when hot; serious burns can occur from the steam and hot coolant. Also, when draining engine coolant, keep in mind that cats and dogs are attracted to ethylene glycol antifreeze and could drink any that is left in an uncovered container or in puddles on the ground. This will prove fatal in sufficient quantities. **Always drain coolant into a sealable container. Coolant should be reused unless it is contaminated or is several years old.**

1. Disconnect the negative battery cable. On vehicles equipped with an air bag, wait at least 90 seconds before proceeding.

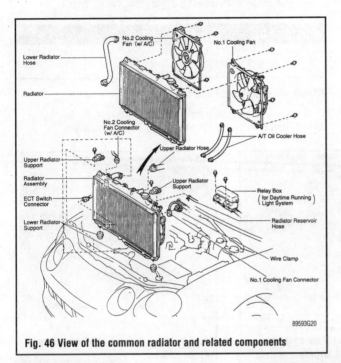

Fig. 46 View of the common radiator and related components

Work must be started after 90 seconds from the time the ignition switch is turned to the LOCK position and the negative battery cable has been disconnected. The SRS is equipped with a back-up power source so that if work is started within 90 seconds of disconnecting the negative battery cable, the SRS may deploy. When the negative terminal cable is disconnected from the battery, memory of the clock and radio will be canceled. Before you start working, make a note of the contents memorized by the audio memory system. When you have finished working, reset the audio systems and adjust the clock. Never use a back-up power supply from outside the vehicle.

2. If necessary, remove the engine undercover.
3. Drain the engine coolant into a suitable container.
4. On Canadian models, remove the two bolts and the Daytime Running Lamp (DRL) relay box.
5. Disconnect the electric cooling fan wiring.
6. Disconnect the upper radiator hose.
7. Separate the lower hose from the water inlet pipe.
8. Disconnect the coolant reservoir hose.
9. If the vehicle is equipped with automatic transmission, disconnect the oil cooler hoses.
10. Disconnect the No. 1 cooling fan connector and wire clamp. If equipped with A/C, disconnect the No. 2 cooling fan connector.
11. Remove the oxygen sensor wire clamps.
12. Remove the two upper radiator support bolts and the two supports.
13. Lift out the radiator assembly being careful not to damage the radiator. Remove the lower radiator supports.
14. If necessary, remove the four bolts and the No. 1 cooling fan. On A/C models, remove the three bolts and the No. 2 cooling fan.

To install:

15. Install the No. 2 cooling fan to the radiator with the three bolts and torque them to 43 inch lbs. (5 Nm).

Fig. 47 Pull off the upper radiator hose and set aside

Fig. 48 Disconnect the lower hose from the radiator

Fig. 49 Lower the hose clamps for the transmission oil cooler lines . . .

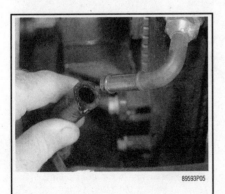

Fig. 50 . . . and slip the hose off

Fig. 51 Note that all the hoses attached to the radiator need to be plugged

Fig. 52 Unbolt the upper radiator supports

16. Install the No. 1 cooling fan to the radiator with the four bolts and torque them to 43 inch lbs. (5 Nm).

17. Install the radiator lower supports and carefully lower the radiator assembly into position.

18. Install the two upper radiator supports with the support bolts. Tighten the support bolts to 9 ft. lbs. (12 Nm). Make sure that the rubber cushions are not distorted.

19. If detached, connect the No. 1 cooling fan connector and the wire clamp.

20. If equipped with A/C, connect the No. 2 cooling fan wiring.

21. On the Celica, connect the two oxygen sensor wire clamps.

22. If the vehicle is equipped with automatic transmission, connect the oil cooler lines.

23. Connect the coolant reservoir hose.

24. Attach the lower radiator hose to the water inlet pipe.

25. Connect the upper radiator hose.

26. Connect the electric cooling fan electrical wiring.

27. Install the DRL relay box and secure it with the two mounting bolts.

28. If removed, install the battery tray, battery and clamp to the engine compartment.

29. Connect the negative battery cable.

30. Refill the cooling system with coolant and bleed the system. Check the cooling system for leaks and proper operation.

31. If the system is OK, install the engine undercover if removed.

Engine Fan

REMOVAL & INSTALLATION

▶ See Figures 46 and 56 thru 61

1. Disconnect the cable at the negative battery terminal. On vehicles equipped with an air bag, wait at least 90 seconds before proceeding.

Fig. 53 Lift the radiator straight up and out of the engine compartment

Fig. 54 Remove the bushings on the bottom of the radiator and inspect or replace

Fig. 55 Attach the coolant reservoir hose to the radiator

Fig. 56 Unclasp the wiring to the cooling fans

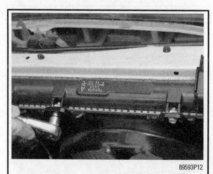

Fig. 57 Remove the upper and lower bolts that retain the engine fan blade and shroud assemblies

Fig. 58 Lift the fan out of the engine compartment and disassemble if necessary

Fig. 59 Insert the fan assembly into the engine compartment

Fig. 60 Attach the wiring connectors for the fans

Fig. 61 Attach the O$_2$ sensor wiring to the bracket on the shroud

❋❋ CAUTION

Work must be started after 90 seconds from the time the ignition switch is turned to the LOCK position and the negative battery cable has been disconnected. The SRS is equipped with a back-up power source so that if work is started within 90 seconds of disconnecting the negative battery cable, the SRS may deploy. When the negative terminal cable is disconnected from the battery, memory of the clock and radio will be canceled. Before you start working, make a note of the contents memorized by the audio memory system. When you have finished working, reset the audio systems and adjust the clock. Never use a back-up power supply from outside the vehicle.

  2. Remove the engine undercovers, as required.
  3. Drain the coolant into a suitable container.
  4. Remove the battery if necessary.
  5. For Canadian models, disconnect the relay box for the Daytime Running Light (DRL) system from the radiator.
  6. Remove the upper radiator hose.
  7. Remove the cooling fan electrical connector clamp then detach the wiring.
  8. Disconnect the O2 sensor wiring harness attached to the fan shroud.
  9. Remove the 4 mounting bolts and the cooling fan.

To install:
  10. Reinstall the cooling fan and attach with the 4 bolts and tighten to 43 inch lbs. (5 Nm).
  11. Reconnect the cooling fan wiring and secure with the clamp.
  12. Reinstall the upper radiator hose.
  13. If removed, install the relay box for the DRL system.
  14. Connect the cable at the negative battery terminal.
  15. Refill the cooling system and bleed.
  16. Check the cooling fan for proper operation.

TESTING

  1. Check the cooling fan operation at a low temperature of 181°F (83°C).
  2. Turn the ignition switch to the **ON** position.
  3. Check that the cooling fan stops. If not, check the cooling fan relay ad the engine coolant temperature switch. Inspect for separated connectors or severed wire between the cooling fan relay and engine coolant switch.
  4. Disconnect the engine coolant temperature switch wiring.
  5. Check that the cooling fan rotates. If not, check the fuses, engine main relay, cooling fan relay, cooling fan, and for a short circuit between the cooling fan relay and engine coolant temperature switch.
  6. Reattach the engine coolant switch wiring.
  7. Start the engine and raise the temperature to above 199°F (93°C). Check that the cooling fan rotates. If not replace the temperature switch.
  8. Disconnect the negative battery cable. Wait at least 90 seconds once the cable is disconnected to hinder airbag deployment.
  9. Disconnect the cooling fan wiring.
  10. Connect the battery and ammeter to the cooling fan wiring.
  11. Check that the cooling fan rotates smoothly, then check the reading on the ammeter. Standard amperage is 5.8–7.4 amps.
  12. Reconnect the wiring for the cooling fan.
  13. Reconnect the negative battery cable.

Water Pump

REMOVAL & INSTALLATION

❋❋ CAUTION

Never open, service or drain the radiator or cooling system when hot; serious burns can occur from the steam and hot coolant. Also, when draining engine coolant, keep in mind that cats and dogs are attracted to ethylene glycol antifreeze and could drink any that is left in an uncovered container or in puddles on the ground. This will prove fatal in sufficient quantities. Always drain coolant into a seal- able container. Coolant should be reused unless it is contaminated or is several years old.

5S-FE Engine

▶ See Figures 62, 63 and 64

  1. Disconnect the negative battery cable. On vehicles equipped with an air bag, wait at least 90 seconds before proceeding.
  2. Raise and safely support the vehicle.
  3. Remove the right engine undercover.
  4. Drain the engine coolant into a suitable container. Disconnect the lower radiator hose from the water outlet.
  5. Remove the timing belt, timing belt tension spring, and the No. 2 idler pulley.
  6. Remove the alternator, drive belt and the adjusting bar if necessary.
  7. Remove the two nuts holding the water pump to the water bypass pipe and remove the three bolts in sequence.
  8. Disconnect the water pump cover from the water bypass pipe and remove the water pump cover assembly.
  9. Remove the gasket and two O-rings from the water pump and the bypass pipe.
  10. Remove the water pump from the water pump cover by removing the three bolts in sequence.

To install:
  11. Cleaned the gasket mating surfaces.
  12. Install a new gasket and assemble the water pump to the water pump cover. Tighten the bolts to 78 inch lbs. (9 Nm) in proper sequence.
  13. Install a new O-ring and gasket to the water pump cover and install a new O-ring on the water bypass pipe. Connect the water pump cover to the water bypass pipe, but do not install the nuts yet.
  14. Install the water pump and tighten the three bolts in sequence. Tighten the bolts to 78 inch lbs. (9 Nm). Install the two nuts holding the water pump cover to the water bypass pipe and torque them to 82 inch lbs. (9 Nm).
  15. Install the alternator drive belt adjusting bar with the bolt and tighten the bolt to 13 ft. lbs. (18 Nm).

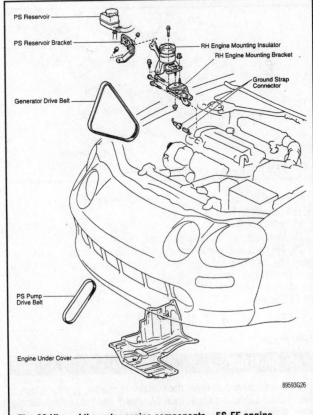

89593G26

Fig. 62 View of the outer engine components—5S-FE engine

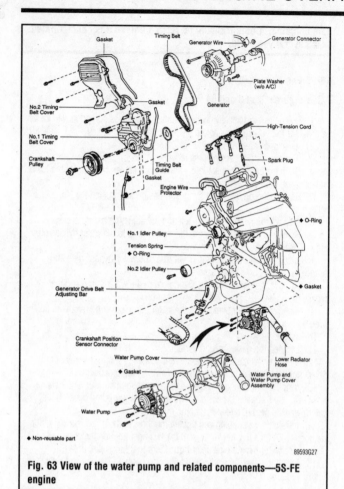

Fig. 63 View of the water pump and related components—5S-FE engine

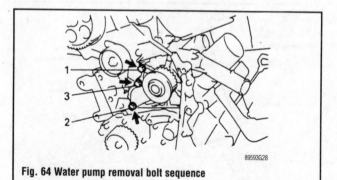

Fig. 64 Water pump removal bolt sequence

16. Install the No. 2 idler pulley and the timing belt tension spring.
17. Connect the lower radiator hose.
18. Install the timing belt.
19. Install the right undercover and safely lower the vehicle.
20. Fill the cooling system with coolant and connect the negative battery cable. Start the engine and bleed the cooling system. Check the cooling system for leaks and proper operation.

7A-FE Engine

▶ See Figures 65, 66, 67, 68 and 69

1994 MODELS

✳✳ CAUTION

Never open, service or drain the radiator or cooling system when hot; serious burns can occur from the steam and hot coolant. Also, when draining engine coolant, keep in mind that cats and dogs are

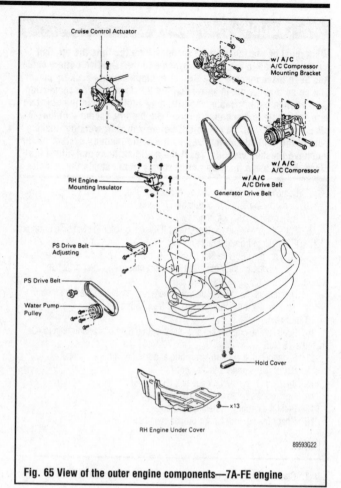

Fig. 65 View of the outer engine components—7A-FE engine

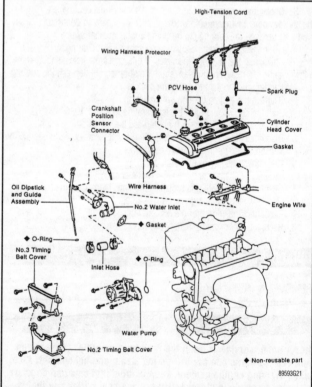

Fig. 66 View of the water pump and related components—7A-FE engine

attracted to ethylene glycol antifreeze and could drink any that is left in an uncovered container or in puddles on the ground. This will prove fatal in sufficient quantities. Always drain coolant into a sealable container. Coolant should be reused unless it is contaminated or is several years old.

1. Disconnect the negative battery cable. On vehicles equipped with an air bag, wait at least 90 seconds before proceeding.

✳✳ CAUTION

Work must be started after 90 seconds from the time the ignition switch is turned to the LOCK position and the negative battery cable has been disconnected. The SRS is equipped with a back-up power source so that if work is started within 90 seconds of disconnecting the negative battery cable, the SRS may deploy. When the negative terminal cable is disconnected from the battery, memory of the clock and radio will be canceled. Before you start working, make a note of the contents memorized by the audio memory system. When you have finished working, reset the audio systems and adjust the clock. Never use a back-up power supply from outside the vehicle.

2. Drain the engine coolant into a suitable container.
3. On models with cruise control, remove the actuator.
4. Raise and support the front of the vehicle, then remove the RH wheel.
5. Unbolt and remove the RH engine under cover.
6. Slightly jack up the engine enough to remove the weight from the engine mounting on the right side. Place a wooden block between the jack and the engine.
7. Remove the RH engine mounting insulator.
8. Stretch the belt tight and loosen the water pump pulley bolts.
9. Remove the alternator drive belt.
10. On models with A/C, remove the compressor without disconnecting the hoses. Suspend and set aside the compressor. Unbolt and remove the compressor mounting bracket.
11. Remove the power steering drive belt and adjusting strut.
12. Remove the 4 bolts, then disconnect the water pump pulley from the pump. Remove the hold cover. Unbolt the front engine insulator to the center member. Carefully jack up the engine and remove the water pump pulley.
13. Unbolt and remove the cylinder head cover.
14. Remove the 6 bolts, No. 3 and No. 2 timing belt covers.

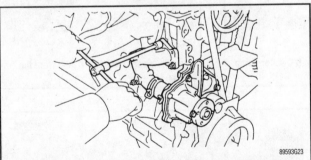

Fig. 67 Unbolt and remove the water pump with the No. 2 inlet

Fig. 68 Position a new O-ring on the block and place the gasket on the head with the upper mark toward the upper side

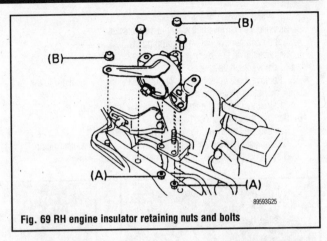

Fig. 69 RH engine insulator retaining nuts and bolts

15. Disconnect the engine wire from the wire clamp. Remove the 3 nuts and disconnect the engine wire.
16. Remove the oil dipstick and guide.
17. Disconnect the engine coolant temperature sensor wiring. Remove the 2 nuts holding the No. 2 water inlet to the cylinder head. Remove the 3 bolts and water pump together with the No. 2 water inlet. Remove the O-ring from the block.
18. Separate the water pump from the No. 2 water inlet.

To install:

19. Install a new O-ring on the block, then place a new gasket in position on the cylinder head so that the upper mark is toward the upper side. Temporarily install the pump and the No. 2 inlet with the bolts and nuts. Tighten them to 10 ft. lbs. (14 Nm).
20. Connect the water temperature sender gauge connector.
21. After applying a small amount of oil to the O-ring, install a new O-ring on the oil dipstick guide. Install the guide mounting bolt and tighten it to 82 inch lbs. (9 Nm).
22. Connect the engine wire with the two nuts and the bolt.
23. Install the No. 2 and No. 3 timing belt covers.
24. Install the cylinder head cover.
25. If equipped with power steering, install the adjusting strut and tighten the two bolts to 29 ft. lbs. (39 Nm).
26. If equipped with power steering, install the drive belt. On A/C models, install the compressor bracket and tighten to 35 ft. lbs. (45 Nm). Attach the compressor to the engine and tighten the bolts to 18 ft. lbs. (25 Nm), then install and adjust the drive belt.
27. Install and adjust the alternator drive belt.
28. Tighten the water pump pulley bolts, stretch the belt and tighten to 8 inch lbs. (9 Nm).
29. Install the engine insulator mounting bolts and tighten the two bolts to 47 ft. lbs. (64 Nm). Tighten nuts **A** to 38 ft. lbs. (52 Nm) and **B** to 21 ft. lbs. (28 Nm).
30. Install and secure the RH engine under cover, then the RH wheel. Lower the vehicle and on models with cruise control, install and secure the actuator.
31. Refill the cooling system with coolant and connect the negative battery cable. Start the engine and bleed the cooling system. Check for cooling system leaks and proper system operation.

1995–98 MODELS

▸ **See Figures 70 thru 77**

1. Disconnect the negative battery cable.

✳✳ CAUTION

Work must be started after 90 seconds from the time the ignition switch is turned to the LOCK position and the negative battery cable has been disconnected. The SRS is equipped with a back-up power source so that if work is started within 90 seconds of disconnecting the negative battery cable, the SRS may deploy. When the negative terminal cable is disconnected from the battery, memory of the clock and radio will be canceled. Before you start working, make a note of the contents memorized by the audio memory system. When you have finished working, reset the audio systems and adjust the clock. Never use a back-up power supply from outside the vehicle.

2. Drain and recycle the engine coolant.
3. Remove the PS drive belt and adjusting bracket.
4. Unbolt and remove the water pump pulley.
5. Remove the engine mounting center member as follows:
   a. Remove the hole cover.
   b. Remove the 2 bolts holding the front of the engine insulator to the engine mounting center member.
   c. Catrefully jack up the engine and remove the pump pulley.
6. Remove the cylinder head cover.
7. Remove the No. 3 and No. 2 timing belt covers.
8. Disconnect the engine wire harness assembly near the water pump.
9. Disconnect the engine coolant temperature sender wiring.

10. Unbolt the oil dipstick guide and dipstick.
11. Remove the nuts holding the No. 2 water inlet to the cylinder head. Remove the three bolts and the water pump together with the No. 2 water inlet. Remove the O-ring from the block.
12. Separate the water pump from the No. 2 water inlet.
To install:
13. Assemble the water pump and No. 2 water pump inlet.
14. Place a new O-ring into position on the block. Place a new gasket on the cylinder head so that the upper mark is toward the upper side. Temporarily install the water pump and the No. 2 inlet with the bolts and nuts. Tighten the bolts and nuts to 11 ft. lbs. (14 Nm).
15. Install the oil dipstick guide and dipstick.

Fig. 70 Unbolt and remove the power steering adjusting bracket

Fig. 71 Lift and disengage the engine wiring harnesses from around the water pump

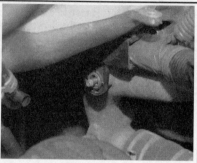

Fig. 72 A bolt or two may hold the engine wiring to the pump also

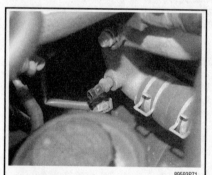

Fig. 73 Pull the engine coolant temperature sensor harness

Fig. 74 Unbolt and remove the water pump with the No. 2 water inlet

Fig. 75 Separate the No. 2 inlet from the pump

Fig. 76 Place a new O-ring into position on the cylinder block

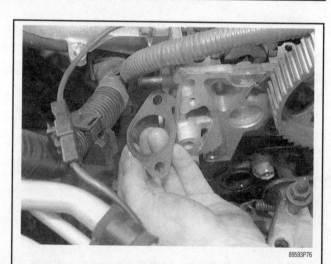

Fig. 77 And don't forget about the new gasket

16. Connect the engine wiring harness and secure.
17. Install the No. 2 and No. 3 timing belt covers. Attach and secure the cylinder head cover also.
18. Install the water pump pulley.
19. Install and secure the engine mounting center member. tighten the bolts to 59 ft. lbs. 980 Nm).
20. Install the PS drive belt adjusting strut and secure the bolts to 29 ft. lbs. (39 Nm). Install and adjust the PS belt.
21. Refill the cooling system.
22. Connect the negative battery cable.
23. Start the engine and check for leaks. Top off the cooling system.

Cylinder Head

REMOVAL & INSTALLATION

5S-FE Engine

▶ **See Figures 78 thru 87**

1. Release the fuel system pressure.
2. Disconnect the negative battery cable. On vehicles equipped with an air bag, wait at least 90 seconds before proceeding to hinder air bag deployment.

> ※ **CAUTION**
>
> **Work must be started after 90 seconds from the time the ignition switch is turned to the LOCKposition and the negative battery cable has been disconnected. The SRS is equipped with a back-up power source so that if work is started within 90 seconds of disconnecting the negative battery cable, the SRS may deploy. When the negative terminal cable is disconnected from the battery, memory of the clock and radio will be canceled. Before you start working, make a note of the contents memorized by the audio memory system. When you have finished working, reset the audio systems and adjust the clock. Never use a back-up power supply from outside the vehicle.**

3. Drain the engine coolant into a suitable container.

> ※ **CAUTION**
>
> **Never open, service or drain the radiator or cooling system when hot; serious burns can occur from the steam and hot coolant. Also, when draining engine coolant, keep in mind that cats and dogs are attracted to ethylene glycol antifreeze and could drink any that is left in an uncovered container or in puddles on the ground. This will prove fatal in sufficient quantities. Always drain coolant into a sealable container. Coolant should be reused unless it is contaminated or is several years old.**

4. Remove the air cleaner and cap assembly.
5. On all models except the 1994–95 non-California models, remove the distributor.
6. Remove the alternator.
7. Remove the front exhaust pipe.
8. Remove the exhaust manifold and front TWC.
9. Unbolt and extract the two O2 sensors from the manifold and TWC.
10. Separate the exhaust manifold from the TWC.
11. Disconnect the oil pressure switch wiring/.
12. Remove the water outlet. Label and disconnect all wring associated.
13. Remove the water bypass pipe.
14. Remove the throttle body.
15. Disconnect the MAP sensor vacuum hose from the gas filter on the manifold. Remove the brake booster vacuum hose from the intake manifold.
16. Remvoe the EGR valve and vacuum modulator.
17. Remove the intake manifold stay.
18. Disconnect the automatic transaxle control cable from the intake manifold.
19. Remove the air tube. Label all hoses attached to the pipe.
20. Disconnect the knock sensor 1 wiring. Disconnect the ground wires. Be sure to label all the wires.

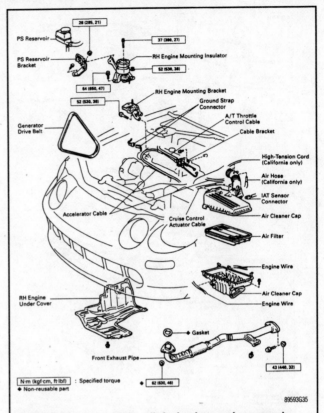

Fig. 78 Exploded view of the cylinder head removal components— 5S-FE engine

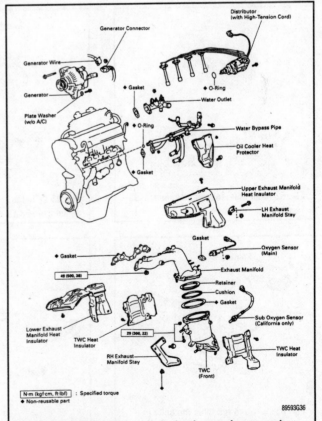

Fig. 79 Exploded view of the cylinder head removal components— 5S-FE engine (continued)

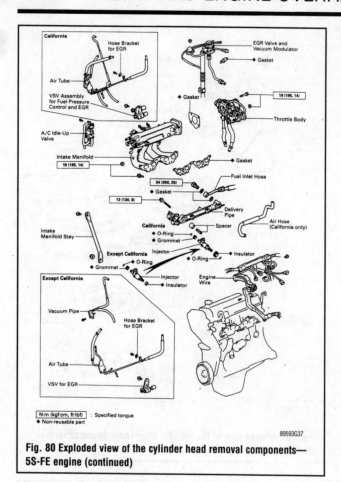

Fig. 80 Exploded view of the cylinder head removal components—5S-FE engine (continued)

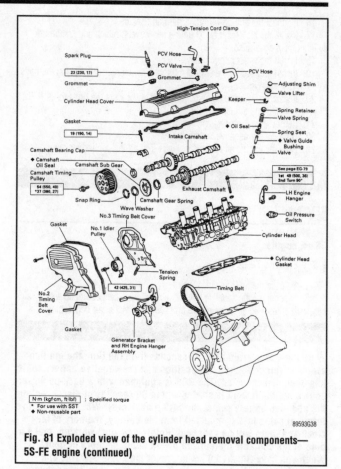

Fig. 81 Exploded view of the cylinder head removal components—5S-FE engine (continued)

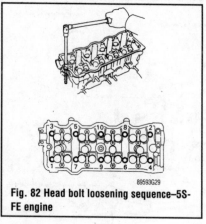

Fig. 82 Head bolt loosening sequence—5S-FE engine

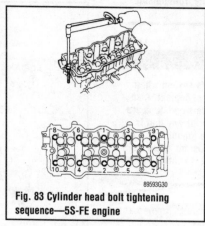

Fig. 83 Cylinder head bolt tightening sequence—5S-FE engine

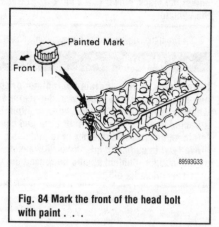

Fig. 84 Mark the front of the head bolt with paint . . .

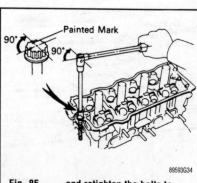

Fig. 85 . . . and retighten the bolts to 90° in order, then make sure the mark is facing front at a 90° angle

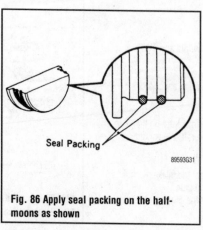

Fig. 86 Apply seal packing on the half-moons as shown

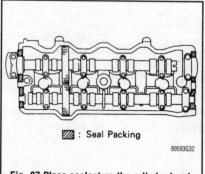

Fig. 87 Place sealant on the cylinder head in these places prior to valve cover installation

21. Remvoe the VSV for the EGR.
22. Disconnect the PCV hose from the intake manifold.
23. Disconnect the accelerator, automatic throttle control cables and bracket from the intake manifold and clamps.
24. Connect the negative battery cable.
25. Remove the union bolt and 2 gaskets, then disconnect the fuel inlet hose from the delivery pipe.
26. Disocnnect the fuel return hose from the return pipe.
27. Remove the intake manifold.
28. On 1994–95 California models, remove the air hose for the air assist system.
29. Remove the delivery pipe and injectors. Refer to Section 5.

❊❊ CAUTION

Observe all applicable safety precautions when working around fuel. Whenever servicing the fuel system, always work in a well ventilated area. Do not allow fuel spray or vapors to come in contact with a spark or open flame. Keep a dry chemical fire extinguisher near the work area. Always keep fuel in a container specifically designed for fuel storage; also, always properly seal fuel containers to avoid the possibility of fire or explosion.

30. Disconnect the timing belt from the camshaft timing pulley.
31. Remove the camshaft timing pulley.
32. Remove the No. 1 idler pulley and tension spring.
33. Remove the No. 3 timing belt cover.

➡ **Support the timing belt, so that the meshing of the crankshaft timing pulley and timing belt does not shift. Do not drop anything inside the timing belt cover.**

34. Remove the engine hangers and alternator bracket.
35. Disconnect the oil pressure sensor wiring and remove the sensor.
36. Remove the 4 nuts, grommets and cylinder head cover.
37. Label the spark plug wires and remove the wires with clamp. Extract the PCV hose and valve from the valve cover.
38. Remove the camshafts. Refer to the procedure later in this section.
39. Uniformily loosen and remove the 10 cylinder head bolts in several passes in the sequence shown.

❊❊ WARNING

Cylinder head warpage or cracking could result from removing the bolts in the incorrect order.

40. Lift the cylinder head from its dowels on the block, and place the head on wooden blocks on a bench.

➡ **If the head is hard to separate from the block, pry between the head and block with a flat-bladed tool to separate. Be careful not to damage the contact surfaces of the cylinder head or block.**

41. Using a gasket scraper, remove all gasket material from the block surface. Using compressed air, blow the carbon and oil from the bolt holes.

❊❊ CAUTION

Protect your eyes from the flying dirt particles when using high pressured air.

42. Clean and inspect the cylinder head if reusing the same one.
To install:
43. Place a new gasket on the block and position the cylinder head over the dowels.
44. Apply a light coat of engine oil on the threads and under the heads of the bolts. Install and uniformly tighten the 10 bolts and plate washers in several passes in the sequence shown. Tighten the bolts to 36 ft. lbs. (49 Nm).

➡ **The bolts are tightened in 2 progressive steps and if any of the bolts has a crack or deformed, it must be replaced.**

   a. Mark the front of the cylinder head bolt head with paint.
   b. Retighten the cylinder head bolts 90°in the order shown.
   c. Check the painted mark is now at the 90°angle in the front.

45. Install the spark plug tubes. Clean the tube holes and remove any oil. Screw the threads of the plug tube coated with adhesive into the head. Using a spark plug tube nut and a 30mm socket, tighten the plug tubes to 29 ft. lbs. (39 Nm).
46. Install the camshafts.
47. Check and adjust the valve clearance. Apply packing to the grooved of the half-moons, then install them into the cylinder head.
48. Install the PCV valve, hose, and spark plug wires clamp.
49. Attach the cylinder head cover.
50. Apply adhesive to the oil pressure switch, install and secure.
51. Install the engine hangers and secure the retaining bolts to 18 ft. lbs. (25 Nm).
52. Install the No. 3 timing belt cover.
53. Temporarily install the No. 1 idler pulley and tension spring.
54. Install the camshaft timing pulley.
55. Connect the timing belt and camshaft timing pulley.
56. Install the injectors and delivery pipe. Refer to Section 5.
57. On California models, if removed, attach the air assist hose.
58. Install the intake manifold. Uniformly tighten the bolts in several passes.
59. Connect the fuel inlet hose-to-delivery pipe. Connect the fuel return hose-to-return hose.
60. Install and secure the engine wire harness.
61. Attach the alternator, A/T throttle cables and bracket.
62. Attach the PCV hose to the intake manifold.
63. Install the Vacuum Switching Valve (VSV) for the EGR.
64. Connect the knocks sensor 1 wiring.
65. Install the ground wires.
66. Install the air tube.
67. Attach the A/T throttle cable to the intake manifold.
68. Install the intake manifold stay and secure the bolt to 15 ft. lbs. (21 Nm) and the nut to 32 ft. lbs. (44 Nm).
69. Attach the EGR valve and vacuum modulator.
70. Connect the MAP sensor and EVAP hoses to their proper locations.
71. Install the throttle body.
72. Attach the water bypass pipe.
73. Install the water outlet and connect all wiring and hoses associated with it.
74. Assemble the exhaust manifold and front TWC.
75. Install the O2 sensor to the exhaust manifold and the other O2 sensor to the front TWC.
76. Attach the exhausts manifold to the TWC with new gaskets. Uniformly tighten the nuts in several passes to specification.
77. Install the front exhaust pipe.
78. Install the alternator, distributor and the air cleaner assembly.
79. Fill the cooling system.
80. Reconnect the negative battery cable, fill the engine with coolant and oil, start the engine, warm up, and check for leaks.
81. Install the RH engine undercover, check ignition timing, and road test for proper operation.

7A-FE Engine

▶ **See Figures 88 thru 97**

❊❊ CAUTION

Fuel injection systems remain under pressure after the engine has been turned OFF. Properly relieve fuel pressure before disconnecting any fuel lines. Failure to do so may result in fire or personal injury.

1. Disconnect the negative battery cable. On vehicles equipped with an air bag, wait at least 90 seconds before proceeding to hinder air bag deployment.
2. Remove the RH engine undercover.
3. Drain the engine coolant into a suitable container.
4. Remove the air cleaner and cap assembly.
5. Remove the spark plug wires and the distributor assembly.
6. Remove the alternator.
7. Disconnect the sub-oxygen and oxygen sensor wiring and remove the front exhaust pipe, the front TWC, and the exhaust manifold.
8. Disconnect the oil pressure switch wiring.
9. Separate the sensor wiring and hoses from the water outlet. Remove the two nuts and gasket; remove the water outlet.

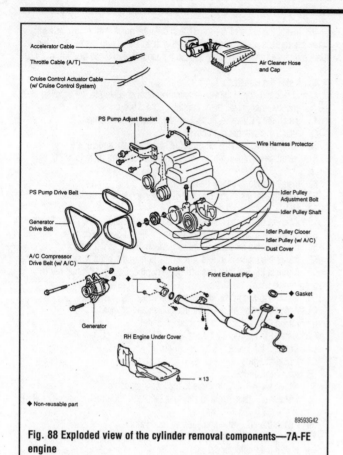

Fig. 88 Exploded view of the cylinder removal components—7A-FE engine

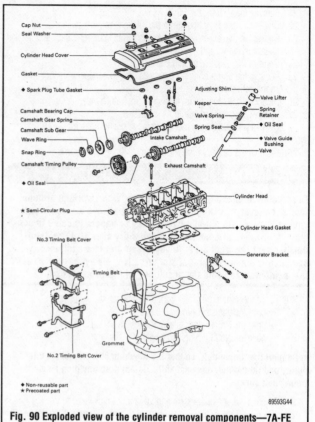

Fig. 90 Exploded view of the cylinder removal components—7A-FE engine (continued)

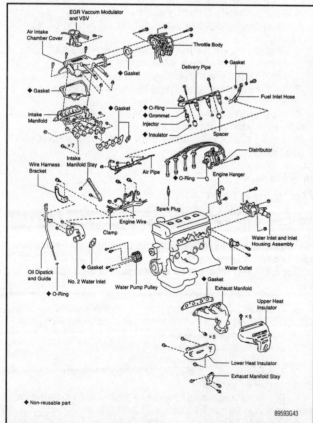

Fig. 89 Exploded view of the cylinder removal components—7A-FE engine (continued)

10. Label and disconnect all wires and hoses attached to the water inlet, then remove the inlet and housing assembly.

11. Disconnect the hoses; remove the heat protector and the water bypass pipe.

12. Remove the throttle body assembly.

13. Separate the vacuum hoses from the intake manifold and remove the A/C idle-up valve.

14. Remove the EGR valve, vacuum modulator, vacuum hoses and gasket.

15. Remove the intake manifold stay and disconnect the A/T throttle control cable.

16. Remove the air hoses from the air tube and remove the air tube assembly.

17. Except California vehicles, disconnect the sensing hoses and remove the vacuum pipe.

18. Disengauge the knock sensor connector, remove the bolt and the ground cable from the intake manifold.

19. On California vehicles, remove the VSV for fuel pressure control and EGR. On all vehicles (except California), remove the VSV for EGR.

20. Disconnect the PCV hose from the intake manifold and disconnect the A/T throttle control cable and bracket from the intake manifold.

21. Disconnect the engine wire harness from the starter bracket. Disengage the VSS sensor connector and the wire harness protector from the LH side of the manifold.

22. Disconnect the fuel inlet hose from the delivery pipe and the fuel return hose from the return pipe.

23. Remove the bolts and nuts, and the intake manifold and discard gasket.

24. On California vehicles, remove the air hose for the air assist system.

25. Remove the fuel delivery pipe and the injectors.

26. Remove the timing belt from the camshaft timing pulley and the camshaft timing pulley.

27. Remove No. 1 idler pulley and tension spring.

28. Remove four bolts and the No. 3 timing belt cover.

➡ **Support the timing belt, so that the meshing of the crankshaft timing pulley and the timing belt does not shift. Be careful not to drop anything inside the timing belt cover.**

29. Remove the engine hangers and the alternator bracket.
30. Remove the oil pressure switch.
31. Remove the cylinder head cover. Remove the spark plug wire clamp, PCV valve and hoses from the cylinder head cover.
32. Remove the camshafts following the proper sequences and procedures in this section.
33. Uniformly loosen and remove the cylinder head bolts in several passes and in the reverse order of the installation sequence. Lift the cylinder head from the cylinder block disengaging the cylinder head from the block dowel pins.

To install:

34. Clean the gasket mating surfaces using care not to damage the aluminum components, replace the gasket, then lower the cylinder head onto the engine. Make sure the dowel pins are aligned and no hoses or wires are between the head and cylinder block.
35. The cylinder head bolts are tightened in three progressive steps. Apply a light coat of engine oil to the cylinder head bolts. Uniformly tighten the 10 cylinder head bolts in several passes and in sequence. The torque for the head bolts is 22 ft. lbs. (29 Nm). Mark the front of the cylinder head bolt with paint. Tighten the cylinder head bolts by 90° in sequence. Tighten an additional 90° and make sure that the paint mark is now positioned toward the rear.

➡ **If any of the bolts does not meet the torque specification, replace the bolt. Cylinder head bolt lengths of 3.54 inch (90mm) and 4.25 inch (108mm). Install the 3.54 inch (90mm) bolts A in the intake manifold side position. Install the 4.25 inch (108mm) bolts B in the exhaust manifold side positions.**

36. Install the camshafts following the proper sequences and procedures.
37. Check and adjust valve clearance.
38. Install sealant to the two new semi-circular seals and install the seals to the cylinder head.
39. Install the PCV valve and hoses and the spark plug wire clamp to the cylinder head cover.
40. Install the cylinder head cover with a new gasket, the four grommets and nuts and uniformly tighten the nuts in several passes. The torque for the nuts is 17 ft. lbs. (23 Nm).

41. Install the oil pressure switch.
42. Install the alternator bracket and the engine hangers.
43. Install the No. 3 timing belt cover and temporarily install the No. 1 idler pulley and tension spring.
44. Install the camshaft timing pulley and install the timing belt to the pulley. Correctly tension the timing belt and make sure that the belt timing is correct.
45. Install the fuel injectors and the delivery pipe.
46. On California cars, install the air hose for the air assist system.
47. Install the intake manifold and insert the engine wire harness between the head and the intake manifold, install a new gaskets the six bolts and two nuts, and tighten the intake manifold to 25 ft. lbs. (34 Nm)
48. Connect the fuel inlet and return hoses to the delivery and return pipes.
49. Install the engine wire protector and harness to the intake manifold and connect the four fuel injector connectors. Connect the VSS connector.
50. Install the cable bracket to the intake manifold and install the accelerator, A/T control cables and bracket.
51. Connect the PCV hose to the intake manifold.
52. On California vehicles, install the VSV assembly for fuel pressure control and EGR.
53. Except for California vehicles, install the VSV for EGR.
54. Connect the knock sensor connector and install the ground cable with the bolt.
55. Except for California vehicles, install the sensing hoses to the vacuum pipe and mount the pipe with the bolt.
56. Install the air tube and the bracket for the EGR. Connect the hoses to the air pipe.
57. Install the A/T throttle control cable to the clamp on the rear side of the intake manifold. Install the manifold stay and tighten the bolt to 15 ft. lbs. (21 Nm) and tighten the nut to 32 ft. lbs. (44 Nm).
58. Install the EGR valve and the vacuum modulator using a new gasket, connect the two vacuum hoses to the VSV for the EGR, and connect the EGR gas temperature sensor connector. Connect the EVAP hose to the charcoal canister.
59. Install the vacuum sensor hose to the gas filter and the brake booster vacuum hose to the intake manifold.

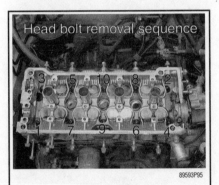

Fig. 91 Cylinder head bolt removal sequence

Fig. 92 Carefully lift the cylinder head off the block

Fig. 93 Lift the head gasket . . .

Fig. 94 . . . place clean shop rags in the piston ports and scrape all old gasket material off the mating areas

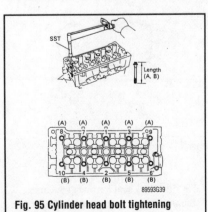

Fig. 95 Cylinder head bolt tightening sequence—7A-FE engine

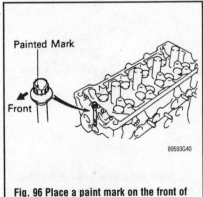

Fig. 96 Place a paint mark on the front of the head bolt as shown

60. Install the A/C idle up valve.
61. Install the throttle body.
62. Connect the water bypass pipe to the water pump cover; install the water bypass pipe and connect the hoses to the water bypass pipe.
63. Install the water outlet with a new gasket and the two nuts and install the water hoses, vacuum hoses, and connect the sensor connectors.
64. Connect the oil pressure switch connector.
65. Assemble the TWC to the exhaust manifold and install the main oxygen sensor to the exhaust manifold. Install the sub oxygen sensor to the TWC.
66. Install the exhaust manifold to the cylinder head and connect the oxygen sensors connectors.
67. Install the front exhaust pipe and install the alternator with the drive belt.
68. Install the distributor assembly and connect the spark plug wires.
69. Install the air cleaner and cap assembly.
70. Connect the negative battery cable, fill the engine with coolant, start the engine, warm up, and check for leaks. Bleed the cooling system and top off coolant as necessary.
71. Install the RH engine undercover, check ignition timing, and road test the vehicle for proper operation.

Oil Pan

REMOVAL & INSTALLATION

➥The engine must be raised and supported to remove the oil pan. A suitable engine hoist must be used.

5S-FE Engine

♦ See Figure 98

1. Disconnect the negative battery cable. On vehicles equipped with an air bag, wait at least 90 seconds before proceeding to hinder air bag deployment.
2. Raise and safely support the vehicle.
3. Drain the engine oil and remove the engine undercovers.

4. Remove the front exhaust pipe.
5. Safely support the engine assembly and remove the engine mounting center member.
6. Remove the Three Way Catalyst.
7. Unbolt and remove the rear end stiffener plate.
8. Remove the oil dipstick and remove the 17 bolts and two nuts attaching the oil pan to the engine.
9. Insert the flat-bladed tool between the oil pan and the cylinder block; cut off the applied sealer and remove the oil pan.

➥Do not use the tool for the oil pump body side and rear oil seal retainer.

To install:
10. Remove any old sealant from the oil pan flange and thoroughly clean both sealing surfaces.
11. Apply a 3–5mm bead of sealant to the oil pan flange.

➥The pan must be installed within 5 minutes of sealant application or the procedure will have to be repeated.

12. Install the oil pan with the 17 bolts and two nuts. Uniformly tighten the bolts and nuts in several passes. Tighten the bolts and nuts to 48 inch lbs. (5 Nm) and install the oil dipstick.
13. Install the rear end stiffener plate.
14. Install and secure the TWC. Use new gaskets.
15. Install the engine mounting center member and safely lower the engine.
16. Install the front exhaust pipe.
17. Fill the engine with oil, connect the negative battery cable and start the engine. Check for leaks.
18. Recheck the engine oil level and reinstall the engine undercovers.

7A-FE Engine

♦ See Figures 99, 100, 101, 102 and 103

1. Disconnect the negative battery cable. On vehicles equipped with an air bag, wait at least 90 seconds before proceeding to hinder air bag deployment.

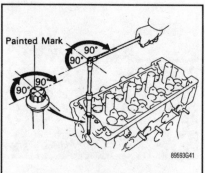

Fig. 97 Next, retighten the bolts, at the end the painted mark should be facing rearward—7A-FE engine

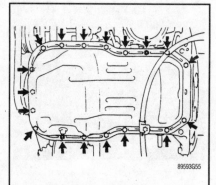

Fig. 98 Oil pan bolt and nut location—5S-FE engine

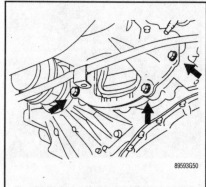

Fig. 99 There are three bolts attaching the No. 1 oil pan to the transaxle

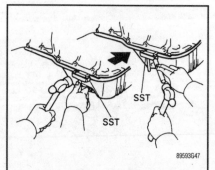

Fig. 100 Insert a blade between the block and oil pan, then cut off the seal and separate the pans

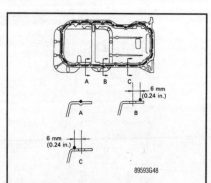

Fig. 101 Apply seal packing to the areas shown in the illustration on the No. 1 oil pan

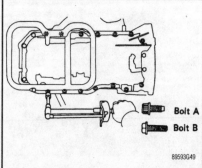

Fig. 102 Attaching the no. 1 oil pan and securing with the bolts in the correct positions

2. With the aid of an assistant, remove the hood.

3. Loosen the RH front wheel lugnuts. Raise and safely support the front of the vehicle.

4. Remove the RH front wheel.

5. Remove the engine undercovers from the vehicle.

6. Drain the engine oil.

7. Remove the front exhaust pipe.

8. If equipped with A/T, disconnect the transaxle control cable from the engine mounting center member.

9. If equipped with A/C, disconnect the A/C pressure pipe from the engine center mounting member.

10. Remove the front exhaust pipe support bracket.

11. Raise and safely support the engine assembly.

12. Remove the rear engine mounting insulator and the engine mounting center member.

13. Install an engine hanger and suspend the engine with a sling device or equivalent.

14. Remove the oil dipstick guide and the dipstick.

15. Remove the 13 bolts and 2 nuts and lower the No. 2 oil pan.

16. Insert a flat-bladed tool between the oil pan and the cylinder block; cut off the applied sealer and remove the oil pan.

➡**Do not use the tool for the oil pump body side and rear oil seal retainer.**

17. Remove the two bolts and nuts securing the baffle plate, then pull the baffle plate from the engine.

18. Remove the three nuts, the oil strainer, and the strainer gasket.

19. Remove the three bolts holding the No. 1 oil pan to the transaxle and remove the six **B** bolts. Remove the 14 bolts and the No. 1 oil pan.

To install:

20. Remove any old sealant from the oil pan flange and thoroughly clean both sealing surfaces.

21. Apply a 3–5mm bead of sealant to the No. 1 oil pan flange.

➡**The pan must be installed within 5 minutes of sealant application or the procedure will have to be repeated.**

22. Install the No. 1 oil pan with 14 new bolts. Tighten the **A** bolts to 12 ft. lbs. (16 Nm). Install the six **B** bolts and tighten the bolts to 69 inch lbs. (8 Nm). Install the three bolts holding the No. 1 oil pan to the transaxle and tighten the bolts to 17 ft. lbs. (23 Nm).

23. Install the oil strainer and gasket with three new nuts. Tighten the nuts to 82 inch lbs. (9 Nm).

24. Install the oil pan baffle plate. Tighten the two bolts and two nuts to 69 inch lbs. (8 Nm).

25. Apply a 3–5mm bead of sealant to the No. 2 oil pan flange.

➡**The pan must be installed within 5 minutes of sealant application or the procedure will have to be repeated.**

26. Install the No. 2 oil pan with the 13 bolts and the two (2) nuts. Tighten the bolts and nuts to 43 inch lbs. (5 Nm).

27. Remove the engine sling device, safely lower the engine, remove the hanger, and install the rear engine mounting insulator and engine mounting center member.

28. Install the remaining components in the reverse order they were removed.

29. Fill the engine with oil and connect the negative battery cable. Start the engine and check for leaks.

30. Install the engine undercovers.

Oil Pump

REMOVAL & INSTALLATION

➡**The engine must be raised and supported to access the oil pump. A suitable engine hoist must be used.**

5S-FE Engine

▶ See Figures 104 and 105

1. Disconnect the negative battery cable. On vehicles equipped with an air bag, wait at least 90 seconds before proceeding to hinder air bag deployment.

2. Raise and safely support the vehicle.

3. Drain the engine oil and remove the engine undercovers.

4. Remove the front exhaust pipe.

5. Safely support the engine assembly and remove the engine mounting center member.

6. Disconnect the sub oxygen sensor wiring. Remove the RH side exhaust manifold stay, TWC with gasket, retainer, and cushion.

7. Remove the rear end stiffener plate.

8. Remove the oil dipstick and oil pan.

9. Insert the flat-bladed tool between the oil pan and the cylinder block; cut off the applied sealer, separate and remove the oil pan.

➡**Do not use the tool for the oil pump body side and rear oil seal retainer.**

10. Remove the oil strainer, baffle plate, and the gasket.

11. Safely support the engine with an engine sling or equivalent.

12. Remove the timing belt.

13. Remove the No. 2 idler pulley and the crankshaft timing pulley.

14. Using a suitable tool, remove the oil pump pulley.

15. Remove the 12 bolts and extract the oil pump and gasket.

To install:

16. Install the oil pump with a new gasket and the 12 mounting bolts. Uniformly tighten the oil pump bolts in several passes. Install the 12 oil pump mounting bolts and tighten them to 78 inch lbs. (9 Nm). The long bolts are **B** 1.38 inch (35mm) long and the short bolts are **A** 0.98 inch (25mm) long.

17. Align the cut outs of the pulley and the shaft and slide on the oil pump pulley. Tighten the pulley nut to 18 ft. lbs. (24 Nm).

18. Install the crankshaft timing pulley and the No. 2 idler pulley.

19. Install the timing belt.

20. Remove the engine sling or equivalent and safely lower the engine.

21. Install a new gasket, the oil strainer and baffle plate with the two bolts and two nuts. Tighten the bolts and nuts to 48 inch lbs. (5 Nm).

22. Remove any old sealant from the oil pan flange and thoroughly clean both sealing surfaces. Apply a new bead (3–5mm) of sealant to the oil pan flange.

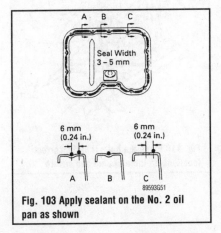

Fig. 103 Apply sealant on the No. 2 oil pan as shown

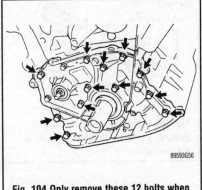

Fig. 104 Only remove these 12 bolts when extracting the oil pump—5S-FE engine

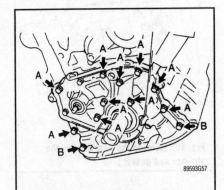

Fig. 105 Place each bolt in the correct location—5S-FE engine

➡ **The pan must be installed within 5 minutes of sealant application or the procedure will have to be repeated.**

23. Install the oil pan and dipstick.
24. Install the rear end stiffener plate.
25. Install the cushion, retainer, and a new gasket to the front TWC. Install the TWC with the three bolts and two nuts. Tighten the bolts and nuts to 21 ft. lbs. (29 Nm). Install the RH side exhaust manifold stay with the two bolts and two new nuts. Tighten the bolts and nuts to 31 ft. lbs. (42 Nm) and connect the sub oxygen sensor connector.
26. Safely support the engine assembly and install the engine mounting center member.
27. Install the front exhaust pipe.
28. Lower the vehicle and fill the engine with oil. Connect the negative battery cable, start the engine, and check for leaks.
29. Recheck the engine oil level and install the engine undercovers.

7A-FE Engine

◆ **See Figures 106, 107, 108, 109 and 110**

1. Properly relieve the fuel system pressure.
2. Disconnect the negative battery cable. On vehicles equipped with an air bag, wait at least 90 seconds before proceeding to hinder air bag deployment.
3. Remove the hood.
4. Raise and safely support the vehicle.
5. Remove the RH front wheel.
6. Remove the undercovers from the vehicle.
7. Drain the engine oil.
8. Remove the front exhaust pipe.
9. If equipped with A/T, disconnect the transaxle control cable from the engine mounting center member.

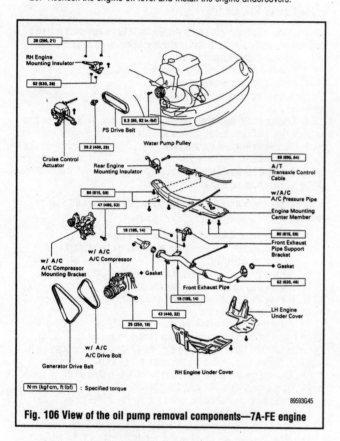

Fig. 106 View of the oil pump removal components—7A-FE engine

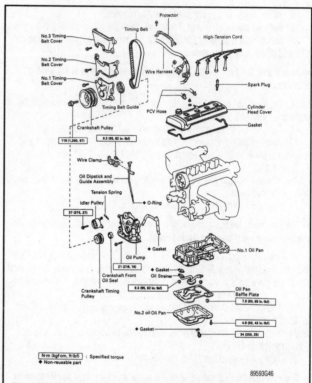

Fig. 107 View of the oil pump and related components—7A-FE engine

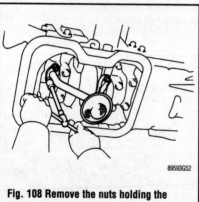

Fig. 108 Remove the nuts holding the strainer and gasket

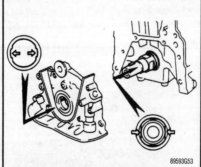

Fig. 109 Engage the spline teeth of the pump drive rotor with the large teeth of the crankshaft

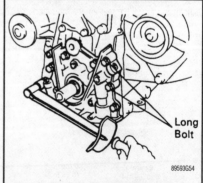

Fig. 110 Place the bolts into the correct locations on the oil pump and secure

10. If equipped w/ A/C, disconnect the A/C pressure pipe from the engine mounting center member.

11. Remove the front exhaust pipe support bracket.

12. Raise and safely support the engine assembly.

13. Remove the rear engine mounting insulator and the engine mounting center member.

14. Install an engine hanger and suspend the engine with an engine sling device or equivalent.

15. Remove the timing belt.

16. Remove the bolt and remove the idler pulley and tension spring.

17. Using a suitable tool, remove the crankshaft timing pulley.

18. Remove the oil dipstick guide and the dipstick.

19. Remove the No. 2 oil pan, baffle plate, oil strainer, and the No. 1 oil pan.

20. Remove the oil pump 7 attaching bolts and by carefully tapping the oil pump body with a plastic tipped hammer, remove the oil pump and gasket.

To install:

21. Place a new gasket on the cylinder block, engage the spline teeth of the oil pump drive rotor with the large teeth of the crankshaft and slide the oil pump on.

22. Install the 7 oil pump mounting bolts and tighten them to 16 ft. lbs. (21 Nm). The long bolts are **B** 1.38 inch (35mm) long and the short bolts are **A** 0.98 inch (25mm) long.

23. Install the No. 1 oil pan, oil strainer, baffle plate and the No. 2 oil pan.

24. Install the timing belt.

25. Remove the engine sling device, safely lower the engine, remove the hanger, and install the rear engine mounting insulator and engine mounting center member.

26. Install the front exhaust pipe support bracket.

27. If equipped with A/C, connect the A/C pressure pipe to engine mounting center member clamp.

28. If equipped with A/T, connect the transaxle control cable to the engine mounting center member.

29. Install the front exhaust pipe.

30. Install the RH front wheel and safely lower the vehicle.

31. Install the hood.

32. Fill the engine with oil, connect the negative battery cable, start the engine, and check for leaks.

33. Recheck the engine oil level and install the engine undercovers.

Crankshaft Seal

REMOVAL & INSTALLATION

➡ **The front oil seal can be removed from the engine without removing the oil pump.**

Pump Installed

▶ **See Figure 111**

1. Disconnect the negative battery cable from the battery. On vehicles equipped with an air bag, wait at least 90 seconds before proceeding to hinder air bag deployment.

2. Remove the timing belt covers and timing belt from the engine.

3. Using a puller, remove the front crankshaft gear from the crankshaft. Make sure not to damage any part of the crankshaft.

4. Using a knife, cut off the oil seal lip.

5. Using a suitable tool, pry out the oil seal. Wrap the edge of the tool with a rag or tape to prevent damaging the crankshaft. Be careful not to damage the crankshaft.

To install:

6. Using a new seal, apply a thin layer of liquid sealer to the outside of the seal.

7. Apply multi purpose grease to the new oil seal lip.

8. Using a oil seal installer and a hammer, tap in the oil seal until its surface is flush with the oil pump body edge.

9. Install the timing belt and the timing belt covers.

10. Install all other components and then connect the negative battery cable to the battery.

11. Start the engine and check for leaks.

Pump Removed

▶ **See Figures 112 and 113**

Remove the oil pump. Using a screwdriver and hammer, tap the old oil seal out of the cover. Apply multi purpose grease to the lip of the seal. Using a seal installer, tap the new one into position flush with the pump body edge. Install the oil pump and related components.

Timing Belt Covers

REMOVAL & INSTALLATION

5S-FE Engine

▶ **See Figures 114 thru 119**

1. Disconnect the negative battery cable. Wait at least 90 seconds once the battery cable is disconnected to disarm the air bag system.

✳✳ CAUTION

Work must be started after 90 seconds from the time the ignition switch is turned to the LOCKposition and the negative battery cable has been disconnected. The SRS is equipped with a back-up power source so that if work is started within 90 seconds of disconnecting the negative battery cable, the SRS may deploy. When the negative terminal cable is disconnected from the battery, memory of the clock and radio will be canceled. Before you start working, make a note of the contents memorized by the audio memory system. When you have finished working, reset the audio systems and adjust the clock. Never use a back-up power supply from outside the vehicle.

2. Remove the alternator.

3. Loosen the RH wheel lugnuts, the raise and support the for of the vehicle.

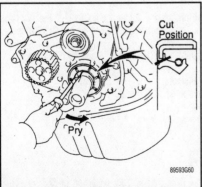

Fig. 111 Using a knife, cut the lip of the seal. With a flat bladed tool, pry it out

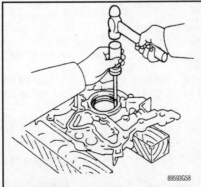

Fig. 112 Using a screwdriver and hammer, tap the old seal out of the cover

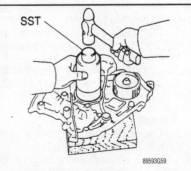

Fig. 113 When installing the new seal, tap until the seal is flush with the pump body edge

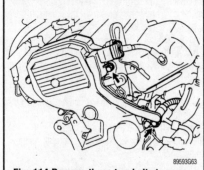

Fig. 114 Remove these two bolts to separate the engine wire protector from the alternator bracket

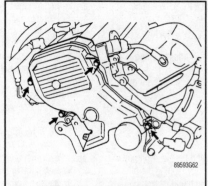

Fig. 115 These four bolts retain the No. 2 timing belt cover—5S-FE engine

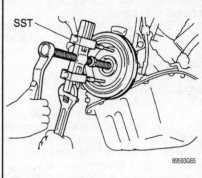

Fig. 116 Use a puller to extract the crankshaft pulley

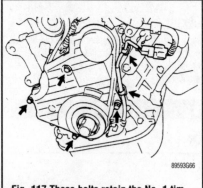

Fig. 117 These bolts retain the No. 1 timing belt cover

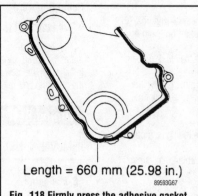

Length = 660 mm (25.98 in.)

Fig. 118 Firmly press the adhesive gasket to the timing belt cover—No. 1

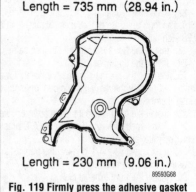

Length = 735 mm (28.94 in.)

Length = 230 mm (9.06 in.)

Fig. 119 Firmly press the adhesive gasket to the timing belt cover—No. 2

4. Unbolt and remove the RH engine under cover.

5. Remove the RH front wheel.

6. Loosen the pivot bolt and adjusting bolts of the PS pump to extract the drive belt.

7. Slightly jack up the engine. Raise the engine enough to remove the weight from the engine mounting on the right side.

8. Disconnect the ground strap wiring.

9. Remove the RH engine mounting insulator.

a. Remove the bolt and nuts holding the insulator to the bracket.

b. Disconnect the PS reservoir from the bracket.

c. Remove the bolt, nut and PS reservoir bracket.

d. Remove the bolts and insulator.

10. Remove the 3 bolts and mounting bracket for the RH side.

➡You will need to raise the engine as far as it will go to remove the RH bracket.

11. If necessary, label and separate the plug wires from the spark plugs.

12. To remove the No. 2 timing belt cover, loosen the 2 bolts and disconnect the engine wire protector from the alternator bracket and adjusting bar. Unbolt and extract the timing belt cover.

13. Using a suitable crankshaft pulley holding tool and bolt, loosen the pulley bolt. Some times a plate washer may be necessary between the bolt and tool.

14. Remove the tool and pulley bolt.

15. Using a puller and wrench remove the crankshaft pulley.

16. Disconnect the 2 clamps of the crankshaft position sensor wire from the timing belt cover. Remove the 4 bolts and No. 1 timing belt cover. Discard the old gaskets.

To install:

17. Check that the timing belt gasket has no cracks or peeling. If the gasket is not reusable do the following:

a. Using a flat-bladed tool and gasket scraper, remove the old gasket material from the cover and mating area.

b. Thoughroughly clean all components to remove all the loose material. Remove the backing paper from the new gasket and install the gasket evenly to the part of the cover shaded black in the illustration.

c. After installing the gasket, press down on it so it seats and the adhesive firmly sticks.

18. Secure the No. 1 cover with the 4 retaining bolts. Install the clamps of the crankshaft position sensor to the timing belt cover.

19. Align the crankshaft pulley key with the groove of the pulley. Using a retaining wrench, install the bolt and tighten to 80 ft. lbs. (108 Nm).

20. Positon the No. 2 timing belt cover gasket. Disconnect the engine protector between the cylinder head cover and the No. 3 timing belt cover.

a. Install the No. 2 belt cover and secure.

b. Attach the engine wire protector to the mounting bolts of the No. 2 cover in the sequence shown. Install the engine wire protector to the alternator bracket and adjusting bar, then secure.

21. If removed, attach the spark plug wires.

22. Install the RH engine mounting bracket and secure the bolts to 38 ft. lbs. (52 Nm).

➡Raise the engine as far as it will go, and place the bracket into position.

23. Attach the RH insulator to the body and bracket. Tighten the bolts to 47 ft. lbs. (64 Nm).

24. Install the PS reservoir bracket and tighten the nut to 21 ft. lbs. (28 Nm).

25. Attach the PS reservoir to the bracket and tighten the bolt to 27 ft. lbs. (37 Nm) and the nut to 38 ft. lbs. (52 Nm).

26. Connect the ground strap wiring. Install the PS belt, then adjust as necessary.

27. Install the RH wheel, alternator and engine undercover.

28. Lower the vehicle and tighten the lug nuts.

29. Double check all wiring and belts.

30. Start the engine and inspect for leaks.

7A-FE Engine

◗ See Figures 120 thru 129

1. Disconnect the negative battery cable. Wait at least 90 seconds once the cable is disconnected to hinder air bad deployment.

Fig. 120 Raise and support the right side of the engine using a floor jack

Fig. 121 Remove the lower nuts for the engine mount

Fig. 122 Extract the mount, inspect and replace if necessary

Fig. 123 Retain the crankshaft pulley with a bolt and . . .

Fig. 124 . . . remove the center bolt

Fig. 125 Use the puller to extract the crankshaft pulley

Fig. 126 Then slide the pulley off the shaft

Fig. 127 These bolts retain the No. 1 timing belt cover

Fig. 128 These four bolts retain the No. 3 timing cover . . .

2. Remove the right front wheel and engine under covers.

3. Slightly jack up the engine on the right side to remove the RH engine mount. Inspect the mount and replace if necessary.

➡The power steering pump and bracket. May need to be removed to access the engine mounting bolts.

4. Remove all drive belts.

5. Remove the valve cover.

6. While retaining the crankshaft pulley, remove the pulley bolt. Extract the crankshaft pulley using a puller.

7. Unbolt all three timing belt covers from the engine.

To install:

8. Check that the timing belt gasket has no cracks or peeling. If the gasket is not reusable do the following:

a. Using a flat-bladed tool and gasket scraper, remove the old gasket material from the cover and mating area.

Fig. 129 Once all the bolts are removed, the covers will come off

b. Thouroughly clean all components to remove all the loose material. Remove the backing paper from the new gasket and install the gasket evenly to the part of the cover shaded black in the illustration.

c. After installing the gasket, press down on it so it seats and the adhesive firmly sticks.

9. Install all three timing belt covers and tighten the bolts to 62 inch lbs. (7 Nm).

10. Install the new valve cover gasket and seal washers to the cylinder head cover.

11. Install the cylinder head cover to the cylinder head; secure with four cap nuts to 53 inch lbs. (6 Nm).

12. Install two PCV hoses to the valve cover; secure with hose clamps.

13. Attach the engine wiring harness to the valve cover, then install the engine wiring harness cover and secure to 53 inch lbs. (6 Nm).

14. Connect the wire and clamp to the alternator.

15. Install and adjust all the drive belts.

16. Install engine mount to body and secure but do not tighten fully. Tighten the following:

- Mounting bracket-to-engine mount bolt to 47 ft. lbs. (64 Nm)
- Mounting bracket-to-engine mount nuts to 38 ft. lbs. (52 Nm)
- Engine mount-to-body bolt **A** to 19 ft. lbs. (25 Nm)
- Engine mount-to-body bolts **B** to 19 ft. lbs. (25 Nm)
- Engine mount-to-body bolt **C** to 19 ft. lbs. (25 Nm), if equipped with cruise control.

17. Install the right engine undercover.

18. Install the right front wheel and lower the vehicle.

19. Connect the negative battery cable.

20. Start the engine and check the ignition timing. Inspect for leaks and check vehicle operation.

Timing Belt and Sprockets

REMOVAL & INSTALLATION

5S-FE Engine

♦ See Figures 130 thru 142

1. Disconnect the negative battery cable. On vehicles equipped with an air bag, wait at least 90 seconds before proceeding.

2. Remove the alternator and alternator bracket.

3. Raise and support the vehicle safely. Remove the right tire and wheel assembly.

4. Remove the right side engine undercover.

5. Remove the power steering belt.

6. Disconnect the ground strap connector.

7. Raise the engine enough to move the right side engine mounting assembly.

8. Remove the spark plugs.

9. Remove the No. 2 timing cover.

10. Position the number one cylinder to TDC on the compression stroke by turning the crankshaft pulley and aligning its groove with the timing mark **0** of the No. 1 timing belt cover. Check that the hole of the camshaft timing pulley is

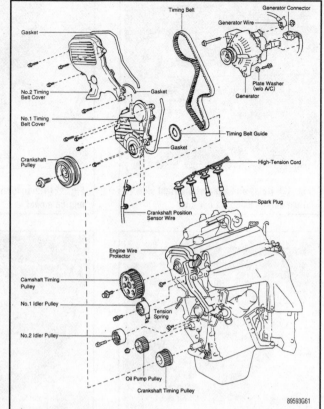

Fig. 130 Exploded view of the timing belt and related components—5S-FE engine

aligned with the alignment mark of the bearing cap. If not, turn the crankshaft one revolution 360°.

11. Remove the timing belt from the camshaft timing pulley.

a. If reusing the belt, place matchmarks on the timing belt and the camshaft pulley. Place matchmarks on the timing belt to match portion **A** of the No. 1 timing belt cover. Loosen the mount bolt of the No. 1 idler pulley and position the pulley toward the left as far as it will go. Tighten the bolt. Remove the belt from the camshaft pulley.

12. Remove the camshaft timing pulley. Use a suitable pulley retaining tool and ratchet and remove the bolt and the camshaft pulley.

13. Remove the crankshaft pulley. Use a suitable crankshaft pulley retaining tool to hold the crankshaft pulley and remove the pulley set bolt and pulley using a puller.

14. If reusing the timing belt, after loosening the pulley bolt, check that the timing belt matchmarks align with the portion **A** of the No. 1 timing belt cover when the crankshaft pulley groove is aligned with the timing mark **0** of the No. 1 cover. If the marks does not align, use the following to do so:

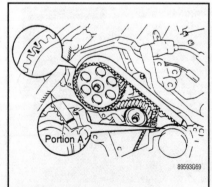

Fig. 131 Matchmark locations for timing belt removal—5S-FE engine

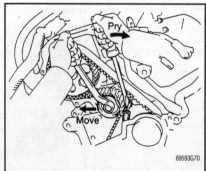

Fig. 132 Loosen the bolt of the No. 1 idler pulley, then shift the it to the left as far as it will go

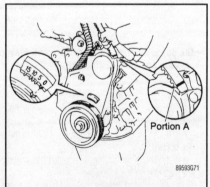

Fig. 133 Checking the alignment of the marks with portion A and No. 1 belt cover

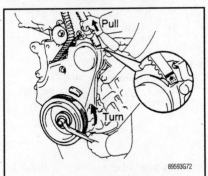

Fig. 134 Misaligned clockwise, pull the belt up and turn the crankshaft pulley counterclockwise . . .

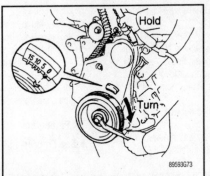

Fig. 135 . . . hold the timing, turn the pulley clockwise to align the groove with the timing mark

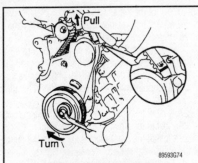

Fig. 136 Misaligned counterclockwise, pull the belt up on the No. 1 idler pulley, while turning the crankshaft pulley clockwise . . .

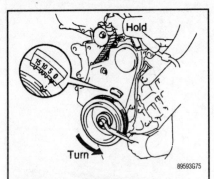

Fig. 137 . . . hold the timing belt, turn the crankshaft pulley counterclockwise and align its groove

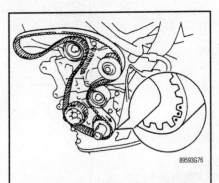

Fig. 138 Place a rotation mark on the timing belt prior to removal if reusing the old belt

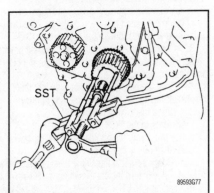

Fig. 139 Remove the crankshaft timing pulley . . .

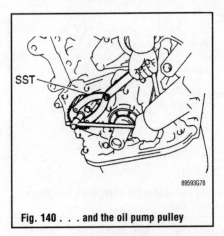

Fig. 140 . . . and the oil pump pulley

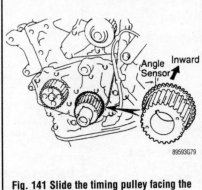

Fig. 141 Slide the timing pulley facing the angle sensor inward

Fig. 142 Align the points marked on the gears and belt during removal!

a. When the matchmark is misaligned clockwise, pull the belt up on the water pump pulley side while turning the crankshaft pulley counterclockwise. After aligning the matchmark, hold the timing belt and turn the crankshaft pulley clockwise. Align its groove with the timing mark **0** of the No. 1 belt cover.

b. If the matchmark is misaligned counterclockwise, align the mark by pulling the timing belt up on the no. 1 idler pulley side while turning the crankshaft pulley clockwise. After the alignment, hold the timing belt. And turn the crankshaft pulley counterclockwise m and align its groove with the timing mark **0** of the No. 1 cover.

c. Remove the timing pulley bolt. Next remove the crankshaft pulley.

15. Unbolt and remove the No. 1 timing belt cover.

16. Remove the timing belt and the belt guide. If reusing the belt mark the belt and the crankshaft pulley in the direction of engine rotation and matchmark for correct installation.

17. Remove the No. 1 idler pulley and the tension spring.

18. Remove the No. 2 idler pulley.

19. Remove the crankshaft timing pulley. If the pulley cannot be removed by hand, use two prying tools with shop rags behind them to prevent damage to the engine.

20. Remove the oil pump pulley.

21. Inspect the belt for defects and replace as required. Inspect the idler pulleys and springs; replace the defective components as required.

To install:

22. Align the cutouts of the oil pump pulley and shaft. Install the oil pump pulley and tighten the retaining nut to 18 ft. lbs. (24 Nm).

23. Install the crankshaft timing pulley.

a. Align the timing pulley set key with the key groove of the pulley.

b. Slide on the timing pulley with the flange side facing inward.

24. Install the No. 2 idler pulley and tighten the bolt to 31 ft. lbs. (42 Nm). Be sure that the pulley moves freely. Use the 1.38 inch (35mm) bolt only.

25. Temporarily install the No. 1 idler pulley and tension spring. Pry the

pulley toward the left as far as it will go. Tighten the bolt. Make sure that the pulley rotates freely. Only use the 1.65 inch (42mm) bolt.

26. Temporarily install the timing belt.

a. Using the crankshaft pulley bolt, turn the crankshaft and align the timing marks of the crankshaft timing pulley and the oil pump body.

b. If reusing the old belt, align the marks made during removal, and install the belt with the arrow pointing in the direction of the engine revolution.

27. Install the timing belt guide with the cup side facing outward.

28. Install the No. 1 timing belt cover.

29. Install the crankshaft pulley. Align the pulley set key with the key groove of the pulley and slide on the pulley. Tighten the bolt to 80 ft. lbs. (108 Nm).

30. Install the camshaft timing pulley.

a. Align the camshaft knock pin with the knock pin groove of the pulley and slide on the timing pulley. Tighten the bolt to 40 ft. lbs. (54 Nm).

31. With the No. 1 cylinder set at TDC on the compression stroke install the timing belt (all timing marks aligned). If reusing the belt, align with the marks made during the removal procedure.

a. Turn the crankshaft pulley, and align its groove with the timing mark **0** of the No. 1 timing belt cover. Make sure the camshaft sprocket hole is aligned with the mark on the bearing cap.

32. Connect the timing belt to the camshaft timing pulley.

33. Check that the matchmark on the timing belt matches the end of the No. 1 timing belt cover.

34. Once the belt is installed be sure that there is tension between the crankshaft timing pulley and the camshaft pulley.

35. Check the valve timing.

a. Loosen the No. 1 idler pulley mount bolt ½ turn. Turn the crankshaft pulley two revolutions from TDC in the clockwise direction. Always turn the crankshaft pulley clockwise.

b. Make sure that the all the timing marks are aligned.

c. Slowly turn the crankshaft pulley 1⅞ revolutions. Align its groove with the mark at 45° BTDC on the No. 1 timing belt cover for the No. 1 cylinder.

d. Tighten the No. 1 idler pulley mount bolt to 31 ft. lbs. (42 Nm).

36. Install the No. 2 timing belt cover.

a. Install the upper gasket to the No. 1 timing belt cover.

b. Disconnect the engine wire protector between the cylinder head cover and the No. 3 timing belt cover.

c. Install the gasket to the timing belt cover.

d. Install the belt cover.

e. Install the engine wire protector to the two mounting bolts of the No. 2 timing belt cover. Install the right side first.

f. Install the engine wire protector to the alternator bracket and adjusting bar.

37. Install the spark plugs and wires.

38. Tighten the right engine mount bracket bolts to 38 ft. lbs. (52 Nm).

39. Lower the engine after installing the bracket.

40. Tighten the engine mount insulator bolt to 47 ft. lbs. (64 Nm). Tighten the through-bolt to 54 ft. lbs. (78 Nm).

41. Install the power steering reservoir bracket, tighten the bolt to 21 ft. lbs. (28 Nm).

42. Install the power steering reservoir to the bracket. Tighten the bolt to 27 ft. lbs. (37 Nm) and the nut to 38 ft. lbs. (52 Nm).

43. Connect the ground strap wiring.

44. Install the power steering pump drive belt.

45. Install the front wheel.

46. Install the alternator.

47. Install the engine undercover.

48. Lower the vehicle and connect the negative battery cable.

49. Check all fluid levels and adjust all drive belts. Perform all necessary engine adjustments. Road test the vehicle for proper operation.

7A-FE Engine

▶ See Figures 143 thru 160

1. Disconnect the negative battery cable. On vehicles equipped with an air bag, wait at least 90 seconds before proceeding.

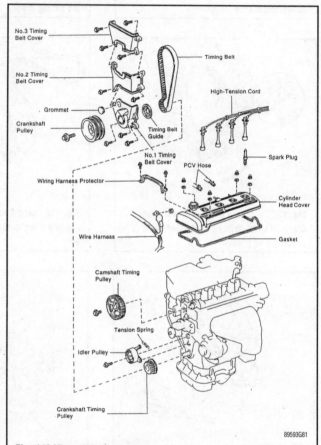

Fig. 143 View of the timing belt, gears and cover along with other related components—7A-FE engine

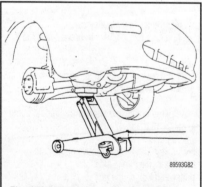

Fig. 144 Jack up the engine enough to remove the weight from the RH mounting

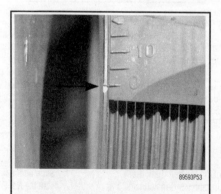

Fig. 145 Verify that the timing mark on the crankshaft pulley is TDC

Fig. 146 Alignment of the hole on the camshaft timing pulley

Work must be started after 90 seconds from the time the ignition switch is turned to the LOCK position and the negative battery cable has been disconnected. The SRS is equipped with a back-up power source so that if work is started within 90 seconds of disconnecting the negative battery cable, the SRS may deploy. When the negative terminal cable is disconnected from the battery, memory of the clock and radio will be canceled. Before you start working, make a note of the contents memorized by the audio memory system. When you have finished working, reset the audio systems and adjust the clock. Never use a back-up power supply from outside the vehicle.

2. Loosen the lugnuts on the right front wheel.

3. If equipped with cruise control, remove the cruise control actuator cover, cruise control electrical connector, control cable and the actuator from the vehicle.

4. Raise and support the vehicle safely.

5. Remove the right front wheel and housing cover.

6. Slightly jack up the engine and remove the right-hand engine mounting insulator.

7. Loosen the water pump pulley bolts.

8. Unbolt and remove the alternator.

9. If equipped with A/C, remove the compressor and bracket.

10. Loosen the power steering pump pivot and lock bolts.

11. Push the power steering pump toward the engine and remove the drive belt.

12. Remove the water pump pulley.

13. Unbolt and separate the wire harness protector from the cylinder head.

14. Remove the spark plug wires and the spark plugs from the cylinder head.

15. Remove the two hose clamps, label and extract the PCV hoses from the valve cover.

16. Remove the four cap nuts, the seal washers, the valve cover, and the gasket from the cylinder head.

17. Turn the crankshaft to align the timing mark on crankshaft pulley at **0**, setting the piston in No. 1 cylinder at Top Dead Center (TDC) on the compression stroke. Check that the hole of the camshaft timing pulley is aligned with the timing mark of the bearing cap. If not, turn crankshaft pulley **1** complete revolution (360 degrees).

18. If necessary, remove the four bolts and retaining the pulley from water pump.

19. While retaining the crankshaft pulley, remove the pulley bolt. Extract the crankshaft pulley using a puller.

20. Unbolt all three timing belt covers from the engine.

21. Slide the timing belt guide from crankshaft.

22. Set the camshaft and crankshaft timing sprockets to align the marks.

➡ Do not turn crankshaft or camshaft independently after removal of timing belt. Binding or damage to engine components could result. If timing belt is to be reused, mark timing belt with arrow showing direction of engine revolution. Put matchmarks where timing belt meets with crankshaft timing sprocket and camshaft timing sprocket to ensure installation in the same position.

23. Remove the timing belt tensioner bolt, tensioner, and the tension spring.

Do not bend, twist or turn the timing belt inside out. Do not allow the belt to come in contact with oil, coolant or steam.

24. Loosen the mounting bolt of the idler pulley and shift the pulley toward the left as far as it will go, them temporarily tighten it.

   a. Remove the timing belt from camshaft and crankshaft timing sprockets.

25. Remove the camshaft timing sprocket bolt while holding the camshaft by the hexagonal wrench head section.

89593P64

Fig. 147 Slide the timing belt guide off the crankshaft

89593P62

Fig. 148 Draw an arrow in the direction of the belt if you are reusing the timing belt

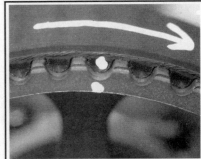

89593P63

Fig. 149 Also mark the points of the belt vs. the gear so the teeth match during installation

89593P65

Fig. 150 Marked crankshaft timing sprocket

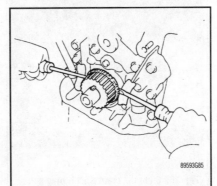

89593G85

Fig. 151 Remove the crankshaft timing pulley by prying it off if necessary

89593P66

Fig. 152 Loosening the idler pulley mounting bolt while moving it to the far left, then . . .

⁂ **WARNING**

Be careful not to damage the cylinder head when holding camshaft in place.

26. Remove crankshaft timing sprocket using 2 flat bladed prybars to pry off. Tape the end of the prybars to prevent damaging the crankshaft.
To install:
27. Check the camshaft and crankshaft timing sprockets to align the marks. Do not turn crankshaft or camshaft independently before installation of the timing belt or engine damage may occur.
28. Install the camshaft timing sprocket. Align the camshaft key with the groove on the sprocket and slide the sprocket on the camshaft; secure with the camshaft timing sprocket bolt. Hold the camshaft at hexagonal wrench head portion to prevent rotation and tighten the camshaft timing sprocket bolt to 43 ft. lbs. (59 Nm).

➡**Inspect the camshaft timing sprocket to ensure mark is still aligned as indicated.**

29. Install the crankshaft timing sprocket. Align the pulley set key with the groove of the pulley. Slide the timing pulley on the crankshaft, facing the flange side inward.

➡**Inspect the crankshaft timing sprocket to ensure mark is still aligned as indicated.**

30. Temporarily install the idler pulley and tension spring. Install the idler pulley with the bolt. Do not tighten the bolt yet. Install the tension spring. Push the pulley toward the left as far as it will go and tighten the bolt.
31. Set the No. 1 cylinder to TDC.
   a. Turn the hexagonal wrench head portion of the camshaft, and align the hole of the camshaft timing pulley with the timing mark of the bearing cap.
   b. Using the crankshaft pulley bolt, turn the crankshaft and align the timing marks of the crankshaft pulley and oil pump body.

32. Install the timing belt. If reinstalling the old belt, observe the match-marks made during removal. Make sure the belt is fully and squarely seated on the sprockets.
33. Check the valve timing as follows:
   a. Loosen the retaining bolt for the timing belt tensioner and allow it to tension the belt.
   b. Temporarily install the crankshaft pulley bolt and turn the crank clockwise 2 full revolutions from TDC to TDC. Insure that each timing mark realigns exactly.
   c. Tighten the timing belt tensioner bolt to 27 ft. lbs. (37 Nm).
34. Measure the timing belt deflection at the **SIDE** point, looking for 0.20–0.24 inch (5–6mm) of deflection at 4.4 pounds of pressure. If the deflection is not correct, adjust with the timing belt tensioner.
35. Install the timing belt guide, remove the temporarily installed crankshaft pulley bolt. Install the guide with the cup side facing outward, onto the crankshaft and install the timing belt covers from the lowest to the highest. Tighten the nine cover bolts to 62 inch lbs. (7 Nm).
36. Install the crankshaft pulley to the crankshaft after aligning the pulley key with the slot on the pulley; secure with the bolt while holding the crankshaft pulley and tighten the pulley bolt to
87 ft. lbs. (118 Nm).
37. Install the new valve cover gasket and seal washers to the cylinder head cover.
38. Install the cylinder head cover to the cylinder head; secure with four cap nuts to 53 inch lbs. (6 Nm).
39. Install two PCV hoses to the valve cover; secure with hose clamps.
40. Install the spark plugs and spark plug wires.
41. Attach the engine wiring harness to the valve cover, then install the engine wiring harness cover and secure to 53 inch lbs. (6 Nm).
42. Install the water pump pulley but do not tighten the bolts at this time.
43. Install the PS pulley and pull the pump back to tighten the drive belt. Tighten the pivot and adjusting bolt to 29 ft. lbs. (39 Nm).

Fig. 153 . . . lift the belt off the gear assemblies

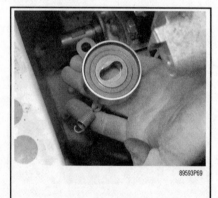
Fig. 154 Then remove the idler pulley

Fig. 155 Hold a hexagonal head wrench portion of the camshaft, then remove the bolt and camshaft timing pulley

Fig. 156 The timing pulley should slide off the end of the camshaft

Fig. 157 Slide the crankshaft timing pulley off by hand if possible

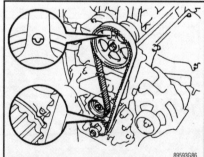
Fig. 158 On valve timing, make sure each pulley aligns with the timing marks, if not remove the belt and reinstall

44. If equipped, install the A/C pipe mounting bracket and tighten the bolts to 35 ft. lbs. (47 Nm).

45. Install the A/C compressor and tighten the bolts to 18 ft. lbs. (25 Nm), then attach the compressor connector.

46. Install and secure the alternator.

47. Install the drive belt with the adjusting bolt and install the idler pulley locknut and tighten the nut and adjusting bolt to 29 ft. lbs. (39 Nm).

48. Install the alternator drive belt and tighten the pivot bolt to 45 ft. lbs. (61 Nm), then the adjusting lock bolt to 14 ft. lbs. (19 Nm).

49. Tighten the water pump pulley bolts to 82 inch. lbs. (9 Nm).

50. Install engine mount to body and secure but do not tighten fully. Tighten the following:
- Mounting bracket-to-engine mount bolt to 47 ft. lbs. (64 Nm).
- Mounting bracket-to-engine mount nuts to 38 ft. lbs. (52 Nm).
- Engine mount-to-body bolt **A** to 19 ft. lbs. (25 Nm).
- Engine mount-to-body bolts **B** to 19 ft. lbs. (25 Nm).
- Engine mount-to-body bolt **C** to 19 ft. lbs. (25 Nm), if equipped with cruise control.

51. Install the right engine undercover.

52. Install the right front wheel and lower the vehicle.

53. If equipped with cruise control, install the actuator.

54. Connect the negative battery cable.

55. Start the engine and check the ignition timing. Inspect for leaks and check vehicle operation.

INSPECTION

Idler Pulley

♦ See Figures 161 and 162

Visually inspect the seal portion of the idler pulley for oil leakage. Check that the idler pulley turns smoothly in each direction. If necessary, replace the pulley.

Tension Spring

♦ See Figure 163

1. Measure the free length of the tension spring. Free length should be:
- 7A-FE engine—1.252 inch (31.8mm)
- 5S-FE engine—1.811 inch (46.0mm)
2. If the free length is not within specifications, replace the tension spring.
3. Measrue the tension of the spring at the specified length. Installed tension should be as follows:
- 7A-FE engine—10.8–11.7 lbf (48–52 N) @ 1.480 inch (37.6mm)
- 5S-FE engine—7.2–8.3 lbf (32–37 N) @ 1.988 inch 950.5mm)
4. If the tension is not within specifications, replace the spring.

Belt

♦ See Figures 164, 165, 166, 167 and 168

✲✲ WARNING

Do not bend or twist the timing belt inside out. Do not allow the timing belt to come in contact with any oil, water or steam.

1. If there are any defects in the timing belt as shown in the illustrations, replace the belt. If premature parting is a concern, check for proper belt installation or the timing cover gasket for damage and improper installation.

2. If the belt teeth are cracked or damaged, check to see if either camshaft or the water pump is locked.

3. If there is noticeable wear or cracks on the belt face, check to see if there are nicks on the side of the idler pulley lock.

4. If there is noticeable wear or damage on only one side of the belt, check the belt guide and the alignment of each pulley.

5. If there is noticeable wear on the teeth, check the timing cover for damage and check that gasket for correct installation. Also inspect for foreign materials on the pulley teeth.

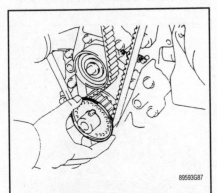

Fig. 159 Install the timing belt guide with the cup side facing outwards

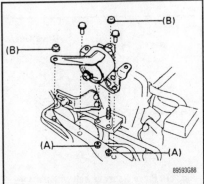

Fig. 160 RH engine mounting nut and bolt locations—7A-FE engine

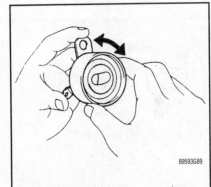

Fig. 161 Check the rotation of the bearing, is it a smooth turn?

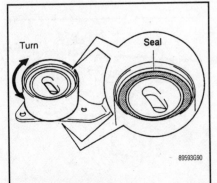

Fig. 162 Inspect the seal of the bearing for any oil seepage

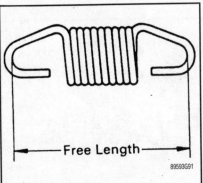

Fig. 163 Measure the free length of the tension spring

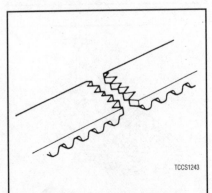

Fig. 164 Check for premature parting of the belt

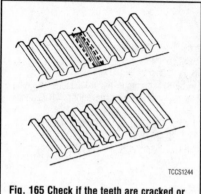

Fig. 165 Check if the teeth are cracked or damaged

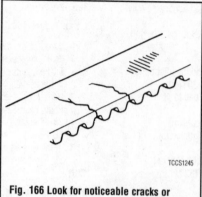

Fig. 166 Look for noticeable cracks or wear on the belt face

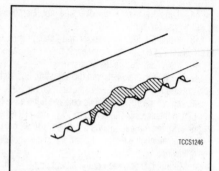

Fig. 167 You may only have damage on one side of the belt; if so, the guide could be the culprit

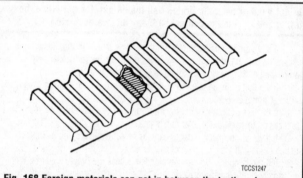

Fig. 168 Foreign materials can get in between the teeth and cause damage

Camshaft, Bearings and Lifters

REMOVAL & INSTALLATION

5S-FE Engine

♦ See Figures 169 thru 181

    1. Disconnect the negative battery cable. On vehicles equipped with an air bag, wait at least 90 seconds before proceeding.

✳✳ CAUTION

Work must be started after 90 seconds from the time the ignition switch is turned to the LOCKposition and the negative battery cable has been disconnected. The SRS is equipped with a back-up power

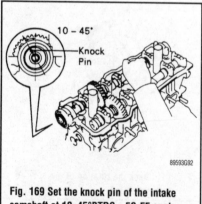

Fig. 169 Set the knock pin of the intake camshaft at 10–45°BTDC—5S-FE engine

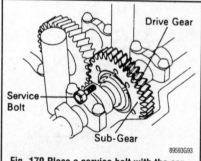

Fig. 170 Place a service bolt with the correct diameter, thread pitch and thread length through the cam sub and drive gears

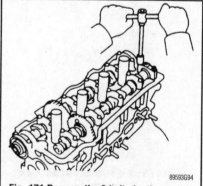

Fig. 171 Remove the 2 bolts for the rear bearing cap first, then . . . . .

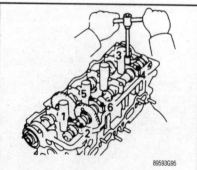

Fig. 172 . . . uniformly remove the No. 1, No. 2 and No. 4 caps in several passes on the exhaust side—5S-FE engine

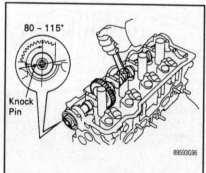

Fig. 173 Set the knock pin of the intake camshaft at 80–115°BTDC of the camshaft angle—5S-FE intake

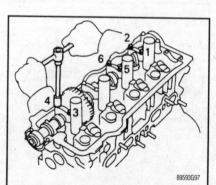

Fig. 174 Uniformly loosen the cap bolts on the No. 1, No. 3 and No. 4 in several passes on the intake side—5S-FE engine

source so that if work is started within 90 seconds of disconnecting the negative battery cable, the SRS may deploy. When the negative terminal cable is disconnected from the battery, memory of the clock and radio will be canceled. Before you start working, make a note of the contents memorized by the audio memory system. When you have finished working, reset the audio systems and adjust the clock. Never use a back-up power supply from outside the vehicle.

2. Label and disconnect the plug wires from the spark plugs. Make note of the proper firing order for installation.

3. Remove the timing belt, gears, and the covers.

4. Remove or disconnect any wire harnesses, clamps, cables, or components necessary in order to remove the cylinder head cover.

5. Remove the four nuts, grommets, head cover, and the gasket.

6. Set the No. 1 cylinder to TDC. Turn the crankshaft pulley and align its groove with the timing mark 0 of the No. 1 timing belt cover. Check that the valve lifters on the No. 1 cylinder are loose and valve lifters on the No. 4 cylinder are tight. If not, rotate the crankshaft 360°.

➡Since the thrust clearance on both the intake and exhaust camshafts is small, the camshafts must be kept level during removal. If the

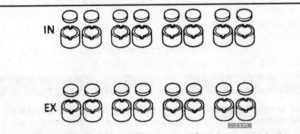

Fig. 175 Always place the lifters and shims together as a set in the correct order

camshafts are removed without being kept level, the camshaft may damage the bearing surface, causing the camshaft to seize during engine operation.

7. To remove the exhaust camshaft proceed as follows:

a. Set the knock pin of the intake camshaft at 10–45°BTDC of camshaft angle on the cylinder head. This angle will help to lift the exhaust camshaft level and evenly by pushing the No. 2 and No. 4 cylinder camshaft lobes of the exhaust camshaft toward their valve lifters evenly.

b. Secure the exhaust camshaft sub-gear to the main gear using a service bolt. The manufacturer recommends a bolt 0.63–0.79 inch (16–20mm) long with a thread diameter of 6.0mm and a 1.0mm thread pitch. When removing the exhaust camshaft be sure that the torsional spring force of the sub-gear has been eliminated.

c. Remove the 2 bolts and the rear bearing cap.

d. Uniformly loosen and remove the bearing cap bolts on the No. 1, No. 2, and No. 4 bearing caps in several passes, in the sequence shown.

➡Do not remove bearing cap bolts to No. 3 bearing cap at this time.

e. Remove the No. 1, 2, and 4 bearing caps.

f. Alternately loosen and remove the bearing cap bolts on the No. 3 bearing cap. As these bolts are loosened check to see that the camshaft is being lifted out straight and level.

➡If the camshaft is not lifted out straight and level, tighten the No. 3 bearing cap bolts. Reverse the order of Steps 7f through 7a and reset the intake camshaft knock pin to 10–45°BTDC, then repeat Steps 7b through 7f. Do not attempt to pry the camshaft from its mounting.

g. Remove the No. 3 bearing cap and exhaust camshaft from the engine.

8. To remove the intake camshaft, proceed as follows:

a. Set the knock pin of the intake camshaft at 80–115°BTDC of the camshaft angle on the cylinder head. This angle will help to lift the intake camshaft level and evenly by pushing No. 1 and No. 3 cylinder camshaft lobes of the intake camshaft toward their valve lifters.

b. Remove the two front bearing cap bolts and extract the front bearing

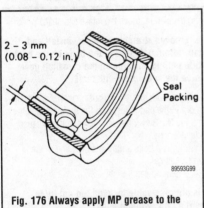

Fig. 176 Always apply MP grease to the bearing caps before installing them

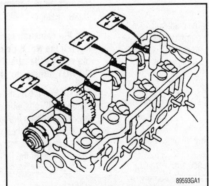

Fig. 177 Install the intake bearing caps in their proper locations—5S-FE exhaust

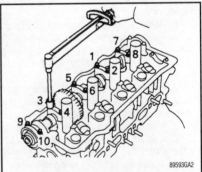

Fig. 178 Uniformly tighten the intake bearing cap bolts in several passes—5S-FE engine

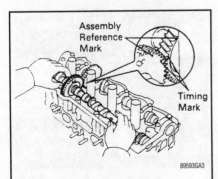

Fig. 179 Engage the exhaust camshaft gear to the intake gear by matching the timing marks—5S-FE exhaust

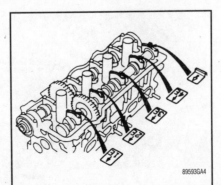

Fig. 180 Place the exhaust bearing caps in the proper locations—5S-FE exhaust

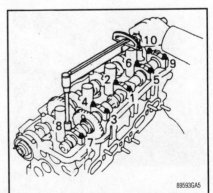

Fig. 181 Exhaust bearing cap tightening sequence—5S-FE exhaust

cap and oil seal. If the cap will not come apart easily, leave it in place without the bolts.

c. Uniformly loosen and remove the bearing cap bolts to No. 1, No. 3, and the No. 4 bearing caps in sequence in several passes. Do not remove bearing cap bolts to the No. 2 bearing cap at this time. Remove No. 1, No. 3, and No. 4 bearing caps.

d. Alternately loosen and remove bearing cap bolts to the No. 2 bearing cap. As these bolts are loosened and after breaking the adhesion on the front bearing cap, check to see that the camshaft is being lifted out straight and level.

➡️**If the camshaft is not lifting out straight and level tighten the No. 2 bearing cap bolts. Reverse Steps 8e through 8a, then start over from Step 8b.**

➡️**Do not attempt to pry the camshaft from its mounting.**

e. Remove the No. 2 bearing cap with the intake camshaft from the engine.

9. Remove the valve lifter shims and hydraulic lifters. Identify each lifter and shim as it is removed so it can be reinstalled in the same position. If the lifters are to be reused, store them upside down in a sealed container.

To install:

10. Install the valve lifters into their original positions and install the shims. Make sure the lifter rotates smoothly by hand.

11. Before installing the intake camshaft, apply multi-purpose grease to the camshaft.

12. To install the intake camshaft, proceed as follows:

a. Position the camshaft at 80–115°BTDC of camshaft angle on the cylinder head.

b. Apply sealant to the No. 1 bearing cap.

c. Coat the bearing cap bolts under the head and on the threads with clean engine oil.

d. Tighten the camshaft bearing caps evenly in sequence and in several passes to 14 ft. lbs. (19 Nm).

e. Apply MP grease to a new oil seal lip, and by using a suitable tool, tap a new oil seal into place.

13. To install the exhaust camshaft, proceed as follows:

a: Set the knock pin of the camshaft at 10–45°BTDC of camshaft angle on the cylinder head.

b. Apply multipurpose grease to the thrust portion of the camshaft.

c. Position the exhaust camshaft gear with the intake camshaft gear so that the timing marks are in alignment with one another. Be sure to use the proper alignment marks on the gears. Do not use the assembly reference marks.

d. Turn the intake camshaft clockwise or counterclockwise little by little until the exhaust camshaft sits in the bearing journals evenly without rocking the camshaft on the bearing journals.

e. Instsall the bearing caps in their proper locations.

f. Coat the bearing cap bolts under the head and to the threads with clean engine oil.

g. Tighten the camshaft bearing caps evenly in sequence and in several passes to 14 ft. lbs. (19 Nm). Remove the service bolt from the assembly.

14. Check and adjust valve clearance. Refer to Section 1.

15. Install the cylinder head cover with the grommets and the four nuts.

16. Install the timing belt and related components.

17. Connect the electrical wiring, cables, brackets, and components attached to the cylinder head cover.

18. Install the spark plug wires and connect the negative battery cable. Start the engine, check for leaks, and road test the vehicle for proper operation.

7A-FE Engine

♦ See Figures 182 thru 191

1. Disconnect the negative battery cable. On vehicles equipped with an air bag, wait at least 90 seconds before proceeding.

2. Disconnect the spark plug wires from the spark plugs. Be sure to make note of the proper firing order for easier installation.

3. Remove the valve cover.

4. Remove the timing belt covers.

5. Remove the timing belt and idler pulley.

6. Set the exhaust camshaft so that the knock pin is slightly above the cylinder head. This angle allows the No. 1 and No. 3 cylinder cam lobes of the intake camshaft to push their valve lifters evenly.

7. Remove the two bolts and the front bearing cap of the intake camshaft.

8. Secure the intake camshaft end gear to the sub-gear with a service bolt. The service bolt should match the following specifications:

- Thread diameter: 6.0mm
- Thread pitch: 1.0mm
- Bolt length: 16mm

9. Uniformly loosen each intake camshaft bearing cap bolt in several passes in the reverse order of the installation sequence.

✳✳ WARNING

The camshaft must be held level while it is being removed. If the camshaft is not kept level, the portion of the cylinder head receiving the thrust may crack or become damaged. In turn, this could cause the camshaft to bind or break. Before removing the intake camshaft, make sure the rotational force has been removed from the sub-gear; that is, the gear should be in a neutral or "unloaded" state.

10. Remove the four bearing caps and remove the intake camshaft.

➡️**If the camshaft cannot be removed straight and level, install and tighten the No. 3 bearing cap. Alternately loosen the bolts on the bearing cap a little at a time while pulling upwards on the camshaft gear. DO NOT attempt to pry or force the cam loose with tools.**

11. With the intake camshaft removed, turn the exhaust camshaft approximately 105°, so that the guide pin in the end is just past the 5 o'clock position. This angle allows the No. 1 and the No. 3 cylinder cam lobes of the exhaust camshaft to push their valve lifters evenly.

12. Loosen the camshaft bearing cap bolts a little at a time and in the reverse order of the installation sequence.

13. Remove the 2 bolts, No. 1 bearing cap and oil seal.

➡️**If the No. 1 bearing cap is not removable by hand, do not try to remove it by force but leave it as it is without bolts.**

Fig. 182 Always remove the No. 1 bearing cap first on the intake side

Fig. 183 Secure the intake camshaft with a service bolt at the end of the sub-gear

Fig. 184 Lift the camshaft out straight and level

Fig. 185 Set the knock pin on the exhaust camshaft slightly counterclockwise from the vertical axis of the cam

Fig. 186 Remove the No. 1 bearing cap off the exhaust side with the oil seal, if hard to remove, do not force it

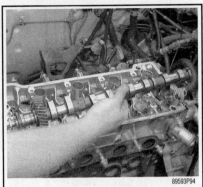

Fig. 187 Remember, remove the camshaft straight and level

Fig. 188 Install the 4 bearing caps on the intake side in their proper locations—7A-FE engine

Fig. 189 Install camshaft bearing tightening sequence—7A-FE engine

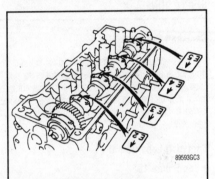

Fig. 190 Position the exhaust 5 bearing caps in there correct locations—7A-FE engine

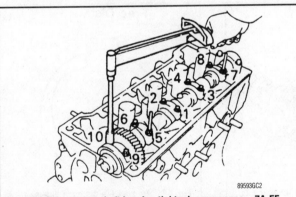

Fig. 191 Exhaust camshaft bearing tightening sequence—7A-FE engine

14. Remove the bearing caps and remove the exhaust camshaft. After removal, label each cap.

➡If the camshaft cannot be removed straight and level, install and tighten the No. 3 bearing cap. Alternately loosen the bolts on the bearing cap a little at a time while pulling upwards on the camshaft gear. DO NOT attempt to pry or force the cam loose with tools.

15. Remove the valve lifter shims and hydraulic lifters. Identify each lifter and shim as it is removed so it can be reinstalled in the same position. If the lifters are to be reused, store them upside down in a sealed container.

To install:

16. Install the valve lifters into their original positions and install the shims. Check valve clearance and replace the shims as necessary.

17. When reinstalling, remember that the camshafts must be handled carefully and kept straight and level to avoid damage.

18. Apply multi-purpose grease to the portion of the camshaft.

19. Place the exhaust camshaft on the cylinder head so that the cam lobes press evenly on the lifters for cylinders Nos. 1 and 3. This will place the guide pin on the camshaft slightly counter clockwise from the vertical axis (about 5 o'clock).

20. Apply a light coat of clean engine oil to the camshaft bearing cap bolts. Install the five bearing caps in position according to the number cast into the cap. The arrow should point towards the pulley end (front) of the motor.

21. Tighten the bearing cap bolts uniformly and in several passes in the proper sequence to 9 ft. lbs. (13 Nm).

22. Apply multi-purpose grease to a new exhaust camshaft oil seal.

23. Install the exhaust camshaft oil seal using a seal driver. Be very careful not to install the seal on a slant or allow it to tilt during installation.

24. Set the exhaust camshaft so that the guide pin is slightly above the cylinder head.

25. Apply multi-purpose grease to the portion of the intake camshaft.

26. Hold the intake camshaft next to the exhaust camshaft and engage the gears by matching the alignment marks on each gear.

➡DO NOT use the TDC timing marks for the timing belt.

27. Keeping the gears engaged, roll the intake camshaft down and into its bearing journals. This angle allows the No. 1 and the No. 3 cylinder cam lobes of the intake camshaft to push their valve lifters evenly.

28. Apply a light coat of clean engine oil to the camshaft bearing cap bolts and install the four bearing caps. Observe the numbers on each cap and make certain the arrows point to the pulley end (front) of the motor.

29. Uniformly tighten each of the eight bearing cap bolts in several passes in the proper sequence. Tighten each bolt to 9 ft. lbs. (13 Nm).

30. Remove any retaining pins or bolts in the intake camshaft gears.

31. Apply a light coat of clean engine oil to the camshaft bearing cap bolts and install the No. 1 bearing cap for the intake camshaft. Tighten the bearing cap bolts to 9 ft. lbs. (13 Nm).

➡️If the No. 1 bearing cap does not fit properly, push the camshaft gear backwards by prying apart the cylinder head and camshaft gear with a suitable tool.

32. Turn the exhaust camshaft clockwise, and set it with the guide pin facing upward. Check that the timing marks of the camshaft gears are aligned. The camshaft assembly installation marks should now be in the 12 o'clock position.

33. Secure the exhaust camshaft and install the timing belt pulley. Tighten the bolt to 43 ft. lbs. (59 Nm).

34. Check and adjust valve clearance.

35. Make sure that both the crankshaft and camshaft positions are set correctly, insuring that they are both set to TDC/compression for No. 1 cylinder.

36. Install the timing belt.

37. Install the timing belt covers and the valve cover.

38. Install the spark plug wires and connect the negative battery cable.

39. Start the engine, check for leaks, and check the ignition timing.

40. Road test the vehicle for proper operation.

INSPECTION

Camshaft Runout

Camshaft runout should be checked when the camshaft has been removed from the engine. An accurate dial indicator is needed for this procedure; engine specialists and most machine shops have this equipment. If you have access to a dial indicator, or can take your camshaft to someone who does, measure the camshaft bearing journal runout. If the runout exceeds the limit replace the camshaft.

Camshaft Lobe Height

▶ See Figure 192

Use a micrometer to check camshaft (lobe) height, making sure the anvil and the spindle of the micrometer are positioned directly on the heel and tip of the camshaft lobe as shown in the accompanying illustration.

Camshaft Journals

▶ See Figure 193

Using a micrometer, measure the journal diameter.
5S-FE:
• 1.0614–1.0620 inch (26.959–26.975mm)
7A-FE:
• Exhaust No. 1—0.9822–0.9829 inch (24.949–24.965mm)
• Others—0.9035–0.9041 inch (22.949–22.965mm)
If the diameters not as specified, check the oil clearance.

Camshaft Gear Spring

▶ See Figure 194

Using a vernier caliper, measure the free distance between the spring ends.
5S-FE:
• 0.886–0.902 inch (22.5–22.9mm)
7A-FE:
• 0.669–0.693 inch (17.0–17.6mm)
If the free distance is not within specifications, replace the gear spring.

Bearing Oil Clearance

▶ See Figures 195, 196, 197 and 198

1. Clean the bearing caps and camshaft journals.
2. Place the camshafts on the cylinder head.
Measure the bearing oil clearance by placing a piece of Plastigage® on each bearing journal. Replace the bearing caps and tighten the bolts to the proper torque.

➡️Do not turn the camshaft.

3. Remove the caps and measure each piece of Plastigage® at its widest point. If the clearance is greater than the values on the Engine Mechanical Specifications chart, replace the camshaft. If necessary, replace the bearing caps and cylinder head as a set.

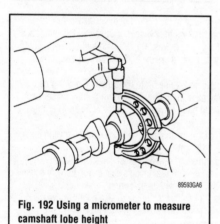

Fig. 192 Using a micrometer to measure camshaft lobe height

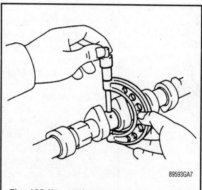

Fig. 193 Use a micrometer to measure the camshaft journals

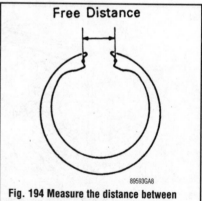
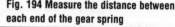

Fig. 194 Measure the distance between each end of the gear spring

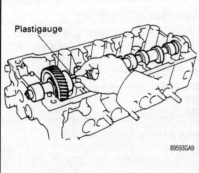

Fig. 195 Lay a strip of Plastigage® across each camshaft journal, then . . . .

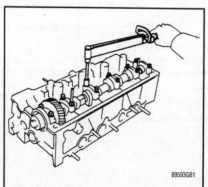

Fig. 196 . . . install the bearing cap and tighten . . .

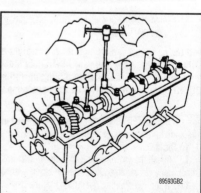

Fig. 197 . . . next remove the caps, then . . .

4. Check the camshaft bearings for flaking and scoring. If the bearings show any signs of damage, replace the bearing caps and the cylinder head as a set.

5. Completely remove the Plastigage®.

Checking Camshaft End-Play

After the camshaft has been installed, end-play should be checked. The camshaft sprocket should **not** be installed on the cam. Use a dial gauge to check the end-play, by moving the camshaft forward and backward in the cylinder head. End-play specifications should be as noted in the Engine Mechanical Specifications chart.

Lifters and Bores

▶ See Figures 199 and 200

Using a caliper gauge, measure the lifter bore diameter of the cylinder head.

5S-FE:
- 1.2205–1.2213 inch (31.000–31.018mm)

7A-FE:
- 1.2205–1.2215 inch (31.000–31.025mm)

Using a micrometer, measure the lifter diameter. Lifter diameter for both engines is 1.2191–1.2195 inch (30.966–30.976mm).

Rear Main Seal

REMOVAL & INSTALLATION

Seal Retainer On Engine

➡ **Use the correct tools. Homemade substitutes may install the seal crooked, resulting in oil leaks and premature seal failure.**

1. Remove the transaxle.
2. Remove the clutch cover assembly and flywheel (manual trans.) or the flexplate (auto. trans.).

3. Use a small sharp knife to cut off the lip of the oil seal. Take great care not to score any metal with the knife.

4. Use a small prytool to pry the old seal from the retaining plate. Be careful not to damage the plate. Protect the tip of the tool with tape and pad the fulcrum point with cloth.

5. Inspect the crankshaft and seal lip contact surfaces for any sign of damage.

To install:

6. Apply a light coat of multi-purpose grease to the lip of a new oil seal. Loosely fit the seal into place by hand, making sure it is not crooked.

7. Use a seal driver of the correct size to install the seal. Tap it into place until the surface of the seal is flush with the edge of the housing.

Seal Retainer Removed

1. Support the retainer on two thin pieces of wood.
2. Use a small prybar to pry the old seal from the retaining plate. Be careful not to damage the plate. Protect the tip of the tool with tape and pad the fulcrum point with cloth.

To install:

3. Apply a light coat of multi-purpose grease to the lip of a new oil seal. Loosely fit the seal into place by hand, making sure it is not crooked.

4. Use a seal driver such as (SST 09223–60010) of the correct size to install the seal. Tap it into place until the surface of the seal is flush with the edge of the housing.

Flywheel/Flexplate

REMOVAL & INSTALLATION

▶ See Figures 201, 202 and 203

1. Remove the transaxle assembly from the vehicle.
2. On manual transaxles, remove the 8 retaining bolts for the flywheel.
3. On automatics, remove the 8 bolts, front plate, drive plate and rear spacer.

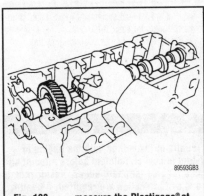

Fig. 198 . . . measure the Plastigage® at its widest point

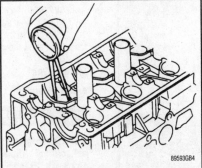

Fig. 199 Using a caliper gauge, measure the lifter bore diameter of the cylinder head

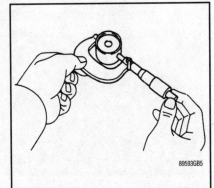

Fig. 200 A micrometer measures the lifter diameter

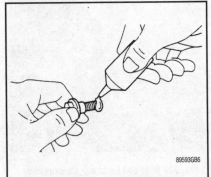

Fig. 201 Apply adhesive to the first 2-3 threads of the bolt

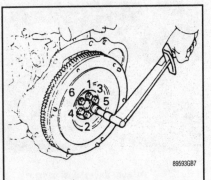

Fig. 202 Tightening sequence of the flywheel on manual transaxles

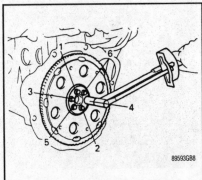

Fig. 203 Driveplate tightening sequence on automatics

To install:

4. On manual transaxles, apply adhesive to the first 2–3 threads of the bolt end. Three bond 1324 or equivalent is recommended.

a. Install the flywheel on the crankshaft.

b. Install and uniformly tighten the 8 bolts in several passes in sequence as shown in the illustration to 65 ft. lbs. (88 Nm).

5. On automatics, apply adhesive to the first 2–3 threads of the bolt end. Three bond 1324 or equivalent is recommended.

a. Install the driveplate on the crankshaft.

b. Install and uniformly tighten the 8 bolts in several passes in sequence as shown in the illustration to 47 ft. lbs. (64 Nm).

EXHAUST SYSTEM

Inspection

▶ See Figures 204, 205 and 206

➡Safety glasses should be worn at all times when working on or near the exhaust system. Older exhaust systems will almost always be covered with loose rust particles which will shower you when disturbed. These particles are more than a nuisance and could injure your eye.

✳✳ CAUTION

DO NOT perform exhaust repairs or inspection with the engine or exhaust hot. Allow the system to cool completely before attempting any work. Exhaust systems are noted for sharp edges, flaking metal and rusted bolts. Gloves and eye protection are required. A healthy supply of penetrating oil and rags is highly recommended.

Your vehicle must be raised and supported safely to inspect the exhaust system properly. By placing 4 safety stands under the vehicle for support should provide enough room for you to slide under the vehicle and inspect the system completely. Start the inspection at the exhaust manifold or turbocharger pipe where the header pipe is attached and work your way to the back of the vehicle. On dual exhaust systems, remember to inspect both sides of the vehicle. Check the complete exhaust system for open seams, holes loose connections, or other deterioration which could permit exhaust fumes to seep into the passenger compartment. Inspect all mounting brackets and hangers for deterioration, some models may have rubber O-rings that can be over stretched and non-supportive. These components will need to be replaced if found. It has always been a practice to use a pointed tool to poke up into the exhaust system where the deterioration spots are to see whether or not they crumble. Some models may have heat shield covering certain parts of the exhaust system, it will be necessary to remove these shields to have the exhaust visible for inspection also.

REPLACEMENT

▶ See Figure 207

There are basically two types of exhaust systems. One is the flange type where the component ends are attached with bolts and a gasket in-between. The other exhaust system is the slip joint type. These components slip into one another using clamps to retain them together.

✳✳ CAUTION

Allow the exhaust system to cool sufficiently before spraying a solvent exhaust fasteners. Some solvents are highly flammable and could ignite when sprayed on hot exhaust components.

Before removing any component of the exhaust system, ALWAYS squirt a liquid rust dissolving agent onto the fasteners for ease of removal. A lot of knuckle skin will be saved by following this rule. It may even be wise to spray the fasteners and allow them to sit overnight.

Flange Type

▶ See Figure 208

✳✳ CAUTION

Do NOT perform exhaust repairs or inspection with the engine or exhaust hot. Allow the system to cool completely before attempting any work. Exhaust systems are noted for sharp edges, flaking metal and rusted bolts. Gloves and eye protection are required. A healthy supply of penetrating oil and rags is highly recommended. Never spray liquid rust dissolving agent onto a hot exhaust component.

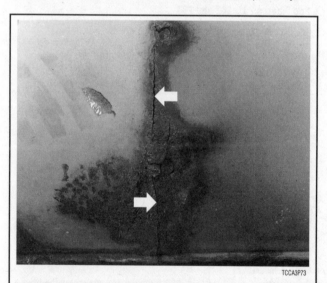

TCCA3P73

Fig. 204 Cracks in the muffler are a guaranteed leak

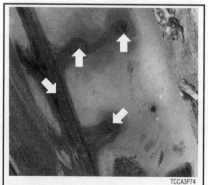

TCCA3P74

Fig. 205 Check the muffler for rotted spot welds and seams

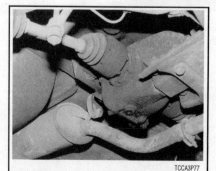

TCCA3P77

Fig. 206 Make sure the exhaust components are not contacting the body or suspension

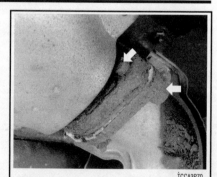

TCCA3P70

Fig. 207 Nuts and bolts will be extremely difficult to remove when deteriorated with rust

Fig. 208 Example of a flange type exhaust system joint

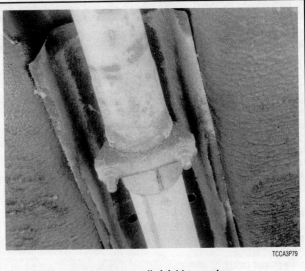

Fig. 209 Example of a common slip joint type system

Before removing any component on a flange type system, ALWAYS squirt a liquid rust dissolving agent onto the fasteners for ease of removal. Start by unbolting the exhaust piece at both ends (if required). When unbolting the headpipe from the manifold, make sure that the bolts are free before trying to remove them. if you snap a stud in the exhaust manifold, the stud will have to be removed with a bolt extractor, which often means removal of the manifold itself. Next, disconnect the component from the mounting; slight twisting and turning may be required to remove the component completely from the vehicle. You may need to tap on the component with a rubber mallet to loosen the component. If all else fails, use a hacksaw to separate the parts. An oxy-acetylene cutting torch may be faster but the sparks are DANGEROUS near the fuel tank, and at the very least, accidents could happen, resulting in damage to the

Slip Joint Type

♦ See Figures 209, 210 and 211

Before removing any component on the slip joint type exhaust system, ALWAYS squirt a liquid rust dissolving agent onto the fasteners for ease of

removal. Start by unbolting the exhaust piece at both ends (if required). When unbolting the headpipe from the manifold, make sure that the bolts are free before trying to remove them. if you snap a stud in the exhaust manifold, the stud will have to be removed with a bolt extractor, which often means removal of the manifold itself. Next, remove the mounting U-bolts from around the exhaust pipe you are extracting from the vehicle. Don't be surprised if the U-bolts break while removing the nuts. Loosen the exhaust pipe from any mounting brackets retaining it to the floor pan and separate the components.

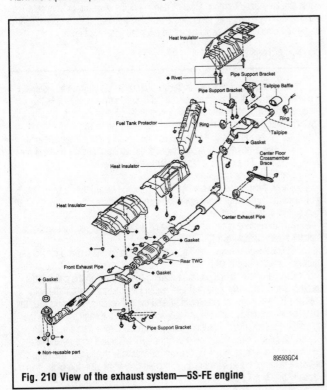

Fig. 210 View of the exhaust system—5S-FE engine

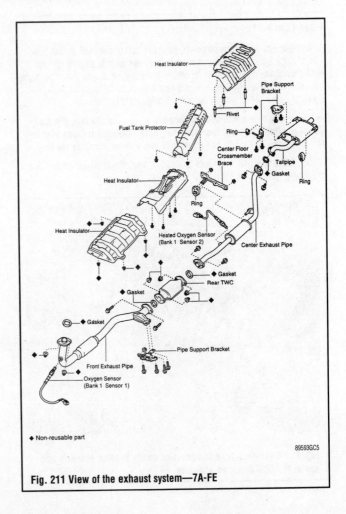

Fig. 211 View of the exhaust system—7A-FE

ENGINE RECONDITIONING

Determining Engine Condition

Anything that generates heat and/or friction will eventually burn or wear out (ie. a light bulb generates heat, therefore its life span is limited). With this in mind, a running engine generates tremendous amounts of both; friction is encountered by the moving and rotating parts inside the engine and heat is created by friction and combustion of the fuel. However, the engine has systems designed to help reduce the effects of heat and friction and provide added longevity. The oiling system reduces the amount of friction encountered by the moving parts inside the engine, while the cooling system reduces heat created by friction and combustion. If either system is not maintained, a break-down will be inevitable. Therefore, you can see how regular maintenance can affect the service life of your vehicle. If you do not drain, flush and refill your cooling system at the proper intervals, deposits will begin to accumulate in the radiator, thereby reducing the amount of heat it can extract from the coolant. The same applies to your oil and filter; if it is not changed often enough it becomes laden with contaminates and is unable to properly lubricate the engine. This increases friction and wear.

There are a number of methods for evaluating the condition of your engine. A compression test can reveal the condition of your pistons, piston rings, cylinder bores, head gasket(s), valves and valve seats. An oil pressure test can warn you of possible engine bearing, or oil pump failures. Excessive oil consumption, evidence of oil in the engine air intake area and/or bluish smoke from the tail pipe may indicate worn piston rings, worn valve guides and/or valve seals. As a general rule, an engine that uses no more than one quart of oil every 1000 miles is in good condition. Engines that use one quart of oil or more in less than 1000 miles should first be checked for oil leaks. If any oil leaks are present, have them fixed before determining how much oil is consumed by the engine, especially if blue smoke is not visible at the tail pipe.

COMPRESSION TEST

▶ **See Figure 212**

A noticeable lack of engine power, excessive oil consumption and/or poor fuel mileage measured over an extended period are all indicators of internal engine wear. Worn piston rings, scored or worn cylinder bores, blown head gaskets, sticking or burnt valves, and worn valve seats are all possible culprits. A check of each cylinder's compression will help locate the problem.

➡A screw-in type compression gauge is more accurate than the type you simply hold against the spark plug hole. Although it takes slightly longer to use, it's worth the effort to obtain a more accurate reading.

1. Make sure that the proper amount and viscosity of engine oil is in the crankcase, then ensure the battery is fully charged.

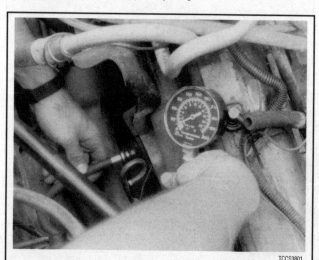

TCCS3801

Fig. 212 A screw-in type compression gauge is more accurate and easier to use without an assistant

2. Warm-up the engine to normal operating temperature, then shut the engine **OFF**.
3. Disable the ignition system.
4. Label and disconnect all of the spark plug wires from the plugs.
5. Thoroughly clean the cylinder head area around the spark plug ports, then remove the spark plugs.
6. Set the throttle plate to the fully open (wide-open throttle) position. You can block the accelerator linkage open for this, or you can have an assistant fully depress the accelerator pedal.
7. Install a screw-in type compression gauge into the No. 1 spark plug hole until the fitting is snug.

✷✷ WARNING

Be careful not to crossthread the spark plug hole.

8. According to the tool manufacturer's instructions, connect a remote starting switch to the starting circuit.
9. With the ignition switch in the **OFF** position, use the remote starting switch to crank the engine through at least five compression strokes (approximately 5 seconds of cranking) and record the highest reading on the gauge.
10. Repeat the test on each cylinder, cranking the engine approximately the same number of compression strokes and/or time as the first.
11. Compare the highest readings from each cylinder to that of the others. The indicated compression pressures are considered within specifications if the lowest reading cylinder is within 75 percent of the pressure recorded for the highest reading cylinder. For example, if your highest reading cylinder pressure was 150 psi (1034 kPa), then 75 percent of that would be 113 psi (779 kPa). So the lowest reading cylinder should be no less than 113 psi (779 kPa).
12. If a cylinder exhibits an unusually low compression reading, pour a tablespoon of clean engine oil into the cylinder through the spark plug hole and repeat the compression test. If the compression rises after adding oil, it means that the cylinder's piston rings and/or cylinder bore are damaged or worn. If the pressure remains low, the valves may not be seating properly (a valve job is needed), or the head gasket may be blown near that cylinder. If compression in any two adjacent cylinders is low, and if the addition of oil doesn't help raise compression, there is leakage past the head gasket. Oil and coolant in the combustion chamber, combined with blue or constant white smoke from the tail pipe, are symptoms of this problem. However, don't be alarmed by the normal white smoke emitted from the tail pipe during engine warm-up or from cold weather driving. There may be evidence of water droplets on the engine dipstick and/or oil droplets in the cooling system if a head gasket is blown.

OIL PRESSURE TEST

Check for proper oil pressure at the sending unit passage with an externally mounted mechanical oil pressure gauge (as opposed to relying on a factory installed dash-mounted gauge). A tachometer may also be needed, as some specifications may require running the engine at a specific rpm.

1. With the engine cold, locate and remove the oil pressure sending unit.
2. Following the manufacturer's instructions, connect a mechanical oil pressure gauge and, if necessary, a tachometer to the engine.
3. Start the engine and allow it to idle.
4. Check the oil pressure reading when cold and record the number. You may need to run the engine at a specified rpm, so check the specifications chart located earlier in this section.
5. Run the engine until normal operating temperature is reached (upper radiator hose will feel warm).
6. Check the oil pressure reading again with the engine hot and record the number. Turn the engine **OFF**.
7. Compare your hot oil pressure reading to that given in the chart. If the reading is low, check the cold pressure reading against the chart. If the cold pressure is well above the specification, and the hot reading was lower than the specification, you may have the wrong viscosity oil in the engine. Change the oil, making sure to use the proper grade and quantity, then repeat the test.

Low oil pressure readings could be attributed to internal component wear, pump related problems, a low oil level, or oil viscosity that is too low. High oil pressure readings could be caused by an overfilled crankcase, too high of an oil viscosity or a faulty pressure relief valve.

Buy or Rebuild?

Now that you have determined that your engine is worn out, you must make some decisions. The question of whether or not an engine is worth rebuilding is largely a subjective matter and one of personal worth. Is the engine a popular one, or is it an obsolete model? Are parts available? Will it get acceptable gas mileage once it is rebuilt? Is the car it's being put into worth keeping? Would it be less expensive to buy a new engine, have your engine rebuilt by a pro, rebuild it yourself or buy a used engine from a salvage yard? Or would it be simpler and less expensive to buy another car? If you have considered all these matters and more, and have still decided to rebuild the engine, then it is time to decide how you will rebuild it.

➡ **The editors at Chilton feel that most engine machining should be performed by a professional machine shop. Don't think of it as wasting money, rather, as an assurance that the job has been done right the first time. There are many expensive and specialized tools required to perform such tasks as boring and honing an engine block or having a valve job done on a cylinder head. Even inspecting the parts requires expensive micrometers and gauges to properly measure wear and clearances. Also, a machine shop can deliver to you clean, and ready to assemble parts, saving you time and aggravation. Your maximum savings will come from performing the removal, disassembly, assembly and installation of the engine and purchasing or renting only the tools required to perform the above tasks. Depending on the particular circumstances, you may save 40 to 60 percent of the cost doing these yourself.**

A complete rebuild or overhaul of an engine involves replacing all of the moving parts (pistons, rods, crankshaft, camshaft, etc.) with new ones and machining the non-moving wearing surfaces of the block and heads. Unfortunately, this may not be cost effective. For instance, your crankshaft may have been damaged or worn, but it can be machined undersize for a minimal fee.

So, as you can see, you can replace everything inside the engine, but, it is wiser to replace only those parts which are really needed, and, if possible, repair the more expensive ones. Later in this section, we will break the engine down into its two main components: the cylinder head and the engine block. We will discuss each component, and the recommended parts to replace during a rebuild on each.

Engine Overhaul Tips

Most engine overhaul procedures are fairly standard. In addition to specific parts replacement procedures and specifications for your individual engine, this section is also a guide to acceptable rebuilding procedures. Examples of standard rebuilding practice are given and should be used along with specific details concerning your particular engine.

Competent and accurate machine shop services will ensure maximum performance, reliability and engine life. In most instances it is more profitable for the do-it-yourself mechanic to remove, clean and inspect the component, buy the necessary parts and deliver these to a shop for actual machine work.

Much of the assembly work (crankshaft, bearings, piston rods, and other components) is well within the scope of the do-it-yourself mechanic's tools and abilities. You will have to decide for yourself the depth of involvement you desire in an engine repair or rebuild.

TOOLS

The tools required for an engine overhaul or parts replacement will depend on the depth of your involvement. With a few exceptions, they will be the tools found in a mechanic's tool kit (see More in-depth work will require some or all of the following:

- A dial indicator (reading in thousandths) mounted on a universal base
- Micrometers and telescope gauges
- Jaw and screw-type pullers
- Scraper
- Valve spring compressor
- Ring groove cleaner
- Piston ring expander and compressor
- Ridge reamer
- Cylinder hone or glaze breaker
- Plastigage®
- Engine stand

The use of most of these tools is illustrated in this section. Many can be rented for a one-time use from a local parts jobber or tool supply house specializing in automotive work.

Occasionally, the use of special tools is called for. See the information on Special Tools and the Safety Notice in the front of this book before substituting another tool.

OVERHAUL TIPS

Aluminum has become extremely popular for use in engines, due to its low weight. Observe the following precautions when handling aluminum parts:

- Never hot tank aluminum parts (the caustic hot tank solution will eat the aluminum.
- Remove all aluminum parts (identification tag, etc.) from engine parts prior to the tanking.
- Always coat threads lightly with engine oil or anti-seize compounds before installation, to prevent seizure.
- Never overtighten bolts or spark plugs especially in aluminum threads.

When assembling the engine, any parts that will be exposed to frictional contact must be prelubed to provide lubrication at initial start-up. Any product specifically formulated for this purpose can be used, but engine oil is not recommended as a prelube in most cases.

When semi-permanent (locked, but removable) installation of bolts or nuts is desired, threads should be cleaned and coated with Loctite® or another similar, commercial non-hardening sealant.

CLEANING

♦ **See Figures 213, 214, 215 and 216**

Before the engine and its components are inspected, they must be thoroughly cleaned. You will need to remove any engine varnish, oil sludge and/or carbon deposits from all of the components to insure an accurate inspection. A crack in the engine block or cylinder head can easily become overlooked if hidden by a layer of sludge or carbon.

Most of the cleaning process can be carried out with common hand tools

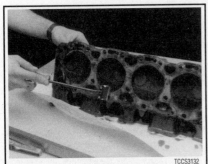

Fig. 213 Use a gasket scraper to remove the old gasket material from the mating surfaces

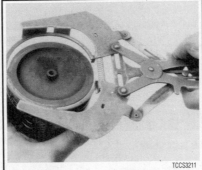

Fig. 214 Use a ring expander tool to remove the piston rings

Fig. 215 Clean the piston ring grooves using a ring groove cleaner tool, or . . .

Fig. 216 . . . use a piece of an old ring to clean the grooves. Be careful, the ring can be quite sharp

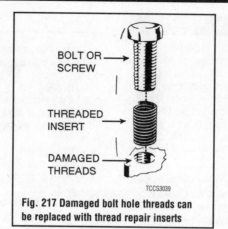

Fig. 217 Damaged bolt hole threads can be replaced with thread repair inserts

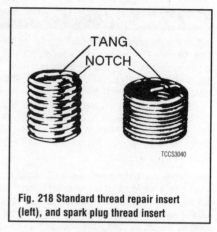

Fig. 218 Standard thread repair insert (left), and spark plug thread insert

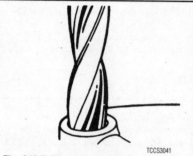

Fig. 219 Drill out the damaged threads with the specified size bit. Be sure to drill completely through the hole or to the bottom of a blind hole

Fig. 220 Using the kit, tap the hole in order to receive the thread insert. Keep the tap well oiled and back it out frequently to avoid clogging the threads

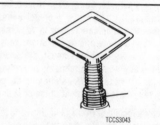

Fig. 221 Screw the insert onto the installer tool until the tang engages the slot. Thread the insert into the hole until it is ¼–½ turn below the top surface, then remove the tool and break off the tang using a punch

and readily available solvents or solutions. Carbon deposits can be chipped away using a hammer and a hard wooden chisel. Old gasket material and varnish or sludge can usually be removed using a scraper and/or cleaning solvent. Extremely stubborn deposits may require the use of a power drill with a wire brush. If using a wire brush, use extreme care around any critical machined surfaces (such as the gasket surfaces, bearing saddles, cylinder bores, etc.). Use of a wire brush is NOT RECOMMENDED on any aluminum components. Always follow any safety recommendations given by the manufacturer of the tool and/or solvent. You should always wear eye protection during any cleaning process involving scraping, chipping or spraying of solvents.

An alternative to the mess and hassle of cleaning the parts yourself is to drop them off at a local garage or machine shop. They will, more than likely, have the necessary equipment to properly clean all of the parts for a nominal fee.

✳✳ CAUTION

Always wear eye protection during any cleaning process involving scraping, chipping or spraying of solvents.

Remove any oil galley plugs, freeze plugs and/or pressed-in bearings and carefully wash and degrease all of the engine components including the fasteners and bolts. Small parts such as the valves, springs, etc., should be placed in a metal basket and allowed to soak. Use pipe cleaner type brushes, and clean all passageways in the components. Use a ring expander and remove the rings from the pistons. Clean the piston ring grooves with a special tool or a piece of broken ring. Scrape the carbon off of the top of the piston. You should never use a wire brush on the pistons. After preparing all of the piston assemblies in this manner, wash and degrease them again.

✳✳ WARNING

Use extreme care when cleaning around the cylinder head valve seats. A mistake or slip may cost you a new seat.

When cleaning the cylinder head, remove carbon from the combustion chamber with the valves installed. This will avoid damaging the valve seats.

REPAIRING DAMAGED THREADS

⬥ See Figures 217, 218, 219, 220 and 221

Several methods of repairing damaged threads are available. Heli-Coil® (shown here), Keenserts® and Microdot® are among the most widely used. All involve basically the same principle—drilling out stripped threads, tapping the hole and installing a prewound insert—making welding, plugging and oversize fasteners unnecessary.

Two types of thread repair inserts are usually supplied: a standard type for most inch coarse, inch fine, metric course and metric fine thread sizes and a spark lug type to fit most spark plug port sizes. Consult the individual tool manufacturer's catalog to determine exact applications. Typical thread repair kits will contain a selection of prewound threaded inserts, a tap (corresponding to the outside diameter threads of the insert) and an installation tool. Spark plug inserts usually differ because they require a tap equipped with pilot threads and a combined reamer/tap section. Most manufacturers also supply blister-packed thread repair inserts separately in addition to a master kit containing a variety of taps and inserts plus installation tools.

Before attempting to repair a threaded hole, remove any snapped, broken or damaged bolts or studs. Penetrating oil can be used to free frozen threads. The offending item can usually be removed with locking pliers or using a screw/stud extractor. After the hole is clear, the thread can be repaired, as shown in the series of accompanying illustrations and in the kit manufacturer's instructions.

Engine Preparation

To properly rebuild an engine, you must first remove it from the vehicle, then disassemble and diagnose it. Ideally you should place your engine on an engine stand. This affords you the best access to the engine components. Follow the manufacturer's directions for using the stand with your particular engine. Remove the flywheel or flexplate before installing the engine to the stand.

Now that you have the engine on a stand, and assuming that you have drained the oil and coolant from the engine, it's time to strip it of all but the necessary components. Before you start disassembling the engine, you may want to take a moment to draw some pictures, or fabricate some labels or containers to mark the locations of various components and the bolts and/or studs which fasten them. Modern day engines use a lot of little brackets and clips which hold wiring harnesses and such, and these holders are often mounted on studs and/or bolts that can be easily mixed up. The manufacturer spent a lot of time and money designing your vehicle, and they wouldn't have wasted any of it by haphazardly placing brackets, clips or fasteners on the vehicle. If it's present when you disassemble it, put it back when you assemble, you will regret not remembering that little bracket which holds a wire harness out of the path of a rotating part.

You should begin by unbolting any accessories still attached to the engine, such as the water pump, power steering pump, alternator, etc. Then, unfasten any manifolds (intake or exhaust) which were not removed during the engine removal procedure. Finally, remove any covers remaining on the engine such as the rocker arm, front or timing cover and oil pan. Some front covers may require the vibration damper and/or crank pulley to be removed beforehand. The idea is to reduce the engine to the bare necessities (cylinder head(s), valve train, engine block, crankshaft, pistons and connecting rods), plus any other `in block' components such as oil pumps, balance shafts and auxiliary shafts.

Finally, remove the cylinder head(s) from the engine block and carefully place on a bench. Disassembly instructions for each component follow later in this section.

Cylinder Head

There are two basic types of cylinder heads used on today's automobiles: the Overhead Valve (OHV) and the Overhead Camshaft (OHC). The latter can also be broken down into two subgroups: the Single Overhead Camshaft (SOHC) and the Dual Overhead Camshaft (DOHC). Generally, if there is only a single camshaft on a head, it is just referred to as an OHC head. Also, an engine with an OHV cylinder head is also known as a pushrod engine.

Most cylinder heads these days are made of an aluminum alloy due to its light weight, durability and heat transfer qualities. However, cast iron was the material of choice in the past, and is still used on many vehicles today. Whether made from aluminum or iron, all cylinder heads have valves and seats. Some use two valves per cylinder, while the more hi-tech engines will utilize a multi-valve configuration using 3, 4 and even 5 valves per cylinder. When the valve contacts the seat, it does so on precision machined surfaces, which seals the combustion chamber. All cylinder heads have a valve guide for each valve. The guide centers the valve to the seat and allows it to move up and down within it. The clearance between the valve and guide can be critical. Too much clearance and the engine may consume oil, lose vacuum and/or damage the seat. Too little, and the valve can stick in the guide causing the engine to run poorly if at all, and possibly causing severe damage. The last component all cylinder heads have are valve springs. The spring holds the valve against its seat. It also returns the valve to this position when the valve has been opened by the valve train or camshaft. The spring is fastened to the valve by a retainer and valve locks (sometimes called keepers). Aluminum heads will also have a valve spring shim to keep the spring from wearing away the aluminum.

An ideal method of rebuilding the cylinder head would involve replacing all of the valves, guides, seats, springs, etc. with new ones. However, depending on how the engine was maintained, often this is not necessary. A major cause of valve, guide and seat wear is an improperly tuned engine. An engine that is running too rich, will often wash the lubricating oil out of the guide with gasoline, causing it to wear rapidly. Conversely, an engine which is running too lean will place higher combustion temperatures on the valves and seats allowing them to wear or even burn. Springs fall victim to the driving habits of the individual. A driver who often runs the engine rpm to the redline will wear out or break the springs faster then one that stays well below it. Unfortunately, mileage takes it toll on all of the parts. Generally, the valves, guides, springs and seats in a cylinder head can be machined and re-used, saving you money. However, if a valve is burnt, it may be wise to replace all of the valves, since they were all operating in the same environment. The same goes for any other component on the cylinder head. Think of it as an insurance policy against future problems related to that component.

Unfortunately, the only way to find out which components need replacing, is

to disassemble and carefully check each piece. After the cylinder head(s) are disassembled, thoroughly clean all of the components.

DISASSEMBLY

◗ See Figures 222 and 223

Whether it is a single or dual overhead camshaft cylinder head, the disassembly procedure is relatively unchanged. One aspect to pay attention to is careful labeling of the parts on the dual camshaft cylinder head. There will be an intake camshaft and followers as well as an exhaust camshaft and followers and they must be labeled as such. In some cases, the components are identical and could easily be installed incorrectly. DO NOT MIX THEM UP! Determining which is which is very simple; the intake camshaft and components are on the same side of the head as was the intake manifold. Conversely, the exhaust camshaft and components are on the same side of the head as was the exhaust manifold.

Cup Type Camshaft Followers

◗ See Figures 224, 225 and 226

Most cylinder heads with cup type camshaft followers will have the valve spring, retainer and locks recessed within the follower's bore. You will need a C-clamp style valve spring compressor tool, an OHC spring removal tool (or equivalent) and a small magnet to disassemble the head.

1. If not already removed, remove the camshaft(s) and/or followers. Mark their positions for assembly.
2. Position the cylinder head to allow use of a C-clamp style valve spring compressor tool.

➥It is preferred to position the cylinder head gasket surface facing you with the valve springs facing the opposite direction and the head laying horizontal.

3. With the OHC spring removal adapter tool positioned inside of the follower bore, compress the valve spring using the C-clamp style valve spring compressor.

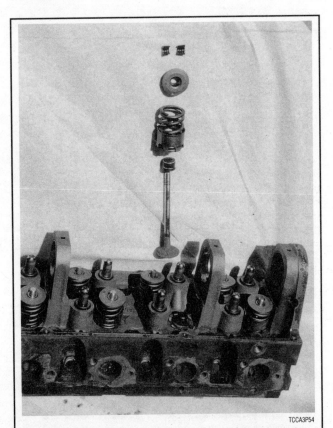

TCCA3P54

Fig. 222 Exploded view of a valve, seal, spring, retainer and locks from an OHC cylinder head

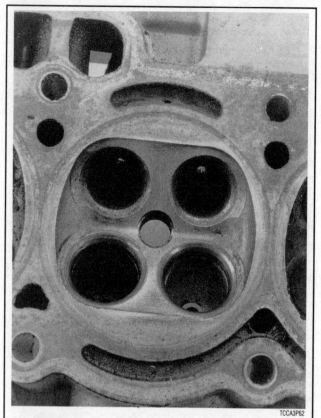

Fig. 223 Example of a multi-valve cylinder head. Note how it has 2 intake and 2 exhaust valve ports

Fig. 224 C-clamp type spring compressor and an OHC spring removal tool (center) for cup type followers

Fig. 225 Most cup type follower cylinder heads retain the camshaft using bolt-on bearing caps

Fig. 226 Position the OHC spring tool in the follower bore, then compress the spring with a C-clamp type tool

4. Remove the valve locks. A small magnetic tool or screwdriver will aid in removal.
5. Release the compressor tool and remove the spring assembly.
6. Withdraw the valve from the cylinder head.
7. If equipped, remove the valve seal.

➡Special valve seal removal tools are available. Regular or needlenose type pliers, if used with care, will work just as well. If using ordinary pliers, be sure not to damage the follower bore. The follower and its bore are machined to close tolerances and any damage to the bore will effect this relationship.

8. If equipped, remove the valve spring shim. A small magnetic tool or screwdriver will aid in removal.
9. Repeat Steps 3 through 8 until all of the valves have been removed.

Rocker Arm Type Camshaft Followers

◆ **See Figures 227 thru 235**

Most cylinder heads with rocker arm-type camshaft followers are easily disassembled using a standard valve spring compressor. However, certain models may not have enough open space around the spring for the standard tool and may require you to use a C-clamp style compressor tool instead.

1. If not already removed, remove the rocker arms and/or shafts and the camshaft. If applicable, also remove the hydraulic lash adjusters. Mark their positions for assembly.
2. Position the cylinder head to allow access to the valve spring.
3. Use a valve spring compressor tool to relieve the spring tension from the retainer.

➡Due to engine varnish, the retainer may stick to the valve locks. A gentle tap with a hammer may help to break it loose.

4. Remove the valve locks from the valve tip and/or retainer. A small magnet may help in removing the small locks.

Fig. 227 Example of the shaft mounted rocker arms on some OHC heads

Fig. 228 Another example of the rocker arm type OHC head. This model uses a follower under the camshaft

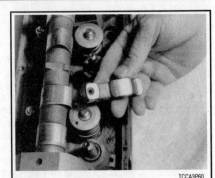

Fig. 229 Before the camshaft can be removed, all of the followers must first be removed . . .

Fig. 230 . . . then the camshaft can be removed by sliding it out (shown), or unbolting a bearing cap (not shown)

Fig. 231 Compress the valve spring . . .

Fig. 232 . . . then remove the valve locks from the valve stem and spring retainer

Fig. 233 Remove the valve spring and retainer from the cylinder head

Fig. 234 Remove the valve seal from the guide. Some gentle prying or pliers may help to remove stubborn ones

Fig. 235 All aluminum and some cast iron heads will have these valve spring shims. Remove all of them as well

5. Lift the valve spring, tool and all, off of the valve stem.

6. If equipped, remove the valve seal. If the seal is difficult to remove with the valve in place, try removing the valve first, then the seal. Follow the steps below for valve removal.

7. Position the head to allow access for withdrawing the valve.

➡**Cylinder heads that have seen a lot of miles and/or abuse may have mushroomed the valve lock grove and/or tip, causing difficulty in removal of the valve. If this has happened, use a metal file to carefully remove the high spots around the lock grooves and/or tip. Only file it enough to allow removal.**

8. Remove the valve from the cylinder head.

9. If equipped, remove the valve spring shim. A small magnetic tool or screwdriver will aid in removal.

10. Repeat Steps 3 though 9 until all of the valves have been removed.

INSPECTION

Now that all of the cylinder head components are clean, it's time to inspect them for wear and/or damage. To accurately inspect them, you will need some specialized tools:

- A 0–1 in. micrometer for the valves
- A dial indicator or inside diameter gauge for the valve guides
- A spring pressure test gauge

If you do not have access to the proper tools, you may want to bring the components to a shop that does.

Valves

▶ See Figures 236 and 237

The first thing to inspect are the valve heads. Look closely at the head, margin and face for any cracks, excessive wear or burning. The margin is the best place to look for burning. It should have a squared edge with an even width all around the diameter. When a valve burns, the margin will look melted and the edges rounded. Also inspect the valve head for any signs of tulipping. This will show as a lifting of the edges or dishing in the center of the head and will usually not occur to all of the valves. All of the heads should look the same, any that seem dished more than others are probably bad. Next, inspect the valve lock grooves and valve tips. Check for any burrs around the lock grooves, especially if you had to file them to remove the valve. Valve tips should appear flat, although slight rounding with high mileage engines is normal. Slightly worn valve tips will need to be machined flat. Last, measure the valve stem diameter with the micrometer. Measure the area that rides within the guide, especially towards the tip where most of the wear occurs. Take several measurements along its length and compare them to each other. Wear should be even along the length with little to no taper. If no minimum diameter is given in the specifications, then the stem should not read more than 0.001 in. (0.025mm) below the specification. Any valves that fail these inspections should be replaced.

Springs, Retainers and Valve Locks

▶ See Figures 238 and 239

The first thing to check is the most obvious, broken springs. Next check the free length and squareness of each spring. If applicable, insure to distinguish between intake and exhaust springs. Use a ruler and/or carpenters square to measure the length. A carpenters square should be used to check the springs for squareness. If a spring pressure test gauge is available, check each springs rating and compare to the specifications chart. Check the readings against the specifications given. Any springs that fail these inspections should be replaced.

The spring retainers rarely need replacing, however they should still be checked as a precaution. Inspect the spring mating surface and the valve lock retention area for any signs of excessive wear. Also check for any signs of cracking. Replace any retainers that are questionable.

Valve locks should be inspected for excessive wear on the outside contact area as well as on the inner notched surface. Any locks which appear worn or broken and its respective valve should be replaced.

Cylinder Head

There are several things to check on the cylinder head: valve guides, seats, cylinder head surface flatness, cracks and physical damage.

VALVE GUIDES

▶ See Figure 240

Now that you know the valves are good, you can use them to check the guides, although a new valve, if available, is preferred. Before you measure anything, look at the guides carefully and inspect them for any cracks, chips or breakage. Also if the guide is a removable style (as in most aluminum heads), check them for any looseness or evidence of movement. All of the guides should appear to be at the same height from the spring seat. If any seem lower (or higher) from another, the guide has moved. Mount a dial indicator onto the spring side of the cylinder head. Lightly oil the valve stem and insert it into the cylinder head. Position the dial indicator against the valve stem near the tip and zero the gauge. Grasp the valve stem and wiggle towards and away from the dial indicator and observe the readings. Mount the dial indicator 90 degrees from

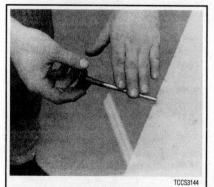

Fig. 236 Valve stems may be rolled on a flat surface to check for bends

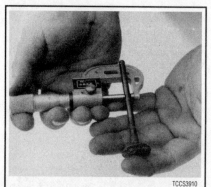

Fig. 237 Use a micrometer to check the valve stem diameter

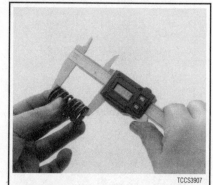

Fig. 238 Use a caliper to check the valve spring free-length

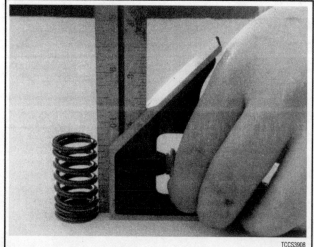

Fig. 239 Check the valve spring for squareness on a flat surface; a carpenter's square can be used

Fig. 240 A dial gauge may be used to check valve stem-to-guide clearance; read the gauge while moving the valve stem

the initial point and zero the gauge and again take a reading. Compare the two readings for a out of round condition. Check the readings against the specifications given. An Inside Diameter (I.D.) gauge designed for valve guides will give you an accurate valve guide bore measurement. If the I.D. gauge is used, compare the readings with the specifications given. Any guides that fail these inspections should be replaced or machined.

VALVE SEATS

A visual inspection of the valve seats should show a slightly worn and pitted surface where the valve face contacts the seat. Inspect the seat carefully for severe pitting or cracks. Also, a seat that is badly worn will be recessed into the cylinder head. A severely worn or recessed seat may need to be replaced. All cracked seats must be replaced. A seat concentricity gauge, if available, should be used to check the seat run-out. If run-out exceeds specifications the seat must be machined (if no specification is given use 0.002 in. or 0.051mm).

CYLINDER HEAD SURFACE FLATNESS

▶ See Figures 241 and 242

After you have cleaned the gasket surface of the cylinder head of any old gasket material, check the head for flatness.

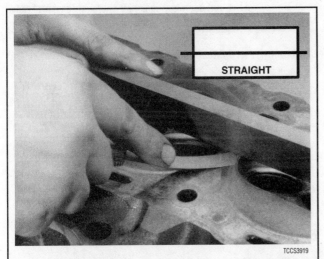

TCCS3919

Fig. 241 Check the head for flatness across the center of the head surface using a straightedge and feeler gauge

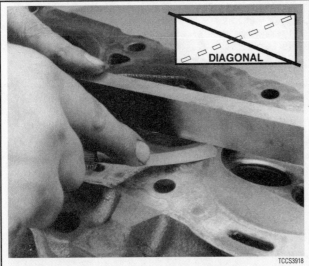

TCCS3918

Fig. 242 Checks should also be made along both diagonals of the head surface

Place a straightedge across the gasket surface. Using feeler gauges, determine the clearance at the center of the straightedge and across the cylinder head at several points. Check along the centerline and diagonally on the head surface. If the warpage exceeds 0.003 in. (0.076mm) within a 6.0 in. (15.2cm) span, or 0.006 in. (0.152mm) over the total length of the head, the cylinder head must be resurfaced. After resurfacing the heads of a V-type engine, the intake manifold flange surface should be checked, and if necessary, milled proportionally to allow for the change in its mounting position.

CRACKS AND PHYSICAL DAMAGE

Generally, cracks are limited to the combustion chamber, however, it is not uncommon for the head to crack in a spark plug hole, port, outside of the head or in the valve spring/rocker arm area. The first area to inspect is always the hottest: the exhaust seat/port area.

A visual inspection should be performed, but just because you don't see a crack does not mean it is not there. Some more reliable methods for inspecting for cracks include Magnaflux®, a magnetic process or Zyglo®, a dye penetrant. Magnaflux® is used only on ferrous metal (cast iron) heads. Zyglo® uses a spray on fluorescent mixture along with a black light to reveal the cracks. It is strongly recommended to have your cylinder head checked professionally for cracks, especially if the engine was known to have overheated and/or leaked or consumed coolant. Contact a local shop for availability and pricing of these services.

Physical damage is usually very evident. For example, a broken mounting ear from dropping the head or a bent or broken stud and/or bolt. All of these defects should be fixed or, if unrepairable, the head should be replaced.

Camshaft and Followers

Inspect the camshaft(s) and followers as described earlier in this section.

REFINISHING & REPAIRING

Many of the procedures given for refinishing and repairing the cylinder head components must be performed by a machine shop. Certain steps, if the inspected part is not worn, can be performed yourself inexpensively. However, you spent a lot of time and effort so far, why risk trying to save a couple bucks if you might have to do it all over again?

Valves

Any valves that were not replaced should be refaced and the tips ground flat. Unless you have access to a valve grinding machine, this should be done by a machine shop. If the valves are in extremely good condition, as well as the valve seats and guides, they may be lapped in without performing machine work.

It is a recommended practice to lap the valves even after machine work has been performed and/or new valves have been purchased. This insures a positive seal between the valve and seat.

LAPPING THE VALVES

➡Before lapping the valves to the seats, read the rest of the cylinder head section to insure that any related parts are in acceptable enough condition to continue.

➡Before any valve seat machining and/or lapping can be performed, the guides must be within factory recommended specifications.

1. Invert the cylinder head.
2. Lightly lubricate the valve stems and insert them into the cylinder head in their numbered order.
3. Raise the valve from the seat and apply a small amount of fine lapping compound to the seat.
4. Moisten the suction head of a hand-lapping tool and attach it to the head of the valve.
5. Rotate the tool between the palms of both hands, changing the position of the valve on the valve seat and lifting the tool often to prevent grooving.
6. Lap the valve until a smooth, polished circle is evident on the valve and seat.
7. Remove the tool and the valve. Wipe away all traces of the grinding compound and store the valve to maintain its lapped location.

Do not get the valves out of order after they have been lapped. They must be put back with the same valve seat with which they were lapped.

Springs, Retainers and Valve Locks

There is no repair or refinishing possible with the springs, retainers and valve locks. If they are found to be worn or defective, they must be replaced with new (or known good) parts.

Cylinder Head

Most refinishing procedures dealing with the cylinder head must be performed by a machine shop. Read the sections below and review your inspection data to determine whether or not machining is necessary.

VALVE GUIDE

➡️**If any machining or replacements are made to the valve guides, the seats must be machined.**

Unless the valve guides need machining or replacing, the only service to perform is to thoroughly clean them of any dirt or oil residue. There are only two types of valve guides used on automobile engines: the replaceable-type (all aluminum heads) and the cast-in integral-type (most cast iron heads). There are four recommended methods for repairing worn guides.
- Knurling
- Inserts
- Reaming oversize
- Replacing

Knurling is a process in which metal is displaced and raised, thereby reducing clearance, giving a true center, and providing oil control. It is the least expensive way of repairing the valve guides. However, it is not necessarily the best, and in some cases, a knurled valve guide will not stand up for more than a short time. It requires a special knurlizer and precision reaming tools to obtain proper clearances. It would not be cost effective to purchase these tools, unless you plan on rebuilding several of the same cylinder head.

Installing a guide insert involves machining the guide to accept a bronze insert. One style is the coil-type which is installed into a threaded guide. Another is the thin-walled insert where the guide is reamed oversize to accept a split-sleeve insert. After the insert is installed, a special tool is then run through the guide to expand the insert, locking it to the guide. The insert is then reamed to the standard size for proper valve clearance.

Reaming for oversize valves restores normal clearances and provides a true valve seat. Most cast-in type guides can be reamed to accept an valve with an oversize stem. The cost factor for this can become quite high as you will need to purchase the reamer and new, oversize stem valves for all guides which were reamed. Oversizes are generally 0.003 to 0.030 in. (0.076 to 0.762mm), with 0.015 in. (0.381mm) being the most common.

To replace cast-in type valve guides, they must be drilled out, then reamed to accept replacement guides. This must be done on a fixture which will allow centering and leveling off of the original valve seat or guide, otherwise a serious guide-to-seat misalignment may occur making it impossible to properly machine the seat.

Replaceable-type guides are pressed into the cylinder head. A hammer and a stepped drift or punch may be used to install and remove the guides. Before removing the guides, measure the protrusion on the spring side of the head and record it for installation. Use the stepped drift to hammer out the old guide from the combustion chamber side of the head. When installing, determine whether or not the guide also seals a water jacket in the head, and if it does, use the recommended sealing agent. If there is no water jacket, grease the valve guide and its bore. Use the stepped drift, and hammer the new guide into the cylinder head from the spring side of the cylinder head. A stack of washers the same thickness as the measured protrusion may help the installation process.

VALVE SEATS

➡️**Before any valve seat machining can be performed, the guides must be within factory recommended specifications.**

➡️**If any machining or replacements were made to the valve guides, the seats must be machined.**

If the seats are in good condition, the valves can be lapped to the seats, and the cylinder head assembled. See the valves section for instructions on lapping.

If the valve seats are worn, cracked or damaged, they must be serviced by a machine shop. The valve seat must be perfectly centered to the valve guide, which requires very accurate machining.

CYLINDER HEAD SURFACE

If the cylinder head is warped, it must be machined flat. If the warpage is extremely severe, the head may need to be replaced. In some instances, it may be possible to straighten a warped head enough to allow machining. In either case, contact a professional machine shop for service.

➡️**Any OHC cylinder head that shows excessive warpage should have the camshaft bearing journals align bored after the cylinder head has been resurfaced.**

Failure to align bore the camshaft bearing journals could result in severe engine damage including but not limited to: valve and piston damage, connecting rod damage, camshaft and/or crankshaft breakage.

CRACKS AND PHYSICAL DAMAGE

Certain cracks can be repaired in both cast iron and aluminum heads. For cast iron, a tapered threaded insert is installed along the length of the crack. Aluminum can also use the tapered inserts, however welding is the preferred method. Some physical damage can be repaired through brazing or welding. Contact a machine shop to get expert advice for your particular dilemma.

ASSEMBLY

The first step for any assembly job is to have a clean area in which to work. Next, thoroughly clean all of the parts and components that are to be assembled. Finally, place all of the components onto a suitable work space and, if necessary, arrange the parts to their respective positions.

CUP TYPE CAMSHAFT FOLLOWERS

◆ **See Figure 243**

To install the springs, retainers and valve locks on heads which have these components recessed into the camshaft follower's bore, you will need a small screwdriver-type tool, some clean white grease and a lot of patience. You will also need the C-clamp style spring compressor and the OHC tool used to disassemble the head.

1. Lightly lubricate the valve stems and insert all of the valves into the cylinder head. If possible, maintain their original locations.
2. If equipped, install any valve spring shims which were removed.

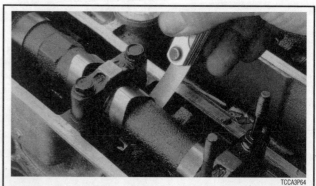

TCCA3P64

Fig. 243 Once assembled, check the valve clearance and correct as needed

3. If equipped, install the new valve seals, keeping the following in mind:
• If the valve seal presses over the guide, lightly lubricate the outer guide surfaces.
• If the seal is an O-ring type, it is installed just after compressing the spring but before the valve locks.

4. Place the valve spring and retainer over the stem.

5. Position the spring compressor and the OHC tool, then compress the spring.

6. Using a small screwdriver as a spatula, fill the valve stem side of the lock with white grease. Use the excess grease on the screwdriver to fasten the lock to the driver.

7. Carefully install the valve lock, which is stuck to the end of the screwdriver, to the valve stem then press on it with the screwdriver until the grease squeezes out. The valve lock should now be stuck to the stem.

8. Repeat Steps 6 and 7 for the remaining valve lock.

9. Relieve the spring pressure slowly and insure that neither valve lock becomes dislodged by the retainer.

10. Remove the spring compressor tool.

11. Repeat Steps 2 through 10 until all of the springs have been installed.

12. Install the followers, camshaft(s) and any other components that were removed for disassembly.

ROCKER ARM TYPE CAMSHAFT FOLLOWERS

1. Lightly lubricate the valve stems and insert all of the valves into the cylinder head. If possible, maintain their original locations.

2. If equipped, install any valve spring shims which were removed.

3. If equipped, install the new valve seals, keeping the following in mind:
• If the valve seal presses over the guide, lightly lubricate the outer guide surfaces.
• If the seal is an O-ring type, it is installed just after compressing the spring but before the valve locks.

4. Place the valve spring and retainer over the stem.

5. Position the spring compressor tool and compress the spring.

6. Assemble the valve locks to the stem.

7. Relieve the spring pressure slowly and insure that neither valve lock becomes dislodged by the retainer.

8. Remove the spring compressor tool.

9. Repeat Steps 2 through 8 until all of the springs have been installed.

10. Install the camshaft(s), rockers, shafts and any other components that were removed for disassembly.

Engine Block

GENERAL INFORMATION

A thorough overhaul or rebuild of an engine block would include replacing the pistons, rings, bearings, timing belt/chain assembly and oil pump. For OHV engines also include a new camshaft and lifters. The block would then have the cylinders bored and honed oversize (or if using removable cylinder sleeves, new sleeves installed) and the crankshaft would be cut undersize to provide new wearing surfaces and perfect clearances. However, your particular engine may not have everything worn out. What if only the piston rings have worn out and the clearances on everything else are still within factory specifications? Well, you could just replace the rings and put it back together, but this would be a very rare example. Chances are, if one component in your engine is worn, other components are sure to follow, and soon. At the very least, you should always replace the rings, bearings and oil pump. This is what is commonly called a "freshen up".

Cylinder Ridge Removal

Because the top piston ring does not travel to the very top of the cylinder, a ridge is built up between the end of the travel and the top of the cylinder bore.

Pushing the piston and connecting rod assembly past the ridge can be difficult, and damage to the piston ring lands could occur. If the ridge is not removed before installing a new piston or not removed at all, piston ring breakage and piston damage may occur.

➡It is always recommended that you remove any cylinder ridges before removing the piston and connecting rod assemblies. If you know that new pistons are going to be installed and the engine block will be bored oversize, you may be able to forego this step. However, some ridges may actually prevent the assemblies from being removed, necessitating its removal.

There are several different types of ridge reamers on the market, none of which are inexpensive. Unless a great deal of engine rebuilding is anticipated, borrow or rent a reamer.

1. Turn the crankshaft until the piston is at the bottom of its travel.

2. Cover the head of the piston with a rag.

3. Follow the tool manufacturers instructions and cut away the ridge, exercising extreme care to avoid cutting too deeply.

4. Remove the ridge reamer, the rag and as many of the cuttings as possible. Continue until all of the cylinder ridges have been removed.

DISASSEMBLY

▶ See Figures 244 and 245

The engine disassembly instructions following assume that you have the engine mounted on an engine stand. If not, it is easiest to disassemble the engine on a bench or the floor with it resting on the bellhousing or transmission mounting surface. You must be able to access the connecting rod fasteners and turn the crankshaft during disassembly. Also, all engine covers (timing, front, side, oil pan, whatever) should have already been removed. Engines which are seized or locked up may not be able to be completely disassembled, and a core (salvage yard) engine should be purchased.

If not done during the cylinder head removal, remove the timing chain/belt and/or gear/sprocket assembly. Remove the oil pick-up and pump assembly and, if necessary, the pump drive. If equipped, remove any balance or auxiliary shafts. If necessary, remove the cylinder ridge from the top of the bore. See the cylinder ridge removal procedure earlier in this section.

Rotate the engine over so that the crankshaft is exposed. Use a number punch or scribe and mark each connecting rod with its respective cylinder number. The cylinder closest to the front of the engine is always number 1. However, depending on the engine placement, the front of the engine could either be the flywheel or damper/pulley end. Generally the front of the engine faces the front of the vehicle. Use a number punch or scribe and also mark the main bearing caps from front to rear with the front most cap being number 1 (if there are five caps, mark them 1 through 5, front to rear).

✺✺ WARNING

Take special care when pushing the connecting rod up from the crankshaft because the sharp threads of the rod bolts/studs will score the crankshaft journal. Insure that special plastic caps are installed over them, or cut two pieces of rubber hose to do the same.

Again, rotate the engine, this time to position the number one cylinder bore (head surface) up. Turn the crankshaft until the number one piston is at the bottom of its travel, this should allow the maximum access to its connecting rod. Remove the number one connecting rods fasteners and cap and place two lengths of rubber hose over the rod bolts/studs to protect the crankshaft from

TCCS3803

Fig. 244 Place rubber hose over the connecting rod studs to protect the crankshaft and cylinder bores from damage

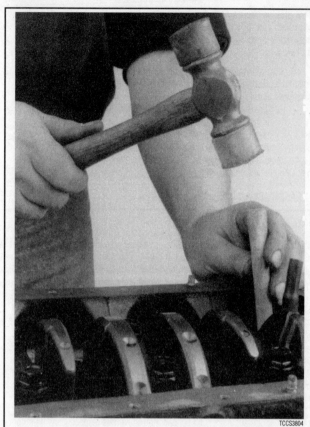

Fig. 245 Carefully tap the piston out of the bore using a wooden dowel

TCCS3804

damage. Using a sturdy wooden dowel and a hammer, push the connecting rod up about 1 in. (25mm) from the crankshaft and remove the upper bearing insert. Continue pushing or tapping the connecting rod up until the piston rings are out of the cylinder bore. Remove the piston and rod by hand, put the upper half of the bearing insert back into the rod, install the cap with its bearing insert installed, and hand-tighten the cap fasteners. If the parts are kept in order in this manner, they will not get lost and you will be able to tell which bearings came form what cylinder if any problems are discovered and diagnosis is necessary. Remove all the other piston assemblies in the same manner. On V-style engines, remove all of the pistons from one bank, then reposition the engine with the other cylinder bank head surface up, and remove that banks piston assemblies.

The only remaining component in the engine block should now be the crankshaft. Loosen the main bearing caps evenly until the fasteners can be turned by hand, then remove them and the caps. Remove the crankshaft from the engine block. Thoroughly clean all of the components.

INSPECTION

Now that the engine block and all of its components are clean, it's time to inspect them for wear and/or damage. To accurately inspect them, you will need some specialized tools:

• Two or three separate micrometers to measure the pistons and crankshaft journals
• A dial indicator
• Telescoping gauges for the cylinder bores
• A rod alignment fixture to check for bent connecting rods

If you do not have access to the proper tools, you may want to bring the components to a shop that does.

Generally, you shouldn't expect cracks in the engine block or its components unless it was known to leak, consume or mix engine fluids, it was severely overheated, or there was evidence of bad bearings and/or crankshaft damage. A visual inspection should be performed on all of the components, but just because you don't see a crack does not mean it is not there. Some more reliable methods for inspecting for cracks include Magnaflux®, a magnetic process or

Zyglo®, a dye penetrant. Magnaflux® is used only on ferrous metal (cast iron). Zyglo® uses a spray on fluorescent mixture along with a black light to reveal the cracks. It is strongly recommended to have your engine block checked professionally for cracks, especially if the engine was known to have overheated and/or leaked or consumed coolant. Contact a local shop for availability and pricing of these services.

Engine Block

ENGINE BLOCK BEARING ALIGNMENT

Remove the main bearing caps and, if still installed, the main bearing inserts. Inspect all of the main bearing saddles and caps for damage, burrs or high spots. If damage is found, and it is caused from a spun main bearing, the block will need to be align-bored or, if severe enough, replacement. Any burrs or high spots should be carefully removed with a metal file.

Place a straightedge on the bearing saddles, in the engine block, along the centerline of the crankshaft. If any clearance exists between the straightedge and the saddles, the block must be align-bored.

Align-boring consists of machining the main bearing saddles and caps by means of a flycutter that runs through the bearing saddles.

DECK FLATNESS

The top of the engine block where the cylinder head mounts is called the deck. Insure that the deck surface is clean of dirt, carbon deposits and old gasket material. Place a straightedge across the surface of the deck along its centerline and, using feeler gauges, check the clearance along several points. Repeat the checking procedure with the straightedge placed along both diagonals of the deck surface. If the reading exceeds 0.003 in. (0.076mm) within a 6.0 in. (15.2cm) span, or 0.006 in. (0.152mm) over the total length of the deck, it must be machined.

CYLINDER BORES

♦ See Figure 246

The cylinder bores house the pistons and are slightly larger than the pistons themselves. A common piston-to-bore clearance is 0.0015–0.0025 in. (0.0381mm–0.0635mm). Inspect and measure the cylinder bores. The bore should be checked for out-of-roundness, taper and size. The results of this inspection will determine whether the cylinder can be used in its existing size and condition, or a rebore to the next oversize is required (or in the case of removable sleeves, have replacements installed).

The amount of cylinder wall wear is always greater at the top of the cylinder than at the bottom. This wear is known as taper. Any cylinder that has a taper of 0.0012 in. (0.305mm) or more, must be rebored. Measurements are taken at a number of positions in each cylinder: at the top, middle and bottom and at two points at each position; that is, at a point 90 degrees from the crankshaft centerline, as well as a point parallel to the crankshaft centerline. The measurements are made with either a special dial indicator or a telescopic gauge and micrometer. If the necessary precision tools to check the bore are not available, take the block to a machine shop and have them mike it. Also if you don't have the tools to check the cylinder bores, chances are you will not have the necessary devices to check the pistons, connecting rods and crankshaft. Take these components with you and save yourself an extra trip.

For our procedures, we will use a telescopic gauge and a micrometer. You will need one of each, with a measuring range which covers your cylinder bore size.

1. Position the telescopic gauge in the cylinder bore, loosen the gauges lock and allow it to expand.

➡Your first two readings will be at the top of the cylinder bore, then proceed to the middle and finally the bottom, making a total of six measurements.

2. Hold the gauge square in the bore, 90 degrees from the crankshaft centerline, and gently tighten the lock. Tilt the gauge back to remove it from the bore.
3. Measure the gauge with the micrometer and record the reading.
4. Again, hold the gauge square in the bore, this time parallel to the crankshaft centerline, and gently tighten the lock. Again, you will tilt the gauge back to remove it from the bore.
5. Measure the gauge with the micrometer and record this reading. The difference between these two readings is the out-of-round measurement of the cylinder.
6. Repeat steps 1 through 5, each time going to the next lower position,

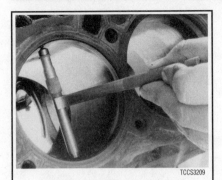

Fig. 246 Use a telescoping gauge to measure the cylinder bore diameter—take several readings within the same bore

Fig. 247 Measure the piston's outer diameter, perpendicular to the wrist pin, with a micrometer

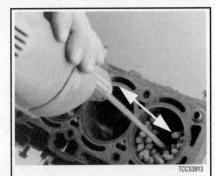

Fig. 248 Use a ball type cylinder hone to remove any glaze and provide a new surface for seating the piston rings

until you reach the bottom of the cylinder. Then go to the next cylinder, and continue until all of the cylinders have been measured.

The difference between these measurements will tell you all about the wear in your cylinders. The measurements which were taken 90 degrees from the crankshaft centerline will always reflect the most wear. That is because at this position is where the engine power presses the piston against the cylinder bore the hardest. This is known as thrust wear. Take your top, 90 degree measurement and compare it to your bottom, 90 degree measurement. The difference between them is the taper. When you measure your pistons, you will compare these readings to your piston sizes and determine piston-to-wall clearance.

Crankshaft

Inspect the crankshaft for visible signs of wear or damage. All of the journals should be perfectly round and smooth. Slight scores are normal for a used crankshaft, but you should hardly feel them with your fingernail. When measuring the crankshaft with a micrometer, you will take readings at the front and rear of each journal, then turn the micrometer 90 degrees and take two more readings, front and rear. The difference between the front-to-rear readings is the journal taper and the first-to-90 degree reading is the out-of-round measurement. Generally, there should be no taper or out-of-roundness found, however, up to 0.0005 in. (0.0127mm) for either can be overlooked. Also, the readings should fall within the factory specifications for journal diameters.

If the crankshaft journals fall within specifications, it is recommended that it be polished before being returned to service. Polishing the crankshaft insures that any minor burrs or high spots are smoothed, thereby reducing the chance of scoring the new bearings.

Pistons and Connecting Rods

PISTONS

◀ See Figure 247

The piston should be visually inspected for any signs of cracking or burning (caused by hot spots or detonation), and scuffing or excessive wear on the skirts. The wristpin attaches the piston to the connecting rod. The piston should move freely on the wrist pin, both sliding and pivoting. Grasp the connecting rod securely, or mount it in a vise, and try to rock the piston back and forth along the centerline of the wristpin. There should not be any excessive play evident between the piston and the pin. If there are C-clips retaining the pin in the piston then you have wrist pin bushings in the rods. There should not be any excessive play between the wrist pin and the rod bushing. Normal clearance for the wrist pin is approx. 0.001–0.002 in. (0.025mm–0.051mm).

Use a micrometer and measure the diameter of the piston, perpendicular to the wrist pin, on the skirt. Compare the reading to its original cylinder measurement obtained earlier. The difference between the two readings is the piston-to-wall clearance. If the clearance is within specifications, the piston may be used as is. If the piston is out of specification, but the bore is not, you will need a new piston. If both are out of specification, you will need the cylinder rebored and oversize pistons installed. Generally if two or more pistons/bores are out of specification, it is best to rebore the entire block and purchase a complete set of oversize pistons.

CONNECTING ROD

You should have the connecting rod checked for straightness at a machine shop. If the connecting rod is bent, it will unevenly wear the bearing and piston, as well as place greater stress on these components. Any bent or twisted connecting rods must be replaced. If the rods are straight and the wrist pin clearance is within specifications, then only the bearing end of the rod need be checked. Place the connecting rod into a vice, with the bearing inserts in place, install the cap to the rod and tighten the fasteners to specifications. Use a telescoping gauge and carefully measure the inside diameter of the bearings. Compare this reading to the rods original crankshaft journal diameter measurement. The difference is the oil clearance. If the oil clearance is not within specifications, install new bearings in the rod and take another measurement. If the clearance is still out of specifications, and the crankshaft is not, the rod will need to be reconditioned by a machine shop.

➡You can also use Plastigage® to check the bearing clearances. The assembling section has complete instructions on its use.

Camshaft

Inspect the camshaft and lifters/followers as described earlier in this section.

Bearings

All of the engine bearings should be visually inspected for wear and/or damage. The bearing should look evenly worn all around with no deep scores or pits. If the bearing is severely worn, scored, pitted or heat blued, then the bearing, and the components that use it, should be brought to a machine shop for inspection. Full-circle bearings (used on most camshafts, auxiliary shafts, balance shafts, etc.) require specialized tools for removal and installation, and should be brought to a machine shop for service.

Oil Pump

➡The oil pump is responsible for providing constant lubrication to the whole engine and so it is recommended that a new oil pump be installed when rebuilding the engine.

Completely disassemble the oil pump and thoroughly clean all of the components. Inspect the oil pump gears and housing for wear and/or damage. Insure that the pressure relief valve operates properly and there is no binding or sticking due to varnish or debris. If all of the parts are in proper working condition, lubricate the gears and relief valve, and assemble the pump.

REFINISHING

◀ See Figure 248

Almost all engine block refinishing must be performed by a machine shop. If the cylinders are not to be rebored, then the cylinder glaze can be removed with a ball hone. When removing cylinder glaze with a ball hone, use a light or penetrating type oil to lubricate the hone. Do not allow the hone to run dry as this may cause excessive scoring of the cylinder bores and wear on the hone. If new pistons are required, they will need to be installed to the connecting rods. This should be performed by a machine shop as the pistons must be installed in the correct relationship to the rod or engine damage can occur.

Pistons and Connecting Rods

▶ **See Figure 249**

Only pistons with the wrist pin retained by C-clips are serviceable by the home-mechanic. Press fit pistons require special presses and/or heaters to remove/install the connecting rod and should only be performed by a machine shop.

All pistons will have a mark indicating the direction to the front of the engine and the must be installed into the engine in that manner. Usually it is a notch or arrow on the top of the piston, or it may be the letter F cast or stamped into the piston.

TCCS3814

Fig. 249 Most pistons are marked to indicate positioning in the engine (usually a mark means the side facing the front)

C-CLIP TYPE PISTONS

1. Note the location of the forward mark on the piston and mark the connecting rod in relation.
2. Remove the C-clips from the piston and withdraw the wrist pin.

➡**Varnish build-up or C-clip groove burrs may increase the difficulty of removing the wrist pin. If necessary, use a punch or drift to carefully tap the wrist pin out.**

3. Insure that the wrist pin bushing in the connecting rod is usable, and lubricate it with assembly lube.
4. Remove the wrist pin from the new piston and lubricate the pin bores on the piston.
5. Align the forward marks on the piston and the connecting rod and install the wrist pin.
6. The new C-clips will have a flat and a rounded side to them. Install both C-clips with the flat side facing out.
7. Repeat all of the steps for each piston being replaced.

ASSEMBLY

Before you begin assembling the engine, first give yourself a clean, dirt free work area. Next, clean every engine component again. The key to a good assembly is cleanliness.

Mount the engine block into the engine stand and wash it one last time using water and detergent (dishwashing detergent works well). While washing it, scrub the cylinder bores with a soft bristle brush and thoroughly clean all of the oil passages. Completely dry the engine and spray the entire assembly down with an anti-rust solution such as WD-40® or similar product. Take a clean lint-free rag and wipe up any excess anti-rust solution from the bores, bearing saddles, etc. Repeat the final cleaning process on the crankshaft. Replace any freeze or oil galley plugs which were removed during disassembly.

Crankshaft

▶ **See Figures 250, 251, 252 and 253**

1. Remove the main bearing inserts from the block and bearing caps.
2. If the crankshaft main bearing journals have been refinished to a definite undersize, install the correct undersize bearing. Be sure that the bearing inserts and bearing bores are clean. Foreign material under inserts will distort bearing and cause failure.
3. Place the upper main bearing inserts in bores with tang in slot.

➡**The oil holes in the bearing inserts must be aligned with the oil holes in the cylinder block.**

4. Install the lower main bearing inserts in bearing caps.
5. Clean the mating surfaces of block and rear main bearing cap.
6. Carefully lower the crankshaft into place. Be careful not to damage bearing surfaces.
7. Check the clearance of each main bearing by using the following procedure:

   a. Place a piece of Plastigage® or its equivalent, on bearing surface across full width of bearing cap and about ¼ in. off center.

   b. Install cap and tighten bolts to specifications. Do not turn crankshaft while Plastigage® is in place.

   c. Remove the cap. Using the supplied Plastigage®scale, check width of Plastigage® at widest point to get maximum clearance. Difference between readings is taper of journal.

   d. If clearance exceeds specified limits, try a 0.001 in. or 0.002 in. under-

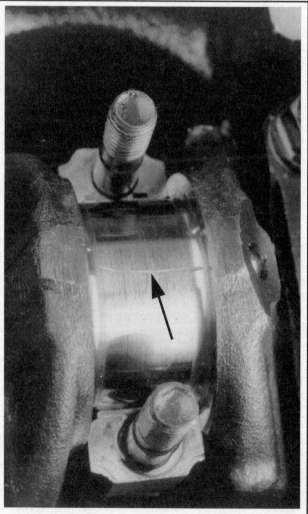

TCCS3243

Fig. 250 Apply a strip of gauging material to the bearing journal, then install and tighten the cap

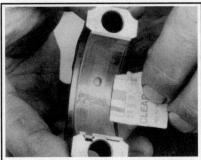

Fig. 251 After the cap is removed again, use the scale supplied with the gauging material to check the clearance

Fig. 252 A dial gauge may be used to check crankshaft end-play

Fig. 253 Carefully pry the crankshaft back and forth while reading the dial gauge for end-play

size bearing in combination with the standard bearing. Bearing clearance must be within specified limits. If standard and 0.002 in. undersize bearing does not bring clearance within desired limits, refinish crankshaft journal, then install undersize bearings.

8. After the bearings have been fitted, apply a light coat of engine oil to the journals and bearings. Install the rear main bearing cap. Install all bearing caps except the thrust bearing cap. Be sure that main bearing caps are installed in original locations. Tighten the bearing cap bolts to specifications.

9. Install the thrust bearing cap with bolts finger-tight.

10. Pry the crankshaft forward against the thrust surface of upper half of bearing.

11. Hold the crankshaft forward and pry the thrust bearing cap to the rear. This aligns the thrust surfaces of both halves of the bearing.

12. Retain the forward pressure on the crankshaft. Tighten the cap bolts to specifications.

13. Measure the crankshaft end-play as follows:

a. Mount a dial gauge to the engine block and position the tip of the gauge to read from the crankshaft end.

b. Carefully pry the crankshaft toward the rear of the engine and hold it there while you zero the gauge.

c. Carefully pry the crankshaft toward the front of the engine and read the gauge.

d. Confirm that the reading is within specifications. If not, install a new thrust bearing and repeat the procedure. If the reading is still out of specifications with a new bearing, have a machine shop inspect the thrust surfaces of the crankshaft, and if possible, repair it.

14. Rotate the crankshaft so as to position the first rod journal to the bottom of its stroke.

15. Install the rear main seal with retainer.

Pistons and Connecting Rods

♦ See Figures 254, 255, 256 and 257

1. Before installing the piston/connecting rod assembly, oil the pistons, piston rings and the cylinder walls with light engine oil. Install connecting rod

bolt protectors or rubber hose onto the connecting rod bolts/studs. Also perform the following:

a. Select the proper ring set for the size cylinder bore.

b. Position the ring in the bore in which it is going to be used.

c. Push the ring down into the bore area where normal ring wear is not encountered.

d. Use the head of the piston to position the ring in the bore so that the ring is square with the cylinder wall. Use caution to avoid damage to the ring or cylinder bore.

e. Measure the gap between the ends of the ring with a feeler gauge. Ring gap in a worn cylinder is normally greater than specification. If the ring gap is greater than the specified limits, try an oversize ring set.

f. Check the ring side clearance of the compression rings with a feeler gauge inserted between the ring and its lower land according to specification. The gauge should slide freely around the entire ring circumference without binding. Any wear that occurs will form a step at the inner portion of the lower land. If the lower lands have high steps, the piston should be replaced.

2. Unless new pistons are installed, be sure to install the pistons in the cylinders from which they were removed. The numbers on the connecting rod and bearing cap must be on the same side when installed in the cylinder bore. If a connecting rod is ever transposed from one engine or cylinder to another, new bearings should be fitted and the connecting rod should be numbered to correspond with the new cylinder number. The notch on the piston head goes toward the front of the engine.

3. Install all of the rod bearing inserts into the rods and caps.

4. Install the rings to the pistons. Install the oil control ring first, then the second compression ring and finally the top compression ring. Use a piston ring expander tool to aid in installation and to help reduce the chance of breakage.

5. Make sure the ring gaps are properly spaced around the circumference of the piston. Fit a piston ring compressor around the piston and slide the piston and connecting rod assembly down into the cylinder bore, pushing it in with the wooden hammer handle. Push the piston down until it is only slightly below the top of the cylinder bore. Guide the connecting rod onto the crankshaft bearing journal carefully, to avoid damaging the crankshaft.

Fig. 254 Checking the piston ring-to-ring groove side clearance using the ring and a feeler gauge

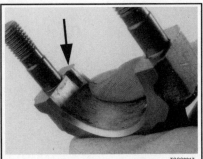

Fig. 255 The notch on the side of the bearing cap matches the tang on the bearing insert

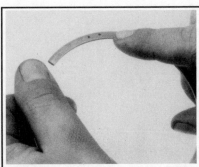

Fig. 256 Most rings are marked to show which side of the ring should face up when installed to the piston

Fig. 257 Install the piston and rod assembly into the block using a ring compressor and the handle of a hammer

6. Check the bearing clearance of all the rod bearings, fitting them to the crankshaft bearing journals. Follow the procedure in the crankshaft installation above.

7. After the bearings have been fitted, apply a light coating of assembly oil to the journals and bearings.

8. Turn the crankshaft until the appropriate bearing journal is at the bottom of its stroke, then push the piston assembly all the way down until the connecting rod bearing seats on the crankshaft journal. Be careful not to allow the bearing cap screws to strike the crankshaft bearing journals and damage them.

9. After the piston and connecting rod assemblies have been installed, check the connecting rod side clearance on each crankshaft journal.

10. Prime and install the oil pump and the oil pump intake tube.

Cylinder Head

1. Install the cylinder head(s) using new gaskets.
2. Install the timing sprockets/gears and the belt/chain assemblies.

Engine Covers and Components

Install the timing cover(s) and oil pan. Refer to your notes and drawings made prior to disassembly and install all of the components that were removed. Install the engine into the vehicle.

Engine Start-up and Break-in

STARTING THE ENGINE

Now that the engine is installed and every wire and hose is properly connected, go back and double check that all coolant and vacuum hoses are connected. Check that you oil drain plug is installed and properly tightened. If not already done, install a new oil filter onto the engine. Fill the crankcase with the proper amount and grade of engine oil. Fill the cooling system with a 50/50 mixture of coolant/water.

1. Connect the vehicle battery.
2. Start the engine. Keep your eye on your oil pressure indicator; if it does not indicate oil pressure within 10 seconds of starting, turn the vehicle off.

✸✸ WARNING

Damage to the engine can result if it is allowed to run with no oil pressure. Check the engine oil level to make sure that it is full. Check for any leaks and if found, repair the leaks before continuing. If there is still no indication of oil pressure, you may need to prime the system.

3. Confirm that there are no fluid leaks (oil or other).
4. Allow the engine to reach normal operating temperature (the upper radiator hose will be hot to the touch).
5. If necessary, set the ignition timing.
6. Install any remaining components such as the air cleaner (if removed for ignition timing) or body panels which were removed.

BREAKING IT IN

Make the first miles on the new engine, easy ones. Vary the speed but do not accelerate hard. Most importantly, do not lug the engine, and avoid sustained high speeds until at least 100 miles. Check the engine oil and coolant levels frequently. Expect the engine to use a little oil until the rings seat. Change the oil and filter at 500 miles, 1500 miles, then every 3000 miles past that.

KEEP IT MAINTAINED

Now that you have just gone through all of that hard work, keep yourself from doing it all over again by thoroughly maintaining it. Not that you may not have maintained it before, heck you could have had one to two hundred thousand miles on it before doing this. However, you may have bought the vehicle used, and the previous owner did not keep up on maintenance. Which is why you just went through all of that hard work. See?

5S-FE ENGINE TORQUE SPECIFICATIONS

Components	English Specifications	Metric Specifications
A/C compressor-to-block	18 ft. lbs.	25 Nm
Alternator bracket-to-cylinder head	18 ft. lbs.	25 Nm
Alternator drive belt adjusting bar-to-cylinder block	20 ft. lbs.	27 Nm
Alternator-to-bracket	40 ft. lbs.	54 Nm
Alternator-to-drive belt adjusting bar	14 ft. lbs.	19 Nm
Camshaft bearing cap-to-cylinder head	14 ft. lbs.	19 Nm
Camshaft timing pulley-to-camshaft	①	①
Center exhaust pipe-to-tailpipe	32 ft. lbs.	43 Nm
Center floor crossmember brace-to-body	19 ft. lbs.	26 Nm
Clutch cover-to-flywheel	14 ft. lbs.	19 Nm
Connecting rod cap-to-connecting rod	②	②
Crankshaft pulley-to-crankshaft	80 ft. lbs.	108 Nm
Cylinder head-to-block	③	③
Delivery pipe-to-cylinder head	9 ft. lbs.	13 Nm
Driveplate-to-crankshaft	61 ft. lbs.	83 Nm
Driveplate-to-torque converter	18 ft. lbs.	25 Nm
EGR pipe-to-cylinder head	43 ft. lbs.	59 Nm
EGR valve-to-cylinder head	9 ft. lbs.	13 Nm
Engine mounting center member-to-body	26 ft. lbs.	35 Nm
Exhaust manifold-to-cylinder head	36 ft. lbs.	49 Nm
Exhaust manifold-to-oxygen sensor	14 ft. lbs.	20 Nm
Exhaust pipe bracket-to-body	10 ft. lbs.	13 Nm
Exhaust pipe support bracket-to-front suspension member	14 ft. lbs.	19 Nm
Exhaust pipe support bracket-to-rear engine mounting insulator	14 ft. lbs.	19 Nm
Flywheel-to-crankshaft	65 ft. lbs.	88 Nm
Front engine insulator-to-mounting bracket	65 ft. lbs.	88 Nm
Front exhaust pipe-to-center pipe-except California	32 ft. lbs.	43 Nm
Front exhaust pipe-to-exhaust pipe bracket	14 ft. lbs.	19 Nm
Front exhaust pipe-to-rear TWC-California	46 ft. lbs.	62 Nm
Front exhaust pipe-to-TWC	22 ft. lbs.	29 Nm
Front TWC-to-exhaust manifold	22 ft. lbs.	29 Nm
Fuel inlet hose-to-fuel filter	25 ft. lbs.	34 Nm
Fuel inlet pipe-to-delivery pipe	14 ft. lbs.	19 Nm
Install manifold-to-mounting bracket	32 ft. lbs.	43 Nm
Intake manifold stay-to-cylinder head	15 ft. lbs.	21 Nm
Intake manifold stay-to-intake manifold	27 ft. lbs.	37 Nm
Knock sensor-to-cylinder block	18 ft. lbs.	25 Nm
LH engine hanger-to-cylinder head	47 ft. lbs.	64 Nm
LH engine mounting insulator-to-bracket	31 ft. lbs.	42 Nm
LH exhaust manifold stay-to-front TWC	29 ft. lbs.	39 Nm
LH exhaust manifold stay-to-transaxle	43 ft. lbs.	59 Nm
Main bearing cap-to-cylinder block	31 ft. lbs.	42 Nm
No. 1 idler pulley-to-cylinder block	31 ft. lbs.	42 Nm
No. 2 idler pulley-to-cylinder block	69 inch lbs.	8 Nm
No. 3 timing belt cover-to-cylinder head	④	④
Oil cooler-to-cylinder block	21 ft. lbs.	28 Nm
Oil pump pulley-to-oil pump drive shaft	32 ft. lbs.	43 Nm
PS pump bracket-to-cylinder block	⑤	⑤
PS pump-to-PS bracket	32 ft. lbs.	44 Nm
Rear end plate stiffener-to-cylinder block	32 ft. lbs.	44 Nm
Rear end plate stiffener-to-transaxle (12mm)	15 ft. lbs.	21 Nm

89593C01

5S-FE ENGINE TORQUE SPECIFICATIONS

Components	English Specifications	Metric Specifications
Rear end plate stiffener-to-transaxle (14mm)	32 ft. lbs.	44 Nm
Rear end plate-to-cylinder block	82 inch lbs.	9 Nm
Rear engine bracket-to-transaxle	58 ft. lbs.	78 Nm
Rear engine mounting insulator-to-bracket	65 ft. lbs.	88 Nm
Rear engine mounting insulator-to-front suspension member	59 ft. lbs.	80 Nm
Rear oil seal retainer-to-cylinder block	9 ft. lbs.	13 Nm
Rear TWC-to-center exhaust pipe-California	32 ft. lbs.	43 Nm
RH engine hanger-to-alternator bracket	18 ft. lbs.	25 Nm
RH engine mounting insulator-to-body	54 ft. lbs.	73 Nm
RH engine mounting insulator-to-bracket	⑥	⑥
RH engine mounting insulator-to-cylinder block	38 ft. lbs.	52 Nm
RH exhaust manifold stay-to-cylinder block	31 ft. lbs.	42 Nm
RH exhaust manifold stay-to-front TWC	31 ft. lbs.	42 Nm
Slave cylinder-to-transaxle	9 ft. lbs.	12 Nm
Spark plug tube-to-cylinder head	29 ft. lbs.	39 Nm
Spark plug-to-cylinder head	13 ft. lbs.	18 Nm
Starter-to-transaxle	29 ft. lbs.	39 Nm
Sub oxygen sensor-to-TWC-California	33 ft. lbs.	44 Nm
Throttle body-to-intake manifold	14 ft. lbs.	19 Nm
Transaxle-to-cylinder block	⑦	⑦
Upper radiator support-to-body	9 ft. lbs.	13 Nm
Valve cover-to-cylinder head	17 ft. lbs.	23 Nm
Water by-pass pipe-to-cylinder head	14 ft. lbs.	19 Nm
Water by-pass pipe-to-water pump cover	78 inch lbs.	9 Nm
Water outlet-to-cylinder head	11 ft. lbs.	15 Nm
Water pump-to-cylinder block	69 inch lbs.	8 Nm

① Torque wrench: 40 ft. lbs.
  Special service tool: 27 ft. lbs. (37 Nm)
② First pass: 18 ft. lbs. (25 Nm)
  First pass: turn additional 90°
③ First pass: 36 ft. lbs. (49 Nm)
  Final pass: turn additional 90°
④ Relief valve: 58 ft. lbs. (78 Nm)
  Nut: 69 inch lbs. (8 Nm)
⑤ Adjusting bolt: 29 ft. lbs. (39 Nm)
  Others: 32 ft. lbs. (43 Nm)
⑥ Bolt: 27 ft. lbs. (37 Nm)
  Nut: 38 ft. lbs. (52 Nm)
⑦ 12mm head: 15 ft. lbs. (21 Nm)
  14mm head: 32 ft. lbs. (44 Nm)

89593C02

7A-FE ENGINE TORQUE SPECIFICATIONS

Components	English Specifications	Metric Specifications
A/C compressor mounting bracket-to-compressor	18 ft. lbs.	25 Nm
Alternator-to-bracket on block	14 ft. lbs.	19 Nm
Alternator-to-bracket on cylinder head	45 ft. lbs.	61 Nm
Camshaft-to-camshaft pulley	43 ft. lbs.	59 Nm
Center exhaust pipe-to-tailpipe	32 ft. lbs.	43 Nm
Center floor crossmember brace-to-body	19 ft. lbs.	26 Nm
Clutch cover-to-flywheel	14 ft. lbs.	19 Nm
Connecting rod cap-to-connecting rod—1994-96	①	①
Connecting rod cap-to-connecting rod—1997-98	②	②
Coolant drain plug-to-block	25 ft. lbs.	34 Nm
Crankshaft-to-crankshaft pulley	87 ft. lbs.	118 Nm
Cylinder block-to-A/C compressor mounting bracket	35 ft. lbs.	47 Nm
Cylinder block-to-head	③	③
Cylinder block-to-idler pulley	27 ft. lbs.	37 Nm
Cylinder head-to-alternator bracket	20 ft. lbs.	26 Nm
Cylinder head-to-camshaft bearing cap	9 ft. lbs.	13 Nm
Cylinder head-to-engine hanger	21 ft. lbs.	28 Nm
Cylinder head-to-IIA distributor	14 ft. lbs.	20 Nm
Cylinder head-to-spark plug	13 ft. lbs.	18 Nm
Cylinder head-to-valve cover	52 inch lbs.	6 Nm
Cylinder head-to-water inlet housing	14 ft. lbs.	20 Nm
Cylinder head-to-water outlet	14 ft. lbs.	20 Nm
Delivery pipe-to-fuel inlet hose	22 ft. lbs.	29 Nm
Driveplate-to-crankshaft	47 ft. lbs.	64 Nm
Driveplate-to-torque converter clutch	18 ft. lbs.	25 Nm
EGR pipe-to-intake manifold	9 ft. lbs.	13 Nm
Engine center mounting bracket-to-transaxle	26 ft. lbs.	35 Nm
Exhaust manifold-to-cylinder head	25 ft. lbs.	34 Nm
Exhaust manifold-to-heat insulator	82 inch lbs.	9 Nm
Exhaust pipe bracket-to-front suspension member	14 ft. lbs.	19 Nm
Exhaust pipe bracket-to-rear engine insulator	14 ft. lbs.	19 Nm
Exhaust pipe support bracket-to-body	10 ft. lbs.	13 Nm
Flywheel-to-crankshaft	58 ft. lbs.	78 Nm
Front engine insulator-to-mounting bracket	65 ft. lbs.	88 Nm
Front exhaust pipe-to-rear TWC	32 ft. lbs.	43 Nm
Front exhaust pipe-to-support bracket	14 ft. lbs.	19 Nm
Front exhaust pipe-to-TWC	46 ft. lbs.	62 Nm
Front TWC-to-exhaust manifold	22 ft. lbs.	29 Nm
Front TWC-to-exhaust manifold stay	29 ft. lbs.	39 Nm
Front TWC-to-heat insulator	78 inch lbs.	9 Nm
Fuel inlet hose-to-fuel filter	22 ft. lbs.	30 Nm
Install manifold stay-to-cylinder block	29 ft. lbs.	39 Nm
Install manifold-to-delivery pipe	11 ft. lbs.	15 Nm
Intake manifold-to-air intake chamber	14 ft. lbs.	19 Nm
Intake manifold-to-cylinder head	14 ft. lbs.	19 Nm
Intake manifold-to-EGR valve	9 ft. lbs.	13 Nm
Intake manifold-to-manifold stay	14 ft. lbs.	19 Nm
Intake manifold-to-throttle body	16 ft. lbs.	22 Nm
Knock sensor-to-block	27 ft lbs.	37 Nm
LH engine insulator-to-body	54 ft. lbs.	73 Nm
LH engine mounting insulator-to-bracket	47 ft. lbs.	64 Nm

89593C03

7A-FE ENGINE TORQUE SPECIFICATIONS

Components	English Specifications	Metric Specifications
Main bearing cap-to-cylinder block	44 ft. lbs.	60 Nm
No. 1 oil pan-to-block	12 ft. lbs.	16 Nm
No. 1 oil pan-to-No. 2 oil pan	69 inch lbs.	8 Nm
No. 1 oil pan-to-oil pump	69 inch lbs.	8 Nm
No. 1 oil pan-to-rear oil seal retainer	69 inch lbs.	8 Nm
No. 1 oil pan-to-transaxle	17 ft. lbs.	23 Nm
No. 2 oil baffle-to-No. 1 oil pan	43 inch lbs.	5 Nm
No. 2 oil pan-to-drain plug	25 ft. lbs.	34 Nm
No. 2 water inlet-to-cylinder head	11 ft. lbs.	15 Nm
No. 2 water inlet-to-oil dipstick guide	82 inch lbs.	9 Nm
Oil pump-to-cylinder block	16 ft. lbs.	21 Nm
Oil strainer-to-oil pump	82 inch lbs.	9 Nm
Oil strainer-to-head	82 inch lbs.	9 Nm
PS pump adjusting bracket-to-pump	29 ft. lbs.	39 Nm
PS pump bracket-to-block (12mm)	14 ft. lbs.	19 Nm
PS pump bracket-to-block (14mm)	29 ft. lbs.	39 Nm
PS pump bracket-to-cylinder block	29 ft. lbs.	39 Nm
Rear end plate-to-block	48 inch lbs.	6 Nm
Rear engine insulator-to-front suspension member	59 ft. lbs.	80 Nm
Rear engine insulator-to-mounting bracket	65 ft. lbs.	88 Nm
Rear engine mounting bracket-to-transaxle	58 ft. lbs.	78 Nm
Rear oil seal retainer-to-block	82 inch lbs.	9 Nm
Rear TWC-to-center exhaust pipe	32 ft. lbs.	43 Nm
RH engine mounting bracket-to-block	38 ft. lbs.	51 Nm
RH engine mounting insulator-to-body	47 ft. lbs.	64 Nm
RH engine mounting insulator-to-mounting bracket (12mm)	21 ft. lbs.	28 Nm
RH engine mounting insulator-to-mounting bracket (14mm)	38 ft. lbs.	52 Nm
Slave cylinder-to-transaxle	9 ft. lbs.	12 Nm
Starter-to-transaxle	29 ft. lbs.	39 Nm
Transaxle-to-engine (14mm)	34 ft. lbs.	46 Nm
Transaxle-to-engine (17mm)	47 ft. lbs.	64 Nm
Upper radiator support-to-body	9 ft. lbs.	13 Nm
Water pump pulley seat-to-pump pulley	82 inch lbs.	9 Nm
Water pump-to-block	11 ft. lbs.	14 Nm

① First pass: 18 ft. lbs. (25 Nm)
　 Final pass: Turn an additional 90°
② First pass: 22 ft. lbs. (29 Nm)
　 Final pass: Turn an additional 90°
③ First pass: 22 ft. lbs. (29 Nm)
　 Second pass: Turn an additional 90°
　 Final pass: Turn an additional 90°

89593C04

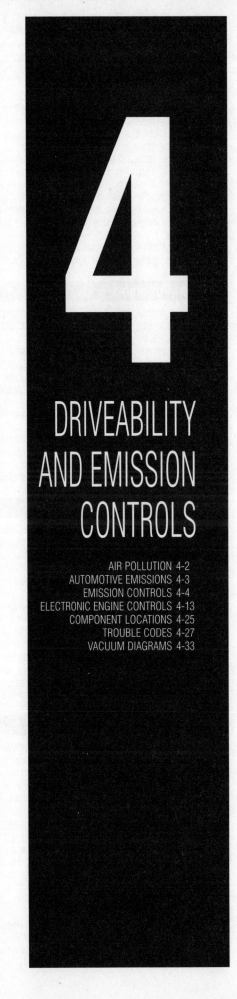

4

DRIVEABILITY AND EMISSION CONTROLS

AIR POLLUTION

The earth's atmosphere, at or near sea level, consists approximately of 78 percent nitrogen, 21 percent oxygen and 1 percent other gases. If it were possible to remain in this state, 100 percent clean air would result. However, many varied sources allow other gases and particulates to mix with the clean air, causing our atmosphere to become unclean or polluted.

Some of these pollutants are visible while others are invisible, with each having the capability of causing distress to the eyes, ears, throat, skin and respiratory system. Should these pollutants become concentrated in a specific area and under certain conditions, death could result due to the displacement or chemical change of the oxygen content in the air. These pollutants can also cause great damage to the environment and to the many man made objects that are exposed to the elements.

To better understand the causes of air pollution, the pollutants can be categorized into 3 separate types, natural, industrial and automotive.

Natural Pollutants

Natural pollution has been present on earth since before man appeared and continues to be a factor when discussing air pollution, although it causes only a small percentage of the overall pollution problem. It is the direct result of decaying organic matter, wind born smoke and particulates from such natural events as plain and forest fires (ignited by heat or lightning), volcanic ash, sand and dust which can spread over a large area of the countryside.

Such a phenomenon of natural pollution has been seen in the form of volcanic eruptions, with the resulting plume of smoke, steam and volcanic ash blotting out the sun's rays as it spreads and rises higher into the atmosphere. As it travels into the atmosphere the upper air currents catch and carry the smoke and ash, while condensing the steam back into water vapor. As the water vapor, smoke and ash travel on their journey, the smoke dissipates into the atmosphere while the ash and moisture settle back to earth in a trail hundreds of miles long. In some cases, lives are lost and millions of dollars of property damage result.

Industrial Pollutants

Industrial pollution is caused primarily by industrial processes, the burning of coal, oil and natural gas, which in turn produce smoke and fumes. Because the burning fuels contain large amounts of sulfur, the principal ingredients of smoke and fumes are sulfur dioxide and particulate matter. This type of pollutant occurs most severely during still, damp and cool weather, such as at night. Even in its less severe form, this pollutant is not confined to just cities. Because of air movements, the pollutants move for miles over the surrounding countryside, leaving in its path a barren and unhealthy environment for all living things.

Working with Federal, State and Local mandated regulations and by carefully monitoring emissions, big business has greatly reduced the amount of pollutant introduced from its industrial sources, striving to obtain an acceptable level. Because of the mandated industrial emission clean up, many land areas and streams in and around the cities that were formerly barren of vegetation and life, have now begun to move back in the direction of nature's intended balance.

Automotive Pollutants

The third major source of air pollution is automotive emissions. The emissions from the internal combustion engines were not an appreciable problem years ago because of the small number of registered vehicles and the nation's small highway system. However, during the early 1950's, the trend of the American people was to move from the cities to the surrounding suburbs. This caused an immediate problem in transportation because the majority of suburbs were not afforded mass transit conveniences. This lack of transportation created an attractive market for the automobile manufacturers, which resulted in a dramatic increase in the number of vehicles produced and sold, along with a marked increase in highway construction between cities and the suburbs. Multi-vehicle families emerged with a growing emphasis placed on an individual vehicle per family member. As the increase in vehicle ownership and usage occurred, so did pollutant levels in and around the cities, as suburbanites drove daily to their businesses and employment, returning at the end of the day to their homes in the suburbs.

It was noted that a smoke and fog type haze was being formed and at times, remained in suspension over the cities, taking time to dissipate. At first this "smog," derived from the words "smoke" and "fog," was thought to result from industrial pollution but it was determined that automobile emissions shared the blame. It was discovered that when normal automobile emissions were exposed to sunlight for a period of time, complex chemical reactions would take place.

It is now known that smog is a photo chemical layer which develops when certain oxides of nitrogen (NOx) and unburned hydrocarbons (HC) from automobile emissions are exposed to sunlight. Pollution was more severe when smog would become stagnant over an area in which a warm layer of air settled over the top of the cooler air mass, trapping and holding the cooler mass at ground level. The trapped cooler air would keep the emissions from being dispersed and diluted through normal air flows. This type of air stagnation was given the name "Temperature Inversion."

TEMPERATURE INVERSION

In normal weather situations, surface air is warmed by heat radiating from the earth's surface and the sun's rays. This causes it to rise upward, into the atmosphere. Upon rising it will cool through a convection type heat exchange with the cooler upper air. As warm air rises, the surface pollutants are carried upward and dissipated into the atmosphere.

When a temperature inversion occurs, we find the higher air is no longer cooler, but is warmer than the surface air, causing the cooler surface air to become trapped. This warm air blanket can extend from above ground level to a few hundred or even a few thousand feet into the air. As the surface air is trapped, so are the pollutants, causing a severe smog condition. Should this stagnant air mass extend to a few thousand feet high, enough air movement with the inversion takes place to allow the smog layer to rise above ground level but the pollutants still cannot dissipate. This inversion can remain for days over an area, with the smog level only rising or lowering from ground level to a few hundred feet high. Meanwhile, the pollutant levels increase, causing eye irritation, respiratory problems, reduced visibility, plant damage and in some cases, even disease.

This inversion phenomenon was first noted in the Los Angeles, California area. The city lies in terrain resembling a basin and with certain weather conditions, a cold air mass is held in the basin while a warmer air mass covers it like a lid.

Because this type of condition was first documented as prevalent in the Los Angeles area, this type of trapped pollution was named Los Angeles Smog, although it occurs in other areas where a large concentration of automobiles are used and the air remains stagnant for any length of time.

HEAT TRANSFER

Consider the internal combustion engine as a machine in which raw materials must be placed so a finished product comes out. As in any machine operation, a certain amount of wasted material is formed. When we relate this to the internal combustion engine, we find that through the input of air and fuel, we obtain power during the combustion process to drive the vehicle. The by-product or waste of this power is, in part, heat and exhaust gases with which we must dispose.

The heat from the combustion process can rise to over 4000°F (2204°C). The dissipation of this heat is controlled by a ram air effect, the use of cooling fans to cause air flow and a liquid coolant solution surrounding the combustion area to transfer the heat of combustion through the cylinder walls and into the coolant. The coolant is then directed to a thin-finned, multi-tubed radiator, from which the excess heat is transferred to the atmosphere by 1 of the 3 heat transfer methods, conduction, convection or radiation.

The cooling of the combustion area is an important part in the control of exhaust emissions. To understand the behavior of the combustion and transfer of its heat, consider the air/fuel charge. It is ignited and the flame front burns progressively across the combustion chamber until the burning charge reaches the cylinder walls. Some of the fuel in contact with the walls is not hot enough to burn, thereby snuffing out or quenching the combustion process. This leaves unburned fuel in the combustion chamber. This unburned fuel is then forced out of the cylinder and into the exhaust system, along with the exhaust gases.

Many attempts have been made to minimize the amount of unburned fuel in the combustion chambers due to quenching, by increasing the coolant temperature and lessening the contact area of the coolant around the combustion area. However, design limitations within the combustion chambers prevent the complete burning of the air/fuel charge, so a certain amount of the unburned fuel is still expelled into the exhaust system, regardless of modifications to the engine.

AUTOMOTIVE EMISSIONS

Before emission controls were mandated on internal combustion engines, other sources of engine pollutants were discovered along with the exhaust emissions. It was determined that engine combustion exhaust produced approximately 60 percent of the total emission pollutants, fuel evaporation from the fuel tank and carburetor vents produced 20 percent, with the final 20 percent being produced through the crankcase as a by-product of the combustion process.

Exhaust Gases

The exhaust gases emitted into the atmosphere are a combination of burned and unburned fuel. To understand the exhaust emission and its composition, we must review some basic chemistry.

When the air/fuel mixture is introduced into the engine, we are mixing air, composed of nitrogen (78 percent), oxygen (21 percent) and other gases (1 percent) with the fuel, which is 100 percent hydrocarbons (HC), in a semi-controlled ratio. As the combustion process is accomplished, power is produced to move the vehicle while the heat of combustion is transferred to the cooling system. The exhaust gases are then composed of nitrogen, a diatomic gas (N_2), the same as was introduced in the engine, carbon dioxide (CO_2), the same gas that is used in beverage carbonation, and water vapor (H_2O). The nitrogen (N_2), for the most part, passes through the engine unchanged, while the oxygen (O_2) reacts (burns) with the hydrocarbons (HC) and produces the carbon dioxide (CO_2) and the water vapors (H_2O). If this chemical process would be the only process to take place, the exhaust emissions would be harmless. However, during the combustion process, other compounds are formed which are considered dangerous. These pollutants are hydrocarbons (HC), carbon monoxide (CO), oxides of nitrogen (NOx) oxides of sulfur (SOx) and engine particulates.

HYDROCARBONS

Hydrocarbons (HC) are essentially fuel which was not burned during the combustion process or which has escaped into the atmosphere through fuel evaporation. The main sources of incomplete combustion are rich air/fuel mixtures, low engine temperatures and improper spark timing. The main sources of hydrocarbon emission through fuel evaporation on most vehicles used to be the vehicle's fuel tank and carburetor float bowl.

To reduce combustion hydrocarbon emission, engine modifications were made to minimize dead space and surface area in the combustion chamber. In addition, the air/fuel mixture was made more lean through the improved control which feedback carburetion and fuel injection offers and by the addition of external controls to aid in further combustion of the hydrocarbons outside the engine. Two such methods were the addition of air injection systems, to inject fresh air into the exhaust manifolds and the installation of catalytic converters, units that are able to burn traces of hydrocarbons without affecting the internal combustion process or fuel economy.

To control hydrocarbon emissions through fuel evaporation, modifications were made to the fuel tank to allow storage of the fuel vapors during periods of engine shut-down. Modifications were also made to the air intake system so that at specific times during engine operation, these vapors may be purged and burned by blending them with the air/fuel mixture.

CARBON MONOXIDE

Carbon monoxide is formed when not enough oxygen is present during the combustion process to convert carbon (C) to carbon dioxide (CO_2). An increase in the carbon monoxide (CO) emission is normally accompanied by an increase in the hydrocarbon (HC) emission because of the lack of oxygen to completely burn all of the fuel mixture.

Carbon monoxide (CO) also increases the rate at which the photo chemical smog is formed by speeding up the conversion of nitric oxide (NO) to nitrogen dioxide (NO_2). To accomplish this, carbon monoxide (CO) combines with oxygen (O_2) and nitric oxide (NO) to produce carbon dioxide (CO_2) and nitrogen dioxide (NO_2). ($CO + O_2 + NO = CO_2 + NO_2$).

The dangers of carbon monoxide, which is an odorless and colorless toxic gas are many. When carbon monoxide is inhaled into the lungs and passed into the blood stream, oxygen is replaced by the carbon monoxide in the red blood cells, causing a reduction in the amount of oxygen supplied to the many parts of the body. This lack of oxygen causes headaches, lack of coordination,

reduced mental alertness and, should the carbon monoxide concentration be high enough, death could result.

NITROGEN

Normally, nitrogen is an inert gas. When heated to approximately 2500°F (1371°C) through the combustion process, this gas becomes active and causes an increase in the nitric oxide (NO) emission.

Oxides of nitrogen (NOx) are composed of approximately 97–98 percent nitric oxide (NO). Nitric oxide is a colorless gas but when it is passed into the atmosphere, it combines with oxygen and forms nitrogen dioxide (NO_2). The nitrogen dioxide then combines with chemically active hydrocarbons (HC) and when in the presence of sunlight, causes the formation of photo-chemical smog.

Ozone

To further complicate matters, some of the nitrogen dioxide (NO_2) is broken apart by the sunlight to form nitric oxide and oxygen. (NO_2 + sunlight = NO + O). This single atom of oxygen then combines with diatomic (meaning 2 atoms) oxygen (O_2) to form ozone (O_3). Ozone is one of the smells associated with smog. It has a pungent and offensive odor, irritates the eyes and lung tissues, affects the growth of plant life and causes rapid deterioration of rubber products. Ozone can be formed by sunlight as well as electrical discharge into the air.

The most common discharge area on the automobile engine is the secondary ignition electrical system, especially when inferior quality spark plug cables are used. As the surge of high voltage is routed through the secondary cable, the circuit builds up an electrical field around the wire, which acts upon the oxygen in the surrounding air to form the ozone. The faint glow along the cable with the engine running that may be visible on a dark night, is called the "corona discharge." It is the result of the electrical field passing from a high along the cable, to a low in the surrounding air, which forms the ozone gas. The combination of corona and ozone has been a major cause of cable deterioration. Recently, different and better quality insulating materials have lengthened the life of the electrical cables.

Although ozone at ground level can be harmful, ozone is beneficial to the earth's inhabitants. By having a concentrated ozone layer called the "ozonosphere," between 10 and 20 miles (16–32 km) up in the atmosphere, much of the ultra violet radiation from the sun's rays are absorbed and screened. If this ozone layer were not present, much of the earth's surface would be burned, dried and unfit for human life.

OXIDES OF SULFUR

Oxides of sulfur (SOx) were initially ignored in the exhaust system emissions, since the sulfur content of gasoline as a fuel is less than $\frac{1}{10}$ of 1 percent. Because of this small amount, it was felt that it contributed very little to the overall pollution problem. However, because of the difficulty in solving the sulfur emissions in industrial pollutions and the introduction of catalytic converter to the automobile exhaust systems, a change was mandated. The automobile exhaust system, when equipped with a catalytic converter, changes the sulfur dioxide (SO_2) into sulfur trioxide (SO_3).

When this combines with water vapors (H_2O), a sulfuric acid mist (H_2SO_4) is formed and is a very difficult pollutant to handle since it is extremely corrosive. This sulfuric acid mist that is formed, is the same mist that rises from the vents of an automobile battery when an active chemical reaction takes place within the battery cells.

When a large concentration of vehicles equipped with catalytic converters are operating in an area, this acid mist may rise and be distributed over a large ground area causing land, plant, crop, paint and building damage.

PARTICULATE MATTER

A certain amount of particulate matter is present in the burning of any fuel, with carbon constituting the largest percentage of the particulates. In gasoline, the remaining particulates are the burned remains of the various other compounds used in its manufacture. When a gasoline engine is in good internal condition, the particulate emissions are low but as the engine wears internally, the particulate emissions increase. By visually inspecting the tail pipe emissions, a determination can be made as to where an engine defect may exist. An engine with light gray or blue smoke emitting from the tail pipe normally indicates an increase in the oil consumption through burning due to internal engine wear. Black smoke would indicate a defective fuel delivery system, causing the engine to operate in a rich mode. Regardless of the color of the smoke, the internal part of the engine or the fuel delivery system should be repaired to prevent excess particulate emissions.

Diesel and turbine engines emit a darkened plume of smoke from the exhaust system because of the type of fuel used. Emission control regulations are mandated for this type of emission and more stringent measures are being used to prevent excess emission of the particulate matter. Electronic components are being introduced to control the injection of the fuel at precisely the proper time of piston travel, to achieve the optimum in fuel ignition and fuel usage. Other particulate after-burning components are being tested to achieve a cleaner emission.

Good grades of engine lubricating oils should be used, which meet the manufacturer's specification. Cut-rate oils can contribute to the particulate emission problem because of their low flash or ignition temperature point. Such oils burn prematurely during the combustion process causing emission of particulate matter.

The cooling system is an important factor in the reduction of particulate matter. The optimum combustion will occur, with the cooling system operating at a temperature specified by the manufacturer. The cooling system must be maintained in the same manner as the engine oiling system, as each system is required to perform properly in order for the engine to operate efficiently for a long time.

Crankcase Emissions

Crankcase emissions are made up of water, acids, unburned fuel, oil fumes and particulates. These emissions are classified as hydrocarbons (HC) and are formed by the small amount of unburned, compressed air/fuel mixture entering the crankcase from the combustion area (between the cylinder walls and piston rings) during the compression and power strokes. The head of the compression and combustion help to form the remaining crankcase emissions.

Since the first engines, crankcase emissions were allowed into the atmosphere through a road draft tube, mounted on the lower side of the engine block. Fresh air came in through an open oil filler cap or breather. The air passed through the crankcase mixing with blow-by gases. The motion of the vehicle and the air blowing past the open end of the road draft tube caused a low pressure area (vacuum) at the end of the tube. Crankcase emissions were simply drawn out of the road draft tube into the air.

To control the crankcase emission, the road draft tube was deleted. A hose and/or tubing was routed from the crankcase to the intake manifold so the blow-by emission could be burned with the air/fuel mixture. However, it was found

that intake manifold vacuum, used to draw the crankcase emissions into the manifold, would vary in strength at the wrong time and not allow the proper emission flow. A regulating valve was needed to control the flow of air through the crankcase.

Testing, showed the removal of the blow-by gases from the crankcase as quickly as possible, was most important to the longevity of the engine. Should large accumulations of blow-by gases remain and condense, dilution of the engine oil would occur to form water, soots, resins, acids and lead salts, resulting in the formation of sludge and varnishes. This condensation of the blow-by gases occurs more frequently on vehicles used in numerous starting and stopping conditions, excessive idling and when the engine is not allowed to attain normal operating temperature through short runs.

Evaporative Emissions

Gasoline fuel is a major source of pollution, before and after it is burned in the automobile engine. From the time the fuel is refined, stored, pumped and transported, again stored until it is pumped into the fuel tank of the vehicle, the gasoline gives off unburned hydrocarbons (HC) into the atmosphere. Through the redesign of storage areas and venting systems, the pollution factor was diminished, but not eliminated, from the refinery standpoint. However, the automobile still remained the primary source of vaporized, unburned hydrocarbon (HC) emissions.

Fuel pumped from an underground storage tank is cool but when exposed to a warmer ambient temperature, will expand. Before controls were mandated, an owner might fill the fuel tank with fuel from an underground storage tank and park the vehicle for some time in warm area, such as a parking lot. As the fuel would warm, it would expand and should no provisions or area be provided for the expansion, the fuel would spill out of the filler neck and onto the ground, causing hydrocarbon (HC) pollution and creating a severe fire hazard. To correct this condition, the vehicle manufacturers added overflow plumbing and/or gasoline tanks with built in expansion areas or domes.

However, this did not control the fuel vapor emission from the fuel tank. It was determined that most of the fuel evaporation occurred when the vehicle was stationary and the engine not operating. Most vehicles carry 5–25 gallons (19–95 liters) of gasoline. Should a large concentration of vehicles be parked in one area, such as a large parking lot, excessive fuel vapor emissions would take place, increasing as the temperature increases.

To prevent the vapor emission from escaping into the atmosphere, the fuel systems were designed to trap the vapors while the vehicle is stationary, by sealing the system from the atmosphere. A storage system is used to collect and hold the fuel vapors from the carburetor (if equipped) and the fuel tank when the engine is not operating. When the engine is started, the storage system is then purged of the fuel vapors, which are drawn into the engine and burned with the air/fuel mixture.

EMISSION CONTROLS

Crankcase Ventilation System

OPERATION

A Positive Crankcase Ventilation (PCV) system is used on all Toyota gasoline engine vehicles sold in the United States. Exhaust blow-by gasses are routed from the crankcase to the intake manifold, where are combined with the fuel/air mixture and burned during combustion. this reduces the amount of hydrocarbons emitted by the exhaust.

A valve (PCV) is used in the line to prevent the gases in the crankcase from being ignited in case of a backfire. The amount of blow-by gasses entering the mixture is also regulated by the PCV valve, which is spring loaded and has a variable orifice.

The important components of the PCV system are the following:
- PCV valve
- Valve cover
- Charcoal canister
- Hoses, connections and gaskets
- Thermal Vacuum Valve (TVV)
- Check valve

COMPONENT TESTING

▶ **See Figures 1, 2 and 3**

Inspect the PCV system hoses and connections at each tune-up and replace any deteriorated hoses. Check the PCV valve at every tune-up and replace it at 30,000 mile (48,000 km) intervals.

The PCV valve is easily checked with the engine running at normal idle speed (warmed up).

1. Remove the PCV valve from the valve cover or intake manifold, but leave it connected to its hose.
2. Start the engine.
3. Place your thumb over the end of the valve to check for vacuum. If there is no vacuum, check for plugged hoses or ports. If these are open, the valve is faulty.
4. With the engine **OFF**, remove the valve completely. Shake it end-to-end, listening for the rattle of the needle inside the valve. If no rattle is heard, the needle is jammed (probably due to oil sludge) and the valve should be replaced.

✳✳ CAUTION

Don't blow directly into the valve; petroleum deposits within the valve can be harmful.

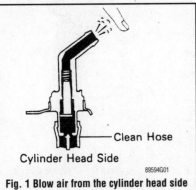

Fig. 1 Blow air from the cylinder head side of the PCV valve, it should flow easily

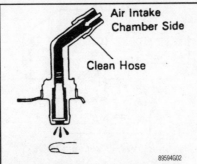

Fig. 2 Blow air from the intake manifold side, check that the air passes with difficulty

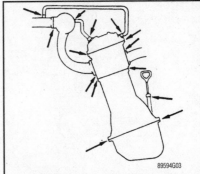

Fig. 3 Leaks from any of these areas can cause the PCV system to malfunction

An engine without crankcase ventilation is quickly damaged. It is important to check the PCV at regular intervals. When replacing a PCV valve you must use the correct one for the engine. Many valves look alike on the outside, but have different mechanical values. Putting the incorrect valve on a vehicle can cause a great deal of driveability problems.

REMOVAL & INSTALLATION

1. Pull the PCV valve from the valve cover.
2. Remove the hose from the valve.
3. Check the valve for proper operation. While the valve is removed, the hoses should be checked for splits, kinks and blockages. Check the vacuum port (that the hoses connect to) for any clogging.
4. Inspect the rubber grommet the PCV valve fits into. If it is in any way deteriorated or oil soaked, replace it.

To install:

5. Insert a new valve into the hose.
6. Push the valve into the rubber grommet. Make sure the valve is firmly into place.

Evaporative Emission Controls

OPERATION

◆ See Figures 4 and 5

The Evaporative Emission Control (EVAP) system is designed to prevent fuel tank vapors from being emitted into the atmosphere. When the engine is not running, gasoline vapors from the tank are stored in a charcoal canister. The charcoal canister absorbs the gasoline vapors and stores them until certain engine conditions are met and the vapors can be purged and burned by the engine. In some vehicles, any liquid fuel entering the canister goes into a reservoir in the bottom of the canister to protect the integrity of the carbon element in the canister above. These systems employ the following components:

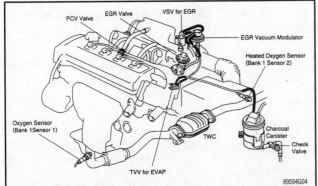

Fig. 4 Evaporative Emission Control (EVAP) system components—5S-FE engine

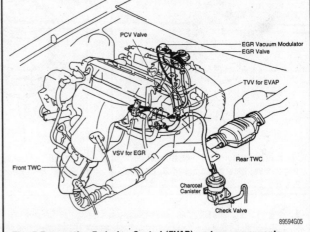

Fig. 5 Evaporative Emission Control (EVAP) system components—7A-FE engine

- Charcoal canister
- Fuel tank cap
- Thermal Vacuum Valve (TVV)
- Check valve
- Heated Oxygen sensors

COMPONENT TESTING

◆ See Figure 6

Before embarking on component removal or extensive diagnosis, perform a complete visual check of the system. Every vacuum line and vapor line (including the lines running to the tank) should be inspected for cracking, loose clamps, kinks and obstructions. Additionally, check the tank for any signs of deformation or crushing. Each vacuum port on the engine or manifold should be checked for restriction by dirt or sludge.

The evaporative control system is generally not prone to component failure in normal circumstances; most problems can be tracked to the causes listed above.

Fuel Filler Cap

◆ See Figure 7

Check that the filler cap seals effectively. Replace the filler cap if the seal is defective.

Charcoal Canister

◆ See Figures 8, 9, 10 and 11

1. Remove the charcoal canister from the vehicle.
2. Visually check the charcoal canister for cracks or damage.

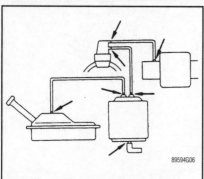

Fig. 6 Always inspect the lines for kinks, cracks and loose connections

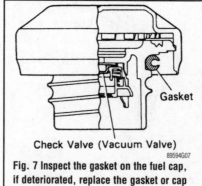

Gasket

Check Valve (Vacuum Valve)

Fig. 7 Inspect the gasket on the fuel cap, if deteriorated, replace the gasket or cap as necessary

Fig. 8 Visually check the charcoal canister for cracks or damage—5S-FE other engines similar

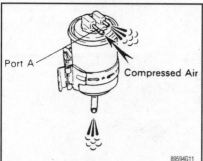

Port A
Compressed Air

Fig. 9 To check for a clogged filter or check valve, blow compressed air into the pipe A . . .

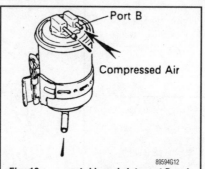

Port B
Compressed Air

Fig. 10 . . . next, blow air into port B and check that air does not flow from the other ports

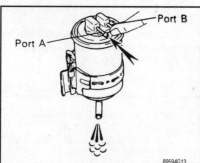

Port B
Port A

Fig. 11 To clean the filter blow compressed air into port A while holding port B closed

3. Check for a clogged filter and stuck check valve. Using low pressure compressed air (0.68 psi. or 4 kPa), blow into the tank pipe **B** and check that the air flows without resistance from the other pipes. Next, blow air into port **B** and check that air does not flow from any other port. If this does not test positive replace the canister.

4. Clean the filter in the canister by blowing no more than 43 psi (294 kPa) of compressed air into the pipe (A) to the outer vent control valve while holding the other upper canister pipes **B** closed.

➡Do not attempt to wash the charcoal canister. Also be sure that no activated carbon comes out of the canister during the cleaning process.

5. Replace or reinstall the canister as needed.

Thermal Vacuum Valve (TVV)

▶ **See Figures 12, 13 and 14**

1. Drain the engine coolant.
2. Remove the TVV valve from the water housing.

➡Be sure to label all hoses leading to the valve.

3. Cool the valve to below 95–104° F (35–40° C) with cool water.
4. Make sure that air does not flow from the upper port to the lower port.
5. Heat the TVV to above 129° F (59° C) with hot water.
6. Check that air flows from the upper port to the lower port of the valve. If the operation is not as specified, replace the TVV valve.

Check Valve

Some check valves are made with two ports and others with three. The two port valves are yellow and black, the three ports are yellow and white.

2 PORT

▶ **See Figures 15, 16 and 17**

1. Label and remove the check valve.
2. Blow air into the yellow port. Check that the air flows from the yellow port to the black port.

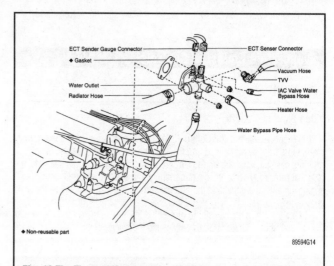

ECT Sender Gauge Connector
♦ Gasket
Water Outlet
Radiator Hose

ECT Senser Connector
Vacuum Hose
TVV
IAC Valve Water Bypass Hose
Heater Hose
Water Bypass Pipe Hose

♦ Non-reusable part

Fig. 12 The Thermal Vacuum valve (TVV) is always located in the water housing on these models

3. Blow air into the yellow port and make sure air does not flow from the black port.
4. Install the check valve with the yellow port facing the body side.

3 PORT

▶ **See Figures 18 and 19**

1. Label and remove the check valve.
2. Blow air into the yellow port. Check that the air flows from the yellow port to the white ports.
3. Cover one of the white ports, then blow air into the other white port and make sure air does not flow from the yellow port.
4. Install the check valve with the yellow port facing the body side.

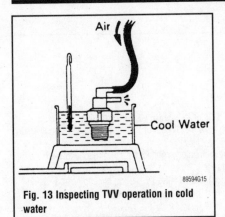

Fig. 13 Inspecting TVV operation in cold water

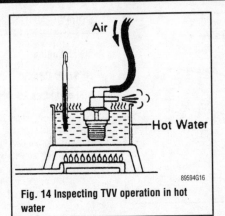

Fig. 14 Inspecting TVV operation in hot water

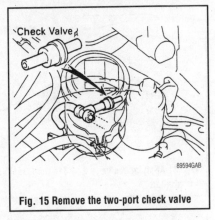

Fig. 15 Remove the two-port check valve

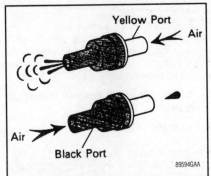

Fig. 16 Blow air into the yellow port and check flow from the black—2 port

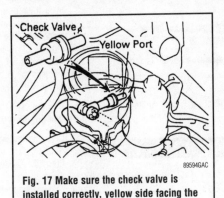

Fig. 17 Make sure the check valve is installed correctly, yellow side facing the body

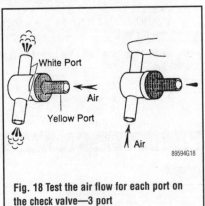

Fig. 18 Test the air flow for each port on the check valve—3 port

Fig. 19 Make sure the check valve is installed correctly, yellow side facing the body

REMOVAL & INSTALLATION

➡When replacing any EVAP system hoses, always use hoses that are fuel-resistant or are marked EVAP. Use of hose which is not fuel-resistant will lead to premature hose failure.

Charcoal Canister

◗ See Figure 20

Label and disconnect the lines running to the canister. On some models the air cleaner lid may need to be removed. Unbolt and extract the charcoal canister from the vehicle. Do not attempt to wash the charcoal canister. Also be sure that no activated carbon comes out of the canister during the cleaning process. Attach the charcoal canister to its mounting bracket and secure. Connect the vacuum hoses in their proper locations.

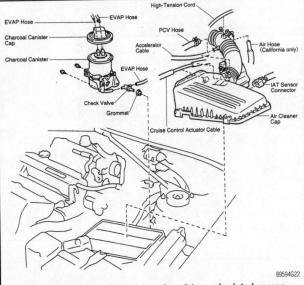

Fig. 20 Exploded view of the charcoal canister and related components—5S-FE engine shown

Thermal Vacuum Valve (TVV)

◗ See Figures 21 and 22

1. Drain the coolant the from the radiator.
2. Disconnect and label the vacuum hoses from the charcoal canister and throttle body.

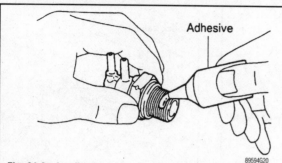

Fig. 21 Apply adhesive to 2 or 3 of the threads of the TVV prior to installation

3. Remove the TVV valve from the engine.

To install:

4. Apply adhesive to 2 or 3 of the threads of the TVV, then tighten the valve to 22 ft. lbs. (29 Nm).

➡On the 5S-FE engine, have the ports facing the direction shown in the illustration.

5. Reattach the vacuum hoses.
6. Refill the engine with coolant. Start the engine, check and top off the fluid level.

Exhaust Gas Recirculation System

OPERATION

The EGR system reduces oxides of nitrogen. This is accomplished by recirculating some of the exhaust gases through the EGR valve to the intake manifold, lowering peak combustion temperatures.

COMPONENT TESTING

5S-FE Engine

SYSTEM CHECK

▶ See Figures 23 thru 28

1. Check and clean the filter in the EGR vacuum modulator. Use compressed air (if possible) to blow the dirt out of the filters and check the filters for contamination or damage.
2. Using a tee (3-way connector), connect a vacuum gauge to the hose between the EGR valve and the VSV.
3. Check the seating of the EGR valve by starting the engine and seeing that it runs at a smooth idle. If the valve is not completely closed, the idle will be rough.
4. Using a jumper wire, connect terminals TE1 and E1 of the DLC1.
5. Inspect the VSV, with the engine coolant temperature below 131°F (55°C), the vacuum gauge should read 0 at 2500 rpm.
6. Inspect the VSV and EGR vacuum modulator, warm the engine to above 140 °F (60 °C). Check the vacuum gauge and confirm low vacuum at 2500 rpm.
7. Disconnect the vacuum hose from the **R** port on the EGR vacuum modulator and, using another piece of hose, connect the **R** port directly to the intake manifold. Check that the vacuum gauge indicates high vacuum at 2500 rpm.

➡Port R is the lower of the two ports. As a large amount of exhaust gas enters, the engine will misfire slightly at this time.

8. Disconnect the vacuum gauge and reattach the vacuum hoses to their proper locations.
9. Check the EGR valve by applying vacuum directly to the valve with the engine at idle. (This may be accomplished either by bridging vacuum directly from the intake manifold or by using a hand-held vacuum pump.) The engine should falter and die as the full load of recalculated gasses enters the engine.
10. If no problem is found with this inspection, the system is OK; otherwise inspect each part.
11. Remove the jumper wire.

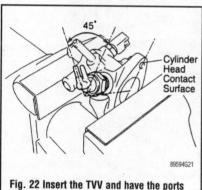

Fig. 22 Insert the TVV and have the ports facing this angle when tightened

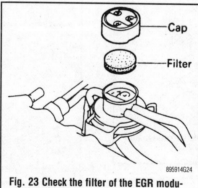

Fig. 23 Check the filter of the EGR modulator for contamination or damage

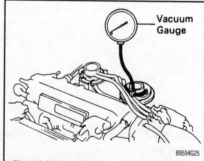

Fig. 24 Place a 3-way union on the EGR valve hose, then connect a vacuum gauge it

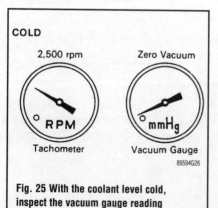

Fig. 25 With the coolant level cold, inspect the vacuum gauge reading

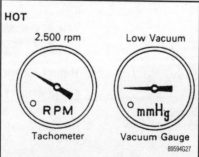

Fig. 26 Inspect the vacuum gauge readings with the engine at normal operating temperature

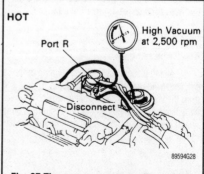

Fig. 27 The vacuum gauge reading at high vacuum should read 2500 rpms

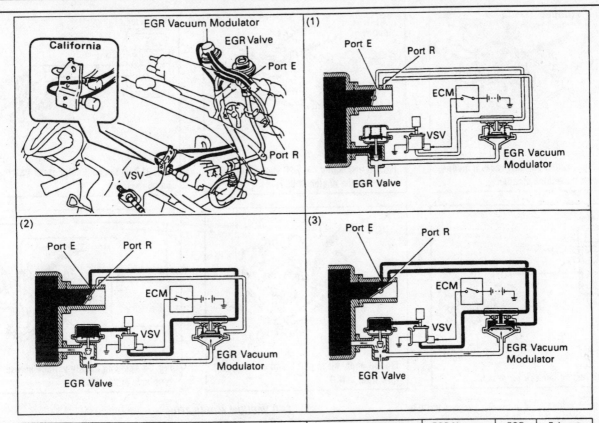

ECT	RPM	PIM (ECM)	VSV	Throttle Valve Opening Aigle	Pressure the EGR Valve Pressure Chamber		EGR Vacuum Modulator	EGR Valve	Exhaust Gas
Below 55°C (131°F)	–	–	CLOSED	–	–		–	CLOSED	Not recirculated
Above 60°C (140°F)	Below 4,000 rpm	OFF	CLOSED	Position below port E	–		–	CLOSED	Not recirculated
		... ON	CLOSED	Position below port E	(1)	–	–	CLOSED	Not recirculated
			OPEN	Positioned between port E and port R	(2) HIGH	*	CLOSES passage to atmosphere	OPEN	Recirculated
			OPEN	Position above port R	(3) HIGH	**	CLOSES passage to atmosphere	OPEN	Recirculated (increase)
	Above 4,000 rpm	OFF	CLOSED	–	–		–	CLOSED	Not recirculated

* Pressure increases ⟶ Modulator closes ⟶ EGR valve opens ⟶ Pressure drops
 EGR valve closes ⟵ Modulator opens ⟵

** When the throttle valve is positioned above port R, the EGR vacuum modulator will close the atmosphere passage and open the EGR valve to increase the exhaust gas, even if the exhaust pressure is insufficiently low.

... If terminals TE1 and E1 of data link connector 1 are connected, the VSV switches ON.

89594G23

Fig. 28 Exhaust Gas Recirculation (EGR) system schematic and operating conditions—5S-FE engine

EGR VALVE

1. Remove the EGR valve. be sure to label all valve vacuum lines.
2. Check the valve for sticking and heavy carbon deposits. If a problem is found, replace the valve.
3. Reinstall the EGR valve with a new gasket.

EGR VACUUM MODULATOR

♦ See Figures 29 and 30

1. Label and disconnect the vacuum hoses from ports **P**, **Q**, and **R** of the EGR vacuum modulator.
2. Plug the **P** and **R** ports with your fingers.
3. Blow air into port **Q**. Check that the air passes freely through the sides of the air filter.

➡ **Port Q is the single port on the one side of the modulator.**

4. Start the engine and maintain 2500 rpm.
5. Repeat the test above. Check that there is a strong resistance to air flow.
6. Reconnect the vacuum hoses to the proper locations.
7. If the operation is not as specified, replace the EGR vacuum modulator.

VACUUM SWITCHING VALVE (VSV)

♦ See Figures 31, 32, 33 and 34

1. Remove the VSV.
2. Using an ohmmeter, check that there is continuity between the terminals. Resistance should read 33–39 ohms @ 68 °F (20 °). If there is no continuity, replace the VSV.
3. Using an ohmmeter, check that there is no continuity between each terminal and the body. If there is, replace the VSV.
4. Check the operation of the VSV, there should be no air flow from ports **E** to **G**.
5. Apply battery voltage across the terminals. Check that air flows from port **E** to the filter.

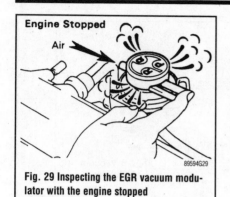

Fig. 29 Inspecting the EGR vacuum modulator with the engine stopped

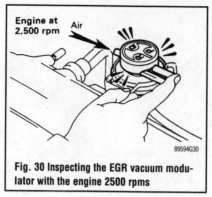

Fig. 30 Inspecting the EGR vacuum modulator with the engine 2500 rpms

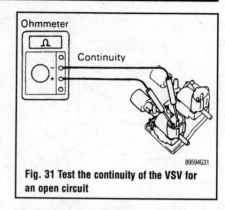

Fig. 31 Test the continuity of the VSV for an open circuit

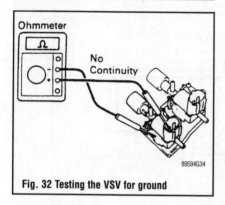

Fig. 32 Testing the VSV for ground

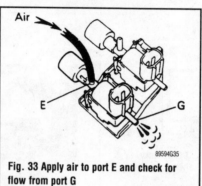

Fig. 33 Apply air to port E and check for flow from port G

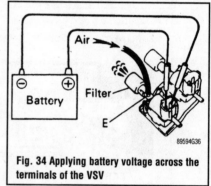

Fig. 34 Applying battery voltage across the terminals of the VSV

6. If the operation is not as specified, replace the VSV.
7. Reinstall or replace the VSV.

7A-FE Engine

SYSTEM CHECK

1. Check and clean the filter in the EGR vacuum modulator. Use compressed air (if possible) to blow the dirt out of the filters and check the filters for contamination or damage.
2. Using a tee (3-way connector), connect a vacuum gauge to the hose between the EGR valve and the EGR vacuum modulator on 1994–95 models and the EGR valve and VSV on 1996–98 models.
3. Check the seating of the EGR valve by starting the engine and seeing that it runs at a smooth idle. If the valve is not completely closed, the idle will be rough.
4. Using a jumper wire, connect terminals TE1 and E1 of the DLC1.
5. Inspect the VSV operation, with the engine coolant temperature below 117°F (47°C), the vacuum gauge should read 0 at 2500 rpm.
6. Inspect the VSV and EGR vacuum modulator operation, warm the engine to above 127 °F (53 °C). Check the vacuum gauge and confirm low vacuum at 2500 rpm.
7. On 1996–98 models, disconnect the vacuum hose from the **R** port on the EGR vacuum modulator and, using another piece of hose, connect the **R** port directly to the intake manifold. Check that the vacuum gauge indicates high vacuum at 2500 rpm. Port R is the lower of the two ports. As a large amount of exhaust gas enters, the engine will misfire slightly at this time.
8. Disconnect the vacuum gauge and reattach the vacuum hoses to their proper locations.
9. Check the EGR valve by applying vacuum directly to the valve with the engine at idle. (This may be accomplished either by bridging vacuum directly from the intake manifold or by using a hand-held vacuum pump.) The engine should falter and die as the full load of recalculated gasses enters the engine.
10. If no problem is found with this inspection, the system is OK; otherwise inspect each part.
11. Remove the jumper wire.

EGR VALVE

1. Remove the EGR valve. be sure to label all valve vacuum lines.
2. Check the valve for sticking and heavy carbon deposits. If a problem is found, replace the valve.
3. Reinstall the EGR valve with a new gasket.

EGR VACUUM MODULATOR

1. Label and disconnect the vacuum hoses from ports **P**, **Q**, and **R** of the EGR vacuum modulator.
2. Plug the **P** and **R** ports with your fingers.
3. Blow air into port **Q**. Check that the air passes freely through the sides of the air filter.

➡**Port Q is the single port on the one side of the modulator.**

4. Start the engine and maintain 2500 rpm.
5. Repeat the test above. Check that there is a strong resistance to air flow.
6. Reconnect the vacuum hoses to the proper locations.
7. If the operation is not as specified, replace the EGR vacuum modulator.

VACUUM SWITCHING VALVE (VSV)

♦ **See Figure 35**

1. Remove the VSV.
2. Using an ohmmeter, check that the continuity is between the terminals. Resistance should read 37–44 ohms @ 68 °F (20 °). If there is no continuity, replace the VSV.
3. Using an ohmmeter, check that there is no continuity between each terminal and the body. If there is, replace the VSV.
4. Check the operation of the VSV, there should be air flow from port **E** to the filter.
5. Apply battery voltage across the terminals. Check that air doers not flow from port **E** to the filter.
6. If the operation is not as specified, replace the VSV.
7. Replace or reinstall the VSV.

REMOVAL & INSTALLATION

Thermal Vacuum Valve (TVV)

♦ **See Figures 21 and 22**

The Thermal Vacuum Valve (TVV) is threaded into the IAC valve bolted to the throttle body. Note the position of the valve prior to removal, it must be facing the same direction on installation.

1. Drain the coolant the from the engine.

Fig. 35 Inspecting the terminal resistance of the EGR VSV

Fig. 36 The EGR VSV is located in the rear of the engine compartment

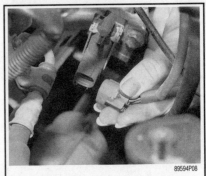

Fig. 37 Disconnect the VSV for the EGR valve wiring harness

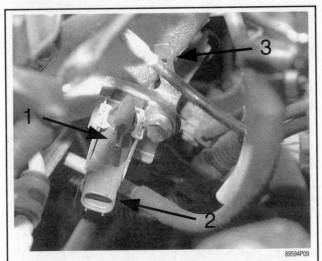

Fig. 38 Vacuum hose port (1), wiring harness connector (2) and harness retainer (3)

2. Disconnect the vacuum hoses from the charcoal canister and throttle body.

3. Remove the TVV from the Intake Air Control (IAC).

To install:

4. Apply adhesive to 2 or 3 of the threads of the TVV, then tighten it to 22 ft. lbs. (29 Nm) on all engines except the 1996–98 7A-FE; 13 ft. lbs. (18 Nm) in the position it was removed from.

5. Reattach the vacuum hoses.

6. Refill the cooling system. Start the engine, check and top off the fluid level.

Vacuum Switching Valve (VSV)

▶ See Figures 36, 37 and 38

Disconnect the wiring from the VSV. Label and removed the vacuum hose(s) from the valve. Loosen the bolt and extract the VSV.

EGR Valve

5S-FE ENGINE

1. Remove the air cleaner hose and cap.

2. Disconnect the throttle body from the intake manifold.

3. Disconnect the EGR gas temperature sensor wiring and unscrew the sensor from the side of the valve.

4. Label and disconnect the hoses from the EGR valve. Remove the 2 union nuts, EGR valve and gasket.

To install:

5. Install a new gasket and the EGR valve and secure the nuts to 9 ft. lbs. (13 Nm).

6. Attach the EGR pipe with the union nuts and tighten to 43 ft. lbs. (59 Nm).

7. Connect the hoses to the EGR valve.

8. Reinstall the EGR gas temperature sensor and tighten to 14 ft. lbs. (20 Nm).

9. Install the throttle body, refer to Section 5.

10. Attach the control cables ad install the air cleaner cap.

7A-FE ENGINE-1994–95 MODELS

▶ See Figures 39 thru 45

1. Turn the ignition switch to the **LOCK** position.

2. Disconnect the negative battery cable. Wait at least 90 seconds from the time the cable is disconnected before working on the vehicle to hinder air bag deployment.

3. Remove the air cleaner hose and cap. Label and disconnect all wiring related to air cleaner removal.

4. Disconnect the accelerator cable bracket from the throttle body.

5. Remove the throttle body from the air intake chamber.

6. Remove the engine hanger, air intake chamber stay and engine vacuum modulator.

7. Loosen the union nut for the EGR pipe.

   a. Label and disconnect the vacuum hose from the EGR valve.

   b. Disconnect the EGR gas temperature sensor wiring.

   c. Remove the EGR gas temperature sensor. Unbolt and remove the EGR valve and pipe. Discard the gaskets.

To install:

8. Clean the EGR valve mating areas. Place a new gasket on the cylinder head, facing the protrusion downward.

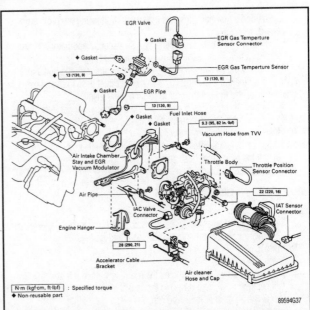

Fig. 39 View of the EGR valve and related components—1994-95 7A-FE engine

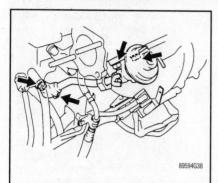

Fig. 40 There are 3 nuts and one bolt retaining the EGR valve and pipe

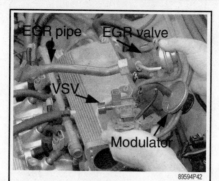

Fig. 41 Extract the EGR valve, pipe and other components as a unit

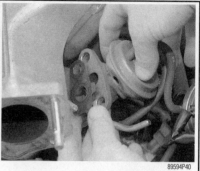

Fig. 42 When extracting the EGR valve, remember to remove the gasket too

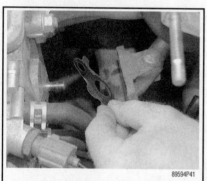

Fig. 43 The EGR pipe is equipped with a gasket at the end of it also

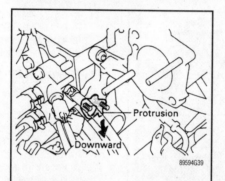

Fig. 44 Position the gasket on the cylinder head with the protrusion facing downward

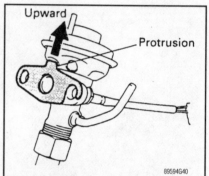

Fig. 45 Place the other gasket on the EGR valve with the protrusion facing upward

a. Set a new gasket on the EGR valve, facing the protrusion upward. check that the gasket clips are firmly fixed in the bolt holes of the EGR valve.

b. Install the EGR valve and pipe with a new bolt and 3 nuts, and tighten to 9 ft. lbs. (13 Nm).

c. Install and secure the EGR gas temperature sensor to 14 ft. lbs. (20 Nm).

d. Connect the wiring to the sensor, then attach the vacuum hose to the EGR valve. tighten the union nut to 43 ft. lbs. (59 Nm).

9. Install the air intake chamber stay, EGR vacuum modulator and engine hanger.

a. Position a new gasket on the intake manifold facing the protrusion downward.

b. Install the air intake chamber stay, EGR vacuum modulator and engine hanger with a nut. Tighten the nut to 21 ft. lbs. (28 Nm).

c. Connect the air pipe to the intake chamber stay with the bolt and tighten to 82 inch lbs. (9 Nm). Connect the fuel inlet hose to the intake chamber stay and tighten the bolt to 82 inch lbs. (9 Nm).

d. Connect the spark plug wire clamp to the engine hanger. Attach the EGR hose and vacuum hose to the EGR valve.

10. Install the throttle body, refer to Section 5.

11. Connect the accelerator cable bracket to the throttle body.

12. Install the air cleaner hose and cap.

13. Connect the negative battery cable.

7A-FE ENGINE—1996–98 MODELS

1. Remove the air cleaner hose and cap.
2. Disconnect and label the vacuum hoses, EGR hose and EGR gas temperature sensor wiring. Remove the nuts, EGR valve and gasket.

To install:

3. Place a new gasket on the cylinder head.
4. Attach the EGR valve and tighten the retaining nuts to 9 ft. lbs. (13 Nm).
5. Connect the hoses and wiring to the sensor and valve.
6. Install the air cleaner hose and cap.

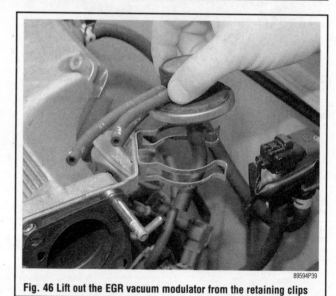

Fig. 46 Lift out the EGR vacuum modulator from the retaining clips

EGR Vacuum Modulator

▶ See Figure 46

1. Unbolt the vacuum modulator bracket and extract.
2. Label and disconnect the hoses attached to the modulator.
3. Pull the clips apart and remove the modulator.

To install:

4. Insert the modulator into the bracket clips.
5. Attach the hoses in their proper positions.
6. Position the bracket/modulator assembly on the engine and secure the mounting bolts to 9 ft. lbs. (12 Nm).

ELECTRONIC ENGINE CONTROLS

The Electronic Fuel Injection (EFI) system precisely controls fuel injection to match engine requirements. This in turn reduces emissions and increases driveability. The ECM receives input from various sensors to determine engine operating conditions. These sensors provide the input to the control unit which determines the amount of fuel to be injected as well as other variables such as idle speed. These inputs and their corresponding sensors include:

- Manifold Absolute Pressure (MAP) sensor
- Intake Air Temperature (IAT) sensor
- Engine Coolant Temperature (ECT) sensor
- Engine speed (RPM)
- Throttle valve opening—Throttle Position Sensor
- Exhaust oxygen content—Oxygen Sensor

Engine Control Module (ECM)

OPERATION

The ECM receives signals from various sensors on the engine. It will then process this information and calculate the correct air/fuel mixture under all operating conditions. The ECM is a very fragile and expensive component. Always follow the precautions when servicing the electronic control system.

PRECAUTIONS

▶ **See Figure 47**

✳✳ CAUTION

Work must be started after 90 seconds from the time the ignition switch is turned to the LOCK position and the negative battery cable has been disconnected. The SRS is equipped with a back-up power source so that if work is started within 90 seconds of disconnecting the negative battery cable, the SRS may deploy. When the negative terminal cable is disconnected from the battery, memory of the clock and radio will be canceled. Before you start working, make a note of the contents memorized by the audio memory system. When you have finished working, reset the audio systems and adjust the clock. Never use a back-up power supply from outside the vehicle.

- Do not permit parts to receive a severe impact during removal or installation. Always handle all fuel injection parts with care, especially the ECM. DO NOT open the ECM cover!
- Before removing the fuel injected wiring connectors, terminals, ect., first disconnect the power by either disconnecting the negative battery cable or turning the ignition switch **OFF**.
- Always check the diagnostic trouble code before disconnecting the terminal cable from the battery.
- Do not be careless during troubleshooting as there are numerous amounts of transistor circuits; even a slight terminal contact can induce troubles.
- When inspecting during rainy days, take extra caution not to allow entry of water in or on the unit. When washing the engine compartment, prevent water from getting on the fuel injection parts and wiring connectors.

Fig. 47 DO NOT drop the ECM!

REMOVAL & INSTALLATION

▶ **See Figure 48**

The ECM is located under the dash on the drivers side near the center console.

1. Disconnect the negative battery cable. Wait at least 90 seconds once the negative battery cable id disconnected to perform work on the vehicle to hinder air bag deployment.

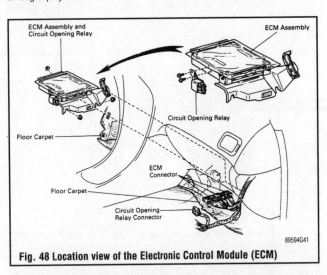

Fig. 48 Location view of the Electronic Control Module (ECM)

✳✳ CAUTION

Work must be started after 90 seconds from the time the ignition switch is turned to the LOCK position and the negative battery cable has been disconnected. The SRS is equipped with a back-up power source so that if work is started within 90 seconds of disconnecting the negative battery cable, the SRS may deploy. When the negative terminal cable is disconnected from the battery, memory of the clock and radio will be canceled. Before you start working, make a note of the contents memorized by the audio memory system. When you have finished working, reset the audio systems and adjust the clock. Never use a back-up power supply from outside the vehicle.

2. Remove any necessary trim panel to gain access to the ECM floor mat bracket bolts.
3. Remove the ECM floor mat bracket bolts.
4. Locate the ECM and release the lock, then pull out the connector. Pull on the connectors only!
5. Unbolt the ECM from its mounting area.

To install:

6. Install the ECM floor mat bracket bolts.
7. Fully insert the connector, then check that it is locked.
8. Install any necessary trim panel. Reconnect the negative battery cable.
9. Start engine and check for proper operation.

Circuit Opening Relay

TESTING

▶ **See Figures 49, 50, 51 and 52**

1. With the ignition switch **OFF**, remove the relay from its mount.
2. Using an ohmmeter, test for continuity between terminals STA and E1. Continuity should be present.
3. There should be continuity between terminals B+ and FC.

4. There should be no continuity between terminals B+ and FP.

5. Apply battery voltage and ground to terminals STA and E1; with voltage applied, continuity should be present at terminals B+ and FP.

6. Apply battery voltage and ground to terminals B and FC; with voltage applied, continuity should be present at terminals B+ and FP.

7. If any test condition is not met, the relay must be replaced.

REMOVAL & INSTALLATION

The circuit opening relay is a attached to the ECM. Removal of the ECM may not be necessary, but refer to the ECM removal sequence to access the relay. Simply disconnect the wiring from the relay and unbolt the relay from the ECM.

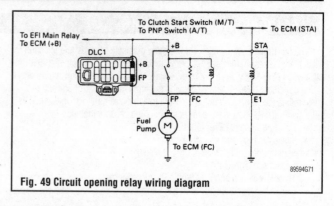

Fig. 49 Circuit opening relay wiring diagram

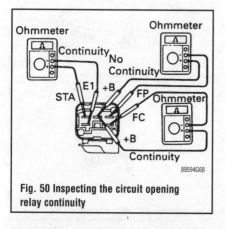

Fig. 50 Inspecting the circuit opening relay continuity

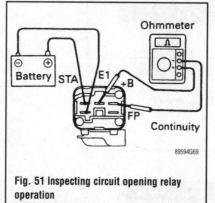

Fig. 51 Inspecting circuit opening relay operation

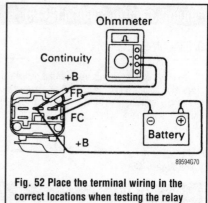

Fig. 52 Place the terminal wiring in the correct locations when testing the relay

Oxygen Sensor

OPERATION

The exhaust oxygen sensor or O2S, is mounted in the exhaust stream where it monitors oxygen content in the exhaust gas. The oxygen content in the exhaust is a measure of the air/fuel mixture going into the engine. The oxygen in the exhaust reacts with the oxygen sensor to produce a voltage which is read by the ECM.

There are two types of oxygen sensors used in these vehicles. They are the single wire oxygen sensor (O2S) and the heated oxygen sensor (HO2S). The oxygen sensor is a spark plug shaped device that is screwed into the exhaust manifold. It monitors the oxygen content of the exhaust gases and sends a voltage signal to the Electronic Control Module (ECM). The ECM monitors this voltage and, depending on the value of the received signal, issues a command to the mixture control solenoid on the throttle body to adjust for rich or lean conditions.

The heated oxygen sensor has a heating element incorporated into the sensor to aid in the warm up to the proper operating temperature and to maintain that temperature.

The proper operation of the oxygen sensor depends upon four basic conditions:

• Good electrical connections. Since the sensor generates low currents, good clean electrical connections at the sensor are a must.

• Outside air supply. Air must circulate to the internal portion of the sensor. When servicing the sensor, do not restrict the air passages.

• Proper operating temperatures. The ECM will not recognize the sensor's signals until the sensor reaches approximately 600°F (316°C).

• Non-leaded fuel. The use of leaded gasoline will damage the sensor very quickly.

TESTING

✳✳ WARNING

Do not pierce the wires when testing this sensor; this can lead to wiring harness damage. Backprobe the connector to properly read the voltage of the HO2S.

Single Wire Sensor

▶ See Figure 53

➡ Use an analog voltmeter or a digital voltmeter with a n analog function to perform this test.

1. Start the engine and bring it to normal operating temperature, then run the engine above 2500 rpm for 90 seconds or more.

2. Connect the voltmeter between terminals TE1 and E1 of the DLC1 and maintain the engine speed of 2500 rpms.

3. Record the number of times the voltmeter fluctuates in 10 seconds.

4. If the needle fluctuates 8 times or more the oxygen sensor is functioning properly.

5. If the needle fluctuates less than 8 times in 10 seconds, check that the engine rpm is still 2500 and repeat the test.

6. If the needle still fluctuates less than 8 times, disconnect the terminals TE1 and E1 of the DLC1 and maintain the engine speed at 2500 rpm.

7. Measure the voltage between terminals VF1 and E1. If the voltage is more than zero volts, replace the sensor.

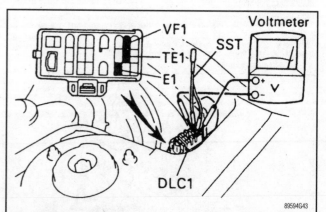

Fig. 53 DLC1 terminal identification for testing the oxygen sensor— 1994–95 models

Heated Oxygen Sensor

♦ **See Figure 54**

1. Remove the scuff plate, cowl side trim, RH front seat and floor carpet.
2. Disconnect the oxygen sensor wiring.
3. Next, connect a high impedance ohmmeter between the HO2S terminals of the heating element and verify that the resistance is 11.0–16.0 ohms at 68° F (20° C).
4. If the HO2S heater resistance is not as specified, the HO2S may be faulty.
5. Reconnect the sensor wiring.

➥**Use an analog voltmeter or a digital voltmeter with a n analog function to perform this test.**

6. Start the engine and bring it to normal operating temperature, then run the engine above 2500 rpm for 90 seconds or more.
7. Connect the voltmeter between terminals TE1 and E1 of the DLC1 and maintain the engine speed of 2500 rpms.
8. Record the number of times the voltmeter fluctuates in 10 seconds.
9. If the needle fluctuates 8 times or more the oxygen sensor is functioning properly.
10. If the needle fluctuates less than 8 times in 10 seconds, check that the engine rpm is still 2500 and repeat the test.
11. If the needle still fluctuates less than 8 times, disconnect the terminals TE1 and E1 of the DLC1 and maintain the engine speed at 2500 rpm.

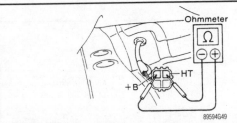

Fig. 54 Testing the terminals of a heated oxygen sensor

12. Measure the voltage between terminals VF1 and E1. If the voltage is more than zero volts, replace the sensor.
13. Reinstall the removed components.

REMOVAL & INSTALLATION

♦ **See Figures 55 thru 60**

The oxygen sensor can be located in several places. Either in the exhaust manifold, front pipe or catalytic converter.

❋❋ WARNING

Care should be used during the removal of the oxygen sensor. Both the sensor and its wire can be easily damaged.

1. The best condition in which to remove the sensor is when the engine is moderately warm. This is generally achieved after two to five minutes (depending on outside temperature) of running after a cold start. The exhaust manifold has developed enough heat to expand and make the removal easier but is not so hot that it has become untouchable. Wearing heat resistant gloves is highly recommended during this repair.
2. With the ignition OFF, unplug the connector for the sensor.
3. Remove the two sensor attaching bolts.
4. Remove the oxygen sensor from its mounting place and discard the gasket.

➥**A special socket is available to remove the sensor.**

To install:
➥**During and after the removal, use great care to protect the tip of the sensor if it is to be reused. Do not allow it to come in contact with fluids or dirt. Do not attempt to clean it or wash it.**

5. Apply a coat of anti-seize compound to the bolt threads but DO NOT allow any to get on the tip of the sensor.
6. Position a new gasket, install and secure the sensor.
7. Reattach the electrical wiring and insure a clean, tight connection.

Fig. 55 Note the manifold mounted sensor is obtained through the heat shield

Fig. 56 Remove the wiring from the sensor located near the radiator

Fig. 57 One oxygen sensor is attached to the front exhaust pipe on all models

Fig. 58 Two nuts retain the O2 sensor on the exhaust manifold

Fig. 59 Extract the sensor from the manifold and . . .

Fig. 60 . . . the gasket

Knock Sensor

OPERATION

▶ See Figure 61

The knock sensor is fitted into the cylinder block to detect engine knocking. This sensor contains a piezoelectric element which generates a voltage when it becomes deformed, which occurs when the cylinder block vibrates due to knocking. If the engine knocking occurs, ignition timing is retarded to suppress it.

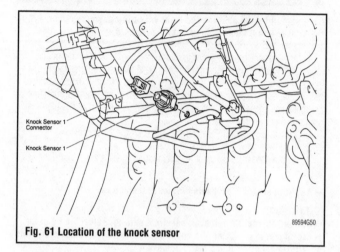

Knock Sensor 1 Connector

Knock Sensor 1

89594G50

Fig. 61 Location of the knock sensor

TESTING

▶ See Figure 62

1. Disconnect the wiring from the knock sensor.
2. Using tool 09816-30010 or an equivalent socket, remove the knock sensor from the vehicle.
3. Using an ohmmeter, check that there is no continuity between the terminal and the body.
4. If there is continuity, replace the sensor.
5. Install the knock sensor with the special tool, tighten securely to 33 ft. lbs. (44 Nm).
6. Connect the sensor wiring.

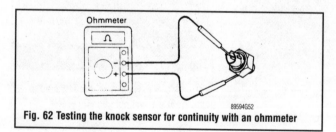

Ohmmeter

89594G52

Fig. 62 Testing the knock sensor for continuity with an ohmmeter

REMOVAL & INSTALLATION

▶ See Figure 63

1. Disconnect the wiring from the knock sensor.
2. Using tool, 09816-30010 or an equivalent socket, remove the knock sensor from the vehicle.
3. Inspect the vacuum hose over its entire length for any signs of cracking or splitting. The slightest leak can cause improper operation.
To install:
4. Install the knock sensor with the special tool, tighten securely to 33 ft. lbs. (44 Nm).
5. Connect the sensor wiring. Inspect the vacuum hose over its entire length for any signs of cracking or splitting. The slightest leak can cause improper operation.

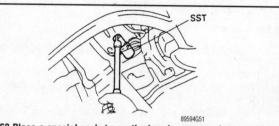

SST

89594G51

Fig. 63 Place a special socket over the knock sensor and remove the sensor

Idle Air Control (IAC) Valve

OPERATION

The ECM is programmed with specific engine speed values to respond to different engine conditions (coolant temperature, air conditioner on/off, etc.). Sensors transmit signals to the ECM which controls the flow of air through the bypass of the throttle valve and adjusts the idle speed to the specified value. Some vehicles use an Idle Speed Control (ISC) valve while others use an Air Valve or Idle Air Control (IAC) valve to control throttle body by-pass air flow.

TESTING

7A-FE Engine

▶ See Figures 64 thru 69

1. Using a jumper wire, connect terminals TE1 and E1 of the DLC1.
   a. After the engine rpm is kept at 900–1300 for about 5 seconds, check that the rpm returns to idle.
   b. If the rpm operation is not as specified, check the IAC valve, wiring and engine ECM.
   c. Remove the jumper wire form the DLC1.
2. Disconnect the IAC valve wiring.
3. Using an ohmmeter, measure the resistance between terminals +B and the other terminals (RSC and RSO).
   a. Resistance should be between:
   • 1994–95 models—19.3–22.3 ohms
   • 1996—17.0–24.5 ohms
4. If the resistance is not within specifications, replace the IAC valve.
5. To check the operation of the IAC valve, the engine should be at normal operating temperature and the transmission in Neutral.
   a. Connect the positive lead of the battery to terminal B+ and the negative lead to terminal RSC, then check that the valve is closed.
   b. Connect the positive lead from the battery to terminal B+ and the negative lead to terminal RSO, then check that the valve is open.
6. If operation is not as specified, replace the IAC valve.

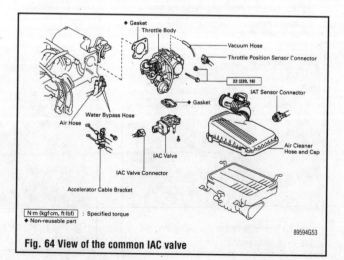

◆ Gasket
Throttle Body
Vacuum Hose
Throttle Position Sensor Connector
22 (220, 16)
IAT Sensor Connector
Water Bypass Hose
Air Hose
◆ Gasket
Air Cleaner Hose and Cap
IAC Valve
IAC Valve Connector
Accelerator Cable Bracket

N·m (kgf·cm, ft·lbf) : Specified torque
◆ Non-reusable part

89594G53

Fig. 64 View of the common IAC valve

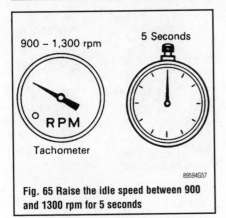

Fig. 65 Raise the idle speed between 900 and 1300 rpm for 5 seconds

Fig. 66 Remove the harness from the IAC valve to test the terminals

Fig. 67 Use an ohmmeter to check the IAC valve resistance between terminals—7A-FE engine

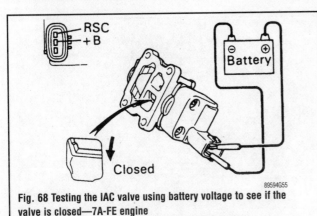

Fig. 68 Testing the IAC valve using battery voltage to see if the valve is closed—7A-FE engine

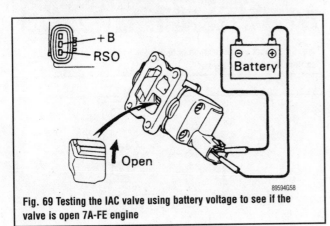

Fig. 69 Testing the IAC valve using battery voltage to see if the valve is open 7A-FE engine

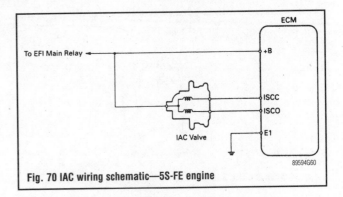

Fig. 70 IAC wiring schematic—5S-FE engine

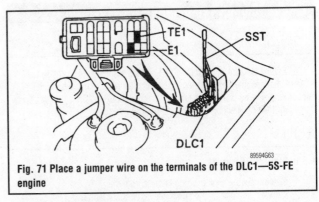

Fig. 71 Place a jumper wire on the terminals of the DLC1—5S-FE engine

a. Connect the positive lead of the battery to terminal B+ and the negative lead to terminal ISCC, then check that the valve is closed.

b. Connect the positive lead from the battery to terminal B+ and the negative lead to terminal ISCO, then check that the valve is open.

4. If operation is not as specified, replace the IAC valve.

REMOVAL & INSTALLATION

▶ See Figures 73, 74 and 75

1. Disconnect the negative battery cable. Wait at least 90 seconds to work on the vehicle once the cable is disconnected to hinder air bag deployment.
2. Drain the engine coolant.
3. Remove the air cleaner cap and disconnect the control cables.
4. Remove the throttle body, refer to Section 5.
5. Remove the 4 retaining screws, IAC valve and gasket.

To install:

6. Position a new gasket on the throttle body. Attach the IAC valve and secure.
7. Attach the throttle body to the engine, refer to Section 5.
8. Attach the control cables, install the air cleaner cap.
9. Fill the cooling system.
10. Start the engine, top off the cooling system and check operation.

5S-FE Engine

▶ See Figures 70, 71 and 72

1. Using a jumper wire, connect terminals TE1 and E1 of the DLC1.
    a. After the engine rpm is kept at 900–1300 for about 5 seconds, check that the rpm returns to idle.
    b. If the rpm operation is not as specified, check the IAC valve, wiring and engine ECM.
    c. Remove the jumper wire from the DLC1.
2. Disconnect the IAC valve wiring.
    a. Using an ohmmeter, measure the resistance between terminals +B and the other terminals ISCC and ISCO.
    b. Resistance should be between:
• 1994–95 models—19.3–22.3 ohms
• 1996–98 models—17.0–24.5 ohms
    c. If the resistance is not within specifications, replace the IAC valve.
3. To check the operation of the IAC valve, the engine should be at normal operating temperature and the transmission in Neutral.

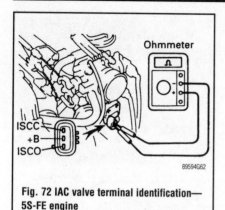

Fig. 72 IAC valve terminal identification—5S-FE engine

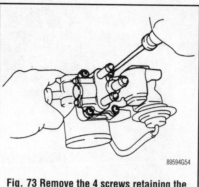

Fig. 73 Remove the 4 screws retaining the IAC valve to the throttle body

Fig. 74 Separate the IAC and remove the gasket

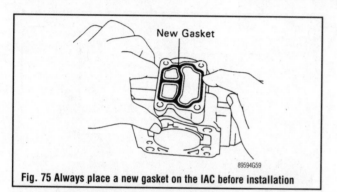

Fig. 75 Always place a new gasket on the IAC before installation

Engine Coolant Temperature (ECT) Sensor

OPERATION

The Engine Coolant Temperature (ECT) sensor's function is to advise the ECM of changes in engine temperature by monitoring the changes in coolant temperature. The sensor must be handled carefully during removal. It can be damaged (thereby affecting engine performance) by impact.

TESTING

▶ **See Figures 76 and 77**

1. Disconnect the engine wiring harness from the ECT sensor.
2. Connect an ohmmeter between the ECT sensor terminals.
3. With the engine cold and the ignition switch in the **OFF** position, measure and note the ECT sensor resistance.
4. Connect the engine wiring harness to the sensor.
5. Start the engine and allow the engine to reach normal operating temperature.
6. Once the engine has reached normal operating temperature, turn the engine **OFF**.
7. Once again, disconnect the engine wiring harness from the ECT sensor.
8. Measure and note the ECT sensor resistance with the engine hot.
9. Compare the cold and hot ECT sensor resistance measurements with the accompanying chart.
10. If readings do not approximate those in the chart, the sensor may be faulty.

REMOVAL & INSTALLATION

▶ **See Figures 78 and 79**

1. Drain the engine coolant.
2. Disconnect the ECT sensor wiring.
3. Remove the sensor and gasket.

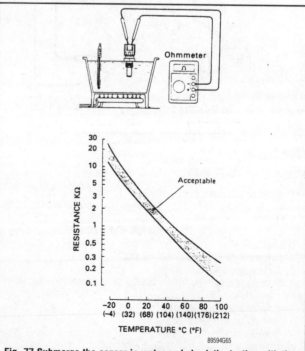

Fig. 76 Inspect the resistance between the terminals of the engine coolant temperature sensor

Fig. 77 Submerge the sensor in water and check the testing with the Engine Coolant Temperature (ECT) sensor chart

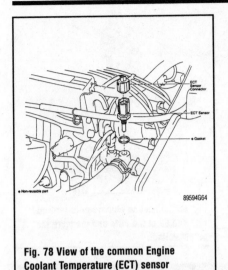

Fig. 78 View of the common Engine Coolant Temperature (ECT) sensor

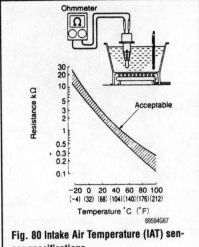

Fig. 79 Place thread sealer on the sensor before installation

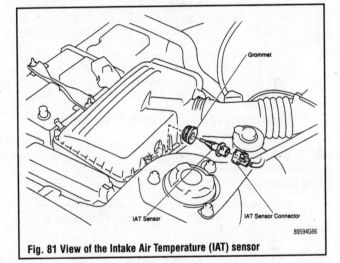

Fig. 80 Intake Air Temperature (IAT) sensor specifications

To install:

4. Install the new sensor with gasket. Tighten the sensor to 17 ft. lbs. (25 Nm).
5. Connect the wiring to the sensor.
6. Refill the engine with coolant and water mixture.

Intake Air Temperature (IAT) Sensor

OPERATION

The IAT sensor is located in the air cleaner housing. The IAT sensor advises the ECM of changes in intake air temperature (and therefore air density). As air temperature of the intake varies, the ECM, by monitoring the voltage change, adjusts the amount of fuel injection according to the air temperature.

TESTING

♦ **See Figure 80**

1. Remove the IAT sensor.
2. Using an ohmmeter, measure the resistance between the terminals. Refer to the graph.
3. If the resistance is not within specifications, replace the sensor.
4. Install the sensor.

REMOVAL & INSTALLATION

♦ **See Figure 81**

Disconnect the wiring from the IAT sensor. Test the sensor using an ohmmeter. If the testing is not within specifications, grasp the sensor and replace as necessary. Inspect the sensor grommet and replace if deteriorated. Insert a new sensor and attach the wiring.

Manifold Air Pressure (MAP) Sensor

OPERATION

This sensor advises the ECM of pressure changes in the intake manifold. It consists of a semi-conductor pressure converting element which converts a pressure change into an electrical signal. The ECM sends a reference signal to the MAP sensor; the change in air pressure changes the resistance within the

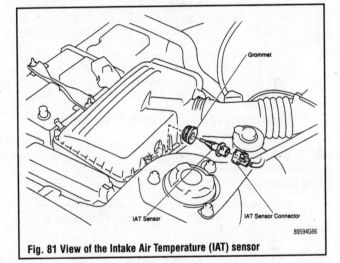

Fig. 81 View of the Intake Air Temperature (IAT) sensor

sensor. The ECM reads the change from its reference voltage and signals its systems to react accordingly.

TESTING

♦ **See Figures 82, 83, 84 and 85**

1. Disconnect the MAP sensor wiring.
2. Turn the ignition switch **ON**.

Applied Vacuum kPa (mmHg) (in.Hg)	13.3 (100) (3.94)	26.7 (200) (7.87)	40.0 (300) (11.81)	53.5 (400) (15.75)	66.7 (500) (19.69)
Voltage drop V	0.3 – 0.5	0.7 – 0.9	1.1 – 1.3	1.5 – 1.7	1.9 – 2.1

Fig. 82 MAP sensor specifications

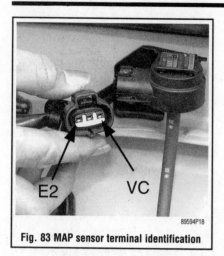

Fig. 83 MAP sensor terminal identification

Fig. 84 Measuring voltage terminals VC and E2 of the MAP sensor

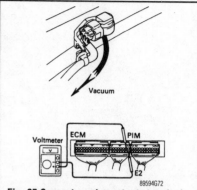

Fig. 85 Connect an ohmmeter to terminals PIM and E2 of the ECM and measure the output voltage

3. Using a voltmeter, measure the voltage between the connector terminals VC and E2 of the wiring harness side. Voltage should be 4.5–5.5 volts.

4. Turn the ignition switch to **LOCK.**

5. Reattach the MAP sensor wiring.

6. To inspect the power output of the sensor, turn the ignition switch to the ON position.

7. Disconnect the vacuum hose from the sensor.

8. Connect the voltmeter to terminals PIM and E2 of the ECM, and measure the output voltage under ambient atmospheric pressure.

9. Apply vacuum to the MAP sensor in 3.94 inch Hg. (13.3 kPa) segments to 19.69 inch Hg. (66.7 kPa).

10. Measure the voltage drop from step 8 above for each segment.

11. Reattach the vacuum hose to the sensor.

REMOVAL & INSTALLATION

▶ **See Figure 86**

Label and disconnect all hoses and wiring to the MAP sensor. Unbolt the sensor from the firewall. Attach ands secure a new sensor, then connect all wires and hoses.

Throttle Position (TP) Sensor

OPERATION

To reduce HC and CO emissions, the Throttle Position (TP) sensor opens the throttle valve to slightly more than the idle position when decelerating. This keeps the air/fuel ratio from becoming excessively rich when the throttle valve is quickly closed. In addition, the TP is used to increase idle rpm when power steering fluid pressure exceeds a calibrated value and/or when a large electrical load is placed on the electrical system (headlights, rear defogger etc).

TESTING

5S-FE Engine

▶ **See Figures 87 thru 92**

1. Apply vacuum to the throttle opener.

2. Insert a 0.020–0.028 inch (0.50–0.70mm) feeler gage between the throttle stop screw and stop lever.

Fig. 86 View of the MAP sensor attached to the firewall

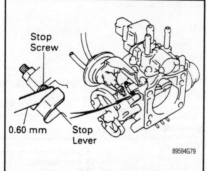

Fig. 87 Insert a feeler gage in between the throttle stop screw and stop lever

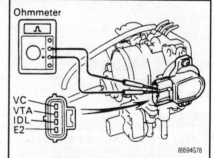

Fig. 88 Measuring the resistance of the throttle position sensor and terminal identification

Clearance between lever and stop screw	Between terminals	Resistance
0 mm (0 in.)	VTA – E2	0.2 – 5.7 kΩ
0.50 mm (0.020 in.)	IDL – E2	2.3 kΩ or less
0.70 mm (0.028 in.)	IDL – E2	Infinity
Throttle valve fully open	VTA – E2	2.0 – 10.2 kΩ
–	VC – E2	2.5 – 5.9 kΩ

Fig. 89 Throttle position sensor chart—1994–95 models

Clearance between lever and stop screw	Between terminals	Resistance
0 mm (0 in.)	VTA – E2	0.2 – 5.7 kΩ
Throttle valve fully open	VTA – E2	2.0 – 10.2 kΩ
–	VC – E2	2.5 – 5.9 kΩ

Fig. 90 Throttle position sensor chart—1996–98 models

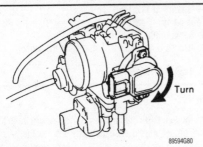

Fig. 91 Gradually turn the sensor clockwise until the ohmmeter deflects, then secure

Clearance between lever and stop screw	Continuity (IDL — E2)
0.50 mm (0.020 in.)	Continuity
0.70 mm (0.028 in.)	No continuity

Fig. 92 Throttle position sensor continuity testing

3. Using an ohmmeter, measure the resistance between each terminal.
4. If necessary adjust the sensor, loosen the 2 screws of the sensor.
5. Insert a 0.024 inch (0.60mm) feeler gauge between the throttle stop screw and stop lever.
6. Connect the tester probe of an ohmmeter to the terminals IDL and E2 of the sensor.
7. Gradually turn the sensor clockwise until the ohmmeter deflects, and secure it with the 2 set screws.
8. Recheck the continuity between terminals IDL and E2.

7A-FE Engine

♦ **See Figures 88 and 93 thru 100**

1. Disconnect the throttle position sensor wiring.
2. Disconnect the throttle opener vacuum hose from the throttle body.
3. Apply vacuum to the throttle opener.
4. Insert a feeler gage between the throttle stop screw and stop lever.
5. Using an ohmmeter, measure the resistance between each terminal.
6. If necessary, adjust the throttle position sensor.
   a. Loosen the 2 set-screws of the sensor.
   b. Apply vacuum to the throttle opener.
   c. Insert a 0.028 inch (0.70mm) feeler gage between the throttle stop screw and stop lever.

Fig. 93 Disengage the throttle position sensor harness

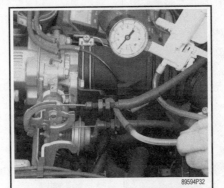

Fig. 94 Apply vacuum to the throttle opener

Fig. 95 Insert a feeler gage between the throttle stop screw and stop lever

Fig. 96 When using this size gauge to test the IDL and E2 terminals of the TPS sensor . . .

Fig. 97 . . . infinity is the result of the testing

Fig. 98 Testing the terminals of the TP sensor for resistance

Clearance between lever and stop screw	Between terminals	Resistance
0 mm (0 in.)	VTA — E2	0.2 — 5.7 kΩ
0.40 mm (0.016 in.)	IDL — E2	2.3 kΩ or less
0.90 mm (0.035 in.)	IDL — E2	Infinity
Throttle valve fully open	VTA — E2	2.0 — 10.2 kΩ
–	VC — E2	2.5 — 5.9 kΩ

Fig. 99 Throttle position sensor terminal identification—7A-FE engine

Clearance between lever and stop screw	Continuity (IDL — E2)
0.40 mm (0.016 in.)	Continuity
0.90 mm (0.035 in.)	No continuity

Fig. 100 Continuity chart between terminals IDL and E2—7A-FE engine

d. Connect the test probe of the ohmmeter to the terminals IDL and E2 of the throttle position sensor.

e. Gradually turn the sensor clockwise until the ohmmeter deflects, and secure it with the set screws.

f. Recheck the continuity between terminals IDL and E2.

7. Reattach the throttle opener vacuum hose to the throttle body.

8. Reconnect the throttle position sensor wiring.

REMOVAL & INSTALLATION

▶ **See Figure 101**

1. Disconnect the harness from the throttle position sensor.
2. Remove the mounting screws and extract the sensor.

To install:

3. Make certain the throttle plate is fully closed. With the throttle body held in its normal orientation, place the sensor onto the throttle body so that the electrical connector is in the correct position.

4. Turn the sensor clockwise as shown and temporarily install the retaining screws.

5. Adjust the throttle position sensor.

Fig. 101 Remove these two screws that attach the throttle position sensor to the throttle body

EGR Gas Temperature Sensor

TESTING

▶ **See Figure 102**

1. Remove the sensor. Place the tip of the sensor in a pot of heated oil.
2. Using an ohmmeter, measure the resistance between the two terminals. It should be as follows:

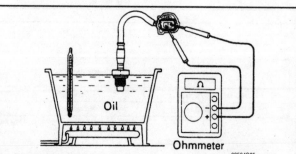

Fig. 102 Submerge the sensor tip in oil and measure the resistance of the sensor

a. 64–97k ohms at 112°F(50°C)

b. 11–16k ohms at 212°F(100°C)

c. 2–4k ohms at 302°F (150°C)

3. If the resistance is not as specified, replace the sensor.

REMOVAL & INSTALLATION

▶ **See Figure 103**

1. With the ignition **OFF**, unplug the electrical connector to the sensor.

2. Using the proper sized wrench, carefully unscrew the sensor from the engine.

To install:

3. Install the sensor.

4. Plug the electrical connector into the sensor.

5. Refill the coolant to the proper level. Road test the vehicle for proper operation.

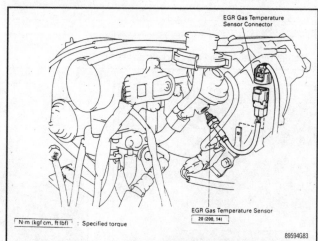

Fig. 103 The EGR temperature sensor located up underneath the EGR valve

A/C Idle-Up System

OPERATION

▶ **See Figures 104 and 105**

An A/C idle-up valve is used on these engines to raise the engine idle when the A/C is turned on.

TESTING

▶ **See Figures 106, 107, 108, 109 and 110**

➡ **The A/C Idle-Up valve can be tested with the valve on or off the engine.**

1. Make sure all accessories are off.

2. Disconnect the idle-up valve wiring.

3. Label and remove the two hoses attached to the valve.

4. Remove the bolts and the valve.

5. Check the valve for and open circuit. Test the A/C idle-up valve using an ohmmeter, check that there is continuity between terminals. Resistance should be around 30–33 ohms at 68°F (20°C).

6. If it is not as specified, replace the VSV.

7. Check the valve for ground, with an ohmmeter, make sure there is not continuity between each terminal and the body.

8. If there is, replace the VSV.

9. Check the valve operation.

10. Check that air does not blow from pipe E to F.

11. Apply positive battery voltage across the terminals. Check that air flows from pipe E to F.

12. If operation is not as specified, replace the VSV.

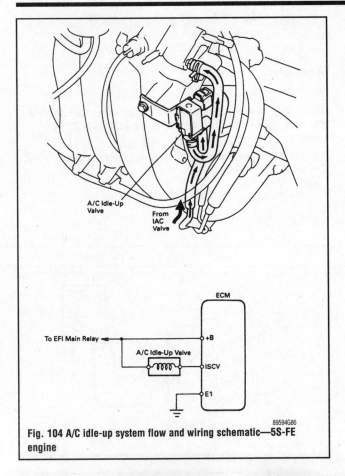

Fig. 104 A/C idle-up system flow and wiring schematic—5S-FE engine

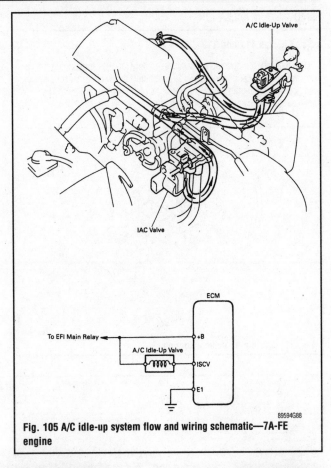

Fig. 105 A/C idle-up system flow and wiring schematic—7A-FE engine

Fig. 106 The A/C Idle-Up valve retaining bolt (1), wiring connector (2) and air hose (3)

Fig. 107 Testing for continuity on the A/C idle-up valve

Fig. 108 Place the negative connector on the body and the positive on the terminal to test for ground

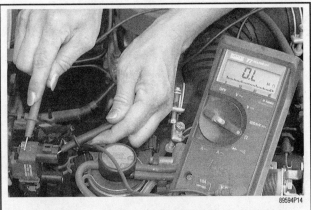

Fig. 109 The same test can be done with the valve on the vehicle

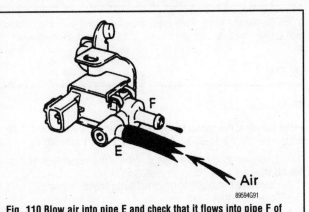

Fig. 110 Blow air into pipe E and check that it flows into pipe F of the VSV

REMOVAL & INSTALLATION

♦ **See Figures 111 and 112**

Replacing the various vacuum switches simply requires unplugging the vacuum and/or electrical connections, then unbolting the switch. Inspect the vacuum hose over its entire length for any signs of cracking or splitting. The slightest leak can cause improper operation.

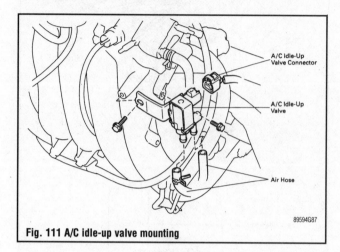

Fig. 111 A/C idle-up valve mounting

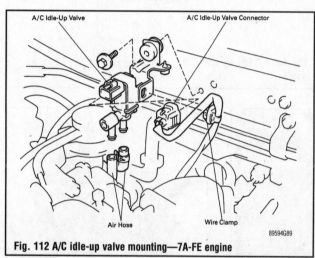

Fig. 112 A/C idle-up valve mounting—7A-FE engine

Crankshaft Position (CKP) Sensor

OPERATION

The Crankshaft Position (CKP) sensor provides a signal through the ignition module which the ECM uses as a reference to calculate rpm and crankshaft position.

TESTING

5S-FE Engine

➡The testing of this sensor is done with the engine hot and cold. Cold is from 14–122°F (–10–50°C), hot is from 122–212°F (50–100°C).

1. Disconnect the crankshaft position sensor wiring from the alternator drive belt adjusting bar.
2. Using an ohmmeter, measure the resistance between terminals.
- Cold—985–1600 ohms
- Hot—1265–1890 ohms

3. If the resistance is not as specified, replace the crankshaft position sensor.
4. Reattach the sensor wiring.

7A-FE Engine

♦ **See Figure 113**

➡The testing of this sensor is done with the engine hot and cold. Cold is from 14–122°F (–10–50°C), hot is from 122–212°F (50–100°C).

1. Disconnect the crankshaft position sensor wiring.
2. Using an ohmmeter, measure the resistance between terminals.
- Cold—1630–2740 ohms
- Hot—2065–3225 ohms

3. If the resistance is not as specified, replace the crankshaft position sensor.
4. Reattach the sensor wiring.

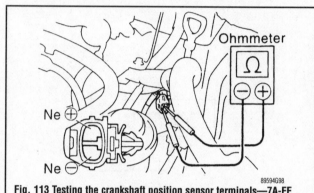

Fig. 113 Testing the crankshaft position sensor terminals—7A-FE engine

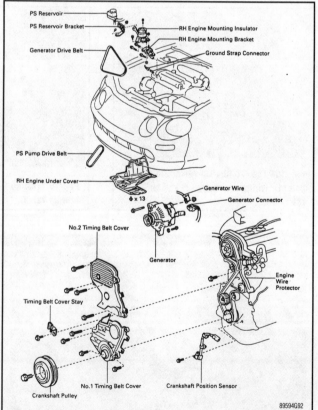

Fig. 114 Crankshaft position sensor and related components—5S-FE engine

REMOVAL & INSTALLATION

▶ **See Figures 114 and 115**

1. Disconnect the crankshaft position sensor wiring.

➡ **On some models the wiring may be attached to the drive belt adjusting bar.**

2. On some engines, remove the RH fender apron seal.
3. On the 5S-FE engine, remove the No. 1 timing belt cover.
4. Remove the bolt and sensor.

To install:

5. Insert the sensor and secure with the retaining bolt to 82 inch lbs. (9 Nm).
6. Install and secure the No. 1 timing belt cover on 5S-FE engines.
7. Install the RH fender apron if removed.
8. Connect the wiring to the sensor.

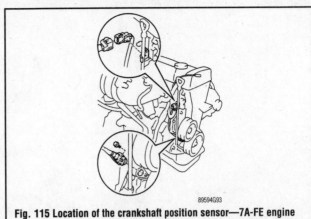

89594G93

Fig. 115 Location of the crankshaft position sensor—7A-FE engine

COMPONENT LOCATIONS

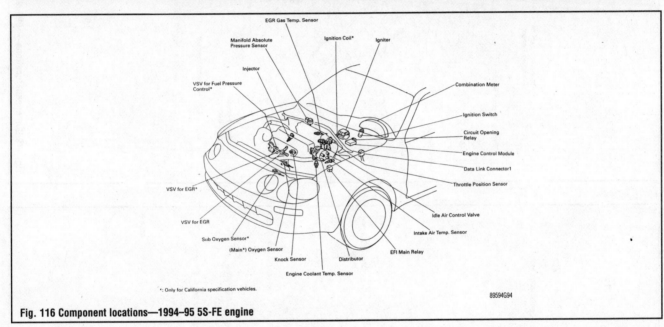

*: Only for California specification vehicles.

89594G94

Fig. 116 Component locations—1994–95 5S-FE engine

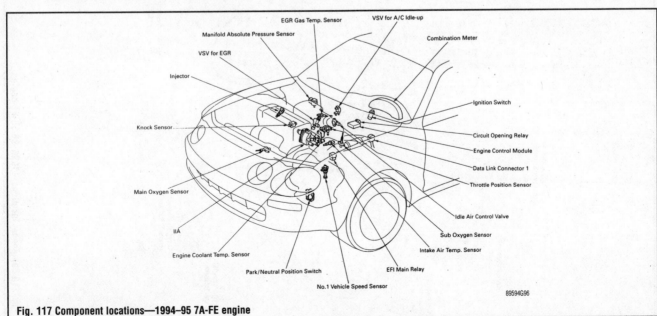

89594G96

Fig. 117 Component locations—1994–95 7A-FE engine

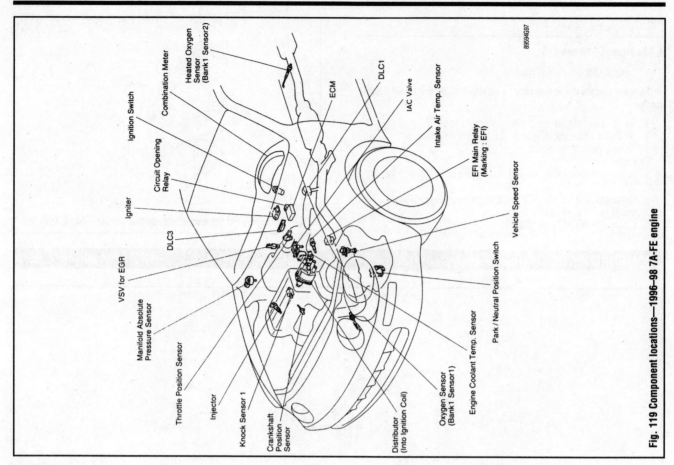

Fig. 119 Component locations—1996–98 7A-FE engine

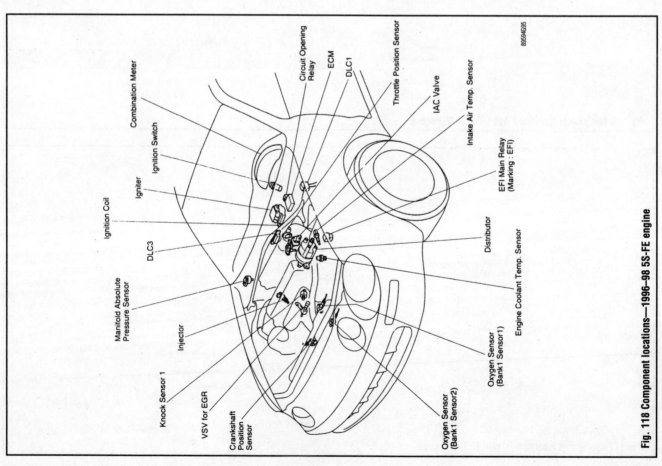

Fig. 118 Component locations—1996–98 5S-FE engine

TROUBLE CODES

General Information

The ECM contains a built-in, self-diagnosis system which detects troubles within the engine signal network. Once a malfunction is detected, the Malfunction Indicator Lamp (MIL), located on the instrument panel, will light.

By analyzing various signals, the ECM detects system malfunctions related to the operating sensors. The ECM stores the failure code associated with the detected failure until the diagnosis system is cleared.

The MIL on the instrument panel informs the driver that a malfunction has been detected. The light will go out automatically once the malfunction has been cleared.

DATA LINK CONNECTOR (DLC)

▶ See Figure 120

The DLC1 is located in the engine compartment. The DLC3 is located in the interior of the vehicle, under the driver's side dash.

Reading Codes

1994–95 MODELS

▶ See Figures 121 thru 135

1. Make sure the battery voltage is at least 11 volts.
2. Make sure the throttle valve is fully closed.

Fig. 120 The Data Link connector 1 (DLC1) is located in the engine compartment near the firewall

3. Place the gear shift lever in Neutral. Turn all accessories off.
4. The engine should be at normal operating temperature.
5. Using a jumper wire, connect terminals TE1 and E1 of the Data Link Connector 1 (DLC1).
6. Turn the ignition switch **ON**, but do not start the engine. Read the diagnostic code by the counting the number of flashes of the malfunction indicator lamp.
7. Codes will flash in numerical order. If no faults are stored, the lamp flashes continuously every ½ second. This is sometimes called the Normal or System Clear signal.8. After the diagnosis check, turn the ignition **OFF** and remove the jumper wire.
9. Compare the codes found to the applicable diagnostic code chart. If necessary, refer to the individual component tests in this section. If the component tests are OK, test the wire harness and connectors for shorts, opens and poor connections.

1996–98 MODELS

➡These models require the use of the Toyota's hand held scan tool or an equivalent OBD II compliant scan tool.

1. Prepare the scan tool according to the manufacturers instructions.
2. Connect the OBD II scan tool, to the DLC3 under the instrument panel.

➡When the diagnosis system is switched from the normal mode to the check mode, it erases all Diagnostic Trouble Codes (DTC) and freeze frame data recorded. Before switching modes, always check the DTC and freeze frame data and write them down.

3. Turn the ignition switch to the **ON** and switch the OBD II scan tool switch on.
4. Use the OBD II scan tool to check the DTC and freeze frame data. Write them down.
5. Compare the codes found to the applicable diagnostic code chart. If necessary, refer to the individual component tests in this section. If the component tests are OK, test the wire harness and connectors for shorts, opens and poor connections.

Clearing Trouble Codes

▶ See Figure 136

After repair of the circuit, the diagnostic code(s) must be removed from the ECM memory. With the ignition turned **OFF**, remove the 15 amp EFI fuse for 30 seconds or more. Once the time period has been observed, reinstall the fuse and check for normal code output.

If the diagnostic code is not erased, it will be retained by the ECM and appear along with a new code in event of future trouble.

Cancellation of the trouble code can also be accomplished by disconnecting the negative battery cable. However, disconnecting the battery cable will erase the other memory systems including the clock and radio settings. If this method is used, always reset these components once the trouble code has been erased.

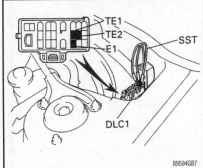

Fig. 121 DLC1 terminal identification for trouble code checking

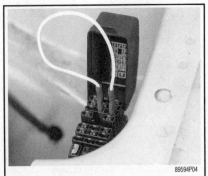

Fig. 122 Use a jumper wire to connect the terminals of the DLC1

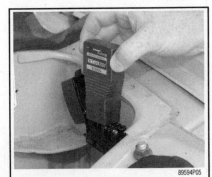

Fig. 123 Special tools are available to check for codes

DTC No.	Number of MIL Blinks	Circuit	Diagnostic Trouble Code Detecting Condition
21	(blink pattern)	(Main*3) Oxygen Sensor Signal	(Main*3) oxygen sensor signal voltage is reduced to between 0.35 V and 0.70 V for 60 sec. under conditions (a) – (d). (2 trip detection logic)*5 (a) Engine coolant temp.: 80°C (176°F) or more. (b) Engine speed: 1,500 rpm or more. (c) Load driving (Ex. A/T in overdrive (5th for M/T), A/C ON, Flat road, 50 mph (80 km/h)). (d) (Main*3) oxygen sensor signal voltage: Alternating above and below 0.45 V.
22	(blink pattern)	Engine Coolant Temp. Sensor Signal	Open or short in engine coolant temp. sensor circuit for 0.5 sec. or more.
24	(blink pattern)	Intake Air Temp. Sensor Signal	Open or short in intake air temp. sensor circuit for 0.5 sec. or more.
25	(blink pattern)	Air-Fuel Ratio Lean Malfunction	(1) (Main*3) oxygen sensor voltage is 0.45 V or less (lean) for 90 sec. under conditions (a) and (b). (2 trip detection logic)*5 (a) Engine coolant temp.: 60°C (140°F) or more. (b) Engine speed: 1,500 rpm or more. (2) Engine speed varies by more than a predetermined rpm over the preceding crankshaft position period during a period of 20 sec. or more under conditions (a) and (b). (2 trip detection logic)*5 (a) Engine speed: Idling (b) Engine coolant temp.: 60°C (140°F) or more.

88594GA2

Fig. 125 Diagnostic codes—1994–95 models

DTC No.	Number of MIL Blinks	Circuit	Diagnostic Trouble Code Detecting Condition
—	(blink pattern)	Normal	No code is recorded.
		G, NE Signal Circuit (No. 1) (Exc. California spec.)	No NE signal to ECM within 2 sec. or more after cranking. No G signal to ECM for 3 sec. or more with engine speed between 600 rpm and 4,000 rpm.
12	(blink pattern)	G, NE Signal Circuit (No. 1) (Only for California spec.)	No NE or G1 and G2 signal to ECM for 2 sec. or more after cranking. Open in G ⊖ circuit
13	(blink pattern)	G, NE Signal Circuit (No. 2)	No NE signal to ECM for 0.3 sec. or more at 1,500 rpm or more. No G signal to ECM while NE signal is input 4 times to ECM when engine speed is between 500 rpm and 4,000 rpm.
			*3 No NE signal to ECM for 0.1 sec. or more at 1,000 rpm or more. *3 NE signal does not pulse 12 times to ECM during the interval between G1 and G2 pulses.
14	(blink pattern)	Ignition Signal Circuit	No IGF signal to ECM for 4 consecutive IGT signals. *3 No IGF signal to ECM for 8 consecutive IGT signals.
16*4	(blink pattern)	A/T Control Signal	Fault in communications between the engine CPU and A/T CPU in the ECM

88594G99

Fig. 124 Diagnostic codes—1994–95 models

DTC No.	Number of MIL Blinks	Circuit	Diagnostic Trouble Code Detecting Condition
26		Air-Fuel Ratio Rich Malfunction	Engine speed varies by more than a predetermined rpm over the preceding crankshaft position period during a period of 20 sec. or more under conditions (a) and (b). (2 trip detection logic)*5 (a) Engine speed: Idling (b) Engine coolant temp.: 60°C (140°F) or more.
27*3		Sub Oxygen Sensor Signal	Main oxygen sensor signal is 0.45 V or more and sub oxygen sensor signal is 0.45 V or less under conditions (a) and (b). (2 trip detection logic)*5 (a) Engine coolant temp.: 80°C (176°F) or more. (b) Engine speed: 1,500 rpm or more. (c) Accel. pedal: Fully depressed for 2 sec. or more.
31		Manifold Absolute Pressure Sensor Signal	Open or short in manifold absolute pressure sensor circuit for 0.5 sec. or more.
41		Throttle Position Sensor Signal	Open or short in throttle position sensor circuit for 0.5 sec. or more.
		No.1 Vehicle Speed Sensor Signal (for A/T)	All conditions below are detected continuously for 8 sec. or more. (a) No.1 vehicle speed sensor signal: 0 mph (km/h) (b) Engine Speed: 3,000 rpm or more. (c) Park/Neutral position switch: OFF
42		No.1 Vehicle Speed Sensor Signal (for M/T)	All conditions below are detected continuously for 8 sec. or more. (a) No.1 vehicle speed sensor signal: 0 mph (km/h) (b) Engine speed: Between 3,100 rpm and 5,000 rpm. (c) Engine coolant temp.: 80°C (176°F) or more. (d) Load driving.

Fig. 126 Diagnostic codes—1994–95 models

DTC No.	Number of MIL Blinks	Circuit	Diagnostic trouble Code Detecting Condition
43		Starter Signal	No starter signal to ECM.
52		Knock Sensor Signal	Open or short in knock sensor circuit with engine speed between 1,200 rpm and 6,000 rpm.
71		EGR System Malfunction	EGR gas temp. is predetermined temp. or below for 50 sec. under conditions (a) and (b). (2 trip detection logic)*5 (a) Engine coolant temp.: 80°C (176°F) or more. (b) EGR operation possible (e.g. A/T in 3rd speed [5th for M/T], 55 ~ 60 mph (88 ~ 96 km/h), Flat road).
51		Switch Condition Signal	(1) 3 sec. or more after engine starts with closed throttle position switch OFF (IDL). (2)*4 Park/Neutral switch OFF (PNP). (Shift position in "R", "D", "2", or "L" positions). (3) A/C switch ON.

Fig. 127 Diagnostic codes—1994–95 models

*1: "ON" displayed in the diagnosis mode column indicates that the malfunction indicator lamp is lighted up when a malfunction is detected. "OFF" indicates that the "CHECK" does not light up during malfunction diagnosis, even if a malfunction is detected. "N.A." indicates that the item is not included in malfunction diagnosis.

*2: "O" in the memory column indicates that a diagnostic trouble code is recorded in the ECM even when a malfunction occurs. "X" indicates that a diagnostic trouble code is not recorded in the ECM memory even if a malfunction occurs. Accordingly, output of diagnostic results in normal or test mode is performed with the IG switch ON.

*3: Only for California specification vehicles.

*4: Only vehicles with A/T.

HINT: Parameters listed in the chart may not be exactly the same as your reading due to the type of instrument or other factors.
If a malfunction code is displayed during the DTC check in check mode, check the circuit for that code listed in the table below. For details of each code, turn to the page referred to under the "See Page" for the respective "DTC No." in the DTC chart.

DTC No.	Detection Item	Trouble Area	MIL*	Memory
P0105	Manifold Absolute Pressure/Barometric Pressure Circuit Malfunction	• Open or short in manifold absolute pressure sensor circuit • Manifold absolute pressure sensor • ECM	○	○
P0106	Manifold Absolute Pressure/Barometric Pressure Circuit Range/Performance Problem	• Manifold absolute pressure sensor	○	○
P0110	Intake Air Temp. Circuit Malfunction	• Open or short in intake air temp. sensor circuit • Intake air temp. sensor • ECM	○	○
P0115	Engine Coolant Temp. Circuit Malfunction	• Open or short in engine coolant temp. sensor circuit • Engine coolant temp. sensor • ECM	○	○
P0116	Engine Coolant Temp. Circuit Range/Performance Problem	• Engine coolant temp. sensor • Cooling system	○	○
P0120	Throttle/Pedal Position Sensor/Switch "A" Circuit Malfunction	• Open or short in throttle position sensor circuit • Throttle position sensor • ECM	○	○
P0121	Throttle/Pedal Position Sensor/Switch "A" Circuit Range/Performance Problem	• Throttle position sensor	○	○
P0125	Insufficient Coolant Temp. for Closed Loop Fuel Control	• Open or short in oxygen sensor circuit • Oxygen sensor	○	○
P0130	Oxygen Sensor Circuit Malfunction (Bank 1 Sensor 1)	• Oxygen sensor • Fuel trim malfunction	○	○
P0133	Oxygen Sensor Circuit Slow Response (Bank 1 Sensor 1)	• Oxygen sensor	○	○

*: ○ ...... MIL lights up

Fig. 129 Diagnostic codes—1996–98 models

If any of the following codes is recorded, the ECM enters fail-safe mode.

DTC No.	Fail-Safe Operation	Fail-Safe Deactivation Conditions
14	Fuel cut	1 IGF detected in consecutive 2 (4*) ignitions.
16	Torque control prohibited.	Returned to normal condition.
22	THW is fixed at 80°C (176°F).	Returned to normal condition.
24	THA is fixed at 20°C (68°F).	Returned to normal condition.

31	• Ignition timing fixed at 5° BTDC.
	• Injection time fixed
	  Starting ...... 12.1 m sec.
	  IDL ON ...... 3.3 m sec.
	  IDL OFF ...... 6.1 m sec.
	• Intake manifold vacuum is fixed at 46.7 kPa.
	  (350 mmHg, 13.8 inHg)
		Returned to normal condition.

41	VTA1 is fixed at 0°.	The following must each be repeated at least 2 time consecutively. • 0.1 V ≦ VTA ≦ 0.95 V • IDL : ON
52	Max. timing retardation.	IG switch OFF.

*: Only for California specification vehicles.

Back-Up Function
If there is trouble with the program in the ECM and the ignition signals (IGT) are not output from microcomputer the ECM controls fuel injection and ignition timing at predetermined levels as a back-up function to make it possible to continue to operate the vehicle.
Furthermore, the injection duration is calculated from the starting signal (STA) and the throttle position signal (IDL). Also, the ignition timing is fixed at the initial ignition timing. 5° BTDC, without relation to the engine speed.
HINT: If the engine is controlled by the back-up function, the malfunction indicator lamp lights up to warn the driver of the malfunction but the diagnostic trouble code is not output.

Fig. 128 Diagnostic codes—1994–95 models

DTC No.	Detection Item	Trouble Area	MIL*	Memory
P0136	Oxygen Sensor Circuit Malfunction (Bank 1 Sensor 2)	• Oxygen sensor		
P0171	System too Lean (Fuel Trim)	• Air intake (hose loose) • Fuel line pressure • Injector blockage • Oxygen sensor malfunction • Manifold absolute pressure sensor • Engine coolant temp. sensor	○	○
P0172	System too Rich (Fuel Trim)	• Fuel line pressure • Injector blockage, leak • Oxygen sensor malfunction • Manifold absolute pressure sensor • Engine coolant temp. sensor	○	○
P0300	Random/Multiple Cylinder Misfire Detected	• Ignition system • Injector • Fuel line pressure • EGR	○	○
P0301 P0302 P0303 P0304	Misfire Detected – Cylinder 1 – Cylinder 2 – Cylinder 3 – Cylinder 4	• Compression pressure • Valve clearance not to specification • Valve timing • Manifold absolute pressure sensor • Engine coolant temp. sensor	○	○
P0325	Knock Sensor 1 Circuit Malfunction	• Open or short in knock sensor 1 circuit • Knock sensor 1 (looseness) • ECM	○	○
P0335	Crankshaft Position Sensor "A" Circuit Malfunction	• Open or short in crankshaft position sensor circuit • Crankshaft position sensor • Starter • ECM	○	○
P0340	Camshaft Position Sensor Circuit Malfunction	• Open or short in camshaft position sensor circuit • Camshaft position sensor • Starter • ECM	○	○

*: ○ .... MIL lights up

Fig. 130 Diagnostic codes—1996–98 models

DTC No.	Detection Item	Trouble Area	MIL*	Memory
P0401	Exhaust Gas Recirculation Flow Insufficient Detected	• EGR valve stuck closed • Open or short in VSV circuit for EGR • Vacuum or EGR hose disconnected • Manifold absolute pressure sensor • EGR VSV open or close malfunction • ECM	○	○
P0402	Exhaust Gas Recirculation Flow Excessive Detected	• EGR valve stuck open • Vacuum or EGR hose is connected to wrong post • Manifold absolute pressure sensor • ECM	○	○
P0420	Catalyst System Efficiency Below Threshold	• Three-way catalytic converter • Open or short in oxygen sensor circuit • Oxygen sensor	○	○
P0500	Vehicle Speed Sensor Malfunction	• Open or short in vehicle speed sensor circuit • Vehicle speed sensor • Combination meter • ECM	○	○
P0505	Idle Control System Malfunction	• IAC valve is stuck or closed • Open or short in IAC valve circuit • Open or short in A/C signal circuit • Air intake (hose loose)	○	○

* - .... MIL does not light up
○ .... MIL lights up

Fig. 131 Diagnostic codes—1996–98 models

DTC No.	Detection Item	Trouble Area	MIL*	Memory
P1300	Igniter Circuit Malfunction	• Open or short in IGF or IGT circuit from igniter to ECM • Igniter • ECM	○	○
P1335	Crankshaft Position Sensor Circuit Malfunction (during engine running)	• Open or short in crankshaft position sensor circuit • Crankshaft position sensor • ECM	-	○
P1500	Starter Signal Circuit Malfunction	• Open or short in starter signal circuit • Open or short in ignition switch or starter relay circuit • ECM	-	○
P1600	ECM BATT Malfunction	• Open in back up power source circuit • ECM	○	○
P1780	Park/Neutral Position Switch Malfunction	• Short in park/neutral position switch circuit • Park/neutral position switch • ECM	○	○

* - .... MIL does not light up
○ .... MIL lights up

Fig. 132 Diagnostic codes—1996–98 models

HINT: Using SST 09843-18020, connect the terminals Tc and E1, and remove the short pin.

If a malfunction code is displayed during the DTC check, check the circuit listed for that code. For details of each code, turn to the page referred to under the "See page" for the respective "DTC No." in the DTC chart.

DTC No. (See page)	Detection Item	Trouble Area
11	Open circuit in ABS solenoid relay circuit	• ABS solenoid relay • Open or short in ABS solenoid relay circuit • ECU
12	Short in ABS solenoid relay circuit	• ABS solenoid relay • B+ short in ABS solenoid relay circuit • ECU
13	Open circuit in ABS motor relay circuit	• ABS motor relay • Open or short in ABS motor relay circuit • ECU
14	Short circuit in ABS motor relay circuit	• ABS motor relay • B+ short in ABS motor relay circuit • ECU
21	Open or short circuit in solenoid circuit for right front wheel	• ABS actuator • Open or short in SFRH or SFRR circuit • ECU
22	Open or short circuit in solenoid circuit for left front wheel	• ABS actuator • Open or short in SFLH or SFLR circuit • ECU
23	Open or short circuit in solenoid circuit for right rear wheel	• ABS actuator • Open or short in SRRH or SRRR circuit • ECU
24	Open or short circuit in solenoid circuit for left rear wheel	• ABS actuator • Open or short in SRLH or SRLR circuit • ECU
31	Right front wheel speed sensor signal malfunction	• Right front, left front, right rear and left rear speed sensor
32	Left front wheel speed sensor signal malfunction	
33	Right rear wheel speed sensor signal malfunction	• Open or short in each speed sensor circuit • ECU
34	Left rear wheel speed sensor signal malfunction	
41	Low battery positive voltage or abnormally high battery positive voltage	• Battery • IC regulator • Open or short in power source circuit • ECU
51	Pump motor is locked Open in pump motor ground	• ABS pump motor • ECU
Always ON	Malfunction in ECU	• ECU

89594GB1

Fig. 135 Diagnostic codes (ABS)

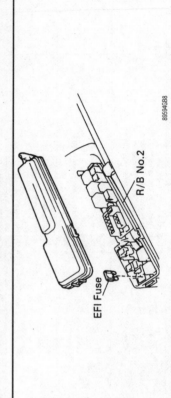

EFI Fuse   R/B No.2

89594GB8

Fig. 136 Removing the EFI fuse will clear the trouble codes retained in the ECM

If any of the following codes is recorded, the ECM enters fail-safe mode.

DTC No.	Fail-Safe Operation	Fail-Safe Deactivation Conditions
P0105	Ignition timing fixed at 5° BTDC	Returned to normal condition
P0110	Intake air temp. is fixed at 68°F (20°C)	Returned to normal condition
P0115	Engine coolant temp. is fixed at 176°F (80°C)	Returned to normal condition
P0120	VTA is fixed at 0°	The following condition must be repeated at least 2 times consecutively: When closed throttle position switch is ON: 0.1 V ≦ VTA ≦ 0.95 V
P0325	Max. timing retardation	Ignition switch OFF
P1300	Fuel cut	IGF signal is detected for 4 consecutive ignitions

89594GB6

Fig. 133 Diagnostic codes—1996-98 models

If a malfunction code is displayed during the DTC check, check the circuit listed for that code in the table below (Proceed to the page given for that circuit).

DTC No. (See page)	Detection Item	Trouble Area	SRS Warning Light
(Normal)	System normal	–	OFF
11	Source voltage drop	• Battery • Center airbag sensor assembly	ON
11	Short in squib circuit or front airbag sensor circuit (to ground)	• Steering wheel pad (D squib) • Front passenger airbag assembly (P squib) • Front airbag sensor • Spiral cable • Center airbag sensor assembly • Wire harness	ON
12	Short in squib circuit (to B+)	• Steering wheel pad (D squib) • Front passenger airbag assembly (P squib) • Front airbag sensor • Spiral cable • Center airbag sensor assembly • Wire harness	ON
13	Short in driver airbag squib circuit	• Steering wheel pad (D squib) • Spiral cable • Center airbag sensor assembly • Wire harness	ON
14	Open in driver airbag squib circuit	• Steering wheel pad (D squib) • Spiral cable • Center airbag sensor assembly • Wire harness	ON
15	Open in front airbag sensor circuit	• Front airbag sensor • Center airbag sensor assembly • Wire harness	ON
24	Half connection in center airbag sensor assembly connector	• Electrical connection check mechanism • Center airbag sensor assembly	ON
31	Center airbag sensor assembly malfunction	• Center airbag sensor assembly	ON
53	Short in front passenger airbag squib circuit	• Front passenger airbag assembly (P squib) • Center airbag sensor assembly • Wire harness	ON
54	Open in front passenger airbag squib circuit	• Front passenger airbag assembly (P squib) • Center airbag sensor assembly • Wire harness	ON

89594GA9

HINT:
• When the SRS warning light remains lit up and the DTC in the normal code, this means a source voltage drop.
  This malfunction is not stored in memory by the center airbag sensor assembly and if the power source voltage returns to normal, after approx. 10 seconds the SRS warning light will automatically go out.
• When 2 or more codes are indicated, the lowest numbered code will appear first.
• If a code not listed on the chart is displayed, then the center airbag sensor assembly is faulty.

Fig. 134 Diagnostic codes (SRS system)

VACUUM DIAGRAMS

Following are vacuum diagrams for most of the engine and emissions package combinations covered by this manual. Because vacuum circuits will vary based on various engine and vehicle options, always refer first to the vehicle emission control information label, if present. Should the label be missing, or should vehicle be equipped with a different engine from the vehicle's original equipment, refer to the diagrams below for the same or similar configuration.

If you wish to obtain a replacement emissions label, most manufacturers make the labels available for purchase. The labels can usually be ordered from a local dealer.

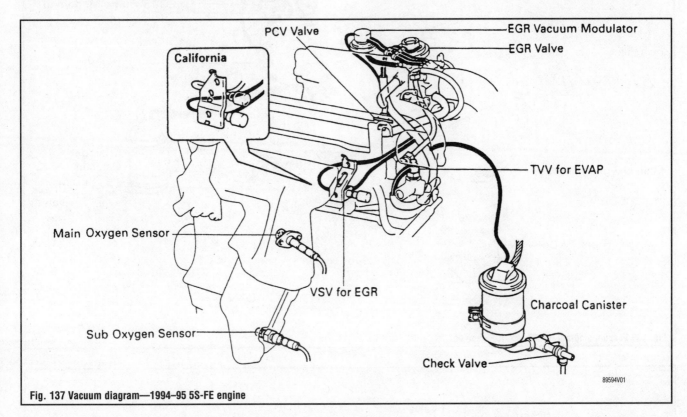

Fig. 137 Vacuum diagram—1994–95 5S-FE engine

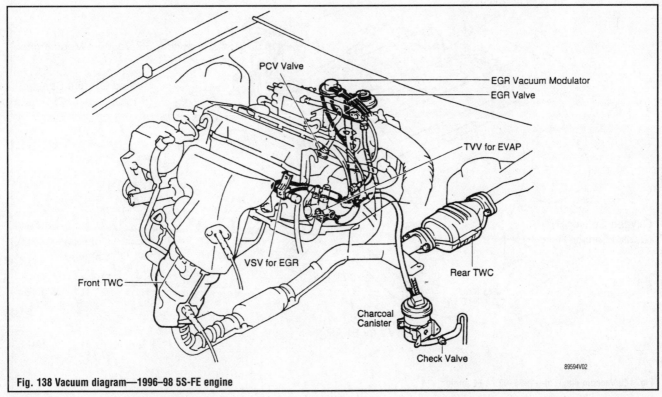

Fig. 138 Vacuum diagram—1996–98 5S-FE engine

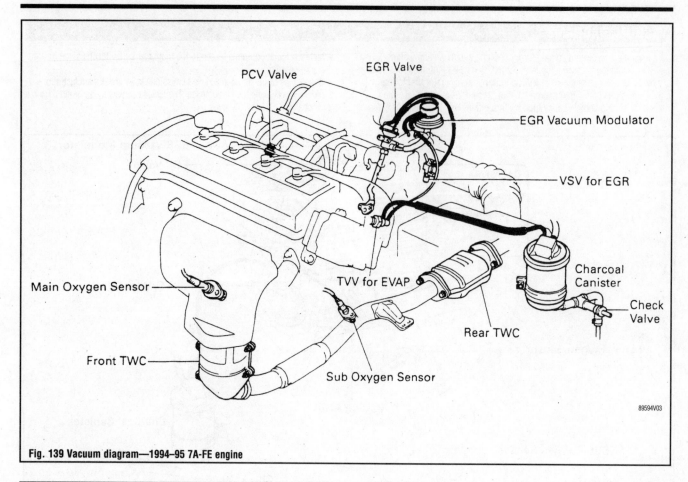

Fig. 139 Vacuum diagram—1994–95 7A-FE engine

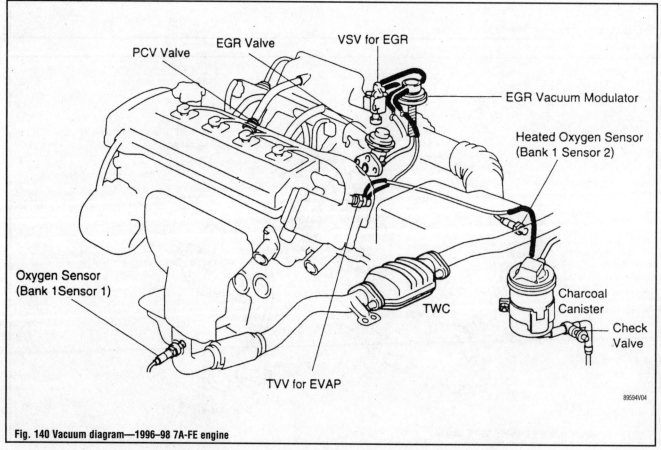

Fig. 140 Vacuum diagram—1996–98 7A-FE engine

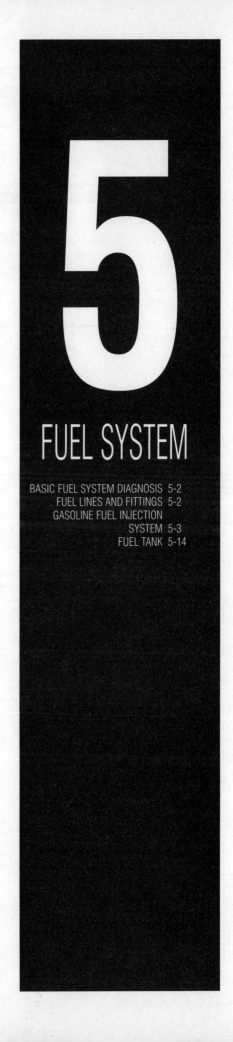

5

FUEL SYSTEM

BASIC FUEL SYSTEM DIAGNOSIS

When there is a problem starting or driving a vehicle, two of the most important checks involve the ignition and the fuel systems. The questions most mechanics attempt to answer first, "is there spark?" and "is there fuel?" will often lead to solving most basic problems. For ignition system diagnosis and testing, please refer to the information on engine electrical components and ignition systems found earlier in this manual. If the ignition system checks out (there is spark), then you must determine if the fuel system is operating properly (is there fuel?).

FUEL LINES AND FITTINGS

♦ See Figures 1, 2 and 3

When working on the fuel system, insect the lines and connections for cracks, leakage and deformation. Inspect the fuel tank vapor vent system hose and connections for looseness, sharp bends or damage. Check the fuel tank for any deformation due to bad driving conditions. Inspect the bands for rust or cracks. The tank bands should be secure and not loose. Check the filler neck for damage or leakage.

Union Bolt Type

REMOVAL & INSTALLATION

♦ See Figures 4 and 5

✳✳ WARNING

When disconnecting the high pressure fuel line, a large amount of gasoline will spill out, so observe the following.

1. Place a container under the connection.
2. Slowly loosen the connection. Have a rag handy to clean up any split fuel.
3. Separate the connection.
4. Plug the connection with a rubber plug.
5. When connecting the union bolt on the high pressure line, always use a new gasket.
6. Always tighten the union bolt by hand. Tighten the bolt to 22 ft. lbs. (29 Nm).

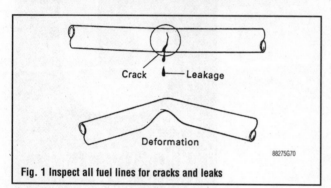

Fig. 1 Inspect all fuel lines for cracks and leaks

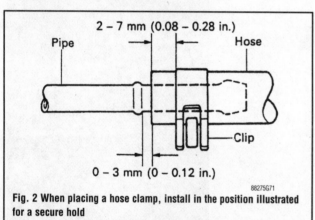

Fig. 2 When placing a hose clamp, install in the position illustrated for a secure hold

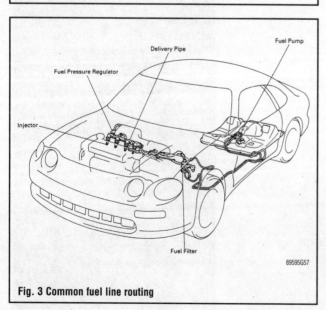

Fig. 3 Common fuel line routing

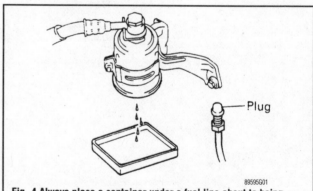

Fig. 4 Always place a container under a fuel line about to being opened to catch any spilt fuel

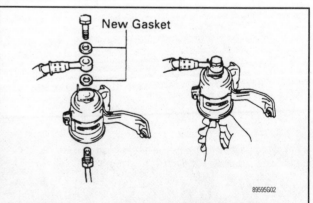

Fig. 5 Always use new gaskets when connecting a fuel line

Flare Nut Type

REMOVAL & INSTALLATION

▶ **See Figure 6**

➡ **Always use a back-up wrench when removing and installing fuel lines.**

Apply a light coat of engine oil to the flare and tighten the flare nut by hand. Using a torque wrench, tighten the flare nut to 17 ft. lbs. (24 Nm) on fuel pump side and 22 ft. lbs. (30 Nm) for all others.

➡ **Use a torque wrench with a fulcrum length of 11.81 inch (30 cm).**

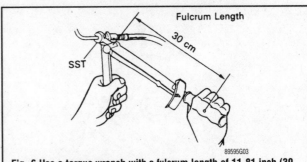

Fig. 6 Use a torque wrench with a fulcrum length of 11.81 inch (30 cm) when tightening the flare nut type lines

GASOLINE FUEL INJECTION SYSTEM

General Information

Fuel injected engines are equipped with the Toyota Computer Control System (TCCS). This integrated control system allows the Engine Control Module (ECM) to control other systems as well as the fuel injection. The control unit is a sophisticated micro-computer, receiving input signals from many sources and locations on the vehicle. It is capable of rapid calculation of many variables and controls several output circuits simultaneously. This system is broken down into 3 major sub-systems: the Fuel System, Air Induction System and the Electronic Control System. Keeping these divisions in mind will shorten troubleshooting and diagnostic time. An electric fuel pump supplies sufficient fuel, under a constant pressure, to the injectors. These injectors allow a metered quantity of fuel into the intake manifold according to signals from the ECM. The air induction system provides sufficient air for the engine operation. This system includes the throttle body, air intake device and idle control system components.

Relieving Fuel System Pressure

✳✳ CAUTION

Failure to relieve fuel pressure before repairs or disassembly can cause serious personal injury and/or property damage.

Fuel pressure is maintained within the fuel lines, even if the engine is **OFF** or has not been run in a period of time. This pressure must be safely relieved before any fuel-bearing line or component is loosened or removed.

1. Place a catch-pan under the joint to be disconnected. A large quantity of fuel will be released when the joint is opened.
2. Wear eye or full face protection.
3. Slowly release the joint using a wrench of the correct size. Counterhold the joint with a second wrench if possible.
4. Allow the pressurized fuel to bleed off slowly before disconnecting the joint.
5. Plug the opened lines immediately to prevent fuel spillage or the entry of dirt.
6. Dispose of the released fuel properly.

Fuel Pump

REMOVAL & INSTALLATION

▶ **See Figures 7 thru 26**

➡ **Before disconnecting fuel system lines, clean the fittings with a spray-type engine cleaner. Follow the instructions on the cleaner. Do not soak fuel system parts in liquid cleaning solvent.**

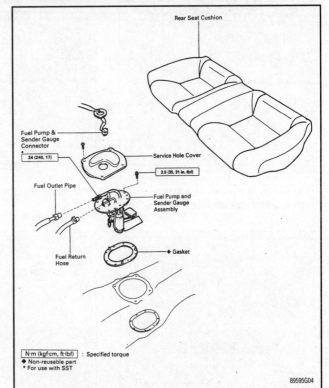

Fig. 7 View of the common electric fuel pump located under the rear seat

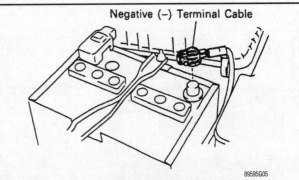

Fig. 8 It is very important to disconnect the negative battery cable whenever removing components on the fuel system

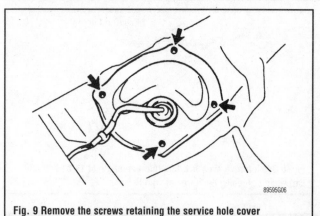

Fig. 9 Remove the screws retaining the service hole cover

✳✳ CAUTION

The fuel injection system is under pressure. Release pressure slowly and contain spillage. Observe "no smoking/no open flame" precautions. Have a Class B-C (dry powder) fire extinguisher within arm's reach at all times.

1. Disconnect the negative battery cable.
2. Remove the rear seat cushion. Refer to Section 10.
3. Unscrew the service hole cover.
4. Disconnect the electrical fuel pump wiring at the pump assembly. Check for any fuel leakage while in there.
5. Remove the gas cap, this will prevent any fuel gas spilling out of any high pressure lines.
6. Using SST 09631–22020 or an equivalent line (flare nut) wrench, disconnect the outlet pipe from the pump bracket.

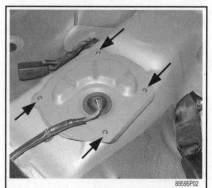

Fig. 10 Only four screws hold the service hole cover into the gas tank

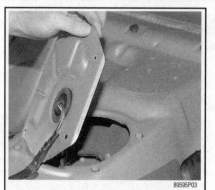

Fig. 11 Lift the service cover up to access the unit

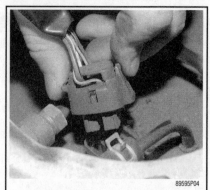

Fig. 12 Disconnect the wiring for the sending unit . . .

Fig. 13 . . . then slide the hose clamps back . . .

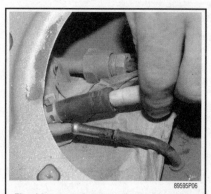

Fig. 14 . . . and remove the fuel hose to the sending unit

Fig. 15 A line wrench (flare-nut) and back-up wrench will be necessary to separate the fuel lines

Fig. 16 Remove the sending unit retaining bolts securing it to the fuel tank

Fig. 17 Lift the pump and sender assembly from the fuel tank

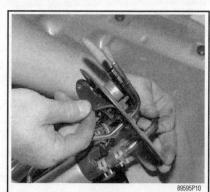

Fig. 18 Inspect the gasket, a good seal is necessary for replacement

7. Remove the pump bracket attaching screws.

8. Disconnect the return hoses from the pump bracket, then pull out the pump/bracket assembly.

9. Remove the nut and spring washer, then disconnect the wires from the pump bracket.

10. Remove the sending unit attaching screws, then pull the unit from the bracket. To disassemble:

　a. Remove the lead wire.

　b. Pull the lower side of the fuel pump from the bracket.

　c. Remove the rubber cushion from the pump.

　d. Disconnect the hose from the pump and extract the pump.

　e. Separate the filter from the pump. Use a small screwdriver to remove the attaching clip.

　f. To remove the sender, disconnect the wiring from the bracket and unscrew the sender. Remove the screws, connector support, connector and gasket.

11. Inspect all of the lines, hoses and fittings for any sign of corrosion, wear or damage to the surfaces. Check the pump outlet hose and the filter for restrictions.

12. When reassembling, ALWAYS replace the sealing gaskets with new ones. Also replace any rubber parts showing any sign of deterioration.

To install:

13. To assemble the pump:

　a. Secure and install a new gasket, connector and support with the screws.

　b. Attach the sensor and secure the screws, connect the wiring to the pump bracket.

　c. Install the pump filter using a new clip.

　d. Connect the outlet hose to the pump.

　e. Install the rubber cushion to the fuel pump. Push the lower side of the pump into place to secure on the bracket.

　f. Engage the connector to the fuel pump.

14. Install the fuel sending unit to the pump bracket.

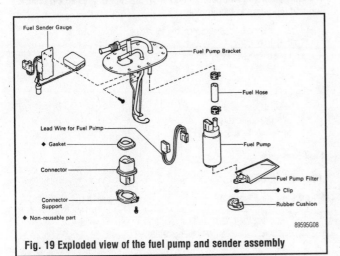

Fig. 19 Exploded view of the fuel pump and sender assembly

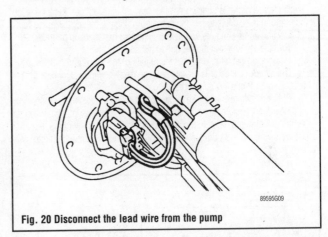

Fig. 20 Disconnect the lead wire from the pump

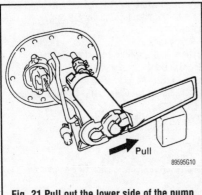

Fig. 21 Pull out the lower side of the pump to extract from the bracket

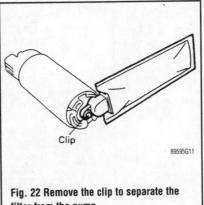
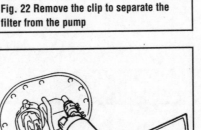

Fig. 22 Remove the clip to separate the filter from the pump

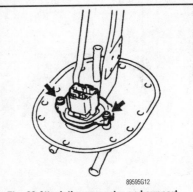

Fig. 23 Attach the connector and support with two screws, then . . .

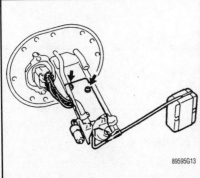

Fig. 24 . . . install the sender gage with two screws to the bracket

Fig. 25 Push the lower side of the pump into the bracket to secure

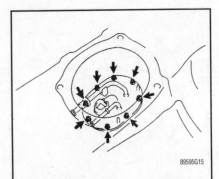

Fig. 26 Tighten all eight pump bracket retaining screws to secure the assembly to the fuel tank

15. Install the fuel pump and bracket assembly onto the tank. Use new gaskets. Tighten the pump bracket retaining screws to 31 inch lbs. (3 Nm).

16. Connect the return hoses to the pump bracket.

17. Install the service hole cover, then the engage the fuel pump and sending unit connector.

18. Connect the negative battery cable.

19. Start the engine and check carefully for any sign of leakage around the tank and lines. Road test the vehicle for proper operation.

20. Install the rear seat cushion.

TESTING

On-Vehicle Inspection

1994–95 MODELS

▶ **See Figures 27, 28, 29 and 30**

Since the fuel pump is concealed within the tank, it is difficult to test directly at the pump. It is possible to test the pump from under the hood, listening for pump function and feeling the fuel delivery lines for the build-up of pressure.

1. Turn the ignition switch **ON**, but do not start the engine.

2. Using a jumper wire, short both terminals of the fuel pump check connector. The check connector is located near the master cylinder. Connect the terminals labeled **FP** and **+B** on the DLC1.

3. Check that there is pressure in the hose running to the delivery pipe. You should hear fuel pressure noise and possibly hear the pump at the rear of the car.

4. If the fuel pump failed to function, it may indicate a faulty pump, but before removing the fuel pump, check the following items within the pump system:

a. All fusible links
b. All fuses
c. H- fuse
d. EFI main relay
e. Fuel pump
f. All wiring connections and grounds.

5. Turn the ignition to OFF.

6. Remove the jumper wire.

1996–98 MODELS

1. Turn the ignition switch to the **ON** position, but do not start the engine.

2. Connect the positive and negative leads from the battery to the fuel pump wiring.

3. Check that there is pressure in the hose from the fuel filter.

➡ **At this point you will hear a noise from the rear of the vehicle indicating that the pump is functioning.**

4. If there is no pressure inspect the following:

a. Fusible link
b. H-Fuse (Main 60A)
c. Fuses (EFI 15A, AM2 30A, ING 7.5A)
d. Circuit opening relay
e. EFI main relay
f. Fuel pump
g. Wiring connections

5. Turn the ignition switch **OFF**.

Fuel Pressure

1994–95 MODELS

▶ **See Figures 31 and 32**

1. Check that the battery voltage is approximately 12 volts.

2. Disconnect the negative battery cable.

3. Relieve the fuel system pressure.

4. Disconnect the hose from the fuel filter outlet.

5. Connect the hose and a fuel pressure gauge to the fuel filter outlet with three new gaskets and the union bolt. Tighten to 22 ft. lbs. (29 Nm).

6. Wipe any spilled gasoline.

7. Connect the negative battery cable.

8. Using a jumper wire, short terminals FP and +B of the DLC1.

9. Turn the ignition switch **ON**, but do not start the car.

10. The fuel pressure should read 38–44 psi (265–304 kPa).

11. If the pressure is too high, the pressure regulator is probably defective. If it is too low, check for the following:

a. Fuel hoses and connections for leaks or restrictions.
b. Defective fuel pump.
c. Clogged fuel filter.
d. Defective pressure regulator.

12. After checking the fuel pressure, turn the ignition **OFF** and remove the jumper wire from the DLC1.

13. Disconnect the negative battery cable.

14. Relieve the fuel system pressure and remove the pressure gauge.

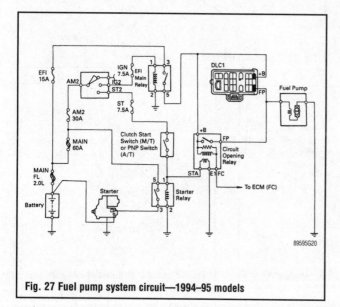

Fig. 27 Fuel pump system circuit—1994–95 models

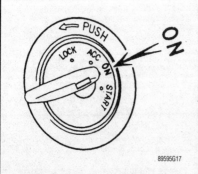

Fig. 28 Turn the ignition switch to the ON position, but do not start the engine

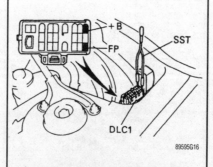

Fig. 29 Using a jumper wire, short both terminals of the fuel pump check connector

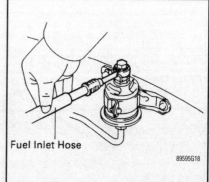

Fig. 30 Feel the high pressure hose at the fuel filter for pressure

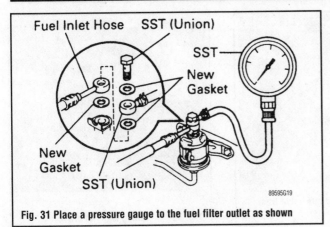

Fig. 31 Place a pressure gauge to the fuel filter outlet as shown

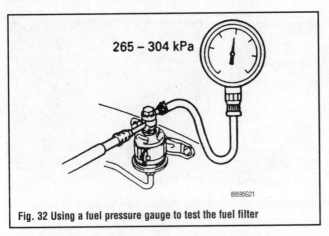

Fig. 32 Using a fuel pressure gauge to test the fuel filter

15. Connect the hose to the fuel filter outlet using new gaskets.
16. Wipe any fuel spillage.
17. Connect the negative battery cable, then start the engine and check for leaks.

1996–98 MODELS

1. Check that the battery voltage is above 12 volts.
2. Disconnect the negative battery cable.

✷✷ WARNING

Make sure you place a suitable container and shop rag under the fuel line to catch any split fuel. The slowly loosen the union bolt.

3. Relieve the fuel system pressure.
4. Remove the union bolt and 2 gaskets, then disconnect the fuel inlet hose from the delivery pipe.
5. Connect the fuel inlet hose and a pressure gauge to the delivery pipe with 3 gaskets and the union bolt. Tighten the bolt to 22 ft. lbs. (29 Nm).
6. Wipe off any split fuel.
7. Turn the ignition switch to the **ON** position but do not start the engine.
8. Connect the positive and negative leads from the battery to the fuel pump wiring.
9. Reconnect the negative terminal cable to the battery.
10. Turn the ignition switch **ON**, but do not start the car.
11. Measure the fuel pressure. Pressure should be between 38–44 psi (265–304 kPa).
12. If the pressure is too high, replace the fuel pressure regulator. If the pressure is too low, check the following:
   a. Fuel hoses
   b. Fuel pump
   c. Fuel filter
   d. Fuel pressure regulator
   e. Injectors

Throttle Body

REMOVAL & INSTALLATION

♦ **See Figures 33 thru 46**

1. Drain and recycle the engine coolant.
2. Remove the air cleaner hose and cap.
3. Disconnect accelerator cable from the throttle linkage. Remove the 2 bolts and the cable bracket.
4. On automatics, disconnect the throttle cable from the throttle linkage.
5. Label and disconnect the vacuum hoses.
6. Carefully remove the throttle position sensor wiring connector.
7. Label and remove the water hoses from the air valve.
8. Depending on the type of mounting refer to the following:
   a. Two bolt and nut; remove the two bolts, two nuts the throttle body with its gasket.
   b. Four bolt; remove the four bolts. Make sure you mark where the bolts go. The bolts are different lengths on the upper and lower sides.
9. Wash and clean the cast metal parts with a soft brush and carburetor cleaner. Use compressed air to blow through all the passages and openings.
10. To check the throttle valve to see that there is NO clearance between the stop screw and the throttle lever when the throttle plate is fully closed.
   a. Apply vacuum to the throttle opener before inserting the feeler gauge between the throttle stop screw and the lever.
11. Inspect the throttle position sensor, refer to Section 4.
To install:
12. Place a new gasket in position and install the throttle body with its two nuts and two bolts. Install the throttle body (with new gasket facing the protrusion downward).
13. Secure the throttle body as follows:
   a. The four bolt type; upper side bolts are 1.77 inch (45mm) and lower side bolts are 2.17 inch (55mm). all bolts are tightened to 14 ft. lbs. (19 Nm).
   b. The two bolt and nut style, install and secure to 14–16 ft. lbs. (19–21 Nm). with the 2 bolts and nuts and tighten.

➡**Make certain everything is properly positioned before securing the unit.**

14. Attach all wiring to each labeled component.
15. Connect the all water and vacuum hoses.
16. Install the air cleaner cap and hose.
17. Connect the wiring to the throttle position sensor.
18. Connect the accelerator cable and its return spring.
19. Refill the coolant to the proper level.
20. Connect the negative battery cable.
21. Start the engine and check operation of the throttle body.

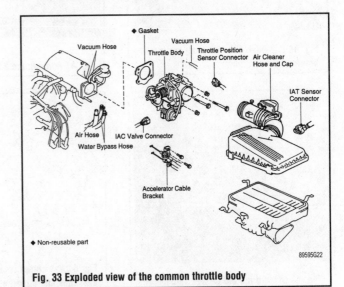

♦ Non-reusable part

Fig. 33 Exploded view of the common throttle body

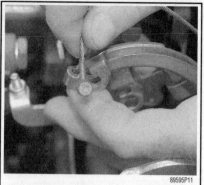

Fig. 34 Disengage the accelerator cable from the linkage . . .

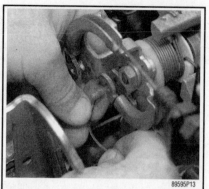

Fig. 35 . . . and the throttle cable from the body . . .

Fig. 36 . . . along with the bracket

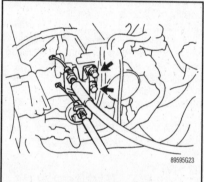

Fig. 37 Remove the bolts retaining the throttle and accelerator cables

Fig. 38 Mark all the vacuum hoses prior to removal

Fig. 39 Disconnect the throttle position and IAC sensor wiring

Fig. 40 It is advised to label all hoses before removing them

Fig. 41 Remove the 2 bolts and nuts . . .

Fig. 42 . . . and lift the throttle body off

Fig. 43 Discard the old gasket from the air chamber

Fig. 44 Use compressed air to clean all passages and openings in the throttle body

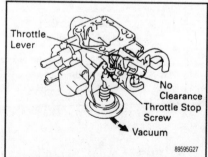

Fig. 45 Check the throttle valve to see that there is NO clearance between the stop screw and the throttle lever when the throttle plate is fully closed

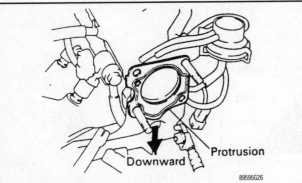

Fig. 46 Place the new gasket on the air intake chamber with the protrusion facing downward

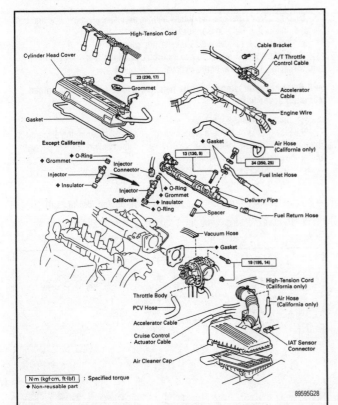

Fig. 47 View of the fuel injector, delivery pipe and related components—5S-FE engine

Fuel Injector(s)

REMOVAL & INSTALLATION

→A small amount of gasoline will be needed to install the O-rings on the injectors. Only replace injectors with NEW insulators and O-rings! If inserting an injector, and it does not seat properly, a new O-ring will be necessary to reinsert the injector.

5S-FE Engine

♦ See Figures 47 thru 54

1. Disconnect the negative battery cable.
2. Remove the air cleaner cap and hose.
3. Remove the throttle body assembly as outlined.
4. If necessary, remove the valve cover assembly. Refer to Section 3. Be sure to label all wiring and hoses.
5. Label and disconnect the vacuum sensing hose from the fuel pressure regulator.
6. On California models, disconnect the air hose for the air assist system from the intake manifold port, then remove the air hose.
7. On all models, remove the bolt and disconnect the engine wire protector from the left side of the intake manifold.
8. Label and disconnect the injector wiring. Label the wiring!
9. Extract the engine wiring protector from the 2 brackets on the front of the intake manifold.
10. Remove the union bolt and 2 gaskets, then disconnect the fuel inlet hoses from the delivery pipe.
11. Disconnect the fuel return hose from the return pipe.
12. Unbolt the delivery pipe from the cylinder head.
13. Disconnect the delivery pipe from the 4 injectors and extract the pipe.
14. Pull the injectors from the pipe, be careful not to drop them.
15. Remove the 4 insulators (except California) and 2 spacers from the intake manifold.
16. On California models, remove the 2 O-rings, insulator and grommet from each injector.
17. On non-California models, remove the O-ring and grommet from each injector.
To install:
18. On California models, install a new insulator and grommet on each injector.
19. On non-California models, install a new grommet on each insulator.
20. Apply a thin coat of gasoline to the O-ring(s) on each injector and then press them into the delivery pipe.
21. Install the spacers and insulators to the intake manifold.
22. Place the delivery pipe between the intake manifold and cylinder head. While turning the injector in a left and right motion, insert them into the delivery pipe. Do this for each injector.

→Position each injector in with the connector facing upward.

23. Attach the injectors and delivery pipe assembly to the cylinder head. Temporarily install the bolts holding the pipe to the cylinder head.

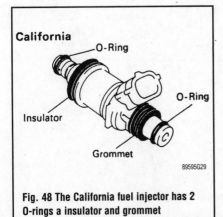

Fig. 48 The California fuel injector has 2 O-rings a insulator and grommet

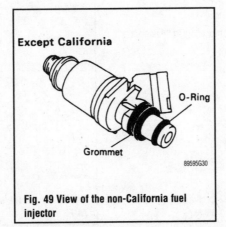

Fig. 49 View of the non-California fuel injector

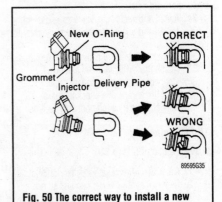

Fig. 50 The correct way to install a new fuel injector O-ring

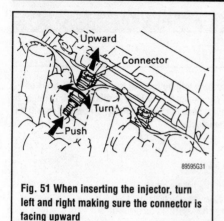

Fig. 51 When inserting the injector, turn left and right making sure the connector is facing upward

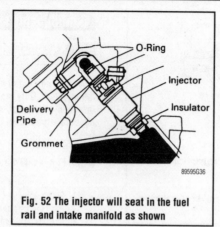

Fig. 52 The injector will seat in the fuel rail and intake manifold as shown

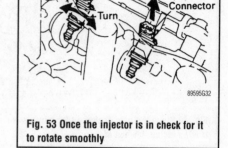

Fig. 53 Once the injector is in check for it to rotate smoothly

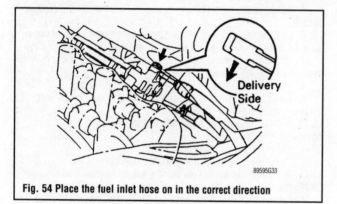

Fig. 54 Place the fuel inlet hose on in the correct direction

24. Check that the injectors rotate smoothly. If they do not rotate smoothly, the O-ring(s) may have been install incorrectly. Replace the O-ring if this occurs.
25. Position the injector wiring connector upward.
26. Tighten the 2 delivery pipe retaining bolts to 9 ft. lbs. (13 Nm).
27. Connect the fuel inlet hose to the delivery pipe with new gaskets and union bolt. Tighten the assembly to 25 ft. lbs. (34 Nm).

➡Be careful of the fuel inlet hose installation direction.

28. Connector the fuel return hose to the return pipe. .
29. Install the engine wire protector to the brackets on the front side of the intake manifold.
30. Connect the injector wiring harnesses.

➡The No. 1 and No. 3 injector wiring are brown and the No. 2 and No. 4 are gray.

31. Attach the engine wire protector to the left side of the intake manifold.
32. Connect the vacuum sensing hose to the fuel pressure regulator.
33. On California models, attach the air hose for the air assist system to the intake manifold port.
34. Install and secure the valve cover assembly.
35. Install and secure the throttle body, refer to the procedure in this section.
36. Connect the control cables to the throttle body.
37. Attach the air cleaner cap and hose.
38. Connect the negative battery cable.
39. Start the engine and check for leaks.
40. Rest any electrical components such as the clock and radio.

7A-FE Engine

▸ See Figures 55 thru 63

1. Disconnect the negative battery cable.
2. Remove the air cleaner cap and air hose.
3. Disconnect the accelerator cable bracket from the throttle body.
4. Disconnect the throttle body from the air intake chamber.

5. If necessary, remove the engine hanger, air intake chamber stay and EGR vacuum modulator. Refer to Section 3 and 4.
6. If equipped, remove the EGR valve and pipe.
7. Remove the air intake chamber cover. Disconnect and label all hoses and wiring incorporated with the removal.

➡A 6mm hexagon wrench will be necessary to remove the air intake chamber cover bolts.

8. Unplug the injector wiring.
9. Slowly loosen and remove the union bolt and 2 gaskets, the disconnect the inlet hose from the delivery pipe. Place s suitable container or shop towel under the pipe to catch any split fuel.
10. Disconnect the fuel return hose from the pressure regulator.
11. Unbolt the fuel rail together with the 4 injectors.

➡Be careful not to drop the injectors when removing the fuel rail.

12. Remove the 4 insulators and 2 spacers from the intake manifold.

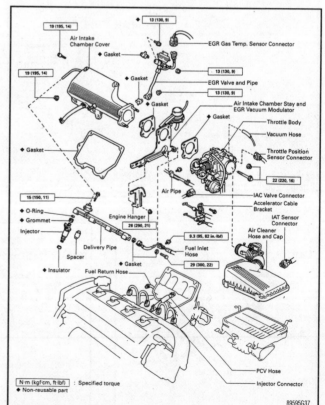

Fig. 55 View of the fuel injector, fuel rail and related components— 7A-FE engine

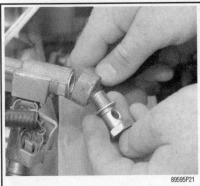

Fig. 56 Unbolt the fuel inlet hose by loosening the union bolt, then . . .

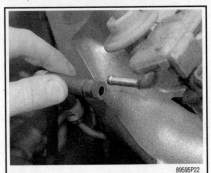

Fig. 57 . . . remove the return hose from the pressure regulator at the other end of the fuel rail

Fig. 58 Remove the bolts attaching the fuel rail to the intake manifold

Fig. 59 Lift the fuel rail carefully so the injectors do not fall out

Fig. 60 An insulator is located at the tip of the injector

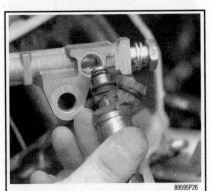

Fig. 61 Pull each injector from the fuel rail, try not to mix them up

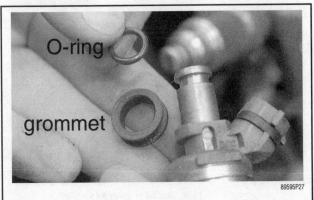

Fig. 62 From each injector, remove the grommet and O-ring

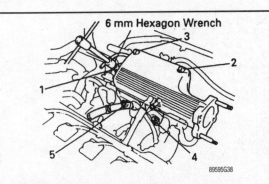

Fig. 63 Air intake chamber cover bolt tightening sequence

13. Pull out the 4 injectors from the delivery pipe.
14. Remove the O-ring and grommet from each injector.
To install:
15. Install a new grommet on each injector.
16. Apply a light coat of gasoline to the new O-ring and install it to the injector.
17. While turning the injector left and right, install it to the delivery pipe. Install each injector in the same manner.
18. Position the injector wiring connector upward.
19. Place new insulators and spacers in position on the intake manifold.
20. Place the injectors and delivery pipe assembly in position on the intake manifold.
21. Check the injectors rotate smoothly.

➡ **If the injectors do not rotate smoothly, the O-rings were probably not installed correctly. Remove the injector and install a new O-ring, then reinsert the injector.**

22. Position the injector connector upward.
23. Tighten the bolts holding the delivery pipe to the intake manifold. Secure the bolts to 11 ft. lbs. (15 Nm).
24. Connect the fuel return hose to the pressure regulator.
25. Attach the fuel inlet hose with the 2 gaskets and union bolt and secure to 22 ft. lbs. (29 Nm).
26. Attach the injector connectors.
27. Install the air intake chamber cover. Secure the bolts in the correct sequence.
28. If removed, install the EGR valve and pipe.
29. If removed, attach the air intake chamber stay, EGR vacuum modulator and engine hanger.
30. Install the throttle body. Refer to the procedure in this section.
31. Connect the accelerator cable bracket to the throttle body.
32. Attach the air cleaner cap and hose.
33. Connect the negative battery cable.

TESTING

On-Vehicle Inspection

CHECK INJECTOR OPERATION

▶ **See Figures 64 and 65**

1. Start the engine.
2. Position the probe of a technicians stethoscope (or finger tip) under the base of the injector connector and have an assistant alternately increase the engine rpm and return it to idle.
3. Listen or feel for a change in the operating sound of the injector. The change should be proportional to the increase in engine rpm.
4. If no sound is heard or if the injector sound is unusual, check the connector wiring, injector, resistor or the signal from the ECU.

CHECK INJECTOR RESISTANCE

▶ **See Figures 66 and 67**

Disconnect the connector from the injector. With an ohmmeter, measure the resistance between the injector terminals. The resistance should be approximately 13.4–14.2 ohms. If the resistance is not as specified, replace the injector. Reconnect the injector connector.

Off-Vehicle Inspection

INJECTOR VOLUME TEST

▶ **See Figures 68 thru 75**

※ CAUTION

To avoid personal injury, do not smoke or use any type of open flame when testing the injectors!

1. Remove the injector(s) from the vehicle and set aside (See Fuel Injectors).
2. Place a rag under the "banjo" fitting and, disconnect the fuel hose from the fuel filter outlet. Remove the gaskets and replace them with new ones.
3. Connect SST No. 09628–41045 (union and hose) to the fuel filter outlet connection with the new gaskets and tighten the union bolt.
4. Remove the fuel pressure regulator.
5. Connect the fuel return hose to the pressure regulator with the service union with a set of new gaskets and tighten the union bolt.
6. Install a new O-ring onto injector.
7. Connect the special service tool (union and hose) to the injector, and hold the injector and union with the clamp.
8. Connect a length of rubber or vinyl hose to the injector tip to prevent fuel splashing and overspray.
9. Place the injector into a graduated cylinder with metric increments.
10. With a jumper wire, short the **+B** and **FP** terminals of the check connector.
11. Reconnect the negative battery cable.
12. Turn the ignition switch **ON** , but DO NOT start the engine.
13. Connect SST No. 09842-30070 (wire) to the injector and battery for 15 seconds.
14. Measure the volume injected into the cylinder during the 15 second period. The volume should be:
   - 3.0–3.6 cu. inch (49–59cc)—5S-FE engine
   - 2.4–3.1 cu inch. (40–50cc)—7A-FE engine

➡ **Test each injector 2 or 3 times.**

15. If all four injectors were tested, there should be no less than 0.3 cu. in. (5cc) difference between each injector. If the actual volume does not agree with the specified volume, replace the injector.

CHECK LEAKAGE RATE

1. Leaving everything as it was from the injection test, disconnect the service tool test probes from the battery.

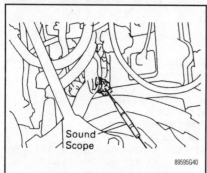

Fig. 64 Place a sound scope under the base of the injector connector to test the operation

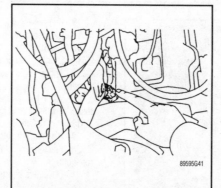

Fig. 65 A finger can be used in place of a sound scope if necessary

Fig. 66 Testing the fuel injector terminals for continuity using an ohmmeter

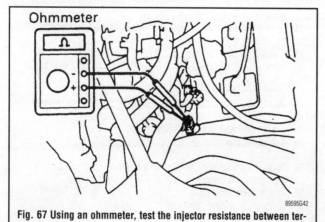

Fig. 67 Using an ohmmeter, test the injector resistance between terminals

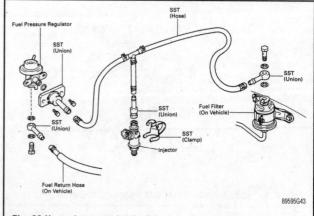

Fig. 68 Hose placement for the injector volume testing

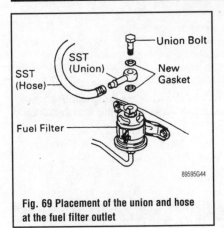

Fig. 69 Placement of the union and hose at the fuel filter outlet

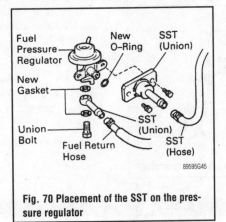

Fig. 70 Placement of the SST on the pressure regulator

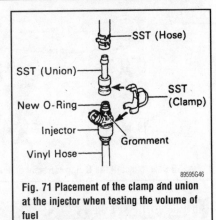

Fig. 71 Placement of the clamp and union at the injector when testing the volume of fuel

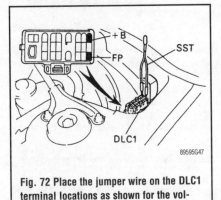

Fig. 72 Place the jumper wire on the DLC1 terminal locations as shown for the volume test

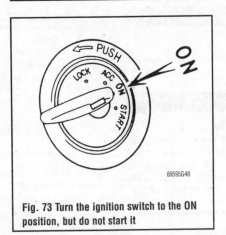

Fig. 73 Turn the ignition switch to the ON position, but do not start it

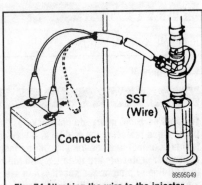

Fig. 74 Attaching the wire to the injector and battery to measure the injection volume

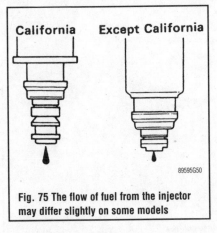

Fig. 75 The flow of fuel from the injector may differ slightly on some models

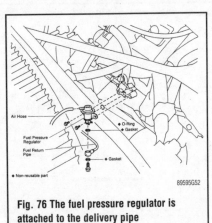

Fig. 76 The fuel pressure regulator is attached to the delivery pipe

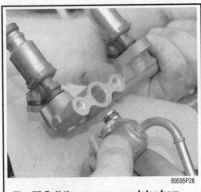

Fig. 77 Pull the pressure regulator from the fuel rail, then . . .

2. Check the injector tip for leakage for a period of one minute. An acceptable leakage rate is one drop.
3. If the leakage exceeds this amount, replace the injector.
4. Disconnect the negative battery cable and remove the all the test equipment.
5. Install the injector(s).

Fuel Pressure Regulator

REMOVAL & INSTALLATION

♦ See Figures 76, 77, 78 and 79

1. Disconnect the air hose from the fuel pressure regulator.
2. Place a suitable container and shop rag under the pressure regulator.
3. To disconnect the fuel return pipe from the fuel pressure regulator, slowly remove the union bolt and gaskets to separate the pipe.

Fig. 78 . . . remove the O-ring

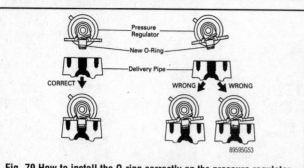

Fig. 79 How to install the O-ring correctly on the pressure regulator

4. Unbolt the regulator and pull the unit out.
5. Remove the O-ring and discard.
To install:
6. Apply a light coat of fuel to the new O-ring, and install the regulator.
7. Attach the regulator to the delivery pipe.
8. Check that the regulator rotates smoothly.

→**If the regulator does not rotate smoothly, the O-ring may be pinched. Remove the regulator and install another new O-ring and reinstall the assembly.**

9. Secure the regulator and tighten the bolts to 48 inch lbs. 95 Nm).

FUEL TANK

Tank Assembly

REMOVAL & INSTALLATION

▶ **See Figure 80**

❊❊ **CAUTION**

To avoid personal injury, do not smoke or use any type of open flame when removing the fuel tank! Always use new gaskets on any fuel tank or fuel line component. During installation, make sure that the rubber protectors are installed with the fuel tank and make sure that all line or plug torque specification are observed. To reduce the amount of fuel that you will have to dispose of, use as much of the fuel as possible before draining the tank.

1. Raise and safely support the vehicle. Disconnect the negative battery cable and properly relieve the fuel system pressure.
2. If equipped with a drain plug position a large capacity waste drain receptacle under the drain plug.
3. Remove the drain plug and gasket. Discard the gasket and purchase a new one.
4. If not equipped with a drain plug obtain an approved pumping device and drain a sufficient amount of fuel from the tank.
5. Remove the luggage compartment mat. Remove the cover over the tank sending unit and hose connections. Disconnect the gauge electrical harness and the vent, feed and fuel return hoses. Disconnect the fuel inlet filler neck.
6. With the aid of an assistant, support the tank and remove the tank strap bolts. Lower the tank and remove it from the vehicle.

→**To make the installation easier, label and tag all fuel lines and electrical connections.**

7. Installation is the reverse of removal. Be careful not to twist or kink any of the hoses. Check for leaks.

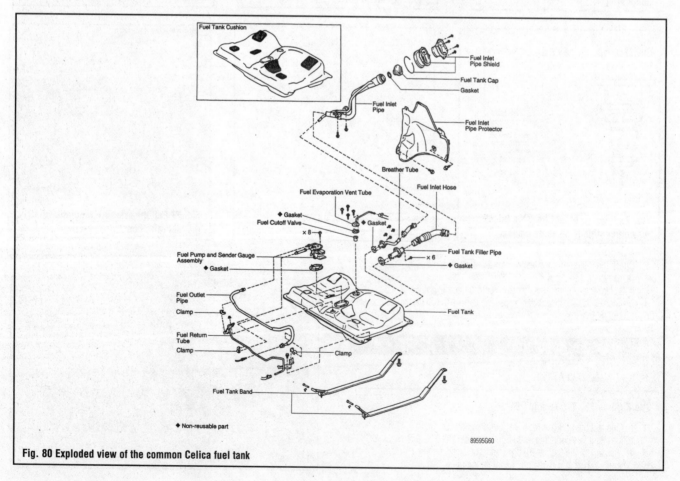

Fig. 80 Exploded view of the common Celica fuel tank

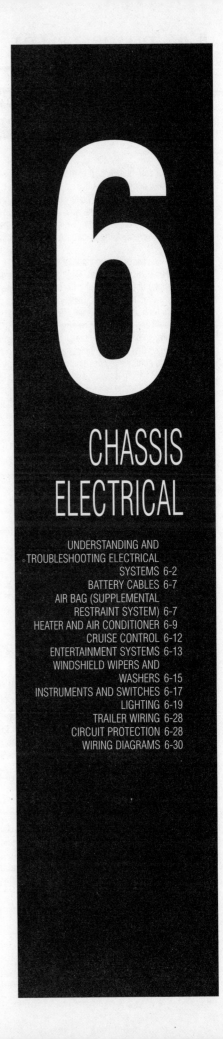

6

CHASSIS
ELECTRICAL

UNDERSTANDING AND TROUBLESHOOTING ELECTRICAL SYSTEMS

Basic Electrical Theory

◆ **See Figure 1**

For any 12 volt, negative ground, electrical system to operate, the electricity must travel in a complete circuit. This simply means that current (power) from the positive (+) terminal of the battery must eventually return to the negative (−) terminal of the battery. Along the way, this current will travel through wires, fuses, switches and components. If, for any reason, the flow of current through the circuit is interrupted, the component fed by that circuit will cease to function properly.

Perhaps the easiest way to visualize a circuit is to think of connecting a light bulb (with two wires attached to it) to the battery-one wire attached to the negative (−) terminal of the battery and the other wire to the positive (+) terminal. With the two wires touching the battery terminals, the circuit would be complete and the light bulb would illuminate. Electricity would follow a path from the battery to the bulb and back to the battery. It's easy to see that with longer wires on our light bulb, it could be mounted anywhere. Further, one wire could be fitted with a switch so that the light could be turned on and off.

The normal automotive circuit differs from this simple example in two ways. First, instead of having a return wire from the bulb to the battery, the current travels through the frame of the vehicle. Since the negative (−) battery cable is attached to the frame (made of electrically conductive metal), the frame of the vehicle can serve as a ground wire to complete the circuit. Secondly, most automotive circuits contain multiple components which receive power from a single circuit. This lessens the amount of wire needed to power components on the vehicle.

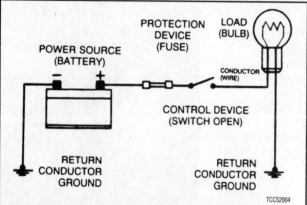

Fig. 1 This example illustrates a simple circuit. When the switch is closed, power from the positive (+) battery terminal flows through the fuse and the switch, and then to the light bulb. The light illuminates and the circuit is completed through the ground wire back to the negative (ñ) battery terminal. In reality, the two ground points shown in the illustration are attached to the metal frame of the vehicle, which completes the circuit back to the battery

HOW DOES ELECTRICITY WORK: THE WATER ANALOGY

Electricity is the flow of electrons-the subatomic particles that constitute the outer shell of an atom. Electrons spin in an orbit around the center core of an atom. The center core is comprised of protons (positive charge) and neutrons (neutral charge). Electrons have a negative charge and balance out the positive charge of the protons. When an outside force causes the number of electrons to unbalance the charge of the protons, the electrons will split off the atom and look for another atom to balance out. If this imbalance is kept up, electrons will continue to move and an electrical flow will exist.

Many people have been taught electrical theory using an analogy with water. In a comparison with water flowing through a pipe, the electrons would be the water and the wire is the pipe.

The flow of electricity can be measured much like the flow of water through a pipe. The unit of measurement used is amperes, frequently abbreviated as amps (a). You can compare amperage to the volume of water flowing through a pipe. When connected to a circuit, an ammeter will measure the actual amount of current flowing through the circuit. When relatively few electrons flow through a circuit, the amperage is low. When many electrons flow, the amperage is high.

Water pressure is measured in units such as pounds per square inch (psi); The electrical pressure is measured in units called volts (v). When a voltmeter is connected to a circuit, it is measuring the electrical pressure.

The actual flow of electricity depends not only on voltage and amperage, but also on the resistance of the circuit. The higher the resistance, the higher the force necessary to push the current through the circuit. The standard unit for measuring resistance is an ohm (Ω). Resistance in a circuit varies depending on the amount and type of components used in the circuit. The main factors which determine resistance are:

• Material-some materials have more resistance than others. Those with high resistance are said to be insulators. Rubber materials (or rubber-like plastics) are some of the most common insulators used in vehicles as they have a very high resistance to electricity. Very low resistance materials are said to be conductors. Copper wire is among the best conductors. Silver is actually a superior conductor to copper and is used in some relay contacts, but its high cost prohibits its use as common wiring. Most automotive wiring is made of copper.

• Size-the larger the wire size being used, the less resistance the wire will have. This is why components which use large amounts of electricity usually have large wires supplying current to them.

• Length-for a given thickness of wire, the longer the wire, the greater the resistance. The shorter the wire, the less the resistance. When determining the proper wire for a circuit, both size and length must be considered to design a circuit that can handle the current needs of the component.

• Temperature-with many materials, the higher the temperature, the greater the resistance (positive temperature coefficient). Some materials exhibit the opposite trait of lower resistance with higher temperatures (negative temperature coefficient). These principles are used in many of the sensors on the engine.

OHM'S LAW

There is a direct relationship between current, voltage and resistance. The relationship between current, voltage and resistance can be summed up by a statement known as Ohm's law.

Voltage (E) is equal to amperage (I) times resistance (R): $E = I \times R$

Other forms of the formula are $R = E/I$ and $I = E/R$

In each of these formulas, E is the voltage in volts, I is the current in amps and R is the resistance in ohms. The basic point to remember is that as the resistance of a circuit goes up, the amount of current that flows in the circuit will go down, if voltage remains the same.

The amount of work that the electricity can perform is expressed as power. The unit of power is the watt (w). The relationship between power, voltage and current is expressed as:

Power (w) is equal to amperage (I) times voltage (E): $W = I \times E$

This is only true for direct current (DC) circuits; The alternating current formula is a tad different, but since the electrical circuits in most vehicles are DC type, we need not get into AC circuit theory.

Electrical Components

POWER SOURCE

Power is supplied to the vehicle by two devices: The battery and the alternator. The battery supplies electrical power during starting or during periods when the current demand of the vehicle's electrical system exceeds the output capacity of the alternator. The alternator supplies electrical current when the engine is running. Just not does the alternator supply the current needs of the vehicle, but it recharges the battery.

The Battery

In most modern vehicles, the battery is a lead/acid electrochemical device consisting of six 2 volt subsections (cells) connected in series, so that the unit is capable of producing approximately 12 volts of electrical pressure. Each subsection consists of a series of positive and negative plates held a short distance apart in a solution of sulfuric acid and water.

The two types of plates are of dissimilar metals. This sets up a chemical reaction, and it is this reaction which produces current flow from the battery when its positive and negative terminals are connected to an electrical load . The power removed from the battery is replaced by the alternator, restoring the battery to its original chemical state.

The Alternator

On some vehicles there isn't an alternator, but a generator. The difference is that an alternator supplies alternating current which is then changed to direct current for use on the vehicle, while a generator produces direct current. Alternators tend to be more efficient and that is why they are used.

Alternators and generators are devices that consist of coils of wires wound together making big electromagnets. One group of coils spins within another set and the interaction of the magnetic fields causes a current to flow. This current is then drawn off the coils and fed into the vehicles electrical system.

GROUND

Two types of grounds are used in automotive electric circuits. Direct ground components are grounded to the frame through their mounting points. All other components use some sort of ground wire which is attached to the frame or chassis of the vehicle. The electrical current runs through the chassis of the vehicle and returns to the battery through the ground (−) cable; if you look, you'll see that the battery ground cable connects between the battery and the frame or chassis of the vehicle.

➡It should be noted that a good percentage of electrical problems can be traced to bad grounds.

PROTECTIVE DEVICES

♦ See Figure 2

It is possible for large surges of current to pass through the electrical system of your vehicle. If this surge of current were to reach the load in the circuit, the surge could burn it out or severely damage it. It can also overload the wiring, causing the harness to get hot and melt the insulation. To prevent this, fuses, circuit breakers and/or fusible links are connected into the supply wires of the electrical system. These items are nothing more than a built-in weak spot in the system. When an abnormal amount of current flows through the system, these protective devices work as follows to protect the circuit:

• Fuse-when an excessive electrical current passes through a fuse, the fuse "blows" (the conductor melts) and opens the circuit, preventing the passage of current.

• Circuit Breaker-a circuit breaker is basically a self-repairing fuse. It will open the circuit in the same fashion as a fuse, but when the surge subsides, the circuit breaker can be reset and does not need replacement.

• Fusible Link-a fusible link (fuse link or main link) is a short length of special, high temperature insulated wire that acts as a fuse. When an excessive electrical current passes through a fusible link, the thin gauge wire inside the link melts, creating an intentional open to protect the circuit. To repair the circuit, the link must be replaced. Some newer type fusible links are housed in plug-in modules, which are simply replaced like a fuse, while older type fusible links must be cut and spliced if they melt. Since this link is very early in the electrical path, it's the first place to look if nothing on the vehicle works, yet the battery seems to be charged and is properly connected.

✸✸ CAUTION

Always replace fuses, circuit breakers and fusible links with identically rated components. Under no circumstances should a component of higher or lower amperage rating be substituted.

SWITCHES & RELAYS

♦ See Figures 3 and 4

Switches are used in electrical circuits to control the passage of current. The most common use is to open and close circuits between the battery and the various electric devices in the system. Switches are rated according to the amount of amperage they can handle. If a sufficient amperage rated switch is not used in a circuit, the switch could overload and cause damage.

Some electrical components which require a large amount of current to operate use a special switch called a relay. Since these circuits carry a large amount of current, the thickness of the wire in the circuit is also greater. If this large wire were connected from the load to the control switch, the switch would have to carry the high amperage load and the fairing or dash would be twice as large to accommodate the increased size of the wiring harness. To prevent these problems, a relay is used.

Relays are composed of a coil and a set of contacts. When the coil has a current passed though it, a magnetic field is formed and this field causes the contacts to move together, completing the circuit. Most relays are normally open, preventing current from passing through the circuit, but they can take any electrical form depending on the job they are intended to do. Relays can be considered "remote control switches." They allow a smaller current to operate devices that require higher amperages. When a small current operates the coil, a larger current is allowed to pass by the contacts. Some common circuits which may use relays are the horn, headlights, starter, electric fuel pump and other high draw circuits.

TCCA6P01

Fig. 2 Most vehicles use one or more fuse panels. This one is located on the driver's side kick panel

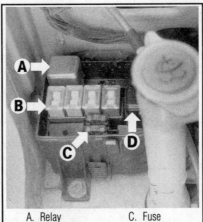

A. Relay   C. Fuse
B. Fusible link D. Flasher

TCCA6P02

Fig. 3 The underhood fuse and relay panel usually contains fuses, relays, flashers and fusible links

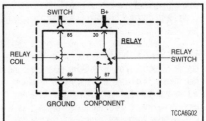

TCCA6G02

Fig. 4 Relays are composed of a coil and a switch. These two components are linked together so that when one operates, the other operates at the same time. The large wires in the circuit are connected from the battery to one side of the relay switch (B+) and from the opposite side of the relay switch to the load (component). Smaller wires are connected from the relay coil to the control switch for the circuit and from the opposite side of the relay coil to ground

LOAD

Every electrical circuit must include a "load" (something to use the electricity coming from the source). Without this load, the battery would attempt to deliver its entire power supply from one pole to another. This is called a "short circuit." All this electricity would take a short cut to ground and cause a great amount of damage to other components in the circuit by developing a tremendous amount of heat. This condition could develop sufficient heat to melt the insulation on all the surrounding wires and reduce a multiple wire cable to a lump of plastic and copper.

WIRING & HARNESSES

The average vehicle contains meters and meters of wiring, with hundreds of individual connections. To protect the many wires from damage and to keep them from becoming a confusing tangle, they are organized into bundles, enclosed in plastic or taped together and called wiring harnesses. Different harnesses serve different parts of the vehicle. Individual wires are color coded to help trace them through a harness where sections are hidden from view.

Automotive wiring or circuit conductors can be either single strand wire, multi-strand wire or printed circuitry. Single strand wire has a solid metal core and is usually used inside such components as alternators, motors, relays and other devices. Multi-strand wire has a core made of many small strands of wire twisted together into a single conductor. Most of the wiring in an automotive electrical system is made up of multi-strand wire, either as a single conductor or grouped together in a harness. All wiring is color coded on the insulator, either as a solid color or as a colored wire with an identification stripe. A printed circuit is a thin film of copper or other conductor that is printed on an insulator backing. Occasionally, a printed circuit is sandwiched between two sheets of plastic for more protection and flexibility. A complete printed circuit, consisting of conductors, insulating material and connectors for lamps or other components is called a printed circuit board. Printed circuitry is used in place of individual wires or harnesses in places where space is limited, such as behind instrument panels.

Since automotive electrical systems are very sensitive to changes in resistance, the selection of properly sized wires is critical when systems are repaired. A loose or corroded connection or a replacement wire that is too small for the circuit will add extra resistance and an additional voltage drop to the circuit.

The wire gauge number is an expression of the cross-section area of the conductor. Vehicles from countries that use the metric system will typically describe the wire size as its cross-sectional area in square millimeters. In this method, the larger the wire, the greater the number. Another common system for expressing wire size is the American Wire Gauge (AWG) system. As gauge number increases, area decreases and the wire becomes smaller. An 18 gauge wire is smaller than a 4 gauge wire. A wire with a higher gauge number will carry less current than a wire with a lower gauge number. Gauge wire size refers to the size of the strands of the conductor, not the size of the complete wire with insulator. It is possible, therefore, to have two wires of the same gauge with different diameters because one may have thicker insulation than the other.

It is essential to understand how a circuit works before trying to figure out why it doesn't. An electrical schematic shows the electrical current paths when a circuit is operating properly. Schematics break the entire electrical system down into individual circuits. In a schematic, usually no attempt is made to represent wiring and components as they physically appear on the vehicle; switches and other components are shown as simply as possible. Face views of harness connectors show the cavity or terminal locations in all multi-pin connectors to help locate test points.

CONNECTORS

▶ See Figures 5 and 6

Three types of connectors are commonly used in automotive applications—weatherproof, molded and hard shell.

• Weatherproof-these connectors are most commonly used where the connector is exposed to the elements. Terminals are protected against moisture and dirt by sealing rings which provide a weathertight seal. All repairs require the use of a special terminal and the tool required to service it. Unlike standard blade type terminals, these weatherproof terminals cannot be straightened once they are bent. Make certain that the connectors are properly seated and all of the sealing rings are in place when connecting leads.

• Molded-these connectors require complete replacement of the connector if found to be defective. This means splicing a new connector assembly into the harness. All splices should be soldered to insure proper contact. Use care when probing the connections or replacing terminals in them, as it is possible to create a short circuit between opposite terminals. If this happens to the wrong terminal pair, it is possible to damage certain components. Always use jumper wires between connectors for circuit checking and NEVER probe through weatherproof seals.

• Hard Shell-unlike molded connectors, the terminal contacts in hard-shell connectors can be replaced. Replacement usually involves the use of a special terminal removal tool that depresses the locking tangs (barbs) on the connector terminal and allows the connector to be removed from the rear of the shell. The connector shell should be replaced if it shows any evidence of burning, melting, cracks, or breaks. Replace individual terminals that are burnt, corroded, distorted or loose.

Test Equipment

Pinpointing the exact cause of trouble in an electrical circuit is most times accomplished by the use of special test equipment. The following describes different types of commonly used test equipment and briefly explains how to use them in diagnosis. In addition to the information covered below, the tool manufacturer's instructions booklet (provided with the tester) should be read and clearly understood before attempting any test procedures.

JUMPER WIRES

✳✳ CAUTION

Never use jumper wires made from a thinner gauge wire than the circuit being tested. If the jumper wire is of too small a gauge, it may overheat and possibly melt. Never use jumpers to bypass high resistance loads in a circuit. Bypassing resistances, in effect, creates a short circuit. This may, in turn, cause damage and fire. Jumper wires should only be used to bypass lengths of wire or to simulate switches.

Jumper wires are simple, yet extremely valuable, pieces of test equipment. They are basically test wires which are used to bypass sections of a circuit. Although jumper wires can be purchased, they are usually fabricated from lengths of standard automotive wire and whatever type of connector (alligator clip, spade connector or pin connector) that is required for the particular application being tested. In cramped, hard-to-reach areas, it is advisable to have insulated boots over the jumper wire terminals in order to prevent accidental grounding. It is also advisable to include a standard automotive fuse in any jumper wire. This is commonly referred to as a "fused jumper". By inserting an in-line fuse holder between a set of test leads, a fused jumper wire can be used for bypassing open circuits. Use a 5 amp fuse to provide protection against voltage spikes.

Jumper wires are used primarily to locate open electrical circuits, on either the ground (−) side of the circuit or on the power (+) side. If an electrical component fails to operate, connect the jumper wire between the component and a good ground. If the component operates only with the jumper installed, the ground circuit is open. If the ground circuit is good, but the component does not operate, the circuit between the power feed and component may be open. By moving the jumper wire successively back from the component toward the power source, you can isolate the area of the circuit where the open is located. When the component stops functioning, or the power is cut off, the open is in the segment of wire between the jumper and the point previously tested.

You can sometimes connect the jumper wire directly from the battery to the "hot" terminal of the component, but first make sure the component uses 12 volts in operation. Some electrical components, such as fuel injectors or sensors, are designed to operate on about 4 to 5 volts, and running 12 volts directly to these components will cause damage.

Fig. 5 Hard shell (left) and weatherproof (right) connectors have replaceable terminals

Fig. 6 Weatherproof connectors are most commonly used in the engine compartment or where the connector is exposed to the elements

Fig. 7 A 12 volt test light is used to detect the presence of voltage in a circuit

TEST LIGHTS

◗ See Figure 7

The test light is used to check circuits and components while electrical current is flowing through them. It is used for voltage and ground tests. To use a 12 volt test light, connect the ground clip to a good ground and probe wherever necessary with the pick. The test light will illuminate when voltage is detected. This does not necessarily mean that 12 volts (or any particular amount of voltage) is present; it only means that some voltage is present. It is advisable before using the test light to touch its ground clip and probe across the battery posts or terminals to make sure the light is operating properly.

> ※※ **WARNING**
>
> **Do not use a test light to probe electronic ignition, spark plug or coil wires. Never use a pick-type test light to probe wiring on computer controlled systems unless specifically instructed to do so. Any wire insulation that is pierced by the test light probe should be taped and sealed with silicone after testing.**

Like the jumper wire, the 12 volt test light is used to isolate opens in circuits. But, whereas the jumper wire is used to bypass the open to operate the load, the 12 volt test light is used to locate the presence of voltage in a circuit. If the test light illuminates, there is power up to that point in the circuit; if the test light does not illuminate, there is an open circuit (no power). Move the test light in successive steps back toward the power source until the light in the handle illuminates. The open is between the probe and a point which was previously probed.

The self-powered test light is similar in design to the 12 volt test light, but contains a 1.5 volt penlight battery in the handle. It is most often used in place of a multimeter to check for open or short circuits when power is isolated from the circuit (continuity test).

The battery in a self-powered test light does not provide much current. A weak battery may not provide enough power to illuminate the test light even when a complete circuit is made (especially if there is high resistance in the circuit). Always make sure that the test battery is strong. To check the battery, briefly touch the ground clip to the probe; if the light glows brightly, the battery is strong enough for testing.

➡**A self-powered test light should not be used on any computer controlled system or component. The small amount of electricity transmitted by the test light is enough to damage many electronic automotive components.**

MULTIMETERS

Multimeters are an extremely useful tool for troubleshooting electrical problems. They can be purchased in either analog or digital form and have a price range to suit any budget. A multimeter is a voltmeter, ammeter and ohmmeter (along with other features) combined into one instrument. It is often used when testing solid state circuits because of its high input impedance (usually 10 megaohms or more). A brief description of the multimeter main test functions follows:

• Voltmeter-the voltmeter is used to measure voltage at any point in a circuit, or to measure the voltage drop across any part of a circuit. Voltmeters usually have various scales and a selector switch to allow the reading of different voltage ranges. The voltmeter has a positive and a negative lead. To avoid damage to the meter, always connect the negative lead to the negative (–) side of the circuit (to ground or nearest the ground side of the circuit) and connect the positive lead to the positive (+) side of the circuit (to the power source or the nearest power source). Note that the negative voltmeter lead will always be black and that the positive voltmeter will always be some color other than black (usually red).

• Ohmmeter-the ohmmeter is designed to read resistance (measured in ohms) in a circuit or component. Most ohmmeters will have a selector switch which permits the measurement of different ranges of resistance (usually the selector switch allows the multiplication of the meter reading by 10, 100, 1,000 and 10,000). Some ohmmeters are "auto-ranging" which means the meter itself will determine which scale to use. Since the meters are powered by an internal battery, the ohmmeter can be used like a self-powered test light. When the ohmmeter is connected, current from the ohmmeter flows through the circuit or component being tested. Since the ohmmeter's internal resistance and voltage are known values, the amount of current flow through the meter depends on the resistance of the circuit or component being tested. The ohmmeter can also be used to perform a continuity test for suspected open circuits. In using the meter for making continuity checks, do not be concerned with the actual resistance readings. Zero resistance, or any ohm reading, indicates continuity in the circuit. Infinite resistance indicates an opening in the circuit. A high resistance reading where there should be none indicates a problem in the circuit. Checks for short circuits are made in the same manner as checks for open circuits, except that the circuit must be isolated from both power and normal ground. Infinite resistance indicates no continuity, while zero resistance indicates a dead short.

> ※※ **WARNING**
>
> **Never use an ohmmeter to check the resistance of a component or wire while there is voltage applied to the circuit.**

• Ammeter-an ammeter measures the amount of current flowing through a circuit in units called amperes or amps. At normal operating voltage, most circuits have a characteristic amount of amperes, called "current draw" which can be measured using an ammeter. By referring to a specified current draw rating, then measuring the amperes and comparing the two values, one can determine what is happening within the circuit to aid in diagnosis. An open circuit, for example, will not allow any current to flow, so the ammeter reading will be zero. A damaged component or circuit will have an increased current draw, so the reading will be high. The ammeter is always connected in series with the circuit being tested. All of the current that normally flows through the circuit must also flow through the ammeter; if there is any other path for the current to follow, the ammeter reading will not be accurate. The ammeter itself has very little resistance to current flow and, therefore, will not affect the circuit, but it will measure current draw only when the circuit is closed and electricity is flowing. Excessive current draw can blow fuses and drain the battery, while a reduced current draw can cause motors to run slowly, lights to dim and other components to not operate properly.

Troubleshooting Electrical Systems

When diagnosing a specific problem, organized troubleshooting is a must. The complexity of a modern automotive vehicle demands that you approach any problem in a logical, organized manner. There are certain troubleshooting techniques, however, which are standard:

• Establish when the problem occurs. Does the problem appear only under certain conditions? Were there any noises, odors or other unusual symptoms? Isolate the problem area. To do this, make some simple tests and observations, then eliminate the systems that are working properly. Check for obvious problems, such as broken wires and loose or dirty connections. Always check the obvious before assuming something complicated is the cause.

• Test for problems systematically to determine the cause once the problem area is isolated. Are all the components functioning properly? Is there power going to electrical switches and motors. Performing careful, systematic checks will often turn up most causes on the first inspection, without wasting time checking components that have little or no relationship to the problem.

• Test all repairs after the work is done to make sure that the problem is fixed. Some causes can be traced to more than one component, so a careful verification of repair work is important in order to pick up additional malfunctions that may cause a problem to reappear or a different problem to arise. A blown fuse, for example, is a simple problem that may require more than another fuse to repair. If you don't look for a problem that caused a fuse to blow, a shorted wire (for example) may go undetected.

Experience has shown that most problems tend to be the result of a fairly simple and obvious cause, such as loose or corroded connectors, bad grounds or damaged wire insulation which causes a short. This makes careful visual inspection of components during testing essential to quick and accurate troubleshooting.

Testing

OPEN CIRCUITS

▶ See Figure 8

This test already assumes the existence of an open in the circuit and it is used to help locate the open portion.

1. Isolate the circuit from power and ground.
2. Connect the self-powered test light or ohmmeter ground clip to the ground side of the circuit and probe sections of the circuit sequentially.
3. If the light is out or there is infinite resistance, the open is between the probe and the circuit ground.
4. If the light is on or the meter shows continuity, the open is between the probe and the end of the circuit toward the power source.

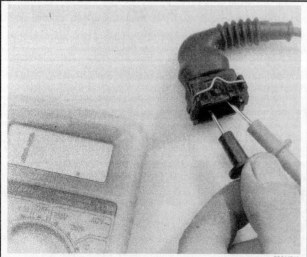

TCCA6P10

Fig. 8 The infinite reading on this multimeter (1 .) indicates that the circuit is open

SHORT CIRCUITS

➡ **Never use a self-powered test light to perform checks for opens or shorts when power is applied to the circuit under test. The test light can be damaged by outside power.**

1. Isolate the circuit from power and ground.
2. Connect the self-powered test light or ohmmeter ground clip to a good ground and probe any easy-to-reach point in the circuit.
3. If the light comes on or there is continuity, there is a short somewhere in the circuit.
4. To isolate the short, probe a test point at either end of the isolated circuit (the light should be on or the meter should indicate continuity).
5. Leave the test light probe engaged and sequentially open connectors or switches, remove parts, etc. until the light goes out or continuity is broken.
6. When the light goes out, the short is between the last two circuit components which were opened.

VOLTAGE

This test determines voltage available from the battery and should be the first step in any electrical troubleshooting procedure after visual inspection. Many electrical problems, especially on computer controlled systems, can be caused by a low state of charge in the battery. Excessive corrosion at the battery cable terminals can cause poor contact that will prevent proper charging and full battery current flow.

1. Set the voltmeter selector switch to the 20V position.
2. Connect the multimeter negative lead to the battery's negative (−) post or terminal and the positive lead to the battery's positive (+) post or terminal.
3. Turn the ignition switch **ON** to provide a load.
4. A well charged battery should register over 12 volts. If the meter reads below 11.5 volts, the battery power may be insufficient to operate the electrical system properly.

VOLTAGE DROP

▶ See Figure 9

When current flows through a load, the voltage beyond the load drops. This voltage drop is due to the resistance created by the load and also by small resistances created by corrosion at the connectors and damaged insulation on the wires. The maximum allowable voltage drop under load is critical, especially if there is more than one load in the circuit, since all voltage drops are cumulative.

1. Set the voltmeter selector switch to the 20 volt position.
2. Connect the multimeter negative lead to a good ground.
3. Operate the circuit and check the voltage prior to the first component (load).
4. There should be little or no voltage drop in the circuit prior to the first component. If a voltage drop exists, the wire or connectors in the circuit are suspect.
5. While operating the first component in the circuit, probe the ground side of the component with the positive meter lead and observe the voltage readings. A small voltage drop should be noticed. This voltage drop is caused by the resistance of the component.
6. Repeat the test for each component (load) down the circuit.
7. If a large voltage drop is noticed, the preceding component, wire or connector is suspect.

RESISTANCE

▶ See Figures 10 and 11

✳✳ WARNING

Never use an ohmmeter with power applied to the circuit. The ohmmeter is designed to operate on its own power supply. The normal 12 volt electrical system voltage could damage the meter!

1. Isolate the circuit from the vehicle's power source.
2. Ensure that the ignition key is **OFF** when disconnecting any components or the battery.
3. Where necessary, also isolate at least one side of the circuit to be checked, in order to avoid reading parallel resistances. Parallel circuit resis-

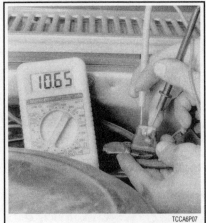

Fig. 9 This voltage drop test revealed high resistance (low voltage) in the circuit

Fig. 10 Checking the resistance of a coolant temperature sensor with an ohmmeter. Reading is 1.04 kilohms

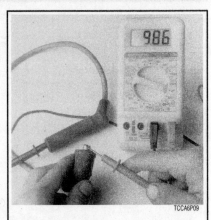

Fig. 11 Spark plug wires can be checked for excessive resistance using an ohmmeter

tances will always give a lower reading than the actual resistance of either of the branches.

4. Connect the meter leads to both sides of the circuit (wire or component) and read the actual measured ohms on the meter scale. Make sure the selector switch is set to the proper ohm scale for the circuit being tested, to avoid misreading the ohmmeter test value.

Wire and Connector Repair

Almost anyone can replace damaged wires, as long as the proper tools and parts are available. Wire and terminals are available to fit almost any need. Even the specialized weatherproof, molded and hard shell connectors are now available from aftermarket suppliers.

Be sure the ends of all the wires are fitted with the proper terminal hardware and connectors. Wrapping a wire around a stud is never a permanent solution and will only cause trouble later. Replace wires one at a time to avoid confusion. Always route wires exactly the same as the factory.

➡If connector repair is necessary, only attempt it if you have the proper tools. Weatherproof and hard shell connectors require special tools to release the pins inside the connector. Attempting to repair these connectors with conventional hand tools will damage them.

BATTERY CABLES

Disconnecting the Cables

♦ See Figure 12

When working on any electrical component on the vehicle, it is always a good idea to disconnect the negative (–) battery cable. This will prevent potential damage to many sensitive electrical components such as the Engine Control Module (ECM), radio, alternator, etc.

➡Any time you disengage the battery cables, it is recommended that you disconnect the negative (–) battery cable first. This will prevent your accidentally grounding the positive (+) terminal to the body of the vehicle when disconnecting it, thereby preventing damage to the above mentioned components.

Before you disconnect the cable(s), first turn the ignition to the **LOCK** position. This will prevent a draw on the battery which could cause arcing (electricity trying to ground itself to the body of a vehicle, just like a spark plug jumping the gap) and, of course, damaging some components such as the alternator diodes.

When the battery cable(s) are reconnected (negative cable last), be sure to check that your lights, windshield wipers and other electrically operated safety components are all working correctly. If your vehicle contains an Electronically Tuned Radio (ETR), don't forget to also reset your radio stations. Ditto for the clock.

Fig. 12 Always disconnect the negative battery cable first to prevent an accidental short circuit

AIR BAG (SUPPLEMENTAL RESTRAINT SYSTEM)

General Information

♦ See Figure 13

The air bag system used on Celica is referred to as Supplemental Restraint System (SRS). The SRS provides additional protection for the driver and front passenger, if a forward collision of sufficient force is encountered. The SRS assists the normal seatbelt restraining system by deploying an air bag, via the steering column.

The center air bag sensor is the heart of the SRS. It consists of safing sensors, ignition control and drive circuit, diagnosis circuit, etc. The center air bag sensor receives signals from the air bag crash sensors and determines whether the air bag must be activated or not. The center air bag sensor is also used to diagnose system malfunctions.

The air bag warning light circuit is equipped with an electrical connection check mechanism which detects when the connector to the center air bag sensor assembly is not properly connected.

All connectors in the air bag system are colored yellow. These connectors use gold-plated terminals with twin-lock mechanism. This design assures positive locking; there-by, preventing the terminals from coming apart.

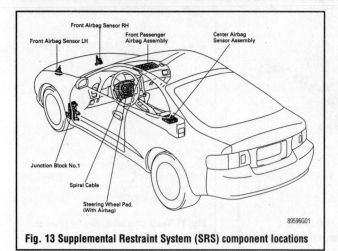

Fig. 13 Supplemental Restraint System (SRS) component locations

SYSTEM OPERATION

When the ignition switch is turn to the **ON** or **ACC** position, the air bag warning lamp will turned on for approximately 6 seconds. If no malfunctions are detected in the system, after the 6 second period have elapse, the warning light will go off.

The safing sensors are designed to go on at a lower deceleration rate than the front or center air bag sensor. When the vehicle is involved in a frontal collision, the shock is great enough to overcome the predetermine level of the front or center air bag sensor. When a safing sensor and a front air bag sensor and/or the center air bag sensor go on simultaneously, it causes the squib of the air bag to ignite and the air bag is deployed automatically. The inflated bag breaks open the steering wheel pad.

After air bag deployment have occurred, the gas is discharged through the discharge holes provided behind the bag. The bag become deflated as a result.

The connector of the air bag contains a short spring plate, which provides an activation prevention mechanism. When the connector is disconnected, the short spring plate automatically connects the power source and grounding terminals of the inflator module (squib).

SYSTEM COMPONENTS

Front Air Bag Sensors

▶ See Figure 13

A front air bag sensor is mounted inside each of the front fenders. The sensor unit is basically a mechanical switch. When the sensor detects a deceleration force above a predetermined level in a collision, the contacts in the sensor close, sending a signal to the center air bag sensor assembly. The sensor cannot be disassembled. If the front fenders on the vehicle are damaged in any way, do a visual check of the sensors even if the air bag is not deployed. Inspect for:

- Bracket deformation
- Peeling of paint
- Cracks, dents or chips in the case
- Cracks, chipping or dents in the wiring connector
- Peeling of the label or damage to the series number

Center Air Bag Sensor

▶ See Figure 13

The center air bag sensor is mounted on the floor inside the console box. The air bag sensor determines whether or not the air bag should be deployed and is also used to diagnose system malfunction.

Spiral Cable

▶ See Figure 13

The spiral cable, part of the combination switch, is used as an electrical joint from the vehicle body to the steering wheel. The spiral cable is referred to as a clock spring.

Drivers Air Bag

▶ See Figure 13

The drivers air bag, located in the steering wheel pad, contains a gas generant which will rapidly inflate the bag in a case of frontal collision.

Passengers Air Bag

▶ See Figure 13

The inflator and bag of the SRS are located in the front of the passengers air bag assembly and can not be disassembled. The air bag will inflate only when the sensor instructs it to do so.

SRS Warning Lamp

▶ See Figure 14

The air bag SRS warning lamp, located on the combination meter, is used to alert the driver of any malfunctions within the air bag system. In normal operating conditions when the ignition switch is turned to the **ON** or **ACC**, the light goes on for about 6 seconds and then goes off.

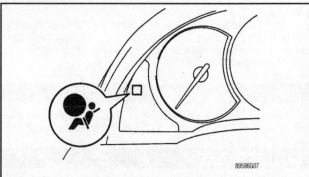

Fig. 14 The air bag warning lamp is located on the combination meter

SRS Connectors

All connectors in the SRS are colored yellow to distinguish them from the other connectors. These connectors have special functions are specifically designed for the SRS. These connectors use durable gold-platted terminals.

TWIN TERMINAL LOCKING MECHANISM

Each connector has a two-piece construction consisting of a housing and a spacer. This secures the locking of the terminal by two locking devices (the spacer and lance) to prevent terminals from coming out.

ACTIVATION SPRING PREVENTION MECHANISM

▶ See Figure 15

Each connector contains a short spring plate. When the connector is disconnected, the short spring plate automatically attaches the power source and grounding terminals of the squib.

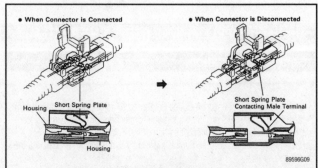

Fig. 15 SRS activation spring plate connection

ELECTRICAL CONNECTION LOCKING MECHANISM

This mechanism is designed to electrically check if the connectors are attached correctly and completely. The connection check mechanism is designed so that the connection detection pin connects with the diagnosis terminals when the housing lock is in the locked position.

CONNECTOR TWIN LOCK MECHANISM

▶ See Figure 16

With this mechanism connectors (male and female) are locked by two devices to increase the connection reliability. If the primary lock is incomplete, ribs interfere and prevent the secondary lock from engaging.

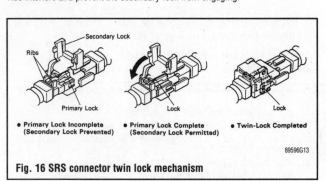

Fig. 16 SRS connector twin lock mechanism

SERVICE PRECAUTIONS

▶ See Figure 17

• In the event that of a minor frontal collision where the air bag does not deploy, the steering wheel pad, front air bag sensors and center air bag sensor assembly should be inspected.
• Never reuse any air bag components involved in a collision when the SRS has deployed.
• Before repairs, remove the air bag sensors if shocks are likely to be applied to the sensors during repairs.
• Never disassemble and repair the steering wheel pad, front air bag sensors or center air bag sensors.
• Do not expose the steering wheel pad, front air bag sensors or center air bag sensor assembly directly to flames or hot air.
• If the steering wheel pad, front air bag sensors or center air bag sensor assembly have been dropped, or there are cracks, dents or other defects in the case, bracket or connectors, have them replaced with new ones.

Fig. 17 Always follow all SRS precautions or this could happen to you while driving down the road

• Information labels are attached to the periphery of the SRS components. Follow the instructions of the notices.
• After arming the system, check for proper operation of the SRS warning light.
• If the wiring harness in the SRS system is damaged, have the entire harness assembly replaced.
• If the vehicle has been in an accident where the air bag has been deployed, always replace all air bag sensors, left, right and center.

DISARMING THE SYSTEM

Work must be started only after 90 seconds from the time the ignition switch is turned to the **LOCK** position and the negative battery cable has been disconnected. The SRS is equipped with a back-up power source so that if work is started within 90 seconds of disconnecting the negative battery cable, the SRS may deploy. When the negative terminal cable is disconnected from the battery, memory of the clock and radio will be canceled. Before you start working, make a note of the contents memorized by the audio memory system. When you have finished work, reset the audio systems as before and adjust the clock. To avoid erasing the memory of each system, never use a back-up power supply from outside the vehicle.

ARMING THE SYSTEM

Reconnect the negative battery cable and perform the airbag warning light check by turning to the **ON** or **ACC** position, the air bag warning lamp will turned on for approximately 6 seconds. If no malfunctions are detected in the system, after the 6 second period has elapsed, the warning light will go off.

HEATER AND AIR CONDITIONER

Blower Motor

REMOVAL & INSTALLATION

▶ See Figure 18

1. Disconnect the negative battery cable.

☀ CAUTION

Work must be started after 90 seconds from the time the ignition switch is turned to the LOCK position and the negative battery cable has been disconnected. The SRS is equipped with a back-up power source so that if work is started within 90 seconds of disconnecting the negative battery cable, the SRS may deploy. When the negative terminal cable is disconnected from the battery, memory of the clock and radio will be canceled. Before you start working, make a note of the contents memorized by the audio memory system. When you have finished working, reset the audio systems and adjust the clock. Never use a back-up power supply from outside the vehicle.

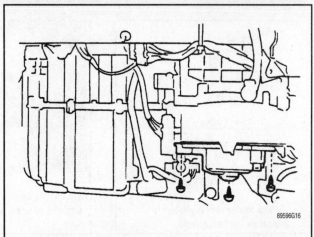

Fig. 18 The heater blower motor is attached to the housing with 3 screws

2. Remove the glove box compartment.
3. Disconnect the wiring attached to the blower motor.
4. Unscrew and extract the motor.

To install:

5. Attach the wiring to the blower motor.
6. Secure the motor to the housing.
7. Install the glove box compartment.
8. Connect the negative battery cable.
9. Test the blower motor operation.

Heater Core

✳✳ CAUTION

Never open, service or drain the radiator or cooling system when hot; serious burns can occur from the steam and hot coolant. Also, when draining engine coolant, keep in mind that cats and dogs are attracted to ethylene glycol antifreeze and could drink any that is left in an uncovered container or in puddles on the ground. This will prove fatal in sufficient quantities. Always drain coolant into a sealable container. Coolant should be reused unless it is contaminated or is several years old.

REMOVAL & INSTALLATION

♦ See Figure 19

➡If your vehicle is equipped with air conditioning, refer to information regarding the implications of servicing your A/C system yourself. Only a MVAC-trained, EPA-certified, automotive technician should service the A/C system or its components.

1. Have the A/C system evacuated by a EPA-certified technician.
2. Remove the cooling unit.
3. Disconnect the suction tube and liquid tube from the cooling unit fitting. Cap all fittings immediately to keep moisture out of the system.
4. Remove the grommets and drain pipe grommet.
5. Remove the glove compartment assembly.
6. Disconnect the wiring from the cooling unit, unbolt and extract the unit.
7. Drain the engine coolant from the radiator.
8. Unbolt the heater control valve, label and disconnect the water hoses.
9. Remove the pipe grommets.
10. Remove the instrument panel and reinforcement.
11. Label and disconnect the heater unit wiring harnesses. Remove the retaining nuts around the heater unit and extract the assembly from the dash.
12. Unscrew the heater air duct and loosen the pipe clamps. Pull the heater core with return pipe out of the unit.
13. Install the components in the reverse order of removal securing all clamps and screws till snug.

14. Fill the cooling system, then start and warm the engine, making sure it stays full. Stop the engine and check for leaks and top off the system if necessary.
15. Have the A/C system charged by a certified automotive technician.
16. Check for proper heater operation.

Heater Water Control Valve

REMOVAL & INSTALLATION

♦ See Figures 20 and 21

1. Partially drain the engine coolant from the radiator.
2. Mark and disconnect the cable from the heater control valve.
3. Disconnect the heater hoses from the heater control valve.

➡Be careful not to pull on the heater core tubes when removing the heater hoses, since the heater core can be easily damaged.

4. Remove the bolt and the heater control valve.

To install:

5. Install the bolt and the heater control valve.
6. Connect the heater hoses to the heater control valve, making sure that the hoses and the clamps are past the outer flaring of the heater control valve tubes. Use new clamps.
7. Install the control cable to its premarked position.
8. Fill the cooling system, then start and warm the engine, making sure it stays full.
9. Stop the engine, pressure test the cooling system and check for leaks. Check for proper heater operation.

Air Conditioning Components

REMOVAL & INSTALLATION

♦ See Figure 22

Repair or service of air conditioning components is not covered by this manual, because of the risk of personal injury or death, and because of the legal ramifications of servicing these components without the proper EPA certification and experience. Cost, personal injury or death, environmental damage, and legal considerations (such as the fact that it is a federal crime to vent refrigerant into the atmosphere), dictate that the A/C components on your vehicle should be serviced only by a Motor Vehicle Air Conditioning (MVAC) trained, and EPA certified automotive technician.

➡If your vehicle's A/C system uses R-12 refrigerant and is in need of recharging, the A/C system can be converted over to R-134a refrigerant (less environmentally harmful and expensive). Refer to Section 1 for

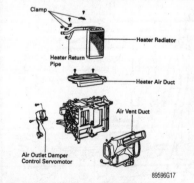

Fig. 19 The heater core (radiator) is located inside the heater unit

Fig. 20 The heater control valve is attached to hoses and linkage on the firewall

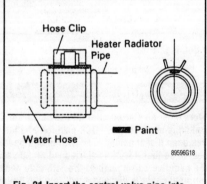

Fig. 21 Insert the control valve pipe into the water hose as far as the ridge

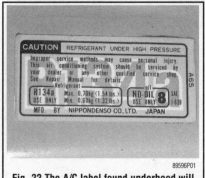

Fig. 22 The A/C label found underhood will indicate the type of refrigerant that is used in your vehicle

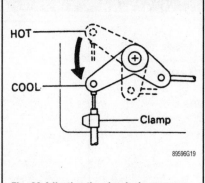

Fig. 23 Adjusting the air mix damper control cable

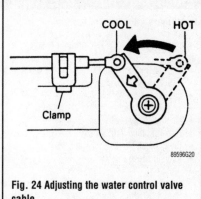

Fig. 24 Adjusting the water control valve cable

additional information on R-12 to R-134a conversions, and for additional considerations dealing with your vehicle's A/C system.

Control Cables

REMOVAL & INSTALLATION

1. Disconnect the negative battery cable. Wait at least 90 seconds from the time that the ignition switch is turned to the **LOCK** position and the battery is disconnected before performing any further work. Refer to Section 7 for all air bag warnings.

✳✳ CAUTION

Work must be started after 90 seconds from the time the ignition switch is turned to the LOCK position and the negative battery cable has been disconnected. The SRS is equipped with a back-up power source so that if work is started within 90 seconds of disconnecting the negative battery cable, the SRS may deploy. When the negative terminal cable is disconnected from the battery, memory of the clock and radio will be canceled. Before you start working, make a note of the contents memorized by the audio memory system. When you have finished working, reset the audio systems and adjust the clock. Never use a back-up power supply from outside the vehicle.

2. Removed the instrument lower finish panel.
3. Unscrew and extract the heater air duct No. 2.
4. Disengage the adjusting clip at the heater/cooling unit end of the cable.
5. Disengage the end of the control cables from the control lever.
6. Remove the cables from the vehicle.
To install:
7. Attach the cables to the end of the lever on the A/C or heater box.
8. Route the cables through the dash to the control levers and secure to the back of the unit.
9. Adjust the cables.
10. Install the control panel and other related components.
11. Connect the negative battery cable.

ADJUSTMENT

Air Mix Door

▶ See Figure 23

1. Disengage the control cable from the lever at the heater/cooling unit end of the cable.
2. Set both the air mix door and the control panel to the COOL position. Then, slide the control cable through the adjusting clip until the eyelet on the cable end can be engaged to the lever. Make sure the cable is secured in the clamps.

3. Move the control levers left and right and check for stiffness or binding through the full range of the levers.
4. Test the control cable operation.

Water Control Valve

▶ See Figure 24

1. Disengage the adjusting clip.
2. Place the water valve lever on the COOL position while pushing the outer cable in the COOL direction. Clamp the outer cable to the water valve bracket with the adjusting clip.
3. Move the control levers left and right and check for stiffness or binding through the full range of the levers.
4. Test the control cable operation.

Control Panel

REMOVAL & INSTALLATION

1. Disconnect the cable at the negative battery terminal. Wait at least 90 seconds once the battery cable is disconnected to perform any work. This will hinder the air bag from deploying.

✳✳ CAUTION

Models covered by this manual are equipped with a Supplemental Restraint System (SRS), which uses an air bag. Whenever working near any of the SRS components, such as the impact sensors, the air bag module, steering column and instrument panel, disable the SRS, as described in this section.

2. Remove the lower finish panel.
3. Unscrew and extract the No. 2 heater air duct.
4. Disconnect the A/C control cables from the heater unit and cable guide.
5. Unscrew and remove the upper console panel.
6. Remove the center cluster panel.
7. Remove the control panel screws and pull the unit from the dash until the wiring connectors are exposed.
8. Disconnect the wiring.
To install:
9. Attach the wiring to the back of the control unit.
10. Position the control assembly into the dash and secure with the retaining screws.
11. Install and secure the center cluster finish panel and upper console panel.
12. Attach the control cables and adjust.
13. Install the No. 2 heater air duct and lower finish panel.
14. Connect the negative battery cable. Reset any electrical components such as the radio and clock.

CRUISE CONTROL

▶ **See Figure 25**

The cruise control system on the Celica models is electronically controlled.

The cruise control system functions by various components such as:
- Cruise control ECU
- Cruise control switch
- Stop light switch
- Neutral safety switch
- Parking brake light switch
- Relay block No. 2-ECU-B fuse
- Vehicle speed sensor
- Actuator

These components together allow the system to work properly. If any of these components fail, the system will not function correctly.

The cruise control system allows you to cruise the vehicle at a desired speed over 25 mph (40 km) even when your foot is off the accelerator pedal. The cruising speed is maintained up or down grades within the limits of the engine performance, although a slight speed change may occur when driving up or down the grades. On steeper hills, a greater speed change will occur so it is better to drive without the cruise control.

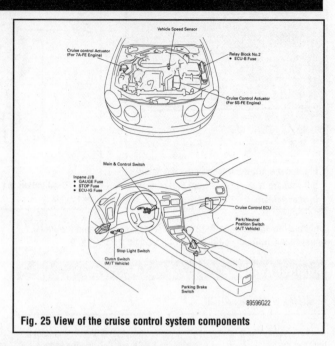

Fig. 25 View of the cruise control system components

CRUISE CONTROL TROUBLESHOOTING

Problem	Possible Cause
Will not hold proper speed	Incorrect cable adjustment
	Binding throttle linkage
	Leaking vacuum servo diaphragm
	Leaking vacuum tank
	Faulty vacuum or vent valve
	Faulty stepper motor
	Faulty transducer
	Faulty speed sensor
	Faulty cruise control module
Cruise intermittently cuts out	Clutch or brake switch adjustment too tight
	Short or open in the cruise control circuit
	Faulty transducer
	Faulty cruise control module
Vehicle surges	Kinked speedometer cable or casing
	Binding throttle linkage
	Faulty speed sensor
	Faulty cruise control module
Cruise control inoperative	Blown fuse
	Short or open in the cruise control circuit
	Faulty brake or clutch switch
	Leaking vacuum circuit
	Faulty cruise control switch
	Faulty stepper motor
	Faulty transducer
	Faulty speed sensor
	Faulty cruise control module

Note: Use this chart as a guide. Not all systems will use the components listed.

TCCA6C01

ENTERTAINMENT SYSTEMS

Radio Receiver/Amplifier/Tape Player/CD Player

REMOVAL & INSTALLATION

▶ **See Figures 26 thru 32**

1. Disconnect the negative battery cable. Wait at least 90 seconds from the time that the ignition switch is turned to the **LOCK** position and the battery is disconnected before performing any further work.

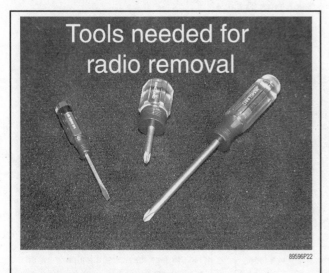

Fig. 26 Required radio removal tools

☆☆ CAUTION

Models covered by this manual are equipped with a Supplemental Restraint System (SRS), which uses an air bag. Whenever working near any of the SRS components, such as the impact sensors, the air bag module, steering column and instrument panel, disable the SRS, as described in this section.

2. Pry and remove the lower console box cover.
3. Remove the two upper trim panel retaining screws, then pry off the upper panel.

➡**It is easier to pry the panels off if you place the flat bladed tool right under the attaching clips.**

4. Disconnect the wiring from the switches (such as clock and hazard warning) in the trim panel.
5. Loosen and remove the retaining screws for the radio.
6. Remove the radio with bracket from the dash until the wiring connectors are exposed.
7. Disconnect the electrical harness and the antenna cable from the body of the radio and withdraw the radio from the vehicle.

To install:

8. Reconnect all the wiring and antenna cable first, then place the radio in position within the dash.
9. Install the attaching screws.
10. Reconnect the wiring harnesses to the switches if so equipped in the trim panel and make sure the switches if so equipped are secure in the panel.
11. Install the trim panel (make sure all the spring clips engage) and secure.
12. Connect the negative battery cable.
13. Check radio system for proper operation. Reset all other electoral components such as the clock if equipped.

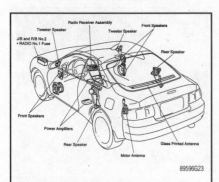

Fig. 27 Exploded view of the radio and speaker locations found on most Celica models

Fig. 28 To remove the upper console trim panel remove these two screws, then pry it off

Fig. 29 Pull the trim panel out far enough to disconnect the wiring behind it

Fig. 30 These four screws hold the radio in the dash

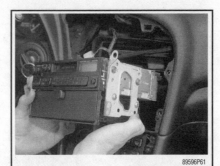

Fig. 31 Remove the screws and extract the radio and bracket enough to disconnect the wiring

Fig. 32 Unplug all wiring in the back of the radio unit

Speakers

REMOVAL & INSTALLATION

▶ See Figure 27

Door Mounted

1. Disconnect the negative battery cable. Wait at least 90 seconds after the battery cable has been disconnected before proceeding, this will hinder air bag deployment.

❋❋ CAUTION

Some models covered by this manual may be equipped with a Supplemental Restraint System (SRS), which uses an air bag. When- ever working near any of the SRS components, such as the impact sensors, the air bag module, steering column and instrument panel, disable the SRS, as described in Section 6.

2. Make sure that the radio is off.
3. If equipped remove the power window switch or manual window handle.
4. Remove the upper door panel, then the lower door panel.
5. Label and disconnect the speaker wires.
6. Remove the 3 screws and the speaker.
7. Installation is the reverse of removal, secure all components.

Rear Mounted

▶ See Figures 33 thru 42

1. Remove the rear seat assembly.
2. Remove the bracket for the rear side trim panel.

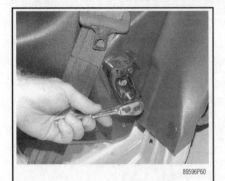

Fig. 33 Remove the bracket on the rear side trim panel

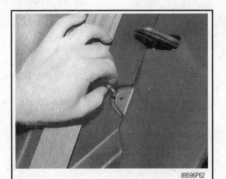

Fig. 34 Farther up the trim panel is a lone screw, remove it

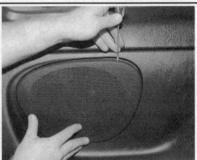

Fig. 35 Tape the end of a tool, and pry off the speaker cover

Fig. 36 Inspect the cover clips, replace any broken ones

Fig. 37 A large bolt is located above the speaker, be careful not to damage the speaker during removal

Fig. 38 Remove any other bolts retaining the side rear trim panel

Fig. 39 Lift up the scuff plate along the carpet edge

Fig. 40 The speaker is mounted to the quarter panel with three bolts

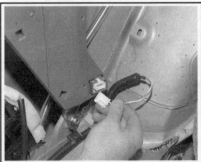

Fig. 41 Push the tab of the connector and pull to disengage

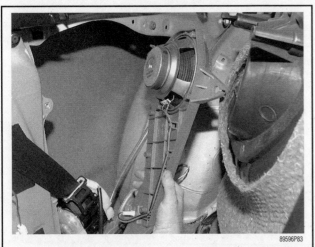

Fig. 42 The speaker and plastic bracket are an assembly on coupes

3. A lone bolt reside farther up the trim panel, remove it.

4. Pry off the speaker cover.

5. A large bolt is located in the upper portion of the speaker, remove this.

6. Remove any bolts retaining the trim panel to the side rear of the vehicle.

7. Lift the scuff plate along the carpets edge.

8. Disconnect the wiring from the speaker, just push in the tab and pull.

9. Unbolt and remove the speaker with attached plastic bracket from the quarter panel.

10. Installation is the reverse of removal, secure all components.

WINDSHIELD WIPERS AND WASHERS

Windshield Wiper Blade and Arm

REMOVAL & INSTALLATION

Front

♦ See Figures 43 thru 48

1. To remove the wiper blades, lift up on the spring release tab on the wiper blade-to-wiper arm connector.

2. Pull the blade assembly off the wiper arm.

3. Press the old wiper blade insert down, away from the blade assembly, to free it from the retaining clips on the blade ends. Slide the insert out of the blade. Slide the new insert into the blade assembly and bend the insert upward slightly to engage the retaining clips.

➠Prior to wiper arm removal, it is wise to mark the windshield-to-blade placement with crayon for installation. This will help with blade height. Next place a paint mark on the nut and shaft of the wiper arm.

4. To replace a wiper arm, first measure the distance between the wiper blade and bottom of the windshield. A small ruler will do just fine.

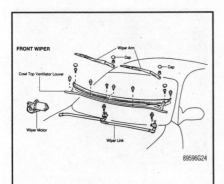

Fig. 43 View of the front wiper blade, arm and related components

Fig. 44 Measure the distance between the wiper blade and windshield before removing the assembly

Fig. 45 Lift the cap off the end of the arm to access the nut

Fig. 46 Use whiteout to place a mark on the wiper arm and nut

Fig. 47 A socket and ratchet will remove the nut from the wiper arm nicely

Fig. 48 Use a rocking motion to lift the arm off the linkage

➡Measuring the distance of the wiperblade and the bottom of the windshield will give you a distance the new blade and arm should sit when you replace the assembly. This way the arm will be seated correctly and not go too far.

5. Remove the cap covering the acorn nut. Loosen and remove the nut.
6. Place paint marks on the wiper arm and nut for installation.
7. Lift the wiper arm and rock with a back and forth motion to remove the arm from the pivot.

To install:

8. Install the arm by placing it on the pivot and tightening the nuts to approximately 15 ft. lbs. (20 Nm).

➡Remember that the arm MUST BE reinstalled in its EXACT previous position or it will not cover the correct area during use.

If one wiper arm does not move when turned on or only moves a little bit, check the retaining nut at the bottom of the arm. The extra effort of moving wet snow or leaves off the glass can cause the nut to come loose—will turn without moving the arm.

Rear

▶ See Figure 49

1. Lift the rear wiper blade spring release tab and pull the blade assembly from the arm.
2. Place a rag under the arm end touching the glass. This will hinder the arm from scratching the glass.
3. Lift the arm retaining nut cap to expose the nut.
4. Place matchmarks on the nut and pivot.
5. Remove the nut and lift the arm off the pivot on a rocking motion.

To install:

6. Place the arm on the pivot with the matchmarks in position.
7. Install the nut, aligning the nut marks with that of the arm and pivot. Tighten the nut to approximately 48 inch lbs. (5 Nm).
8. Attach the blade to the arm.

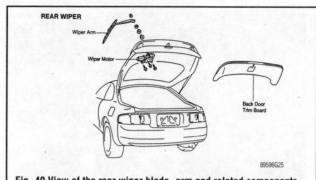

Fig. 49 View of the rear wiper blade, arm and related components

9. Align the wiper arm. Operate the arm and blade assembly and turn off the switch while the arm is in the upright position.
10. The wiper blade should be approximately an inch from the edge of the glass as shown in the illustration.

Windshield Wiper Motor and Linkage

REMOVAL & INSTALLATION

Front

▶ See Figures 50 thru 56

➡For easy removal of the wiper arms, operate the wipers and turn the ignition switch OFF when the wiper arms are half-way in a downward sweep (10 o'clock position).

1. Remove the front wiper arms.
2. Lift off the cowl top ventilator louver.

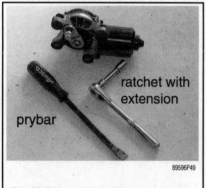

Fig. 50 Tool needed to remove the wiper motor from the linkage

Fig. 51 Place the wipers in the 10 o'clock position

Fig. 52 Unbolt and set aside the wiring harness in front of the wiper motor . . .

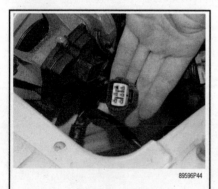

Fig. 53 . . . then disconnect the wiper motor wiring harness

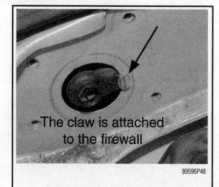

Fig. 54 Note the way the claw is clipped to the firewall to retain the linkage

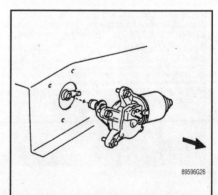

Fig. 55 Pull the motor out to separate from the linkage

3. Remove the 6 bolts of the wiper linkage.

4. Disconnect the wiring, then loosen the wiper motor bolts.

5. Removing the wiring harness with bracket in front of the wiper motor will aide in removal of one of the motor bolts.

6. Clip the claw of the wiper link on to the panel. Disconnect the motor from the wiper link, then pull the motor forward to remove.

➡A large pry bar will be necessary to separate the wiper motor from the linkage. The claw of the linkage should be secured on the firewall to separate the components.

7. Pull the wiper link through the service hole.

To install:

8. Insert the linkage through the service hole. Secure with the retaining bolts.

9. Clip the claw of the wiper link on the panel.

10. Connect the motor to the wiper link. Tighten the bolts to 48 inch lbs. (5 Nm).

11. Install the cowl top ventilator louver.

12. Install the wiper arm and blade assembly. Adjust the position of the arm and blade and tighten the nuts to 15 ft. lbs. (21 Nm).

Rear

◗ See Figure 49

1. Remove the wiper arm and blade.

2. Carefully remove the rear door inner panel. Inspect all trim panel clips and replace any that may have been damaged during removal.

3. Disconnect the wiper motor wring and loosen the retaining bolts.

4. Extract the motor through the hole in the door.

To install:

5. Insert the wiper motor through the opening in the door. Place the motor over the mounting holes and secure with the bolts.

6. Attach the wring to the motor.

7. Place the trim cover on the door and press down hard enough to engage the clips.

8. Close the rear door and attach the wiper arm and blade assembly.

9. Align the wiper arm. Operate the arm and blade assembly and turn off the switch while the arm is in the upright position.

INSTRUMENTS AND SWITCHES

Instrument Cluster

REMOVAL & INSTALLATION

◗ See Figures 57 thru 65

1. Disconnect the negative battery cable. Wait at least 90 seconds once the battery cable is disconnected to work on the vehicle. this will hinder air bag deployment.

➡It may be easier to work on the instrument panel if the steering wheel is removed.

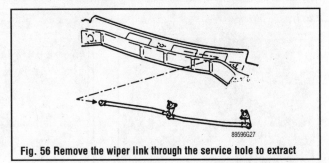

Fig. 56 Remove the wiper link through the service hole to extract

10. The wiper blade should be approximately an inch from the edge of the glass as shown in the illustration.

Windshield Washer Motor

REMOVAL & INSTALLATION

The windshield washer reservoir motor (pump) is located in the washer reservoir. The same pump is used for the front and rear washers.

1. Remove the washer reservoir/motor assembly from the vehicle.

2. Separate the washer fluid motor wiring from the harness.

3. Pull the motor from the rubber grommet retaining it to the washer reservoir.

➡The motor may be slightly hard to extract. Turning the motor side to side will ease removal.

To install:

4. Inspect the rubber grommet for deterioration and replace if necessary.

5. Apply petroleum jelly to the motor before inserting it into the grommet.

6. Attach the harness to the pump.

7. Secure the washer reservoir into the engine compartment.

8. Connect the negative battery cable and test the washer pump for operation.

2. Remove the steering wheel.

3. Remove the front pillar lower garnish, front pillar garnish and door scuff inside plate. Carefully pry away the cowl side trim board.

4. Unscrew and pull off the steering wheel column cover.

5. Using a taped flatbladed tool, carefully pry the lower console trim panel around the edges near the clip locations.

6. If necessary, under the steering column, remove the No. 1 lower finish panel, finish panel and the heater-to-register duct No. 2.

7. Pulling off the combination switch assembly may aide in removal if you are stuck in a tight situation.

8. Around the upper trim panel are screws retaining it to the instrument panel, remove them.

Fig. 57 Carefully pry the lower console trim panel at the clip locations

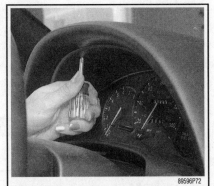

Fig. 58 Remove the upper trim panel screws from above the instrument panel

Fig. 59 Remove the bolts under the lower dash piece . . .

Fig. 60 . . . and remove the cluster lower finish panel to access the instrument cluster screws

Fig. 61 The lower bolts for the instrument panel are located behind the panel just removed

Fig. 62 Lift out the upper instrument panel trim, then you can access the combination meter retaining bolts

Fig. 63 Four bolts hold the combination meter in place

Fig. 64 Slight maneuvering is necessary to extract the meter

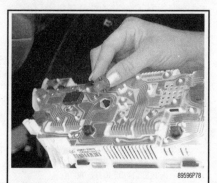

Fig. 65 Unscrew the socket and extract a bulb if necessary

9. On the lower dash trim, remove the bolts and pull the panel off to access the cluster screws.

10. Remove the bolts around the finish panel for the cluster.

11. Remove the four bolts holding the combination meter into the dash.

12. Carefully maneuver the assembly from the dash.

13. Disconnect any harnesses from the back of the meter.

14. If bulb replacement is necessary, now is the time to do it. Simply pop out or unscrew the bulbs or socket to replace them.

15. Installation is the reverse order of removal. Be sure to attach all electrical wiring to each component snug. Secure all components and connect the negative battery cable.

16. Start the engine and make sure all components work properly. Are all the bulbs in working order?

Gauges

REMOVAL & INSTALLATION

▶ **See Figure 66**

The fuel gauge works when the ignition switch is **ON** and indicates approximately the quantity of fuel remaining the gas tank. **F** indicates that the tanks is nearly full and **E** indicates nearly empty.

The engine coolant gauge indicates the engine coolant temperature when the ignition switch is **ON**. The engine temperature will vary with the changes in weather and engine load. If the needle moves into the red zone (H), your engine is too hot. Stop the car and allow it to cool off.

The tachometer indicates the engine speed in rpms (revolutions per minute). Use it while driving to select the correct shift timing and to prevent the engine from lugging and over-revving. Do not allow the needle to enter the red zone of the tachometer gage, this may cause severe engine damage.

The odometer shows the total distance the vehicle has been driven. The trip meter shows the distance the vehicle has been driven since the last time it was set to zero. The trip meter knob resets the trip meter to zero.

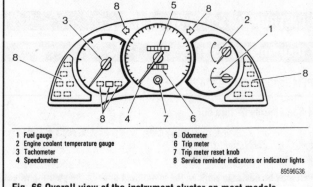

1 Fuel gauge	5 Odometer
2 Engine coolant temperature gauge	6 Trip meter
3 Tachometer	7 Trip meter reset knob
4 Speedometer	8 Service reminder indicators or indicator lights

Fig. 66 Overall view of the instrument cluster on most models

The gauges on all the models covered here can be replaced in the same basic manner. First, remove the instrument cluster and the front lens. Then, remove the gauge's attaching screws on either the front or the back of the cluster.

When replacing a speedometer or odometer assembly, the law requires the odometer reading of the replacement unit to be set to register the same mileage as the prior odometer. If the mileage cannot be set, the law requires that the replacement be set at zero and a proper label be installed on the drivers door frame to show the previous odometer reading and date of replacement.

Windshield Wiper/Washer Switch

REMOVAL & INSTALLATION

The windshield wiper/washer switch is part of the Combination Switch Assembly. Refer to Turn Signal/Combination Switch services procedures in Section 8 for additional information.

Headlight Switch

REMOVAL & INSTALLATION

The headlight switch is part of the Combination Switch Assembly. Refer to Turn Signal/Combination Switch services procedures in Section 8 for additional information.

Dash-Mounted Switches

REMOVAL & INSTALLATION

Most dash-mounted switches can be removed using the same basic procedure. Remove the trim panel which the switch is secured to. Trim panels are usually secured by a series of screws and/or clips. Make sure you remove all attaching screws before attempting to pull on the panel. Do not use excessive force as trim panels are easily damaged. Once the trim panel has been removed, unplug the switch connector, then remove its retaining screws or pry it from the mounting clip. Always disconnect the negative battery cable first.

Clock

REMOVAL & INSTALLATION

⬧ **See Figures 67, 68, 69 and 70**

1. Disconnect the negative battery cable. Wait at least 90 seconds once the battery cable is disconnected to work on the vehicle. this will hinder air bag deployment.

2. Remove the finish panel on the lower console. There should just be clips retaining the console cover.
3. Remove the two bolts from the finish panel over the clock/radio area. Pull the panel off far enough to disconnect the wiring of any switches.
4. Carefully detach each tab on either side of the clock to extract.
5. Pop a new clock into place securing the tabs.
6. Install the finish plate and secure with clips and screws.
7. Attach the lower console cover.
8. Connect the negative battery cable.
9. Turn the ignition key to the ACC position and test the clock.

Fig. 67 Pull the upper console panel from the dash to access the clock

Fig. 68 Disconnect the clock—wiring from the upper panel

Fig. 69 Carefully pry the sides of the clock around the clips . .

Fig. 70 . . . . to extract the unit

LIGHTING

Headlights

REMOVAL & INSTALLATION

⬧ **See Figures 71 thru 77**

1. Open the vehicle's hood and secure it in an upright position.
2. Disconnect the wiring from the back of the bulb socket.
3. Unfasten the locking ring which secures the bulb and socket assembly, then withdraw the assembly rearward.
4. If necessary, gently pry the socket's retaining clip over the projection on the bulb (use care not to break the clip.) Pull the bulb from the socket.
   To install:
5. Before installing a light bulb into the socket, ensure that all electrical contact surfaces are free of corrosion or dirt.

6. Line up the replacement headlight bulb with the socket. Firmly push the bulb onto the socket until the spring clip latches over the bulb's projection.

❉❉ WARNING

Do not touch the glass bulb with your fingers. Oil from your fingers can severely shorten the life of the bulb. If necessary, wipe off any dirt or oil from the bulb with rubbing alcohol before completing installation.

7. To ensure that the replacement bulb functions properly, activate the applicable switch to illuminate the bulb which was just replaced. (If this is a combination low and high beam bulb, be sure to check both intensities.) If the replacement light bulb does not illuminate, either it too is faulty or there is a problem in the bulb circuit or switch. Correct if necessary.
8. Position the headlight bulb and secure it with the locking ring.
9. Aim the headlights.

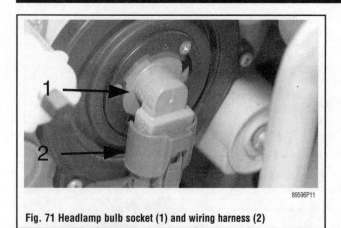

Fig. 71 Headlamp bulb socket (1) and wiring harness (2)

AIMING THE HEADLIGHTS

▶ **See Figures 78 thru 86**

The headlights must be properly aimed to provide the best, safest road illumination. The lights should be checked for proper aim and adjusted as necessary. Certain state and local authorities have requirements for headlight aiming; these should be checked before adjustment is made.

✴✴ CAUTION

About once a year, when the headlights are replaced or any time front end work is performed on your vehicle, the headlight should be accurately aimed by a reputable repair shop using the proper equipment. Headlights not properly aimed can make it virtually impossible to see and may blind other drivers on the road, possibly causing an accident. Note that the following procedure is a tempo-

Fig. 72 The clasp is part of the connector attached to the socket

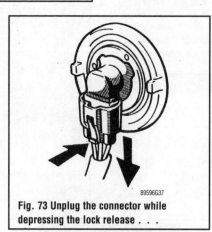

Fig. 73 Unplug the connector while depressing the lock release . . .

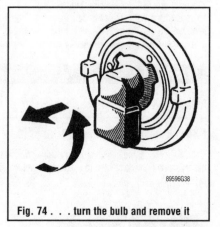

Fig. 74 . . . turn the bulb and remove it

Fig. 75 Do not hold the lamp by the bulb, this will ruin a good bulb from the oils on your hand

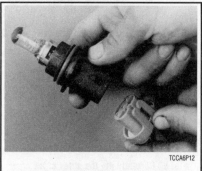

Fig. 76 Carefully pull the halogen headlight bulb from its socket. If applicable, release the retaining clip

Fig. 77 Insert the new bulb and connector into the mounting hole, then turn to secure

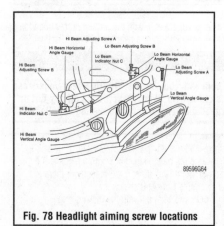

Fig. 78 Headlight aiming screw locations

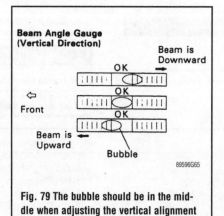

Fig. 79 The bubble should be in the middle when adjusting the vertical alignment

Fig. 80 Note the bubble in the middle, this means the lamp is aligned correctly

Fig. 81 Headlight aiming adjustment bubble and alignment markings

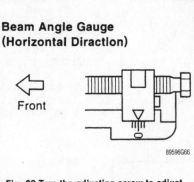

Fig. 82 Turn the adjusting screw to adjust the headlight within specifications

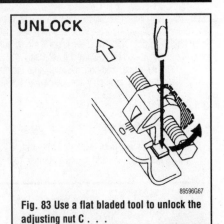

Fig. 83 Use a flat bladed tool to unlock the adjusting nut C . . .

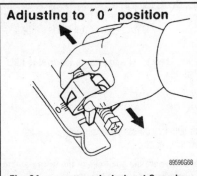

Fig. 84 . . . once unlocked, nut C can be moved to achieve the correct headlight aiming mark then . . .

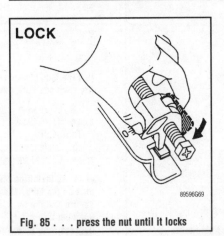

Fig. 85 . . . press the nut until it locks

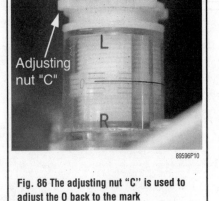

Fig. 86 The adjusting nut "C" is used to adjust the O back to the mark

rary fix, until you can take your vehicle to a repair shop for a proper adjustment.

Headlight adjustment may be temporarily made using a wall, as described below, or on the rear of another vehicle. When adjusted, the lights should not glare in oncoming car or truck windshields, nor should they illuminate the passenger compartment of vehicles driving in front of you. These adjustments are rough and should always be fine-tuned by a repair shop which is equipped with headlight aiming tools. Improper adjustments may be both dangerous and illegal.

For most of the vehicles covered by this manual, horizontal and vertical aiming of each sealed beam unit is provided by two adjusting screws which move the retaining ring and adjusting plate against the tension of a coil spring. There is no adjustment for focus; this is done during headlight manufacturing.

Before removing the headlight bulb or disturbing the headlamp in any way, note the current settings in order to ease headlight adjustment upon reassembly. If the high or low beam setting of the old lamp still works, this can be done using the wall of a garage or a building:

1. Park the vehicle on a level surface, with a filled fuel tank and with the vehicle empty of all extra cargo (unless normally carried). The vehicle should be facing a wall which is no less than 6 feet (1.8m) high and 12 feet (3.7m) wide. The front of the vehicle should be about 25 feet from the wall.

2. Bounce the vehicle several times.

➡If aiming is to be performed outdoors, it is advisable to wait until dusk in order to properly see the headlight beams on the wall. If done in a garage, darken the area around the wall as much as possible by closing shades or hanging cloth over the windows.

3. To adjust the headlight in the vertical alignment perform the following:
   a. Using the adjusting screw **A**, adjust the headlight aim to within specifications. Refer to the illustration.
   b. Make sure the gage bubble is within the acceptable range.
   c. If the bubble is outside the acceptable range, check that the vehicle is parked on a level spot. Readjust the headlight aim after parking the vehicle on the level spot.

4. To adjust the headlight in horizontal alignment perform the following:
   a. Using the adjusting screw **B**, adjust the headlight aim to within specifications.
   b. Using a flat-bladed tool, unlock the adjusting nut **C**. Lift and turn to adjust.
   c. Slide the nut **C** to align the top of the triangle mark to the zero position.
   d. Press the indicator nut **C** until it locks securely.

Signal and Marker Lights

REMOVAL & INSTALLATION

♦ See Figure 87

Turn Signal And Parking Lights

♦ See Figures 88, 89, 90, 91 and 92

1. Unscrew and remove the lamp assembly from the front of the lens housing.
2. To remove a light bulb with retaining pins from its socket, grasp the bulb, then gently depress and twist it 1/8 turn counterclockwise, and pull it from the socket.
   To install:
3. Before installing a light bulb into the socket, ensure that all electrical contact surfaces are free of corrosion or dirt.

➡Before installing the light bulb, note the positions of the two retaining pins on the bulb. They will likely be at different heights on the bulb, to ensure that the bulb is installed correctly. If, when installing the bulb, it does not turn easily, do not force it. Remove the bulb and rotate it 180 degrees from its former position, then reinsert it into the bulb socket.

4. Insert the light bulb into the socket and, while depressing the bulb, twist it 1/8 turn clockwise until the two pins on the light bulb are properly engaged in the socket.

5. To ensure that the replacement bulb functions properly, activate the applicable switch to illuminate the bulb which was just replaced. If the replacement light bulb does not illuminate, either it too is faulty or there is a problem in the bulb circuit or switch. Correct if necessary.

6. Install the socket and bulb assembly into the rear of the lens housing.

7. Insert the lamp assembly and secure with the retaining screw.

Side Marker Light

▶ See Figures 93 thru 98

1. Remove the lens from the body of the vehicle.
2. Disengage the bulb and socket assembly from the lens housing.

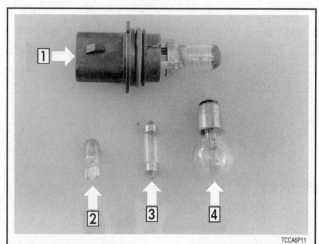

TCCA6P11

1. Halogen headlight bulb
2. Side marker light bulb
3. Dome light bulb
4. Turn signal/brake light bulb

Fig. 87 Examples of various types of automotive light bulbs

3. Gently grasp the light bulb and pull it straight out of the socket.

To install:

4. Before installing the light bulb into the socket, ensure that all electrical contact surfaces are free of corrosion or dirt.

5. Line up the base of the light bulb with the socket, then insert the light bulb into the socket until it is fully seated.

6. To ensure that the replacement bulb functions properly, activate the applicable switch to illuminate the bulb which was just replaced. If the replacement light bulb does not illuminate, either it too is faulty or there is a problem in the bulb circuit or switch. Correct as necessary.

7. Install the socket and bulb assembly into the lens housing.

Brake Light

▶ See Figures 99 thru 107

1. Open the trunk lid and from inside remove the nuts holding the trim panel over the lamp assembly.

2. From the outside of the vehicle, pull out the lamp far enough to disconnect the sockets from the lens.

3. Label each socket prior to removal. Twist each socket one at a time to replace a bulb.

➡ If the lens is being replaced. label all wiring prior to removal to identify each one during installation.

4. To remove a light bulb with retaining pins from its socket, grasp the bulb, then gently depress and twist it 1/8 turn counterclockwise, and pull it from the socket.

To install:

5. Before installing a light bulb into the socket, ensure that all electrical contact surfaces are free of corrosion or dirt.

➡ Before installing the light bulb, note the positions of the two retaining pins on the bulb. They will likely be at different heights on the bulb, to ensure that the bulb is installed correctly. If, when installing the bulb, it does not turn easily, do not force it. Remove the bulb and rotate it 180 degrees from its former position, then reinsert it into the bulb socket.

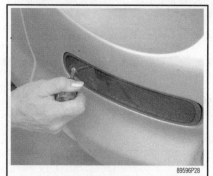

89596P28

Fig. 88 Remove the retaining screw holding the lamp into position

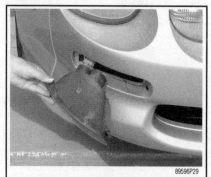

89596P29

Fig. 89 Extract the lamp and twist the socket assembly from the lamp

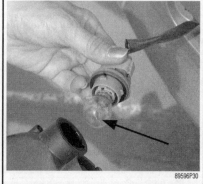

89596P30

Fig. 90 Inspect the light bulb filaments

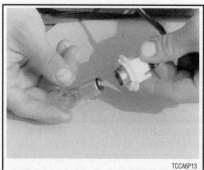

TCCA6P13

Fig. 91 Depress and twist this type of bulb counterclockwise, then pull the bulb straight from its socket

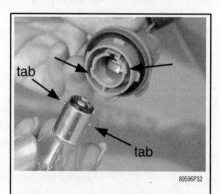

tab

tab

89596P32

Fig. 92 When inserting the new bulb, place the tabs into the socket and turn

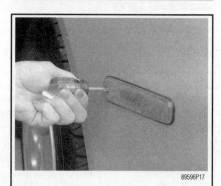

89596P17

Fig. 93 Use a Phillips head screwdriver to remove the screws on the side marker

Fig. 94 Pull back and out to remove the lens and socket assembly

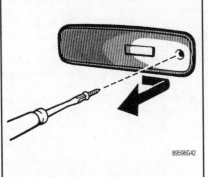

Fig. 95 Remove the side marker lens, then . . .

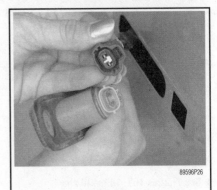

Fig. 96 . . . separate the wiring harness and socket from the lens

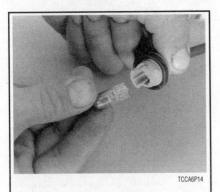

Fig. 97 Simply pull this side marker light bulb straight from its socket

Fig. 98 Inspect the bulb for broken elements and replace as necessary

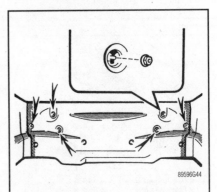

Fig. 99 Inside the trunk, remove the nuts holding the trim cover to the body

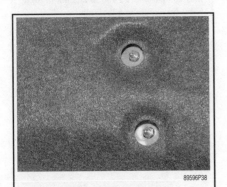

Fig. 100 Two of the nuts are within view . . .

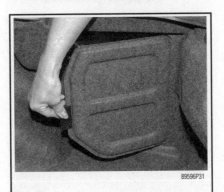

Fig. 101 . . . pull back the side door in the trunk . . .

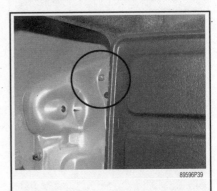

Fig. 102 . . . and the other nut is behind the door on the side

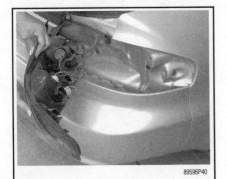

Fig. 103 Outside the vehicle, pull the lamp out far enough to access the sockets

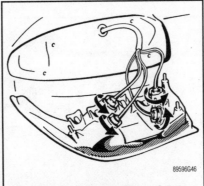

Fig. 104 Twist each one of the sockets to replace either the bulbs or lens

Fig. 105 Inspect the filaments and replace any bad bulbs

6. Insert the light bulb into the socket and, while depressing the bulb, twist it 1/8 turn clockwise until the two pins on the light bulb are properly engaged in the socket.

7. To ensure that the replacement bulb functions properly, activate the applicable switch to illuminate the bulb which was just replaced. If the replacement light bulb does not illuminate, either it too is faulty or there is a problem in the bulb circuit or switch. Correct if necessary.

8. Install the socket and bulb assembly into the rear of the lens housing.

9. Insert the lamp assembly and secure with the retaining screw.

10. Place the trim panel over the socket assembly and secure with the retaining nuts.

Dome Light

▶ **See Figures 108, 109, 110 and 111**

1. Remove the retaining screw for the dome lamp.

2. Using a small prytool, carefully remove the cover lens from the lamp assembly.

3. Remove the bulb from its retaining clip contacts. If the bulb has tapered ends, gently depress the spring clip/metal contact and disengage the light bulb, then pull it free of the two metal contacts.

To install:

4. Before installing the light bulb into the metal contacts, ensure that all electrical conducting surfaces are free of corrosion or dirt.

5. Position the bulb between the two metal contacts. If the contacts have small holes, be sure that the tapered ends of the bulb are situated in them.

6. To ensure that the replacement bulb functions properly, activate the applicable switch to illuminate the bulb which was just replaced. If the replacement light bulb does not illuminate, either it is faulty or there is a problem in the bulb circuit or switch. Correct as necessary.

7. Install the cover lens until its retaining tabs are properly engaged.

High-Mount Brake Light

▶ **See Figures 112 thru 119**

1. On the coupe, pull the third brake light cover off the housing.
   a. Remove the screws holding the housing to the back dash panel.
   b. Lift the housing out of the dash and remove the bulb to replace.

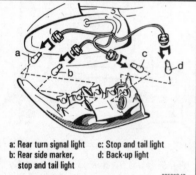

a: Rear turn signal light c: Stop and tail light
b: Rear side marker, d: Back-up light
   stop and tail light

89596G47

Fig. 106 Lamp identification—coupe and convertible

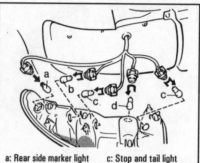

a: Rear side marker light c: Stop and tail light
b: Rear turn signal light d: Back-up light

89596G48

Fig. 107 Liftback rear tail lamp socket identification

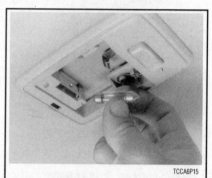

TCCA6P15

Fig. 108 Disengage the spring clip which retains one tapered end of this dome light bulb, then withdraw the bulb

89596P71

Fig. 109 Unscrew the dome lamp from in between the sun visors

89596P70

Fig. 110 Pull the lamp from the roof panel

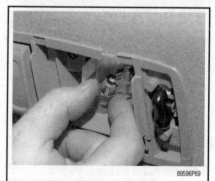

89596P69

Fig. 111 Extract the bulb from the socket of the dome lamp

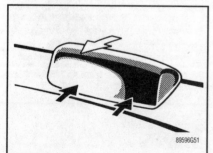

89596G51

Fig. 112 On the coupe, lift off the cover from the third brake light in the back dash, then . . .

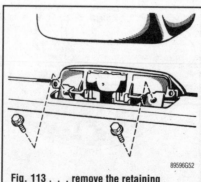

89596G52

Fig. 113 . . . remove the retaining screws . . .

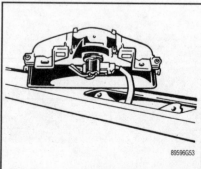

89596G53

Fig. 114 . . . then lift the housing out and twist the socket to extract the bulb

2. On the liftback models, lift the trunk lid and remove the trim panel by sliding it out and down. Be careful not to damage the tabs.

   a. Twist the socket from inside the lamp housing to access the bulb.

   b. Twist the bulb from the socket and replace as needed.

3. Install all components in the reverse order of removal.

License Plate Lights

▶ See Figures 120, 121, 122 and 123

Remove the Phillips head screws holding the lens from the license plate lamp. Carefully twist the bulb from its socket and replace if necessary.

Fog/Driving Lights

REMOVAL & INSTALLATION

▶ See Figures 124 thru 130

1. Loosen the retaining screw an pull out the beam unit.
2. Turn the cover counterclockwise and remove it.
3. Disconnect the wiring.
4. Release the bulb retaining spring and remove the bulb.

To install:

5. Align the cutouts of the bulb with the protrusions of the mounting hole and insert the new bulb. Secure with the spring.

Fig. 115 Pull the bulb straight out of the socket to replace

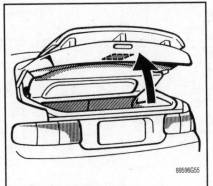

Fig. 116 On liftbacks, raise the trunk lid . . .

Fig. 117 . . . pull the cover out from inside the trunk compartment . . .

Fig. 118 . . . twist the socket . . .

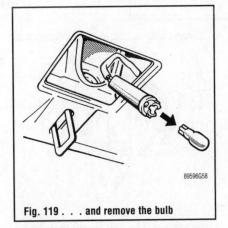

Fig. 119 . . . and remove the bulb

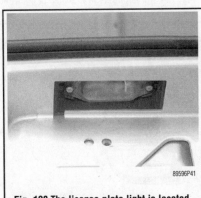

Fig. 120 The license plate light is located just above the plate assembly

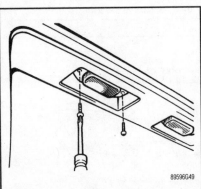

Fig. 121 Remove the lens screws to access the license plate bulb

Fig. 122 Pull the lens off the lamp to access the bulb

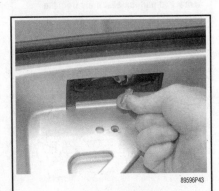

Fig. 123 Carefully pull on the bulb to extract it from the socket

6. Connect the wiring, install the cover and turn it clockwise so that the two triangles are aligned.
7. Plug the connector together.
8. Install the beam unit and secure with the screw.
9. Adjust the fog lights using the vertical adjusting screw located behind the lamp.

Light bulb application chart

Light Bulbs	Bulb No.	W	Type
Headlights (low beam)	9006	55	A
Headlights (high beam)	9005	65	B
Front fog light	—	55	C
Parking and front turn signal lights	1157	27/8	C
Front side marker lights	194	3.8	D
Rear side marker, stop and tail lights (coupe)	1157	27/8	C
Rear side marker lights (liftback)	194	4.9	D
Rear turn signal lights	1156	27	C
Stop and tail lights	1157	27/8	C
Back-up lights	1156	27	C
License plate lights	168	5	D
High mounted stoplight	921	18	D
Interior light (with moon roof)	—	10	C
Interior lights (without moon roof)	—	8	C
Personal lights	—	5	E
Glovebox light	—	1.2	D
Door courtesy lights	—	3.8	D
Luggage compartment light	—	5	E
Trunk light	—	3.8	D

A : HB4 halogen bulbs
B : HB3 halogen bulbs
C : Single end bulbs
D : Wedge base bulbs
E : Double end bulbs

89596C01

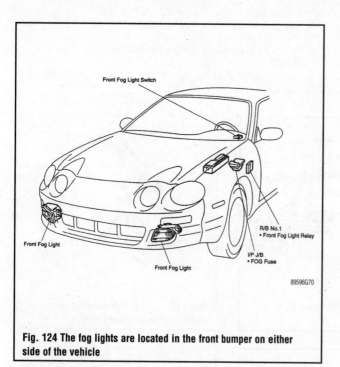

Fig. 124 The fog lights are located in the front bumper on either side of the vehicle

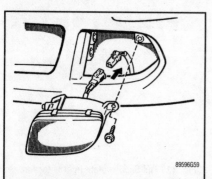

Fig. 125 Remove the fog lamp retaining screw and pull the assembly from the bumper

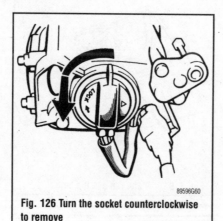

Fig. 126 Turn the socket counterclockwise to remove

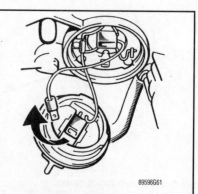

Fig. 127 Carefully disengage the wiring from the back of the lamp

Fig. 128 Removing and I stalling the fog light bulb

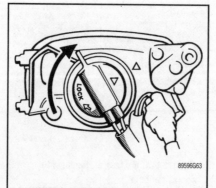

Fig. 129 Turn the socket of the fog lamp clockwise to lock

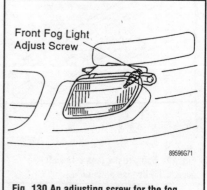

Fig. 130 An adjusting screw for the fog lights is located behind the lamp

Lighting System Troubleshooting—Continued

Trouble	Parts name
"Lo—Beam" does not light. (ALL)	1. Headlight Dimmer Switch 2. D.R.L. Relays (R/B No.6) 3. Wire Harness
"Lo—Beam" does not light. (ONE SIDE)	1. HEAD LO (LH) Fuse (J/B and R/B No.2) 2. HEAD LO (RH) Fuse (J/B and R/B No.2) 3. Headlight Bulb 4. Wire Harness
"Hi—Beam" does not light. (ALL)	1. Headlight Dimmer Switch 2. D.R.L. Relays (R/B No.6) 3. Wire Harness
"Hi—Beam" does not light. (ONE SIDE)	1. HEAD HI (LH) Fuse (R/B No.6) 2. HEAD HI (RH) Fuse (R/B No.6) 3. Headlight Bulb 4. Wire Harness
"Flash" does not light.	1. Headlight Dimmer Switch 2. D.R.L. Relays (R/B No.6) 3. Wire Harness
"Auto Turn—off System" does not operate.	1. Integration Relay (I/P J/B) 2. GAUGE Fuse (I/P J/B) 3. D.R.L. Relays (R/B No.6) 4. Door Courtesy Switch (Driver's) 5. Wire Harness
Headlight does not light with light control SW in HEAD.	1. Integration Relay (I/P J/B) 2. Light Control Switch 3. D.R.L. Relays (R/B No.6) 4. Wire Harness
Headlight does not go out with light Control SW in OFF.	1. Headlight Relay (J/B and R/B No.2) 2. D.R.L. Relays (R/B No.6) 3. Wire Harness
Taillight does not light with light control SW in TAIL.	1. Taillight Relay (I/P J/B) 2. Light Control Switch 3. D.R.L. Relays (R/B No.6)
Taillight does not go out with light control SW in OFF.	1. Taillight Relay (I/P J/B) 2. Light Control Switch 3. Wire Harness
Headlight and Taillight do not light with engine running and light control SW in OFF.	1. GAUGE Fuse (I/P J/B) 2. D.R.L. Relays (R/B No.6) 3. Generator L Terminal 4. Parking Brake Switch 5. Wire Harness

89596C03

Lighting System Troubleshooting

The table below will be useful for you in troubleshooting these electrical problems. The most likely causes of the malfunction are shown in the order of their probability. Inspect each part in the order shown, and replace the part when it is found to be faulty.

USA:

Trouble	Parts name
Headlight does not light. (Taillight is normal)	1. HEAD Fuse (LH, RH) (J/B and R/B No.2) 2. Headlight Relay (J/B and R/B No.2) 3. Headlight Dimmer Switch 4. Light Control Switch 5. Integration Relay (I/P J/B) 6. Headlight Bulb 7. Wire Harness
Headlight does not light. (Taillight does not light up.)	1. Light Control Switch 2. Integration Relay (I/P J/B) 3. Headlight Bulb 4. Wire Harness
Only one side light does not light.	1. HEAD Fuse (LH, RH) (J/B and R/B No.2) 2. Headlight Bulb 3. Wire Harness
"Lo—Beam" does not light.	1. Light Control Switch
"Hi—Beam" does not light.	1. Headlight Dimmer Switch 2. Wire Harness
"Flash" does not light.	1. Headlight Dimmer Switch 2. Wire Harness

CANADA:

Trouble	Parts name
Headlight does not light. (Taillight is normal)	1. Headlight Relay (J/B and R/B No.2) 2. D.R.L. Relays (R/B No.6) 3. Headlight Dimmer Switch 4. Light Control Switch 5. Headlight Bulb 6. Wire Harness
Headlight does not light. (Taillight does not light up.)	1. Light Control Switch 2. D.R.L. Relays (R/B No.6) 3. Integration Relay (I/P J/B) 4. Wire Harness
Only one side light does not light.	1. Headlight Bulb 2. Wire Harness

89596C02

TRAILER WIRING

Wiring the vehicle for towing is fairly easy. There are a number of good wiring kits available and these should be used, rather than trying to design your own.

All trailers will need brake lights and turn signals as well as tail lights and side marker lights. Most areas require extra marker lights for overwide trailers. Also, most areas have recently required back-up lights for trailers, and most trailer manufacturers have been building trailers with back-up lights for several years.

Additionally, some Class I, most Class II and just about all Class III and IV trailers will have electric brakes. Add to this number an accessories wire, to operate trailer internal equipment or to charge the trailer's battery, and you can have as many as seven wires in the harness.

Determine the equipment on your trailer and buy the wiring kit necessary. The kit will contain all the wires needed, plus a plug adapter set which includes the female plug, mounted on the bumper or hitch, and the male plug, wired into, or plugged into the trailer harness.

When installing the kit, follow the manufacturer's instructions. The color coding of the wires is usually standard throughout the industry. One point to note: some domestic vehicles, and most imported vehicles, have separate turn signals. On most domestic vehicles, the brake lights and rear turn signals operate with the same bulb. For those vehicles with separate turn signals, you can purchase an isolation unit so that the brake lights won't blink whenever the turn signals are operated, or, you can go to your local electronics supply house and buy four diodes to wire in series with the brake and turn signal bulbs. Diodes will isolate the brake and turn signals. The choice is yours. The isolation units are simple and quick to install, but far more expensive than the diodes. The diodes, however, require more work to install properly, since they require the cutting of each bulb's wire and soldering in place of the diode.

One, final point, the best kits are those with a spring loaded cover on the vehicle mounted socket. This cover prevents dirt and moisture from corroding the terminals. Never let the vehicle socket hang loosely; always mount it securely to the bumper or hitch.

CIRCUIT PROTECTION

Fuses

REPLACEMENT

◆ See Figures 131 thru 138

There are several fuse blocks. They are located in the engine compartment and under the dash instrument panel.

If any light or electrical component in the vehicle does not work, its fuse may be blown. To determine the fuse that is the source of the problem, look on the lid of the fuse box as it will give the name and the circuit serviced by each fuse. To inspect a suspected blown fuse, pull the fuse straight out with the pull-out tool and look at the fuse carefully. If the thin wire that bridges the fuse terminals is broken, the fuse is bad and must be replaced. On a good fuse, the wire will be intact.

Sometimes it is difficult to make an accurate determination. If this is the case, try replacing the fuse with one that you know is good. If the fuse blows repeatedly, then this suggests that a short circuit lies somewhere in the electrical system and you should have the system checked.

✷✷ CAUTION

When making emergency replacements, only use fuses that have an equal or lower amperage rating than the one that is blown, to avoid damage and fire.

Fig. 131 Lift the fuse block lid while pulling back on the clamp

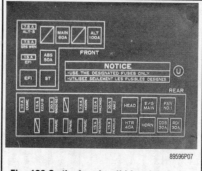

Fig. 132 On the fuse box lid is a label of all recommended amperage fuses and relay locations

Fig. 133 Lift up and pull the fuse lid on the interior to remove

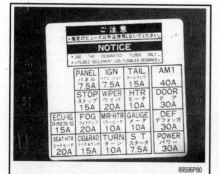

Fig. 134 Common fuse cover listing on interior fuses

Fig. 135 A fuse puller will make the removal much easier

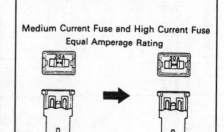

Fig. 136 The larger type fuse are a medium and high amperage rating . . .

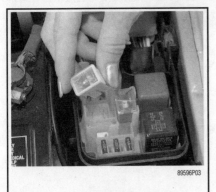

Fig. 137 . . . and can be removed with your fingers by simply pulling upward

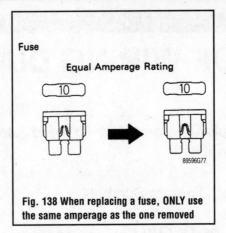

Fig. 138 When replacing a fuse, ONLY use the same amperage as the one removed

Fig. 139 Resetting a circuit breaker

When installing a new fuse, use one with the same amperage rating as the one being replaced. To install the a new fuse, first turn off all the electrical components and the ignition switch. Always use the fuse pull-out tool and install the fuse straight. Twisting of the fuse could cause the terminals to separate too much which may result in a bad connection. It may be a good idea to purchase some extra fuses and put them in the box in case of an emergency.

Fusible Links

In case of an overload in the circuits from the battery, the fusible links are designed to melt before damage to the engine wiring harness occurs. Headlight and other electrical component failure usually requires checking the fusible links for melting. Fusible links are located in the engine compartment next to the battery.

The fusible link is replaced in a similar manner as the regular fuse, but a removal tool is not required.

✳ CAUTION

Never install a wire in place of a fusible link. Extensive damage and fire may occur.

Circuit Breakers

In the event the rear window defogger, environmental control system, power windows, power door locks, power tail gate lock, sunroof or automatic shoulder belt does not work, check its circuit breaker. Circuit breakers are located in the passenger's or driver's side kick panel with the fuses.

REPLACEMENT

1. Turn the ignition switch to the **OFF** position.
2. Disconnect the negative battery cable. Wait at least 90 seconds before working on models with SRS system.
3. Remove the circuit breaker by unlocking its stopper and pulling it from its socket.

To install:

4. Carefully snap the breaker into place and be sure to secure.

➡**Always use a new circuit breaker with the same amperage as the old one. If the circuit breaker immediately trips or the component does not operate, the electrical system must be checked.**

5. Connect the negative battery cable.

RESETTING

♦ **See Figure 139**

1. Insert a thin object into the reset hole and push until a click is heard.
2. Using an ohmmeter, check that there is continuity between both terminals of the circuit breaker. If continuity is not as specified, replace the circuit breaker.

Fuse Types

Illustration	Symbol	Part Name	Abbreviation
		FUSE	FUSE
		MEDIUM CURRENT FUSE	M-FUSE
		HIGH CURRENT FUSE	H-FUSE
		FUSIBLE LINK	FL
		CIRCUIT BREAKER	CB

89596C05

INDEX OF WIRING DIAGRAMS

98596W01

WIRING DIAGRAM SYMBOLS

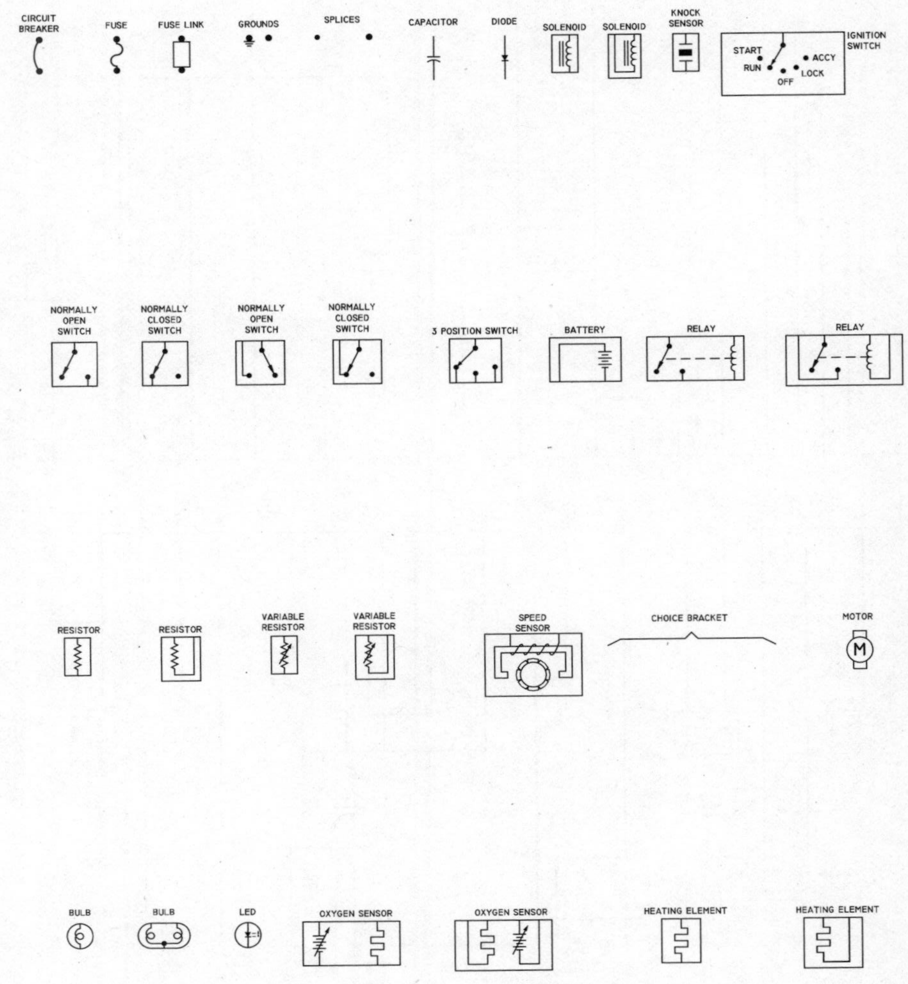

TCCA6W02

CIRCUIT BREAKER	FUSE	FUSE LINK	GROUNDS	SPLICES	CAPACITOR	DIODE	SOLENOID	SOLENOID	KNOCK SENSOR	IGNITION SWITCH
NORMALLY OPEN SWITCH	NORMALLY CLOSED SWITCH	NORMALLY OPEN SWITCH	NORMALLY CLOSED SWITCH	5 POSITION SWITCH	BATTERY	RELAY	RELAY		
RESISTOR	RESISTOR	VARIABLE RESISTOR	VARIABLE RESISTOR		SPEED SENSOR	CHOICE BRACKET	MOTOR		
BULB	BULB	LED			OXYGEN SENSOR	OXYGEN SENSOR	HEATING ELEMENT	HEATING ELEMENT	

DIAGRAM 2

SAMPLE DIAGRAM: HOW TO READ & INTERPRET WIRING DIAGRAMS

WIRE COLOR ABBREVIATIONS

BLACK	B OR BLK	PINK	PK OR PNK
BROWN	BR OR BRN	PURPLE	P OR PPL
RED	R OR RED	GREEN	G OR GRN
ORANGE	O OR ORG	WHITE	W OR WHT
YELLOW	Y OR YEL	LIGHT BLUE	LBL OR LT BLU
GRAY	GY OR GRY	LIGHT GREEN	LG OR LT GRN
VIOLET	V OR VIO	DARK GREEN	DG OR DK GRN
BLUE	BL OR BLU	DARK BLUE	DBL OR DK BLU
TAN	T OR TAN	-NO COLOR AVAILABLE-	NCA

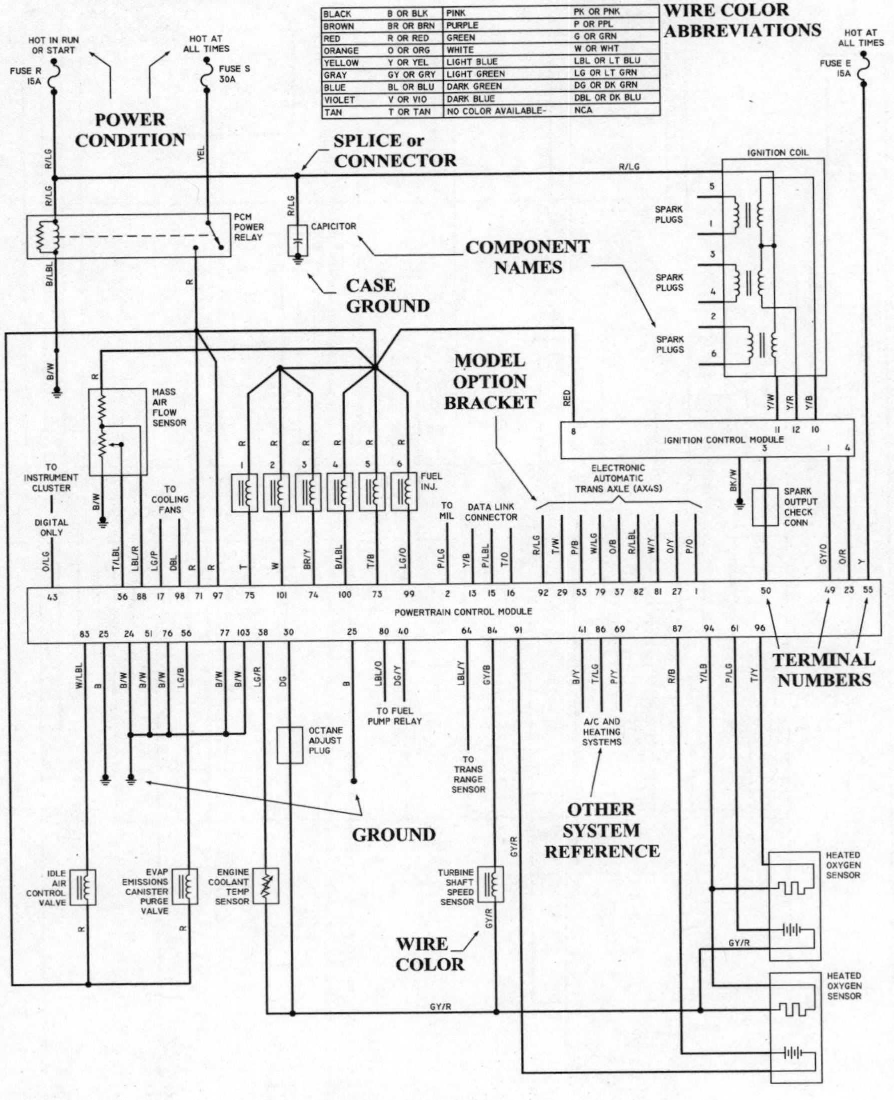

POWER CONDITION

SPLICE or CONNECTOR

COMPONENT NAMES

CASE GROUND

MODEL OPTION BRACKET

TERMINAL NUMBERS

OTHER SYSTEM REFERENCE

GROUND

WIRE COLOR

IGNITION COIL

SPARK PLUGS

IGNITION CONTROL MODULE

SPARK OUTPUT CHECK CONN

ELECTRONIC AUTOMATIC TRANS AXLE (A/AXS)

POWERTRAIN CONTROL MODULE

TO DATA LINK CONNECTOR

TO MIL

FUEL INJ.

TO INSTRUMENT CLUSTER DIGITAL ONLY

MASS AIR FLOW SENSOR

TO COOLING FANS

PCM POWER RELAY

FUSE S 30A

FUSE R 15A

FUSE E 15A

HOT AT ALL TIMES

HOT IN RUN OR START

CAPICITOR

OCTANE ADJUST PLUG

TO FUEL PUMP RELAY

TO TRANS RANGE SENSOR

A/C AND HEATING SYSTEMS

HEATED OXYGEN SENSOR

HEATED OXYGEN SENSOR

TURBINE SHAFT SPEED SENSOR

ENGINE COOLANT TEMP SENSOR

EVAP EMISSIONS CANISTER PURGE VALVE

IDLE AIR CONTROL VALVE

DIAGRAM 1

TCCA6W01

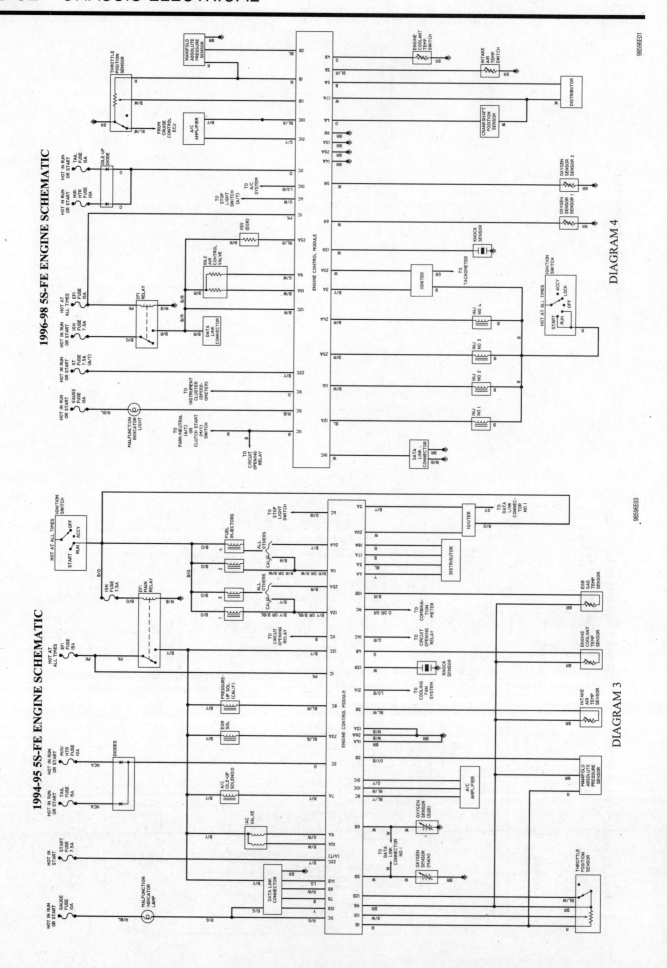

1996-98 5S-FE ENGINE SCHEMATIC

DIAGRAM 4

1994-95 5S-FE ENGINE SCHEMATIC

DIAGRAM 3

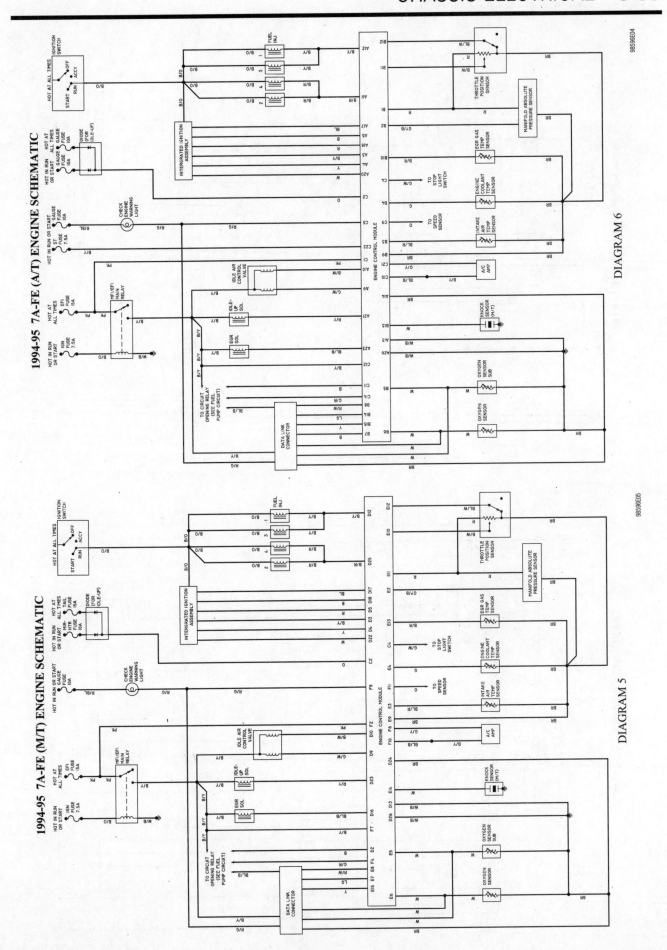

DIAGRAM 6

DIAGRAM 5

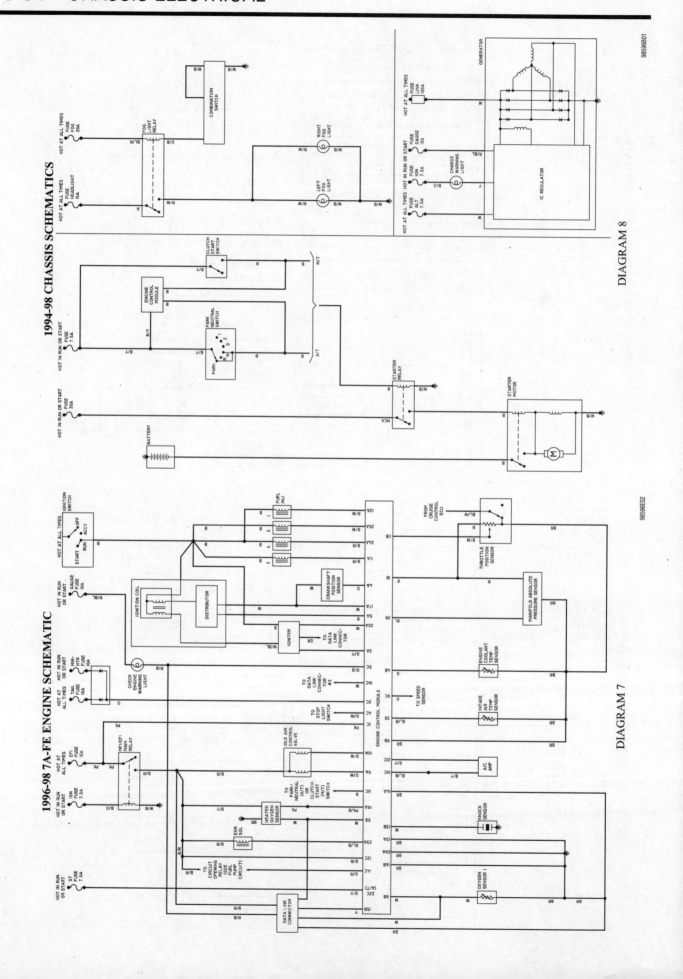

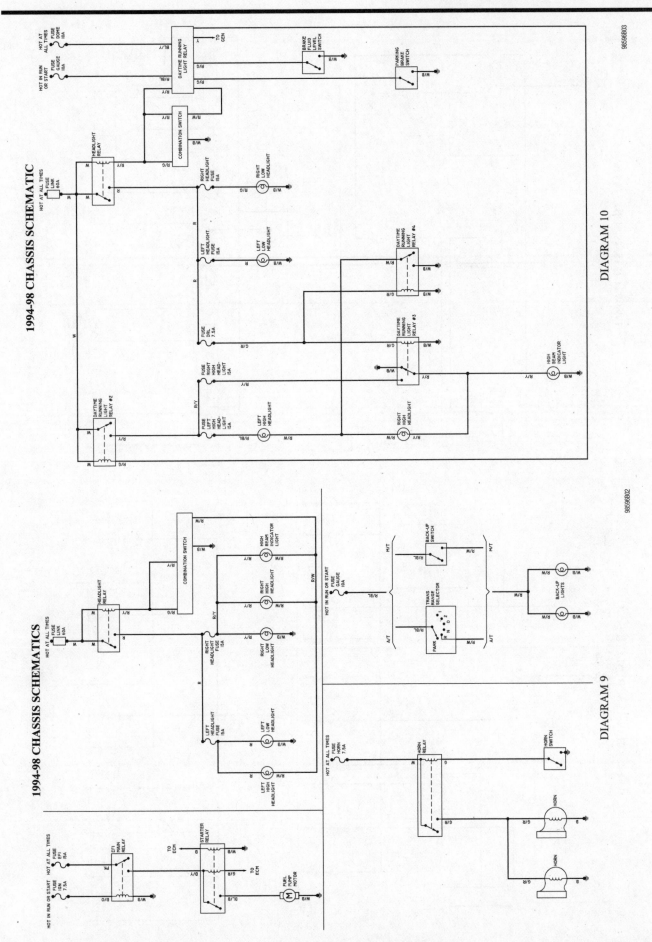

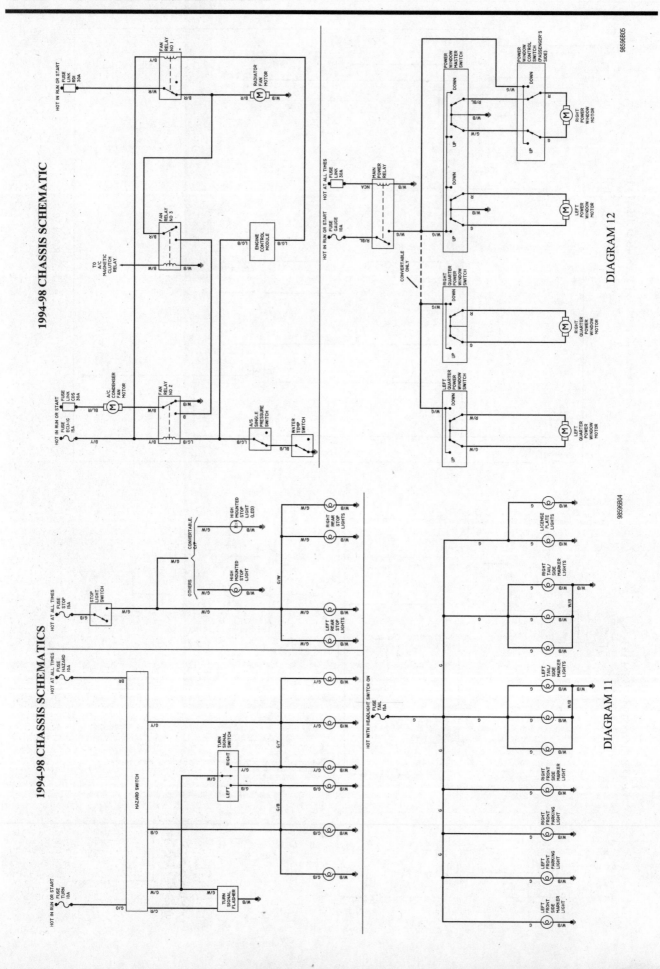

1994-98 CHASSIS SCHEMATIC

1994-98 CHASSIS SCHEMATICS

DIAGRAM 12

DIAGRAM 11

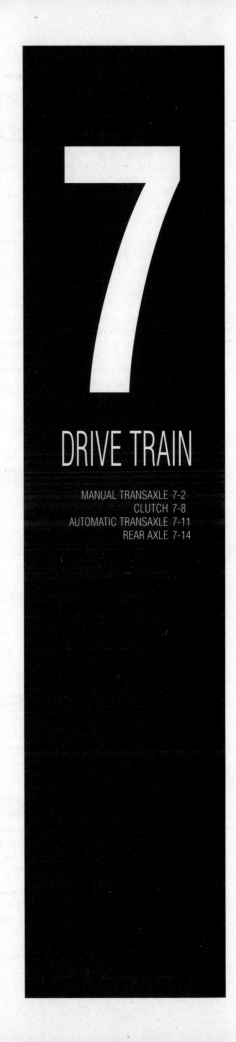

7

DRIVE TRAIN

MANUAL TRANSAXLE

Understanding the Manual Transaxle

Because of the way an internal combustion engine breathes, it can produce torque, or twisting force, only within a narrow speed range. Most modern, overhead valve pushrod engines must turn at about 2500 rpm to produce their peak torque. By 4500 rpm they are producing so little torque that continued increases in engine speed produce no power increases. The torque peak on overhead camshaft engines is generally much higher, but much narrower.

The manual transaxle and clutch are employed to vary the relationship between engine speed and the speed of the wheels so that adequate engine power can be produced under all circumstances. The clutch allows engine torque to be applied to the transaxle input shaft gradually, due to mechanical slippage. Consequently, the vehicle may be started smoothly from a full stop. The transaxle changes the ratio between the rotating speeds of the engine and the wheels by the use of gears. The gear ratios allow full engine power to be applied to the wheels during acceleration at low speeds and at highway/passing speeds.

In a front wheel drive transaxle, power is usually transmitted from the input shaft to a mainshaft or output shaft located slightly beneath and to the side of the input shaft. The gears of the mainshaft mesh with gears on the input shaft, allowing power to be carried from one to the other. All forward gears are in constant mesh and are free from rotating with the shaft unless the synchronizer and clutch is engaged. Shifting from one gear to the next causes one of the gears to be freed from rotating with the shaft and locks another to it. Gears are locked and unlocked by internal dog clutches which slide between the center of the gear and the shaft. The forward gears employ synchronizers; friction members which smoothly bring gear and shaft to the same speed before the toothed dog clutches are engaged.

Back-up Light Switch

➡The back-up light switch is mounted on top of the manual transaxle assembly.

REMOVAL & INSTALLATION

1. Disconnect the electrical harness from the back-up switch, which is mounted on the transaxle case.
2. Loosen and remove the back-up light switch from the transaxle case.
3. Remove the gasket. Discard the gasket.
To install:
4. Install the new gasket onto the switch.
5. Screw the switch with gasket into the transaxle case and tighten to 33 ft. lbs. (44 Nm).
6. Attach the back-up light switch electrical connector.

Manual Transaxle Assembly

REMOVAL & INSTALLATION

▶ See Figures 1, 2, 3, 4 and 5

1. Disconnect the negative battery cable.

✳✳ CAUTION

All models covered by this manual are equipped with a Supplemental Restraint System (SRS), which uses an air bag. Whenever working near any of the SRS components, such as the impact sensors, the air bag module, steering column and instrument panel, disable the SRS, as described in Section 6.

2. Remove the battery and air cleaner assembly with hose.
3. On models with cruise control, unbolt and remove the cruise control actuator.
4. Remove the starter.
5. Unbolt and unclamp the clutch slave cylinder release cable.
6. Remove the ground cable.
7. Disconnect the back-up light switch wiring.

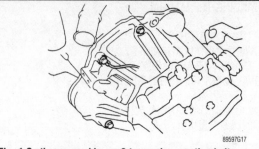

Fig. 1 On the upper side are 3 transaxle mounting bolts

89597G17

8. Disengage the transaxle control cables from the linkage.
9. Disconnect the speed sensor connector.
10. Remove the 3 bolts on the upper side of the transaxle case.
11. Unbolt and remove the nuts on the left engine mounting for the upper side.
12. Attach an engine support fixture.
13. Remove the front wheels.
14. Raise the front of the vehicle and support it securely.
15. Remove the engine under covers.
16. Drain the transaxle oil.
17. Remove the left and right driveshafts.
18. Unbolt and pull down the front exhaust pipe and support bracket. on some models the O2 sensor will need to be removed.
19. Unbolt and remove the starter.
20. On the C52 transaxle, unbolt and remove the engine center crossmember.
21. Remove the engine front mounting as follows:
22. Remove the hole plug.
    a. Extract the nut and bolt.
    b. Remove the 4 bolts and lower the mount.
23. Remove the engine rear engine mounting as follows:
    a. Remove the 2 hole plugs.
    b. Remove the through bolt.
    c. Remove the 4 bolts, 2 nuts and the engine rear mount.
24. Remove the engine left mount bolt from the lower side.
25. On the S54 transaxles, unbolt the engine center crossmember.
26. Remove the stiffener plate held in by 6 bolts and a nut.
27. Jack up the transaxle slightly and support it.
28. Remove the transaxle mounting bolts and lower the engine on the left side and pull the transaxle from the engine.
29. To install, align the input shaft spline with the clutch disc and install the transaxle to the engine. Tighten the mounting bolts on the manual transaxle to:
    • S54—**A** 47 ft. lbs. (64 Nm)
    • S54—**B** bolts to 34 ft. lbs. (46 Nm)
    • C52—47 ft. lbs. (64 Nm)
30. Install all the remaining components in the reverse order of removal and tighten to specifications in the end of this section.
31. Install the air cleaner assembly with hose.
32. Fill the transaxle to specifications. Refer to the chart in Section 1
33. Connect the negative battery cable.
34. Inspect the front end alignment.
35. Perform a road test. check for abnormal noises and smooth shifting.

Halfshafts

REMOVAL & INSTALLATION

▶ See Figures 6 thru 18

✳✳ WARNING

The hub bearing can be damaged if it is subjected to the vehicle weight, such as when moving the vehicle with the driveshaft removed. Therefore, if it is not absolutely necessary to place the vehicle weight on the hub bearing, first support it.

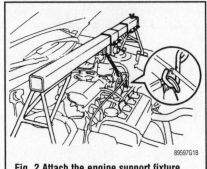

Fig. 2 Attach the engine support fixture and use the hook located on the engine to secure

89597G18

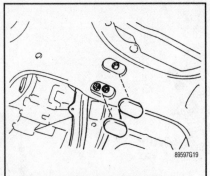

Fig. 3 Pop out the center hole plugs to access the crossmember bolt and nuts

89597G19

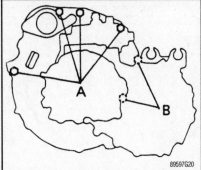

89597G20

Fig. 4 Tighten the transaxle mounting bolts A and B—S54

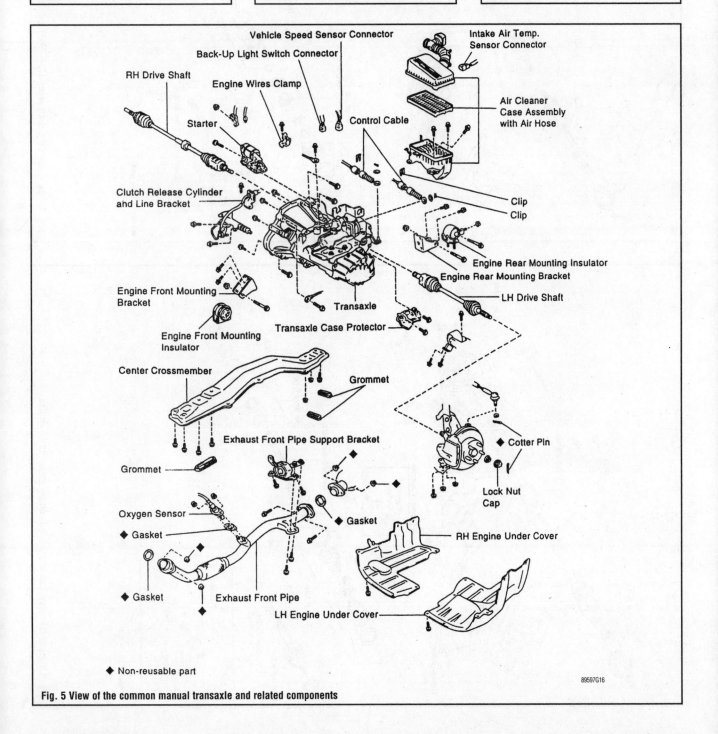

Vehicle Speed Sensor Connector
Back-Up Light Switch Connector
Intake Air Temp. Sensor Connector
RH Drive Shaft
Engine Wires Clamp
Control Cable
Starter
Air Cleaner Case Assembly with Air Hose
Clutch Release Cylinder and Line Bracket
Clip
Clip
Engine Rear Mounting Insulator
Engine Rear Mounting Bracket
Engine Front Mounting Bracket
Transaxle
LH Drive Shaft
Engine Front Mounting Insulator
Transaxle Case Protector
Center Crossmember
Grommet
Cotter Pin
Exhaust Front Pipe Support Bracket
Grommet
Lock Nut Cap
Oxygen Sensor
Gasket
RH Engine Under Cover
Gasket
Gasket
Exhaust Front Pipe
LH Engine Under Cover

◆ Non-reusable part

89597G16

Fig. 5 View of the common manual transaxle and related components

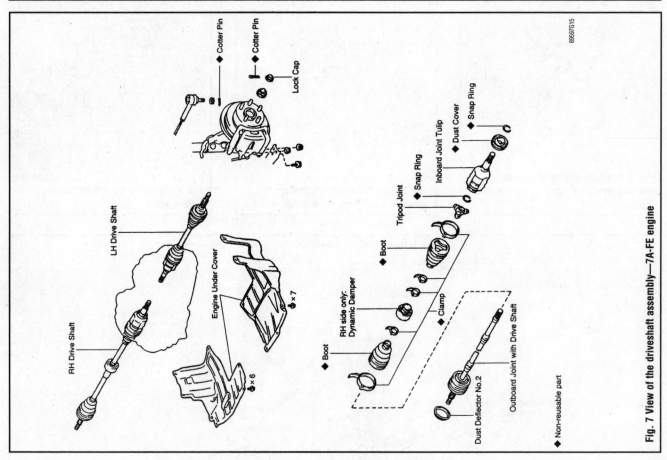

Fig. 7 View of the driveshaft assembly—7A-FE engine

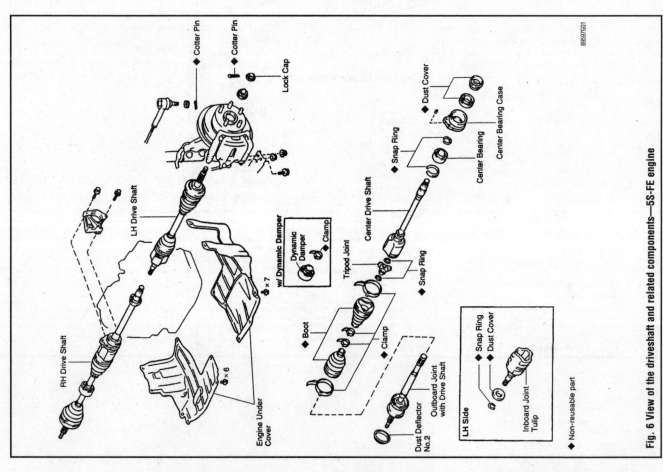

Fig. 6 View of the driveshaft and related components—5S-FE engine

➥On models with ABS, after disconnecting the driveshaft from the axle hub, work carefully so as not to damage the sensor rotor serration's on the driveshaft.

1. Jack up the vehicle and remove the front wheel.
2. Remove the engine under covers.
3. Drain the gear oil (manual) or ATF (automatic) from the transaxle.
4. Remove the cotter pin and lock cap nut. loosen the bearing lock nut while depressing the brake pedal/
5. Disconnect the tie rod end from the steering knuckle by pulling the cotter pin and nut off. Using a puller, separate the tie rod end from the knuckle.
6. Remove the nut and disconnect the stabilizer bar link from the lower control arm.

➥If the ball joint stud turns together with the nut, use a hexagon wrench to hold the stud.

7. Disconnect the lower ball joint from the lower control arm.
8. Using a plastic hammer, carefully disconnect the drive shaft from the axle hub.

➥Be careful not to damage the inner seal, boots and ABS speed sensor rotor.

9. Pull the hub and disc away from the shaft.
10. On the left side driveshaft perform the following:
   a. Cover a hub nut wrench with cloth and using the wrench and a hammer handle or equivalent, pry between the shaft and transaxle, then pull out the driveshaft. Be careful not to damage the dust cover.
   b. Remove the snapring on the end of the shaft.
11. On the right hand drive shaft perform the following:
   a. Remove the 2 bolts of the center bearing bracket, then pull out the right driveshaft together with the center bearing case and center driveshaft.
   b. Remove the center driveshaft with the right driveshaft to the transaxle through the bearing bracket.

To install:

➥Whether or not the driveshaft is making contact with the pinion shaft can be know by the sound of the feeling when driving in it.

12. To install the left side driveshaft perform the following:

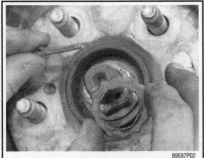
Fig. 8 Remove the castellated washer and cotter pin on the axle shaft, discard the cotter pin

Fig. 9 Retain the rotor and loosen the shaft nut

Fig. 10 Remove the three bolts for the lower control arm, then . . .

Fig. 11 . . . pull the arm away form the steering knuckle

Fig. 12 Carefully tap the end of the half-shaft to separate it from the hub

Fig. 13 The rotor and hub assembly can now be pulled away from the shaft

Fig. 14 Prying at the groove on the CV joint will ease halfshaft removal

Fig. 15 Use both hands to maneuver the halfshaft from the transaxle

Fig. 16 Inspect the seal and replace it if necessary

a. Before installing the driveshaft, using a snapring expander, set the snapring opening side facing downward and install the new snapring.

b. Coat gear oil on the inboard joint tulip and differential case sliding surface.

c. Using a brass bar and hammer, tap in the driveshaft until it makes contact with the pinion shaft.

d. Inspect the installation, there should be 0.08–0.12 inch (2–3mm) of play in the axial direction. Check that the driveshaft will not come out by trying to pull it completely out by hand.

13. Install the right side driveshaft by performing the following:

a. Coat gear oil to the inboard joint tulip and differential case sliding surface.

b. Install the center driveshaft with the right side to the transaxle through the bearing bracket.

c. Install the 2 bolts and tighten them to 47 ft. lbs. (64 Nm).

14. Connect the driveshaft to the axle hub. Attach the outboard joint side of the driveshaft to the axle hub.

15. Connect the lower ball joint to the lower control arm.

16. Attach the stabilizer bar link to the lower control arm.

17. Connect the tie rod end to the steering knuckle and tighten the nut.

18. Connect the tie rod end to the steering knuckle.

19. Install a new bearing lock nut, lock nut cap and new cotter pin. Tighten the lock nut to 159 ft. lbs. (216 Nm).

20. Fill the transaxle with gear oil (manual) or ATF (automatic).

21. Install the engine undercover.

22. Install the front wheel and lower the vehicle.

23. Check and adjust the front wheel alignment.

24. On ABS models, check the speed sensor signal.

CV-JOINTS OVERHAUL

5S-FE Engine

▶ See Figures 19 thru 30

➡Whenever the halfshaft is held in a vise, use pieces of wood in the jaws to protect the components from damage or deformation.

1. Remove the driveshaft.

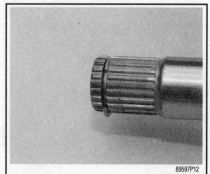

Fig. 17 Snaprings are located on the end of the halfshaft

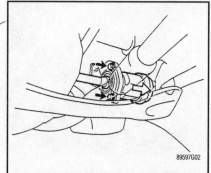

Fig. 18 Remove the 2 bolts of the center bracket on the right side driveshaft.

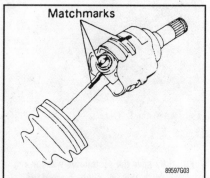

Fig. 19 Place matchmarks on the tripod and outboard joints

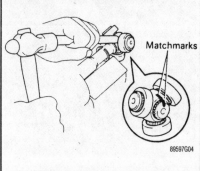

Fig. 20 With matchmarks on the tripod, tap the joint for the driveshaft

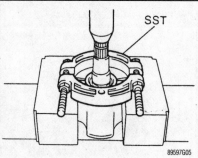

Fig. 21 Using a press, remove the dust cover from the center driveshaft on the left side

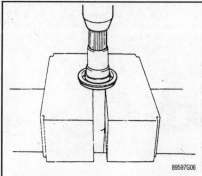

Fig. 22 Use a press to drive the old dust cover out of the right side center driveshaft

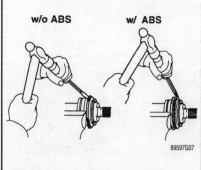

Fig. 23 Removing the no. 2 dust deflector on models with and without ABS

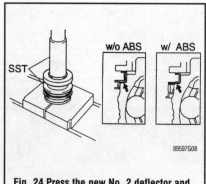

Fig. 24 Press the new No. 2 deflector and seat it properly

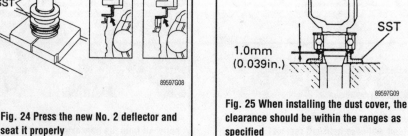

Fig. 25 When installing the dust cover, the clearance should be within the ranges as specified

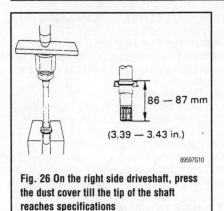

Fig. 26 On the right side driveshaft, press the dust cover till the tip of the shaft reaches specifications

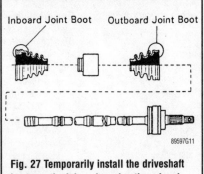

Fig. 27 Temporarily install the driveshaft boots on the inboards and outboard and dynamic damper

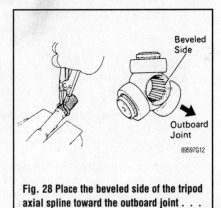

Fig. 28 Place the beveled side of the tripod axial spline toward the outboard joint . . .

2. On the inboard joint tulip, using a flatbladed tool, remove the boot clamps. Slide the inboard joint boot toward the outboard joint.

   a. Place matchmarks on the tripod and inboard joint tulip or center drive-shaft.

➡**Do not punch the marks.**

   b. Remove the inboard joint tulip or center driveshaft from the drive-shaft.

3. On the tripod, use snapring expander, temporarily, slide the snapring toward the outboard joint side.

   a. Place matchmarks on the driveshaft and tripod.

➡**Do not punch the marks.**

   b. Use a brass bar and hammer, remove the tripod from the driveshaft.

   c. Use a snapring expander and remove the snapring.

4. Remove the inboard joint boot.

5. On the right side with dynamic damper, remove the clamps from the damper and extract the unit.

6. Remove the clamps from the outboard joint. Pull the boot from the out-board joint.

➡**Do not disassemble the outboard joint.**

7. Remove the dust cover as follows:

   a. On the left side, press the dust cover from the inboard joint tulip.

   b. On the right side, use a press to remove the dust cover from the center driveshaft.

8. On the right side, remove the snapring and press the bearing from the case.

   a. Next press the dust cover and remove the snapring with expanders.

   b. Press the bearing from the shaft and remove the other snapring. Using a pin punch and hammer, remove the straight pin.

9. On the No. 2 dust deflector, mount the outboard joint shaft in a soft jaw vise. Next, pry out the No. 2 dust deflector.

➡**Be careful not to damage the ABS speed sensor.**

To assemble:

10. On the right side, assemble the center driveshaft by inserting the straight pin into the bearing case.

   a. Using a press, install a new bearing into the case.

   b. Use a flatbladed tool, and install a new snapring.

   c. Using a press and retaining devise, insert a new bearing into the case assembly to the center driveshaft.

   d. Use a snapring expander and install the new snapring.

   e. Press in the new dust cover. The clearance between the dust cover and bearing should be kept in the ranges in the illustration.

11. Install the dust cover as follows:

   a. On the left side, use a press and insert the new dust cover.

   b. On the right side, using a steel plate and press, press in a new dust cover until the distance from the tip of the center driveshaft to the cover reaches the specification as shown.

12. Temporarily install boots and the damper. Before installing the outboard joint, wrap vinyl tape around the spline of the driveshaft to prevent damaging the boots and damper.

   a. Temporarily install the new outboard boot onto the driveshaft.

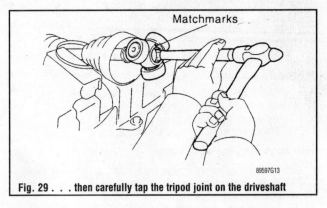

Fig. 29 . . . then carefully tap the tripod joint on the driveshaft

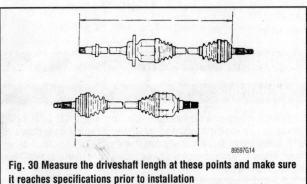

Fig. 30 Measure the driveshaft length at these points and make sure it reaches specifications prior to installation

   b. On the dynamic damper, temporarily install the damper to the drive-shaft.

   c. Temporarily install a new inboard joint to the driveshaft.

13. Install the tripod joint as follows:

   a. Use a snapring expander and insert a new snapring.

   b. Place the beveled side of the tripod joint axial spline toward the out-board joint.

   c. Align the matchmarks placed before removal.

   d. Using a brass bar and hammer, carefully tap the tripod joint to the driveshaft.

➡**Do not tap the roller.**

   e. Using snapring expanders, install a new snapring.

14. Install the boot to the outboard joint. Before assembling the boot, fill grease into the outboard joint and boot. Special grease (usually black) is sup-plied with the boot kits. Grease capacity is 4.2–4.6 oz (120–130 g).

15. Install the inboard joint tulip to the front driveshaft. Pack grease (usually yellow) into the boot and inboard joint tulip.

   a. Align the matchmarks placed before removal, then install the inboard joint tulip onto the driveshaft.

   b. Attach the boot to the inboard joint tulip.

16. Assemble the boot clamps to both boots as follows:

a. Be sure the boot is on the shaft groove.

b. Insure that the boot is not stretched or contracted when the driveshaft is standard length.

The standard driveshaft length is as follows:

- Automatic left—22.516–22.910 inch (571.7–581.7mm)
- Automatic right—33.74–34.13 inch (857.0–867.0mm)
- Manual left—22.34–22.73 inch (525.5–577.4mm)
- Manual right—33.56–33.95 inch (852.5–862.5mm)

a. Bend the band of the clamp and lock onto the boot.

17. On the dynamic damper attach the clamp is on the shaft groove. Check the distance as shown in the illustration. Correct distance should be 7.677–8.071 inch (195.0–205.0mm).

a. Using a screwdriver, tighten the band of the clamp and lock it.

7A-FE Engine

1. Remove the driveshaft.
2. Remove the inboard joint boot clamps as follows:
   a. Using a flatbladed tool, unclasp the clamps.
   b. Slide the inboard joint toward the outboard joint.
3. Remove the inboard joint tulip as follows:
   a. Place matchmarks on the inboard joint tulip, tripod and driveshaft.

➡**Do not punch the marks.**

   b. Remove the inboard joint tulip from the driveshaft.
4. Remove the tripod joint as follows:
   a. Using snapring expanders, remove the snapring.
   b. Place a matchmark on the shaft and tripod.

➡**Do not place a punch on the mark.**

   c. Using a brass bar and hammer, remove the tripod joint from the driveshaft. Do not tap the roller.
5. Remove the inboard joint boot.
6. On the dynamic damper (right side), remove the clamp from the damper.
   a. Remove the dynamic damper.
7. Remove the outboard joint boot, but do not disassemble the joint.

8. Separate the dust cover from the inboard joint tulip using a press.

To assemble:

9. Press a new dust cover onto the inboard joint tulip.
10. Temporarily install boots and the right damper. Before installing the outboard joint boot, wrap vinyl tape around the spline of the driveshaft to prevent damaging the boots and damper.
   a. Temporarily install a new outboard boot to the driveshaft.
   b. On the right side, install the dynamic damper to the driveshaft.
   c. Temporarily install the new inboard joint boot to the driveshaft.
11. Install the tripod joint as follows:
   a. Place the beveled side of the tripod joint axial spline toward the outboard joint..
   b. Align the matchmarks placed before removal.
   c. Using a brass bar and hammer, tap the tripod joint to the driveshaft. Do not tap the roller.
   d. Using snapring expanders, install a new snapring.
12. Install the boot to the outboard joint.
   a. Before assembling the boot, fill it with the grease (black), supplied with the kit, into the outboard joint and boot.
13. Install the inboard joint tulip to the front driveshaft. Pack grease into the inboard joint tulip and boot. The grease should be yellow in color and supplied with the boot kit.
   a. Align the matchmarks place before removal.
   b. Install the inboard joint tulip to the driveshaft.
   c. Temporarily install the boot to the inboard joint tulip.
14. Assemble the boot clamps on both boots as follows:
   a. Be sure the boots are on the shaft groove. Set the driveshaft length to the standard:
- 1994–98 left—21.81–22.21 inch (554.2–564.2mm)
- 1994 right—33.46–33.85 inch (849.9–859.9mm)
- 1995–98 right—34.33–34.73 inch (872.25–882.2mm)
   b. Using a screwdriver, bend the band and lock it.
15. On the right side driveshaft, place the clamp on in the shaft groove. Check that the distance is within specifications. Distance should be 15.25–15.65 inch (387.5–397.5mm).
   a. Using a screwdriver, bend the band and lock it.

CLUTCH

✳✳ CAUTION

The clutch driven disc may contain asbestos, which has been determined to be a cancer causing agent. Never clean clutch surfaces with compressed air! Avoid inhaling any dust from any clutch surface! When cleaning clutch surfaces, use a commercially available brake cleaning fluid.

Understanding the Clutch

✳✳ CAUTION

The clutch driven disc may contain asbestos, which has been determined to be a cancer causing agent. Never clean clutch surfaces with compressed air! Avoid inhaling any dust from any clutch surface! When cleaning clutch surfaces, use a commercially available brake cleaning fluid.

The purpose of the clutch is to disconnect and connect engine power at the transaxle. A vehicle at rest requires a lot of engine torque to get all that weight moving. An internal combustion engine does not develop a high starting torque (unlike steam engines) so it must be allowed to operate without any load until it builds up enough torque to move the vehicle. Torque increases with engine rpm. The clutch allows the engine to build up torque by physically disconnecting the engine from the transaxle, relieving the engine of any load or resistance.

The transfer of engine power to the transaxle (the load) must be smooth and gradual; if it weren't, drive line components would wear out or break quickly. This gradual power transfer is made possible by gradually releasing the clutch pedal. The clutch disc and pressure plate are the connecting link between the engine and transaxle. When the clutch pedal is released, the disc and plate con-

tact each other (the clutch is engaged) physically joining the engine and transaxle. When the pedal is pushed inward, the disc and plate separate (the clutch is disengaged) disconnecting the engine from the transaxle.

Most clutches utilize a single plate, dry friction disc with a diaphragm-style spring pressure plate. The clutch disc has a spliced hub which attaches the disc to the input shaft. The disc has friction material where it contacts the flywheel and pressure plate. Torsion springs on the disc help absorb engine torque pulses. The pressure plate applies pressure to the clutch disc, holding it tight against the surface of the flywheel. The clutch operating mechanism consists of a release bearing, fork and cylinder assembly.

The release fork and actuating linkage transfer pedal motion to the release bearing. In the engaged position (pedal released) the diaphragm spring holds the pressure plate against the clutch disc, so engine torque is transmitted to the input shaft. When the clutch pedal is depressed, the release bearing pushes the diaphragm spring center toward the flywheel. The diaphragm spring pivots the fulcrum, relieving the load on the pressure plate. Steel spring straps riveted to the clutch cover lift the pressure plate from the clutch disc, disengaging the engine drive from the transaxle and enabling the gears to be changed.

The clutch is operating properly if:

1. It will stall the engine when released with the vehicle held stationary.
2. The shift lever can be moved freely between 1st and reverse gears when the vehicle is stationary and the clutch disengaged.

Driven Disc and Pressure Plate

REMOVAL & INSTALLATION

◆ **See Figures 31 thru 37**

1. Remove the transaxle from the vehicle.
2. Place matchmarks on the flywheel and clutch cover.

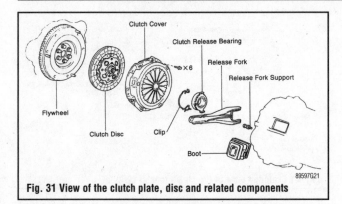

Fig. 31 View of the clutch plate, disc and related components

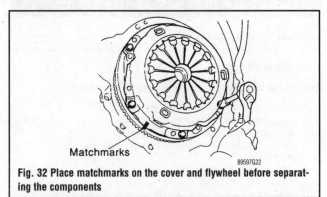

Fig. 32 Place matchmarks on the cover and flywheel before separating the components

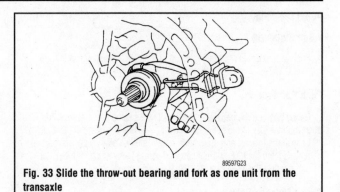

Fig. 33 Slide the throw-out bearing and fork as one unit from the transaxle

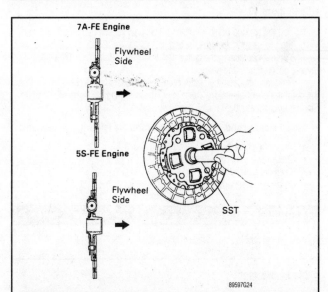

Fig. 34 Insert an guide tool into the disc and set the cover and disc on the flywheel

3. Loosen each set bolt one turn at a time until the spring tension is released.

4. Remove the set bolts, then pull off the clutch cover with the disc.

➡**Do not drop the clutch disc.**

5. Remove the throw-out bearing and fork form the transaxle. Separate the two components.

6. Inspect the components.

To install:

7. Install the clutch disc with a guide tool, then set the clutch cover in position.

8. Align the matchmarks on the cover and flywheel. Tighten the bolts on the cover in the order shown to 14 ft. lbs. (19 Nm).

9. Temporarily tighten the No. 1 and No. 2 bolts.

10. Check the diaphragm spring alignment with a dial indicator with a roller instrument. Alignment should be 0.020 inch (0.5mm).

   a. If alignment is not as specified, using a diaphragm spring alignment tool, position the components correctly.

11. Apply molybdenum disulphide lithium based grease (NLGI No. 2) to the release fork and hub contact points, release fork and push rod contact point, release fork pivot point and the clutch disc spline.

12. Place the throw-out on the release fork, then install the assembly on the transaxle.

13. Attach the transaxle to the engine and secure the components.

ADJUSTMENTS

♦ **See Figure 38**

Pedal Height

1. Measure clutch pedal height from the floor to the top of the pedal pad, along the line of pedal travel. The height should be:
   - 1994—5.86–6.25 inch (148.8–158.9mm)
   - 1995–98–5.70–6.10 inch (144.9–154.9mm)

2. Adjust the pedal height, if necessary, by loosening the locknut and turning the adjusting bolt or rotating clutch switch, and retighten the locknut. Now adjust the pedal free-play.

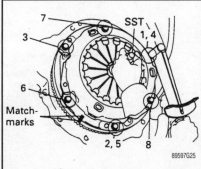

Fig. 35 Line up the matchmarks and tighten the clutch cover bolts in this sequence

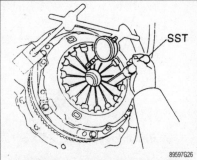

Fig. 36 Using a dial indicator with a roller instrument, check the diaphragm spring tip alignment

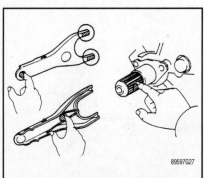

Fig. 37 Apply NLGI No. 2 hub grease on the following contact points

Pedal Free-Play

♦ See Figure 39

Push in the pedal until the beginning of the clutch resistance is felt. Resistance is 0.197–0.59 inch (5–15mm).

Push Rod Free-Play

Gently push on the pedal until the resistance begins to increase a little. The push rod free-play at the pedal top should be 0.039–0.197 inch (1.0–5.0mm)

Loosen the locknut and push the rod until the free play and push rod play are correct. Tighten the lock nut, then after adjusting the play, check the pedal height. connect the air duct and install the finish panel.

Clutch Release Point

♦ See Figure 40

1. Pull the parking brake lever and install a wheel stopper.
2. Start the engine and idle the engine.
3. Without depressing the clutch pedal, slowly shift the shift lever into reverse position until the gears contact.
4. Gradually depress the clutch pedal and measure the stroke distance from the point the gear noise stops (release point) up to the full stroke end position. Standard distance is 0.98 inch (25mm) or more.

➡**If the distance is not as specified, perform the following inspections:**

- Check the pedal height
- Check the push rod play and height
- Bleed the clutch line
- Check the cover and disc

Master Cylinder

REMOVAL & INSTALLATION

♦ See Figure 41

➡**A syringe, container and shop rags are needed to aid in master cylinder replacement.**

1. Draw the fluid from the master cylinder out with a syringe.

➡**A turkey baster can substitute for a syringe to remove the fluid.**

2. Using a line wrench, disconnect the line leading to the clutch master cylinder.
3. Remove the clip and clevis pin.
4. Loosen the mounting nuts and pull the unit out. Discard the gasket.
To install:
5. Insert the master cylinder and secure the clip and clevis pin.
6. Tighten the mounting nuts to 8 ft. lbs. (12 Nm).
7. Attach the clutch line and tighten to 11 ft. lbs. (15 Nm).
8. Add fluid to the master cylinder and bleed the system.
9. Test the clutch system.

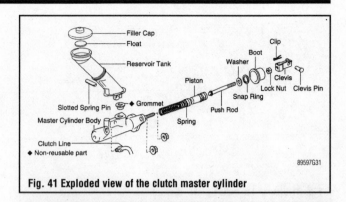

Fig. 41 Exploded view of the clutch master cylinder

Slave Cylinder

REMOVAL & INSTALLATION

♦ See Figure 42

➡**The clutch slave cylinder usually located on the transaxle.**

1. Located the slave cylinder and remove the bolt and clamp.
2. Using a line wrench, disconnect the line from the cylinder. Have a container and rags handy to catch the spilt brake fluid.
3. Remove the 2 bolts and pull out the slave cylinder.
To install:
4. Attach the slave cylinder with the two bolts. Hand tighten the bolts.
5. Attach the line and tighten to 11 ft. lbs. (15 Nm).
6. Tighten the two bolts to 8 ft. lbs. (12 Nm) to secure the cylinder.
7. Attach the clamp with the bolt and secure to 43 inch lbs. (5 Nm).
8. Bleed the system.

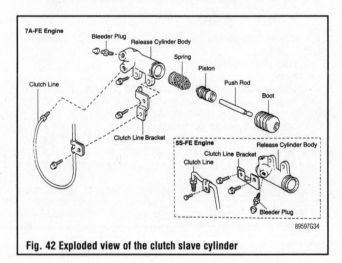

Fig. 42 Exploded view of the clutch slave cylinder

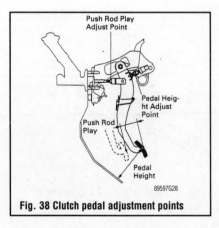

Fig. 38 Clutch pedal adjustment points

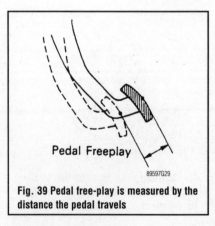

Fig. 39 Pedal free-play is measured by the distance the pedal travels

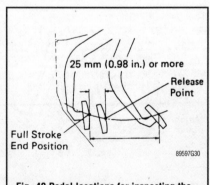

Fig. 40 Pedal locations for inspecting the clutch release point

HYDRAULIC SYSTEM BLEEDING

♦ See Figures 43 and 44

➡An assistant is necessary to bleed the clutch system. If any work is performed on the clutch system or is any air is suspected in the clutch lines, bleed the system of air through the bleeder plug on the slave cylinder.

✳✳ WARNING

Clean, high quality brake fluid is essential to the safe and proper operation of the clutch system. You should always buy the highest quality brake fluid that is available. If the brake fluid becomes cont-

aminated, drain and flush the system, then refill the master cylinder with new fluid. Never reuse any brake fluid. Any brake fluid that is removed from the system should be discarded. Also, do not allow any brake fluid to come in contact with a painted surface; it will damage the paint.

1. Fill the clutch reservoir with brake fluid.
2. Connect a see-through vinyl tube to the bleeder plug and insert the other half of the tube into a half full container of brake fluid.
3. Have an assistant, slowly pump the clutch pedal several times.
4. While pressing on the pedal, loosen the bleeder plug on the slave cylinder until the fluid starts to run out. Then close the plug.
5. Repeat this procedure until there are no more air bubbles in the fluid.

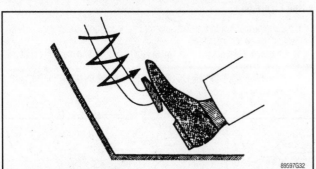

Fig. 43 Have an assistant pump the clutch pedal several times while you loosen the bleeder plug

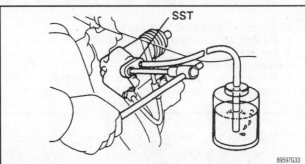

Fig. 44 When loosening the bleeder plug, allow the fluid to flow into the container until no more bubbles are seen

AUTOMATIC TRANSAXLE

Understanding the Automatic Transaxle

The automatic transaxle allows engine torque and power to be transmitted to the front wheels within a narrow range of engine operating speeds. It will allow the engine to turn fast enough to produce plenty of power and torque at very low speeds, while keeping it at a sensible rpm at high vehicle speeds (and it does this job without driver assistance). The transaxle uses a light fluid as the medium for the transmission of power. This fluid also works in the operation of various hydraulic control circuits and as a lubricant. Because the transaxle fluid performs all of these functions, trouble within the unit can easily travel from one part to another. For this reason, and because of the complexity and unusual operating principles of the transaxle, a very sound understanding of the basic principles of operation will simplify troubleshooting.

Neutral Safety Switch

♦ See Figure 45

The neutral safety switch is connected to the throttle cable and the manual shift lever on the transaxle. The switch, in addition to preventing vehicle start with the transaxle in gear, also actuates the back-up warning lights.

REMOVAL & INSTALLATION

A140E

♦ See Figure 46

1. Raise and support the vehicle.
2. Disconnect the neutral start switch harness.
3. With a pair of needle nose pliers, remove the clip that connects the manual control cable to the manual shift lever.
4. Unstake the lock nut and remove the manual shift lever.
5. Remove the neutral start switch with the seal gasket.
To install:
6. Install the neutral start switch making sure that the lip of the seal gasket is facing inward.
7. Install the manual shift lever.

Fig. 45 The neutral safety switch is located on the side of the automatic transaxle

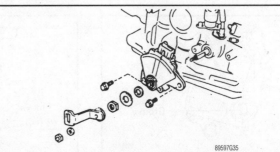

Fig. 46 The neutral safety switch is held in with these components in this order

8. Install the locknut and tighten to 61 inch lbs. (7 Nm). Stake the nut with the locking plate.
9. Connect the switch harness. Adjust the neutral start switch.
10. Connect the transmission shift cable and install the clip.
11. Adjust the transmission shift cable.
12. Lower the vehicle.
13. Check the operation of the switch and adjust as necessary.

A246E

♦ See Figures 47 thru 54

1. Raise an support the front of the vehicle.
2. On some models it may be necessary to remove the No. 2 engine under cover.
3. Disconnect the shift cable from the manual shift lever. A nut retains the cable.
4. Remove the nut and extract the manual shift lever.
5. Pry off the lock plate and remove the manual valve shaft nut.
6. Remove the 2 bolts and pull out the switch.

To install:

7. Position the neutral safety switch on the manual valve shaft.
8. Install a new lock plate and tighten the nut till secure.

9. Using a screwdriver, stake the nut with the lock plate.
10. Temporarily install the manual shift lever.
11. Turn the lever counterclockwise until it stops, then turn it 2 notches.
12. Remove the manual shift lever.
13. Adjust the switch.

➡ **Use the groove to align the basic line.**

14. Install and tighten the 2 bolts to 48 inch lbs. (5 Nm).
15. Install and secure the manual shift lever.
16. Connect the shift cable to the manual shift lever.
17. Install the No. 2 engine under cover and lower the vehicle.

ADJUSTMENT

♦ See Figure 55

If the engine starts with the shift selector in any position except Park or Neutral, adjust the switch as follows:
1. Loosen the two neutral start switch retaining bolts and move the shift selector to the Neutral range.
2. Align the groove and the neutral basic line. Maintain the alignment and tighten the bolts to 48 inch lbs. (5 Nm).

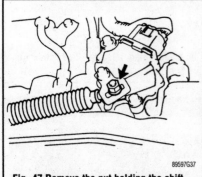

Fig. 47 Remove the nut holding the shift cable to the manual shift lever

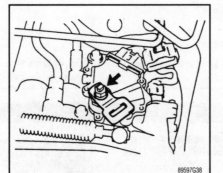

Fig. 48 Remove the nut from the shift lever attaching it to the neutral safety switch

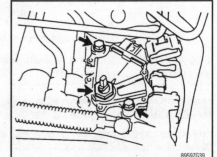

Fig. 49 Pry off the lock plate, then remove the 2 bolts holding the neutral safety switch to the transaxle

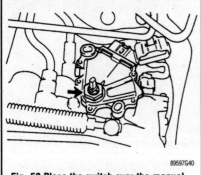

Fig. 50 Place the switch over the manual valve shaft

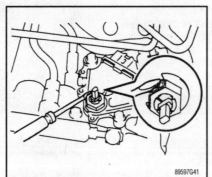

Fig. 51 With a screwdriver, stake the nut with the lock plate

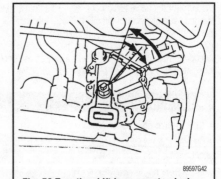

Fig. 52 Turn the shift lever counterclockwise until it stops, then turn it 2 notches

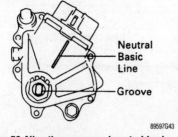

Fig. 53 Align the groove and neutral basic line of the neutral safety switch

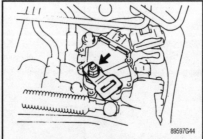

Fig. 54 Next, place the manual shift lever into position

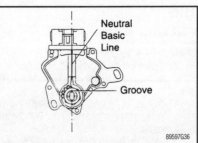

Fig. 55 Align the groove and the neutral basic line, then tighten the bolt

Back-up Light Switch

REMOVAL & INSTALLATION

The neutral start switch functions as the back-up light switch. See removal, installation and adjustment procedures for the neutral safety switch as previously detailed in this section.

Automatic Transaxle Assembly

REMOVAL & INSTALLATION

See Figures 56, 57, 58, 59 and 60

CAUTION

All models covered by this manual are equipped with a Supplemental Restraint System (SRS), which uses an air bag. Whenever working near any of the SRS components, such as the impact sensors, the air bag module, steering column and instrument panel, disable the SRS, as described in Section 6.

1. Disconnect the negative battery cable. Wait at least 90 seconds once the battery cable is disconnected to perform any work on the vehicle. this will hinder air bag deployment.
2. Remove the battery.
3. Unbolt and extract the filler tube.
4. Disconnect the throttle cable.
5. On A246E models equipped with cruise control, remove the actuator.
6. Remove the air cleaner.
7. Remove the engine left mounting upper side bolt(s).
8. Remove the throttle cable and ground cable mounting bolts.
9. Remove the starter.
10. Disconnect the neutral safety switch, speed sensor and solenoid wiring.
11. Disconnect the oil cooler hoses.
12. On the A246E, disconnect the intermediate shaft.
13. Disconnect the pressure and return lines.
14. Install an engine support fixture.
15. Raise and support the vehicle.
16. Remove the engine under covers., then drain the transaxle fluid.
17. Remove the left and right driveshafts. Refer to the procedure in this section.
18. Jack up the transaxle with a jack and support it securely.
19. Remove the engine rear mounting bolt.
20. Extract the front exhaust pipe from the engine.
21. Unbolt and remove the engine suspension members.
22. On the A140E, remove the stiffener plate and No. 1 manifold stay.
23. Remove the converter clutch cover. Turn the crankshaft to gain access to the bolts. Hold the crankshaft pulley set bolt and remove the 6 bolts.
24. On the A140E, remove the 3 bolts and the transaxle.
25. On the A246E, remove the 2 engine left mounting lower side bolts, then the 5 bolts and the transaxle.
26. Installation is the reverse order of removal, but keep these important steps in mind:

a. If the torque converter has been drained and washed, refill with new ATF.

b. Using calipers and a straight edge, measure the installed surface to the front surface of the transaxle housing. Correct distance should be:

- A246E—0.898 inch (22.8mm)
- 1994–95 A140E—0.898 inch (22.8mm)
- 1996–98 A140E—0.512 inch (13.0mm)

c. Jack up the transaxle and align the 2 knock pins on the block with the converter housing and secure the bolts as follows:

A246E-

- A—17 ft. lbs. (23 Nm)
- B—34 ft. lbs. (46 Nm)

A140E

- 10mm—34 ft. lbs. (46 Nm)
- 12mm—47 ft. lbs. (64 Nm)
- Other 6 bolts—28 ft. lbs. (25 Nm)

27. Secure the crossmember bolts and nuts as follows:

A140E

- A—26 ft lbs. (35 Nm)
- B—59 ft. lbs. (80 Nm)
- C—130 ft. lbs. (175 Nm)
- D—94 ft. lbs. (127 Nm)
- E—123 ft. lbs. (167 Nm)
- Nut—59 ft. lbs. (80 Nm)

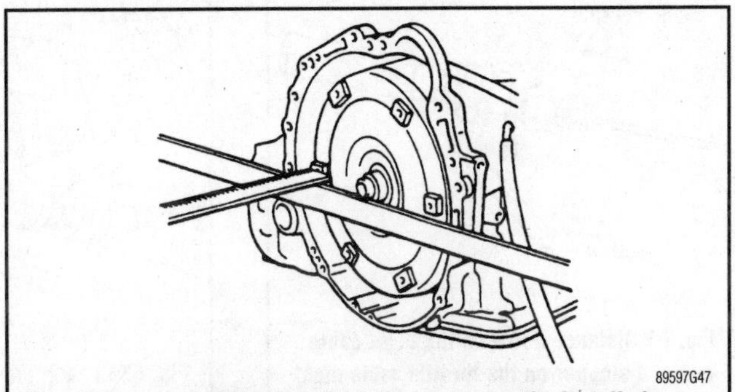

Fig. 56 Using a scale and straight edge, measure the installed surface of the transaxle housing

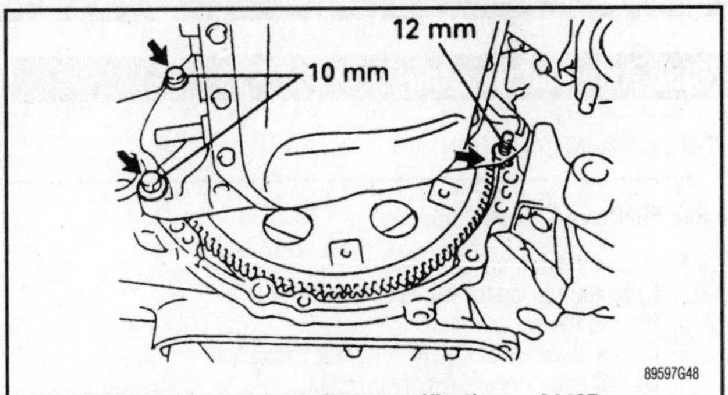

Fig. 57 Tighten these three bolts to specifications—A140E

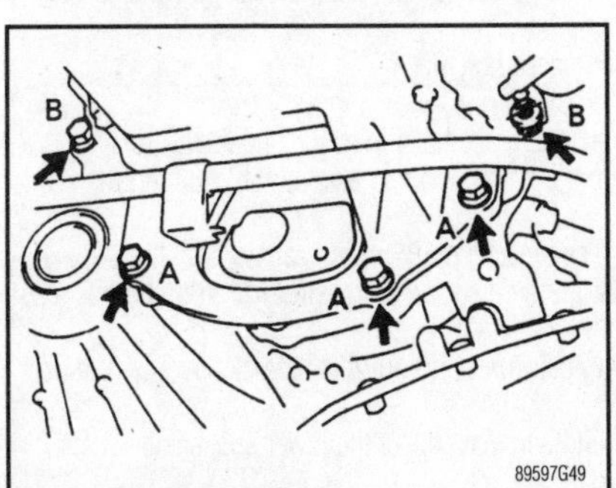

Fig. 58 Tighten these five bolts A and B to specifications—A246E

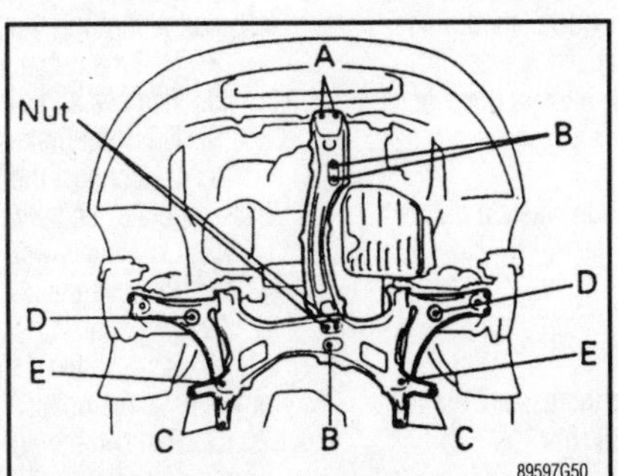

Fig. 59 Crossmember bolt tightening locations—A140E

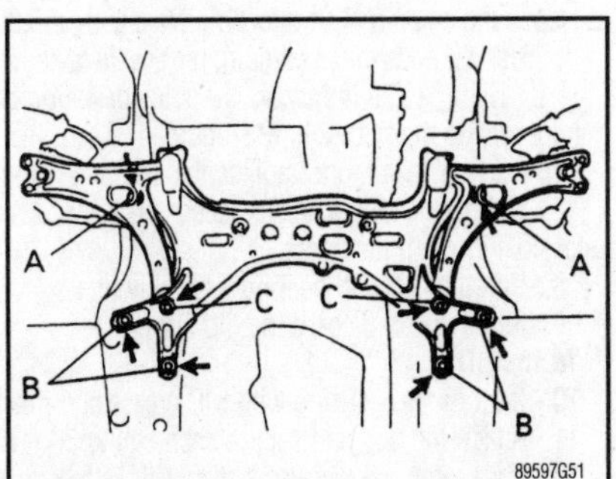

Fig. 60 Crossmember bolt tightening locations—A246E

A246E

- A—94 ft. lbs. (127 Nm)
- B—130 ft. lbs. (175 Nm)
- C—127 ft. lbs. (167 Nm)

28. After installation, adjust the throttle cable, shaft cable and neutral safety switch. Fill the automatic transaxle and check the fluid level.

    a. Test drive the vehicle.

ADJUSTMENTS

Throttle Cable

▶ **See Figure 61**

1. Check that the throttle valve is fully closed.
2. Check that the inner cable is not slack.
3. Measure the distance between the outer cable end and stopper on the cable. Standard boot and cable stopper distance should be 0–0.04 inch 90–1mm).
4. If the distance is not within specifications, adjust the cable using the adjusting nuts.

Shift Cable

▶ **See Figures 62 and 63**

When shifting the lever from the **N** position to the other positions, check that the lever can be shifted smoothly and accurately to each position and that the position indicator correctly indicates the position. If the indicator is not aligned with the correct position, carry out the adjustment procedure.

1. Loosen the swivel nut on the manuals shift lever.
2. Push the control shaft lever fully toward the right side of the vehicle.
3. Return the control shaft lever 2 notches to the **N** position.
4. Set the shift lever to the **N** position.
5. While holding the shift lever lightly toward the **R** position side, tighten the shift lever nut to 10 ft. lbs. (13 Nm).

Halfshafts

➡ **For procedures of the halfshafts and related components, refer to Manual Transaxle in this section.**

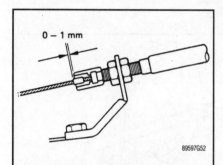

Fig. 61 Distance between the outer cable end and stopper on the throttle cable must be as specified or adjustment is required

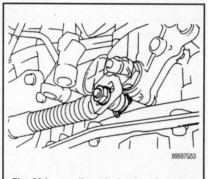

Fig. 62 Loosen the swivel nut on the manuals shaft lever, then . . .

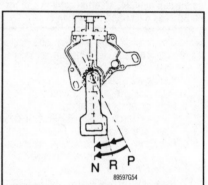

Fig. 63 . . . push the lever fully toward the right side of the vehicle

REAR AXLE

Stub Axle and Bearing

REMOVAL & INSTALLATION

▶ **See Figures 64, 65 and 66**

1. Loosen the rear lugnuts.
2. Raise and support the rear of the vehicle.
3. Remove the rear wheel.
4. On disc brake models, remove the disc and caliper.
5. On rear drum models, remove the drum.
6. Check the bearing backlash and axle hub deviation.

    a. Place a dial indicator near the center of the axle hub and check the backlash in the bearing shaft direction. Maximum is 0.0020 inch (0.05mm). If the backlash exceeds the maximum, replace the axle hub and bearing assembly.

    b. Using a dial indicator, check the deviation at the surface of the axle hub outside the hub bolt. Maximum is 0.0028 inch (0.07mm). If the deviation exceeds maximum, replace the axle hub with bearing.

7. Unbolt the stub axle. To access the bolts , turn the hub where a bolt is accessible through the holes.
8. Pull the hub and bearing assembly off .
9. Remove and discard the old O-ring.

To install:

10. Coat the new O-ring with MP grease and insert into the back of the hub.
11. Attach the hub and secure each bolt to 59 ft. lbs. (80 Nm).
12. Install the brake drum or disc with caliper.
13. Install the wheel, hand-tighten the lug nuts.
14. Lower the vehicle and secure the lug nuts to 76 ft. lbs. (103 Nm).

Axle Carrier Assembly

REMOVAL & INSTALLATION

▶ **See Figure 67**

1. Loosen the rear lugnuts.
2. Raise and support the rear of the vehicle.
3. Remove the rear wheel.
4. On disc brake models, remove the disc and caliper.
5. On rear drum models, remove the drum.
6. Check the bearing backlash and axle hub deviation.
7. Unbolt the stub axle. To access the bolts , turn the hub where a bolt is accessible through the holes.
8. Pull the hub and bearing assembly off .
9. Remove and discard the old O-ring.
10. On drum brakes, remove the brake hose from the shock absorber.
11. Disconnect the backing plate from the rear axle carrier. Support the backing plate securely.
12. On models with ABS, disconnect the ABS speed sensor from the rear axle.
13. Remove the nut and bolt, then disconnect the strut rod from the rear axle carrier.
14. Remove the 2 nuts from the lower portion of the shock absorber but do not remove the bolts.
15. Remove the nut and bolt, then disconnect the lower suspension arms from the carrier.
16. Pull out the 2 bolts from the shock absorber, then remove the rear axle carrier.

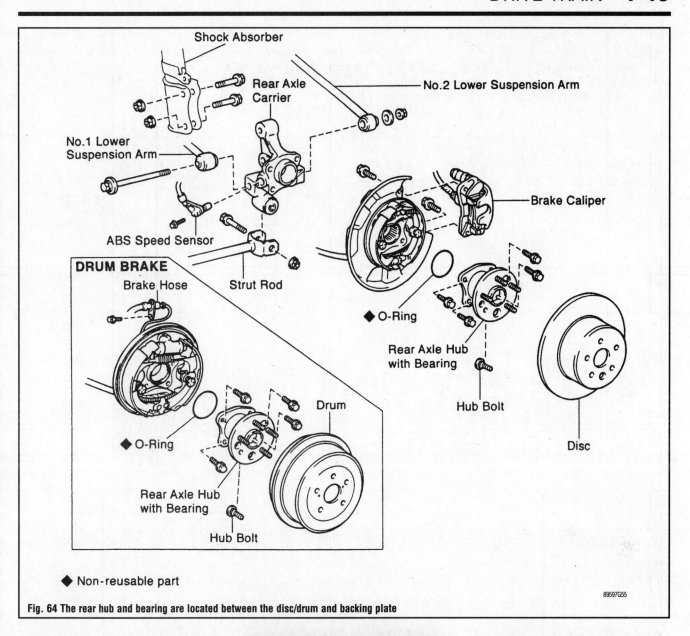

Fig. 64 The rear hub and bearing are located between the disc/drum and backing plate

◆ Non-reusable part

89597G55

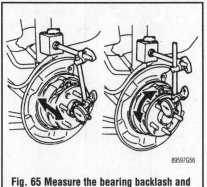

Fig. 65 Measure the bearing backlash and axle hub deviation

89597G56

Fig. 66 Remove all four hub bolts and lift the unit from the car

89597P13

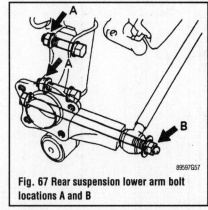

Fig. 67 Rear suspension lower arm bolt locations A and B

89597G57

To install:

17. Position the axle carrier and stabilize the suspension then secure the lower suspension arms to the carrier. Tighten (nut B) to 145 ft. lbs. (197 Nm).

18. Secure the suspension and attach the shock absorber lower set bolts and tighten (nut A) to 188 ft. lbs. (255 Nm).

19. With the suspension stabilized, attach the strut rod to the axle carrier and secure the bolt and nut to 83 ft. lbs. (113 Nm).

20. On ABS models attach the speed sensor and tighten the bolt to 71 inch lbs. (8 Nm).

21. Attach the remaining components, check the ABS signal and have a rear wheel alignment.

TORQUE SPECIFICATIONS

Components	English Specifications	Metric Specifications
Clutch		
Bleeder plug	74 inch lbs.	8 Nm
Clutch cover-to-flywheel	14 ft. lbs.	19 Nm
Clutch line union	11 ft. lbs.	15 Nm
Clutch master cylinder-to-mounting bracket	9 ft. lbs.	12 Nm
Flywheel (5S-FE)	65 ft. lbs.	88 Nm
Flywheel (7A-FE)	58 ft. lbs.	78 Nm
Release fork support (5S-FE)	29 ft. lbs.	39 Nm
Release fork support (7A-FE)	27 ft. lbs.	37 Nm
Slave (release) cylinder	9 ft. lbs.	12 Nm
Manual Transaxle - C52		
Back-up light switch	30 ft. lbs.	40 Nm
Back-up light switch	33 ft. lbs.	44 Nm
Center crossmember-to-body	26 ft. lbs.	35 Nm
Center crossmember-to-rear engine mounting insulator	59 ft. lbs.	80 Nm
Center crossmember-to-front engine mounting insulator	59 ft. lbs.	80 Nm
Center member-to-body	38 ft. lbs.	52 Nm
Center member-to-engine mounting	47 ft. lbs.	64 Nm
Clutch release fork support	27 ft. lbs.	37 Nm
Control shaft cover	27 ft. lbs.	37 Nm
Engine mounting through bolt	64 ft. lbs.	87 Nm
Filler and drain plug	36 ft. lbs.	49 Nm
Filler and drain plugs	29 ft. lbs.	39 Nm
Front engine mounting bracket-to-insulator	64 ft. lbs.	87 Nm
Front engine mounting bracket-to-transaxle	57 ft. lbs.	77 Nm
Grommet-to-body	43 inch lbs.	5 Nm
Heat insulator-to-body	48 inch lbs.	5 Nm
Left engine mounting bracket-to-insulator	47 ft. lbs.	64 Nm
Manual Transaxle - S54		
No. 1 and No. 2 oil receiver set bolt	13 ft. lbs.	17 Nm
Rear engine mounting bracket-to-insulator	64 ft. lbs.	87 Nm
Rear engine mounting bracket-to-transaxle	57 ft. lbs.	77 Nm
Selecting bellcrank-to-transmission case	27 ft. lbs.	37 Nm
Shift lever-to-body	9 ft. lbs.	12 Nm
Shift select lever shaft-to-transmission case	14 ft. lbs.	20 Nm
Slave cylinder-to-transaxle	9 ft. lbs.	12 Nm
Slave cylinder-to-transaxle	9 ft. lbs.	12 Nm
Starter-to-transaxle	29 ft. lbs.	39 Nm
Starter-to-transaxle	29 ft. lbs.	39 Nm
Stiffener plate-to-engine	32 ft. lbs.	43 Nm
Stiffener plate-to-transaxle	15 ft. lbs.	21 Nm
Transmission case-to-case cover	22 ft. lbs.	29 Nm
Transmission case-to-transaxle case	22 ft. lbs.	29 Nm
Transaxle case oil, receiver	65 inch lbs.	7 Nm
Transaxle case receiver-to-transaxle case	8 ft. lbs.	11 Nm
Transaxle-to-engine (10mm)	47 ft. lbs.	64 Nm
Transaxle-to-engine (10mm)	34 ft. lbs.	46 Nm
Transaxle-to-engine (12mm)	34 ft. lbs.	46 Nm
Transaxle-to-engine (12mm)	47 ft. lbs.	64 Nm
Transaxle-to-engine mounting	57 ft. lbs.	77 Nm
Transmission case cover-to-case	13 ft. lbs.	18 Nm

TORQUE SPECIFICATIONS

Components	English Specifications	Metric Specifications
Manual Transaxle - S54 (continued)		
Transmission case protector	13 ft. lbs.	18 Nm
Transmission case-to-transaxle case	22 ft. lbs.	29 Nm
Vehicle speed sensor	8 ft. lbs.	11 Nm
Automatic Transaxle - A140E		
Driveplate-to-crankshaft	61 ft. lbs.	83 Nm
Engine left mounting	47 ft. lbs.	64 Nm
Front lower sub-frame w/steering gear-to-exhaust pipe	14 ft. lbs.	19 Nm
Neutral safety switch-to-case (bolt)	48 inch lbs.	5 Nm
Neutral safety switch-to-case (nut)	61 inch lbs.	7 Nm
Oil pan	43 inch lbs.	5 Nm
Oil pan drain plug	36 ft. lbs.	49 Nm
Oil strainer	8 ft. lbs.	11 Nm
Rear engine mounting-to-exhaust pipe stay	14 ft. lbs.	19 Nm
Rear engine mounting-to-transaxle	64 ft. lbs.	88 Nm
Right driveshaft-to-bracket	47 ft. lbs.	64 Nm
Shift control cable	9 ft. lbs.	12 Nm
Stiffener plate (12mm)	15 ft. lbs.	21 Nm
Stiffener plate (14mm)	32 ft. lbs.	43 Nm
Suspension members (A)	26 ft. lbs.	35 Nm
Suspension members (B)	59 ft. lbs.	80 Nm
Suspension members (C)	130 ft. lbs.	175 Nm
Suspension members (D)	94 ft. lbs.	127 Nm
Suspension members (E)	123 ft. lbs.	167 Nm
Suspension members (nut)	59 ft. lbs.	80 Nm
Testing plug	65 inch lbs.	7 Nm
Torque converter clutch-to-drive plate	18 ft. lbs.	25 Nm
Transaxle housing-to-engine (10mm)	34 ft. lbs.	46 Nm
Transaxle housing-to-engine (12mm)	47 ft. lbs.	64 Nm
Valve body-to-transaxle case	8 ft. lbs.	11 Nm
Automatic Transaxle - A246E		
Driveshaft-to-axle hub	159 ft. lbs.	216 Nm
Engine left mounting bolts	38 ft. lbs.	52 Nm
Engine-to-transaxle lower housing (A)	17 ft. lbs.	23 Nm
Engine-to-transaxle lower housing (B)	34 ft. lbs.	46 Nm
Engine-to-transaxle upper housing	47 ft. lbs.	64 Nm
Front lower sub-frame-to-body (A)	94 ft. lbs.	127 Nm
Front lower sub-frame-to-body (B)	130 ft. lbs.	175 Nm
Front lower sub-frame-to-body (C)	127 ft. lbs.	167 Nm
Lower center member-to-body	26 ft. lbs.	35 Nm
Neutral safety switch-to-manual shift lever	9 ft. lbs.	12 Nm
Neutral safety switch-to-transaxle case	48 inch lbs.	5 Nm
Oil pan drain plug	13 ft. lbs.	17 Nm
Starter-to-transaxle case	29 ft. lbs.	39 Nm
Torque converter-to-driveplate	18 ft. lbs.	25 Nm
Transaxle case-to-oil pan	48 inch lbs.	55 Nm
Halfshaft		
Drive shaft locknut	159 ft. lbs.	216 Nm
ABS speed sensor set bolt	69 inch lbs.	8 Nm
Right driveshaft-to-transaxle (5S-FE)	47 ft. lbs.	64 Nm

89597C02

89597C01

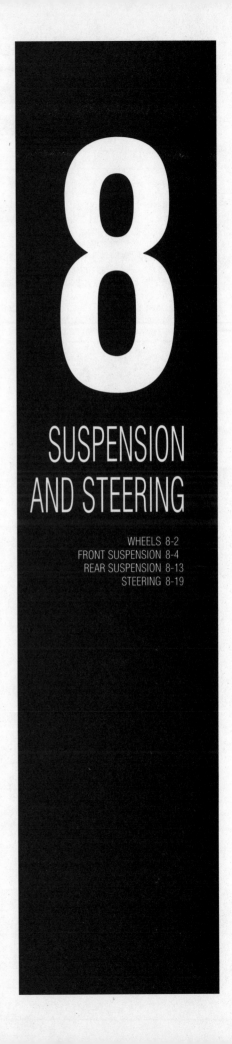

SUSPENSION
AND STEERING

WHEELS

Wheel Assembly

REMOVAL & INSTALLATION

▶ **See Figures 1 thru 7**

1. Park the vehicle on a level surface.
2. Remove the jack, tire iron and, if necessary, the spare tire from their storage compartments.
3. Check the owner's manual or refer to Section 1 of this manual for the jacking points on your vehicle. Then, place the jack in the proper position.
4. If equipped with lug nut trim caps, remove them by either unscrewing or pulling them off the lug nuts, as appropriate. Consult the owner's manual, if necessary.
5. If equipped with a wheel cover or hub cap, insert the tapered end of the tire iron in the groove and pry off the cover.

6. Apply the parking brake and block the diagonally opposite wheel with a wheel chock or two.

➡ **Wheel chocks may be purchased at your local auto parts store, or a block of wood cut into wedges may be used. If possible, keep one or two of the chocks in your tire storage compartment, in case any of the tires has to be removed on the side of the road.**

7. If equipped with an automatic transaxle, place the selector lever in **P** or Park; with a manual transaxle, place the shifter in Reverse.
8. With the tires still on the ground, use the tire iron/wrench to break the lug nuts loose.

➡ **If a nut is stuck, never use heat to loosen it or damage to the wheel and bearings may occur. If the nuts are seized, one or two heavy hammer blows directly on the end of the bolt usually loosens the rust. Be careful, as continued pounding will likely damage the brake drum or rotor.**

Fig. 1 Place the jack at the proper lifting point on your vehicle

Fig. 2 Before jacking the vehicle, block the diagonally opposite wheel with one or, preferably, two chocks

Fig. 3 With the vehicle still on the ground, break the lug nuts loose using the wrench end of the tire iron

Fig. 4 After the lug nuts have been loosened, raise the vehicle using the jack until the tire is clear of the ground

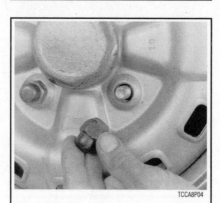

Fig. 5 Remove the lug nuts from the studs

Fig. 6 Remove the wheel and tire assembly from the vehicle

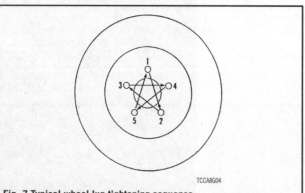

Fig. 7 Typical wheel lug tightening sequence

9. Using the jack, raise the vehicle until the tire is clear of the ground. Support the vehicle safely using jackstands.
10. Remove the lug nuts, then remove the tire and wheel assembly.

To install:

11. Make sure the wheel and hub mating surfaces, as well as the wheel lug studs, are clean and free of all foreign material. Always remove rust from the wheel mounting surface and the brake rotor or drum. Failure to do so may cause the lug nuts to loosen in service.
12. Install the tire and wheel assembly and hand-tighten the lug nuts.
13. Using the tire wrench, tighten all the lug nuts, in a crisscross pattern, until they are snug.
14. Raise the vehicle and withdraw the jackstand, then lower the vehicle.
15. Using a torque wrench, tighten the lug nuts in a crisscross pattern to 76 ft. lbs. (103 Nm). Check your owner's manual or refer to Section 1 of this manual for the proper tightening sequence.

Do not overtighten the lug nuts, as this may cause the wheel studs to stretch or the brake disc (rotor) to warp.

16. If so equipped, install the wheel cover or hub cap. Make sure the valve stem protrudes through the proper opening before tapping the wheel cover into position.

17. If equipped, install the lug nut trim caps by pushing them or screwing them on, as applicable.

18. Remove the jack from under the vehicle, and place the jack and tire iron/wrench in their storage compartments. Remove the wheel chock(s).

19. If you have removed a flat or damaged tire, place it in the storage compartment of the vehicle and take it to your local repair station to have it fixed or replaced as soon as possible.

INSPECTION

Inspect the tires for lacerations, puncture marks, nails and other sharp objects. Repair or replace as necessary. Also check the tires for treadwear and air pressure as outlined in Section 1 of this manual.

Check the wheel assemblies for dents, cracks, rust and metal fatigue. Repair or replace as necessary.

Wheel Lug Studs

REMOVAL & INSTALLATION

With Disc Brakes

▶ **See Figures 8, 9 and 10**

1. Raise and support the appropriate end of the vehicle safely using jackstands, then remove the wheel.

2. Remove the brake pads and caliper. Support the caliper aside using wire or a coat hanger. For details, please refer to Section 9 of this manual.

3. Remove the outer wheel bearing and lift off the rotor. For details on wheel bearing removal, installation and adjustment, please refer to Section 1 of this manual.

4. Properly support the rotor using press bars, then drive the stud out using an arbor press.

➡**If a press is not available, CAREFULLY drive the old stud out using a blunt drift. MAKE SURE the rotor is properly and evenly supported or it may be damaged.**

To install:

5. Clean the stud hole with a wire brush and start the new stud with a hammer and drift pin. Do not use any lubricant or thread sealer.

6. Finish installing the stud with the press.

➡**If a press is not available, start the lug stud through the bore in the hub, then position about 4 flat washers over the stud and thread the lug nut. Hold the hub/rotor while tightening the lug nut, and the stud should be drawn into position. MAKE SURE THE STUD IS FULLY SEATED, then remove the lug nut and washers.**

7. Install the rotor and adjust the wheel bearings.

8. Install the brake caliper and pads.

9. Install the wheel, then remove the jackstands and carefully lower the vehicle.

10. Tighten the lug nuts to the proper torque.

With Drum Brakes

▶ **See Figures 11, 12 and 13**

1. Raise the vehicle and safely support it with jackstands, then remove the wheel.

2. Remove the brake drum.

3. If necessary to provide clearance, remove the brake shoes, as outlined in Section 9 of this manual.

4. Using a large C-clamp and socket, press the stud from the axle flange.

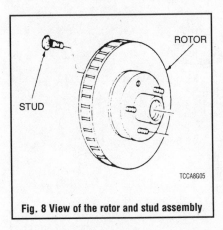

Fig. 8 View of the rotor and stud assembly

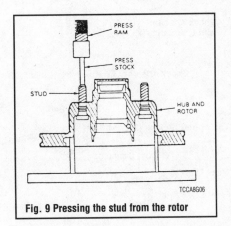

Fig. 9 Pressing the stud from the rotor

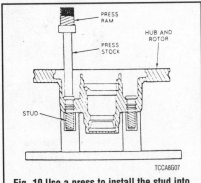

Fig. 10 Use a press to install the stud into the rotor

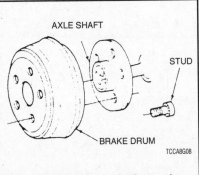

Fig. 11 Exploded view of the drum, axle flange and stud

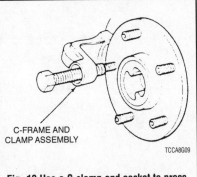

Fig. 12 Use a C-clamp and socket to press out the stud

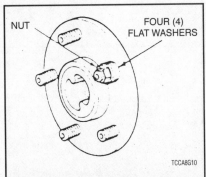

Fig. 13 Force the stud onto the axle flange using washers and a lug nut

5. Coat the serrated part of the stud with liquid soap and place it into the hole.

To install:

6. Position about 4 flat washers over the stud and thread the lug nut. Hold the flange while tightening the lug nut, and the stud should be drawn into position. MAKE SURE THE STUD IS FULLY SEATED, then remove the lug nut and washers.

FRONT SUSPENSION

MacPherson Struts

REMOVAL & INSTALLATION

▶ **See Figures 14 thru 20**

1. Loosen the lug nuts on the side of the vehicle you are replacing the strut.
2. Raise and support the vehicle.
3. Remove the front wheel
4. Detach the speed sensor (ABS models) and brake hose from the shock absorber.

7. If applicable, install the brake shoes.
8. Install the brake drum.
9. Install the wheel, then remove the jackstands and carefully lower the vehicle.
10. Tighten the lug nuts to the proper torque.

5. Remove the 2 nuts ad bolts then disconnect the strut from the steering knuckle.
6. Loosen and remove the 3 nuts from the upper side of the shock tower.
7. From below, lower the shock and coil assembly from the wheel well.
8. Remove the 3 nuts which secure the upper shock absorber mounting plate to the top of the wheel arch and remove the shock absorber with coil spring.

To install:

9. Align the hole in the upper suspension support with the shock absorber piston or end, so they fit properly.
10. Always use a new nut and nylon washer on the shock absorber piston rod end when securing it to the upper suspension support. Tighten the nut to 35 ft. lbs. (47 Nm).

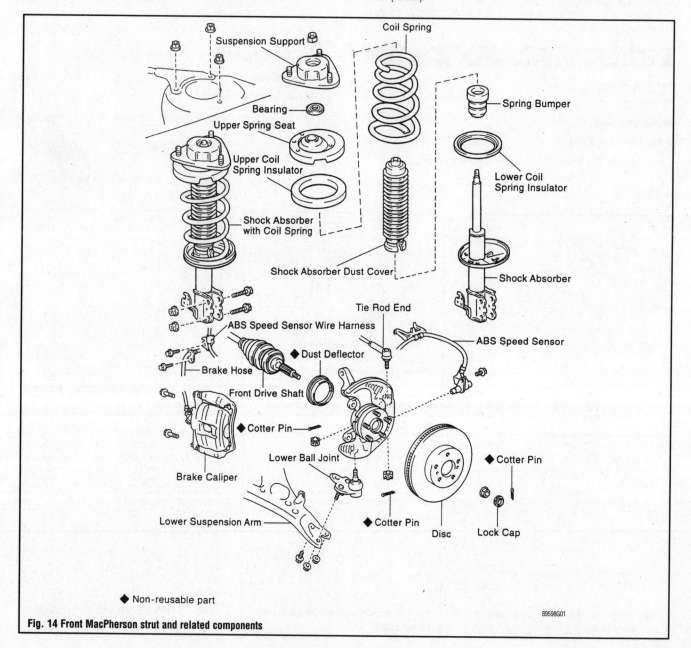

◆ Non-reusable part

Fig. 14 Front MacPherson strut and related components

FRONT SUSPENSION COMPONENTS

1. Lower control arm
2. Ball joint
3. Axle driveshaft
4. Strut assembly
5. Tie rod end
6. Stabilizer bar
7. Sub-frame
8. Center crossmember
9. Stabilizer bar link

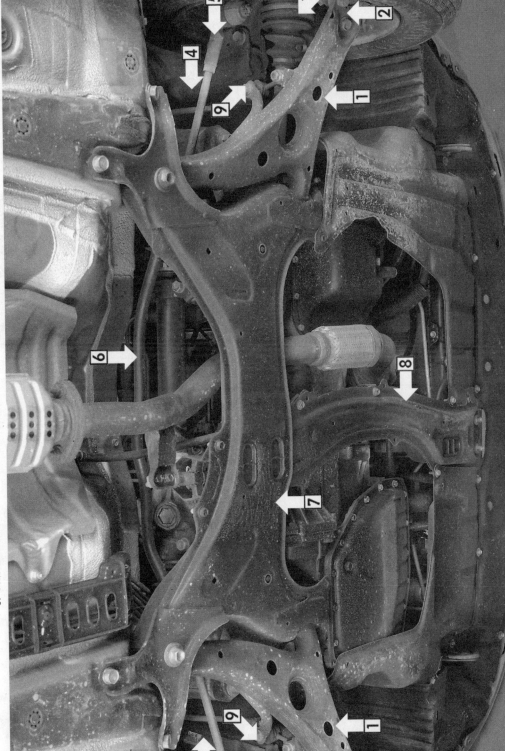

89598P60

Fig. 15 Separate the brake hose from the strut assembly at the bracket

Fig. 16 Front strut/shock lower mounting bolt location

Fig. 17 Unbolt the upper and lower bolts attaching the strut to the knuckle

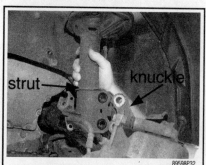

Fig. 18 Carefully pull back on the knuckle to separate the strut assembly from the unit

Fig. 19 Three nuts retain the upper portion of the strut tower

Fig. 20 Remove the strut with coil assembly from under the wheel well

➡ **Do not use an impact wrench to tighten the nut.**

11. Coat the suspension support bearing with multipurpose grease prior to installation. Pack the space in the upper support with multipurpose grease, also, after installation.

12. Tighten the 3 suspension support-to-wheel arch nuts to 59 ft. lbs. (80 Nm).

13. Tighten the shock absorber-to-steering knuckle arm bolts to 113 ft. lbs. (153 Nm).

14. Install the ABS speed sensor and the brake hose to the shock absorber, if equipped.

15. Install the front tire and wheel assembly. Tighten the lug nuts to 76 ft. lbs. (103 Nm).

16. Have the front wheel alignment checked.

OVERHAUL

▶ **See Figures 21 thru 30**

1. Remove the shock absorber assembly with coil spring out from under the vehicle.

2. To disassemble the shock absorber from the coil spring, install 2 nuts and a bolt to the bracket at the lower part of the shock absorber and secure it in a vice.

3. Using a special coil spring compressor, such as 09727–30020 or equivalent, compress the coil spring. Do not use an impact wrench, it will damage the compression tool.

4. Remove the cap from the suspension support. Using a retaining tool to hold the seat, such as 09729–22031 or equivalent remove the nut.

5. Remove the following components:
- Suspension support
- Bearing
- Upper spring seat
- Upper insulator and coil spring
- Dust cover
- Spring bumper
- Lower insulator

➡ **When removing or installing the shock absorber, if the bearing becomes separated in any way, it must be replaced by a new bearing.**

To install:

6. Install the lower insulator onto the shock

7. Using the compressor tool, such as 09727–30020 or equivalent, compress the coil spring. Install the coil spring to the shock absorber. Do not use an impact wrench, it will damage the compressor tool.

➡ **Fit the lower end of the coil spring into the gap of the spring seat of the shock absorber.**

8. Install the spring bumper to the piston rod.

9. Place the upper coil spring insulator on the upper spring seat. Place the dust cover on the spring seat.

10. Align the **OUT** mark on the upper spring seat with the dust cover to the shock.

11. Install the bearing and suspension support.

12. Install the retaining tool, such as 09729–22031 or equivalent to hold the spring seat, install a new nut. Tighten the nut to 34–36 ft. lbs. (47–49 Nm). Install the cap and remove the compression tool.

➡ **Check that the bearing fits into the recess in the suspension support.**

13. Pack the upper suspension support with MP grease.

14. Install the coil and shock absorber assembly into the vehicle.

Lower Ball Joint

INSPECTION

▶ **See Figure 31**

Flip the ball joint stud back and forth several times before installing the nut. Using a torque wrench turn the nut continuously one turn each 2–4 seconds and take the torque reading on the 5th turn. Tightening torque should be 9–26 inch lbs. (1–3 Nm).

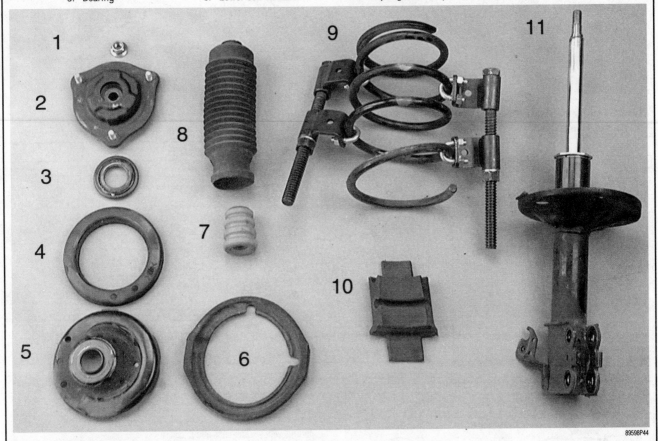

FRONT MACPHERSON STRUT

1. Nut
2. Suspension support
3. Bearing
4. Upper coil insulator
5. Upper spring seat
6. Lower coil insulator
7. Spring bumper
8. Dust cover
9. Coil spring with compressor
10. Spacer
11. Shock absorber

Fig. 21 Exploded view of the front strut assembly

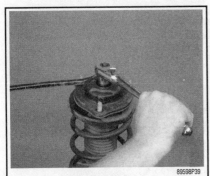

Fig. 22 Securing the strut in a vise, and loosening the retaining nut

spring compressor tool

Fig. 23 A spring compressor tool is used to remove the coil spring

Fig. 24 Use care when using a spring compressor tool, follow all warnings from the manufacturer

REMOVAL & INSTALLATION

▶ See Figures 32, 33 and 34

1. Remove the cotter pin from the lower ball joint. Discard the cotter pin.
2. Remove the ball joint retaining bolts securing it to the lower control arm.
3. Position a puller over the lower control arm and separate the ball joint from the arm.

To install:
4. Install the lower ball joint and tighten the nut to 76 ft. lbs. (103 Nm).
5. Insert a new cotter pin and bend the end to secure.

Stabilizer Bar and Links

REMOVAL & INSTALLATION

▶ See Figures 35, 36 and 37

1. Using a special Torx® head, remove the stabilizer bar link bolts.
2. Lower the stabilizer bar link.
3. Unbolt the stabilizer bar brackets located near the center of the bar.
4. Remove the brackets and bushings.

Fig. 25 Once the spring is compressed, the nut can be removed

Fig. 26 Remove and inspect the bearing if reusing

Fig. 27 Now each one of the components can be extracted from the strut assembly

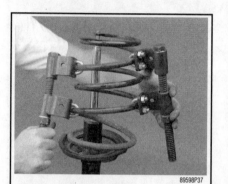

Fig. 28 Lift the coil with tool over the strut . . . .

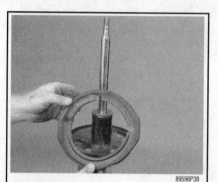

Fig. 29 . . . and remove the lower coil spring insulator

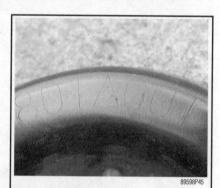

Fig. 30 Align the OUT mark to point outward from the vehicle when installed

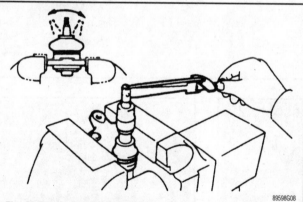

Fig. 31 Flip the ball joint stud back and forth several times to inspect the rotation condition

5. From the left side of the vehicle, twist and maneuver the bar out from the engine compartment.

To install:

6. Maneuver the stabilizer bar into the engine compartment and secure temporarily with the bushings and brackets.

7. Attach the stabilizer bar links and tighten the retaining nuts to 33 ft. lbs. (44 Nm).

8. Secure the stabilizer bar bracket nuts to 14 ft. lbs. (19 Nm).

Lower Control Arm

REMOVAL & INSTALLATION

▶ See Figures 38 thru 43

➡An assistant will be needed to remove the lower control arm.

1. Loosen the lug nuts on the side of the vehicle that the arm will be removed.

Fig. 32 Remove the cotter pin from the lower ball joint

Fig. 33 Place a puller on the ball joint . . .

Fig. 34 . . . to separate it from the lower control arm

Fig. 35 Using a Torx® head driver, remove the bolts from the stabilizer linkage

Fig. 36 Two brackets retain the stabilizer bar once the links are removed

Fig. 37 Slip the stabilizer bar linkage through the hole in the lower control arm

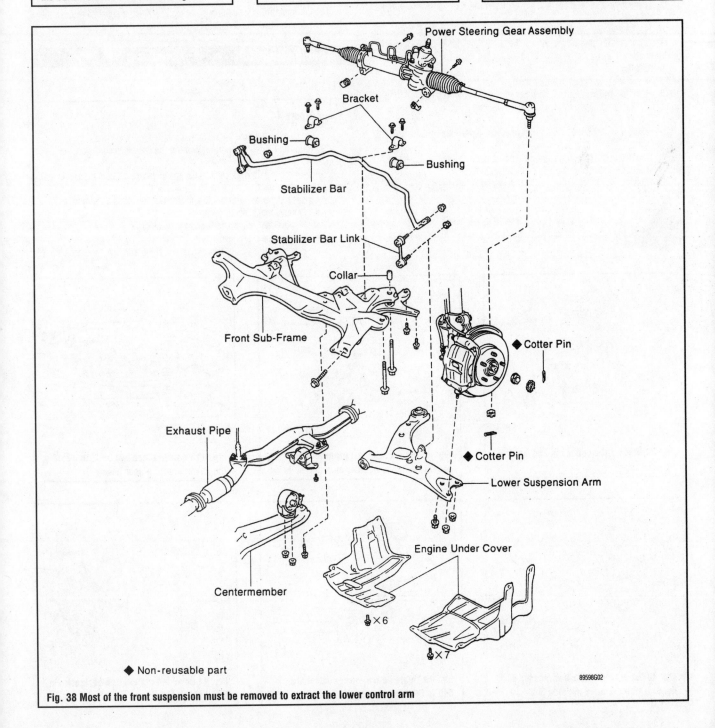

Power Steering Gear Assembly

Bracket

Bushing

Bushing

Stabilizer Bar

Stabilizer Bar Link

Collar

Front Sub-Frame

Cotter Pin

Cotter Pin

Lower Suspension Arm

Exhaust Pipe

Engine Under Cover

Centermember

×6

×7

◆ Non-reusable part

Fig. 38 Most of the front suspension must be removed to extract the lower control arm

2. Raise and safely support the front of the vehicle securely on jackstands.

3. Remove the front wheel.

4. Unbolt and extract the engine under covers.

5. Remove the cotter pin and lock cap for the wheel, then while an assistant is applying the brakes, remove the nut.

6. Disconnect the tie rod end from the steering knuckle.

7. Separate the stabilizer bar from the lower control arm.

8. Unbolt and remove the ball joint from the lower control arm.

9. Remove the three bolts from the lower control arm, they are two different sizes.

10. Support the transaxle with a jack.

11. Remove the 2 exhaust pipe support bracket set bolts. Pull out the grommets and remove the center crossmember set bolt.

12. Loosen and remove the center crossmember set nuts.

13. Unbolt the power steering gear assembly.

14. Support the sub-frame with a jack.

15. Remove both of the bolts and slightly lower the front sub-frame with the control arm attached.

16. Unbolt and remove the stabilizer bar brackets.

17. On the lower control arm, remove the collar, then unbolt and disconnect the lower control arm.

To install:

18. Attach the lower control arm to the front sub-frame.

19. Place the collar into place, then raise the sub-frame with control arms into place. Stabilize the assembly and tighten the control arm bolts to 116 ft. lbs. (157 Nm).

20. Install and attach the stabilizer bar brackets, tighten the set bolts to 14 ft. lbs. (19 Nm).

21. Double check the suspension is stabilized, then secure the sub-frame with the set bolts and tighten them to 94 ft. lbs. (127 Nm).

22. Attach the power steering gear assembly and tighten the set bolts to 94 ft. lbs. (127 Nm).

23. Install and secure the crossmember set nuts and set bolts to 59 ft. lbs. (80 Nm). Next place the grommets over the set bolts and nuts.

24. Attach the exhaust pipe support bracket and secure. Tighten the bolts to 14 ft. lbs. (19 Nm).

25. Double check all bolts for security and lower the jack supporting the sub-frame.

26. once the assembly is stabilized, tighten the lower control arm 3 bolts to **A** 123 ft. lbs. (167 Nm) and **B** 130 ft. lbs. (175 Nm).

27. Install and secure the lower ball joint and stabilizer bar link to the control arm.

28. Attach the tie rod end to the steering knuckle.

29. Tighten the drive shaft lock nut to 159 ft. lbs. (216 Nm), then place the lock cap and new cotter pin over the nut.

30. Place the engine under covers on the vehicle.

31. Install the wheel, hand-tighten the lug nuts and lower the vehicle.

32. Tighten the lug nuts to 76 ft. lbs. (103 Nm). Bounce the front end several times and test drive the vehicle.

CONTROL ARM BUSHING REPLACEMENT

The lower control arm bushing is not replaceable as a separate piece. If the bushing does go bad, the complete control arm must be replaced.

Knuckle and Hub

REMOVAL & INSTALLATION

▶ **See Figure 44**

1. Loosen the lug nuts on the front wheel.

2. Raise and safely support the front of the vehicle securely on jackstands.

3. On models with ABS, remove the speed sensor set bolt and clamp and extract the component.

4. Inspect the bearing backlash and axle hub deviation as follows:

   a. Remove the 2 caliper set bolts.

   b. Remove the caliper and support it securely.

   c. Remove the brake disc.

   d. Place a dial indicator near the center of the axle hub and check the

Fig. 39 Discard the cotter pin and remove the lock cap

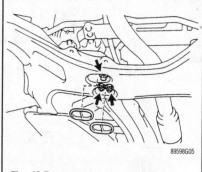

Fig. 40 Remove the two grommets to access the crossmember nuts and bolts

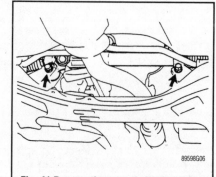

Fig. 41 Remove these two bolts that retain the power steering gear assembly

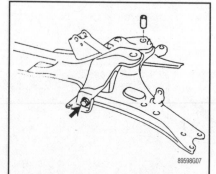

Fig. 42 Extract the collar from the top of the arm, then remove the side bolt

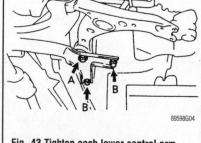

Fig. 43 Tighten each lower control arm bolt to the correct specification

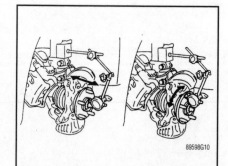

Fig. 44 Checking the bearing backlash and axle hub deviation

backlash in the bearing shaft direction. Maximum is 0.0031 inch (0.08mm). If the backlash exceeds the maximum, replace the bearing.

    e. Using a dial indicator, check the deviation at the surface of the axle hub outside the hub bolt. Maximum should be 0.0028 inch (0.07mm). If the deviation is not within specifications, replace the axle hub.

5. Install the disc and caliper.

6. Remove the cotter pin and lock cap. Have an assistant apply the brakes as you remove the nut.

7. Remove the caliper and brake disc.

8. Loosen the 2 nuts on the lower side of the shock, but do not remove them at this time.

9. Remove the cotter pin and remove the nut from the tie rod end. Using a puller, disconnect the tie rod from the steering knuckle.

10. Disconnect the stabilizer bar link from the lower control arm.

11. Separate the ball joint from the lower control arm.

12. Remove the 2 nuts and bolts on the lower side of the shock and extract the steering knuckle with the axle hub.

To install:

13. Coat the nut threads of the axle hub with engine oil.

14. Place the steering knuckle and axle hub assembly into place and hand-tighten the nuts on the lower side of the shock.

15. Attach the ball joint to the lower control arm and tighten the nuts to 94 ft. lbs. (127 Nm).

16. Place the stabilizer link to the lower control arm and tighten the nuts to 33 ft. lbs. (44 Nm).

17. Attach the tie rod to the steering knuckle, use a new cotter pin and tighten the nut to 36 ft. lbs. (49 Nm).

18. Install the two nuts on the lower side of the shock and tighten them to 113 ft. lbs. (153 Nm).

19. Install the disc and caliper, then install the drive shaft lock nut and tighten to 159 ft. lbs. (216 Nm). Slide the lock cap on, then insert and secure a new cotter pin.

20. Install the ABS speed sensor if removed.

21. Install the wheel, lower the vehicle and tighten the lug nuts to 76 ft. lbs. (103 Nm).

Front Bearing

REMOVAL & INSTALLATION

◆ **See Figures 45 thru 53**

1. Remove the hub and knuckle assembly from the vehicle. Refer to the procedure earlier in this section.

2. Place the knuckle portion in a vise.

3. Using a taped pry tool, remove the dust deflector from the hub.

4. Insert a seal puller into the hub and pull out the inner oil seal.

5. Remove the cotter pin and nut, then use a separator tool and extract the ball joint.

6. Using a puller (09520–00031), remove the axle hub from the knuckle. Next use the puller and race replacer (09550–40010 and 09550–60010) to remove the inner race (outside) from the axle hub.

7. Using a Torx® wrench, remove the 4 bolts and dust cover.

➡ **The Torx® wrench is the T30 type (09042–00010) or locally manufactured tool.**

8. Using snapring pliers, remove the snapring.

9. Set the knuckle into position the a vise so that a puller can be used to extract the outer oil seal.

10. Retain the knuckle and using snapring pliers, remove the snapring and the press out the bearing from the knuckle.

To assemble:

11. Press the new bearing into the steering knuckle.

12. Use snapring pliers to insert a new snapring over the bearing.

13. Using a Torx® wrench, install a dust cover with the 4 bolts and tighten them to 74 inch lbs. (8 Nm).,

14. Insert the axle hub using a press into the knuckle.

15. Attach the lower ball joint and tighten the nut to 76 ft. lbs. (103 Nm). Insert a new cotter pin.

16. Using a seal installer, insert the dust deflector and tap it into place.

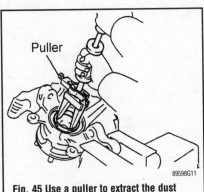

Fig. 45 Use a puller to extract the dust seal from the hub

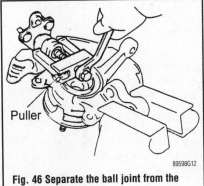

Fig. 46 Separate the ball joint from the end of the knuckle

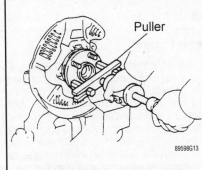

Fig. 47 Secure a puller on the end of the hub and separate the two components

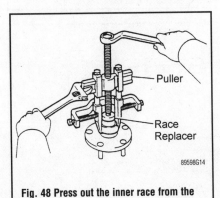

Fig. 48 Press out the inner race from the hub

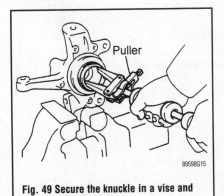

Fig. 49 Secure the knuckle in a vise and pull out the outer oil seal

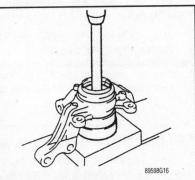

Fig. 50 Use a press to extract the bearing out of the steering knuckle

Fig. 51 Turn the knuckle in the opposite direction and press a new bearing into place

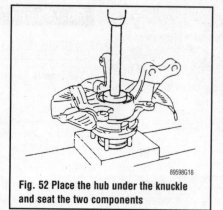

Fig. 52 Place the hub under the knuckle and seat the two components

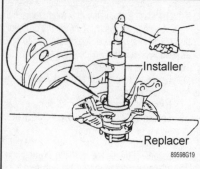

Fig. 53 Tap the dust deflector in carefully and evenly

Make sure to align the holes for the ABS speed sensor in the dust deflector and knuckle on models equipped with ABS.

17. Install the steering knuckle and hub assembly. Refer to the procedure earlier in this section.

Wheel Alignment

If the tires are worn unevenly, if the vehicle is not stable on the highway or if the handling seems uneven in spirited driving, the wheel alignment should be checked. If an alignment problem is suspected, first check for improper tire inflation and other possible causes. These can be worn suspension or steering components, accident damage or even unmatched tires. If any worn or damaged components are found, they must be replaced before the wheels can be properly aligned. Wheel alignment requires very expensive equipment and involves minute adjustments which must be accurate; it should only be performed by a trained technician. Take your vehicle to a properly equipped shop.

Following is a description of the alignment angles which are adjustable on most vehicles and how they affect vehicle handling. Although these angles can apply to both the front and rear wheels, usually only the front suspension is adjustable.

CASTER

▶ See Figure 54

Looking at a vehicle from the side, caster angle describes the steering axis rather than a wheel angle. The steering knuckle is attached to a control arm or strut at the top and a control arm at the bottom. The wheel pivots around the line between these points to steer the vehicle. When the upper point is tilted back, this is described as positive caster. Having a positive caster tends to make the wheels self-centering, increasing directional stability. Excessive positive caster makes the wheels hard to steer, while an uneven caster will cause a pull to one side. Overloading the vehicle or sagging rear springs will affect caster, as will raising the rear of the vehicle. If the rear of the vehicle is lower than normal, the caster becomes more positive.

CAMBER

▶ See Figure 55

Looking from the front of the vehicle, camber is the inward or outward tilt of the top of wheels. When the tops of the wheels are tilted in, this is negative camber; if they are tilted out, it is positive. In a turn, a slight amount of negative camber helps maximize contact of the tire with the road. However, too much negative camber compromises straight-line stability, increases bump steer and torque steer.

TOE

▶ See Figure 56

Looking down at the wheels from above the vehicle, toe angle is the distance between the front of the wheels, relative to the distance between the back of the wheels. If the wheels are closer at the front, they are said to be toed-in or to have negative toe. A small amount of negative toe enhances directional stability and provides a smoother ride on the highway.

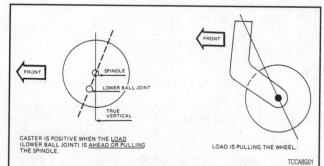

Fig. 54 Caster affects straight-line stability. Caster wheels used on shopping carts, for example, employ positive caster

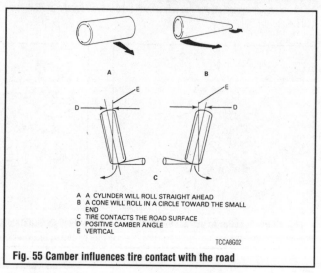

A A CYLINDER WILL ROLL STRAIGHT AHEAD
B A CONE WILL ROLL IN A CIRCLE TOWARD THE SMALL END
C TIRE CONTACTS THE ROAD SURFACE
D POSITIVE CAMBER ANGLE
E VERTICAL

Fig. 55 Camber influences tire contact with the road

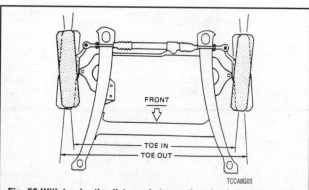

Fig. 56 With toe-in, the distance between the wheels is closer at the front than at the rear

REAR SUSPENSION

REAR SUSPENSION COMPONENTS

1. Strut rod
2. Stabilizer bar link
3. No. 1 lower suspension arm
4. No. 2 lower suspension arm
5. Shock absorber
6. Rear axle carrier

MacPherson Struts

REMOVAL & INSTALLATION

▶ See Figures 57, 58, 59 and 60

1. On the coupe models, remove the rear seat and package trim tray.
2. Loosen the rear lug nuts. Raise and support the vehicle and remove the wheel.
3. Disconnect the ABS speed sensor wiring harness and remove the brake hose from the shock absorber.
4. Disconnect the stabilizer link from the shock.

➡If the ball joint stud turns together with the nut, use a hexagon wrench to hold the stud.

5. Loosen the nuts on the lower side of the shock, and do not remove the bolts.
6. Support the rear axle carrier with a jack.
7. On liftback models, remove the service hole cover and remove the 3 suspension support nuts.
8. Lower the rear axle carrier and remove the 2 bolts.
9. Remove the shock and coil spring.

To install:

10. Reinsert the shock and coil assembly into the vehicle. On the liftback, tighten the 3 support nuts to 29 ft. lbs. (39 Nm). Tighten the nuts on the lower side of the shock to 188 ft. lbs. (255 Nm).
11. Install the stabilizer bar link, refer to the procedure earlier in this section.
12. Connect the brake hose and tighten the bolt to 14 ft. lbs. (19 Nm) On models with ABS, tighten the wire bolt to 44 inch lbs. (5 Nm).
13. Install the rear wheel, lower the vehicle and tighten the lug nuts to 76 ft. lbs. (103 Nm).
14. On coupe models, install the rear seat and package tray.

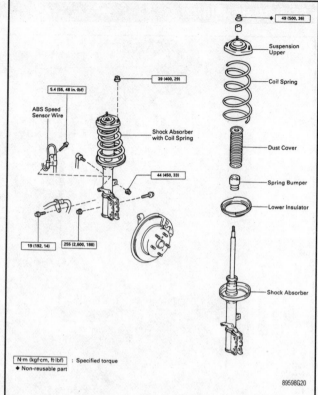

Fig. 57 View of the rear shock with coil spring assembly and related axle components

Fig. 58 The strut is retained by bolts on each end of the assembly

Fig. 59 Loosen the two nuts on the lower portion of the rear shock

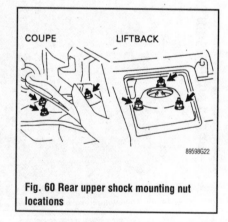

Fig. 60 Rear upper shock mounting nut locations

OVERHAUL

▶ See Figures 61 and 62

1. Remove the shock and coil spring.
2. Install 2 nuts and a bolt to the bracket at the lower portion of the shock and secure it in a vise.
3. Use a spring compressor and compress the coil, spring.

➡Do not use an impact wrench, it will damage the compressor tool.

4. Using a retaining tool to hold the suspension support, remove the nut.
5. Remove the following:
• Collar and suspension support
• Coil spring
• Dust cover
• Spring bumper
• Lower insulator

To install:
6. Install the lower coil spring insulator onto the shock.

➡Fit the gap of the lower coil spring insulator.

7. Install the spring bumper on the piston rod.
8. Compress the coil spring and install it on the shock. Fit the lower end of the spring into the gap of the lower spring insulator.
9. Install the dust cover and suspension support to the piston rod.
   a. Install the collar.
   b. Use a retaining tool to hold the suspension support, then install a new nut. Tighten the nut to 36 ft. lbs. (49 Nm).
   c. Rotate the suspension support and set it in the direction with the paint mark facing outwards.
   d. Remove the compressor tool from the spring and shock assembly. After removing the tool, recheck the direction of the support.
10. Reinsert the shock and coil assembly into the vehicle. On the liftback, tighten the 3 support nuts to 29 ft. lbs. (39 Nm). Tighten the nuts on the lower side of the shock to 188 ft. lbs. (255 Nm).

Suspension Arms

REMOVAL & INSTALLATION

◆ **See Figures 63 thru 70**

1. Loosen the rear wheel lug nuts.
2. Raise and safely support the rear of the vehicle securely on jack-stands.

3. Remove the rear wheel.
4. Remove the nut from the axle carrier. Remove the mounting bolts from the strut rod and disconnect from the carrier.
5. Remove the 2 nuts and washers for the No. 2 lower control arm.
6. Support the suspension member with a jack. Remove the 4 nuts and 2 nuts from the suspension member. Lower the suspension member.
7. Remove the No. 1 arm with the 2 bolts and washer.

To install:

8. Install the No. 1 arm with the washer and two bolts. Face the paint mark towards the rear. Do not tighten at this time.

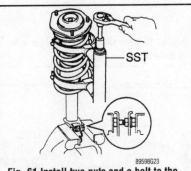

Fig. 61 Install two nuts and a bolt to the bracket at the lower part of the shock and secure in a vise to disassemble

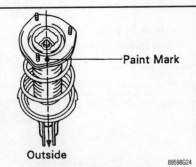

Fig. 62 Rotate the suspension support and set it in the direction with the paint mark facing outwards

Fig. 63 Always keep in mind which suspension arm goes where before removing them; mark them if you're not sure

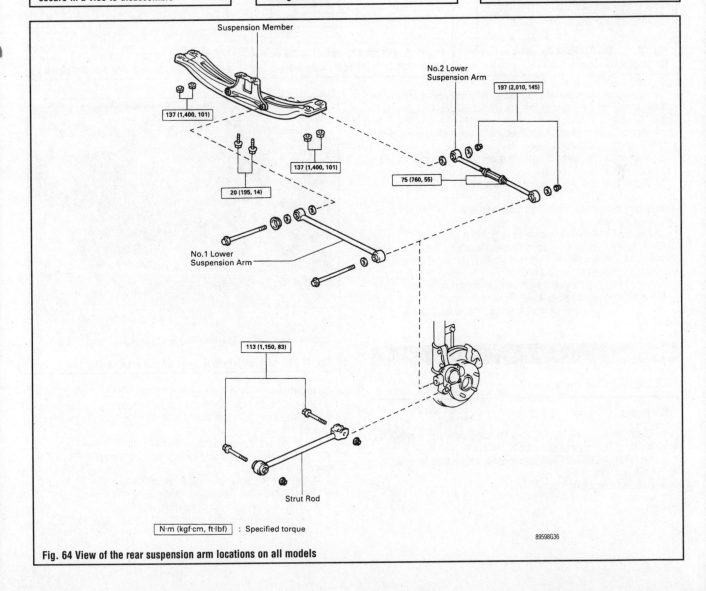

Fig. 64 View of the rear suspension arm locations on all models

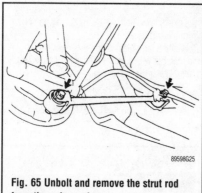

Fig. 65 Unbolt and remove the strut rod from the axle carrier

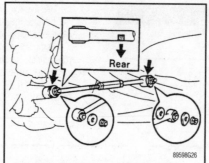

Fig. 66 On the No. 2 suspension arm, remove the nuts and washers and pull the arm off

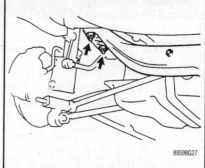

Fig. 67 Remove the 2 bolts on either side of the suspension member, and . . .

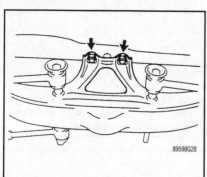

Fig. 68 . . . the 2 bolts in the center of the suspension member

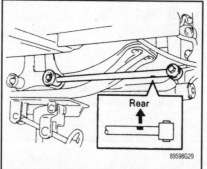

Fig. 69 A paint mark is located on the rear suspension arms, place it facing rearward

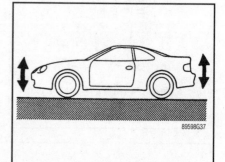

Fig. 70 Stabilizing the suspension is important when replacing rear components

9. Jack up the suspension member. Install the member and secure with the nuts and bolts. Tighten the bolts to 14 ft. lbs. (20 Nm). Tighten the nuts to 101 ft. lbs. (137 Nm).

10. Face the paint mark on the No. 2 suspension arm toward the rear of the vehicle. Temporarily install the two lock nuts.

11. Connect the strut bar to the axle carrier and temporarily install the bolt and nut.

12. Tighten the nut on the outside of the lower arms to 145 ft. lbs. (197 Nm).

13. Install the rear wheels and lower the vehicle. Bounce the suspension up and down a few times.

14. Jack up the vehicle and support the body with stands.

15. Remove the rear wheel. Support the rear axle carrier with a jack. Tighten the nut on the outside of the lower arm to 145 ft. lbs. (197 Nm). Tighten the strut rod set bolts to 83 ft. lbs. (113 Nm).

16. Install the rear wheel and lower the vehicle. Tighten the lug nuts.

17. Inspect and adjust the rear wheel alignment.

18. Tighten the No. 2 lower arm and locknuts to 145 ft. lbs. (197 Nm) if necessary.

Strut Rod

REMOVAL & INSTALLATION

▶ See Figure 71

1. Loosen the rear wheel lug nuts. Raise the rear of the vehicle with a floor jack and support the body with safety stands. Remove the rear wheels.

2. Disconnect the strut rod from the axle carrier and the body by removing the two nuts and bolts.

3. Remove the strut rod.

Fig. 71 The strut rod is held in by a bolt and nut on either end

To install:

4. Position the strut rod onto the body and axle carrier and install the nuts and bolts finger tight. Make sure that the lip of the nut is resting on the flange of the bracket.

5. Install the rear wheels and remove the safety stands.

6. Lower the vehicle and bounce the rear end a few to times to allow the rear suspension to stabilize.

7. Tighten the mounting bolts to 83 ft. lbs. (113 Nm).

8. Have the rear wheel alignment checked.

Stabilizer Bar and Links

REMOVAL & INSTALLATION

▶ See Figures 72, 73, 74, 75 and 76

1. Loosen the rear wheel lug nuts. Raise the rear of the vehicle with a floor jack and support the body with safety stands. Remove the rear wheels.
2. Remove the exhaust tail pipe.
3. On some vehicles, it may be necessary to support the fuel tank and remove the tank band from the body.
4. Remove the 4 nuts and 2 stabilizer bar links. If the ball joint turns when removing the nut, use a wrench to stabilize the stud.
5. Disconnect the stabilizer bar from the body by removing the nuts. Remove the stabilizer bar from the vehicle with bushings and brackets. If the bushings appear to be worn or cracked, replace them.

To install:

➡Install the bushing to the outside of the pant line. Install the bushing to the stabilizer bar so that the cutout of the bushings faces the front of the vehicle.

6. Temporarily connect the stabilizer bar to the body with the bushings, brackets and bolts.
7. Connect the stabilizer bar links to the No. 1 suspension arm with the retainers, cushions and nuts. Tighten the center bracket bolts to 14 ft. lbs. (19 Nm). Tighten the stabilizer-to-body bolts to 14 ft. lbs. (19 Nm) and the stabilizer link to stabilizer bar bolts to 33 ft. lbs. (44 Nm).
8. Install the right side fuel tank band and tighten the bolts to 30 ft. lbs. (40 Nm).

9. Install the rear exhaust tail pipe. Tighten the retaining nuts and bolts to 32 ft. lbs. (43 Nm).
10. Install the rear wheels and remove the safety stands.
11. Lower the vehicle and bounce the rear end a few to times to allow the rear suspension to stabilize.
12. Have the rear wheel alignment checked.

Hub and Carrier

REMOVAL & INSTALLATION

▶ See Figures 77, 78 and 79

1. Loosen the rear wheel lug nuts.
2. Raise and safely support the rear of the vehicle securely on jackstands.
3. Remove the rear wheels.
4. On models with rear disc brakes, remove the caliper and brake disc.
5. On models with rear drum brakes, remove the brake drum.
6. Check the bearing backlash and axle hub deviation.
   a. Place a dial indicator near the center of the axle hub and check the backlash in the bearing shaft direction. Maximum is 0.0020 inch (0.05mm). If the backlash exceeds the maximum, replace the axle hub with bearing.
   b. Using a dial indicator, check the deviation at the surface of the axle hub outside the hub bolt. Maximum deviation is 0.0028 inch (0.07mm). If the deviation exceeds maximum, replace the axle hub with bearing.
7. Remove the 4 bolts and rear axle. The bolts are accessed through the hole provided in the hub. Turn the hub to access each one of the bolts.
8. Pull the hub off and remove the O-ring on the back of the unit.

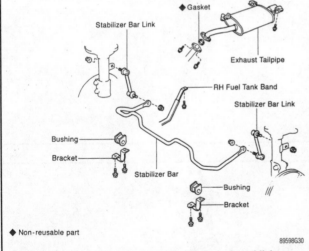

Fig. 72 The rear stabilizer bar is attached to the body and links on either side

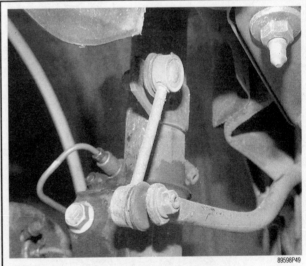

Fig. 73 The links are attached to the stabilizer bar

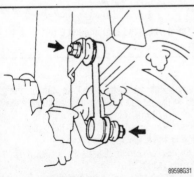

Fig. 74 Unbolt and remove both of the stabilizer links

Fig. 75 The stabilizer bar has brackets on either side to be removed

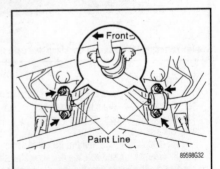

Fig. 76 Place the bushings on the stabilizer bar in the correct locations with the paint marks on the inside

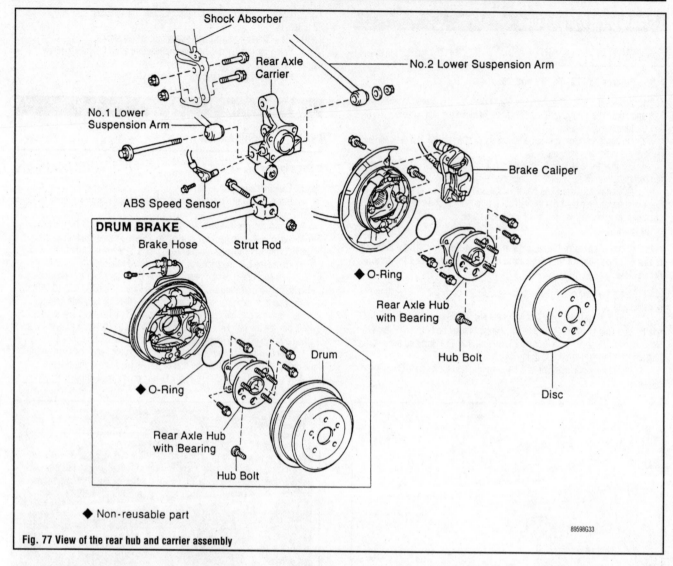

Fig. 77 View of the rear hub and carrier assembly

◆ Non-reusable part

89598G33

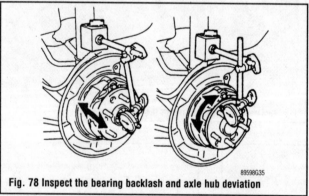

Fig. 78 Inspect the bearing backlash and axle hub deviation

89598G35

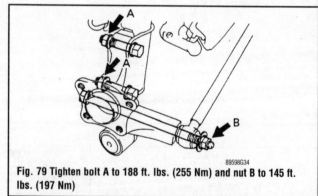

Fig. 79 Tighten bolt A to 188 ft. lbs. (255 Nm) and nut B to 145 ft. lbs. (197 Nm)

89598G34

To install:

9. Coat the O-ring with MP grease and insert into the back of the hub.

10. On models with drum brakes, remove the brake hose from the shock.

11. Disconnect the backing plate from the rear axle carrier. Support the backing plate securely.

12. On models with ABS, remove the speed sensor.

13. Remove the nut and bolt, the disconnect the strut trod from the rear axle carrier. Remove the 2 nuts from the shock lower set bolts, but do not remove the bolts.

14. Disconnect the lower suspension arms from the axle carrier. Pull out the 2 bolts from the shock and remove the rear axle carrier.

To install:

15. Attach the carrier to the shock absorber. Attach the lower control arms to the axle carrier. Bounce the vehicle up and down several times and tighten the suspension arms **B** to 145 ft. lbs. (197 Nm).

16. Install the shock absorber lower set bolts nuts, bounce the vehicle up and down and tighten the nuts **A** to 188 ft. lbs. (255 Nm).

17. Attach the strut rod to the rear axle carrier, stabilize the suspension and tighten the nut and bolt to 83 ft. lbs. (113 Nm).

18. On models with ABS, attach the speed sensor and secure to 71 inch lbs. (8 Nm).

19. Attach the backing plate to the rear axle carrier.

20. On drum brake models, install and secure the brake hose. Tighten the bolt to 14 ft. lbs. (19 Nm).

21. Coat the new O-ring on the back of the axle hub with MP grease and insert into the groove.

22. Place the hub on the backing plate and in a sequential fashion tighten the hub bolts to 59 ft. lbs. (80 Nm).

23. On drum brakes install the brake drum.

24. On disc brake models, install the disc and caliper. tighten the caliper set bolts to 34 ft. lbs. (47 Nm).

25. Install the rear wheel, hand-tighten the lug nuts and lower the vehicle.

26. Tighten the lug nuts to 76 ft. lbs. (103 Nm).

27. Bounce the vehicle up and down to stabilize the suspension several times and double check each suspension components torque.

Wheel Bearings

REMOVAL & INSTALLATION

On all models the rear wheel bearing can not be separated from the rear hub. If the bearing is bad, the entire hub must be replaced.

STEERING

Steering Wheel

REMOVAL & INSTALLATION

▶ See Figures 80 thru 94

1. Place the ignition in the **LOCK** position and disconnect the negative battery cable. Wait at least 90 seconds once the batter cable is disconnected to hinder the air bag deployment.

❊❊ CAUTION

Models covered by this manual may be equipped with a Supplemental Restraint System (SRS), which uses an air bag. Whenever working near any of the SRS components, such as the impact sensors, the air bag module, steering column and instrument panel, disable the SRS, as described in Section 6.

2. Place the front wheels straight ahead.

3. Remove the No. 2 and No. 3 covers from the side of the steering wheel.

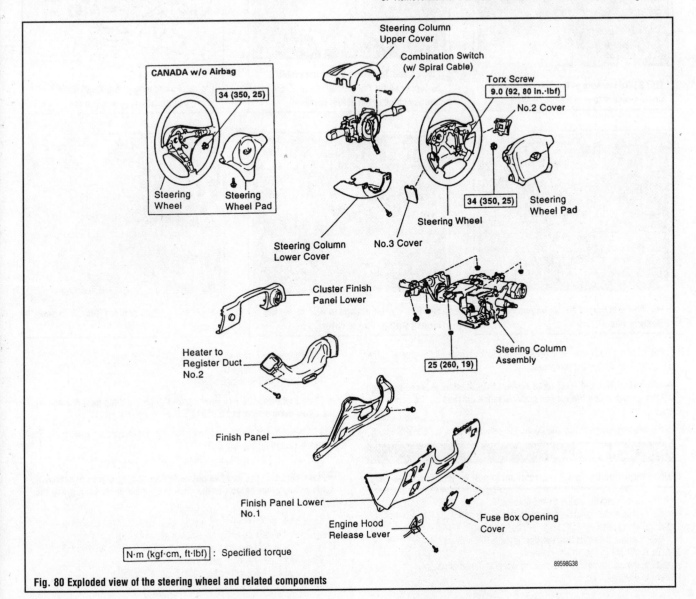

N·m (kgf·cm, ft·lbf) : Specified torque

89598G38

Fig. 80 Exploded view of the steering wheel and related components

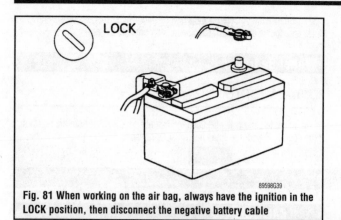

Fig. 81 When working on the air bag, always have the ignition in the LOCK position, then disconnect the negative battery cable

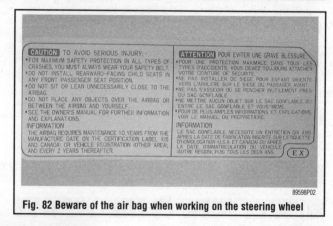

Fig. 82 Beware of the air bag when working on the steering wheel

Fig. 83 On the side of the steering wheel, pry the covers to remove

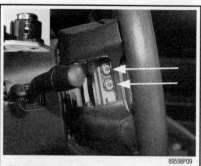

Fig. 84 The T30 Torx® head screws must be loosened till the groove of the circumference catches the screw case

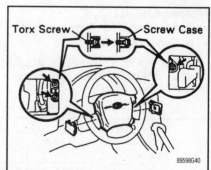

Fig. 85 Positioning of the Torx® head screws in the steering wheel pad

Fig. 86 Carefully lift the air bag off the steering wheel . . .

Fig. 87 . . . far enough to disconnect the air bag wiring, lift the cover . . .

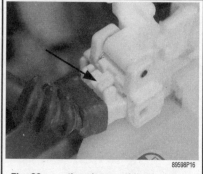

Fig. 88 . . . then depress this tab to separate

4. Using a Torx® wrench, loosen the T30 Torx® screws till the groove of the circumference catches the screw case.

➡When removing the Torx® head screws, they must be loosened enough till the groove along the screws circumference catches on the screw case.

5. Pull the pad out from the steering wheel and disconnect the SRS wiring.

✳✳ WARNING

When removing the pad, be careful not to pull on the air bag harness.

6. Disconnect the wiring for the horn ect.
7. Place matchmarks on the steering wheel nut and shaft. Remove the steering wheel nut.
8. Using a puller, remove the steering wheel.

To install:

Align the matchmarks on the steering wheel and main shaft, then install the wheel to the shaft.

9. Tighten the center wheel nut to 25 ft. lbs. (34 Nm).
10. Connect the horn wiring.
11. Attach the SRS wiring.

➡When installing the pad, make sure the wiring does not interfere with the other parts and is not pinched between other parts.

12. Install the pad after confirming that the circumference groove of the Torx screws is caught on the screw case.
13. Using a Torx® wrench, tighten the screws to 80 inch lbs. (9 Nm).

➡Make sure that the pad has not been dropped, or there are cracks, dents or any other defects in the case or connection. If so, replace the pad with a new one.

14. Check the steering wheel center point. Have the tires pointed straight ahead, rock the steering wheel gently back and forth with light finger pressure. Freeplay should not be more than 1.18 inch (30mm). If incorrect repair.
15. Connect the negative battery cable.
16. Reset any electrical components such as the radio.

Fig. 89 Never lay the air bag with the pad facing down!

Turn Signal (Combination) Switch

REMOVAL & INSTALLATION

▶ See Figures 95 and 96

1. Place the ignition switch in the **LOCK** position. Disconnect the negative battery cable. Wait at least 90 seconds before working on the vehicle to hinder air bag deployment.

✳✳ CAUTION

Some models covered by this manual may be equipped with a Supplemental Restraint System (SRS), which uses an air bag. Whenever working near any of the SRS components, such as the impact sensors, the air bag module, steering column and instrument panel, disable the SRS, as described in Section 6.

2. Remove the steering wheel, as outlined in this section.
3. Remove the upper and lower steering column covers.
4. Disconnect the combination switch wiring.
5. Disconnect the cable wiring, remove the spiral cable housing attaching screws and slide the cable assembly from the front of the combination switch.
6. Remove the screws that attach the combination switch to its mounting brackets and extract the assembly from the vehicle.

To install:

7. Position the combination switch onto the mounting bracket and install the retaining screws.

Fig. 90 Remove the center steering wheel nut, then . . .

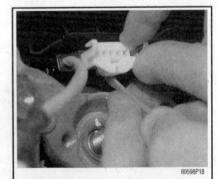

Fig. 91 . . . matchmark the shaft and wheel with whiteout or paint

Fig. 92 Disconnect the horn wiring harness above the steering wheel

Fig. 93 Position a steering wheel puller in place . . .

Fig. 94 . . . and pull the steering wheel carefully off the shaft

8. Connect the electrical wiring.

9. Install the upper/lower column covers.

10. Turn the spiral cable on the combination switch counterclockwise by hand until it becomes harder to turn (roughly 3 turns). Then rotate the cable clockwise about 3 turns to align the alignment mark.

➡**The spiral cable will rotate about 3 turns to either the left or the right of the center.**

11. Install the steering wheel onto the shaft and tighten nut to 25 ft. lbs. (34 Nm).

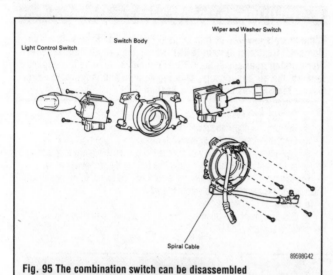

Fig. 95 The combination switch can be disassembled

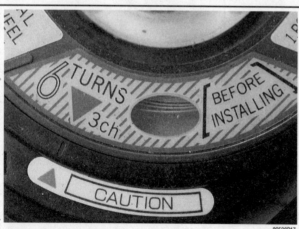

Fig. 96 When installing the turn signal switch, be sure the spiral cable is turned 6 turns

12. Connect the air bag wiring and install the steering pad as outlined.

13. Connect the negative battery cable.

14. Check all combination switch functions for proper operation.

15. Check the steering wheel center point. Have the tires pointed straight ahead, rock the steering wheel gently back and forth with light finger pressure. Freeplay should not be more than 1.18 inch (30mm). If incorrect repair.

Ignition Lock Cylinder

REMOVAL & INSTALLATION

◆ **See Figures 97, 98, 99 and 100**

1. Place the ignition switch in the **LOCK** position. Disconnect the negative battery cable. Wait at least 90 seconds before working on the vehicle to hinder air bag deployment.

✳✳ CAUTION

Some models covered by this manual may be equipped with a Supplemental Restraint System (SRS), which uses an air bag. Whenever working near any of the SRS components, such as the impact sensors, the air bag module, steering column and instrument panel, disable the SRS, as described in Section 6.

2. Disconnect the negative battery cable. Wait at least 90 seconds once the cable has been disconnected before

3. Remove the cover over the lock cylinder.

4. Place the key in the **ACC** position, then push the pin located on the top of the cylinder in and pull.

Fig. 97 Remove the ring around the outside of the lock cylinder

Fig. 98 Place the ignition key in the ACC position, then . . .

Fig. 99 . . . push in the pin located on the top of the cylinder . . .

Fig. 100 . . . and pull the using the key to extract the lock assembly

To install:

5. Insert the lock assembly. Align the pin and the assembly should just slip right into place.

6. Install the ring over the lock cylinder.

7. Test the key movements.

8. Connect the negative battery cable.

Steering Linkage

REMOVAL & INSTALLATION

Tie Rod Ends

▶ See Figures 101 thru 106

1. Loosen the front wheel lug nuts.
2. Raise the front of the vehicle and support the body with safety stands.
3. Remove the front wheels.
4. With a wire brush remove all the dirt and grease from the tie rod end, clamp bolt or lock nut and threads.
5. Remove the cotter pin from the tie rod end and discard.
6. Use white crayon or similar marker to place alignment marks on the tie rods and rack ends.
7. Loosen but do not remove the castellated nut from the tie rod end.
8. Place a suitable puller around the ball of the tie rod end and force the shaft out.
9. Lift the tie rod out of the control arm and inspect the nut threads.
10. Count the number of turns it takes to completely free the tie rod end from the steering rack, this is a good reference for installation of the tie rod to its original position.

To install:

11. Install the lock nut or clamp bolt. Screw the tie rod end onto the rack until the marks on the tie rod are aligned with the marks on the rack. The tie rod ends must be screwed equally on both sides of the rack.

12. Adjust the toe-in.

13. On tie rod ends with clamps, tighten the clamp nut to 14 ft. lbs. (19 Nm). On tie rod ends with lock nuts, tighten the nut to 36 ft. lbs. (49 Nm).

14. Connect the tie rod ends to the steering knuckle arm and tighten the nuts to 36 ft. lbs. (49 Nm). Install a new cotter pin and wrap the prongs firmly around the flats of the nuts.

15. Install the front wheels and lower the vehicle.

Power Steering Gear

REMOVAL & INSTALLATION

▶ See Figures 107 thru 114

➡When disconnecting the intermediate shaft No. 2 during removal of the gear housing, remove the steering wheel and center the spiral cable. If the centering is done without removing the steering wheel, use the procedure below to make the steering wheel firmly fixed in position and make sure it cannot turn.

1. Raise and support the front of the vehicle.
2. Remove the engine under covers.
3. Disconnect the tie rod ends. Refer to the procedure earlier in this section.
4. On some models the oxygen sensor must be removed.
5. Remove the front exhaust pipe.
6. Place the front wheels facing straight ahead.
   a. Using a seat belt from the drivers side, fix the steering wheel so that it does not turn.
   b. Place matchmarks on the No. 2 shaft and control valve shaft.
   c. Loosen bolt A and remove bolt B.
   d. Disconnect the shaft.
7. Loosen the unions from the pressure feed and return tubes.
8. Using an engine support device, support the engine.
9. Disconnect the right and left lower control arms from the ball joints.
10. Separate the two engine mountings, on the front, remove the bolt and nut, on the rear, just remove the bolt.

Fig. 101 Always discard the cotter pin when removed from any component

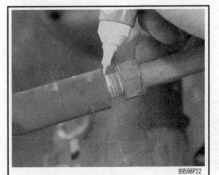

Fig. 102 Place a paint mark on the threads where the tie rod sits on the shaft

Fig. 103 Loosen but do not remove the castellated nut from the tie rod end

Fig. 104 Install a puller around the tie rod end and force the components apart

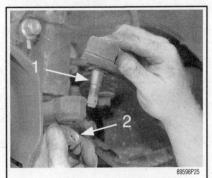

Fig. 105 Tie rod end (1) and castellated nut (2)

Fig. 106 Count the number of turns when removing the tie rod end form the steering shaft

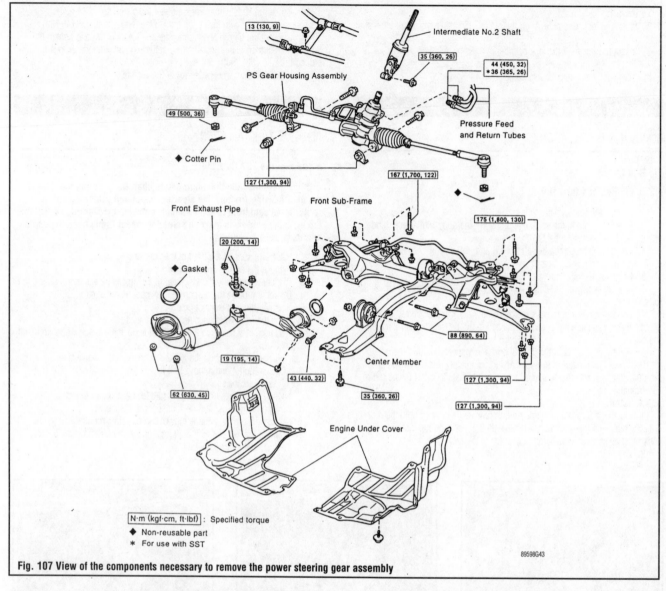

Fig. 107 View of the components necessary to remove the power steering gear assembly

Fig. 108 Retain the steering wheel using the seat belt if it is not removed

11. Unbolt the front sub-frame with the power steering gear assembly and lower it from the vehicle. There should be 10 bolts.

To install:

12. Set the housing assembly so that it matches the dimensions shown in the illustration. The housing assembly at the center point:

- Dimension A—1.20 inch (30.5mm)
- Dimension B—17.78 inch (451.5mm)

  a. Install the housing assembly to the front sub-frame and tighten the bolts and nuts to 94 ft. lbs. (127 Nm).

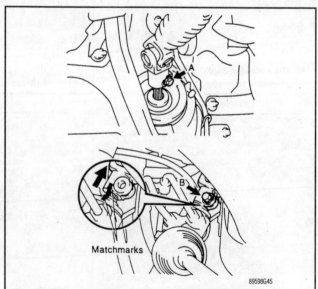

Fig. 109 Place matchmarks on the No. 2 shaft and control valve, then loosen the following bolts

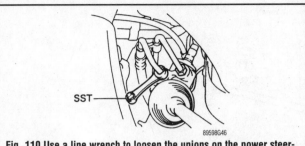

Fig. 110 Use a line wrench to loosen the unions on the power steering lines

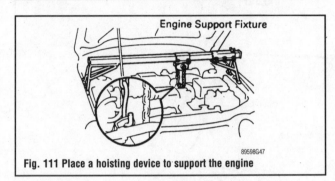

Fig. 111 Place a hoisting device to support the engine

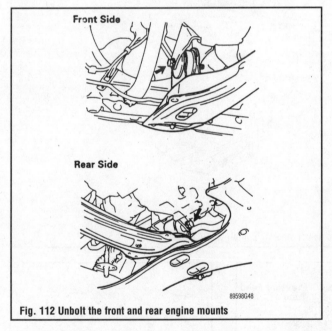

Fig. 112 Unbolt the front and rear engine mounts

13. Attach the pressure feed and return lines. Secure the union nuts to 26 ft. lbs. (36 Nm). Use a fulcrum wrench with the length of 11.81 inch (300mm).

14. Connect the intermediate shaft No. 2. Align the matchmarks on the shaft and control valve shaft, then tighten the bolts to 26 ft. lbs. (35 Nm).

15. If the steering wheel has been removed, or the wheel was moved at all during the operation, always center the spirals cable.

16. Bleed the power steering system.

17. Check the steering wheel center point. Have the tires pointed straight ahead, rock the steering wheel gently back and forth with light finger pressure. Freeplay should not be more than 1.18 inch (30mm). If incorrect repair.

18. Check the toe-in.

Power Steering Pump

REMOVAL & INSTALLATION

5S-FE Engine

♦ See Figures 115, 116, 117, 118 and 119

1. Remove the right side engine undercover.
2. On models with ABS, disconnect the speed sensor wiring harness clamp.
3. Remove the right side driveshaft.
4. Disconnect and labile the two vacuum hoses on the pump. Do not allow fluid to spill on the drive belt.
5. Disconnect the return hose.
6. Remove the drive belt.
7. Remove the 2 tube clamp bracket set bolts on the feed tube.
   a. Remove the tube clamp bracket and grommets from the tube.
   b. Loosen the union and separate the tube from the pump.

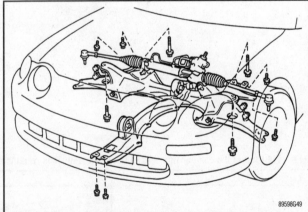

Fig. 113 Remove these 10 bolts to lower the sub-frame and power steering gear assembly

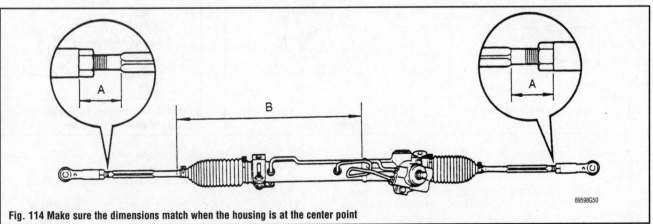

Fig. 114 Make sure the dimensions match when the housing is at the center point

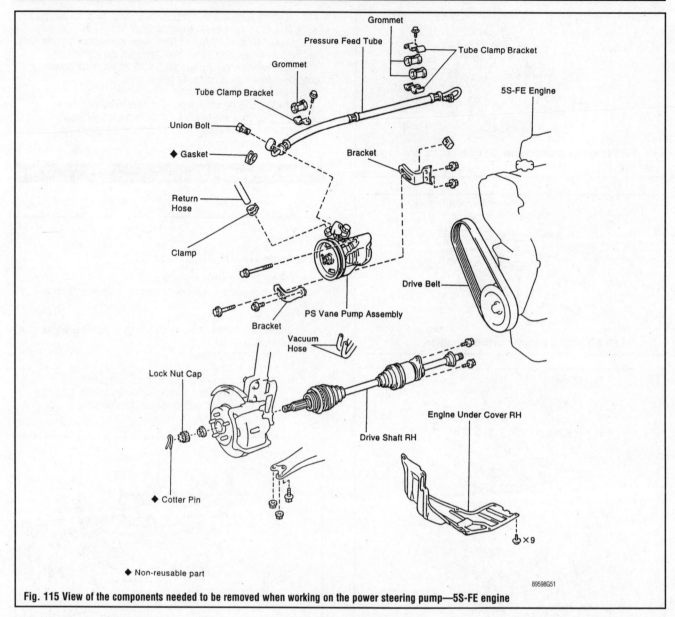

Fig. 115 View of the components needed to be removed when working on the power steering pump—5S-FE engine

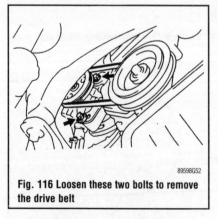

Fig. 116 Loosen these two bolts to remove the drive belt

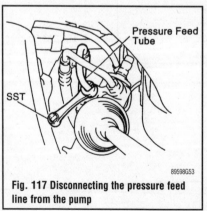

Fig. 117 Disconnecting the pressure feed line from the pump

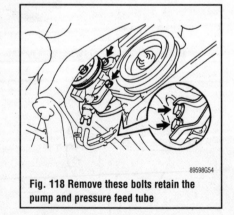

Fig. 118 Remove these bolts retain the pump and pressure feed tube

8. Unbolt the pump and extract the pump with bracket.
9. Remove the pressure feed tube.

To install:

10. Attach the pressure feed tube to the pump, be sure to install the gasket. tighten the union bolt to 38 ft. lbs. (52 Nm). Make sure the stopper of the pressure feed tube is touching the tube, then tighten the bolt.

11. Temporarily install the brackets to the pump and position the assembly on the vehicle. tighten the mounting bolts to 32 ft. lbs. (43 Nm).

12. Install the 3 pressure feed tube clamp brackets and grommets. Tighten the tube clamp bracket set bolts.

13. Using a line wrench, attach the tube and secure. Tighten the union to 26 ft. lbs. (36 Nm).

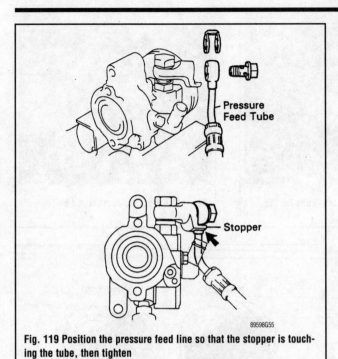

Fig. 119 Position the pressure feed line so that the stopper is touching the tube, then tighten

➥**Use a torque wrench with a fulcrum length of 11.81 inch (300mm). This value is effective in case the tool is parallel to a torque wrench.**

14. Install the drive belt and adjust the tension. Tighten the bolts to 32 ft. lbs. (43 Nm).
15. Connect the return hose and two vacuum hoses.
16. Install the right side driveshaft.
17. If removed, connect the ABS speed sensor harness clamp.
18. Install the engine under cover. Bleed the power steering system.
19. Check the ABS speed sensor signal if equipped.

7A-FE Engine

▶ **See Figures 120, 121, 122 and 123**

1. Remove the right side engine under cover.
2. Disconnect the return and feed tubes. Do not allow the fluid to spill on the drive belt.
3. Label and disconnect the vacuum hoses.
4. Unbolt and remove the power steering pump with the bracket.
5. Remove the bracket from the pump.
6. Install the components in the reverse order of removal. Tighten the 12mm pump bolts to 14 ft. lbs. (19Nm) and the 14mm bolts to 29 ft. lbs. (39 Nm).
7. Attach the pressure feed tube to the pump, be sure to install the gasket. tighten the union bolt to 38 ft. lbs. (52 Nm). Make sure the stopper of the pressure feed tube is touching the tube, then tighten the bolt.
8. Install the drive belt and adjust the tension.
9. Bleed the power steering system.

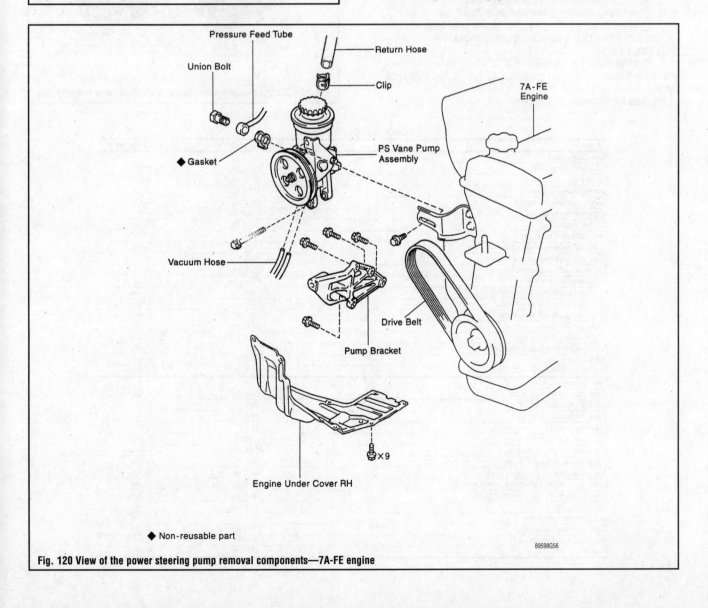

◆ Non-reusable part

Fig. 120 View of the power steering pump removal components—7A-FE engine

Fig. 121 Remove the four bolts on the outside of the power steering pump . . .

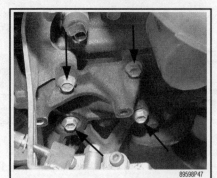

Fig. 122 . . . and the four bolts for the bracket

Fig. 123 Extract the bracket and pulley attached

BLEEDING

▶ **See Figure 124**

1. Inspect the fluid level.
2. Jack the front of the vehicle up and support it on jackstands. Block the rear wheels.
3. Turn the steering wheel slowly from lock to lock several times.
4. Lower the vehicle.
5. Start the engine and run at idle for a few minuets.
6. While the engine is idling, turn the wheel to the left and right full lock and keep it there for about 2–3 seconds, then turn the wheel to the opposite full lock and keep it there for 2–3 seconds. Repeat this several times.
7. Stop the engine.
8. Check for foaming or emulsification. If the system has been bled twice specifically because of foaming or emulsification, check for fluid leaks in the system.
9. Check the fluid level.

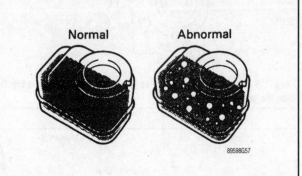

Fig. 124 Check the power steering for emulsification or foaming

TORQUE SPECIFICATIONS

Components	English Specifications	Metric Specifications
Front Suspension:		
Tie rod end locknut (1994)	41 ft. lbs.	56 Nm
Tie rod end locknut (1995-98)	54 ft. lbs.	74 Nm
Steering knuckle-to-shock	113 ft. lbs.	153 Nm
Steering knuckle-to-tie rod end	36 ft. lbs.	49 Nm
ABS speed sensor set bolt	69 inch lbs.	8 Nm
Axle hub-to-driveshaft	159 ft. lbs.	216 Nm
Lower ball joint-to-lower control arm	94 ft. lbs.	127 Nm
Lower ball joint-to-steering knuckle	76 ft. lbs.	103 Nm
Upper strut suspension support-to-body	59 ft. lbs.	80 Nm
Strut piston rod-to-suspension support	35 ft. lbs.	47 Nm
ABS speed sensor-to-strut	48 inch lbs.	5 Nm
Lower control arm-to sub-frame (front)	116 ft. lbs.	157 Nm
Lower control arm-to-sub-frame (rear)	123 ft. lbs.	167 Nm
Center crossmemeber-to-sub-frame	59 ft. lbs.	80 Nm
Front sub-frame center-to-body	94 ft. lbs.	127 Nm
Front sub-frame rear-to-body	130 ft. lbs.	175 Nm
Power steering gear-to-front sub-frame	94 ft. lbs.	127 Nm
Stabilizer bar-to-link	33 ft. lbs.	44 Nm
Stabilizer bar bushing retainer-to-front sub-frame	14 ft. lbs.	19 Nm
Rear Suspension:		
Brake caliper-to-rear axle carrier	34 ft. lbs.	47 Nm
Axle hub with bearing set bolt	59 ft. lbs.	80 Nm
Shock-to-rear axle carrier	188 ft. lbs.	255 Nm
Brake hose-to-shock	14 ft. lbs.	19 Nm
ABS speed sensor set bolt	69 inch lbs.	8 Nm
ABS speed sensor wire-to-shock	48 inch lbs.	5 Nm
Suspension upper support-to-body	29 ft. lbs.	39 Nm
Suspension upper support-to-piston rod	36 ft. lbs.	49 Nm
Lower No. 1 and No. 2 arm-to-suspension member	145 ft. lbs.	197 Nm
Lower No. 1 and No. 2 arm-to-rear axle carrier	145 ft. lbs.	197 Nm
Strut rod-to-body	83 ft. lbs.	113 Nm
Strut rod-to-rear axle carrier	83 ft. lbs.	113 Nm
Suspension member-to-body	101 ft. lbs.	137 Nm
Stabilizer bar bushing retainer	14 ft. lbs.	19 Nm
Stabilizer bar link	33 ft. lbs.	44 Nm

89598C01

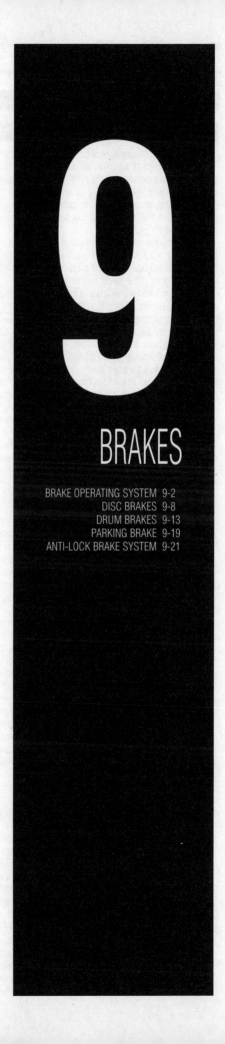

9

BRAKES

BRAKE OPERATING SYSTEM

Basic Operating Principles

Hydraulic systems are used to actuate the brakes of all modern automobiles. The system transports the power required to force the frictional surfaces of the braking system together from the pedal to the individual brake units at each wheel. A hydraulic system is used for two reasons.

First, fluid under pressure can be carried to all parts of an automobile by small pipes and flexible hoses without taking up a significant amount of room or posing routing problems.

Second, a great mechanical advantage can be given to the brake pedal end of the system, and the foot pressure required to actuate the brakes can be reduced by making the surface area of the master cylinder pistons smaller than that of any of the pistons in the wheel cylinders or calipers.

The master cylinder consists of a fluid reservoir along with a double cylinder and piston assembly. Double type master cylinders are designed to separate the front and rear braking systems hydraulically in case of a leak. The master cylinder coverts mechanical motion from the pedal into hydraulic pressure within the lines. This pressure is translated back into mechanical motion at the wheels by either the wheel cylinder (drum brakes) or the caliper (disc brakes).

Steel lines carry the brake fluid to a point on the vehicle's frame near each of the vehicle's wheels. The fluid is then carried to the calipers and wheel cylinders by flexible tubes in order to allow for suspension and steering movements.

In drum brake systems, each wheel cylinder contains two pistons, one at either end, which push outward in opposite directions and force the brake shoe into contact with the drum.

In disc brake systems, the cylinders are part of the calipers. At least one cylinder in each caliper is used to force the brake pads against the disc.

All pistons employ some type of seal, usually made of rubber, to minimize fluid leakage. A rubber dust boot seals the outer end of the cylinder against dust and dirt. The boot fits around the outer end of the piston on disc brake calipers, and around the brake actuating rod on wheel cylinders.

The hydraulic system operates as follows: When at rest, the entire system, from the piston(s) in the master cylinder to those in the wheel cylinders or calipers, is full of brake fluid. Upon application of the brake pedal, fluid trapped in front of the master cylinder piston(s) is forced through the lines to the wheel cylinders. Here, it forces the pistons outward, in the case of drum brakes, and inward toward the disc, in the case of disc brakes. The motion of the pistons is opposed by return springs mounted outside the cylinders in drum brakes, and by spring seals, in disc brakes.

Upon release of the brake pedal, a spring located inside the master cylinder immediately returns the master cylinder pistons to the normal position. The pistons contain check valves and the master cylinder has compensating ports drilled in it. These are uncovered as the pistons reach their normal position. The piston check valves allow fluid to flow toward the wheel cylinders or calipers as the pistons withdraw. Then, as the return springs force the brake pads or shoes into the released position, the excess fluid reservoir through the compensating ports. It is during the time the pedal is in the released position that any fluid that has leaked out of the system will be replaced through the compensating ports.

Dual circuit master cylinders employ two pistons, located one behind the other, in the same cylinder. The primary piston is actuated directly by mechanical linkage from the brake pedal through the power booster. The secondary piston is actuated by fluid trapped between the two pistons. If a leak develops in front of the secondary piston, it moves forward until it bottoms against the front of the master cylinder, and the fluid trapped between the pistons will operate the rear brakes. If the rear brakes develop a leak, the primary piston will move forward until direct contact with the secondary piston takes place, and it will force the secondary piston to actuate the front brakes. In either case, the brake pedal moves farther when the brakes are applied, and less braking power is available.

All dual circuit systems use a switch to warn the driver when only half of the brake system is operational. This switch is usually located in a valve body which is mounted on the firewall or the frame below the master cylinder. A hydraulic piston receives pressure from both circuits, each circuit's pressure being applied to one end of the piston. When the pressures are in balance, the piston remains stationary. When one circuit has a leak, however, the greater pressure in that circuit during application of the brakes will push the piston to one side, closing the switch and activating the brake warning light.

In disc brake systems, this valve body also contains a metering valve and, in some cases, a proportioning valve. The metering valve keeps pressure from traveling to the disc brakes on the front wheels until the brake shoes on the rear wheels have contacted the drums, ensuring that the front brakes will never be used alone. The proportioning valve controls the pressure to the rear brakes to lessen the chance of rear wheel lock-up during very hard braking.

Warning lights may be tested by depressing the brake pedal and holding it while opening one of the wheel cylinder bleeder screws. If this does not cause the light to go on, substitute a new lamp, make continuity checks, and, finally, replace the switch as necessary.

The hydraulic system may be checked for leaks by applying pressure to the pedal gradually and steadily. If the pedal sinks very slowly to the floor, the system has a leak. This is not to be confused with a springy or spongy feel due to the compression of air within the lines. If the system leaks, there will be a gradual change in the position of the pedal with a constant pressure.

Check for leaks along all lines and at wheel cylinders. If no external leaks are apparent, the problem is inside the master cylinder.

DISC BRAKES

Instead of the traditional expanding brakes that press outward against a circular drum, disc brake systems utilize a disc (rotor) with brake pads positioned on either side of it. An easily-seen analogy is the hand brake arrangement on a bicycle. The pads squeeze onto the rim of the bike wheel, slowing its motion. Automobile disc brakes use the identical principle but apply the braking effort to a separate disc instead of the wheel.

The disc (rotor) is a casting, usually equipped with cooling fins between the two braking surfaces. This enables air to circulate between the braking surfaces making them less sensitive to heat buildup and more resistant to fade. Dirt and water do not drastically affect braking action since contaminants are thrown off by the centrifugal action of the rotor or scraped off the by the pads. Also, the equal clamping action of the two brake pads tends to ensure uniform, straight line stops. Disc brakes are inherently self-adjusting. There are three general types of disc brake:

1. A fixed caliper.
2. A floating caliper.
3. A sliding caliper.

The fixed caliper design uses two pistons mounted on either side of the rotor (in each side of the caliper). The caliper is mounted rigidly and does not move.

The sliding and floating designs are quite similar. In fact, these two types are often lumped together. In both designs, the pad on the inside of the rotor is moved into contact with the rotor by hydraulic force. The caliper, which is not held in a fixed position, moves slightly, bringing the outside pad into contact with the rotor. There are various methods of attaching floating calipers. Some pivot at the bottom or top, and some slide on mounting bolts. In any event, the end result is the same.

DRUM BRAKES

Drum brakes employ two brake shoes mounted on a stationary backing plate. These shoes are positioned inside a circular drum which rotates with the wheel assembly. The shoes are held in place by springs. This allows them to slide toward the drums (when they are applied) while keeping the linings and drums in alignment. The shoes are actuated by a wheel cylinder which is mounted at the top of the backing plate. When the brakes are applied, hydraulic pressure forces the wheel cylinder's actuating links outward. Since these links bear directly against the top of the brake shoes, the tops of the shoes are then forced against the inner side of the drum. This action forces the bottoms of the two shoes to contact the brake drum by rotating the entire assembly slightly (known as servo action). When pressure within the wheel cylinder is relaxed, return springs pull the shoes back away from the drum.

Most modern drum brakes are designed to self-adjust themselves during application when the vehicle is moving in reverse. This motion causes both shoes to rotate very slightly with the drum, rocking an adjusting lever, thereby causing rotation of the adjusting screw. Some drum brake systems are designed to self-adjust during application whenever the brakes are applied. This on-board adjustment system reduces the need for maintenance adjustments and keeps both the brake function and pedal feel satisfactory.

POWER BOOSTERS

Virtually all modern vehicles use a vacuum assisted power brake system to multiply the braking force and reduce pedal effort. Since vacuum is always available when the engine is operating, the system is simple and efficient. A vacuum diaphragm is located on the front of the master cylinder and assists the driver in applying the brakes, reducing both the effort and travel he must put into moving the brake pedal.

The vacuum diaphragm housing is normally connected to the intake manifold by a vacuum hose. A check valve is placed at the point where the hose enters the diaphragm housing, so that during periods of low manifold vacuum brakes assist will not be lost.

Depressing the brake pedal closes off the vacuum source and allows atmospheric pressure to enter on one side of the diaphragm. This causes the master cylinder pistons to move and apply the brakes. When the brake pedal is released, vacuum is applied to both sides of the diaphragm and springs return the diaphragm and master cylinder pistons to the released position.

If the vacuum supply fails, the brake pedal rod will contact the end of the master cylinder actuator rod and the system will apply the brakes without any power assistance. The driver will notice that much higher pedal effort is needed to stop the car and that the pedal feels harder than usual.

Vacuum Leak Test

1. Operate the engine at idle without touching the brake pedal for at least one minute.
2. Turn **OFF** the engine and wait one minute.
3. Test for the presence of assist vacuum by depressing the brake pedal and releasing it several times. If vacuum is present in the system, light application will produce less and less pedal travel. If there is no vacuum, air is leaking into the system.

System Operation Test

1. With the engine **OFF**, pump the brake pedal until the supply vacuum is entirely gone.
2. Put light, steady pressure on the brake pedal.
3. Start the engine and let it idle. If the system is operating correctly, the brake pedal should fall toward the floor if the constant pressure is maintained.

Power brake systems may be tested for hydraulic leaks just as ordinary systems are tested.

Brake Light Switch

REMOVAL & INSTALLATION

▶ **See Figure 1**

1. If necessary, remove the lower instrument finish panel and heater to No. 2 register duct.
2. Disconnect the wiring from the stop light switch.
3. Loosen the stop light switch lock nut and remove the assembly.
To install:
4. Position the switch and turn it until it lightly contacts the pedal stopper.
5. Turn the stop light switch back one turn.

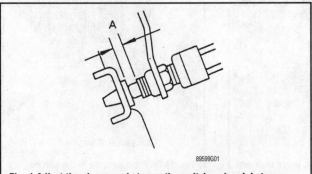

89599G01

Fig. 1 Adjust the clearance between the switch and pedal stopper

6. Adjust the clearance **A** of the switch. This can be done by turning the switch assembly. Clearance between the switch and the brake pedal stopper should be 0.02–0.09 inch (0.5–2.4mm).
7. Tighten the switch lock nut.
8. Attach the wiring to the switch.
9. Install the finish panel and heater duct.
10. Check the operation of the switch. Turn the ignition key to **ON** but do not start the engine. Have an assistant observe the brake lights at the rear while you push lightly on the brake pedal. The lights should come on just as the brake pedal passes the point of free-play.
11. Adjust the switch as necessary to get the correct response from the lights. The small amount of free-play in the pedal should not trigger the brake lights; if the switch is set incorrectly, the brake lights will flicker due to pedal vibration on road bumps.

Master Cylinder

REMOVAL & INSTALLATION

▶ **See Figures 2 thru 16**

✳ WARNING

Clean, high quality brake fluid is essential to the safe and proper operation of the brake system. You should always buy the highest quality brake fluid that is available. If the brake fluid becomes contaminated, drain and flush the system, then refill the master cylinder with new fluid. Never reuse any brake fluid. Any brake fluid that is removed from the system should be discarded.

1. Disconnect the negative battery cable from the battery. Wait at least 90 seconds once the cable is disconnected to perform any work, this will hinder air bag deployment.

✳ CAUTION

Models covered by this manual are equipped with a Supplemental Restraint System (SRS), which uses an air bag. Whenever working near any of the SRS components, such as the impact sensors, the air bag module, steering column and instrument panel, disable the SRS, as described in Section 6.

2. Remove the 2 bolts and 4 nuts holding the upper suspension brace over the master cylinder.
3. Temporarily fasten the strut with the 4 nuts.
4. Remove the air cleaner assembly.
5. On models without ABS, remove the wiring harness clamp.

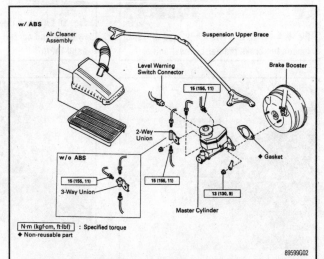

89599G02

Fig. 2 To extract the brake master cylinder, these other components must be removed

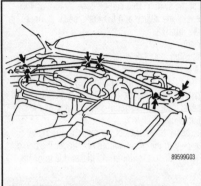

Fig. 3 The suspension upper brace is located above the brake master cylinder

Fig. 4 Unbolt the wiring harness clamp attached to the side of the strut tower

Fig. 5 If equipped, disengage the level warning switch wiring from the master cylinder

Fig. 6 Remove the cap and pull out the strainer to siphon the fluid from the reservoir

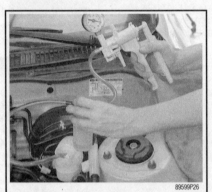

Fig. 7 Use a siphoning device to draw the fluid from the master cylinder reservoir

Fig. 8 The brake master cylinder has several lines attached to it

Fig. 9 A 10mm line wrench is used to loosen the brake master cylinder nuts

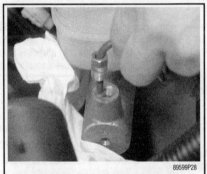

Fig. 10 Lift each line from the master cylinder and carefully put aside. Do not bend them

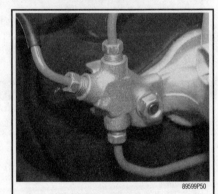

Fig. 11 A union is attached to the one side of the brake master cylinder . . .

Fig. 12 . . . remove the lines from the union if necessary . . .

Fig. 13 . . . and unbolt the union then set aside

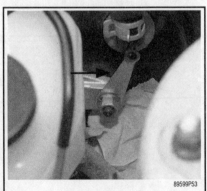

Fig. 14 On the other side of the master cylinder is a small arm to be removed

Fig. 15 Unbolt and lift the master cylinder off the brake booster

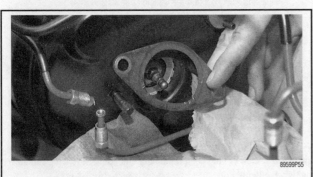
Fig. 16 Extract the gasket and discard

6. If equipped, disconnect the level warning switch connector from the master cylinder.

7. Remove the master cylinder cap and strainer. Next using a syringe, remove the brake fluid from the master cylinder.

➟Do not let brake fluid remain on painted surfaces for very long, wash off immediately.

8. Place paper towels or rags under and around the brake master cylinder to catch any spilt fluid. Using a line wrench, disconnect the brake lines from the master cylinder and union.

9. Remove the master cylinder-to-power booster mounting nuts.

10. Separate the master cylinder and gasket from the power brake unit.

➟It is recommended to discard the old gasket if the unit has never been removed.

To install:

11. Adjust the length of the brake booster push rod as follows:
   a. Install a new gasket on the master cylinder.
   b. Install a vacuum booster push rod depth gage such as (09737–00010) or equivalent, on the master cylinder gasket and lower the pin until its tip slightly touches the piston.
   c. Turn the tool upside down and position it on the brake booster.
   d. Measure the clearance between the booster push rod and the pin head on the depth gage tool.
   e. Clearance should be zero. If not, adjust the booster push rod length until the push rod lightly touches the pin head.

➟When adjusting the push rod, depress the brake pedal so that the push rod sticks out.

12. Remove the tool and install the master cylinder to the brake booster using a new gasket.

13. Install the master cylinder four nuts and tighten the nuts to 9 ft. lbs. (13 Nm).

14. Carefully connect each brake line to its port on the master cylinder. Start each by hand, making sure that the fitting is at 90° to the port before starting to turn it. Once threaded one or two turns by hand, a line wrench may be used to tighten each fitting to 11 ft. lbs. (15 Nm).

15. Connect the level warning switch wiring.

16. Fill the brake reservoir with brake fluid and bleed the brake system.

17. Check and adjust brake pedal.

18. Attach and secure the upper suspension brace.

19. Connect the negative battery cable and rest electrical components such as the radio stations.

20. Test drive the vehicle.

Power Brake Booster

REMOVAL & INSTALLATION

1. Disconnect the negative battery cable. Wait at least 90 seconds once the battery cable is disconnected before working on the vehicle. This will hinder the deployment of the air bags.

2. Loosen the left front wheel lug nuts.

3. Raise and safely support the front of the vehicle securely on jackstands.

4. Remove the left front wheel.

5. Unbolt and remove the master cylinder. Be sure to label all brake lines.

6. Label and disconnect the vacuum hose from the brake booster.

7. Remove the lower pad.

8. Remove the pedal return spring. Do not stretch the spring.

9. Detach the clip and clevis pin from the booster.

10. Unbolt and remove the ignition coil and igniter assembly.

11. Using a line wrench and a spanner, disconnect the brake line from the flexible hose of the left hand brake.

12. Extract the brake line grommet from the body.

13. Unbolt and remove the 3 brake lines from the No. 1 line clamp.

14. From inside the vehicle, remove the 4 nuts and clevis then pull out the brake booster along with gasket.

To install:

15. Position a new gasket on the end of the brake booster and mount on the firewall.

16. Connect the hoses.

17. Install the clevis to the operating rod.

18. Install and tighten the booster nuts to 9 ft. lbs. (13 Nm).

19. Insert the clevis pin into the clevis and brake pedal, then secure the clevis pin with the clip.

20. Engage the pedal return spring.

21. Attach the brake lines to the No. 1 clamp, then tighten to 48 inch lbs. (5 Nm).

22. Insert the brake line grommet to the body.

23. Adjust the length of the brake booster push rod as follows:
   a. Install a new gasket on the master cylinder.
   b. Install a vacuum booster push rod depth gage such as (09737–00010) or equivalent, on the master cylinder gasket and lower the pin until its tip slightly touches the piston.
   c. Turn the tool upside down and position it on the brake booster.
   d. Measure the clearance between the booster push rod and the pin head on the depth gage tool.
   e. Clearance should be zero. If not, adjust the booster push rod length until the push rod lightly touches the pin head.

➟When adjusting the push rod, depress the brake pedal so that the push rod sticks out.

24. Install the brake master cylinder.

25. Connect the vacuum hose to the brake booster.

26. Fill the brake booster reservoir with fluid and bleed the system.

27. Check for leaks.

28. Check and adjust the brake pedal, then tighten the clevis lock nut to 19 ft. lbs. (25 Nm).

29. Perform a system operational test:
   a. Depress the brake pedal several times with the engine **OFF** and check that there is no change in the pedal reserve distance.

b. Depress the brake pedal and start the engine. If the pedal goes down slightly, operation is normal.

Proportioning Valve

A proportioning valve is used to reduce the hydraulic pressure to the rear brakes because of weight transfer during high speed stops. This helps to keep the rear brakes from locking up by improving front to rear brake balance.

REMOVAL & INSTALLATION

➡️**The proportioning valve is located in the center of the firewall under heater hoses.**

1. Disconnect the brake lines from the valve unions.
2. Remove the valve mounting nuts, if used, and remove the valve.

➡️**If the proportioning valve is defective, it must be replaced as an assembly; it cannot be rebuilt.**

To install:
3. Place the valve in line and attach with the mounting nuts.
4. Attach all brake lines to the valve.
5. Bleed the brake system.
6. Test drive the vehicle for proper operation.

Brake Hoses and Pipes

REMOVAL & INSTALLATION

◆ See Figures 17 thru 25

✳️ WARNING

Clean, high quality brake fluid is essential to the safe and proper operation of the brake system. You should always buy the highest quality brake fluid that is available. If the brake fluid becomes contaminated, drain and flush the system, then refill the master cylinder with new fluid. Never reuse any brake fluid. Any brake fluid that is removed from the system should be discarded.

Metal lines and rubber brake hoses should be checked frequently for leaks and external damage. Metal lines are particularly prone to crushing and kinking under the vehicle. Any such deformation can restrict the proper flow of fluid and therefore impair braking at the wheels. Rubber hoses should be checked for cracking or scraping; such damage can create a weak spot in the hose and it could fail under pressure.

Any time the lines are removed or disconnected, extreme cleanliness must be observed. Clean all joints and connections before disassembly (use a stiff bristle brush and clean brake fluid); be sure to plug the lines and ports as soon as they are opened. New lines and hoses should be flushed clean with brake fluid before installation to remove any contamination.

1. Disconnect the negative battery cable.
2. Raise and safely support the vehicle on jackstands.
3. Remove any wheel and tire assemblies necessary for access to the particular line you are removing.
4. Thoroughly clean the surrounding area at the joints to be disconnected.
5. Place a suitable catch pan under the joint to be disconnected.
6. Using two wrenches (one to hold the joint and one to turn the fitting), disconnect the hose or line to be replaced.
7. Disconnect the other end of the line or hose, moving the drain pan if necessary. Always use a back-up wrench to avoid damaging the fitting.
8. Disconnect any retaining clips or brackets holding the line and remove the line from the vehicle.

➡️**If the brake system is to remain open for more time than it takes to swap lines, tape or plug each remaining clip and port to keep contaminants out and fluid in.**

To install:
9. Install the new line or hose, starting with the end farthest from the master cylinder. Connect the other end, then confirm that both fittings are correctly threaded and turn smoothly using finger pressure. Make sure the new line will

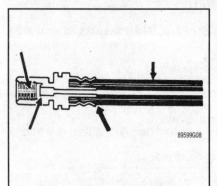
Fig. 17 Inspect the hoses for damage, cracks or swelling, next inspect

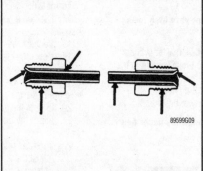
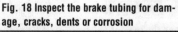
Fig. 18 Inspect the brake tubing for damage, cracks, dents or corrosion

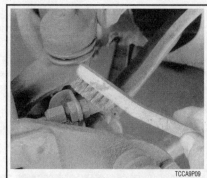
Fig. 19 Use a brush to clean the fittings of any debris

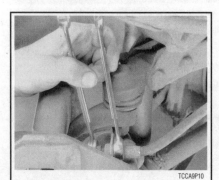
Fig. 20 Use two wrenches to loosen the fitting. If available, use flare nut type wrenches

Fig. 21 Some hoses may have clips that retain them in the mounting brackets

Fig. 22 A bolt may hold the entire hose and line to the rear shock . . .

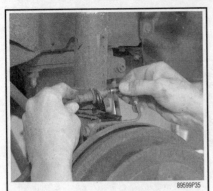

Fig. 23 . . .then the two components may be separated

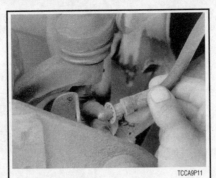

Fig. 24 Any gaskets/crush washers should be replaced with new ones during installation

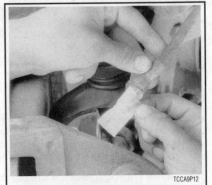

Fig. 25 Tape or plug the line to prevent contamination

not rub against any other part. Brake lines must be at least 1/2 in. (13mm) from the steering column and other moving parts. Any protective shielding or insulators must be reinstalled in the original location.

✳✳ WARNING

Make sure the hose is NOT kinked or touching any part of the frame or suspension after installation. These conditions may cause the hose to fail prematurely.

10. Using two wrenches as before, tighten each fitting.
11. Install any retaining clips or brackets on the lines.
12. If removed, install the wheel and tire assemblies, then carefully lower the vehicle to the ground.
13. Refill the brake master cylinder reservoir with clean, fresh brake fluid, meeting DOT 3 specifications. Properly bleed the brake system.
14. Connect the negative battery cable.

Bleeding the Brake System

✳✳ CAUTION

Brake fluid contains polyglycol ethers and polyglycols. Avoid contact with the eyes and wash your hands thoroughly after handling brake fluid. If you do get brake fluid in your eyes, flush your eyes with clean, running water for 15 minutes. If eye irritation persists, or if you have taken brake fluid internally, IMMEDIATELY seek medical assistance.

On vehicles equipped with anti-lock brakes (ABS), please refer to the appropriate procedure in a later section of this Section.

➡If any maintenance or repairs were performed on the brake system, or if air is suspected in the system, the system must be bled. If the master cylinder has been overhauled or if the fluid reservoir was run dry, start the bleeding procedure with the master cylinder. Otherwise (and after bleeding the master cylinder), start with the wheel cylinder which is farthest from the master cylinder (longest hydraulic line).

✳✳ WARNING

Clean, high quality brake fluid is essential to the safe and proper operation of the brake system. You should always buy the highest quality brake fluid that is available. If the brake fluid becomes contaminated, drain and flush the system, then refill the master cylinder with new fluid. Never reuse any brake fluid. Any brake fluid that is removed from the system should be discarded. Also, do not allow any brake fluid to come in contact with a painted surface; it will damage the paint.

MASTER CYLINDER

◗ See Figures 26, 27 and 28

✳✳ CAUTION

Brake fluid contains polyglycol ethers and polyglycols. Avoid contact with the eyes and wash your hands thoroughly after handling brake fluid. If you do get brake fluid in your eyes, flush your eyes with clean, running water for 15 minutes. If eye irritation persists, or if you have taken brake fluid internally, IMMEDIATELY seek medical assistance.

1. Check the fluid level in the master cylinder reservoir and add fluid as required to bring to the proper level.
2. Disconnect the brake lines from the master cylinder. Place a few shop rags around the master cylinder port holes.
3. Have an assistant depress the brake pedal and hold it in the down position, fluid will spew from the cylinder.

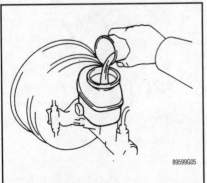

Fig. 26 Add brake fluid to the master cylinder to the full position

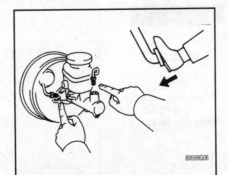

Fig. 27 Once the brake lines are disconnected, have an assistant depress and hold the pedal down

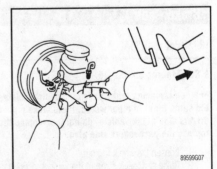

Fig. 28 Place your fingers on the cylinder port holes to keep fluid from spewing out while the pedal is depressed

4. While the pedal is depressed, block the port holes of the master cylinder with your finger.

5. Repeat the procedure three or four times.

6. Bleed the brake system, if needed.

BRAKE SYSTEM

▶ **See Figures 29, 30, 31 and 32**

➡**Start the brake system bleeding procedure on the wheel cylinder that is the furthest away from the master cylinder. To bleed the brakes you will need a supply of brake fluid, a long piece of clear vinyl tubing and a small container that is half full of brake fluid.**

1. Clean all the dirt and grease from the caliper or wheel cylinder bleeder plug and remove the protective cap. Connect one end of a clear vinyl tube to the fitting.

2. Insert the other end of the tube into a jar which is half filled with brake fluid.

3. Have an assistant slowly depress the brake pedal while you open the bleeder plug ⅓ to ½ of a turn. Fluid should run out of the tube. When the pedal is at its full range of travel, close the bleeder plug.

4. Have your assistant slowly pump the brake pedal. Repeat Step 3 until there are no more air bubbles in the fluid.

5. Repeat the procedure for each wheel cylinder. Add brake fluid to the master cylinder reservoir every few pumps, so that it does not completely drain during bleeding.

Fig. 29 Remove the rubber plug from the bleeder screw

Fig. 30 Attach a hose to the bleeder screw and a see-thru container

Fig. 31 Remove the bleeder plug rubber cap, then . . .

Fig. 32 . . . attach a hose with a clear container to the wheel cylinder bleeder and loosen to drain

DISC BRAKES

✳✳ CAUTION

Brake pads or shoes may contain asbestos, which has been determined to be cancer causing agent. Never clean the brake surfaces with compressed air! Avoid inhaling any dust from any brake surface! When cleaning brake surfaces, use a commercially available brake cleaning fluid.

Brake Pads

REMOVAL & INSTALLATION

▶ **See Figures 33 thru 46**

➡**When replacing brake pads on a vehicle, always replace both sides at the same time. In other words, if the brake pads are worn only on the drivers side of the vehicle, do not just replace the drivers side pads, replace the passengers side also.**

1. Loosen the wheel lug nuts.
2. Raise and safely support the vehicle securely on jackstands.
3. Remove the wheel.
4. On front brake pads, temporarily retain the brake disc with a couple of lug nuts.

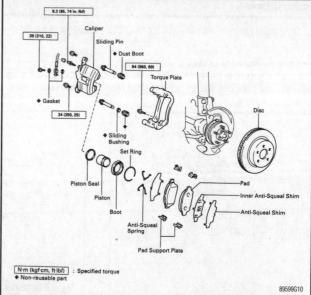

Fig. 33 Exploded view of the front brake pads and related components—7A-FE engine

5. On rear brake pads, remove the brake hose mounting bracket attached to the strut.

6. Siphon a sufficient quantity of brake fluid from the master cylinder reservoir to prevent any brake fluid from overflowing the master cylinder when removing or installing new pads. This is necessary as the piston must be forced into the caliper bore to provide sufficient clearance when installing the pads.

7. Hold the caliper sliding pin on the bottom and loosen the installation bolt.

8. Grasp the caliper from behind and carefully pull it to seat the piston in its bore.

9. On some models it will be necessary to remove the 2 caliper mounting pins (bolts), then remove the caliper assembly. Suspend the caliper with a wire. On other calipers, remove just the lower bolt and lift the caliper up and suspend it from a wire. Do not disconnect the brake line.

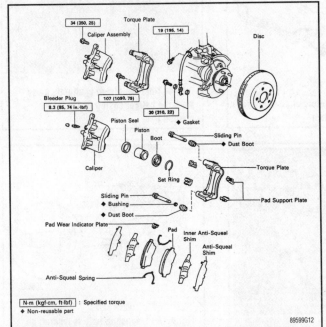

Fig. 34 Exploded view of the front brake pads and related components—5S-FE engine

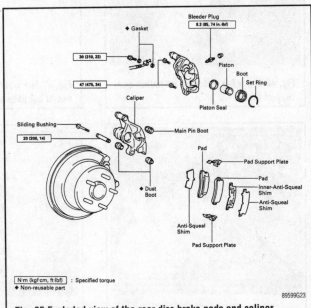

Fig. 35 Exploded view of the rear disc brake pads and caliper assembly

Fig. 36 Using a slim line wrench, loosen the installation bolt and use another wrench to retain the sliding pin

Fig. 37 Once removed, inspect the bolt threads

Fig. 38 Raise the outer portion of the caliper

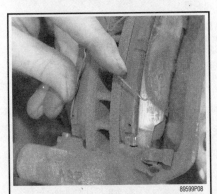

Fig. 39 Unclasp and remove the anti-squeal springs . . .

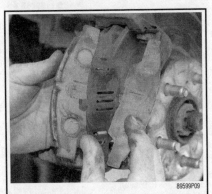

Fig. 40 . . . and slide the brake pads and shims out of the caliper

Fig. 41 Inspect the tabs on the shims, be sure they are in good condition for reuse

Fig. 42 Check the pad wear indicators and support plates

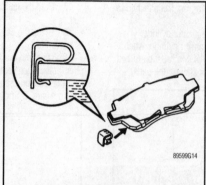

Fig. 43 The wear indicators slide over the end of the pads as shown

Fig. 44 Note the piston is slightly away from the caliper casing and must be pushed in

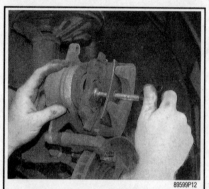

Fig. 45 Seat the piston back into its bore using a clamp

Fig. 46 Now the piston is flush with the caliper case

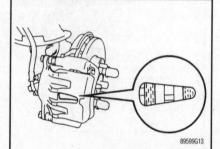

Fig. 47 An inspection hole is located on the side of the caliper to check brake pad lining thickness

10. Slide out the old brake pads along with any anti-squeal shims, springs, pad wear indicators and pad support plates. Make sure to note the position of all assorted pad hardware.

To install:

11. Check the brake disc (rotor) for thickness and run-out. Inspect the caliper and piston assembly for breaks, cracks, fluid seepage or other damage. Overhaul or replace as necessary.

12. Install the pad support plates into the torque plate.

13. Install the pad wear indicators onto the pads. Be sure the arrow on the indicator plate is pointing in the direction of rotation.

14. Apply brake grease to both sides of the inner anti squeal shim. Install the anti-squeal shims on the outside of each pad and then install the pad assemblies into the torque plate.

➡**There should be no grease or oil adhering to the friction surfaces of the pads or disc.**

15. Position the caliper back down over the pads. If it won't fit, use a C-clamp or hammer handle and carefully force the piston into its bore.

16. Install the caliper over the brake disc.

17. Hold the sliding pin and tighten the installation bolt on the front to 25 ft. lbs. (34 Nm) and rear to 14 ft. lbs. (20 Nm.).

18. Attach the rear brake hose bracket and tighten the bolt to 22 ft. lbs. (30 Nm).

19. Install the wheels and lower the vehicle. Check the brake fluid level. Before moving the vehicle, make sure to pump the brake pedal to seat the pads against the rotors.

INSPECTION

▶ **See Figure 47**

If you hear a squealing noise coming from the brakes while driving, check the brake lining thickness and pad wear indicator by looking into the inspection hole on the brake cylinder with the wheels removed and the vehicle properly supported. The wear indicator is designed to emit the squealing noise when the brake pad wears down to 2.5mm at which time the pad wear plate and the rotor disc rub against each other. If there are traces of the pad wear indicator contacting the rotor disc, the brake pads should be replaced.

To inspect the brake lining thickness, look through the inspection hole and measure the lining thickness using a machinists rule. Also looks for signs of uneven wear. Standard thickness is 10mm. The **minimum** allowable thickness is 0.039 inch. (1mm) at which time the brake pads must be replaced.

➡**Always replace the pads on both wheels. When inspecting or replacing the brake pads, check the surface of the disc rotors for scoring, wear and runout. The rotors should be resurfaced if badly scored or replaced if badly worn.**

Brake Caliper

REMOVAL & INSTALLATION

▶ **See Figures 48, 49 and 50**

1. Loosen the wheel lug nuts slightly.
2. Raise and support the vehicle safely.
3. Remove the wheels.
4. Disconnect the brake hose from the caliper. Plug the end of the hose to prevent loss of fluid. Some brake lines have a union bolt and gasket type line attached to the caliper. Do not loose the washers.

➡**Have a container handy to catch brake fluid from the disconnected lines.**

5. Hold the sliding pin and remove the bolts that attach the caliper to the torque plate.
6. With two hands, lift up and remove the caliper assembly.

To install:

7. Grease the caliper pins and bolts with Lithium grease or equivalent. Temporarily install the caliper on the torque plate with the installation bolts.

8. Hold the sliding pin and tighten the installation bolts to 25 ft. lbs. (34 Nm) on the front wheels, and 14 ft. lbs. (20 Nm) in the rear.

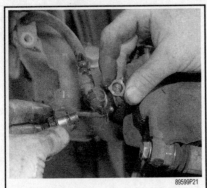

Fig. 48 Remove the brake hose union bolt with gaskets from the caliper

Fig. 49 Remove the two bolts that attach the caliper to the backing plate

Fig. 50 The sliding pins should be greased with Lithium before installation

9. Attach the flexible brake hose to the caliper with new gaskets. Tighten the hose to 22 ft. lbs. (30 Nm).

➡Install the brake hose lock securely in the lock hole, in the caliper.

10. Fill and bleed the system.
11. Install the wheel, lower the vehicle and tighten the lug nuts.
12. Before moving the vehicle, make sure to pump the brake pedal to seat the pads against the rotors.
13. Check for leaks.

OVERHAUL

♦ See Figures 51 thru 58

➡Some vehicles may be equipped dual piston calipers. The procedure to overhaul the caliper is essentially the same with the exception of multiple pistons, O-rings and dust boots.

1. Remove the caliper from the vehicle and place on a clean workbench.

✳✳ CAUTION

NEVER place your fingers in front of the pistons in an attempt to catch or protect the pistons when applying compressed air. This could result in personal injury!

➡Depending upon the vehicle, there are two different ways to remove the piston from the caliper. Refer to the brake pad replacement procedure to make sure you have the correct procedure for your vehicle.

2. The first method is as follows:
a. Stuff a shop towel or a block of wood into the caliper to catch the piston.
b. Remove the caliper piston using compressed air applied into the caliper inlet hole. Inspect the piston for scoring, nicks, corrosion and/or

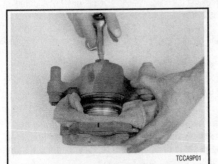

Fig. 51 For some types of calipers, use compressed air to drive the piston out of the caliper, but make sure to keep your fingers clear

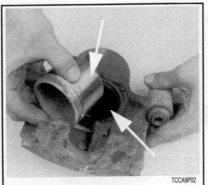

Fig. 52 Withdraw the piston from the caliper bore

Fig. 53 On some vehicles, you must remove the anti-rattle clip

Fig. 54 Use a prytool to carefully pry around the edge of the boot . . .

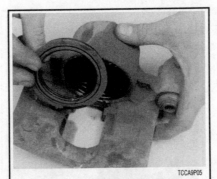

Fig. 55 . . . then remove the boot from the caliper housing, taking care not to score or damage the bore

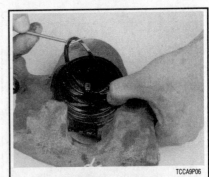

Fig. 56 Use extreme caution when removing the piston seal; DO NOT scratch the caliper bore

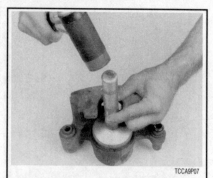

Fig. 57 Use the proper size driving tool and a mallet to properly seal the boots in the caliper housing

TCCA9P07

Fig. 58 There are tools, such as this Mighty-Vac, available to assist in proper brake system bleeding

TCCA9P08

Fig. 59 Place two bolts in the threaded area to retain the rotor to the hub

89599P17

worn or damaged chrome plating. The piston must be replaced if any of these conditions are found.

3. For the second method, you must rotate the piston to retract it from the caliper.

4. If equipped, remove the anti-rattle clip.

5. Use a prytool to remove the caliper boot, being careful not to scratch the housing bore.

6. Remove the piston seals from the groove in the caliper bore.

7. Carefully loosen the brake bleeder valve cap and valve from the caliper housing.

8. Inspect the caliper bores, pistons and mounting threads for scoring or excessive wear.

9. Use crocus cloth to polish out light corrosion from the piston and bore.

10. Clean all parts with denatured alcohol and dry with compressed air.

To assemble:

11. Lubricate and install the bleeder valve and cap.

12. Install the new seals into the caliper bore grooves, making sure they are not twisted.

13. Lubricate the piston bore.

14. Install the pistons and boots into the bores of the calipers and push to the bottom of the bores.

15. Use a suitable driving tool to seat the boots in the housing.

16. Install the caliper in the vehicle.

17. Install the wheel and tire assembly, then carefully lower the vehicle.

18. Properly bleed the brake system.

Brake Disc (Rotor)

REMOVAL & INSTALLATION

▶ **See Figures 59, 60, 61 and 62**

1. Loosen the wheel lugs, then raise and safely support the of the car. Remove the wheel(s) and temporarily attach the rotor disc with two bolts.

➡ **There are two spots to place bolts for retaining the rotor to the hub.**

2. Remove the caliper from the rotor and suspend on wire from the coil spring.

3. Remove the two wheel bolts and pull the disc from the axle hub.

To install:

4. Place the rotor into position and retain with the two bolts.

5. Attach the caliper to the rotor.

6. Remove the bolts from the rotor and install the wheel.

7. Hand tighten the lug nuts, lower the vehicle and tighten the lug nuts.

INSPECTION

Front

▶ **See Figure 63**

Examine the disc. If it is worn, warped or scored, it must be replaced. Check the thickness of the disc against the specifications given in the Disc and Pad Specifications chart. If it is below specifications, replace it. Use a micrometer to measure the thickness.

The disc run-out should be measured before the disc is removed and again, after the disc is installed. Use a dial indicator mounted on a magnet type stand (attached to the shock absorber shaft) to determine runout. Position the dial so the stylus is 0.394 inch (10mm) from the outer edge of the rotor disc. The maximum allowable runout is 0.05 inch (0.20mm). If runout exceeds the specification, replace the disc.

➡ **Be sure that the wheel bearing nut is properly tightened. If it is not, an inaccurate run-out reading may be obtained. If different run-out readings are obtained with the same disc, between removal and installation, this is probably the cause.**

Rear

Examine the disc. If it is worn, warped or scored, it must be replaced. Check the thickness of the disc against the specifications given in the Disc and Pad

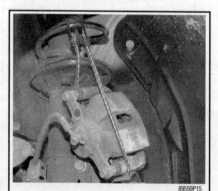

Fig. 60 Once removed, support the caliper on the coil spring with bungie cords or wire

89599P15

Fig. 61 Remove the two bolts in the rotor . . .

89599P16

Fig. 62 . . . and pull the rotor off with two hands, it may be heavy

89599P18

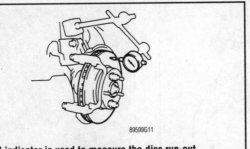

Fig. 63 A dial indicator is used to measure the disc run-out

Specifications chart. If it is below specifications, replace it. Use a micrometer to measure the thickness.

The disc run-out should be measured before the disc is removed and again, after the disc is installed. Use a dial indicator mounted on a magnet type stand (attached to the shock absorber shaft) to determine runout. Position the dial so the stylus is 0.394 inch (10mm) from the outer edge of the rotor disc. The maximum allowable runout 0.0059 inch (0.15mm). If the runout exceeds the specification, replace the disc.

DRUM BRAKES

✳✳ CAUTION

Brake pads or shoes may contain asbestos, which has been determined to be cancer causing agent. Never clean the brake surfaces with compressed air! Avoid inhaling any dust from any brake surface! When cleaning brake surfaces, use a commercially available brake cleaning fluid.

Brake Drums

➡ When servicing drum brakes, only dissemble and assemble one side at a time, leaving the remaining side intact for reference.

REMOVAL & INSTALLATION

◗ **See Figures 64, 65, 66, 67 and 68**

1. Loosen the rear wheel lug nuts slightly. Release the parking brake.
2. Block the front wheels, raise the rear of the car, and safely support it with jackstands.
3. Remove the lug nuts and the wheel.
4. One way to remove the drum is to tap the drum lightly with a mallet to free the drum if resistance is felt. Sometimes brake drums are stubborn. If the drum is difficult to remove, perform the following:

   a. Insert the end of a bent wire (a coat hanger will do nicely) through the hole in the brake drum and hold the automatic adjusting lever away from the adjuster.

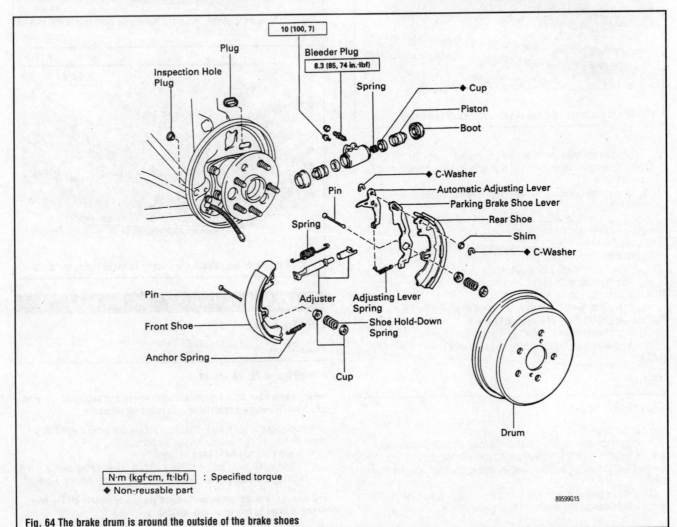

N·m (kgf·cm, ft·lbf) : Specified torque
◆ Non-reusable part

Fig. 64 The brake drum is around the outside of the brake shoes

Fig. 65 Access the shoe adjustment through this hole in the backing plate

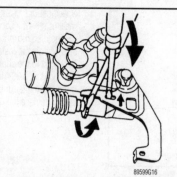

Fig. 66 Insert a bent wire or brake tool through the hole in the drum and hold the adjuster lever away from the lever

Fig. 67 Insert two bolts and tighten them down till a popping noise is heard

Fig. 68 Lift the drum off using two hands, they can be heavy

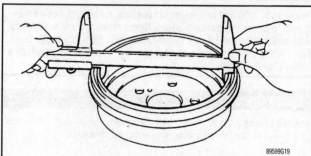

Fig. 69 Using an H-gauge, measure the inside diameter of the brake drum

Fig. 70 The drum specification is usually stamped inside the drum

  b. Reduce the brake shoe adjustment by turning the adjuster bolt with a brake adjuster tool. The drum should now be loose enough to remove without much effort.

  5. Another way to remove the brake drum is to insert a bolt in each of the two holes in the drum.

  a. Tighten the bolts down, a popping sound should be heard, this is the drum separating from the backing plate.

  b. Pull the drum from the backing plate.

To install:

  6. Clean the drum and inspect it as detailed in this Section.

  7. Hold the brake drum so that the hole on the drum is aligned with the large hole on the axle carrier and install the drum.

  8. If the adjuster was loosened to remove the drum, turn the adjuster bolt to adjust the length to the shortest possible amount.

  9. Install the rear wheels, tighten the lug nuts and lower the vehicle.

  10. Retighten the lug nuts and pump the brake pedal before moving the vehicle.

INSPECTION

♦ See Figures 69 and 70

  1. Clean the drum.

  2. Inspect the drum for scoring, cracks, grooves and out-of-roundness. Replace the drum or have it "turned" at a machine or brake specialist shop, as required. Light scoring may be removed by dressing the drum with fine emery cloth.

  3. Measure the inside diameter of the drum. A tool called a H-gauge caliper is used. See the Brake Specifications chart for your vehicle.

Brake Shoes

♦ See Figure 71

INSPECTION

♦ See Figures 72, 73 and 74

➡When servicing drum brakes, only dissemble and assemble one side at a time, leaving the remaining side intact for reference.

  A hole is located in the back of the back plate under and inspection plug, check the shoe lining thickness through the hole.

  1. Inspect all parts for rust and damage.

  2. Measure the lining thickness. The minimum allowable thickness is 0.039 inch (1.0mm). If the lining does not meet the minimum specification, replace it.

➡If one of the brake shoes needs to be replaced, replace all the rear shoes in order to maintain even braking.

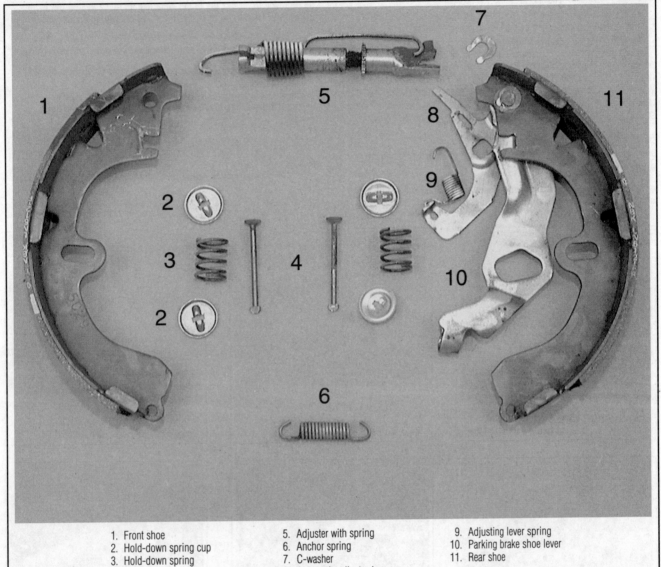

1. Front shoe
2. Hold-down spring cup
3. Hold-down spring
4. Pin

5. Adjuster with spring
6. Anchor spring
7. C-washer
8. Automatic adjuster lever

9. Adjusting lever spring
10. Parking brake shoe lever
11. Rear shoe

89599P29

Fig. 71 Exploded view of the common rear brake shoe components

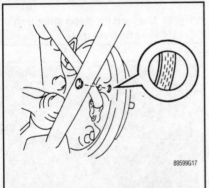

89599G17

Fig. 72 Remove the inspection plug to check the brake shoe lining thickness

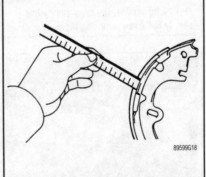

89599G18

Fig. 73 Using a ruler, measure the shoe lining thickness

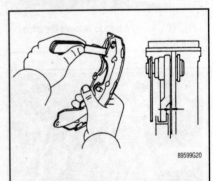

89599G20

Fig. 74 A feeler gauge is used to measure the clearance between the brake shoe and lever

3. Measure inside diameter of the drum as detailed in this Section.

4. Place the shoe into the drum and check that the lining is in proper contact with the drum's surface. If the contact is improper, repair the lining with a brake shoe grinder or replace the shoe.

5. To measure the clearance between brake shoe and parking brake lever, temporarily install the parking brake and automatic adjusting levers onto the rear shoe, using a new C-washer/shim. Replace the shim with the correct size, check the chart. With a feeler gauge, measure the clearance between the shoe and the lever. The clearance should be 0.0138 inch (0.35mm). If the clearance is not as specified, use a shim to adjust it. When the clearance is correct, stake the C-washer with pliers.

REMOVAL & INSTALLATION

◆ **See Figures 75 thru 85**

➡ **When servicing drum brakes, only dissemble and assemble one side at a time, leaving the remaining side intact for reference. The hub can** be removed to access the brake components much easier, but is not necessary. The hub has been removed for photographic reasons.

1. Loosen the rear wheel lug nuts slightly. Release the parking brake.
2. Block the front wheels, raise the rear of the vehicle, and safely support it with jackstands.
3. Remove the wheel lug nuts and the wheel.
4. Remove the brake drum.

➡**Do not depress the brake pedal once the brake drum has been removed.**

5. Carefully unhook the return spring from the leading (front) brake shoe.
6. Press the hold-down spring retainer in and turn the pin on the front brake shoe.
7. Remove the hold-down spring, retainers and the pin for the front brake shoe.
8. Pull out the brake shoe and unhook the anchor spring from the lower edge.

Fig. 75 Overall view of the brake shoe components attached to the backing plate

Fig. 76 Using a special brake spring tool, remove the return spring from the front brake shoe

Fig. 77 Insert the brake tool into the grooves of the hold-down retainer . . .

Fig. 78 . . . and turn to remove the cups and spring

Fig. 79 Be careful, the cups and spring can fly out when removing them

Fig. 80 Disconnect the anchor spring from the bottom of the brake shoes

Fig. 81 Use needle-nose pliers to remove the spring over the adjuster

Fig. 82 Separate the parking brake cable from the rear shoe using a flat bladed tool

Fig. 83 Sometimes the rear shoe will have a portion of the adjuster attached to it, simply remove it afterwards

Fig. 84 Pull the parking brake lever all the way up until a clicking sound is no longer heard when checking the adjuster mechanism

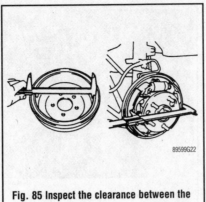

Fig. 85 Inspect the clearance between the brake shoes and drum using a caliper tool

Fig. 86 Loosen the brake line attached to the wheel cylinder from behind

9. Remove the hold-down spring, cups and pin from the trailing (rear) shoe. Pull the shoe out with the adjuster, automatic adjuster assembly and springs attached. Disconnect the parking brake cable. Remove the tension/return and anchor springs from the rear shoe.

10. Remove the c-washer, automatic adjusting lever, other c-washer, then extract the adjusting lever and parking brake lever from he rear shoe.

To install:

11. Inspect the shoes for signs of unusual wear or scoring.

12. Check the wheel cylinder for any sign of fluid seepage or frozen pistons.

13. Clean and inspect the brake backing plate and all other components. Check that the brake drum inner diameter is within specified limits. Lubricate the backing plate at the positions the brakes come in contact with the backing plate. Also lubricate the anchor plate.

14. Mount the automatic adjuster assembly onto a new rear brake shoe.

15. Using pliers, connect the parking brake cable to the lever, then set the adjuster and return spring. Install the adjusting lever spring. Position the rear shoe so the lower end rides in the anchor plate and the upper end is against the boot of the wheel cylinder.

16. Install the pin and the hold-down spring. Press the retainer down over the pin and rotate the pin so the crimped edge is held by the retainer.

➡ **Do not allow oil or grease to get on the rubbing face.**

17. Place the front brake into position and install the anchor spring between the front and rear shoes. Stretch the spring enough so the front shoe will fit as the rear did. Install the hold-down spring, pin and retainer to the front brake shoe.

18. Connect the return spring to the front brake shoe.

19. Check the operation of the automatic adjuster mechanism:
   a. Apply the parking brake lever and verifying the adjusting bolt turns.
   b. Adjust the strut to where it is the shortest possible length.
   c. Install the brake drum.
   d. Apply the parking brake lever until the clicking sound can no longer be heard.

20. Check the clearance between the brake shoes and drum:
   a. Remove the brake drum.
   b. Measure the brake drum inside diameter and diameter of the brake shoes. The difference is "Shoe-to-drum clearance" and should be approximately 0.024 inch (0.6mm). If incorrect, check the parking brake system.

➡ **A special brake caliper tool is required to gauge the brake drum inside diameter and "Shoe-to-drum clearance". However it is not required to perform brake shoe adjustment.**

21. Install the brake drum.

22. Adjust the brake pedal until a slight drag is felt when the drum is spun by hand.

23. Pull the parking lever all the way up until a clicking sound can no longer be heard. Check the clearance between brake shoes and brake drum.

24. Install the rear wheels, tighten the wheel lug nuts and lower the vehicle.

25. Retighten the wheel lug nuts and pump the brake pedal a few times before moving the vehicle. Adjust the rear brakes again if necessary.

26. Check the level of brake fluid in the master cylinder, then perform a test drive.

ADJUSTMENTS

All models are equipped with self-adjusting rear drum brakes. Under normal conditions, adjustment of the rear brake shoes should not be necessary. However, if an initial adjustment is required insert the blade of a brake adjuster tool or a screw driver into the hole in the brake drum and turn the adjuster slowly. The tension is set correctly if the tire and wheel assembly will rotate approximately 3 times when spun with moderate force. Do not over adjust the brake shoes. Before adjusting the rear drum brake shoes, make sure emergency brake is in the OFF position, and all cables are free.

Wheel Cylinders

✳✳ WARNING

Clean, high quality brake fluid is essential to the safe and proper operation of the brake system. You should always buy the highest quality brake fluid that is available. If the brake fluid becomes contaminated, drain and flush the system, then refill the master cylinder with new fluid. Never reuse any brake fluid. Any brake fluid that is removed from the system should be discarded.

REMOVAL & INSTALLATION

▶ **See Figures 86, 87 and 88**

1. Plug the master cylinder inlet to prevent hydraulic fluid from leaking. Raise and safely support the vehicle.

✳✳ CAUTION

Brake fluid contains polyglycol ethers and polyglycols. Avoid contact with the eyes and wash your hands thoroughly after handling brake fluid. If you do get brake fluid in your eyes, flush your eyes with clean, running water for 15 minutes. If eye irritation persists, or if you have taken brake fluid internally, IMMEDIATELY seek medical assistance.

2. Remove the brake drums and shoes.

3. Working from behind the backing plate, disconnect the hydraulic line from the wheel cylinder.

4. Unfasten the screws retaining the wheel cylinder and withdraw the cylinder.

To install:

5. Attach the wheel cylinder to the backing plate. Tighten the bolts to 7 ft. lbs. (10 Nm).

6. Connect the hydraulic line to the wheel cylinder and tighten it.

7. Install the brake shoes and drums. Make all the necessary adjustments.

8. Fill the master cylinder to the proper level with clean brake fluid bleed the brake system. Check the brake system for leaks.

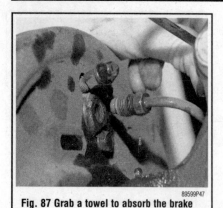

Fig. 87 Grab a towel to absorb the brake fluid

Fig. 88 Remove the screws and pull out the wheel cylinder

Fig. 89 Remove the outer boots from the wheel cylinder

OVERHAUL

▶ See Figures 89 thru 98

Wheel cylinder overhaul kits may be available, but often at little or no savings over a reconditioned wheel cylinder. It often makes sense with these components to substitute a new or reconditioned part instead of attempting an overhaul.

If no replacement is available, or you would prefer to overhaul your wheel cylinders, the following procedure may be used. When rebuilding and installing wheel cylinders, avoid getting any contaminants into the system. Always use clean, new, high quality brake fluid. If dirty or improper fluid has been used, it will be necessary to drain the entire system, flush the system with proper brake fluid, replace all rubber components, then refill and bleed the system.

1. Remove the wheel cylinder from the vehicle and place on a clean workbench.

2. First remove and discard the old rubber boots, then withdraw the pistons. Piston cylinders are equipped with seals and a spring assembly, all located behind the pistons in the cylinder bore.

3. Remove the remaining inner components, seals and spring assembly. Compressed air may be useful in removing these components. If no compressed air is available, be VERY careful not to score the wheel cylinder bore when removing parts from it. Discard all components for which replacements were supplied in the rebuild kit.

4. Wash the cylinder and metal parts in denatured alcohol or clean brake fluid.

❊❊ WARNING

Never use a mineral-based solvent such as gasoline, kerosene or paint thinner for cleaning purposes. These solvents will swell rubber components and quickly deteriorate them.

5. Allow the parts to air dry or use compressed air. Do not use rags for cleaning, since lint will remain in the cylinder bore.

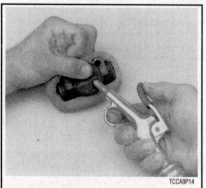

Fig. 90 Compressed air can be used to remove the pistons and seals

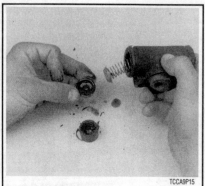

Fig. 91 Remove the pistons, cup seals and spring from the cylinder

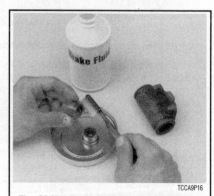

Fig. 92 Use brake fluid and a soft brush to clean the pistons . . .

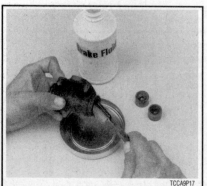

Fig. 93 . . . and the bore of the wheel cylinder

Fig. 94 Once cleaned and inspected, the wheel cylinder is ready for assembly

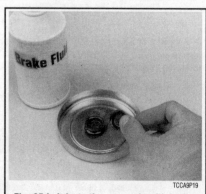

Fig. 95 Lubricate the cup seals with brake fluid

Fig. 96 Install the spring, then the cup seals in the bore

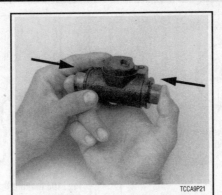

Fig. 97 Lightly lubricate the pistons, then install them

Fig. 98 The boots can now be installed over the wheel cylinder ends

6. Inspect the piston and replace it if it shows scratches.
7. Lubricate the cylinder bore and seals using clean brake fluid.
8. Position the spring assembly.
9. Install the inner seals, then the pistons.

10. Insert the new boots into the counterbores by hand. Do not lubricate the boots.
11. Install the wheel cylinder.

PARKING BRAKE

Cable(s)

REMOVAL & INSTALLATION

▶ See Figure 99

1. Loosen the rear wheel lugnuts on the side of the vehicle you are performing work on.
2. Raise and support the rear of the vehicle. Remove the wheel.
3. Remove the rear caliper assembly.
4. Pull off the rear brake disc.
5. Remove the parking brake shoes.

6. Using pliers, disconnect the parking brake cable form the parking brake shoe lever.
To install:
7. Connect the parking brake cable to the parking brake shoe lever of the rear shoe.
8. Install the parking brake shoes.
9. Install the rear brake disc. Adjust the parking brake shoe clearance.
10. Attach the rear caliper assembly.
11. Install the wheel, lower the vehicle and settle the parking brake shoes and disc.
12. Recheck and adjust the parking brake lever.

ADJUSTMENT

▶ See Figures 100 and 101

Adjusting the parking brake cables can be done from inside the vehicle.
1. Pull the parking brake lever all the way up and count the number of clicks. The correct number of clicks should be 4–7.

➡Before adjusting the parking brake, make sure the rear shoe clearance has been adjusted. for shoe clearance adjustment, refer to the procedure later in this section.

2. Remove the console box.
3. Loosen the locknut and turn the adjusting nut until the lever travel is correct.
4. Tighten the locknut to 48 inch lbs. (5 Nm).
5. Install the console box.

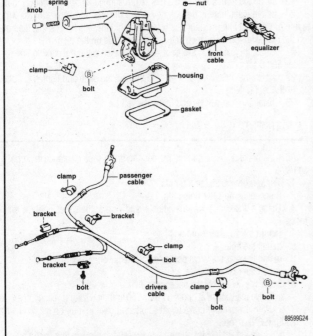

Fig. 99 The parking lever controls all three parking cables

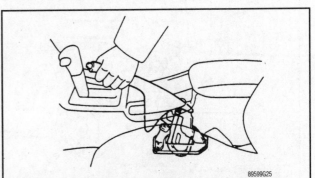

Fig. 100 Pull the parking brake lever all the way and count the clicks

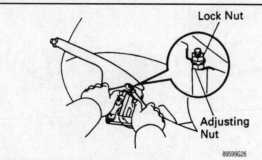

Fig. 101 Loosen the locknut and tune the adjusting nut until the lever travel is correct

Brake Shoes

REMOVAL & INSTALLATION

▶ See Figures 102 and 103

1. Remove the rear wheels.
2. Place matchmarks on the axle hub and disc, then pull the disc from the hub.
3. If necessary, turn the shoe adjuster until the wheel turns freely.
4. Using a pair of needle-nose pliers, remove the shoe return springs.
5. Slide the shoe strut with spring form the brake adjustment.
6. Slide the front shoe and remove the adjuster. Disconnect the tension spring and remove the front shoe.
7. Slide the rear shoe out, then remove the tension spring from the shoe.
   a. Disconnect the parking brake cable from the parking brake shoe lever.
   b. Using a suitable spring tool, remove the hold-down spring cups, springs and pins.
8. Inspect all disassembled parts for wear, rust or damage.
9. Using a scale, measure the thickness of the brake shoe lining. Standard thickness is 0.079 inch (2.0mm) and minimum thickness is 0.039 inch (1.0mm). If the lining thickness is at the minimum thickness or less, or if there is uneven wear of the shoes, replace the brake shoes.
10. Using a vernier caliper, measure the inside diameter of the disc. Standard inside diameter is 6.69 inch (170.0mm) and maximum inside diameter is 6.73 inch (171.0mm). Replace the brake disc if the inside diameter is at the maximum value or more. Replace the disc or grind it with a lathe if the disc is scored or worn unevenly.
11. To inspect the parking brake lining or disc for correct contact, apply chalk to the inside of the disc. Grind down the brake shoe lining to fit. If the contact between the disc and brake shoe lining is incorrect, repair it using a brake shoe grinder or replace the shoe assemblies.
12. Measure the distance between the parking brake shoe and lever. Using a feeler gage, measure the clearance. Standard is 0.0138 inch (0.35mm). If the

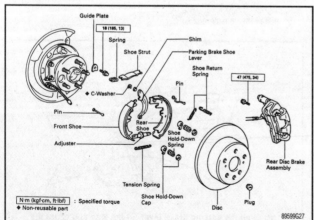

Fig. 102 Parking brake shoes are only equipped on models with rear disc brakes

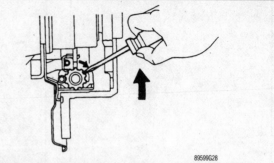

Fig. 103 Moving the wheel adjuster to separate the parking brake shoes from the disc

clearance is not within specifications, replace the shim, with one of the correct size. Check your local parts wholesaler or dealer for the correct shim. Shims usually come in these sizes:
- 0.012 inch (0.3mm)
- 0.024 inch (0.6mm)
- 0.035 inch (0.9mm)

13. If replacing the shim is necessary, removed the parking brake lever and install the correct size shim. Install the parking brake shoe lever with a new c-washer. Remeasure the clearance.
14. Lubricate all shoe sliding surfaces of the backing plate and the threads and head of the adjuster with a high temperature Lithium grease or equivalent.
15. Connect the parking brake cable to the to the rear shoe lever. Install the shoe hold down springs, cups and pins.
16. Slide the rear shoe in between the hold down spring cup and the backing plate.

✷✷ CAUTION

Do not allow the brake shoe rubbing surface to come in contact with the grease on the backing plate.

17. Hook the one end of the tension spring to the rear shoe and connect the front shoe to the other end of the spring. Install the adjuster between the front and rear shoes. Slide the front shoe in between the hold-down spring cup and the backing plate.
18. Install the strut so that the spring end is forward.
19. Install the front and then the rear return springs using the removal tool.
20. Before installing the disc, lightly polish the disc and shoe surfaces with a fine grit emery cloth. Position the rotor disc onto the axle hub so that the hole on the rear axle shaft is aligned with the service hole on the disc.
21. Adjust the parking brake shoe clearance, then settle the parking brake shoes and disc.
22. Attach the disc brake assembly to the backing plate and tighten the bolt to 34 ft. lbs. (47 Nm).
23. Install the rear wheels and lower the vehicle.

ADJUSTMENT

After the brake disc is installed, the parking brake shoe clearance must be adjusted.
1. Temporarily install the lug nuts.
2. Remove the adjuster hole plug.
3. Using a brake tool, turn the adjuster and expand the shoes until the disc locks.
4. Return the adjuster eight notches.
5. Install the hole plug.
6. Install the rear brake caliper assembly, remove the lugnuts.
7. Install the rear wheel.
8. Settle the parking brake shoes and disc as follows:
   a. Drive the vehicle at about 31 mph (50 km) on a safe, level and dry road.
   b. With the parking brake release button pushed in, pull on the lever with 20 lbf (98N) of force.
   c. Drive the vehicle for about ¼ miles (400 meters) in this condition.
   d. Repeat the procedure 2 or 3 times.
9. Recheck and adjust the parking brake lever travel.

ANTI-LOCK BRAKE SYSTEM

General Information

♦ See Figure 104

The system is designed to prevent wheel lock-up during hard or emergency braking. By preventing wheel lock-up, maximum braking effort is maintained while preventing loss of directional control. Additionally, some steering capability is maintained during the stop. The ABS system will operate regardless of road surface conditions.

There are conditions for which the ABS system provides no benefit. Hydroplaning is possible when the tires ride on a film of water, losing contact with the paved surface. This renders the vehicle totally uncontrollable until road contact is regained. Extreme steering maneuvers at high speed or cornering beyond the limits of tire adhesion can result in skidding which is independent of vehicle braking. For this reason, the system is named anti–lock rather than anti–skid.

Under normal braking conditions, the ABS system functions in the same manner as a standard brake system. The system is a combination of electrical and hydraulic components, working together to control the flow of brake fluid to the wheels when necessary.

The Anti-lock Brake System Electronic Control Unit (ABS ECU) is the electronic brain of the system, receiving and interpreting speed signals from the speed sensors. The ABS ECU will enter anti-lock mode when it senses impending wheel lock at any wheel and immediately controls the brake line pressure(s) to the affected wheel(s). The actuator assembly is separate from the master cylinder and booster. It contains the wheel circuit valves used to control the brake fluid pressure to each wheel circuit.

During anti-lock braking, line pressures are controlled or modulated by the rapid cycling of electronic valves within the actuator. These valves can allow pressures within the system to increase, remain constant or decrease depending on the needs of the moment as registered by the ABS ECU.

The operator may hear a popping or clicking sound as the pump and/or control valves cycle on and off during normal operation. The sounds are due to normal operation and are not indicative of a system problem. Under most conditions, the sounds are only faintly audible. If ABS is engaged, the operator may notice some pulsation in the body of the vehicle during a hard stop; this is generally due to suspension shudder as the brake pressures are altered rapidly and the forces transfer to the vehicle.

Although the ABS system prevents wheel lock–up under hard braking, as brake pressure increases, wheel slip is allowed to increase as well. This slip will result in some tire chirp during ABS operation. The sound should not be interpreted as lock–up but rather than as indication of the system holding the wheel(s) just outside the point of lock–up. Additionally, the final few feet of an ABS–engaged stop may be completed with the wheels locked; the system does not operate below 4 mph.

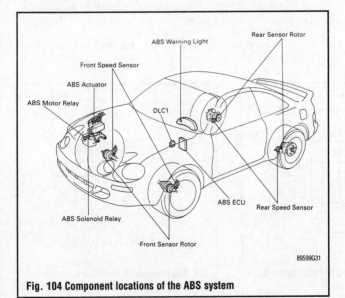

Fig. 104 Component locations of the ABS system

SYSTEM COMPONENTS

Wheel Speed Sensors

The speed of each wheel is monitored by a sensor. A toothed wheel (sensor rotor) rotates in front of the sensor, generating a small AC voltage which is transmitted to the ABS controller. The ABS computer compares the signals and reacts to rapid loss of wheel speed at a particular wheel by engaging the ABS system. Each speed sensor is individually removable. In most cases, the toothed wheels may be replaced if damaged, but disassembly of other components such as hub and knuckle, constant velocity joints or axles may be required.

ABS ECU

This computer-based unit interprets inputs from the speed sensors, the brake lights and the brake warning lamp circuit. After processing the inputs, the unit controls output electrical signals to the hydraulic control solenoids, causing them to increase, decrease or hold brake line pressures.

Additionally, the controller oversees operation of the pump motor and the ABS warning lamp. Additionally, the controller constantly monitors system signals, performs a system actuation test immediately after engine start-up and can assign and store diagnostic fault codes if any errors are noted.

ABS Actuator

Also called the hydraulic unit, the actuator contains the control solenoids for each brake circuit. The pump which maintains the system pressure during ABS braking is also within this unit. The control relay is mounted externally near the actuator. The ABS actuator can only be replaced as a unit; with the exception of the relay, individual components cannot be replaced.

ABS Warning Lamp

♦ See Figure 105

The ABS dashboard warning lamp is controlled by the ABS controller. The lamp will illuminate briefly when the ignition switch is turned **ON** as a bulb check. The lamp should then extinguish and remain out during vehicle operation. If only the ABS warning lamp illuminates while driving, the controller has noted a fault within the ABS system. ABS function is halted, but normal braking is maintained.

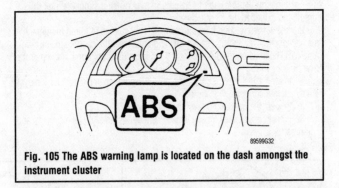

Fig. 105 The ABS warning lamp is located on the dash amongst the instrument cluster

Diagnosis and Testing

SYSTEM PRECAUTIONS

- Certain components within the ABS system are not intended to be serviced or repaired. Only those components with service procedures should be repaired.
- Do not use rubber hoses or other parts not specifically specified for the ABS system. When using repair kits, replace all parts included in the kit. Partial or incorrect repair may lead to functional problems and require the replacement of components.
- Lubricate rubber parts with clean, fresh brake fluid to ease assembly. Do not use lubricated shop air to clean parts; damage to rubber components may result.

- Use only DOT 3 brake fluid from an unopened container.
- If any hydraulic component or line is removed or replaced, it may be necessary to bleed the entire system.
- A clean repair area is essential. Always clean the reservoir and cap thoroughly before removing the cap. The slightest amount of dirt in the fluid may plug an orifice and impair the system function. Use denatured alcohol to clean components.
- Do not allow ABS components to come into contact with any substance containing mineral oil; this includes used shop rags.
- The ABS ECU is a microprocessor similar to other computer units in the vehicle. Ensure that the ignition switch is **OFF** before removing or installing controller harnesses. Avoid static electricity discharge at or near the controller.
- If any arc welding is to be done on the vehicle, the ABS controller should be disconnected before welding operations begin.
- If the vehicle is to be baked after paint repairs, disconnect and remove the ABS ECU from the vehicle.

DEPRESSURIZING THE SYSTEM

The system operates on low hydraulic pressure and requires no special system depressurization prior to the opening of hydraulic lines or other system repairs. Simply verify the ignition switch is **OFF** and pump/motor is not running.

DIAGNOSTIC CODES

If a malfunction occurs, the system will identify the problem and the computer will assign and store a fault code for the fault(s). The dashboard warning lamp will be illuminated to inform the driver that a fault has been found.

During diagnostics, the system will transmit the stored code(s) by flashing the dashboard warning lamp. If two or more codes are stored, they will be displayed from lowest number to highest, regardless of the order of occurrence. The system does not display the diagnostic codes while the vehicle is running.

INITIAL CHECKS

Visual Inspection

Before diagnosing an apparent ABS problem, make absolutely certain that the normal braking system is in correct working order. Many common brake problems (dragging parking brake, seepage, etc.) will affect the ABS system. A visual check of specific system components may reveal problems creating an apparent ABS malfunction. Performing this inspection may reveal a simple failure, thus eliminating extended diagnostic time.

Also check battery condition; approximately 12 volts is required to operate the system. Turn the ignition switch **ON** and check that the dashboard warning lamp (ABS) comes on for 3-4 seconds. If the lamp does not come on, repair the fuse, bulb or wiring.

1. Inspect the tire pressures; they must be approximately equal for the system to operate correctly.
2. Inspect the brake fluid level in the reservoir.
3. Inspect brake lines, hoses, master cylinder assembly, brake calipers and cylinders for leakage.

4. Visually check brake lines and hoses for excessive wear, heat damage, punctures, contact with other parts, missing clips or holders, blockage or crimped.
5. Check the calipers or wheel cylinders for rust or corrosion. Check for proper sliding action if applicable.
6. Check the caliper and wheel cylinder pistons for freedom of motion during application and release.
7. Inspect the wheel speed sensors for proper mounting and connections.
8. Inspect the sensor wheels for broken teeth or poor mounting.
9. Inspect the wheels and tires on the vehicle. They must be of the same size and type to generate accurate speed signals.
10. Confirm the fault occurrence with the operator. Certain driver induced faults, such as not releasing the parking brake fully, will set a fault code and trigger the dash warning light(s). Excessive wheel spin on low-traction surfaces, high speed acceleration or riding the brake pedal may also set fault codes and trigger a warning lamp. These induced faults are not system failures but examples of vehicle performance outside the parameters of the control unit.
11. Many system shut–downs are due to loss of sensor signals to or from the controller. The most common cause is not a failed sensor but a loose, corroded or dirty connector. Incorrect adjustment of the wheel speed sensor will cause a loss of wheel speed signal. Check harness and component connectors carefully.

DATA LINK CONNECTORS (DLC)

The DLC1 is located in the engine compartment. The DLC3 is located in the lower portion of the dash on the driver's side.

READING CODES

♦ See Figures 106, 107, 108 and 109

1. Make sure the battery voltage is about 12 volts.
2. Turn the ignition switch to the **ON** position.
3. Check that the ABS warning light illuminates for about 3 seconds. If not, inspect and repair or replace the fuse, bulb or wiring harness.
4. Remove the short pin from the DLC1.
5. Using a jumper wire connect terminals Tc to E1 of the DLC1.
6. Turn the ignition switch **ON**.
7. In the event that there is a malfunction, 4 seconds later the warning light will begin to blink. Read the number of blinks.

➡The first number of blinks will equal the first digit of as two digit code. After a 1.5 second pause, the 2nd number of blinks will equal the 2nd number of the two digit code. If there are more than two or more codes, there will be a 2.5 second pause between codes. The indication will begin after a 4.0 second pause from the smaller value and continue in order to larger.

8. If the system is operating normally with no malfunctions, the warning light will blink once every 0.5 seconds.
9. Repair the system.
10. After the malfunction occurs, and components have been repaired, clear the codes stored in the ECM.

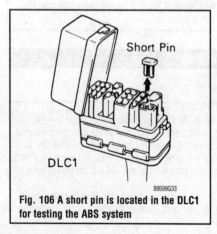

Fig. 106 A short pin is located in the DLC1 for testing the ABS system

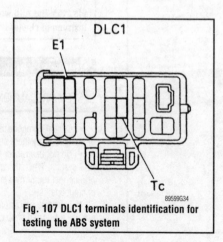

Fig. 107 DLC1 terminals identification for testing the ABS system

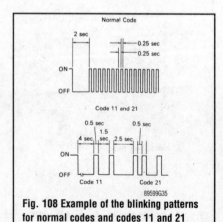

Fig. 108 Example of the blinking patterns for normal codes and codes 11 and 21

DTC No.	Detection Item	Trouble Area
11	Open circuit in ABS solenoid relay circuit	• ABS solenoid relay • Open or short in ABS solenoid relay circuit
12	Short in ABS solenoid relay circuit	• ABS solenoid relay • B+ short in ABS solenoid relay circuit
13	Open circuit in ABS motor relay circuit	• ABS motor relay • Open or short in ABS motor relay circuit
14	Short circuit in ABS motor relay circuit	• ABS motor relay • B+ short in ABS motor relay circuit
21	Open or short circuit in solenoid circuit for right front wheel	• ABS actuator • Open or short in SFRH or SFRR circuit
22	Open or short circuit in solenoid circuit for left front wheel	• ABS actuator • Open or short in SFLH or SFLR circuit
23	Open or short circuit in solenoid circuit for right rear wheel	• ABS actuator • Open or short in SRRH or SRRR circuit
24	Open or short circuit in solenoid circuit for left rear wheel	• ABS actuator • Open or short in SRLH or SRLR circuit
31	Right front wheel speed sensor signal malfunction	• Right front, left front right rear and left rear speed sensor • Open or short in each speed sensor circuit • Sensor rotor
32	Left front wheel speed sensor sirnal malfunction	
33	Right rear wheel speed sensor signal malfunction	
34	Left rear wheel speed sensor signal malfunction	
41	Low battery positive voltage	• Battery • IC regulator • Open or short in power source circuit
51	Pump motor is locked Open in pump motor ground	• ABS pump motor
Always ON	Malfunction in ECU Abnormally high battery positive voltage	• ECU • Battery

Fig. 109 ABS diagnostic trouble code chart

CLEARING TROUBLE CODES

1. Using a jumper wire, connect terminals Tc and E1 of the DLC1 and remove the short pin.
2. Turn the ignition switch to the **ON** position.
3. Depress the brake pedal 8 or more times within 3 seconds.
4. Cheek that the warning light shows a normal code.
5. Remove the jumper wire and connect the short pin.

➥**Cancellation can also be done by removing the ECU-B fuse, but in this case, other memory systems will be canceled out.**

ABS Actuator

▶ See Figure 110

REMOVAL & INSTALLATION

1. Disconnect the negative battery cable. Wait at least 90 seconds once the battery cable is disconnected before working on the vehicle. This will hinder the deployment of the air bags.

✳✳ CAUTION

All models covered by this manual are equipped with a Supplemental Restraint System (SRS), which uses an air bag. Whenever working near any of the SRS components, such as the impact sensors, the air bag module, steering column and instrument panel, disable the SRS, as described in Section 6.

2. Label and disconnect the electrical harnesses.
3. Disconnect the hydraulic lines from the brake actuator. Plug the ends of the lines to prevent loss of fluid.
4. Detach the hydraulic fluid pressure differential switch wiring connectors.
5. Unfasten the nuts and remove the ABS actuator assembly.
To install:
6. Before tightening the mounting nuts and bolts, screw the hydraulic line into the cylinder body a few turns.
7. Install the actuator and tighten the ABS assembly bolts to 14 ft. lbs. (19 Nm).
8. Attach and tighten the hydraulic lines to 11 ft. lbs. (15 Nm).
9. Fill the brake master cylinder reservoir with new brake fluid. Bleed the system and check for leaks.

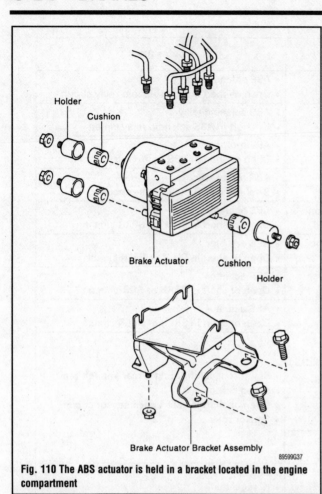

Fig. 110 The ABS actuator is held in a bracket located in the engine compartment

Speed Sensors

TESTING

1. To perform the speed sensor signal check, turn the ignition switch to the **OFF** position.
2. Using a jumper wire, connect terminals Ts and E1 of the DLC1.
3. Start the engine.
4. Check that the ABS warning light blinks.

➡ **If the light does not blink, inspect the ABS wring light circuit.**

5. Drive the vehicle straight forward at 28 mph (45 km) for a short distance (several seconds).

6. Stop the vehicle.
7. Using another jumper wire, connect terminals Tc and E1 of the DLC1.
8. Read the number of blinks of the ABS warning light. If every second is normal, a normal code will be output.

➡ **A cycle of 0.25 seconds ON and 0.25 seconds OFF is repeated. If 2 or more malfunctions are indicated at the same time, the lowest numbered code will be displayed first.**

9. After performing the check, disconnect the two jumper wires from the DLC1 and turn the ignition switch **OFF**.

REMOVAL & INSTALLATION

Front

▶ **See Figures 111 and 112**

1. Remove the fender shield.
2. Disconnect the speed sensor wiring.
3. Remove the 3 clamp bolts holding the sensor harness from the body and shock absorber.
4. Remove the speed sensor retaining bolt from the steering knuckle.
5. Remove the clamp from the speed sensor.

To install:

6. Install the sensor to the steering knuckle and tighten the bolt to 71 inch lbs. (8 Nm).

➡ **Make sure that there are no foreign objects on the sensor or the part of the knuckle where it seats. The sensor should be seated flat against the knuckle when you tighten the bolt.**

7. Install the clamp to the shock bracket until a clicking is heard.
8. Install the sensor harness with the 3 bolts.
9. Connect the wiring to the sensor,.
10. Perform the speed sensor signal check.

Rear

▶ **See Figures 113, 114 and 115**

1. On liftback models, remove the rear seat back and deck trim panel.
2. On coupes, remove the luggage compartment trim cover.
3. Disconnect the wiring and pull out the sensor wire with grommet.
4. Remove the 2 clamp bolts holding the sensor wire harness from the body and the shock.
5. Remove the speed sensor from the axle carrier.

To install:

6. Install the sensor and tighten the bolt to 71 inch lbs. (8 Nm).

➡ **Make sure that there are no foreign objects on the sensor or the part of the knuckle where it seats. The sensor should be seated flat against the knuckle when you tighten the bolt.**

7. Feed the harness connector back inside the vehicle and connect.
8. On the liftbacks, install the deck trim side panel and rear seat back.

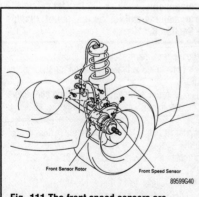

Fig. 111 The front speed sensors are located around the strut assembly

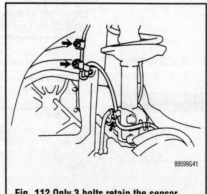

Fig. 112 Only 3 bolts retain the sensor harness to the body and strut

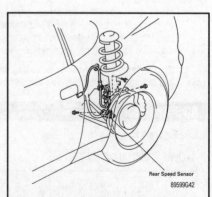

Fig. 113 Rear speed sensor harness routing

9. On coupes, install the luggage compartment trim cover.
10. Install the grommet securely.
11. Attach the sensor harness with the 2 clamps and bolts.
12. Perform the speed sensor signal check.

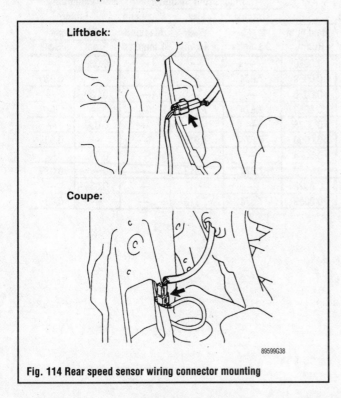

Fig. 114 Rear speed sensor wiring connector mounting

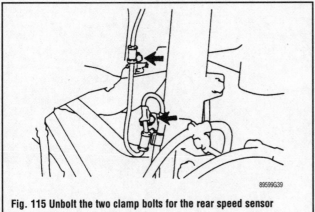

Fig. 115 Unbolt the two clamp bolts for the rear speed sensor

Filling the System

▶ See Figure 116

The brake fluid reservoir is located on top of the master cylinder. While no special procedures are needed to fill the fluid, the reservoir cap and surrounding area must be wiped clean of all dirt and debris before removing the cap. The slightest dirt in the fluid can cause a system malfunction. Use only DOT 3 fluid from an unopened container. Use of old, polluted or non-approved fluid can seriously impair the function of the system.

Bleeding the ABS System

❋❋ WARNING

Clean, high quality brake fluid is essential to the safe and proper operation of the brake system. You should always buy the highest quality brake fluid that is available. If the brake fluid becomes contaminated, drain and flush the system, then refill the master cylinder with new fluid. Never reuse any brake fluid. Any brake fluid that is removed from the system should be discarded.

Bleeding is performed in the usual manner, using either a pressure bleeder or the 2-person manual method. If a pressure bleeder is used, it must be of the diaphragm type with an internal diaphragm separating the air chamber from the fluid. Tighten each bleeder plug to 74 inch lbs. (8 Nm).

Always begin the bleeding with the longest brake line, then the next longest, and so on. If the master cylinder has been repaired or if the reservoir has been emptied, the master cylinder will need to be bled before the individual lines and calipers. During any bleeding procedure, make certain to maintain the fluid level above the MIN line on the reservoir. When the bleeding procedure is complete, fill the reservoir to the MAX line before reinstalling the cap.

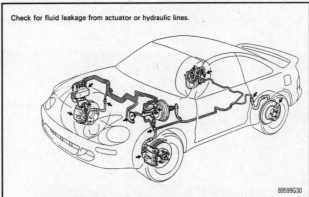

Fig. 116 When filling the system, remember to check for leaks in the lines, specifically these areas

BRAKE SPECIFICATIONS
All measurements in inches unless noted

Year	Model		Master Cylinder Bore	Brake Disc			Brake Drum Diameter			Minimum Lining Thickness	
				Original Thickness	Minimum Thickness	Maximum Runout	Original Inside Diameter	Max. Wear Limit	Maximum Machine Diameter	Front	Rear
1994	Celica	F	—	①	②	0.0020	—	—	—	0.039	—
	Celica	R	—	0.354	0.314	0.0059	7.874	7.913	—	—	0.039
1995	Celica	F	—	①	②	0.0028	—	—	—	0.039	—
	Celica	R	—	0.354	0.314	0.0059	7.874	7.913	—	—	0.039
1996	Celica	F	—	①	②	0.0028	—	—	—	0.039	—
	Celica	R	—	0.354	0.314	0.0059	7.874	7.913	—	—	0.039
1997	Celica	F	—	①	②	0.0028	—	—	—	0.039	—
	Celica	R	—	0.354	0.314	0.0059	7.874	7.913	—	—	0.039
1998	Celica	F	—	①	②	0.0028	—	—	—	0.039	—
	Celica	R	—	0.354	0.314	0.0059	7.874	7.913	—	—	0.039

① 5S-FE: 1.102 inch, 7A-FE: 0.984 inch
② 5S-FE: 1.024 inch, 7A-FE: 0.986 inch

89599C01

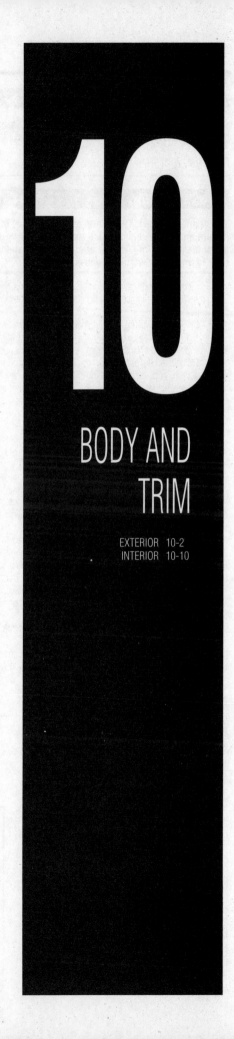

10

BODY AND TRIM

EXTERIOR

Doors

REMOVAL & INSTALLATION

✳✳ WARNING

The doors are heavier than they appear. Support the door from the bottom and use a helper during removal and installation. Do not allow the door to sag while partially attached and do not subject the door to impact or twisting motions.

1. If equipped with power door locks, windows or any other power option located on the door, remove the inner door panel and disconnect the electrical component.
2. Remove the wire harness retainers and extract the harness from the door.
3. Use a floor jack padded with rags or soft lumber to support the door at its lower midpoint. Use a felt tip marker to outline the hinge position on the door.
4. Disconnect the door check rod. To prevent the rod from falling inside the door, install the retainer into the hole in the end of the check rod.
5. Have a helper support the door, keeping it upright at all times. Remove the bolts holding the upper and lower hinge to the door.
6. Using two people, lift the door clear of the car.
7. The door hinge may be removed from the body if necessary.

To install:

8. If the door hinge is removed from the body, reinstall it and tighten the bolts to 24 ft. lbs. (32 Nm).
9. Place the door in position and support it. Use the jack to fine tune the position until the bolt holes and matchmark (hinge outline) align.
10. Apply an appropriate amount of multipurpose grease to the lower hinge and cam sliding area. Using engine oil, lubricate between the lower hinge pin and the roller.
11. Install the hinge bolts and nuts. Tighten the bolts to 21 ft. lbs. (28 Nm).
12. If all has gone well, the door should almost be in the original position. Refer to the door adjustment procedures to align the door and body. It may be necessary to loosen the hinge bolts and reposition the door; remember to retighten them each time or the door will shift out of place.
13. Once adjusted, connect the door check lever and install the pin. Install the hinge covers if any were removed.
14. Route the wiring harness(es) into the body and connect them to their leads.
15. Test the operation of any electrical components in the door (locks, mirrors, speakers, etc.) and test drive the car, checking the door for air leaks and rattles.

ADJUSTMENT

▶ See Figures 1, 2 and 3

To adjust the door in forward, rearward and vertical directions, perform the following adjustment:
1. Loosen the body side hinge bolts or nuts.
2. Adjust the door to the desired position.

3. Secure the body side hinge bolts or nuts and check the door for proper alignment. Tighten the bolts to 21 ft. lbs. (28 Nm).
To adjust the door in left, right and vertical directions, perform the following adjustments:
4. Loosen the door side hinge bolts slightly.
5. Adjust the door to the desired position.
6. Secure the door side hinge bolts and check the door for proper alignment. Tighten the bolts to 21 ft. lbs. (28 Nm).
To adjust the door lock striker, perform the following procedure:
7. Check that the door fit and the door lock linkages are adjusted properly.
8. Slightly loosen the striker mounting screws and tap striker with a hammer until the desired position is obtained.
9. Tighten the striker mounting screws to 19 ft. lbs. (26 Nm).

Hood

REMOVAL & INSTALLATION

▶ See Figures 4, 5 and 6

1. Open the hood completely, then prop the hood in the upright position.
2. Protect the cowl panel and hood from scratches during this operation. Apply protection tape or cover body surfaces before starting work.
3. Disconnect the hoses attached to the hood for the windshield wipers.
4. Scribe a mark showing the location of each hinge on the hood to aid in alignment during installation.
5. Have an assistant help hold the hood while you remove the hood-to-hinge bolts. Use care not to damage hood or vehicle during hood removal.
6. Lift the hood off of the vehicle.

To install:

7. Position he hood on hinges and align with the scribe marks.
8. Install and tighten the mounting bolts with enough torque to hold hood in place.
9. Close the hood slowly to check for proper alignment. Do not slam the hood closed, alignment is normally required.
10. Open the hood and adjust so that all clearances are the same and the hood panel is flush with the body.
11. After all adjustments are complete, tighten hinge mounting bolts to 10 ft. lbs. (14 Nm).

ALIGNMENT

▶ See Figures 7, 8, 9, 10 and 11

Since the centering bolt, which has a chamfered shoulder, is used as the hood hinge and the lock set bolt, the hood and lock can't be adjusted with it on. To adjust properly, remove the hinge centering bolt and substitute a bolt with a washer for the centering bolt.
To adjust the hood forward or rearward and left or right directions, adjust the hood by loosening the side hinge bolts and moving the hood to the desired position. Secure the hinge bolts to 10 ft. lbs. (14 Nm).
To adjust the front edge of the hood in a vertical direction, turn the cushions as required.

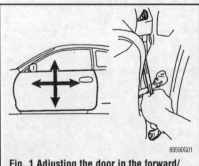

89590G01

Fig. 1 Adjusting the door in the forward/ rearward and vertical directions

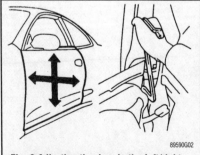

89590G02

Fig. 2 Adjusting the door in the left/right and vertical directions

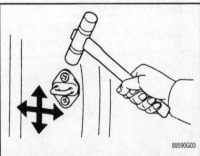

89590G03

Fig. 3 Tap the striker once loosened gently with a plastic ended hammer to adjust

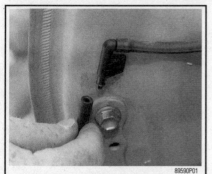

Fig. 4 Disconnect the hose from the windshield wipers on the hood

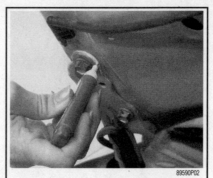

Fig. 5 Mark the placement of the hood hinges with paint or chalk

Fig. 6 Loosen and remove these bolts on the hood hinge. Have an assistant holds the hood for support

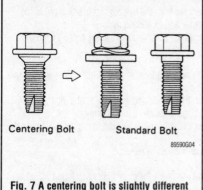

Fig. 7 A centering bolt is slightly different than other bolts

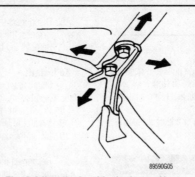

Fig. 8 Adjust the hood in the forward/rearward and left/right directions by loosening the bolts

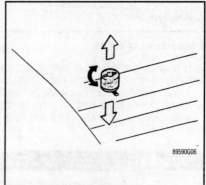

Fig. 9 Turn the cushions on the hood for front edge adjustment

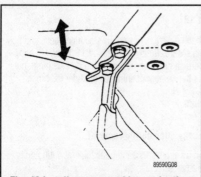

Fig. 10 Install or remove shims under the hinge bolts to adjust the vertical direction of the rear edge

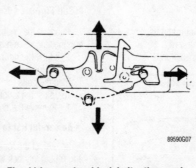

Fig. 11 Loosen hood lock bolts, then position the lock bolts to adjust. Secure at the desired location

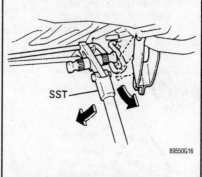

Fig. 12 Push down the tool, then pull the trunk hinge from the torsion bar

Adjust the rear edge of the hood in the vertical direction by increasing or decreasing the number of washers.

To adjust the hood lock, remove the clips holding the radiator upper seal to the upper radiator support. Remove the upper seal from the vehicle and adjust the lock by loosening the lock retainer bolts. Tighten the hood lock mounting bolts to 69 inch lbs. (8 Nm) and reinstall the radiator upper seal when adjustment is complete.

Sedan Trunk Lid

REMOVAL & INSTALLATION

▶ **See Figures 12 and 13**

1. Remove the luggage compartment trim to access the hinge bolts.
2. Using a pry tool or SST 09804–24010, push down on the torsion bar at one end and pull the luggage compartment lid hinge from the torsion bar.

3. Slowly lift the tool and remove the torsion bar from the bracket.
4. Repeat the last 2 steps for the other side of the trunk lid to remove that torsion bar.
5. Prop the lid in the upright position and scribe the hinge locations in the trunk lid.
6. Remove the hinge-to-trunk lid mounting bolts and remove the trunk lid from the vehicle.
   To install:
7. Position the trunk lid on the vehicle and loosely install the retainer bolts.
8. Align the scribe marks on the tailgate and secure the fasteners.
9. Install the torsion bar to the side and center brackets, and the pry tool or SST 09804–24010, install the torsion bar to the hinges.
10. Install the luggage compartment trim that was removed to access the hinge bolts.

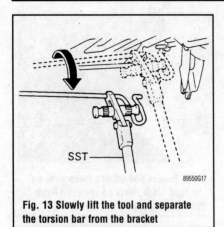

Fig. 13 Slowly lift the tool and separate the torsion bar from the bracket

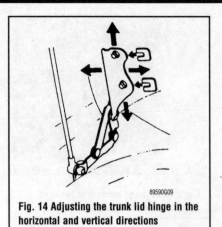

Fig. 14 Adjusting the trunk lid hinge in the horizontal and vertical directions

Fig. 15 Adjust the lock position by slightly loosening the bolts and tap the lock with a hammer and brass bar

ALIGNMENT

▶ See Figures 14 and 15

To adjust the door in horizontal direction, loosen the hinge bolts and position the tailgate as required. Tighten the hinge bolts to 69 inch lbs. (8 Nm).

To adjust the tailgate lock striker, loosen the mounting bolts and using a plastic hammer and a brass bar, tap the striker to the desired position.

Vertical adjustment of the door edge is made by removing or adding washes to shim the hinge bolts.

Liftback Lid

REMOVAL & INSTALLATION

▶ See Figure 16

1. Open the tailgate completely.
2. Remove the inner trim panels.
3. Disengage the electrical connector from the wiper motor and third brake light as required. Remove the harness and position out of the way.
4. Scribe the hinge location on the tailgate to aid in installation.

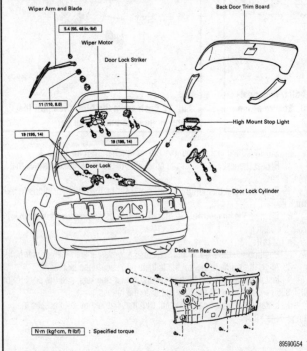

Fig. 16 View of the rear liftback door interior components

5. Disconnect the damper stay from the tailgate and position out of the way. Disconnect the rear defroster wiring, if equipped.
6. Remove the tailgate-to-hinge bolts and remove the tailgate from the vehicle.

To install:

7. Install any components removed from the old tailgate such as the wiper blade assembly, motor, striker etc.
8. Position the tailgate on the vehicle and align the scribe marks.
9. Install the tailgate-to-hinge bolts and secure tightly.
10. Install the damper stay to the tailgate attaching the upper end to the tailgate first.
11. Reconnect the electrical harness as required.
12. Install the interior trim panel.
13. Close the tailgate slowly to check for proper alignment, and adjust as required.

ALIGNMENT

▶ See Figures 17, 18 and 19

To adjust the door in horizontal direction, loosen the side hinge bolts and position the tailgate as required and secure. Tighten the bolts to 11 ft. lbs. (14 Nm).

To adjust the door in the vertical direction, loosen the body side hinge nuts to adjust. Increase or decrease the number of shims used under the hinge. Tighten the bolts to 15 ft. lbs. (21 Nm).

To adjust the tailgate lock striker:

1. Remove the deck rear trim cover.

➡ Be careful not to damage the clips during removal.

2. Adjust the lock position by slightly loosening the lock mounting bolts, and hitting the lock with a hammer and brass bar.

➡ Do not tap the lock too hard.

3. Install the deck rear trim cover.

Outside Mirrors

REMOVAL & INSTALLATION

Both left and right outside mirrors may be either manual, manual remote (small lever on the inside to adjust the mirror) or electric remote. If the mirror glass is damaged, replacements may be available through your dealer or a reputable glass shop in your area. If the plastic housing is damaged or cracked, the entire unit will need to be replaced.

Manual

1. Remove the set screw and the adjustment knob, if equipped.
2. Remove the delta cover; that's the triangular black inner cover. It can be removed with a blunt plastic or wooden tool. Don't use a metal prytool; the plastic will be marred.
3. Depending on the style of mirror, there may be concealment plugs or other minor parts under the delta cover—remove them.

Fig. 17 Loosen the tailgate hinge bolts and adjust the horizontal position

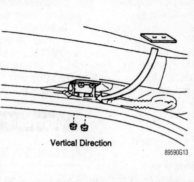

Fig. 18 Loosen the body side hinge nuts to adjust the vertical direction

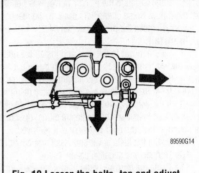

Fig. 19 Loosen the bolts, tap and adjust the lock in the direction desired, but do not tap too hard

4. Support the mirror housing from the outside and remove the bolts or nuts holding the mirror to the door.

5. Remove the mirror assembly.

To install:

6. Fit the mirror to the door and install the nuts and bolts to hold it. Pay particular attention to the placement and alignment of any gaskets or weather-strips around the mirror; serious wind noises may result from careless work.

7. Install any concealment plugs, dust boots or seals which were removed.

8. Install the delta cover and install the adjustment knob, if it was removed.

9. Cycle the mirror several times to make sure that it works properly.

Power

▶ **See Figures 20, 21, 22, 23 and 24**

1. Turn the ignition key to the OFF position. Disconnect the negative battery cable. Wait at least 90 seconds from the time the negative battery was disconnected to start work.

✷✷ CAUTION

All models covered by this manual may be equipped with a Supplemental Restraint System (SRS), which uses an air bag. Whenever working near any of the SRS components, such as the impact sensors, the air bag module, steering column and instrument panel, disable the SRS, as described in Section 6.

2. Remove the delta cover; that's the triangular black inner cover. It can be removed with a blunt plastic or wooden tool. Don't use a metal prytool; the plastic will be marred.

3. Depending on the style of mirror, there may be concealment plugs or other minor parts under the delta cover—remove them.

4. You may need to remove the door inner panel to access the electrical wiring harness for the mirror.

5. Support the mirror housing from the outside and remove the three bolts or nuts holding the mirror to the door.

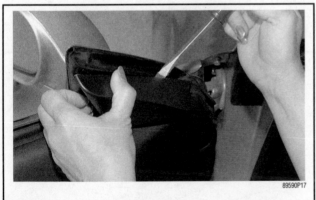

Fig. 20 Carefully pry off the trim cover over the mirror screws

Fig. 21 Only three bolts retain the mirror to the door frame

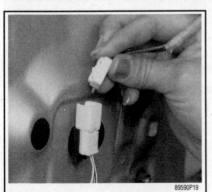

Fig. 22 Unclasp the wiring for electric mirrors located along the inner door skin

Fig. 23 Hold the mirror with one hand while removing the bolts retaining the unit

Fig. 24 Next, pull the wiring through the hole in the door skin

6. If the wiring to the electric mirror was not disconnected previously, detach it now. Some connectors can only be reached after the mirror is free of the door. Remove the mirror assembly.

To install:

7. Fit the mirror to the door and install the nuts and bolts to hold it. Connect the wiring harnesses if they are on the outside of the door. Pay particular attention to the placement and alignment of any gaskets or weather-strips around the mirror; serious wind noises may result from careless work.

8. If the wiring connectors are on the inside of the door, plug them back together and install any concealment plugs, dust boots or seals which were removed. Attach the door inner panel if removed.

9. Install the delta cover and install the control lever, if it was removed.

10. Connect the negative battery cable.

11. Cycle the mirror several times to make sure that it works properly.

Antenna

REPLACEMENT

❊❊ CAUTION

All models covered by this manual are equipped with a Supplemental Restraint System (SRS), which uses an air bag. Whenever working near any of the SRS components, such as the impact sensors, the air bag module, steering column and instrument panel, disable the SRS, as described in Section 6.

Manual

If your antenna mast is the type where you can unscrew the mast from the fender, simply do so with a pair of pliers. Most damaged antennas are simply the result of a car wash or similar mishap, in which the mast is bent.

Disconnect the antenna cable at the radio by pulling it straight out of the set. Depending on access, this may require loosening the radio and pulling it out of the dash. Working under the instrument panel, disengage the cable from its retainers.

➡ **On some models, it may be necessary to remove the instrument panel pad to get at the cable.**

Outside, unsnap the cap from the antenna base. Remove the screw(s) and lift off the antenna base, pulling the cable with it, carefully. When reinstalling, make certain the antenna mount area is clean and free of rust and dirt. The antenna must make a proper ground contact through its base to work properly. Install the screws and route the cable into the interior. Make certain the cable is retained in the clips, etc. Attach the cable to the radio; reinstall the radio if it was removed.

Power

Some models are equipped with a power antenna located in the trunk.

1. Turn the ignition key to the **LOCK** position. Disconnect the negative battery cable. Wait at least 90 seconds from the time the negative battery was disconnected to start work.

2. To access the antenna, simply remove the trim panel from the interior of the vehicle.

3. Detach the electrical wiring harness from the component. Unbolt the unit.

4. The antenna may have a mounting nut retaining it to the outside of the quarter panel. Remove this nut and retainer to slip the unit out from inside the car. Pull the unit out from the vehicle.

5. Installation is the reverse to install. Connect the negative battery cable and check component operation.

Fenders

REMOVAL & INSTALLATION

1. Remove the inner liner from the fender to be removed.
2. Remove of disconnect all electrical items attached to the fender.
3. If necessary, remove the front bumper assembly.
4. Remove all bolts attaching the fender and the brace to the firewall and the radiator/grille panel.

5. Remove the rear attaching bolts through the pillar opening and remove the fender from the vehicle.

To install:

6. Attach the fender to the vehicle with the mounting bolts and tighten securely. Make sure the fender is aligned correctly with all other panels.

7. If removed, attach the front bumper.

8. Install and connect all electrical components removed.

9. Attach the inner fender liner.

Convertible Top

REMOVAL & INSTALLATION

▶ **See Figures 25 thru 41**

1. Remove the rear seat back and cushion.

2. On the quarter panel, remove the 3 screws, clip and trim upper panel. Extract the 2 screws, clip and lower trim panel.

3. Remove the headliner as follows:

   a. Using a clip removal tool, pull out the 3 clips.

   b. Remove the screw, the release the fastener tapes of the headliner from the No. 1 bow and the rear top cover.

   c. Remove the headliner from the No. 2 and No. 3 bow.

   d. Remove the headliner molding by sliding the No. 4 bow to the right.

➡ **When sliding the molding, be careful not to forcibly pull on the headliner. Otherwise the top cover will be torn off.**

4. Remove the quarter and back belt molding as follows:

   a. Remove the quarter glass.

   b. Unscrew the quarter belt outer weather-strip. Using a short driver, remove the 2 screws on the side.

➡ **Perform these operations with the top cover half open and its quarter part loose.**

   c. Using a short driver again, remove the 2 screws on the inner side and the 4 screws in the back.

   d. Disconnect the third brake light wiring. Extract the quarter and back belt molding from the vehicle.

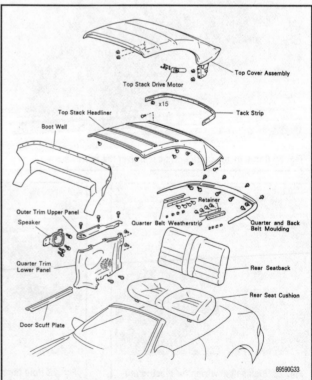

Fig. 25 View of the convertible top cover and related components

89590G33

5. Disconnect the rear defogger and remove the rear boot well. The boot is held in by 15 retainers.

6. Loosen the 15 nuts holding on the tack strip. Be very careful when removing it, it may bend quite easily.

7. Unscrew and pull out the speaker, the disconnect the wiring.

8. Unbolt the drive stack motor.

9. On the top cover, remove the 4 nuts and pull off the top.

10. Replace all the components in the reverse order of removal. Pay particular attention to the following.

11. When sliding the headliner, be careful not to force it, otherwise damage can occur to the top cover.

12. Tighten all nuts and screws securely, and double check all fasteners once the job is complete.

13. Adjust the position of the top stack unstop by loosening the nut and turning the bolt when the bow control link is closed.

14. Inspect the position of the bow control link downstop. With the top fully closed, measure the height of the front seal carrier from the quarter belt rear molding. Measurement height should be 3.93–4.09 inch (100–104mm).

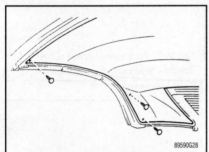

Fig. 26 On the inside of the headliner, remove the three clips on the side . . .

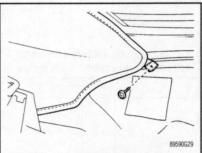

Fig. 27 . . . and the one screw in the upper corner

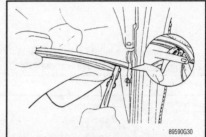

Fig. 28 Next, pry out the fastener tapes from the No. 1 bow and rear top cover of the headliner

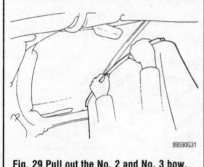

Fig. 29 Pull out the No. 2 and No. 3 bow, then . . .

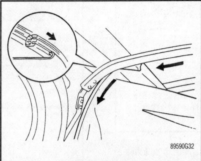

Fig. 30 . . . slide the headliner molding by removing the No. 4 bow to the right

Fig. 31 On the side quarter molding, remove the 4 screws and outer weatherstrip

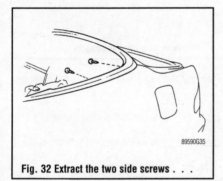

Fig. 32 Extract the two side screws . . .

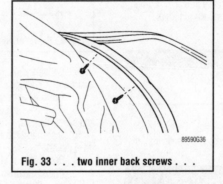

Fig. 33 . . . two inner back screws . . .

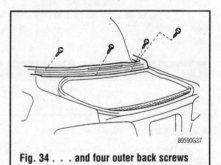

Fig. 34 . . . and four outer back screws from the molding

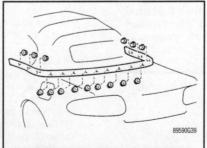

Fig. 35 Lift up the rear quarter and back belt molding

Fig. 36 Fifteen nuts retain the tack strip in the back of the vehicle

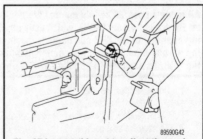

Fig. 37 Loosen this nut to adjust the position of the top stack unstop while the bow control link is closed

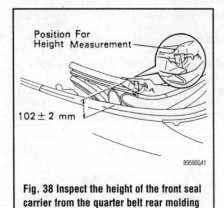

Fig. 38 Inspect the height of the front seal carrier from the quarter belt rear molding

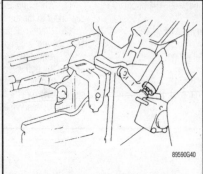

Fig. 39 Loosen the nut to turn the unstop bolt when the bow control link is opened

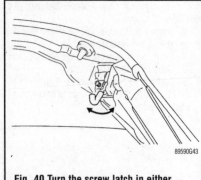

Fig. 40 Turn the screw latch in either direction to adjust

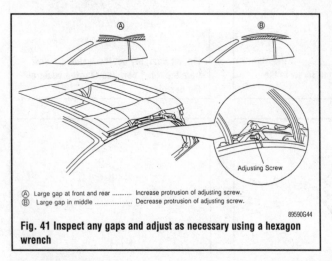

Ⓐ Large gap at front and rear .... Increase protrusion of adjusting screw.
Ⓑ Large gap in middle .... Decrease protrusion of adjusting screw.

Fig. 41 Inspect any gaps and adjust as necessary using a hexagon wrench

15. Adjust the position of the top stack downstop, loosen the nut to turn the downstop bolt when the bow control link is opened.

16. To adjust the latch assembly, if there's clearance or level difference between the windshield from and the front edge of the top cover when the top cover is fully closed, adjust it by turning the screw.

17. If a gap existed between the bow control link weatherstrip and the front door glass of the quarter window glass, use a hexagon wrench to turn the adjusting screw.

Power Sunroof

REMOVAL & INSTALLATION

♦ **See Figures 42, 43, 44, 45 and 46**

1. Disconnect the negative battery cable. Wait at least 90 seconds from the time the negative battery was disconnected to start work.

❊❊ CAUTION

All models covered by this manual are equipped with a Supplemental Restraint System (SRS), which uses an air bag. Whenever working near any of the SRS components, such as the impact sensors, the air bag module, steering column and instrument panel, disable the SRS, as described in Section 6.

2. On the liftback, remove the package tray trim panel, luggage compartment mat and deck trim cover.

3. On all models, remove the rear seatback and cushion.

4. Remove the side garnish.

5. Remove the front and rear garnish using a tapped screwdriver.

6. Apply tape to the vehicle to protect the finish and remove the screws holding the glass into the roof.

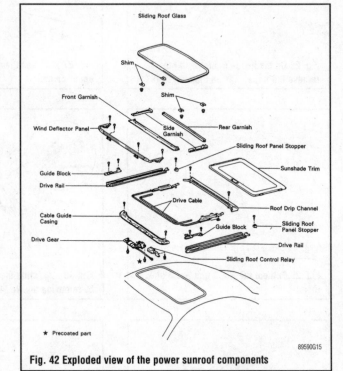

Fig. 42 Exploded view of the power sunroof components

7. Unbolt and remove the inner rear view mirror, sun visors, and the front assist grip, if equipped.

8. Remove the headliner.

9. Disconnect the wiring for the sliding roof control relay. Remove the bolt and extract the relay.

10. Disconnect the electrical wiring, remove the fasteners and remove the drive motor.

11. Remove the roof drip channel and wind deflector panel.

12. Adjust the drive rail to a closed and tilted down position. Using a flat bladed tool, slide the link forward or rearward and align the 2 marks as shown.

13. Slide the drive cable forwards and remove the 12 screws. Apply adhesive tape to protect the body. Pull the cable guide casing assembly forward to remove.

To install:

14. Installation is the reverse of removal. Position the roof onto the vehicle from above. Take notice of shim positioning and install in original location.

15. Secure the screws holding the glass into the roof.

16. Install the side guide rail trim covers.

17. Turn the driveshaft with a screwdriver to align the housing and gear point mark. Apply adhesive to the installation bolts, then connect the electrical wiring, install the drive motor and install the fasteners.

18. Install the sliding roof control relay.

19. Install the wind deflector and secure on the vehicle with the retaining screws.

20. Install the front side of the headliner and install the front pillar garnishes. Install the upper and the lower side garnishes, if removed.

21. Install the inner rear view mirror, sun visors, and the front assist grip, if equipped.

22. Install the roof switch and cover.

23. Connect the negative battery cable.

ADJUSTMENTS

◆ See Figures 47 thru 52

1. Before making any roof adjustments, remove the left and right sliding roof garnishes. After the adjustment, reinstall the garnishees.

2. To adjust the level difference:

a. Adjust by increasing or decreasing the number if shims between the sliding roof.

3. To adjust the forward/rearward adjustment:

a. Adjust by loosening the sliding roof installation nuts, and move the roof bracket forwards and backwards.

b. When the front or rear alignment is not correct, remove the glass and adjust the drive rail.

c. Using a flat bladed tool, slide the link forwards or backwards and align the marks.

4. To adjust the right or left:

a. Adjust by loosening the roof glass installation nuts, then move the roof to the right or left.

5. To adjust the clearance:

a. Loosen the roof installation nuts and readjust the roof to the proper location.

6. Inspect the alignment:

a. Start the engine and check the operation of the sliding roof. Time should be approximately 6 seconds.

b. Check for abnormal noises or binding heard during operation.

c. With the roof fully closed, check for water leakage.

d. Check for the difference in level between the roof, weather-strip and roof panel.

- Front end——0.059–0.059 inch (–1.5–1.5mm)
- Rear end——0.059–0.059 inch (1.5–1.5mm)

e. If the sliding roof does not operate, remove the control switch cover and the large screw inside. Manually operate the roof by inserting a screwdriver into the hole and turning the driveshaft.

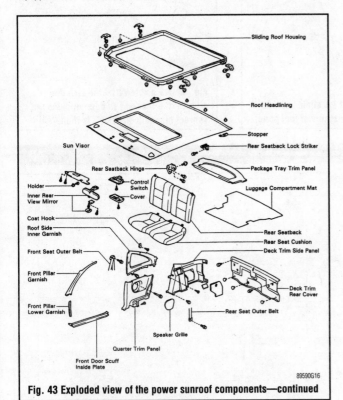

Fig. 43 Exploded view of the power sunroof components—continued

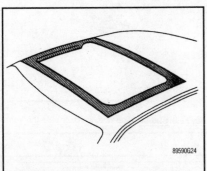

Fig. 44 Apply tape to protect the body of the vehicle, then . . .

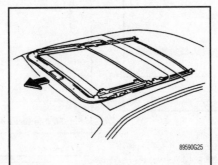

Fig. 45 . . . pull the cable guise casing forward and remove the assembly

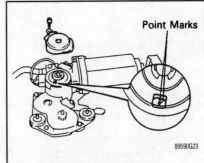

Fig. 46 Align the point marks of the sunroof motor

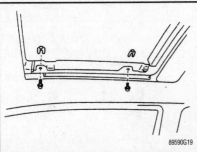

Fig. 47 Adjusting the level difference by increasing or decreasing the amount of shims used

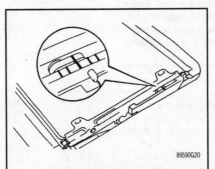

Fig. 48 Adjusting the forward and rearward by aligning the adjustment marks

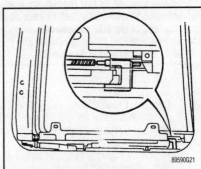

Fig. 49 Slide the link forwards or backwards to align the marks

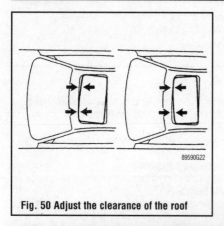

Fig. 50 Adjust the clearance of the roof

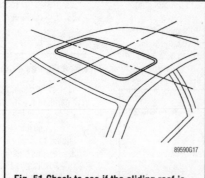

Fig. 51 Check to see if the sliding roof is level with the weather-strip and roof panel

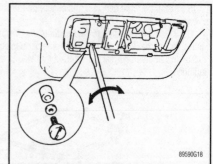

Fig. 52 Use a screwdriver to turn the driveshaft either way to open or close the sunroof manually in case it is inoperable

INTERIOR

Instrument Panel and Pad

♦ See Figures 53, 54 and 55

Always apply protection tape to the body adjacent to the component when removing or installing. When prying off the body components with a screwdriver or scraper, etc. be sure to apply protection tape to the tip of the blade to prevent damage to the component or paint. This will not be a sure way to keep the component from being damaged. Careful use of a tool in this matter is necessary. There are tools specifically made to remove trim pieces of a vehicle that can be purchased at your local parts store.

Fig. 53 If a special trim removal tool is not accessible, tape the end of the prytool and use with care

REMOVAL & INSTALLATION

♦ See Figures 56 thru 62

1. Turn the ignition key to the **LOCK** position. Disconnect the negative battery cable. Wait at least 90 seconds from the time the negative battery was disconnected to start work.

✳✳ CAUTION

All models covered by this manual are equipped with a Supplemental Restraint System (SRS), which uses an air bag. Whenever working near any of the SRS components, such as the impact sensors, the air bag module, steering column and instrument panel, disable the SRS, as described in Section 6.

2. Remove the front pillar garnishes and the scuff plates from the inner door wells.
3. Remove the steering wheel. Refer to the procedure in Section 8.
4. Unscrew and remove the cowl side trim boards and steering column cover.
5. Unsecure the upper console panel, make sure to tape the end of the tool prior to removal.
6. Remove the screws to extract the console box. Watch out for the clips.
7. Remove the combination switch, lower center cluster finish panel, cluster finish panel and No. 1 register.
8. Unbolt and extract the instrument cluster. Refer to Section 6.

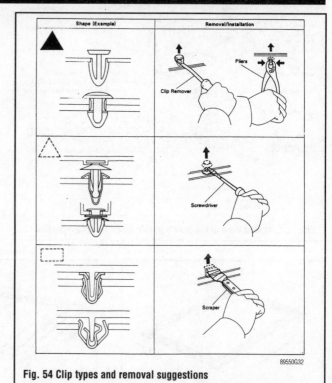

Fig. 54 Clip types and removal suggestions

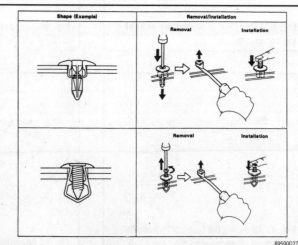

Fig. 55 Clip types and removal suggestions—continued

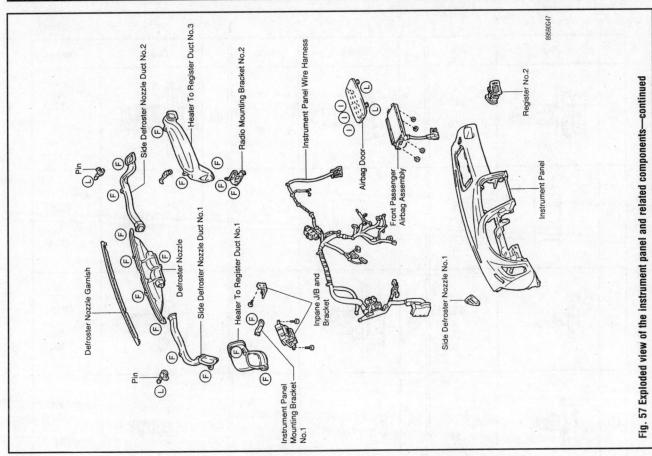

Fig. 57 Exploded view of the instrument panel and related components—continued

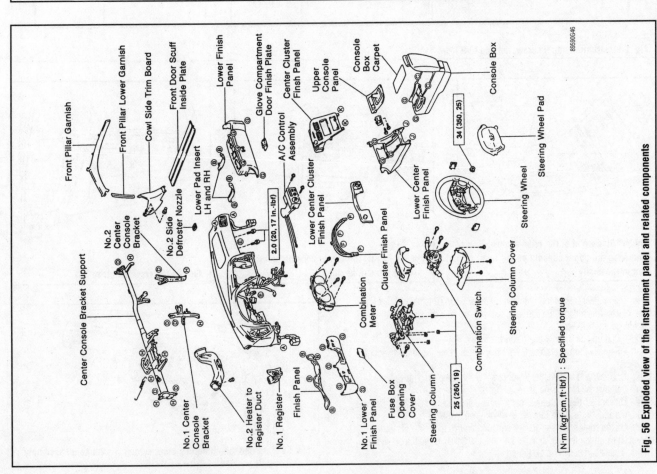

N·m (kgf·cm, ft·lbf) : Specified torque

Fig. 56 Exploded view of the instrument panel and related components

mm (in.)

	Shape	Size		Shape	Size		Shape	Size
A		ϕ = 6 (0.24) L = 20 (0.79)	B		ϕ = 6 (0.24) L = 20 (0.79)	C		ϕ = 8 (0.31) L = 22 (0.98)
D		ϕ = 8 (0.31)	E		ϕ = 6 (0.24)	F		ϕ = 5 (0.20) L = 14 (0.55)
G		ϕ = 5.22 (0.2055) L = 16 (0.63)	H		ϕ = 8 (0.31) L = 15 (0.59)	I		ϕ = 6 (0.24) L = 16 (0.63)
J		ϕ = 5 (0.20) L = 14 (0.55)	K		ϕ = 5.22 (0.2055) L = 20 (0.79)	L		ϕ = 4.5 (0.177) L = 12

89590G48

Fig. 58 Instrument panel screw, nut and bolt types

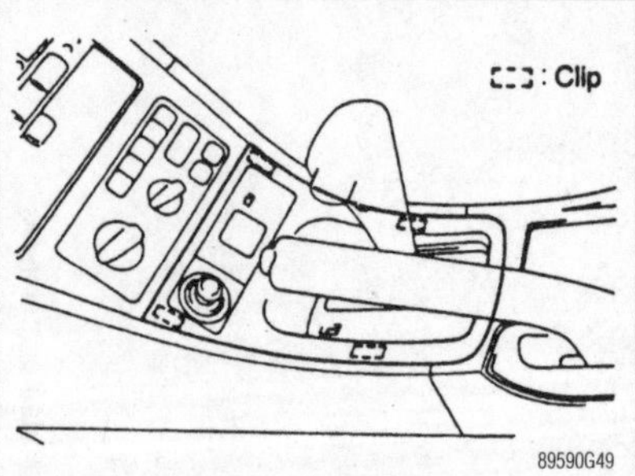

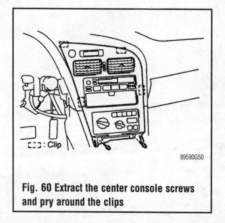

Fig. 59 Be careful of the clips when removing the upper console panel, they can break easily

89590G49

Fig. 60 Extract the center console screws and pry around the clips

89590G50

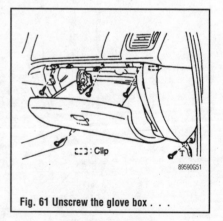

Fig. 61 Unscrew the glove box . . .

89590G51

9. Using a flat bladed tool, remove the screws and clips then extract the center cluster finish panel. Be careful when working near the air bag wiring, do not damage the harness.

    a. Pull up and disconnect the air bag wiring.

    b. Remove the screws and lower finish panel, then unbolt the lower pad inserts.

10. Unscrew and remove the lower center finish panel with glove box.

11. Remove the No. 2 side defroster nozzle.

12. Disconnect the instrument panel wiring, and label if necessary. Remove the 9 bolts and 2 nuts, then pull out the instrument panel.

13. On the center console bracket support, remove the bolt, nuts and bracket. Next unbolt the No. 2 center console bracket. Remove the brake spring, 6 bolts, 2 nuts and center bracket support.

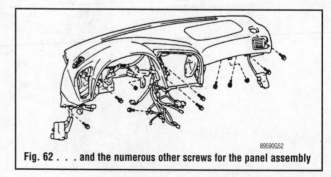

89590G52

Fig. 62 . . . and the numerous other screws for the panel assembly

14. Installation is the reverse of removal. Attach the instrument panel wiring to the appropriate harnesses. Place the panel into position and tighten the bolts and nuts to 69 inch lbs. (8 Nm).
15. Attach the No. 2 side defroster nozzle.
16. Attach the passengers side airbag. Refer to the airbag precautions in Section 5. Tighten the bolts. Tighten the instrument panel reinforcement bolts to 15 ft. lbs. (21 Nm).
17. Attach the No. 2 heater duct register.
18. Install the heater control assembly, combination meter and radio.
19. Install and secure the No. 1 and No. 2 heater duct registers.
20. Install the cluster finish panel, and the center cluster finish panel.
21. Install the front console box and lower instrument panel. Position the no. 2 under cover and secure into position.
22. Install the combination switch.
23. Position the instrument panel lower pad and secure the mounting bolts. Insert he coin box.
24. Install the rear console box and upper console panel secure.
25. Attach the steering column cover and steering wheel. Install the drivers side air bag. Refer to Steering Wheel Removal and Installation in Section 8.
26. Install all of the remaining components in the reverse order. Make sure all components are secure.
27. Connect the negative battery cable.
28. Reset all of the electrical components such as radio and clock.

Center Console

REMOVAL & INSTALLATION

▶ See Figure 59

1. Disconnect the negative battery cable. Wait at least 90 seconds from the time the negative battery was disconnected to start work.

✳✳ CAUTION

All models covered by this manual are equipped with a Supplemental Restraint System (SRS), which uses an air bag. Whenever working near any of the SRS components, such as the impact sensors, the air bag module, steering column and instrument panel, disable the SRS, as described in Section 6.

2. Remove the floor console upper trim panel to gain access to the mounting screws.
3. Remove the mounting screws in the front floor console and in the rear console box.
4. Remove the floor console from the vehicle.
5. Reverse the removal procedure to install.

Door Panels

REMOVAL & INSTALLATION

▶ See Figures 63 thru 75

1. Remove the mirror/speaker cover, it should pop right off.
2. Pop off the door handle cover.
3. On vehicles without power windows, place a soft cloth under the window regulator handle and pull upwards on the cloth to release the snapring. Remove the regulator handle and plate.
4. Remove the arm rest screw, the angle is slightly awkward.
5. Remove all the screws located around the door panel.
6. Some clips and screws are hidden, watch for them it makes panel removal difficult.
7. Remove the door lamp lens using a taped small prytool.
8. Remove the door switch assembly and disconnect the wiring.
9. Once all components are removed from the door panel, carefully separate the panel form the door.
To install:
10. Connect the electrical wiring, if equipped, and install the trim panel onto the door.

11. Secure the trim panel with the mounting screws, then install screw caps and speaker cover(s).
12. Install the armrest and secure with the mounting screw. Install the power window switch as required.
13. Install the door courtesy lamp. Install the inside handle bezel.
14. Install the outside rear view mirror cover and retainer. On manual mirrors, install the knob and setting screw.
15. Connect the inside handle to the control link. Install the handle, slide it rearward and install the screw.
16. With the door window fully closed, install the window regulator handle.

Door Locks

REMOVAL & INSTALLATION

▶ See Figure 63

1. Turn the ignition key to the **LOCK** position. Disconnect the negative battery cable. All models are equipped with an air bag, so wait at least 90 seconds from the time the negative battery was disconnected to start work.

✳✳ CAUTION

All models covered by this manual are equipped with a Supplemental Restraint System (SRS), which uses an air bag. Whenever working near any of the SRS components, such as the impact sensors, the air bag module, steering column and instrument panel, disable the SRS, as described in Section 6.

2. Remove the door panel and watershield. Remove the service hole cover.
3. Disconnect the door outside opening linkage. Remove the two mounting bolts and remove the door handle if in need of replacement.
4. Disconnect the lock cylinder control linkage.
5. Remove the lock knob and the child protector lock lever knob.
6. Remove the three lock assembly retaining screws and the door lock. If equipped with power locks, disconnect the electrical wiring.
7. To remove the lock cylinder, remove the lock cylinder retaining clip and pull the cylinder from the door.
To install:
8. Coat all the door lock sliding surfaces with multi-purpose grease.
9. Install the outside handle with the two retaining bolts, if removed.
10. Install the door lock solenoid linkage to the door lock.
11. Connect the link to the outside handle.
12. Install the lock knob and the child protector lock lever knob.
13. Install the door opening control link.
14. Install the door lock cylinder control linkage.
15. Install the door panel and watershield.
16. Reconnect the negative battery cable.

Tailgate Lock

REMOVAL & INSTALLATION

▶ See Figure 16

1. Remove the back door inside garnish.
2. Remove the link protector.
3. Disconnect the links from the door control and door lock cylinder.
4. Remove the bolts and the door lock control with the solenoid.
5. To remove the door lock cylinder, remove the retaining screws and then remove the cylinder.
To install:
6. Install the door lock cylinder and secure with the retaining screws.
7. Install the bolts and the door lock control with the solenoid.
8. Connect the links to the door control and door lock cylinder.
9. Install the link protector.
10. Install the back door inner garnish.

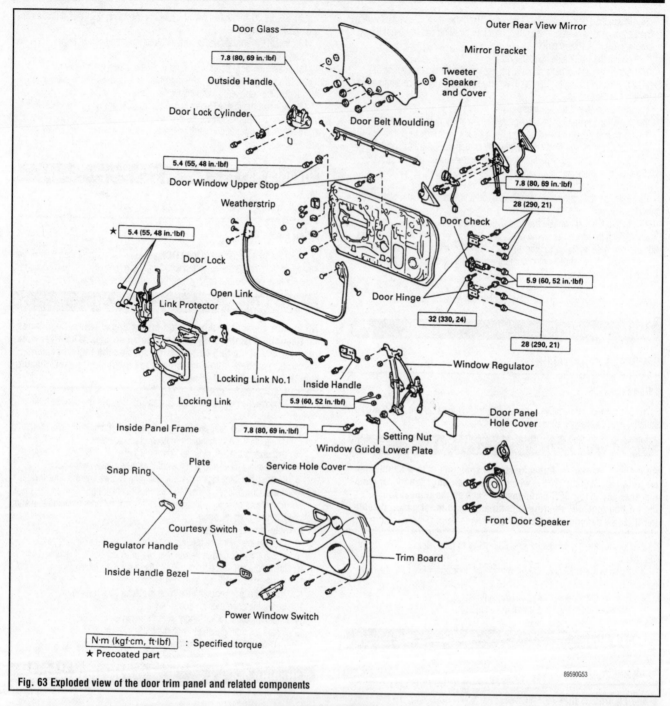

Door Glass

7.8 (80, 69 in.·lbf)

Outside Handle

Door Lock Cylinder

5.4 (55, 48 in.·lbf)

Door Window Upper Stop

Weatherstrip

Door Belt Moulding

Outer Rear View Mirror

Mirror Bracket

Tweeter Speaker and Cover

7.8 (80, 69 in.·lbf)

28 (290, 21)

Door Check

Door Hinge

5.9 (60, 52 in.·lbf)

32 (330, 24)

28 (290, 21)

★ 5.4 (55, 48 in.·lbf)

Door Lock

Open Link

Link Protector

Locking Link No.1

Inside Handle

Locking Link

Inside Panel Frame

Window Regulator

5.9 (60, 52 in.·lbf)

7.8 (80, 69 in.·lbf)

Setting Nut

Window Guide Lower Plate

Door Panel Hole Cover

Service Hole Cover

Front Door Speaker

Snap Ring

Plate

Courtesy Switch

Regulator Handle

Inside Handle Bezel

Trim Board

Power Window Switch

N·m (kgf·cm, ft·lbf) : Specified torque
★ Precoated part

89590G53

Fig. 63 Exploded view of the door trim panel and related components

89590P22

Fig. 64 First, remove the door handle trim held in by one screw

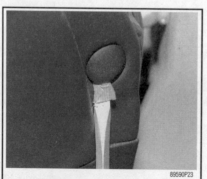

89590P23

Fig. 65 Tape the end of a screwdriver and pop off the screw trim covers

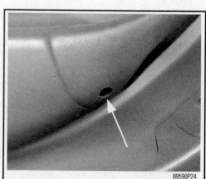

89590P24

Fig. 66 Remove the arm rest retaining screw

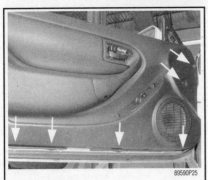

Fig. 67 There are several screws around the door panel to be removed

Fig. 68 On the side of the door, there are push-pin type clips. Use a thin bladed tool . . .

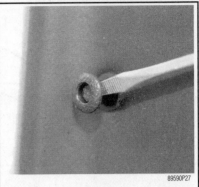

Fig. 69 . . . to pop them out

Fig. 70 If any clips become damaged, replace them (this one is not)

Fig. 71 Remove the screw near the door handle

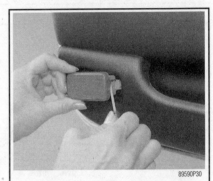

Fig. 72 The small interior lamp lens can be pried out

Fig. 73 Use a taped tool to pry out the door switch assembly

Fig. 74 Next disconnect the wiring

Fig. 75 Now you can lift up and remove the door panel

Sedan Trunk Lock

REMOVAL & INSTALLATION

Remove the inside trunk garnish. Remove the bolts and the door lock control with the solenoid, if equipped. The installation is the reverse of the removal procedure.

Door Glass and Regulator

REMOVAL & INSTALLATION

▶ See Figures 76 thru 81

1. Remove the door panel to gain access to the regulator assembly.
2. Remove the service hole cover.
3. Lower the regulator until the door glass is in the fully open position.
4. Remove the glass channel mount bolts.
5. Pull the glass up and out of the door.
6. If equipped, unbolt and remove the inside door panel frame.
7. If equipped with power windows, disconnect the electrical wiring.
8. Remove the equalizer arm bracket mounting bolts.
9. Remove the window regulator mounting nuts and extract the regulator (with the power window motor attached) through the service hole.

To install:

10. Coat all the window regulator sliding surfaces with multi-purpose grease.
11. Place the regulator (with the power window motor) through the service hole and install the mounting nuts. Connect the power window connector if equipped.
12. Place the glass into the door cavity.
13. Connect the glass to the regulator with the channel mount bolts.
14. With the equalizer arm, raise the glass to the almost closed position and make sure that the leading and trailing edges of the glass are equidistant from the top of the glass channel. If not, adjust the equalizer arm to achieve an even fit.

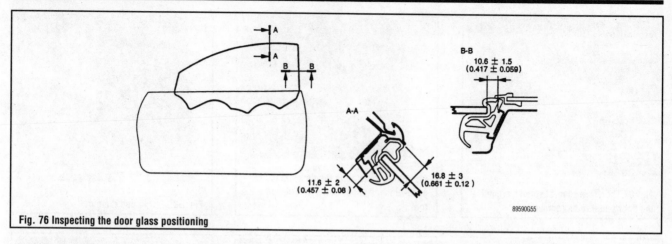

Fig. 76 Inspecting the door glass positioning

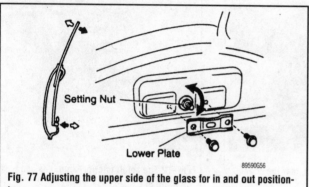

Fig. 77 Adjusting the upper side of the glass for in and out positioning

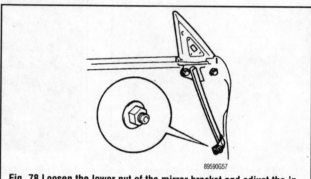

Fig. 78 Loosen the lower nut of the mirror bracket and adjust the in and out by turning the stud bolt

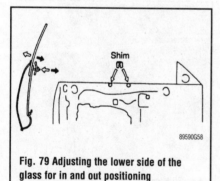

Fig. 79 Adjusting the lower side of the glass for in and out positioning

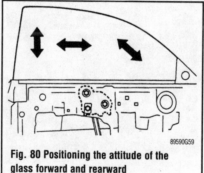

Fig. 80 Positioning the attitude of the glass forward and rearward

Fig. 81 Adjusting the door glass upper stops for vertical attitude

15. Check the door glass as follows:

   a. If when closing the door with the glass fully closed, the A-A and B-B sections are in the same condition as shown in the illustration.

   b. When you push the glass in firmly from inside, the glass stops at the roof drip molding and does not move.

   c. When you close the door with the glass fully closed, the glass is not caught in the outside lip of the weatherstrip and does not touch the roof drip molding.

   d. With the door shut the glass moves smoothly. The upper edge of the glass can not be seen from the outside of the vehicle.

16. If any of these conditions is not met, adjust the glass as follows:

   a. Upper side of the glass—in and out—Remove the 2 lower plate bolts and lower plate.

   b. Adjust the glass by turning the setting nut. Reinstall the lower plate and tighten the bolts to 69 inch lbs. (8 Nm).

   c. In case the glass doers not fit the mirror bracket, loosen the lower nut of the bracket.

   d. Using a hexagon wrench, adjust the mirror bracket to the in/out position by turning the stud bolt. Tighten the bolt to 69 inch lbs. (8 Nm).

17. To adjust the lower side of the glass—in and out perform the following:

   a. Loosen the 2 nuts for the window regulator.

   b. Using a shim, adjust the glass to the in/out direction. The shim thickness should be 0.039 inch (1.0mm) or 0.079 inch (2.0mm).

18. To position the forward/rearward and attitude of the glass perform the following:

   a. Loosen the 3 bolts of the carrier plate and adjust. Tighten the bolts to 69 inch lbs. (8 Nm).

19. To position the vertical attitude of the glass perform the following:

   a. Adjust the door window upper stops. Tighten the bolts to 48 inch lbs. (5 Nm).

20. Install the service hole cover.

21. Install the door panel.

Electric Window Motor

The power window motor, if equipped, is attached to the window regulator. If service is required, remove the window regulator from the inside of the door panel and detach the motor from the regulator. Removal and installation of the regulator is described in this section.

Windshield and Fixed Glass

REMOVAL & INSTALLATION

If your windshield, or other fixed window, is cracked or chipped, you may decide to replace it with a new one yourself. However, there are two main reasons why replacement windshields and other window glass should be installed only by a professional automotive glass technician: safety and cost.

The most important reason a professional should install automotive glass is for safety. The glass in the vehicle, especially the windshield, is designed with safety in mind in case of a collision. The windshield is specially manufactured from two panes of specially-tempered glass with a thin layer of transparent plastic between them. This construction allows the glass to "give" in the event that a part of your body hits the windshield during the collision, and prevents the glass from shattering, which could cause lacerations, blinding and other harm to passengers of the vehicle. The other fixed windows are designed to be tempered so that if they break during a collision, they shatter in such a way that there are no large pointed glass pieces. The professional automotive glass technician knows how to install the glass in a vehicle so that it will function optimally during a collision. Without the proper experience, knowledge and tools, installing a piece of automotive glass yourself could lead to additional harm if an accident should ever occur.

Cost is also a factor when deciding to install automotive glass yourself. Performing this could cost you much more than a professional may charge for the same job. Since the windshield is designed to break under stress, an often life saving characteristic, windshields tend to break VERY easily when an inexperienced person attempts to install one. Do-it-yourselfers buying two, three or even four windshields from a salvage yard because they have broken them during installation are common stories. Also, since the automotive glass is designed to prevent the outside elements from entering your vehicle, improper installation can lead to water and air leaks. Annoying whining noises at highway speeds from air leaks or inside body panel rusting from water leaks can add to your stress level and subtract from your wallet. After buying two or three windshields, installing them and ending up with a leak that produces a noise while driving and water damage during rainstorms, the cost of having a professional

do it correctly the first time may be much more alluring. We here at Chilton, therefore, advise that you have a professional automotive glass technician service any broken glass on your vehicle.

WINDSHIELD CHIP REPAIR

▶ See Figures 82 thru 96

➡ Check with your state and local authorities on the laws for state safety inspection. Some states or municipalities may not allow chip repair as a viable option for correcting stone damage to your windshield.

Although severely cracked or damaged windshields must be replaced, there is something that you can do to prolong or even prevent the need for replace-

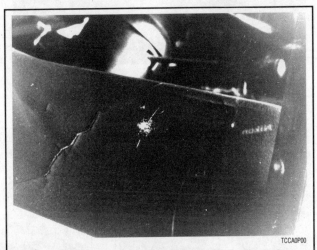
TCCA0P00
Fig. 82 Small chips on your windshield can be fixed with an after-market repair kit, such as the one from Loctite®

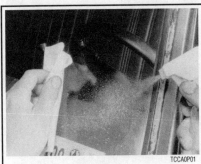
TCCA0P01
Fig. 83 To repair a chip, clean the windshield with glass cleaner and dry it completely

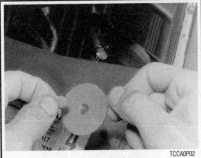
TCCA0P02
Fig. 84 Remove the center from the adhesive disc and peel off the backing from one side of the disc . . .

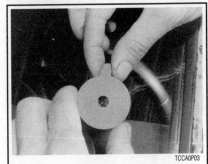
TCCA0P03
Fig. 85 . . . then press it on the windshield so that the chip is centered in the hole

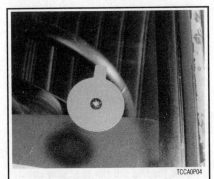
TCCA0P04
Fig. 86 Be sure that the tab points upward on the windshield

TCCA0P05
Fig. 87 Peel the backing off the exposed side of the adhesive disc . . .

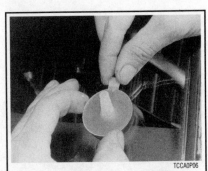
TCCA0P06
Fig. 88 . . . then position the plastic pedestal on the adhesive disc, ensuring that the tabs are aligned

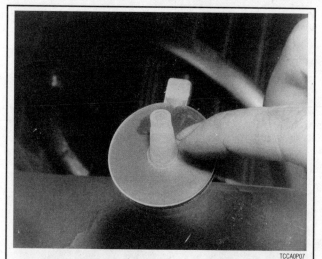

Fig. 89 Press the pedestal firmly on the adhesive disc to create an adequate seal . . .

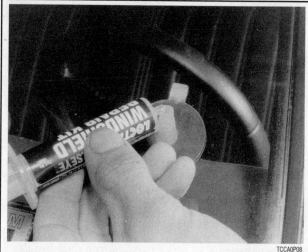

Fig. 90 . . . then install the applicator syringe nipple in the pedestal's hole

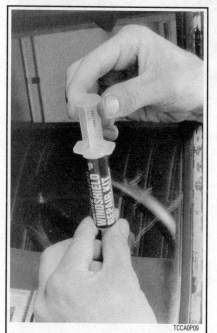

Fig. 91 Hold the syringe with one hand while pulling the plunger back with the other hand

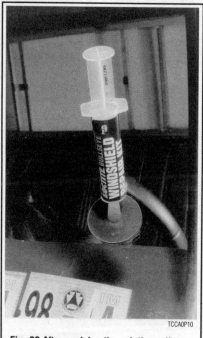

Fig. 92 After applying the solution, allow the entire assembly to sit until it has set completely

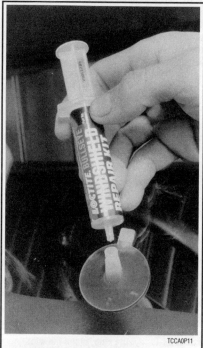

Fig. 93 After the solution has set, remove the syringe from the pedestal . . .

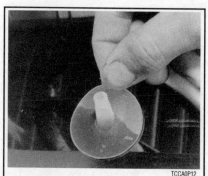

Fig. 94 . . . then peel the pedestal off of the adhesive disc . . .

Fig. 95 . . . and peel the adhesive disc off of the windshield

Fig. 96 The chip will still be slightly visible, but it should be filled with the hardened solution

ment of a chipped windshield. There are many companies which offer windshield chip repair products, such as Loctite's® Bullseye™ windshield repair kit. These kits usually consist of a syringe, pedestal and a sealing adhesive. The syringe is mounted on the pedestal and is used to create a vacuum which pulls the plastic layer against the glass. This helps make the chip transparent. The adhesive is then injected which seals the chip and helps to prevent further stress cracks from developing. Refer to the sequence of photos to get a general idea of what windshield chip repair involves.

➡**Always follow the specific manufacturer's instructions.**

Inside Rear View Mirror

REPLACEMENT

▶ **See Figure 97**

The inside mirror is held to its bracket by screws. Usually these are covered by a colored plastic housing which must be removed for access. These covers can be stubborn; take care not to gouge the plastic during removal.

Once exposed, the screws are easily removed. The mirror mounts are designed to break away under impact, thus protecting your head and face from serious injury in an accident.

Reassembly requires only common sense (which means you can do it wrong—pay attention); make sure everything fits without being forced and don't overtighten any screws or bolts.

Seats

REMOVAL & INSTALLATION

▶ **See Figures 98 thru 113**

Front seats are held to the floor with four bolts each.

The convertible rear set is held in by 4 bolts and nuts with a retainer bracket.

1. The sedan rear seat is retained by clips, bolts and hinges. The side trim may need to be removed on some models. On liftback models, the rear seat cushion is retained by four bolts, while the seat back is bolted to its hinges. Refer to the following for reference:

   a. Lift and pull up the lower rear seat cushion.

   b. From in the trunk area, unsnap the rear seatback cover from the four clips.

   c. Unbolt the upper and lower seat assembly at the center support attached to the trunk floor.

   d. From the inside of the vehicle, remove the side bracket bolts.

   e. Grab the upper and lower seat cushion assembly and remove it from the vehicle.

When installing the seats, tighten the bolts to specifications. Refer to the chart at the end of this section.

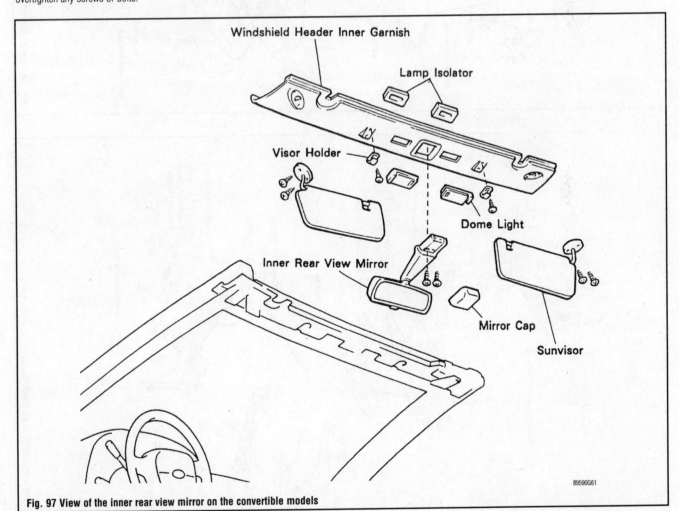

Fig. 97 View of the inner rear view mirror on the convertible models

89590G61

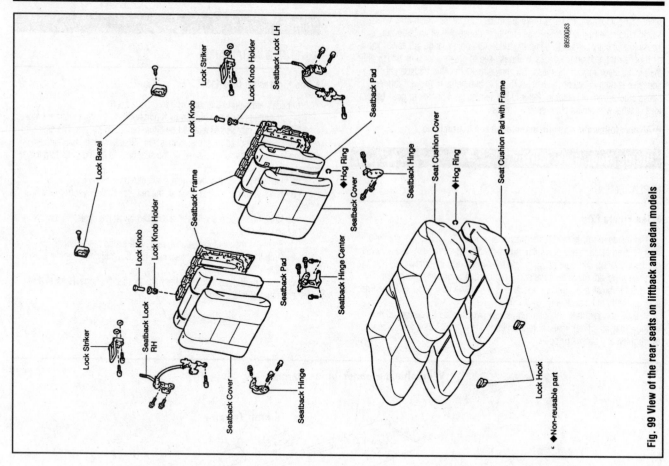

Fig. 99 View of the rear seats on liftback and sedan models

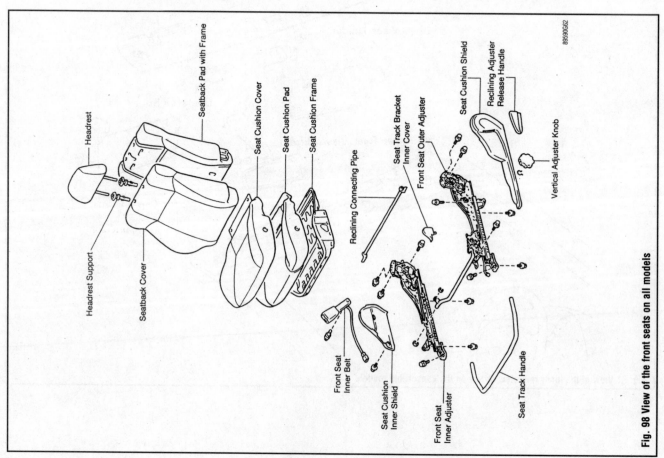

Fig. 98 View of the front seats on all models

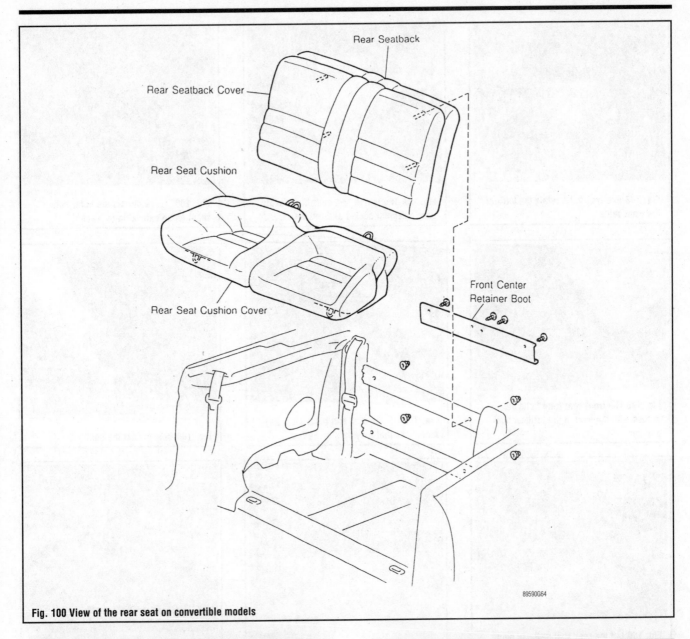

Fig. 100 View of the rear seat on convertible models

Rear Seatback

Rear Seatback Cover

Rear Seat Cushion

Rear Seat Cushion Cover

Front Center
Retainer Boot

Tools required to remove the front seats

Fig. 101 Tools required to remove the front seats of your Celica

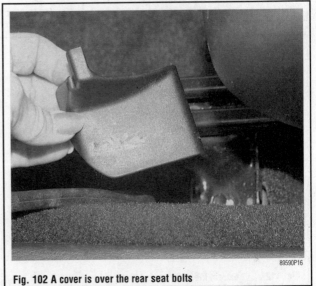

Fig. 102 A cover is over the rear seat bolts

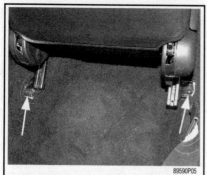

Fig. 103 Two rear bolts retain the back of the front seats

Fig. 104 The inside bolt near the console uses a regular socket and ratchet . . .

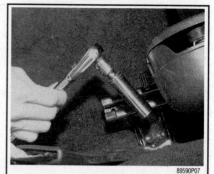

Fig. 105 . . . whereas the outer bolt requires an extension to reach it

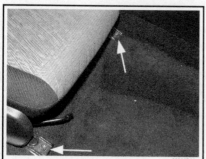

Fig. 106 The front seat front bolts are access with the seat in the farthest back position

Fig. 107 Lift the seat and disconnect any harnesses that may be attached

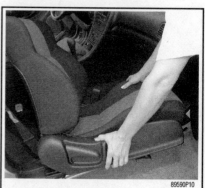

Fig. 108 Now extract the seat

Fig. 109 Lift the rear seat at these points where latches are located

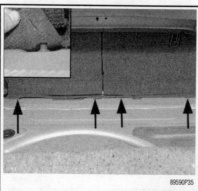

Fig. 110 Unsnap the floor seatback cover

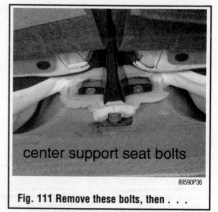

Fig. 111 Remove these bolts, then . . .

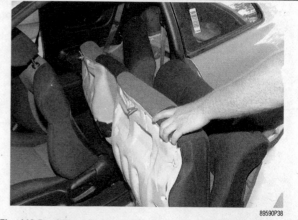

Fig. 112 . . . extract the side bracket bolts

Fig. 113 Bend the seat assembly enough to extract it from the vehicle

TORQUE SPECIFICATIONS

Components	English Specifications	Metric Specifications
Front Bumper:		
Reinforcement-to-body	10 ft. lbs.	13 Nm
Cover-to-body	48 inch lbs.	5 Nm
Hood:		
Hinge-to-hood	10 ft. lbs.	13 Nm
Lock-to-hood	69 inch lbs.	8 Nm
Rear Bumper:		
Reinforcement-to-body	70 ft. lbs.	95 Nm
Reinforcement-to-body	48 inch lbs.	5 Nm
Front Door:		
Check-to-body	24 ft. lbs.	32 Nm
Hinge-to-body	21 ft. lbs.	28 Nm
Hinge-to-panel	21 ft. lbs.	28 Nm
Lock striker-to-body	19 ft. lbs.	26 Nm
Lock-to-panel	48 inch lbs.	5 Nm
Glass-to-window regulator	69 inch lbs.	8 Nm
Window regulator-to-panel	52 inch lbs.	6 Nm
Guide lower plate-to-panel	69 inch lbs.	8 Nm
Window upper stop-to-panel	48 inch lbs.	5 Nm
Mirror bracket-to-panel	69 inch lbs.	8 Nm
Back Door:		
Door hinge-to-body	15 ft. lbs.	21 Nm
Door hinge-to-door	11 ft. lbs.	14 Nm
Lock-to-body	14 ft. lbs.	19 Nm
Striker-to-door	14 ft. lbs.	19 Nm
Damper stay-to-body	78 inch lbs.	9 Nm
Damper stay-to-door	78 inch lbs.	9 Nm
Luggage Compartment:		
Door hinge-to-body	48 inch lbs.	5 Nm
Door hinge-to-compartment door	48 inch lbs.	5 Nm
Door Lock-to-body	48 inch lbs.	5 Nm
Damper stay-to-body	19 ft. lbs.	26 Nm
Damper stay-to-luggage compartment door	19 ft. lbs.	26 Nm
Sliding Roof:		
Drive gear-to-body	48 inch lbs.	5 Nm
Instrument Panel:		
Steering column-to-center console bracket support	19 ft. lbs.	25 Nm
Passengers air bag-to-console bracket support	15 ft. lbs.	21 Nm
Steering wheel-to-steering column	25 ft. lbs.	34 Nm
Steering wheel pad-to-steering wheel	80 inch lbs.	9 Nm
Front Seat:		
Seat adjuster-to-body	27 ft. lbs.	37 Nm
Adjuster-to-seatback	13 ft. lbs.	18 Nm
Adjuster-to-cushion	13 ft. lbs.	18 Nm
Rear Seat:		
Seatback hinge LH and RH-to-body	71 inch lbs.	8 Nm
Seatback hinge center-to-body	13 ft. lbs.	18 Nm
Seatback-to-hinge	13 ft. lbs.	18 Nm
Lock striker-to-body	14 ft. lbs.	19 Nm
Lock-to-seatback	14 ft. lbs.	19 Nm
Front Seat Belt:		
Outer belt shoulder anchor-to-body	32 ft. lbs.	43 Nm
Outer belt floor anchor-to-body	32 ft. lbs.	43 Nm
Retractor-to-body (upper)	69 inch lbs.	8 Nm
Retractor-to-body (lower)	32 ft. lbs.	43 Nm
Inner belt-to-seat	32 ft. lbs.	43 Nm
Rear Seat Belt:		
Outer shoulder belt anchor-to-body	32 ft. lbs.	43 Nm
Outer belt floor anchor-to-body	32 ft. lbs.	43 Nm
Retractor-to-body	32 ft. lbs.	43 Nm
Inner belt-to-body	32 ft. lbs.	43 Nm

89590CA1

GLOSSARY

AIR/FUEL RATIO: The ratio of air-to-gasoline by weight in the fuel mixture drawn into the engine.

AIR INJECTION: One method of reducing harmful exhaust emissions by injecting air into each of the exhaust ports of an engine. The fresh air entering the hot exhaust manifold causes any remaining fuel to be burned before it can exit the tailpipe.

ALTERNATOR: A device used for converting mechanical energy into electrical energy.

AMMETER: An instrument, calibrated in amperes, used to measure the flow of an electrical current in a circuit. Ammeters are always connected in series with the circuit being tested.

AMPERE: The rate of flow of electrical current present when one volt of electrical pressure is applied against one ohm of electrical resistance.

ANALOG COMPUTER: Any microprocessor that uses similar (analogous) electrical signals to make its calculations.

ARMATURE: A laminated, soft iron core wrapped by a wire that converts electrical energy to mechanical energy as in a motor or relay. When rotated in a magnetic field, it changes mechanical energy into electrical energy as in a generator.

ATMOSPHERIC PRESSURE: The pressure on the Earth's surface caused by the weight of the air in the atmosphere. At sea level, this pressure is 14.7 psi at 32°F (101 kPa at 0°C).

ATOMIZATION: The breaking down of a liquid into a fine mist that can be suspended in air.

AXIAL PLAY: Movement parallel to a shaft or bearing bore.

BACKFIRE: The sudden combustion of gases in the intake or exhaust system that results in a loud explosion.

BACKLASH: The clearance or play between two parts, such as meshed gears.

BACKPRESSURE: Restrictions in the exhaust system that slow the exit of exhaust gases from the combustion chamber.

BAKELITE: A heat resistant, plastic insulator material commonly used in printed circuit boards and transistorized components.

BALL BEARING: A bearing made up of hardened inner and outer races between which hardened steel balls roll.

BALLAST RESISTOR: A resistor in the primary ignition circuit that lowers voltage after the engine is started to reduce wear on ignition components.

BEARING: A friction reducing, supportive device usually located between a stationary part and a moving part.

BIMETAL TEMPERATURE SENSOR: Any sensor or switch made of two dissimilar types of metal that bend when heated or cooled due to the different expansion rates of the alloys. These types of sensors usually function as an on/off switch.

BLOWBY: Combustion gases, composed of water vapor and unburned fuel, that leak past the piston rings into the crankcase during normal engine operation. These gases are removed by the PCV system to prevent the buildup of harmful acids in the crankcase.

BRAKE PAD: A brake shoe and lining assembly used with disc brakes.

BRAKE SHOE: The backing for the brake lining. The term is, however, usually applied to the assembly of the brake backing and lining.

BUSHING: A liner, usually removable, for a bearing; an anti-friction liner used in place of a bearing.

CALIPER: A hydraulically activated device in a disc brake system, which is mounted straddling the brake rotor (disc). The caliper contains at least one piston and two brake pads. Hydraulic pressure on the piston(s) forces the pads against the rotor.

CAMSHAFT: A shaft in the engine on which are the lobes (cams) which operate the valves. The camshaft is driven by the crankshaft, via a belt, chain or gears, at one half the crankshaft speed.

CAPACITOR: A device which stores an electrical charge.

CARBON MONOXIDE (CO): A colorless, odorless gas given off as a normal byproduct of combustion. It is poisonous and extremely dangerous in confined areas, building up slowly to toxic levels without warning if adequate ventilation is not available.

CARBURETOR: A device, usually mounted on the intake manifold of an engine, which mixes the air and fuel in the proper proportion to allow even combustion.

CATALYTIC CONVERTER: A device installed in the exhaust system, like a muffler, that converts harmful byproducts of combustion into carbon dioxide and water vapor by means of a heat-producing chemical reaction.

CENTRIFUGAL ADVANCE: A mechanical method of advancing the spark timing by using flyweights in the distributor that react to centrifugal force generated by the distributor shaft rotation.

CHECK VALVE: Any one-way valve installed to permit the flow of air, fuel or vacuum in one direction only.

CHOKE: A device, usually a moveable valve, placed in the intake path of a carburetor to restrict the flow of air.

CIRCUIT: Any unbroken path through which an electrical current can flow. Also used to describe fuel flow in some instances.

CIRCUIT BREAKER: A switch which protects an electrical circuit from overload by opening the circuit when the current flow exceeds a predetermined level. Some circuit breakers must be reset manually, while most reset automatically.

COIL (IGNITION): A transformer in the ignition circuit which steps up the voltage provided to the spark plugs.

COMBINATION MANIFOLD: An assembly which includes both the intake and exhaust manifolds in one casting.

COMBINATION VALVE: A device used in some fuel systems that routes fuel vapors to a charcoal storage canister instead of venting them into the atmosphere. The valve relieves fuel tank pressure and allows fresh air into the tank as the fuel level drops to prevent a vapor lock situation.

COMPRESSION RATIO: The comparison of the total volume of the cylinder and combustion chamber with the piston at BDC and the piston at TDC.

CONDENSER: 1. An electrical device which acts to store an electrical charge, preventing voltage surges. 2. A radiator-like device in the air conditioning system in which refrigerant gas condenses into a liquid, giving off heat.

CONDUCTOR: Any material through which an electrical current can be transmitted easily.

CONTINUITY: Continuous or complete circuit. Can be checked with an ohmmeter.

COUNTERSHAFT: An intermediate shaft which is rotated by a mainshaft and transmits, in turn, that rotation to a working part.

CRANKCASE: The lower part of an engine in which the crankshaft and related parts operate.

CRANKSHAFT: The main driving shaft of an engine which receives reciprocating motion from the pistons and converts it to rotary motion.

CYLINDER: In an engine, the round hole in the engine block in which the piston(s) ride.

CYLINDER BLOCK: The main structural member of an engine in which is found the cylinders, crankshaft and other principal parts.

CYLINDER HEAD: The detachable portion of the engine, usually fastened to the top of the cylinder block and containing all or most of the combustion chambers. On overhead valve engines, it contains the valves and their operating parts. On overhead cam engines, it contains the camshaft as well.

DEAD CENTER: The extreme top or bottom of the piston stroke.

DETONATION: An unwanted explosion of the air/fuel mixture in the combustion chamber caused by excess heat and compression, advanced timing, or an overly lean mixture. Also referred to as "ping".

DIAPHRAGM: A thin, flexible wall separating two cavities, such as in a vacuum advance unit.

DIESELING: A condition in which hot spots in the combustion chamber cause the engine to run on after the key is turned off.

DIFFERENTIAL: A geared assembly which allows the transmission of motion between drive axles, giving one axle the ability to turn faster than the other.

DIODE: An electrical device that will allow current to flow in one direction only.

DISC BRAKE: A hydraulic braking assembly consisting of a brake disc, or rotor, mounted on an axle, and a caliper assembly containing, usually two brake pads which are activated by hydraulic pressure. The pads are forced against the sides of the disc, creating friction which slows the vehicle.

DISTRIBUTOR: A mechanically driven device on an engine which is responsible for electrically firing the spark plug at a predetermined point of the piston stroke.

DOWEL PIN: A pin, inserted in mating holes in two different parts allowing those parts to maintain a fixed relationship.

DRUM BRAKE: A braking system which consists of two brake shoes and one or two wheel cylinders, mounted on a fixed backing plate, and a brake drum, mounted on an axle, which revolves around the assembly.

DWELL: The rate, measured in degrees of shaft rotation, at which an electrical circuit cycles on and off.

ELECTRONIC CONTROL UNIT (ECU): Ignition module, module, amplifier or igniter. See Module for definition.

ELECTRONIC IGNITION: A system in which the timing and firing of the spark plugs is controlled by an electronic control unit, usually called a module. These systems have no points or condenser.

END-PLAY: The measured amount of axial movement in a shaft.

ENGINE: A device that converts heat into mechanical energy.

EXHAUST MANIFOLD: A set of cast passages or pipes which conduct exhaust gases from the engine.

FEELER GAUGE: A blade, usually metal, or precisely predetermined thickness, used to measure the clearance between two parts.

FIRING ORDER: The order in which combustion occurs in the cylinders of an engine. Also the order in which spark is distributed to the plugs by the distributor.

FLOODING: The presence of too much fuel in the intake manifold and combustion chamber which prevents the air/fuel mixture from firing, thereby causing a no-start situation.

FLYWHEEL: A disc shaped part bolted to the rear end of the crankshaft. Around the outer perimeter is affixed the ring gear. The starter drive engages the ring gear, turning the flywheel, which rotates the crankshaft, imparting the initial starting motion to the engine.

FOOT POUND (ft. lbs. or sometimes, ft.lb.): The amount of energy or work needed to raise an item weighing one pound, a distance of one foot.

FUSE: A protective device in a circuit which prevents circuit overload by breaking the circuit when a specific amperage is present. The device is constructed around a strip or wire of a lower amperage rating than the circuit it is designed to protect. When an amperage higher than that stamped on the fuse is present in the circuit, the strip or wire melts, opening the circuit.

GEAR RATIO: The ratio between the number of teeth on meshing gears.

GENERATOR: A device which converts mechanical energy into electrical energy.

HEAT RANGE: The measure of a spark plug's ability to dissipate heat from its firing end. The higher the heat range, the hotter the plug fires.

HUB: The center part of a wheel or gear.

HYDROCARBON (HC): Any chemical compound made up of hydrogen and carbon. A major pollutant formed by the engine as a byproduct of combustion.

HYDROMETER: An instrument used to measure the specific gravity of a solution.

INCH POUND (inch lbs.; sometimes in.lb. or in. lbs.): One twelfth of a foot pound.

INDUCTION: A means of transferring electrical energy in the form of a magnetic field. Principle used in the ignition coil to increase voltage.

INJECTOR: A device which receives metered fuel under relatively low pressure and is activated to inject the fuel into the engine under relatively high pressure at a predetermined time.

INPUT SHAFT: The shaft to which torque is applied, usually carrying the driving gear or gears.

INTAKE MANIFOLD: A casting of passages or pipes used to conduct air or a fuel/air mixture to the cylinders.

JOURNAL: The bearing surface within which a shaft operates.

KEY: A small block usually fitted in a notch between a shaft and a hub to prevent slippage of the two parts.

MANIFOLD: A casting of passages or set of pipes which connect the cylinders to an inlet or outlet source.

MANIFOLD VACUUM: Low pressure in an engine intake manifold formed just below the throttle plates. Manifold vacuum is highest at idle and drops under acceleration.

MASTER CYLINDER: The primary fluid pressurizing device in a hydraulic system. In automotive use, it is found in brake and hydraulic clutch systems and is pedal activated, either directly or, in a power brake system, through the power booster.

MODULE: Electronic control unit, amplifier or igniter of solid state or integrated design which controls the current flow in the ignition primary circuit based on input from the pick-up coil. When the module opens the primary circuit, high secondary voltage is induced in the coil.

NEEDLE BEARING: A bearing which consists of a number (usually a large number) of long, thin rollers.

OHM: (Ω) The unit used to measure the resistance of conductor-to-electrical flow. One ohm is the amount of resistance that limits current flow to one ampere in a circuit with one volt of pressure.

OHMMETER: An instrument used for measuring the resistance, in ohms, in an electrical circuit.

OUTPUT SHAFT: The shaft which transmits torque from a device, such as a transmission.

OVERDRIVE: A gear assembly which produces more shaft revolutions than that transmitted to it.

OVERHEAD CAMSHAFT (OHC): An engine configuration in which the camshaft is mounted on top of the cylinder head and operates the valve either directly or by means of rocker arms.

OVERHEAD VALVE (OHV): An engine configuration in which all of the valves are located in the cylinder head and the camshaft is located in the cylinder block. The camshaft operates the valves via lifters and pushrods.

OXIDES OF NITROGEN (NOx): Chemical compounds of nitrogen produced as a byproduct of combustion. They combine with hydrocarbons to produce smog.

OXYGEN SENSOR: Use with the feedback system to sense the presence of oxygen in the exhaust gas and signal the computer which can reference the voltage signal to an air/fuel ratio.

PINION: The smaller of two meshing gears.

PISTON RING: An open-ended ring with fits into a groove on the outer diameter of the piston. Its chief function is to form a seal between the piston and cylinder wall. Most automotive pistons have three rings: two for compression sealing; one for oil sealing.

PRELOAD: A predetermined load placed on a bearing during assembly or by adjustment.

PRIMARY CIRCUIT: the low voltage side of the ignition system which consists of the ignition switch, ballast resistor or resistance wire, bypass, coil, electronic control unit and pick-up coil as well as the connecting wires and harnesses.

PRESS FIT: The mating of two parts under pressure, due to the inner diameter of one being smaller than the outer diameter of the other, or vice versa; an interference fit.

RACE: The surface on the inner or outer ring of a bearing on which the balls, needles or rollers move.

REGULATOR: A device which maintains the amperage and/or voltage levels of a circuit at predetermined values.

RELAY: A switch which automatically opens and/or closes a circuit.

RESISTANCE: The opposition to the flow of current through a circuit or electrical device, and is measured in ohms. Resistance is equal to the voltage divided by the amperage.

RESISTOR: A device, usually made of wire, which offers a preset amount of resistance in an electrical circuit.

RING GEAR: The name given to a ring-shaped gear attached to a differential case, or affixed to a flywheel or as part of a planetary gear set.

ROLLER BEARING: A bearing made up of hardened inner and outer races between which hardened steel rollers move.

ROTOR: 1. The disc-shaped part of a disc brake assembly, upon which the brake pads bear; also called, brake disc. 2. The device mounted atop the distributor shaft, which passes current to the distributor cap tower contacts.

SECONDARY CIRCUIT: The high voltage side of the ignition system, usually above 20,000 volts. The secondary includes the ignition coil, coil wire, distributor cap and rotor, spark plug wires and spark plugs.

SENDING UNIT: A mechanical, electrical, hydraulic or electro-magnetic device which transmits information to a gauge.

SENSOR: Any device designed to measure engine operating conditions or ambient pressures and temperatures. Usually electronic in nature and designed to send a voltage signal to an on-board computer, some sensors may operate as a simple on/off switch or they may provide a variable voltage signal (like a potentiometer) as conditions or measured parameters change.

SHIM: Spacers of precise, predetermined thickness used between parts to establish a proper working relationship.

SLAVE CYLINDER: In automotive use, a device in the hydraulic clutch system which is activated by hydraulic force, disengaging the clutch.

SOLENOID: A coil used to produce a magnetic field, the effect of which is to produce work.

SPARK PLUG: A device screwed into the combustion chamber of a spark ignition engine. The basic construction is a conductive core inside of a ceramic insulator, mounted in an outer conductive base. An electrical charge from the spark plug wire travels along the conductive core and jumps a preset air gap to a grounding point or points at the end of the conductive base. The resultant spark ignites the fuel/air mixture in the combustion chamber.

SPLINES: Ridges machined or cast onto the outer diameter of a shaft or inner diameter of a bore to enable parts to mate without rotation.

TACHOMETER: A device used to measure the rotary speed of an engine, shaft, gear, etc., usually in rotations per minute.

THERMOSTAT: A valve, located in the cooling system of an engine, which is closed when cold and opens gradually in response to engine heating, controlling the temperature of the coolant and rate of coolant flow.

TOP DEAD CENTER (TDC): The point at which the piston reaches the top of its travel on the compression stroke.

TORQUE: The twisting force applied to an object.

TORQUE CONVERTER: A turbine used to transmit power from a driving member to a driven member via hydraulic action, providing changes in drive ratio and torque. In automotive use, it links the driveplate at the rear of the engine to the automatic transmission.

TRANSDUCER: A device used to change a force into an electrical signal.

TRANSISTOR: A semi-conductor component which can be actuated by a small voltage to perform an electrical switching function.

TUNE-UP: A regular maintenance function, usually associated with the replacement and adjustment of parts and components in the electrical and fuel systems of a vehicle for the purpose of attaining optimum performance.

TURBOCHARGER: An exhaust driven pump which compresses intake air and forces it into the combustion chambers at higher than atmospheric pressures. The increased air pressure allows more fuel to be burned and results in increased horsepower being produced.

VACUUM ADVANCE: A device which advances the ignition timing in response to increased engine vacuum.

VACUUM GAUGE: An instrument used to measure the presence of vacuum in a chamber.

VALVE: A device which control the pressure, direction of flow or rate of flow of a liquid or gas.

VALVE CLEARANCE: The measured gap between the end of the valve stem and the rocker arm, cam lobe or follower that activates the valve.

VISCOSITY: The rating of a liquid's internal resistance to flow.

VOLTMETER: An instrument used for measuring electrical force in units called volts. Voltmeters are always connected parallel with the circuit being tested.

WHEEL CYLINDER: Found in the automotive drum brake assembly, it is a device, actuated by hydraulic pressure, which, through internal pistons, pushes the brake shoes outward against the drums.

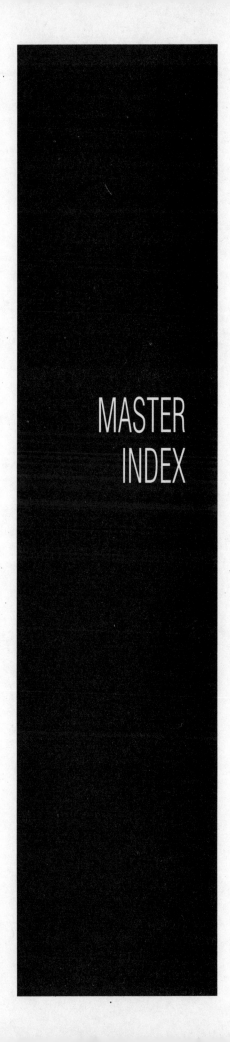

MASTER

INDEX

Total Car Care, continued

Sentra/Pulsar/NX 1982-96
PART NO. 8263/52700
Stanza/200SX/240SX 1982-92
PART NO. 8262/52750
240SX/Altima 1993-98
PART NO. 52752
Datsun/Nissan Z and ZX 1970-88
PART NO. 8846/52800

RENAULT
Coupes/Sedans/Wagons 1975-85
PART NO. 58300

SATURN
Coupes/Sedans/Wagons 1991-98
PART NO. 8419/62300

SUBARU
Coupes/Sedan/Wagons 1970-84
PART NO. 8790/64300
Coupes/Sedans/Wagons 1985-96
PART NO. 8259/64302

SUZUKI
Samurai/Sidekick/Tracker 1986-98
PART NO. 66500

TOYOTA
Camry 1983-96
PART NO. 8265/68200
Celica/Supra 1971-85
PART NO. 68250
Celica 1986-93
PART NO. 8413/68252

Celica 1994-98
PART NO. 68254
Corolla 1970-87
PART NO. 8586/68300
Corolla 1988-97
PART NO. 8414/68302
Cressida/Corona/Crown/MkII 1970-82
PART NO. 68350
Cressida/Van 1983-90
PART NO. 68352
Pick-ups/Land Cruiser/4Runner 1970-88
PART NO. 8578/68600
Pick-ups/Land Cruiser/4Runner 1989-98
PART NO. 8163/68602
Previa 1991-97
PART NO. 68640

Tercel 1984-94
PART NO. 8595/68700

VOLKSWAGEN
Air-Cooled 1949-69
PART NO. 70200
Air-Cooled 1970-81
PART NO. 70202
Front Wheel Drive 1974-89
PART NO. 8663/70400
Golf/Jetta/Cabriolet 1990-93
PART NO. 8429/70402

VOLVO
Coupes/Sedans/Wagons 1970-89
PART NO. 8786/72300
Coupes/Sedans/Wagons 1990-98
PART NO. 8428/72302

SELOC MARINE MANUALS

OUTBOARDS
Chrysler Outboards, All Engines 1962-84
PART NO. 018-7(1000)
Force Outboards, All Engines 1984-96
PART NO. 024-1(1100)
Honda Outboards, All Engines 1988-98
PART NO. 1200
Johnson/Evinrude Outboards, 1.5-40HP,
2-Stroke 1956-70
PART NO. 007-1(1300)
Johnson/Evinrude Outboards, 1.25-60HP,
2-Stroke 1971-89
PART NO. 008-X(1302)
Johnson/Evinrude Outboards, 1-50 HP, 2-Stroke
1990-95
PART NO. 026-8(1304)
Johnson/Evinrude Outboards, 50-125 HP,
2-Stroke 1958-72
PART NO. 009-8(1306)
Johnson/Evinrude Outboards,
60-235 HP, 2-Stroke 1973-91
PART NO. 010-1(1308)
Johnson/Evinrude Outboards,
80-300 HP, 2-Stroke 1992-96
PART NO. 040-3(1310)
Mariner Outboards, 2-60 HP, 2-Stroke 1977-89
PART NO. 015-2(1400)

Mariner Outboards, 45-220 HP, 2 Stroke
1977-89
PART NO. 016-0(1402)
Mercury Outboards, 2-40 HP, 2-Stroke 1965-91
PART NO. 012-8(1404)
Mercury Outboards, 40-115 HP,
2-Stroke 1965-92
PART NO. 013-6(1406)
Mercury Outboards, 90-300 HP,
2-Stroke 1965-91
PART NO. 014-4(1408)
Mercury/Mariner Outboards, 2.5-25 HP,
2-Stroke 1990-94
PART NO. 035-7(1410)
Mercury/Mariner Outboards, 40-125 HP,
2-Stroke 1990-94
PART NO. 036-5(1412)
Mercury/Mariner Outboards, 135-275 HP,
2-Stroke 1990-94
PART NO. 037-3(1414)
Mercury/Mariner Outboards, All Engines
1995-99
PART NO. 1416
Suzuki Outboards, All Engines 1985-99
PART NO. 1600

Yamaha Outboards, 2-25 HP, 2-Stroke
and 9.9 HP, 4-Stroke 1984-91
PART NO. 021-7(1700)
Yamaha Outboards, 30-90 HP, 2-Stroke
1984-91
PART NO. 022-5(1702)
Yamaha Outboards, 115-225 HP,
2-Stroke 1984-91
PART NO. 023-3(1704)
Yamaha Outboards, All Engines 1992-98
PART NO. 1706

STERN DRIVES
Marine Jet Drive 1961-96
PART NO. 029-2(3000)
Mercruiser Stern Drive Type 1, Alpha,
Bravo I, II, 1964-92
PART NO. 005-5(3200)
Mercruiser Stern Drive Alpha 1
Generation II 1992-96
PART NO. 039-X(3202)
Mercruiser Stern Drive Bravo I, II, III 1992-96
PART NO. 046-2(3204)
OMC Stern Drive 1964-86
PART NO. 004-7(3400)
OMC Cobra Stern Drive 1985-95
PART NO. 025-X(3402)

Volvo/Penta Stern Drives 1968-91
PART NO. 011-X(3600)
Volvo/Penta Stern Drives 1992-93
PART NO. 038-1(3602)
Volvo/Penta Stern Drives 1992-95
PART NO. 041-1(3604)

INBOARDS
Yanmar Inboard Diesels 1988-91
PART NO. 7400

PERSONAL WATERCRAFT
Kawasaki 1973-91
PART NO. 032-2(9200)
Kawasaki 1992-97
PART NO. 042-X(9202)
Polaris 1992-97
PART NO. 045-4(9400)
Sea Doo/Bombardier 1988-91
PART NO. 033-0(9000)
Sea Doo/Bombardier 1992-97
PART NO. 043-8(9002)
Yamaha 1987-91
PART NO. 034-9(9600)
Yamaha 1992-97
PART NO. 044-6(9602)

"...and even more from CHILTON"

General Interest / Recreational Books

ATV Handbook
PART NO. 9123
Auto Detailing
PART NO. 8394
Auto Body Repair
PART NO. 7898
Briggs & Stratton Vertical Crankshaft
Engine
PART NO. 61-1-2
Briggs & Stratton Horizontal
Crankshaft Engine
PART NO. 61-0-4
Briggs & Stratton Overhead Valve
(OHV) Engine
PART NO. 61-2-0
Easy Car Care
PART NO. 8042

Motorcycle Handbook
PART NO. 9099
Snowmobile Handbook
PART NO. 9124
Small Engine Repair (Up to 20 Hp)
PART NO. 8325

Total Service Series

Automatic Transmissions/Transaxles
Diagnosis and Repair
PART NO. 8944
Brake System Diagnosis and Repair
PART NO. 8945
Chevrolet Engine Overhaul Manual
PART NO. 8794
Engine Code Manual
PART NO. 8851
Ford Engine Overhaul Manual
PART NO. 8793
Fuel Injection Diagnosis and Repair
PART NO. 8946

COLLECTOR'S SERIES HARD-COVER MANUALS

Chilton's Collector's Editions are perfect for enthusiasts of vintage or rare cars. These hard-cover manuals contain repair and maintenance information for all major systems that might not be available elsewhere. Included are repair and overhaul procedures using thousands of illustrations. These manuals offer a range of coverage from as far back as 1940 and as recent as 1997, so you don't need an antique car or truck to be a collector.

MULTI-VEHICLE SPANISH LANGUAGE MANUALS

Chilton's Spanish language manuals offer some of our most popular titles in Spanish. Each is as complete and easy to use as the English-language counterpart and offers the same maintenance, repair and overhaul information along with specifications charts and tons of illustrations.

TOTAL SERVICE SERIES / SYSTEM SPECIFIC MANUALS

These innovative books offer repair, maintenance and service procedures for automotive related systems. They cover today's complex vehicles in a user-friendly format, which places even the most difficult automotive topic well within the reach of every Do-It-Yourselfer. Each title covers a specific subject from Brakes and Engine Rebuilding to Fuel Injection Systems, Automatic Transmissions and even Engine Trouble Codes.

For the titles listed, visit your local Chilton® Retailer
For a Catalog, for information, or to order call toll-free: 877-4CHILTON.

 **NP|CHILTON'S®** 1020 Andrew Drive, Suite 200 • West Chester, PA 19380-4291
www.chiltononline.com

2P2VerB